THE GOVERNMENT
OF AMERICAN CITIES

BY THE SAME AUTHOR

THE GOVERNMENT OF EUROPEAN CITIES
MUNICIPAL GOVERNMENT AND ADMINISTRATION (2 VOLS.)
THE GOVERNMENTS OF EUROPE
THE GOVERNMENT OF THE UNITED STATES
CURRENT PROBLEMS IN CITIZENSHIP
PERSONALITY IN POLITICS

THE GOVERNMENT OF AMERICAN CITIES

BY

WILLIAM BENNETT MUNRO, Ph.D., LL.B.

JONATHAN TRUMBULL PROFESSOR OF AMERICAN HISTORY
AND GOVERNMENT IN HARVARD UNIVERSITY

FOURTH EDITION

New York
THE MACMILLAN COMPANY
1928

All rights reserved

COPYRIGHT, 1912, 1916, AND 1926,
BY THE MACMILLAN COMPANY

Set up and electrotyped. Published November, 1912.
Fourth Edition, July, 1926.

PRINTED IN THE UNITED STATES OF AMERICA BY
THE BERWICK & SMITH CO.

To
My Mother

"*Municipal institutions constitute the strength of free nations. A nation may establish a system of free government, but without municipal institutions it cannot have the spirit of liberty.*"

Alexis de Tocqueville.

PREFACE TO THE FOURTH EDITION

It is the purpose of this volume to describe, in a general way, the organization of city government in the United States. The book presents an historical outline of American municipal government, explains the relation of the city to the state, describes the different forms and organs of city administration, treats of the legal powers of the city as a municipal corporation, examines municipal administration as a business proposition, suggests some criteria for judging whether the government of a city is good or bad, and describes in detail the government of four large American cities.

For the most part, however, the volume deals with the governmental rather than with the administrative problems of the municipality. It endeavors to explain what the organs of municipal government are, rather than what they do. It discusses the mechanism of city government rather than functions or activities. This is not because the latter are deemed less important, but because the author has already dealt with them in other volumes. This book, in short, provides a general introduction to a large and complicated subject, namely the methods by which more than thirty million Americans are now being governed in their respective local communities.

This fourth edition embodies a complete revision and rewriting of the original volume which appeared fourteen years ago. Several new chapters have been added. Elsewhere in the book the emphasis has been greatly changed. Various charts and diagrams have been inserted. The general overhauling has been so extensive, indeed, that the book is virtually a new one, especially in its point of view. That is not surprising, for American city government is quite a different thing from what it was in days before the war.

I am indebted to Dr. Luther Gulick of New York City, Hon. Clinton Rogers Woodruff of Philadelphia, Mr. George C. Sikes of Chicago, and Mr. George H. McCaffrey of Boston for various

viii   PREFACE TO THE FOURTH EDITION

criticisms and suggestions. Mr. Joseph Wright, Superintendent of the Bureau for Municipal Research at Harvard University, has helped me greatly in the collection of material, and I am also under obligation to Miss Gladys E. Campbell for assistance in preparing the manuscript.

May 1, 1926.

W. B. M.

CONTENTS

CHAPTER		PAGE
I.	THE CITY AS A PROBLEM IN GOVERNMENT	1
II.	AMERICAN MUNICIPAL DEVELOPMENT	21
III.	THE SOCIAL STRUCTURE OF THE CITY	46
IV.	THE CITY AND THE STATE	71
V.	THE CITY CHARTER	92
VI.	LEGAL PHASES OF CITY GOVERNMENT	112
VII.	THE MUNICIPAL ELECTORATE	133
VIII.	POLITICAL PARTIES: THEIR PURPOSE AND ORGANIZATION	151
IX.	THE METHODS OF NOMINATION IN CITIES	170
X.	MUNICIPAL ELECTIONS AND ELECTION PROCEDURE	186
XI.	PRACTICAL POLITICS	203
XII.	URBAN PUBLIC OPINION	220
XIII.	THE INITIATIVE, REFERENDUM, AND RECALL	238
XIV.	THE FORMS OF CITY GOVERNMENT	255
XV.	MAYOR AND COUNCIL GOVERNMENT	
	A. THE MAYOR	267
	B. THE CITY COUNCIL	284
XVI.	THE COMMISSION FORM OF GOVERNMENT	302
XVII.	THE CITY MANAGER FORM OF GOVERNMENT	321
XVIII.	THE ADMINISTRATIVE DEPARTMENTS	343
XIX.	MUNICIPAL EMPLOYEES AND THE CIVIL SERVICE SYSTEM	363
XX.	THE MUNICIPAL COURTS	387
XXI.	CITY GOVERNMENT AS BUSINESS	402
XXII.	MUNICIPAL REFORM AND REFORMERS	420
XXIII.	THE CRITERIA OF GOOD CITY GOVERNMENT	434
XXIV.	THE GREATER CITIES	447
INDEX		481

THE GOVERNMENT
OF AMERICAN CITIES

THE GOVERNMENT OF AMERICAN CITIES

CHAPTER I

THE CITY AS A PROBLEM IN GOVERNMENT

The life that men live in the city gives the measure of their civilization. The city, in other words, is merely an organized and improved cross-section of the country in which it is located. Whenever large numbers of people are crowded into a limited area they must inevitably raise their plane of life above that of the surrounding territory. Otherwise they would not be able to continue their existence. If a large city, for example, had no better sanitation than the average rural district it would soon be overwhelmed by epidemics. If it had no better protection against fire it would soon be in ashes. If it had no better facilities for transporting goods its people would starve. The great city, in short, cannot rest content with those simple measures for the care of the public health, for fire and police protection, for recreation, for the handling of traffic, for water supply, and for education which satisfy the countryside. It must make more and better provision for all these things as the price of its existence and progress. The city population is driven to a different plane of life by reason of the exigencies which arise from the massing of people together. *The city's place in civilization.*

It has always been so. The cities have been in the vanguard at all stages in the history of civilization. All great cultures have been city-born. The ancient city-states of Greece were the pioneers of Hellenic culture and progress. They outdistanced the rural territories. The great Roman empire owed its strength to the cities which it contained, particularly to the capital city. The whole ancient world, indeed, was a world of cities; its civilization was the handiwork of people who *1. In ancient times.*

1

lived close together and managed to solve the problems which arise from the hum and shock of men.

2. During the Middle Ages.

But the collapse of Roman power brought the day of the ancient city to a close and during the next few centuries the old centers of urban life went into decay. Many of them disappeared altogether. This decline of city life went hand in hand with the relapse of civilization to barbarism. There could be no advance in the amenities of life under conditions which made it impossible for cities to grow and prosper. These Dark Ages, from the sixth century to the twelfth, ought to teach the student of history and government an impressive lesson. They prove that what we call "urban civilization" is after all a very fragile thing. It will not stand mishandling. A Roman in the second century would have scouted the idea that his mighty empire could ever be brought to the dust, its armies disbanded, its commerce disappear, its splendid roads grow rank with weeds, its massive buildings crumble into ruins, and its far-flung culture become the mockery of barbarians. Yet it all came to pass. Ancient civilization went into total eclipse. Ten generations of men were born and died before the first glimmer of light reappeared. Let us not be too confident that modern civilization, as ensconsed in the great urban centers of today, can safely withstand the roughest usage.

3. In modern times.

The collapse of the Roman empire was perhaps the greatest catastrophe in human history. The world was a long time recovering from it. Eventually, however, there came a revival in city life. With the suppression of banditry and pillage the towns began to flourish again, particularly those of the Mediterranean region. Later the free cities of Northwestern Europe came in for their share of the new prosperity, and between these two areas the civic revival gradually spread. With it came a renaissance in European culture, disclosing once more the close relation between city growth and national power. The modern world, like the ancient, began its march to urbanization, a progress that was slow at first but has been gradually speeded up. Cities grew more rapidly in the eighteenth century than in the seventeenth, and still more rapidly in the nineteenth than in the eighteenth. With the twentieth century entering its second quarter there is every indication that city growth will keep on accelerating its pace. With this growth has come

THE CITY AS A PROBLEM IN GOVERNMENT 3

an enormously increased complexity in life, in civic institutions, and in the problems which have to be solved.

The American city of today provides a fine example of institutional evolution. It begins as a little village. Even Chicago, with its three million people, was a frontier settlement ninety years ago. Los Angeles, with its million or more people, was a little hamlet clustered around an old Spanish mission in 1875. The village becomes a town, doubling or trebling in population, and with this evolution into townhood some new problems arise. Its people call for better streets, for a public water supply, for sewerage, for regular police and fire protection. With another trebling of the population the town becomes a city, and here again there is a rapid development of new problems. The people now demand not only streets, water, sewerage, and protection, but parks, playgrounds, civic centers, specialized schools, traffic officers, public libraries, and organized recreation. Finally, as the city expands into a metropolis, the need for larger and better public services grows at an increased pace. A vastly more intricate scheme of municipal administration is required to handle the diversified problems of law, finance, engineering, and philanthropy. The people, by reason of the crowded conditions under which they live, must be more rigidly subjected to control by the public authorities. On the whole they welcome this paternalism and in the end we find the super-city taking over many of the functions which in a smaller community belong to the home. Size brings complexity, and complexity brings paternalism. This paternalism engenders docility, and in the end we have great masses of people whose inclination is to depend for everything upon social effort and control.

What city growth means.

The problem of governing great cities is an old one in Europe but a relatively new one in America. It gave the Fathers of the Republic no concern one hundred and forty years ago. If you read the debates which took place in the Constitutional Convention of 1787 you will find scarcely a word concerning the possible growth of great cities or the problems which this might bring with it. Alexander Hamilton, a few years later, expressed the hope that the country would some day become industrially self-sufficient, but he did not seem to realize that this would entail the urbanization of the country. Jefferson, on the other hand, had a definite premonition of what would happen in the

The municipal problem in America.

Jefferson's forebodings.

ages to come, and he did not look upon the growth of cities with complacency. It was his prediction that democracy would be subjected to its greatest strain by the urban proletariate of the country whenever this element had sufficiently developed in numbers and in strength. The great Virginian was right. It is the larger cities that have given us, during the past fifty years, our most acute difficulties in the way of keeping government honest, efficient, responsible, democratic.

The comments of Tocqueville.

Nearly a hundred years ago a shrewd Frenchman, Alexis de Tocqueville, came to the United States and made a study of political conditions here. Tocqueville embodied his conclusions and observations in a notable book which even today is worth reading. But the seven hundred pages which are incorporated in Tocqueville's two volumes contain only a single paragraph bearing on the problems of municipal government.[1] He did not find that the American people were giving any thought to this matter although more than half a million people in 1830 were living in the cities of the new world. Tocqueville, however, could not be oblivious to the lessons of history in his own country. He knew that the larger cities of France had been trouble-makers on a considerable scale, and he feared that America would have a similar experience. Consequently he went so far as to predict that in time it might be necessary for the national government to use armed force in repressing the turbulence of these great urban mobs. A century after Tocqueville's day it has hardly come to that. We have devised a better way of holding the cities in check, namely, by rigid state control over their charters and government.

Bryce in 1888 and in 1921.

It is interesting to compare the writings of Tocqueville with those of another sagacious foreign student of American institutions, James Bryce (afterwards Lord Bryce), who wrote his remarkable volumes a half century later. Bryce found the problem of city government so urgent and so interesting that he devoted three whole chapters to a discussion of it.[2] He began with the lament that "the growth of great cities has been among the most significant and the least fortunate changes in the character of

---

[1] Alexis de Tocqueville, *Democracy in America* (Reeve's translation, 2 vols., New York, 1904), Vol. I, p. 311. In addition there are a couple of footnotes in which mention of city problems is made.

[2] James Bryce, *The American Commonwealth* (2 vols., New York, 1888), Vol. I, ch. l-lii (i.e. 50-52).

THE CITY AS A PROBLEM IN GOVERNMENT 5

the population" and concluded with the oft-quoted remark that the government of cities was "the one conspicuous failure" of the American people. The conditions of the time (1888) probably justified this indictment, but Americans were more alive to the urgencies of the problem than Bryce seemed to realize. They were getting ready to deal with it in an aggressive and effective way. So great a degree of success has attended the efforts of municipal reformers during the interval that Lord Bryce in 1921 confessed himself "astonished at the change."[1] The American people as a whole have become steadily more conscious of the municipal problem, its difficulties and its implications. They have also become more determined to deal with it in a vigorous and comprehensive way.

It is well that they should have this determination, for nowhere has the problem been growing to such dimensions as in the United States. Today more than a third of the American people live in cities of over 100,000, that is, in an environment which has become thoroughly urbanized. Fifty years ago the proportion was hardly one-tenth. This drift of the people into the cities, moreover, shows no signs of slackening; on the contrary, the indications are that it will keep on and perhaps be accelerated. The exodus, if it continues, can have but one result. In time it will virtually denude the rural districts of their population and transform the United States into a land of cities as England and Belgium have already become. It will do to the whole expanse of the United States what time and circumstance have done to Rhode Island and Eastern Massachusetts. This possibility, of course, suggests some interesting questions. When that time comes, where will the country get its food supply? And where will three or four hundred million people, massed in the ten thousand cities of the country, find a market for the products which they make? The same questions were asked in England seventy-five years ago, when statisticians predicted that the sceptered isle would in time become one great sprawling metropolis. Less than half the people of England lived in cities then; today the proportion is 85 per cent. More than one-sixth of the English people now live in Greater London alone. Yet England, with thirty-five of her forty million people concentrated into cities, has managed to provide herself with food, and under

The future of this problem.

[1] *Modern Democracies* (2 vols., New York, 1921), Vol. II, p. 154.

normal conditions to find a market for her manufactures. America, when the time comes, will no doubt be successful in doing the same.

<small>Some causes of city growth.</small>

Now what are the causes of this steady influx into the cities of the United States? It is not enough to say that the country as a whole is gaining in population and that the cities naturally take their share. The cities are growing in population at a much more rapid rate than the Union as a whole. It is true that a national increase helps to make city growth possible; but it is by no means the fundamental cause. Owing to the restrictions on immigration the increase of population in the United States as a whole will probably be smaller in the present decade than it was in the three preceding ten-year periods, but there is no likelihood that the relative growth of the cities will be slackened in proportion.

In the earlier centuries many cities owed their original location and most of their subsequent growth to facilities for defense or to political considerations. Athens grew because she could protect her people, and so did Rome. The expansion of Rome to a city of a million inhabitants was largely due to her position as the political capital of a world empire. Paris, Berlin, Vienna, and Madrid have owed much of their growth to similar considerations. But neither defense nor politics now plays much part in the location and growth of great communities. There is not a single large city in the United States that owes its location to a defensible position, and only one (Washington) that owes its growth to politics. Trade and industry, in the main, are the determining factors of today.

<small>1. Agriculture.</small>

The rate of city growth now depends for the most part on the progress of agriculture, industry, and commerce. Agriculture is important in this connection, for paradoxical as it may sound, its progress has helped to depopulate the country and to enrich the town. Better agricultural implements and better methods of farming have released a large amount of farm labor for migration to the cities. It has been estimated that by reason of tractors and other improved machinery, about fifteen per cent of the farm labor in the United States has been set free during the past twenty-five years. Bear in mind, moreover, that every day's work on the farm gives employment to one or more workers in the city. The western farmer who raises wheat or cattle is

THE CITY AS A PROBLEM IN GOVERNMENT 7

providing work for men in the flour mills of Minneapolis and the packing plants of Chicago. More than that, he is providing employment, indirectly, for men who work on railroads, in banks, and in other institutions of credit or exchange. The products of the farm have to be transported, marketed, and financed during the whole process which intervenes from production to final sale. Hence it is that the agricultural regions are the real backbone of our national economy. They furnish the cities with food, work, and immigrants. The farmer has been one of our chief city-builders, although he does not seem to be proud of it.

Industry is a still more important factor in city growth. The city is a logical place for the factories. This is because of its superior transportation facilities, its elastic labor supply, and its appeal to the average factory worker as a place in which to live. The factories go to the cities, and where the factories go the workers must follow. People go where they can find employment, and there is a much more diversified opportunity for work in the large city than in the rural village. Probably nine-tenths of the drift to the city is motivated by the desire to find congenial and profitable work. It should be mentioned, in passing, that industries of the same, or of an allied character, tend to congregate. It is not by mere accident that the motor industry is so heavily concentrated in Detroit, the steel industry in Pittsburgh, the furniture industry in Grand Rapids, the rubber industry in Akron, and the ready-made clothing industry in New York City. Birds of a feather flock together in industry as in everything else. New factories go where older establishments of the same nature are already located, and this for various reasons which will come to mind on a moment's reflection. Subsidiary trades likewise congregate around the main industries. A group of automobile factories, for example, is sure to attract various shops which make batteries, magnetos, tires, tubes, windshields, spark-plugs, tops, cushions, and all manner of automobile accessories. The shoe factories draw around them a variety of subsidiary establishments which manufacture heels, laces, shoe polish, shoe trees, shoe boxes, and so on.

Proximity to the raw materials of industry has had something to do with the rise of various manufacturing communities. Pittsburgh, for example, owes much to the coal fields which are close

2. Industry.

at hand. Chicago, Kansas City, and Omaha have become great centers of the meat-packing industry by reason of their geographical advantages. The same is true of Minneapolis with respect to flour-making. But the development of the textile and shoe industries in New England indicates that proximity to the source of raw materials is not always essential—for New England imports her wool, cotton, and leather over long distances. Akron is as far from the source of raw rubber supply as any American city. Detroit began with no more advantages for the development of her motor industry than were possessed at the time by Toledo, Cleveland, or Buffalo. Rapid industrial progress is the outcome of various forces which operate together—proximity to raw materials, nearness to a large market, good transportation facilities, financial resources, abundant and flexible labor supply, local initiative, and sometimes to individual personalities. No two industrial cities owe their growth to these various factors in precisely the same degree.

The satellite cities. Some years ago it was suggested that the crowding of factories into the large cities would in time produce its own reaction. Land in the downtown industrial areas would become so expensive, it was said, that the factories would drift back into the the smaller places once more. To a certain extent this has proved to be the case as is shown by their present tendency to locate in the outskirts of larger cities rather than in the downtown sections. Hence we have Norwoods and Ivorydales, Flints and Sugar Creeks, Fairfields and Bessemers, Hammonds and Garys, springing up within range of the big centers where the industries can obtain all the advantages of a metropolitan location while retaining the advantage of cheap land and room for expansion. These "satellite cities," as they are called, begin with the establishment of one or more industries; then come houses for the workmen, stores, and all the other accoutrements of a full-sized town. Gary, an hour's run from Chicago, is a striking example of a made-to-order industrial satellite. Twenty-five years ago its site was a stretch of rolling sand dunes along the lake, but the United States Steel Corporation took the place in hand and today it has a population of nearly 100,000. The impulse toward cheap land, low taxes, and elbow room is now driving the industries out of the big cities, but not into the rural districts,—merely into the outer suburban rings. Two or three decades ago the usual

THE CITY AS A PROBLEM IN GOVERNMENT 9

expansion of the city was by the creation of new residential suburbs. Now we are creating industrial suburbs as well.

Commerce, likewise, has much to do with the growth of American cities during the past fifty years. Look at a map of the United States and see where the big cities are. Of the twenty largest centers (all of them with populations exceeding 300,000), seven are on the Atlantic, five on the Great Lakes, six on the Mississippi or the Ohio, and two on the Pacific Coast. Every one of them is located on navigable water. This is not a mere coincidence; it proves that facilities for water-borne commerce are virtually essential to growth beyond a certain size. In America we think of the railroads as the great carriers of trade, and are inclined to look upon navigation as of secondary importance; but the figures of urban population and growth lend no support to this impression. On the contrary it would appear that proximity to navigable water is an absolute essential if a city expects to gain a place among the leaders. The history of Europe points to the same conclusion. With the exception of a few national capitals, all the great cities of the old continent are located at tidewater or on the great rivers.

3. Commerce.

Agriculture, industry and commerce are thus the primary factors in city growth, but there are secondary causes as well. In America the cities have gained more than their share of the immigrants (for reasons which will be explained a little later) and this alien accretion has in some cases contributed handsomely to their growth in population. Political considerations have had something to do with the expansion of a few American cities (such as Albany, Hartford, and Sacramento) which are the headquarters of state government. But the fact that a city becomes a state capital does not of itself suffice to bring any great increase in size, as witness the examples of Tallahassee, Augusta, Salem, and Harrisburg. The social lure of the city must also be reckoned among the secondary causes of urban growth. The large city draws heavily upon the leisure class, upon those who, having accumulated a competence, desire to be where comfort and luxury prevail. It also draws from the other end of the economic scale, taking into its ranks the jobless, the outcasts, the flotsam and jetsam of society. Strangely enough, most wage-earners and their families likewise prefer to live in large cities despite the higher cost of living there. The educa-

4. Other factors in city growth.

tional advantages, the amusements, and the whirling "life" of the city are forces not easy to resist. Country life, notwithstanding all that has been done to improve it, still seems to most people isolated, and in a sense monotonous. It lacks that variety which is spice to the lives of men. Some of the reputed attractions of city life are new; others are as old as civilization itself. Man, after all, is a gregarious animal, hence it is not surprising that he should seek the close contact with his fellows which the city provides. The city affords full scope for every type of ability, inclination, whim, or caprice. Its call is strong, and its allurements seductive. Its combined attractions are enough, at any rate, to sweep thousands from the rural areas into its vortex every year.

<small>Is city life unnatural?</small> We are often told that city life is unnatural, artificial, debilitating. The idea is embodied in the old saying that "God made the country and man made the town," a saying commonly attributed to Cowper, but probably far antedating him. But it is by no means certain that primitive man lived off by himself rather than with his fellows. When we come upon the most primitive tribes of today we find them huddled together in tree-dwellings or rude huts or in caves, with less elbow-room than civilized men have in a modern apartment house. Simeon Strunsky maintains, indeed, although perhaps not over-seriously, that the one-room-and-kitchenette of today is merely a throwback to the era of the tree-dwellers. Certain it is, at any rate, that the Iroquois Indians dwelt in "long houses" when the Europeans first came upon them, several families occupying the same rude structure. It is possible to set up a good historical argument for the proposition that man's earliest habitations were urban, and that only when he emerged from the primitive stage did he move out of his crowded quarters to set up a detached hut for himself. He could not safely do this until he had made some provision for his own defense. Philosophers have usually visualized man "in a state of nature" as a rural man, but they have no historical warrant for so doing. It is not unnatural for men to live close to their fellows, or, if it is, mankind has always lived unnaturally. There has been too much denouncing of the modern city as a social abomination, which by all the evidence it is not.

How may our cities of today be classified? There have been

THE CITY AS A PROBLEM IN GOVERNMENT 11

many classifications of cities—according to size into big, medium, and small, according to character into industrial and residential, or according to location into seaport cities and inland cities. But these classifications do not help us much because they take into account only one aspect of the city. What we need is a classification that takes into account the economic and social individuality of each city, their interdependence, and the relation of each to its environment—in other words, what biologists (in speaking of organisms) would call an "ecological" classification.[1] The classification of cities.

Now one of the first things that will impress anyone who studies the structure of many cities, big and little, is the fact that each has one or more sources to which it owes its origin and progress. These sources form the city's economic base. As the base broadens, the city grows and prospers; if by any chance the base narrows, the city will decline. Take an illustration. Los Angeles, fifty years ago, had its sole *raison d'être* in the fact that it was a distributing point for a relatively small cultivable area. Its economic base was narrow and the town was small. But industries developed; the base broadened, and the city grew. Later a harbor was built and commerce sprang up. Again a broadening of the base and we have the metropolis of the Pacific Southwest. On the other hand, we have seen cities come into existence as the result of a mining or oil boom, and thrive mightily on this slender economic base—for a time. But with the closing of the mines or wells these places have gone stagnant.

One might, therefore, classify cities according to their economic bases in some such fashion as this:

First. The community which depends for its growth and prosperity upon a single, restricted source—for example, the large country town which serves merely as a local center for the distribution of agricultural products and finished goods. Or the place which depends on mining, oil wells, lumbering, or fisheries. Gloucester, in Massachusetts, will serve as an example of the last-named. In the same category we might place those cities which depend upon the fact that they are political capitals, or favorite places of resort by reason of climatic or scenic advantages, or are the location of state universities or other great

[1] See the chapter on "The Ecological Approach" in R. E. Park, E. W. Burgess, and R. D. McKenzie *The City* (Chicago, 1925).

educational institutions. Cities which fall in this class can never become very large unless they broaden the basis on which they stand.

2. The industrialized city.

Second, there is the community which is becoming, or has become, industrialized. It is not only a local distributing point but a producer on its own account. We should distinguish, however, between two subdivisions in this class, namely, the one-industry cities and the cities with diversified industries. In the former, one type of manufacture is dominant and far outdistances all the rest—cash registers in Dayton, furniture in Grand Rapids, shoes in Brockton, and collars in Troy. Or the city may have multiple industries organized on a relatively small scale. The latter, of course, is the broader and safer economic base.

3. The industro-commercial city.

Third, we have the city that adds commerce to industry. The two naturally go together when a city has reached a certain point. This further broadening of the groundwork is of great advantage in promoting urban growth. Take such a city as Providence. It is a local distributing point for Rhode Island, yet as such alone it would never have amounted to much. But it is also the state capital and the seat of a university. It has many diversified industries, and last, but by no means least, it is something of a seaport. That explains why the smallest state in the Union can support a city of nearly 300,000 people.

4. The metropolitan city.

Finally, there is the metropolitan city, of which more will be said later on.[1] It has all the advantages of cities in the two preceding classes with the additional one of serving as the economic focus of a wide surrounding area. Its possibilities in the way of growth are limited only by the potentialities of this encircling area or hinterland. The latter may easily provide an economic base for a city of a million or more.

No city can grow unless its base broadens.

Every American city, wherever located, and whether large or small, has its corps of boosters. They will assure you that the place is destined to be another Chicago. But reflect a moment and ask yourself what is the groundwork, present or future, upon which this growth is likely to be built. Will industries come and why? Will commerce develop and for what reason? Will the surrounding area do economic homage to the place in time? These questions will usually answer themselves. A small community, remote from the highways of maritime commerce, with-

[1] See *below*, Chapter xxiv.

THE CITY AS A PROBLEM IN GOVERNMENT 13

out mineral resources close at hand, not a political capital or an educational center and not likely to be—such a place may dream of a great urban future but it is only a dream. "We have a wonderful future here," declaims the orator at rotary club luncheons amid loud applause, but post-prandial rhetoric is perhaps the least among all the factors which help to make a city great.

At any rate the city has become a very important factor in the national life and seems destined to become an even bigger one. But if asked to frame a definition of the city how would you do it? Offhand one might say that it is a large body of people living in a relatively small area. That, however, would be a very inadequate definition, for it would convey no intimation of the fact that the city has a peculiar legal status, a distinct governmental organization, a highly complicated economic structure, and a host of special problems which do not arise when an equal number of people live less compactly together. A comprehensive definition of the modern city must indicate that it is a legal, political, economic, and social unit all rolled into one. It is a large body of people, possessing some striking social characteristics, massed in a small area, chartered as a municipal corporation, having its own local government, carrying on various economic enterprises, and busily engaged in trying to solve the multifarious problems which its own crowded life puts upon it. The modern city is a many-sided thing. It affords a field of study for the jurist, the political scientist, the economist, the sociologist, and the engineer. Problems of law, government, finance, health, transportation, social welfare, and education come persistently forward every day in the year. No man, though he devote his whole life to the task, can hope to master them all. Let us look for a moment at some of the different phases of municipal organization and life. *The varied aspects of the modern city.*

First of all, the city is a corporation at law, a municipal corporation as we call it. It is endowed with an artificial personality. It may sue and be sued, hold property, make contracts, and do in its corporate capacity most of the things that a natural person or individual may do. It employs officials or agents, and in some cases assumes legal liability for what these employees do. In other cases it is immune from such liability.[1] The city, as a municipal corporation, may levy taxes, and the *1. Legal.*

---
[1] For a discussion of municipal liability see *below*, Chapter vi.

power to tax is the most far-reaching power that a corporation can possess. It has power to borrow money, and to give in pledge the private property of its citizens. The bonded indebtedness of a city constitutes in effect a first mortgage on every piece of property within its boundaries, no matter by whomsoever owned. It has the right of eminent domain, the right to take private property for public use, against the will of the owner, on payment of just compensation. All these things the city can do, and does, in its capacity as a municipal corporation at law. A study of such legal powers and their exercise is what chiefly interests the lawyer.

2. Political. Second, the city is a unit of government. It is an agency which the state uses, as a matter of convenience, for the better government of its people. A city may be older than the state in which it is located, but it is the creature of the state nevertheless. New York City is nearly a hundred years older than New York State, yet the subordination of the metropolis to the larger entity is beyond dispute. The state endows the city with a charter, which is its warrant for existence. It may permit the people of the city to frame their own charter, as some states do; but the state retains the ultimate power, control, and responsibility. No city in the United States has a charter which the higher authorities cannot revoke or take away.[1] The city is the agent of the state, holding a delegated authority to perform certain governmental functions on the state's behalf, and for the sole reason that these functions can be more conveniently performed by the municipality than by the state itself.

In order to carry on the work thus delegated to it by the state, the city is provided with a frame of government. It has a mayor and council, or an elective commission, or a council and city manager. It has a variety of administrative boards and appointive officials, likewise a large number of subordinate municipal employees. The duties of these various authorities are prescribed by the city charter, or by the general statutes of the state, or by municipal ordinances. There is a city electorate which nominates and elects the higher officials, and these in turn appoint the lower ones. This mechanism, which is sometimes very elaborate, constitutes the city government. A study

[1] In some cases, however, such action would involve amending the state constitution.

THE CITY AS A PROBLEM IN GOVERNMENT 15

of these powers, functions, relations, and personalities is what chiefly interests political scientists.

But the city is much more than a political division of the commonwealth. It is more than a governmental agency. Its competence extends beyond the making of ordinances, the levying of taxes, and the maintenance of law and order. The modern city is an agency of economic enterprise, engaged in work which is by no means strictly governmental in its nature. It is a purveyor of water (and sometimes of gas, electricity, and transportation), an employer of labor, a purchaser of supplies and materials, a seller of service. Much of what the modern city does is business, not government.[1] It consists in providing services which would be furnished by private enterprise were it not that the municipality, for one reason or another, has seen fit to assume the task. It is work that ought to be performed in strict compliance with business principles, but usually it cannot be so performed because it is vested in the hands of authorities who are under the continuous pressure of political influences. Thus economic and political considerations frequently come into conflict, and when they do the latter often get the best of it.

3. Economic.

Nor is this all. The city government comes into contact with many economic organizations and enterprises which it does not directly control. It deals not only with its own municipal water service but with privately-owned gas and electric plants, street railways, bus lines, and telephone companies. It has dealings with banks and other financial institutions, for it is a large collector, depositor, spender, and borrower of money. It enters into relations with contractors and others for all sorts of work or service. It regulates, by licensing or otherwise, a long category of trades and vocations. These things give the city, as a unit of government, a considerable rôle in the economic life of the community, and the student of economics finds interest in this phase of its activity.

Finally the city is an agency for the promotion of the social welfare. Its officials are engaged not only in governmental and economic enterprises but in work of social amelioration as well. They provide from the public taxes free education, health protection, poor relief, and public recreation. More than one-third of the average city's annual expenditures is now devoted to

4. Social.

[1] See *below*, Chapter xvii.

these social welfare undertakings, including the public schools. Indirectly, of course, these things have an economic significance, but they are not of the nature of business enterprises. They cannot be conducted according to business principles as the private industrialist understands them. Nor, on the other hand, should they be subjected to the sinister influences of politics. Together they form a phase of the city's work which broader considerations than those of either business or politics ought to dominate. This is a matter of importance because the social or welfare activities of the city are expanding rapidly year by year. There is everywhere an insatiable demand that the city shall do more for its people along lines of education, philanthropy, health protection, recreation, and amusement. We are steadily transferring responsibilities from the home to the school, to the public playground, to the neighborhood house, or to the civic center. You will find on the payroll of some municipalities today a "city mother," whose duty it is to look after the welfare of youngsters whose parents are not properly attending to it! Thus have we passed the stage of paternalism and are moving to maternalism in the work which the city is being asked to perform. There is no forecasting where this absorption of new welfare activities will ultimately lead the municipality. Certain it is, in any event, that we must look for an uninterrupted expansion of the city's work in this field, for the crowding of people into great centers is bound to bring social responsibilities which cannot be evaded. A great throbbing wen of human beings, in which common needs demand satisfaction by means of social effort and control—that is the city as the sociologist sees it.

Summary. In summary, then, the modern city is not merely a problem in government (using the term in its ordinary sense), but a problem in law, in economics, and in sociology. That is why its solution presents so many difficulties. Often the municipality would do its work of government more satisfactorily were it not limited by the range of its powers at law. It could better preserve the integrity of its politics were it not that economic considerations (often of a sinister sort) tend to break this integrity down. When a city operates its own gas or electric plant, the political authorities are under steadfast pressure from the employees and their friends. When it does not own them, a private company will sometimes supply temptations which the municipal authori-

THE CITY AS A PROBLEM IN GOVERNMENT 17

ties find equal difficulty in resisting. And as for the welfare enterprises, with their considerable range of patronage, they have virtually no objective tests of efficiency. How can we tell whether a city is getting full value for the money that it spends on public recreation? It is largely a matter of individual opinion. In determining municipal policy it often happens that political, economic, and social motives do not run parallel but at opposing angles. Sound principles of economics or of social ethics seem to advise one course, while considerations of practical politics dictate something altogether different. It is this conflict of motives and of pressure that makes the whole problem of city government so difficult.

The failure of the American people to achieve a greater degree of success in the government of large cities is not due to political incompetence or apathy. It is partly accounted for by the inherent difficulties of the problem. No cities in the world are so hard to govern efficiently as are the cities of the United States. Yet even with proper allowance for all this there has been more urban misgovernment in America than we have had a right to expect. The reasons for this are not altogether clear, and they have been widely misunderstood. Why have we made so poor a showing in this field of government? If you ask the ordinary citizen this question, he will usually give you some explanations that do not explain. He will probably assert (if he be himself a native American) that municipal misgovernment in the United States has been largely due to the presence of great masses of foreign population in the cities. This concentration of foreigners, he will argue, has demoralized the quality of the electorate and has given the self-seeking politicians their opportunity to get control. *[Why have we not done better in governing our cities?]*

Much has been written about the way in which the foreign-born voters allow themselves to be hoodwinked by demagogues, and some of it is true. It is beyond denial that foreign-born voters (and native-born also) have sometimes permitted themselves to be misled by the sophistry of politicians. But the inadequacy of this explanation is shown by the fact that those American cities which contain the largest proportion of foreign-born voters are not the ones which have been most steadily misgoverned. Chicago, on the whole, has not been worse governed than Philadelphia. Boston does not suffer in comparison with *[Is the alien voter to blame?]*

Baltimore. Cleveland need pay no homage to Los Angeles as respects the efficiency of city government. There has been plenty of corruption and inefficiency in cities where the electorate is largely made up of native-born Americans. It is easy to cast the blame on the newcomers, but a careful study of the political situation in cities throughout the United States does not indicate that they are in any large measure entitled to it.

Has municipal misgovernment been due to the very rapid growth of our cities?

Again, it is sometimes asserted that American cities have been unable to maintain high standards of municipal administration because of their rapid growth. Our cities are growing so fast, we are told, that government has not been able to keep pace with the problems which this rapid expansion brings with it. In a whirl of growth and prosperity things have to be done hastily, without careful planning. The result is that they are done poorly and wastefully. To a certain extent this has been the case in parts of the country where the increase of urban population during the past fifty years has been phenomenal. It has necessitated a huge outpouring of public funds for new streets and public buildings, for water supply, sewerage systems, parks, and all the rest. But here again we come face to face with the awkward fact that the most rapidly-growing cities have not been more wasteful or more corruptly administered than the slow-growing or stagnant ones. Cities like Detroit, Cleveland, and Los Angeles have grown much more rapidly during the past fifteen years than Baltimore, Boston, and Philadelphia, for example; but there is no ground for the assertion that their public affairs have been less competently handled. Rapidity of growth does not seem to be in itself a cause of civic deterioration. On the contrary, it seems to inspire the people to higher ideals and better standards. Some of the best-governed American cities have been expanding by leaps and bounds during the past two decades, while some of the worst-governed have been moving ahead very slowly or not moving at all.

The real source of the trouble.

What, then, is the true reason for the failure of American cities to maintain standards of government equal to those of the nation and the states? One may hazard the suggestion that clumsiness of governmental machinery has had something to do with it. Most American cities have had too much governmental apparatus. Mayors, aldermen, councilors, commissioners, members of boards, and heads of departments have created a

THE CITY AS A PROBLEM IN GOVERNMENT 19

network in which they have themselves become hopelessly entangled. There has been too much division of power and too little concentration of responsibility. The ordinary citizen, when things have gone wrong, has not known where to place the blame. He has had a long ballot placed in his hands, and he has had to vote it blindly because there have been too many offices to be filled and too many candidates. In order to control any government the voters must first be able to understand it; they must know what functions they are electing officials to perform. This, in many instances, they have not known. The voter has been blamed for perverseness, or for indifference, when the real fault has lain in our not giving him a fair chance. There are very few people who consciously choose to be misgoverned. But there are a great many who can be baffled into making that choice.

City government in the United States has been considerably improved during the past twenty-five years by simplifying it, by reducing the number of elective officials, by defining more exactly the powers of the various officers, and by shortening the ballot. In these ways the voters have been enabled to place the responsibility for misgovernment where it belongs. These improvements point the way to still better things. What we need is to keep on making city government more simple in its mechanism, more intelligible to the ordinary voter, and hence more truly responsible to the people. The cure for the ills of democracy is not more democracy (as we sometimes are told), but a better-functioning democracy with fewer complications.

REFERENCES

The subject dealt with in the foregoing chapter is touched upon in many books. On the forces which have promoted the growth of cities the best discussions are in Henri Pirenne's *Mediæval Cities* (Princeton, 1925); A. F. Weber's *Growth of Cities in the Nineteenth Century* (New York, 1909), Chapter iii; N. S. B. Gras's *Introduction to Economic History* (New York, 1922); Graham R. Taylor's *Satellite Cities* (New York, 1915), and in the volume by R. Pearl and L. J. Reed on the *Predicted Growth of Population of New York and Its Environs* (New York, 1923). Mention should also be made of Pierre Clerget's "Urbanism: A Historic, Geographic, and Economic Study," in the Annual Report of the Smithsonian Institution for 1912, *passim*. Karl Bücher's *Industrial Revolution* (translated by S. Morley Wickett, New York,

1901) deals with the relation of the modern city to industry. Many other references may be found in the bibliography (by Louis Wirth) which is appended to the book on *The City* by R. E. Park, E. W. Burgess, and R. D. McKenzie (Chicago, 1925). Attention should be called to the discussion of "Urban Life and Modern Civilization" by Eugene McQuillin, and of "The City as It Is and as it Might Be" by Frederic Harrison, both of which are reprinted in Joseph Wright's *Selected Readings in Municipal Problems* (Boston, 1925), pp. 934-950. There are chapters on the city as a governmental problem in William Anderson's *American City Government* (New York, 1925), pp. 3-17; in Chester C. Maxey's *Outline of Municipal Government* (New York, 1924), pp. 1-13, and in the same author's *Readings in Municipal Government*, pp. 1-8. See also the references at the close of Chapter iii (*below*, p. 70).

CHAPTER II

AMERICAN MUNICIPAL DEVELOPMENT

To understand the American city of today, one must know something about the American city of yesterday, for its present organization owes a good deal to the past. The American system of municipal government did not originate in America; it was borrowed from England and has been gradually changed through the process of adaptation in a new environment. This series of adaptations has now covered a period of nearly two hundred and fifty years, a period which has been prolific in municipal experiments of every sort. Step by step the cities of the United States have departed from the English governmental pattern until the external resemblances are now very slight indeed. This process of almost unceasing change has made America the world's principal laboratory of experimentation in municipal government. There are very few governmental devices which have not been given a trial by some city of the United States during the past seventy-five years. This stands in marked contrast with the countries of Europe, where relatively few changes in the general frame of municipal government have taken place during the past three quarters of a century. The cities of Great Britain, France, Germany, and Italy are today governed by much the same mechanism that they possessed in 1850; in the United States the changes that have taken place during the interim amount to a virtual revolution. Nevertheless there are some features of the American municipal system that have remained substantially unaltered, and there are certain traditions which have become established, hence it is well that these be explained before any attempt is made to deal with the American city of today. *The significance of municipal history.*

The beginnings of the American municipal system are to be found in the incorporation of the colonial boroughs during the latter half of the seventeenth century. In this New York was the pioneer, receiving its first city charter from Governor Dongan *Boroughs of the colonial era.*

in 1686.[1] Albany followed a few months later in the same year, its first charter being substantially the same as that granted to New York. Both charters continued in force until the revolution. Other rising colonial towns received similar recognition in due course,—Philadelphia in 1691, Annapolis in 1696, Norfolk in 1736, Richmond in 1742, and Trenton, the last of the colonial list, in 1746. A dozen others of less importance, scattered through the middle and southern colonies, also obtained their charters during this interval. There were no active chartered boroughs in the New England colonies, for there the system of town government seemed to be sufficient and satisfactory. In Massachusetts no city charter was granted prior to the Boston charter of 1822, and this change was made only because the community had become too populous to be any longer governed as a town, not because new corporate powers were needed; [2] for the New England town had, without any specific grant, substantially all the powers and privileges that a borough charter could confer. The town required no charter to give it powers, and desired none to set limitations upon local freedom. Hence it did not want to be a city.

From first to last the governors of the thirteen colonies gave charters to twenty boroughs, or cities, as some places were called

[1] A burgher government, after the model of that maintained in the free cities of Holland, had been established by Governor Stuyvesant in 1656; but in 1665 the town passed into English hands and the government was changed to that of an English municipal corporation, although no formal charter was issued. The burgomaster and schepens of New Amsterdam gave place to the mayor, aldermen and common councillors of New York. Dongan granted a regular charter in 1686 at the request of the mayor and aldermen. This charter, which in its printed form covers only fourteen pages, is still preserved in the archives of the comptroller in New York City. A copy may be found in the *Colonial Laws of New York* (5 vols., New York, 1897), I, 181. Its provisions are summarized in A. E. Peterson's *New York as an Eighteenth Century Municipality Prior to 731* (New York, 1917), pp. 14-19. Some doubts having arisen as to the validity of this charter, it was reissued under the royal seal in 1730. This confirmation, which made no very important changes, is commonly known as the Montgomery charter.

[2] The population of Boston in 1822 had passed the 40,000 mark, and the qualified voters numbered about 7,000. "When a town-meeting was held on any exciting subject in Fanueil Hall, those only who obtained places near the moderator could even hear the discussion. A few busy or interested individuals easily obtained the management of the most important affairs, in an assembly in which the greater number could have neither voice nor hearing. When the subject was not generally exciting, town-meetings were usually composed of the selectmen, the town-officers, and thirty or forty inhabitants."—Joseph Quincy, *Municipal History of Boston* (Boston, 1852), 28.

AMERICAN MUNICIPAL DEVELOPMENT

from the outset.[1] Fifteen of these were towns of considerable importance. It will be noticed that the charters were given by the governors and not by the colonial legislatures, a local adaptation of the practice existing in England, where the incorporation of boroughs was always made by royal grant rather than by act of parliament. The governor acted upon the request of the inhabitants, and the charters were sometimes submitted to the latter for their acceptance before being put into operation.

<small>Charters before the Revolution.</small>

There is no evidence that the people of any colonial town ever had a borough charter forced upon them by the governor against their own desires. In the drafting of these charters no single model was followed. In general, however, all the boroughs were provided with a frame of government which approximated that of the English municipal corporation in the days before the era of reform. In each case provision was made for a governing body, to which were given the corporate powers of the community. This governing body, usually styled "the mayor, aldermen, and commonalty" of the borough, consisted of a single council made up of a mayor, a small number of aldermen, and a larger number of councilmen, all sitting together. Except in the three close corporations, Annapolis, Norfolk, and Philadelphia, the councilmen were chosen at regular intervals by the freemen or freeholders of the town, and so were the aldermen as a rule; but the mayor was usually named by the governor of the colony. There were, in addition, some other borough officers, such as the recorder and the treasurer. None of these had any burdensome administrative tasks to perform, for the boroughs were small and provided for their inhabitants no public services of much account.

New York, two hundred years ago, had only about 8000 inhabitants. Boston, from its foundation in 1630 until after the middle of the eighteenth century, was the most populous community in the new world. Philadelphia then took the lead, and retained it till after the Revolution. On the eve of the revolutionary war there were only five cities and towns with populations exceeding 8000, and the combined strength of these was less than 100,000.[2] When it is remembered that these five places contained less than three per cent of the total population

---

[1] The list, with dates of grant and details, may be found in J. A. Fairlie's *Essays in Municipal Administration* (New York, 1908), Chapter iv.
[2] Philadelphia, New York, Boston, Charleston, and Newport.

of the thirteen colonies, the large part which their citizens took in the military and political events of the war period becomes the more remarkable. Even at this time the urban population was doing more than its proportionate share in moulding the course of national development.

New York as a colonial borough. How was New York governed two centuries ago? In 1726 it had a mayor, recorder, aldermen and assistants who exercised the corporate powers of the city. The mayor and the recorder were appointed by the governor; the others were elected by the voters of the six city wards. All sat together as a common council. The common council made "the laws, ordinances, and constitutions" of the city and appropriated from the municipal revenues such money as was needed for current expenses. The entire revenue, however, was less than four thousand dollars per year. Virtually all of it came from fees and tolls, for the city charter gave the common council no power to levy taxes. The annual cost of city government was only fifty cents per capita in these days, for there were almost no municipal services calling for the expenditure of money. Only a few streets were paved—and these with stone flags or cobble stones. There was no system of public street-cleaning, or street lighting. There was no public water supply and no public sewers. There was no regular police system and nothing but a volunteer bucket brigade to afford protection against fire. The common council made some regulations, chiefly with reference to the use of the markets and the keeping of the peace; its mayor and aldermen held court when necessary; they also appointed various subordinate officers such as constables, surveyors, beadles and billmen, most of whom were unpaid. Beyond this they did little for the inhabitants.

Summary. In a few sentences the salient features of American municipal government during the colonial period may be summed up as follows: About twenty places, all of them small, were chartered as boroughs or cities. The charters came from the governors but the right to levy taxes had to be obtained from the colonial legislatures which were very niggardly about granting such power. In general the charters were modelled upon those of the English boroughs of the period. They established in each case a municipal corporation and vested the powers of the corporation in a common council, made up of a mayor, recorder, aldermen and assistants (or councillors) sitting together. The mayor and recorder were appointed. The aldermen and councillors were elected, in most cases, by the freeholders of the town. The council had very little revenue and even in the most important boroughs provided no public services of much consequence. There were numerous minor officials, as in a New England town of today; but their duties were relatively unimportant. All in all, we find a somewhat complex frame of government performing very few and simple functions.

Then came the breach with England, ushering in the second period of American municipal development. The successful outcome of the revolution and the adoption of the new state constitutions served to bring about great changes in both the form and the spirit of government. Municipal charters were henceforth granted, not by the governor alone, but by the state legislature. In other words, the city charter became a statute, which might be amended or repealed like any other statute. This involved a radical change in the relation existing between the city and the state. Under their colonial charters the boroughs had enjoyed almost entire freedom from legislative interference; under the new dispensation they went completely under the domination of the state legislature. This change in status ought to have special emphasis, for it is of great importance. Prior to the revolution no charter was imposed on any town against the desires of its inhabitants. But after the revolution the state legislatures were free to do in this matter as they pleased. Municipal home rule did not come in with the revolution but went out with it.

Some of the boroughs that had received charters before 1775 now abandoned them and received new grants from the legislatures of their respective states. These new municipal constitutions differed considerably from the old ones. The old idea of the borough as a "close corporation" was discarded, for instance, and the new order rested upon the idea that admission to citizenship should be made easy. Nevertheless the new charter of Philadelphia, issued in 1789, indicated that no sweeping changes in the old system were deemed essential.[1] By the provisions of

Effects of the revolution.

The new charters.

---

[1] The charter of 1789 is printed in *Laws of the Commonwealth of Pennsylvania* (ed. A. J. Dallas, 2 vols., Philadelphia, 1793-1797). A summary of its provisions is given by E. P. Allison and Boies Penrose, *History of Philadelphia* (Philadelphia, 1887), 60-62.

this charter the government of the city continued to be vested in the hands of the mayor, aldermen, and common councillors, sitting together in one body. Fifteen aldermen were to be elected for a seven-year term by the owners of freehold property, and thirty councillors were to be chosen for a three-year term by the "freemen." Aldermen and councillors were to sit together. The mayor was to be chosen by the aldermen from among their own number, his post to be no more than that of a presiding officer. Such officials as might from time to time be found necessary were to be chosen by the council.

Departures from the old pattern.

Before long, however, the charters of other cities began to show a greater tendency to depart from the old pattern. One reason for this may be found in the influence of the federal analogy—in other words, the influence of those ideas which had been embodied in the federal constitution of 1787. The new national government started on a wave of enthusiasm and national prosperity. Its principles rapidly gained a hold on the imagination of the people, and it was natural that these principles should gradually have worked their way into state constitutions and city charters. More especially the principle of division of powers, of checks and balances, now became gradually influential upon the framers of city charters.

The Baltimore charter of 1797.

The first clear indication of this appeared in the Baltimore charter of 1797 which provided for a mayor and a bicameral city council. The lower branch of this council was to be composed of two members elected annually from each of the eight city wards; the upper branch was to contain one member from each of these wards. The mayor was to be chosen by an electoral college, the members of which were to be separately elected by the voters of each ward. This was a very striking illustration of the attempt to make the charter a reproduction in miniature of the national constitution. So, likewise, was the provision that resolutions of the council should be subject to the mayor's veto but might be repassed by a two thirds vote.

A new model that was not at once copied.

Other cities, for the moment, made no haste to follow the Baltimore example. Several important charters were issued during the early years of the nineteenth century but in none of them was the influence of the federal analogy made so clear. Nevertheless, as the national government grew stronger and gained a firmer hold upon the confidence of the people, the acceptance of

AMERICAN MUNICIPAL DEVELOPMENT

its basic principles became almost universal. The doctrine of checks and balances was looked upon as gospel. Men did not stop to enquire whether an idea that was sound in its application to the national government would be equally applicable to the states or the cities. They tacitly assumed that if checks and balances were good in one branch of government they must be good in all. At any rate the doctrine that legislative and executive powers ought to be kept separate gradually gained converts and recognition; it became an "American political principle" (although it was as old as Aristotle); and ultimately it determined the main channels of governmental development in the states and the cities alike. The independent mayor, the double-chambered city council, the confirmation of appointments, and the executive veto—all of these features in city government were the progeny of the national constitution. The men who sat in the convention of 1787 at Philadelphia were making city charters as well as a national constitution, although they did not realize it.

During the fifty years which followed the close of the revolutionary war the cities of the United States did not grow with great rapidity. In 1770, as has been said, there were six cities and towns of more than 8000 population; in 1820 there were only thirteen. But some of these municipalities were forging ahead at great speed. New York, for example, had passed the 150,000 mark, quite outstripping Boston and Philadelphia which had larger populations a half century before. Virtually all of these thirteen urban centers were on the Atlantic seaboard. They owed their early prosperity to trade, and not to industry, for very little industrial development took place before 1820. In the main they were markets where the products of the soil were exchanged for manufactured goods brought in from Europe. *City growth from 1770 to 1820.*

After 1820, however, the growth of the cities was greatly accelerated. Immigrants now began to flock in from Europe. The building of canals and turnpikes stimulated internal trade. Factories commenced to hum in the older sections of the country. The opening of the new west contributed to the general prosperity. The thirteen cities of over 8000 population increased to forty-four in 1840 and the largest ones were now comparable with the great urban centers of Europe. New York, at the close of "the roaring forties," had passed the half-million mark. These were boom years in the young Republic, with new towns springing into *From 1820 to 1840.*

existence as the frontier passed. Chicago had less than 5000 inhabitants in 1840, but this figure rose above 100,000 before the Civil War began.

<small>Important changes in the municipal system:
1. The elective mayor.</small>

During these first five or six decades of the national era several new and important developments took place in the American municipal system. First of all, the mayors became elective. During the colonial era, and for a time thereafter, they had been appointed by the governor. Then it became the practice to have them selected by the city council, usually from among its own members. But the Boston and St. Louis charters of 1822 provided that the mayor should be elected by direct popular vote, and the Detroit charter of 1824 contained a similar provision. One by one the other cities followed suit until the elective mayoralty became general.[1]

<small>Significance of this change.</small>

This change in the method of selecting the mayor was not made the occasion for any substantial increase in the powers of the chief municipal executive. Neither the Boston nor St. Louis charters gave the mayor any authority to appoint city officials, nor did they bestow upon him the right to veto acts of the council. But in giving the mayor the function of presiding at council meetings, and of appointing all its committees, these charters paved the way for the exercise of strong mayoral influence on administration. This was made clear by Josiah Quincy, the second mayor of Boston, who managed to become the dominant factor in every branch of the city's work by appointing himself chairman of all the important council committees.[2] Being elected by the people, and responsible to them alone, the mayor now occupied a strategic position. Josiah Quincy was merely the first to make use of its possibilities: he was a utilizer of things present and a prophet of things to come. A further significant step in the direction of making the mayor a co-ordinate branch of city government was taken when New

---

[1] Philadelphia in 1826, Baltimore in 1833, New York in 1834. From 1821 to 1834 the mayor of New York was chosen by the city council.

[2] This action drew much criticism upon Mayor Quincy's shoulders. "The mayor assumes too much himself," declared his critics. "He places himself at the head of all committees. He prepares all reports. He permits nothing to be done but by his own agency. He does not sit solemn and dignified in his chair, and leave general superintendence to others; but he is everywhere and about everything,—in the street, at the docks, among the common sewers;—no place but what is vexed by his presence." Three Quincy's were mayors of Boston during the nineteenth century, father, son, and great-grandson.

AMERICAN MUNICIPAL DEVELOPMENT

York City definitely gave him the veto power. One by one other cities did likewise.

A second development which had its beginning during this period was the popular election of administrative officials other than the mayor. Everywhere, down to about 1824, these officials (assessors, collectors of taxes, constables and so on) had been chosen by the council. The Detroit charter of 1824 provided for their election by popular vote. Other cities were slow to follow this precedent and for some years the council managed, throughout the country, to retain its appointing power. The rising tide of democracy, however, gradually undermined this plan, especially in the newer cities which sprang up west of the Alleghenies. There was a feeling that administration ought to be kept close to the people by giving the voters direct control over the election of all their local officers.

2. The election of administrative officers.

The widening of the suffrage is the third feature of the period. There is widespread popular impression in the United States that manhood suffrage came into vogue throughout the country on the heels of the Revolution. Had the actions of the Fathers been as revolutionary as their theories this doubtless would have been the case; but in no one of the thirteen states were the pronouncements of the Declaration carried to their logical conclusion. Restrictions upon the suffrage continued to exist in nearly all the states until the nineteenth century was well under way.[1] During the Jacksonian era, however, a movement for the abolition of all restrictions upon manhood suffrage gained great momentum and most of the barriers were speedily broken down. In the new Chicago charter of 1837, for example, the taxpaying qualification was reduced to three dollars, and in 1841 it was abolished altogether.

3. The extension of the suffrage.

Finally, the spoils system made its *début* in local politics at

---

[1] In some the requirement was that voters should own at least fifty acres of land or an equivalent amount of property in some tangible form. In others the suffrage was confined to taxpayers. These requirements applied to municipal and state elections alike. Within a decade after the close of the Revolution one or two states abandoned the property requirements and admitted all taxpayers to voting rights. Vermont, which came into the Union in 1791, was the first state to establish full manhood suffrage; Kentucky and New Hampshire followed during the next year. Other states were created in the ensuing three decades but not all of them were ready to go so far. The anti-suffragists of these days waged a bitter struggle, hard-fought all the way. It has been estimated that not more than twenty per cent of the adult male population of the cities possessed voting rights in 1830.

30 THE GOVERNMENT OF AMERICAN CITIES

4. Rise of the spoils system.

this stage of American municipal development. Commonly attributed to Andrew Jackson, the introduction of party patronage was in reality an older feature of American political life. Jackson and his friends merely called it by its right name and avowed their allegiance to it openly. In the cities the practice of appointing to office men who had rendered party service, and of displacing from office men who had incurred the antagonism of the political leaders—these practices far antedated Jackson's first term. As early as 1816 the spoils system was flourishing in New York City.[1] The power to appoint municipal officers rested for the most part with boards of aldermen everywhere, although in a few cities some of the higher administrative officials were chosen by direct popular vote. The aldermen acted, as a rule, on the recommendation of an appointment committee which did its work on the principle that each ward should have a share of the patronage. City elections were fought out on straight lines, with no distinction between local and national issues. The New York municipal election of 1831 was waged entirely upon the issue of Andrew Jackson's popularity. Tammany capitalized this popularity and won. Elections in most of the cities were held annually and overturns were frequent. This, combined with the current notion that there should be rotation in office, took away all chance of stability in local administration. Rarely was any municipal officer permitted to remain at his post long enough to develop an adequate acquaintance with his duties.

Summary

These four features, namely, the elective mayor, the election of other administrative officials, the extension of the suffrage, and the genesis of the spoils system, gave American city government some dominant characteristics which it retained throughout the remainder of the nineteenth century. They charted the course for the next fifty years. By 1840 there had been a complete departure from the old colonial traditions, and even from the system of borough government which had existed during the years immediately following the Revolution. The cities had definitely committed themselves to the system of checks and balances, the fusion of state and city politics, and the spoils system—three distinctively American contributions to the art of government.

The Civil War, while it lasted, naturally placed a damper upon

---

[1] Gustavus Myers, *History of Tammany Hall* (2d ed., New York, 1917), pp. 37-38.

city growth, although it was not so much of a handicap as might have been expected. The stream of immigration from abroad became smaller than it doubtless would have been; yet the immigration was larger in 1863 than in any of the years immediately preceding the war. Sea-borne commerce declined, but most of the factories kept working at full speed. The clash of arms did not reach far into the regions of industry. Industrially the North was more active and more prosperous than ever before; the output of raw material from the farms, the mines, and the forests was unusual; the growth of manufacturing and transportation was extraordinary; all departments of economic enterprise were speeded up.[1] With the exception of the cotton mills, which found great difficulties in obtaining raw material, the factories everywhere increased their production. Woolen goods, boots and shoes, agricultural machinery, hardware, as well as munitions of war, were in great demand. The progress of the woolen mills, many of them located in New England and New York, was especially remarkable; their output more than doubled during the years 1861-1865. On the other hand, the great conflict, along with the vicissitudes of reconstruction, greatly impeded the progress of cities in the South.

Effects of the Civil War on city growth.

With the end of the Civil War, moreover, conditions were ripe for an epoch of city growth such as the world had never seen. Great tracts of western land were open for settlement. The era of railroad building on a giant scale was just about to begin. The country had committed itself to the policy of protecting its industries by means of a high tariff. Scarcely a session passed but the duties were raised a notch higher. Prices were high; so were wages, and the high level of wages was bound to attract immigrants from Europe. Finally, the country was in an optimistic mood; it had survived a crucial test and had learned to do things in a big way. All this pointed to a great industrial boom, and the signs proved to be correct. The rapidity of the expansion during the eight years following the war was so great that it produced the inevitable reaction, and in 1873 the country found itself in the throes of a severe industrial crisis. But this setback was only for the moment. The march of

After the Civil War.

---

[1] See the abundant data on this point in E. D. Fite, *Social and Industrial Conditions in the North during the Civil War* (New York, 1910), especially pp. 78-104.

progress was soon renewed and with a few minor interruptions it outlasted the nineteenth century.

The Dark Ages, 1870-1900.

When cities grow too rapidly the progress of municipal institutions and services usually fails to keep pace. It was so in the United States during the second half of the nineteenth century and particularly so during the three decades which followed the Civil War. This was the era in which many of the large communities had their stiffest fight to overcome governmental inefficiency, to eradicate corruption in municipal office, and to secure a scheme of administration which would promote rather than retard the common progress. It was a prolonged battle and not until after 1900 did the ultimate outcome appear in sight. These years from 1870 to 1900 are the Dark Ages of American municipal history.

Important developments since 1870:

1. Rise of the independent administrative department.

Three important features mark the evolution of the municipal system during this period. The first was the rise of the independent administrative department. The city council, as has been pointed out, was the sole administrative authority provided for in the earlier charters. Its administrative functions were performed through various committees, one for each branch of the municipal service. This plan, so long as the cities were small, served well enough; but as they grew in size and presented more difficult problems of administration the committee system proved altogether too clumsy. The introduction of manhood suffrage lowered the caliber of the councilmen; the committees were appointed by a process of log-rolling; their main quest was for patronage in all its forms. In New York the committees spent much of their time "wrangling over appointments and cribbing at the public treasury."[1] The streets were an abomination of filth. Owing to the lack of sanitation and the inadequacy of the public water supply the city had several epidemics of cholera and typhoid. The general dissatisfaction with the committee system caused the New York charter of 1830 to provide that administrative business should be conducted, not by the council's own committees, but by independent officials and commissions.

New York's earlier experience in this field.

---

[1] These committee meetings, according to one chairman of the time, were made the occasion for "unreasonable and costly suppers at the city's expense." At these festivities, he continues, the committeemen consumed "such wines as they never in their lives tasted before; choice wines that cost $40 a dozen." Gustavus Myers, *History of Tammany Hall* (2d ed., New York, 1917), p. 69.

AMERICAN MUNICIPAL DEVELOPMENT 33

These officials and boards were to be appointed by the council, however, and hence were in a sense under the council's control. In 1849 the next step was taken by providing that they should be chosen by popular vote. In this way the divorce of administrative from legislative functions was gradually accomplished.

The example of New York in making this separation was presently followed by other cities. In Cleveland, owing to the failure of the council committees to keep pace with the need for public works, a board of public improvements was established by a charter amendment in 1852, this board being composed of the mayor, the city engineer and three elective commissioners. Thus the entire control of public works was withdrawn from the council and vested in an administrative board. The next forty years witnessed a great extension of this plan. Boards of public works, park commissioners, water boards, sewerage boards, lighting boards, and health were set up in cities all over the country. The members of these various bodies were in nearly all cases elected by popular vote for short terms. This development added greatly to the clumsiness of municipal organization; it parcelled the administrative responsibilities among many different authorities, and resulted in much friction among them. *Experience in other cities.*

The system of administration by elective boards was an improvement over its predecessor; but nowhere did it prove entirely satisfactory. Men who enjoyed popularity with the electorate, but who were altogether without administrative skill or experience, sought and obtained election to these various commissions. Once elected they used their official positions to serve personal ends. As the members of each board were usually elected at different times and often by different political parties, there was no cohesion, no unity within the board itself. Unable to agree on positive action it frequently wound up by doing nothing at all. The people of the cities were inclined to blame the mayor when things went wrong; but the mayor had no direct means of controlling officials whom he did not appoint and could not remove. After some costly experience along these lines, accordingly, the cities took the next logical step, namely, that of vesting the appointment of these officials in the mayor. They did this with some reluctance, for it seemed to be a stroke of counter-democracy, rendering the dependence of city administra- *Elective boards prove unsatisfactory.*

Supplanted by appointive boards.

tion upon the people less direct and immediate. And since it was regarded as dangerous to give the mayor the appointing power without placing any restraint upon him, the necessity of obtaining confirmation from the upper chamber of the city council was added as a measure of precaution.

It is difficult to fix any exact date for this transfer of power to the mayor. The tendency antedates the middle of the century, but the actual shifting of authority did not come until after 1850. New York City inaugurated the plan of mayoral appointments with confirmation in 1857, and here, again, the example of the metropolis was soon followed by other cities.[1] The concentration of control in the mayor's hands proved to be a distinct improvement; but the plan of aldermanic confirmation did not, on the whole, function to advantage. Brooklyn in 1882 was the first city to abolish this requirement—a bold stroke it was thought to be at the time. Few cities had the courage to follow Brooklyn's lead until the end of the nineteenth century. Thereafter they began to do it quite generally.

The balance of power shifts to the mayor.

By these successive steps, covering an interval of sixty years, the dominant influence over administrative affairs passed from the council to the mayor. The shift was due to many causes, but to two in particular. First was the failure of the council, either by its own committees or through its appointive boards, to provide honest or efficient public services. The second outstanding reason may be found in the influence of the federal analogy. In the national government the President appointed all the officers of administration and was responsible for their work. Why not a similar arrangement in the municipalities? The separation of administrative from legislative functions seemed to be, by reason of experience in the higher fields of government, a good principle to follow.

2. State interference in city affairs.

The subordination of the city to the state began with the winning of national independence; but state interference in city affairs was relatively infrequent until after 1850. It was tacitly assumed that although the legislature had power to intervene in local matters if it so desired, nevertheless it ought not to do so

[1] "Out of twelve representative cities five made some progress toward vesting the mayor with various measures of authority over appointments, and four of them vested in him either complete or partial supervisory powers over administration." R. M. Story, *The American Municipal Executive* (Urbana, 1918), pp. 30-31.

AMERICAN MUNICIPAL DEVELOPMENT 35

"except when requested by the municipality."[1] But as the cities grew, both in population and importance, they came face to face with problems which were not altogether local in scope. One city, for example, desired to bring its water supply from outside the city limits; another wanted to empty its sewage into some waterway which it did not control. Various cities in the same region sometimes depended for their lighting upon the same gas company; yet no one municipality could effectively control the rates or service. It often happened, moreover, that policing, fire protection, and other civic functions failed to keep pace with the growth of the cities. Finally, the temptation to dip its fingers into the rich patronage provided by municipal offices, contracts, and franchises was more than some of the legislators could resist. The spoils seemed too valuable to be left wholly to the local authorities. The legislators desired a share for themselves. For good reasons and bad, therefore, the practice of legislative intervention was gradually extended. *Reasons for it.*

It is not easy to designate the exact date at which this practice of unsolicited legislative interference in city affairs began; but there were several instances of it before the Civil War. In 1857 the legislature of New York abolished municipal control of police in New York City and established a metropolitan police district (comprising New York, Brooklyn and adjacent municipalities) which it placed in charge of a state board.[2] Three years later the Maryland legislature took over the police of Baltimore, and state control over the police of both St. Louis and Chicago followed soon thereafter. The police department was the first to feel the brunt of state control for two reasons, to wit, because it was the most inefficient among all the city departments and because it provided the largest amount of political patronage. The spoils system was now triumphant; the cities were strategic points in the struggle for patronage; hence to get them under control was a matter of great importance to the party leaders. *Some examples of drastic intervention.*

But the action of the states in withdrawing powers from the city did not make things much better. In some instances it made *The reaction against it.*

---

[1] A judge of one of the New York courts, in the course of a decision rendered in 1815, spoke of this as being "almost the invariable course of proceedings." Mayor, etc., of New York v. Ordrenan, 12 *John* (New York), 122, cited by H. L. McBain, *The Law and the Practice of Municipal Home Rule* (New York, 1916).

[2] A state park commission for New York City was also established in the same year.

them worse. State control, furthermore, was a constant source of irritation to the citizen. The current of public opinion on this point rose so strongly that a reaction was produced and most of the state commissions were abolished. New York took this step in 1870. To afford protection against undue state interference in local affairs some other states adopted the plan of framing constitutional provisions against it. As a rule these provisions merely stipulated that there should be no legislative interference in matters of purely municipal concern; but two states—Missouri and California—provided that the cities should have the right to make their own charters. Thus began the municipal home rule movement which eventually gained a strong footing in more than a dozen of the states.[1]

Some other features of the Dark Ages, 1870-1890. The twenty years following the close of the Civil War may be said to have marked the lowest point in the morale of American city government. The nefarious activities of the Tweed Ring and other plundering groups gave the impression that the cities of the United States were the worst governed in the world. Still these cities kept growing at a marvelous pace; the value of real estate mounted so rapidly that fortunes were often made in a few months. The people were so busy in the promotion of their own private interests that public affairs got scant attention save from the professional politicians. Everywhere the problem of securing good service at reasonable cost was met in a makeshift and haphazard way. No state of the Union had any fixed policy as respects its cities; every problem was dealt with in opportunist fashion as it arose. The municipal reform movements of this period were directed against individual abuses; reformers did not venture to urge a complete and thorough overhauling of the municipal system. Honest men in the larger communities were on the verge of giving up in despair. It seemed as if city government in the United States were destined to remain the conspicuous failure that Mr. Bryce had frankly avowed that it was.

The emergence into light. Toward the close of the nineteenth century, however, there were some gleams of light. The introduction of the civil service system in some of the larger municipalities began to have its effects. The plan of putting increased responsibility upon the mayor seemed to work to such advantage that nearly all the

[1] See *below*, pp. 80-82.

larger cities adopted it.[1] Placing large powers in the hands of the mayor did not ensure efficient departmental administration, but it at least provided a focus of responsibility when things went wrong. Moreover, it secured a better organization of the departments and a certain amount of team play among them. Some of the most flagrant evils in city administration now disappeared.

With all its persisting problems and its apparent inability to find solution for most of them, the American municipal system underwent noticeable improvement during the quarter-century preceding 1900. Some of the more flagrant abuses were greatly diminished, some of the lesser ills disappeared. From time to time during the period there were spasms of civic virtue. Public indignation in this or that large city would arise, shake off its wonted apathy, and turn a remiss administration out of office; then it would usually allow itself to be lulled into false security while the old régime gradually worked itself back into full operation. Reform movements encountered serious obstacles, for the public temper was not yet ready to brook any root-and-branch demolition of existing municipal institutions. Proposals for improvements had, accordingly, to reckon with an intense loyalty to the principle of division of powers in city government, and such of them as secured adoption were invariably inadequate to the desired ends. The cause of municipal reform suffered greatly in the public estimation through its frequent championship of halfway measures, which were put through with great expenditure of energy but which accomplished very little after their acceptance. To gain support for their proposals, reformers had to promise more civic improvement than their measures could ever achieve; and this constant discrepancy between prediction and performance brought a natural loss in public prestige.

An era of general improvements.

The latest period in the growth of the American municipal system, extending from about 1890 to the present time, has been in many ways the most important and the most interesting of all. It began with somewhat indistinct tremors of an awakening civic conscience. During the nineties, however, the old municipal framework suffered little impairment; for the assaults of reform were directed against particular features of it rather than against

The civic renaissance since 1890.

[1] Boston, for example, in 1885, and Cleveland in 1891.

its general principles of construction. The spoils system, for example, became a favorite target, and with excellent results. Soon after civil-service reform had proved its profitableness in national administration, the agitation for its extension to state and municipal appointments brought tangible results in New York and Massachusetts, the former state enacting its first civil-service law in 1883, and the latter in 1884. After an interval of about a decade three other states, Illinois, Wisconsin, and Indiana, followed in 1895. Since that date many of the other states have been added to the list, until at the present time about two-thirds of them have civil-service reform laws of one sort or another. In some instances the cities have secured legislation putting certain of their officials and employees under civil-service rules even before the policy has gained acceptance in the state administration. There are now very few municipalities of any considerable size in which civil-service reform has not gained some footing. It would be difficult to overestimate the beneficent political reaction which the introduction of the merit system, even upon a narrow scale, has exercised in American cities. Not all municipal abuses can be related to the vice of political patronage; but a great many of them are very closely connected with it, and it is certain that where patronage has been eliminated, or even restricted, some of the worst evils have disappeared.

1. Civil service reform.

Other improvements in municipal methods during the nineties deserve mention. One was a return to the early practice of holding state and city elections upon different dates, a procedure which made possible the divorce of local from state issues. This method was not followed by all the larger cities, however; for it always has to brave the opposition of party organizations, and its adoption necessarily involves considerable extra expense. The abolition of the two-chambered council, the reduction in size of the municipal legislature, the substitution of election at large for election by wards, the abolition of aldermanic checks upon the mayor's appointing power,—all these features gained favor in some cities prior to 1900.

2. Other reforms.

But the real renaissance in American city government has come during the last twenty-five years and may be said to have begun with the Galveston experiment of 1901, although somewhat connected with the general movement for the concentra-

3. The reconstruction of the municipal framework.

AMERICAN MUNICIPAL DEVELOPMENT 39

tion of power in the mayor. The genesis of government of commission and its remarkable growth in popularity throughout the United States are matters that will be discussed in a later chapter.[1] It ought to be emphasized at this point, however, that the advocates of the commission plan were the first group of municipal reformers to bring forth a proposal to abolish the traditional separation of legislative and administrative powers, and consequently the first to urge a complete reorganization, on a simplified basis, of the whole municipal framework. The plan spread rapidly and led people to re-examine the fundamentals of city government. Of itself the commission plan was not an unqualified success, but it paved the way for a still newer form of government, known as the commission-manager or city manager plan.

4. Reform in the electoral mechanism.

With the adoption of new charters, moreover, most cities have used the opportunity to make other organic changes. The introduction of the initiative, referendum and recall has accompanied these charter revisions in many parts of the country.[2] The open, direct, non-partisan primary as a means of putting candidates in nomination for municipal offices has also found its way into many of the charters. The abolition of party designations on the municipal ballot, the simplification and shortening of the ballots itself by reduction in the number of elective officers, the provision of new securities for fairness at elections,—all these reforms have made unparalleled headway during the past twenty-five years. Finally, some American cities are now experimenting with a system of proportional representation, the aim of which is to make the city council truly and proportionally representative of all elements in the electorate.

5. Administrative improvements.

Improvements in internal administration have gone hand in hand with these organic changes. The routine methods of city business have been vastly bettered. Improved budget procedure, better methods of municipal accounting and auditing, a closer scrutiny of all payments out of the municipal treasury, the elimination of padded payrolls, non-competitive contracts, and patronage purchases, the proper safeguarding of the city's interests in all dealings with public-service corporations,—these are

[1] See *below*, Chapter xvi.
[2] *Below*, Chapter x.
[3] *Below*, Chapter ix.

but a few examples of the progress toward greater efficiency and economy made by many of the cities of the United States within recent years.

6. Improvements in municipal services. Noteworthy improvements in both the scope and the efficiency of various municipal services have been made in the last two decades. In 1900 there was little or no public interest in city planning, or, indeed, in any of these later-day movements which have for their aim the æsthetic improvement of cities. Municipal works were undertaken with little regard to what had gone before, and with less regard to what was likely to come after. All this has changed, or is changing. So, too, there has been a great advance along the lines of municipal sanitation and care for the public health; arrangements for the protection of life and property have been better organized; and lighting and transportation systems have made more progress in efficiency during the last twenty years than they did in the preceding fifty.

7. And in the tone of public opinion. Finally, the civic conscience has been brought from apathy to activity, and the whole tone and temper of municipal life has been raised thereby. Public opinion in American cities is healthier today than it has been for three-quarters of a century; it will not tolerate doings which it freely condoned a generation ago. In the late eighties and early nineties it was in many large cities practically impossible to secure a fair election. Impersonation, repeating, intimidation, and kindred offences against the election laws were committed with impunity, in some cases with the aid or the connivance of the police officials of the municipality. All that has passed away, or nearly so. Organized crookedness in politics, as in business, has become unprofitable.

Where the credit belongs. Much of the credit for this improved tone in city affairs is due to the host of local organizations whose officers and members have labored unceasingly to leaven the whole electoral lump. The cause of municipal reform, like all reform causes, has produced its due quota of misguided zealots who would fain reap where they have not sown, and who, accordingly, have aimed to hurry the cities into righteousness without that preliminary education of the electorate which is the only safe foundation upon which to build. Yet, on the whole, the great majority of civic organizations, as a subsequent chapter is designed to show, have done their work patiently and to good ultimate end.

AMERICAN MUNICIPAL DEVELOPMENT 41

During the last decade, moreover, there has been more team play among the organizations, and a greater readiness to coördinate their various activities so that energy may not be wasted.

In point of city growth the last twenty-five years constitute the most remarkable period in American history. In 1900 the urban population of the United States formed 40.5 per cent of the whole; in 1910 it rose to 46.3 per cent, and in 1920 to 51.4 per cent. It should be explained, however, that these census percentages include as "urban population" all those who live in incorporated places, villages, towns, boroughs or cities of 2500 inhabitants or more. Whether this figure is too high or too low is a matter on which there may be differences of opinion; but it any case it is now (1926) a conservative statement that at least half the American people live under conditions that are more properly termed urban than rural. Great as the interests of agriculture still are, we have ceased to be a predominately agricultural country. In 1900 there were 19 cities with populations exceeding 200,000; in 1910 there were 28 and today there are 34. In 1900 there were 37 cities with more than 100,000 and 77 with over 50,000; in 1920 these numbers had risen to 68 and 144 respectively. Even more striking is the rate at which some individual cities have been expanding. During the decade 1910-1920 more than 90 American cities showed increases of population ranging from 100 per cent upward. Today we have about fifteen cities with over half a million people and if we take all our cities of over 25,000 the total number is nearly 300.

<small>City growth since 1900.</small>

All this seems to prove that the great urbanizing forces which made the nineteenth century the classic era of city expansion are still at work with undiminished vigor. The continued development of production on a large scale, the centripetal influence of steam power, the greater facilities which the large city gives to industry in the matter of transportation, the better opportunities that it offers for the profitable utilization of by-products, the elasticity of the labor market in urban centers, the advantages derivable from a considerable market close at hand,—all this is compelling the concentration of industries in the cities, and particularly in the larger cities. Time was when industries went where the water power happened to be placed by nature; but nowadays great industries are rarely, if ever, ready to sacrifice for the sake of this single feature the other great

<small>Prospects for the future.</small>

advantages offered by an urban location. It is the combination of cheap fuel for motive power, cheap labor, and cheap transportation which now determines the location and governs the growth of great cities.

<small>Will the drift to the cities continue?</small>
Is there no stopping this denuding of the rural districts? Is the village doomed in America as was the English village in Goldsmith's day? More than eighty per cent of the population of England is now massed in the cities; in the United States the pendulum has already passed the dead center, yet the exodus shows no sign of abating. The cry of "back to the land" has been raised from time to time but few there be that heed it. Some years ago it was freely predicted that the boom in city-building would collapse with the restriction of immigration. But the operations of the new immigration law have not slackened city growth to any noticeable extent, nor has national prohibition, despite some solemn warnings that it would. The cityward movement is an inevitable outcome of our economic and social organization; it will not be stemmed until this organization undergoes a radical change, and perhaps not even then. In Belgium, which is the most congested of all countries, cheap transportation has induced large bodies of urban workers to live in the country. But they remain city-dwellers to all intents, just as the Boston business man, who commutes to his home in Newton or Milton, remains a Bostonian in everything that counts. Country life will be improved, no doubt, and farming will become more profitable. The telephone, the radio, and the automobile have already softened the isolation of the countryside. Future inventions may do more to the same end. It is conceivable that the bucolic life will widen its appeal and draw more recruits from the crowded centers. A strange paradox it is that when a farmer makes his fortune he retires to live in a town; but when a townsman grows rich he finds pleasure in having a country home. At any rate there are possibilities which may serve somewhat to stem the hegira citywards, but there is no probability that it will succeed in turning the current the other way.

<small>How big can a city become?</small>
This being the case, one may well propound the query: Is there any limit to the size of a city? Most human groups, if they continue to grow, eventually reach a point where they slacken, then stop altogether, and finally fall off. Ancient philosophers looked upon the ideal city as one having not more

AMERICAN MUNICIPAL DEVELOPMENT

than 10,000 population. Today this figure is looked upon as the minimum and not the maximum of cityhood. For many centuries it seemed easy to prove, from the experience of Nineveh, Babylon, Carthage, and Rome that all leviathan cities were foredoomed to deflation, and when London and Paris began to reckon their populations by the hundreds of thousands, as they did in the latter part of the eighteenth century, the statisticians began to grow pessimistic.[1] But to no avail, for the cities kept growing at an accelerated pace. The metropolitan London of today has about eight times the maximum population of ancient Rome, yet London with all her bulk is far more manageable than Rome ever was. She is easier to govern and easier to keep supplied with food. It has been estimated that New York City, at the close of the twentieth century, will have about 15,000,000 people within her present boundaries and an equal number within the metropolitan area outside. Thirty million people in one urban area, or more than the entire population of the United States on the eve of the Civil War! Chicago, in the year 2000, should have seven or eight millions. In the United States as a whole there will probably be at least twenty cities with over a million inhabitants.

But all this assumes that economic progress will continue without serious interruption. A general breakdown of industry, commerce, transportation, and credit or a prolonged and exhausting war would interrupt the growth of both nation and cities, might even cause the population to decline. Cities are extremely sensitive to any reversal in the normal progress of industrial and commercial life. They feel the effects far more acutely than the rural districts do. Every student of history can recall how the discovery of America, and of the new all-water route to the Orient via the Cape of Good Hope gave the maritime cities of Italy a set-back from which it took them a long time to recover. There is a possibility that changes in the drift of trade may some day make history repeat itself in the new world. Certainly no one can affirm that all American cities have equal prospects

---

[1] The renowned English statistician, Sir William Petty, for example, calculated in 1686 that for reasons which he set forth in detail, London's population could not possibly go above 5,000,000. In the course of his figuring he demonstrated that a city of 5,000,000 would require 600,000 houses and thus cover a circle with a radius of about thirty-five miles. To supply such a place with food, he felt, would be virtually impossible. *Essays on Mankind and Political Arithmetic*, pp. 27-52.

44   THE GOVERNMENT OF AMERICAN CITIES

of future growth. Some will grow much more rapidly than others; some will fail to grow at all—it will largely depend upon the turns which industry and commerce may take. No wise man will venture predictions in this field.

REFERENCES

There is no monograph covering the history of city government in the United States, although one is much to be desired. The nearest approach to anything of the sort is the long introductory chapter on the rise and progress of municipal institutions (pp. 1-159) in the first volume of Eugene McQuillin's *Treatise on the Law of Municipal Corporations* (8 vols., Chicago, 1911-1913). Mention may also be made of the chapter on the "Development of American Municipal Organization" in T.-S. Chang's *History and Analysis of the Commission Plan*, etc. (Iowa City, 1918). Several numbers of the Johns Hopkins University Studies in Historical and Political Science deal with the development of municipal institutions in various sections of the country; among these mention may be made of Dr. Albert Shaw's *Local Government in Illinois* (1883); E. R. L. Gould's *Local Government in Pennsylvania* (1883), and W. P. Holcomb's *Pennsylvania Boroughs* (1886); E. W. Bemis's *Local Government in the South and Southwest* (1893); D. E. Spencer's *Local Government in Wisconsin* (1890) and D. F. Wilcox's *Municipal Government in Michigan and Ohio* (New York, 1896).

Much has also been written on the municipal history of the various larger American cities. Among these may be mentioned A. E. Peterson and G. W. Edwards, *New York as an Eighteenth Century Municipality* (2 vols., New York, 1917); J. G. Wilson, *Memorial History of the City of New York* (4 vols., New York, 1892-1893); Theodore Roosevelt, *New York* (New York, 1891); J. W. Leonard, *History of the City of New York, 1609-1909* (New York, 1910); A. T. Andreas, *History of Chicago* (3 vols., Chicago, 1885); S. E. Sparling, *Municipal History and Present Organization of the City of Chicago* (Madison, 1898); H. S. Grosser, *Chicago: a Review of its Governmental History* (Chicago, 1906); E. P. Allison and Boies Penrose, *History of Philadelphia* (Baltimore, 1887); University of Pennsylvania, Wharton School of Finance and Economics, *The City Government of Philadelphia* (Philadelphia, 1893); J. T. Scharf, *History of St. Louis* (2 vols., Philadelphia, 1883); Josiah Quincy, *Municipal History of Boston* (Boston, 1852); H. H. Sprague, *The City Government of Boston, its Rise and Development* (Boston, 1890); Nathan Matthews, *City Government of Boston* (Boston, 1895); J. H. Hollander, *Financial History of Baltimore* (Baltimore, 1899); Bernard Moses, *The Establishment of City Government in San*

Francisco (Baltimore, 1889); Charles Snavely, *History of the City Government of Cleveland* (Baltimore, 1902); C. C. Williamson, *The Finances of Cleveland* (New York, 1907); W. W. Howe, *Municipal History of New Orleans;* Clyde L. King, *The History of the Government of Denver* (Denver, 1911); L. M. Larson, *Financial and Administrative History of Milwaukee* (Madison, 1908); and W. B. Bryan, *History of the National Capital* (2 vols., New York, 1914). Further references may be found in the *Bibliography of Municipal Government,* ed. W. B. Munro (Cambridge, Mass., 1915).

The best brief outlines of municipal development in the United States are those given in J. A. Fairlie's *Municipal Administration* (New York, 1901), ch. v, the same author's *Essays in Municipal Administration* (New York, 1908), ch. iv. and in William Anderson's *American City Government and Administration* (New York, 1925); ch. ii, xii.

Statistics relating to city growth in America may be found in the publication entitled *A Century of Population Growth, 1790-1900,* issued by the Bureau of the Census, in the volume on *Population* published in 1921 and based on the Fourteenth Census, and in the *Statistics of Cities of over 30,000,* which has been issued annually since 1905 by the same Bureau. The *Statistical Abstract* published by the Census Bureau is also useful. A. F. Weber's *Growth of Cities in the Nineteenth Century* (New York, 1899) is a study covering a large portion of the field. An interesting discussion of future urban growth may be found in R. Pearl and L. J. Reed's *Predicted Growth of Population of New York and its Environs* (New York, 1923).

CHAPTER III

THE SOCIAL STRUCTURE OF THE CITY

The city as a social fact.
It is not enough to say that a city is a large body of people massed in a small area. Even as a social fact it is a good deal more than that; it is a body of population with a peculiar social texture. It possesses measurable characteristics that differentiate it from the general mass of the nation's inhabitants. In other words, if we take as one unit the 200,000 individuals who may constitute the population of a present-day American city, and compare this with another unit made up of 200,000 individuals drawn at random from the length and breadth of the land, from city and country alike, the two units will show differences, more or less marked, at all points at which their respective social characteristics can be statistically compared. In such matters as the numerical proportion of the sexes, the distribution of population according to age, the variety and nature of occupation, the birth, marriage, and death rates, the average earning power of individuals, the proportion of the propertied to the non-propertied class, the relative prevalence of illiteracy, pauperism, and crime,—if we make such a comparison of the two units it will reveal differences which, in their totality, warrant the conclusion that the modern city is a social phenomenon of unique interest and significance.

Some differences between urban and rural populations.
There is every reason to believe, moreover, that urban and rural populations differ just as much, or even more, in features which do not lend themselves to statistical comparison. Are the people of the city more radical in their habits of mind, less conservative in their points of view? Is there a difference in ethical standards between the city and the country populations? In which of the two areas are religious convictions deeper and more influential upon daily life and conduct? Is the urban mentality more enterprising, optimistic, progressive? These questions cannot be answered by quoting figures from the census

THE SOCIAL STRUCTURE OF THE CITY 47

reports, but every sociologist, and indeed every casual observer, has his own opinions as to the right answer in each case.

In the United States, as in all other new countries, the males outnumber the females in the national population as a whole; but in many cities this is reversed, the excess of females being quite pronounced.[1] This reversal of the ratio in many urban sections of the country is explained by the fact that the normal proportion of the sexes is dependent upon the prevailing occupations of the people. In agricultural and mining districts males predominate strongly; in certain industrial centres the reverse is likely to be true. The city is such a centre; and upon the nature of its industries depends, of course, the strength of the female excess. In the factory cities of New England, which are strongholds of the textile industry, the predominance of females ranges from three to four per hundred of population. Washington, the national capital, shows an excess of females because of the large number of clerical positions open to women workers. Of itself, this difference in the ratio of the sexes may now be regarded as a matter of no considerable importance; but the steady opening of new occupations to women may make it otherwise in time. Agriculture, under American conditions, can hardly be expected to afford a greatly enlarged scope for the employment of women, but industry and trade offer vast possibilities in that direction as was demonstrated during the war emergency. May it not be that we shall have, at some future time, a marked excess of females in all our larger cities? And if so, what will be the effect upon city life in general? Would the change help to improve our political standards and our social ethics?

1. Distribution by sex.

A national population, not affected in its growth by immigration or emigration, and regarded from the standpoint of its distribution by age, is commonly plotted on the census charts in the form of an irregular pyramid. At the base are the infants, at the apex the aged. The base is broad, and the more rapid the increase of population the broader this base becomes. The sides of the pyramid converge sharply for a short distance above the

2. Distribution by age.

---

[1] According to the fourteenth (1920) census, there were 2,090,242 more males than females in the national population, or about two more in every hundred; but in many of the large cities the females were found to be in the majority. Among the sixty-eight cities of over 100,000 population the females predominated in nearly half.

base, because the mortality of infant years is heavy; the convergence which portrays the more moderate mortality rates of youth and middle life is more gradual; and finally the lines close rapidly in the years above threescore and ten. Such a population is normally strongest in persons of immature age, and weakens in each succeeding decennial age period; but in the United States the foreign influx has introduced a new element, with the result that the national population, taken as a whole, has shown its chief strength in the early middle-age periods. In the figures of city population this is especially the case. Glance for a moment at the accompanying chart which shows the distribution by age-groups in the population of the City of Chicago and the State of Illinois respectively.

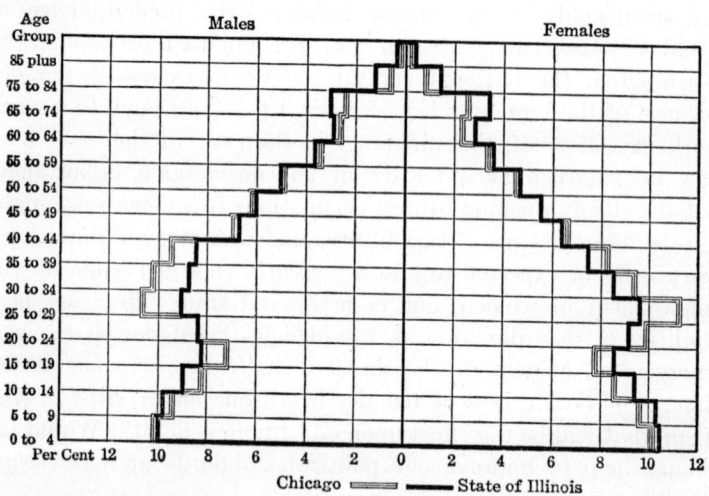

Explanation of the foregoing chart.

It will be noted that, according to the census of 1920, the midwestern metropolis is distinctly weaker in persons (both male and female) under twenty years of age. Then it is stronger in persons of both sexes between the ages of twenty and fifty. Finally it becomes weaker in the age-periods above sixty. Relatively more children are born in the city; but the higher infant death rate offsets this advantage. At about the age of twenty and thereafter, on the other hand, the city gets the benefit of an influx from outside—young men and women who come to it seeking employment, with high hopes of fame and fortune. Hence the city's age-pyramid bulges during the stretch from twenty

THE SOCIAL STRUCTURE OF THE CITY 49

to forty, after which it begins to deflate again. In other words, the city acquires, mainly at the expense of the rural areas, an undue strength in persons of productive age, a fact which forms one of the chief contributory causes of its great economic capacity per head of population.

American cities, particularly the larger ones, have possessed this magnetism in marked degree. They have drawn far more than their share of young aliens, and at the same time have laid heavy toll upon the country districts of the land.[1] The call of the city is heard most readily by the able-bodied young man or woman; infants and persons of advanced years do not ordinarily migrate to a populous community save as dependents upon individuals of the productive age. It is the young and rugged who take their way to the throbbing centres of trade, industry, education, recreation, and opportunity.

The rural influx.

"And at night along the dusty highway, near and nearer drawn,
    Sees in heaven the lights of London, flaring like a dreary dawn."

The drain which the city makes upon the rural areas cannot, then, be measured merely by counting heads. Those who seek the city's opportunities, its fellowship, its comforts, and its human interest are the best blood of the race, the vigorous, the ambitious, and the firm-willed of both sexes; it is the crippled, the dull, the shiftless, and the morons who remain behind. The city ought, therefore, to make a superior showing in wealth and income per head—which it does. It ought to display superior qualities of enterprise and initiative; its achievements per individual should be greater than those of rural areas, for it contains more persons of achieving age.

The United States is commonly regarded as the land *par excellence* of alien accumulation, and in truth the resort to these shores during the past five decades has presented a phenomenon unparalleled in human history. The census of 1910 showed that 14.5 per cent of the whole national population was foreign-born; ten years later (owing to the slackening of emigration during the world war) it had dropped to a little over 13 per cent. The native-born element is thus gaining in the country

3. Distribution by race and nationality.

---

[1] The great bulk of alien immigration has been composed of persons between the ages of 15 and 44. As will be pointed out a little later, most of the immigrants during the past forty years have gone to the cities.

as a whole, and will certainly continue to do so if we maintain our present restrictions on the incoming of aliens. But the foreign-born are relatively much stronger in the cities than in the national population. In the cities of over 25,000 the foreign-born constituted, in 1920, over 25 per cent of the population; in those of over 100,000 the ratio was nearly 35 per cent, and in a few cities it went to nearly 40 per cent. But here again the percentages represented a decrease from those of the thirteenth census, ten years previously.

<small>Reasons for strength of foreign-born element in cities.</small>   The reasons for the strength of the foreign-born element in the larger cities are easy enough to find. It is not, as might be superficially supposed, that large cities are usually ports of entry for European immigrants, and that the immigrant settles down at his first point of arrival; for this would not explain the presence of great alien elements in cities like Chicago, Milwaukee, or San Francisco. The true reasons are numerous, and they are chiefly economic. Immigrants of some nationalities do go, and go in large numbers, to the rural districts. Whole agricultural regions of the West, for example, are peopled by Scandinavians. But the greater part of the alien influx during the last few decades has come from the countries of Eastern, Middle, and Southern Europe. These races—Slavs, Poles, Lithuanians, Italians, Greeks, and Armenians—drift very largely to the urban centres, mainly because many of them come with neither the capital nor the skill necessary to enable them to do anything else. Although most of them come from the agricultural regions of their own lands, few bring any knowledge of farming that would be of much service to them under American conditions. It takes a little knowledge to be even an agricultural laborer; and for an immigrant to become a farmer in America on his own account requires some capital as well as some knowledge, whereas to obtain a place as a sewer-digger or as an unskilled laborer in one of the cities does not require either.

Most immigrants come to America to find work; and they go, accordingly, wherever the work which they can do is to be found. So long as industry concentrates itself in the large cities, and so long as great industries present a steady demand for cheap, unskilled labor, both of men and of women, the large cities will naturally get more of those aliens who come without either skill or sustenance. About the only great industry employing large

THE SOCIAL STRUCTURE OF THE CITY 51

quantities of unskilled labor and situated outside the larger cities is that of mining. This industry does draw great numbers of newly-arrived aliens into its vortex. It is chiefly for this reason that Pennsylvania usually ranks next to New York in the statistics of immigration.

Social as well as economic motives have their influence. Aliens, who cannot speak English, like to be among their own people in a strange land; and in any event their passage to America is very often paid for by friends or relatives already here. When a colony of any alien race is once started in a large American city, therefore, the social motive comes quickly into play. It grows like a cottonwood tree. Hence we find, in many of the large centres, an Italian quarter, a Jewish quarter, a Polish quarter, and so on. All these things have been so fully elaborated, however, by writers upon the ethnic factors in city government that they need no further discussion here.[1] It should be pointed out, nevertheless, that the strength of the foreign-born population is not directly related to the size of the city or to its location. New York, in 1920, had only 35.4 per cent foreign born inhabitants, while New Bedford, a textile city in Massachusetts, had more than 40 per cent. In the cities of the southern and southwestern states the percentage of foreign-born is almost everywhere small, sometimes as low as 5 per cent. There are two reasons for this, first, the relative absence of industrial development until quite recently, and, second, the presence of cheap negro labor. It is industrial opportunity that lures the alien to the city.

<small>Social motives in alien concentration</small>

At any rate the problem of governing the state and the nation remains primarily a problem of governing native Americans; but the task of administering the affairs of the industrial cities has become a problem of making political and administrative

<small>Has the alien influx accentuated the difficulty of our municipal problems?</small>

---

[1] Well-known books on the general topic of immigration are J. R. Commons, *Races and Immigrants in America* (New York, 1907); Edith Abbott, *Immigration: Select Documents and Case Records* (Chicago, 1924); J. W. Jenks and W. Jett Lauck, *The Immigrant Problem* (New York, 1922); Mary Antin, *The Promised Land* (Boston, 1917); Edward A. Steiner, *From Alien to Citizen* (New York, 1914); Peter Roberts, *The New Immigration* (New York, 1912); F. J. Warne, *The Tide of Immigration* (New York, 1916); J. P. Gavitt, *Americans by Choice* (New York, 1922); H. P. Fairchild, *Immigration; A World Movement and its American Significance* (New York, 1925); and E. A. Ross, *The Old World in the New* (New York, 1914). See also the report of the National Industrial Conference Board (New York, 1923).

provision for units of population which have come to America without sound and well-fixed political traditions. This is not to say that the alien element is wholly or even mainly responsible for the fact that the government of great cities has so often been inefficient or corrupt. If you look over the large cities of the country you will not find that those with many foreign-born have been better governed than those with few. Baltimore, Philadelphia, Indianapolis, and Denver, with relatively low percentages of foreign-born, have not been noticeably better governed than Boston, Chicago, Detroit, or San Francisco. Something of this sort has been said in a previous chapter, but it will bear repetition. Nevertheless, the fact that the alien-born bulk so large in many of the bigger American cities does complicate the problems of municipal government. It can hardly be true that heredity affects the business aptitudes, the tastes, and even the ideals of races, but is wholly without influence upon their political ideals or capacities.

The alien in politics. There is an undoubted relation between chromosomes and politics. A considerable proportion of those who have come to America during the past half-century are men and women who did not possess voting rights in their own lands, and whose fathers before them did not have such rights. Government, in their native countries, went on over their heads, in a sort of rarified stratum which they were never privileged to enter. To these newcomers, on becoming naturalized, we have given the ballot, forgetting that the discreet use of this powerful weapon of democracy cannot be learned in a few years. You cannot "give" to any one, whether native-born or alien, the capacity for sober self-government. The capacity has to be earned, acquired, and slowly-developed. To make a "hundred per center" of any nationality you have to begin with his grandfather. Hence, while the alien is trying to get his right bearings, the political exploiter of his own race goes after him with an appeal to his preconceptions and his prejudices which often proves irresistible.

The new citizen has inherited political traditions which do not fit the American environment. There are many things that he does not understand. Being unable to go to sure sources of information concerning his new political duties, he must take what comes to him from the hired henchman of his own race,

THE SOCIAL STRUCTURE OF THE CITY 53

from the newspaper of his own language (which is frequently kept in existence by patronage from the party in power), or from the native-born political roundsmen who cultivate the newcomer's confidence for their own ends. All these make it appear to him that his own immediate advantage can be best served by following the counsel which they give; and being led to believe that individual interest is the only motive which actuates American-born voters, he is liable to let himself be thus exploited.

We have the testimony of seasoned campaigners that the alien-born voter is inclined to think for himself if he gets the opportunity, but too often he does not secure even that small amount of reliable information which is necessary as a basis for forming opinions of his own. As a rule, practically all that he gets concerning the facts of the municipal situation comes to him in such form that it leads to one conclusion only. It is not that the foreign-born voter is undiscriminating, or that he always prefers to vote for one of his own race or religion. Experience has proved that he cannot regularly be stampeded by appeals to class prejudice, or delivered blindly to the support of some political faction. Given a fair chance, he is, according to authoritative testimony, a voter of at least normal independence. He does not consciously choose to be misgoverned. If he has too often proved to be the prey of the exploiter, it is largely because he is made the goal of an almost irresistible drive by the political machines of the ward or the city. These organizations concentrate their blandishments upon him from the day that he arrives. They do it with a persistence that is worthy of a better cause. Now if it were somebody's business to enlighten the foreign-born voter as to the real nature of the issues and the personalities, there would be some chance of counteracting these efforts of the political machine—but it is nobody's business. The ward boss and his satellites, on the other hand, are on the job throughout the year.

In any case, the presence of a large alien element in urban areas gives the cities of the united states a prime interest in the terms of the naturalization law, and in the rigid enforcement of this law, likewise in all regulations pertaining to the selection of immigrants, and, indeed, in every matter relating to the immigration policy of the nation. The enormous assimilating power of the American people has often been commented upon by students of sociology; but it is not by the American people as a whole that this process is being steadily performed. Most of the task falls upon the industrial cities of the country, and it would therefore be surprising if their municipal standards did not in some degree give way under the strain.

The dynamics of urban population:

A unit of population constituting a large city, when contrasted with a unit of equal size drawn from rural districts, shows marked differences in its birth, marriage, and death rates.[1] In the matter of births it seems to be generally true that the number per thousand of population is almost always greater in cities than in rural communities. Indeed, it has been laid down as a working rule that the birth-rate varies directly with density of population in all parts of the country, and this holds true in the main, although there are occasional exceptions. A superficial explanation of this may be found in the fact that aliens, among whom the birth-rate is high, are numerous in urban populations; but that would not explain why the birth-rate is larger among the native-born in cities than among the same element in rural districts. The real explanation of this disparity, as of many other social phenomena, is probably economic. Since the national birth-rate is to a considerable extent dependent upon general economic conditions, rising in times of prosperity and falling in times of depression, it is more than likely that the higher birth-rate of the urban community connects itself with the city's superiority over the rural district in point of wage-earning power per capita.[2]

1. Birth-rates.

2. Marriage-rates.

The urban marriage-rate per 10,000 of population is also considerably higher than the rural. This is accounted for in part by the fact that the city is proportionately stronger in persons of marriageable age, in part by the greater accuracy with which the marriage records and statistics are kept in the cities, and in part by the fact that many marriages which ought to go into the rural statistics are credited to the city in which the ceremony happens to have been performed. The economic factor of

---

[1] Accurate statistics relating to vital progress (that is, to the birth, marriage, and death rates) are not available for the whole United States, but only for what is officially termed the "registration area." This area, which covers most of the Eastern and Middle, some of the Western, and parts of a few Southern states, comprises slightly over three-fourths of the total population of the Union.

[2] It should also be recalled that the city is relatively stronger in persons of child-rearing age. See *above*, p. 48.

THE SOCIAL STRUCTURE OF THE CITY 55

greater income-earning power per individual also has a considerable influence.

The city, as is well known, has a death-rate per thousand very much above that of the country. This is a statistical discrepancy which seems to be characteristic of all periods and of all countries. It was the decimating urban death-rate of the middle ages and the early modern centuries that kept the cities from making substantial headway in growth of population. In London the normal death-rate during the seventeenth century is estimated to have been about fifty persons per thousand of population each year; and it was not till about 1800 that London's annual death-rate went below her birth-rate, thereby permitting the city to achieve some growth through natural increase.[1] In this respect London was not unique among European cities; on the contrary, her showing was probably better than that of the other great centres. Nor was the situation very different in America. In 1880 the death-rate of Boston was thirty per thousand; in 1925 it was only thirteen per thousand. The enormous advances made by the science of medicine, including improvements in sanitation, and progress in personal hygiene, in arrangements for preventing the spread of infectious diseases, and in preventive medical science generally,—all this has cut down the urban death-rate in every large American city during the last four decades.[2]

3. Death-rates.

But, with it all, the city death-rate continues at every stage of human life to be higher than that of the rural district. Especially is this true, as one might expect, among children under five years of age. In larger cities (taking richer and poorer sections together) the child mortality is twice that of rural areas having an equal number of children; in the case of infants under one year of age the discrepancy is even greater. Roughly

Causes of the high urban death-rate.

[1] In 1685 there were 23,222 deaths in London and only 14,732 births.
[2] The decline of the average death-rates of some large American cities may be seen in the following table of deaths per thousand of population. The figures for 1924 are from the *United States Public Health Reports*, Vol. XL, No. 4 (January 23, 1925).

City	1886 to 1890	1891 to 1895	1896 to 1900	1901 to 1905	1906 to 1910	1924
New York	25.8	24.6	20.3	18.9	16.9	11.8
Chicago	19.5	20.6	15.2	14.2	14.9	11.2
Philadelphia	20.6	21.1	19.2	18.1	17.7	13.1
Boston	23.5	23.6	20.9	18.8	17.9	14.1

about ten per cent of the children born in a large city do not survive their first year of life. Many circumstances combine to bring about this situation. The poverty, the cramped quarters, and the general lack of even elementary necessities in the congested tenement districts have much to do with it. It is the overpopulated wards of the large city that make the figures of infant mortality what they are. The employment of married women, particularly of the poorer classes, in fatiguing industrial occupations is also a factor of importance, as is shown by the heavy infant mortality of those cities in which textile industries prevail.[1] In any event, much of the heavy loss of population in its earlier years is admittedly preventable; its continuance is due largely to public failure to realize the seriousness of the situation and to the small amount of money available for public health work. It has been demonstrated, for example, that the annual infant mortality in large cities can be greatly reduced by strict inspection and control of the milk supply, by the education of mothers in child hygiene, and by the provision of more playgrounds. The accidental death-rate among both children and adults is also larger than it ought to be. Automobile fatalities nowadays form quite an item in the total, due mainly to overspeeding, violations of the traffic rules, and the readiness of pedestrians to take chances. Little by little, however, the number of deaths due to these causes is being reduced.

The death-rate as a barometer of administrative efficiency. Of all conservation measures none can be more worthy than those which have for their end the conservation of human life. It is in the infant mortality of the cities, large and small, that the greatest saving can be made; for in some respects the infant death-rate is a good barometer of the efficiency of a city's administration in matters of health and sanitation. The water-supply service, the sewerage arrangements, the parks and recreation grounds, the system of medical inspection in the schools, the street railway system in so far as it operates to relieve density, the public health department, the street-cleaning service, the inspection of food and milk,—nearly every branch of city administration reflects its efficiency or its inefficiency in the figures of child mortality. Much as these services have been improved, and the improvement has shown itself in the lower mortality

---

[1] See the interesting table printed in F. J. Goodnow and F. G. Bates, *Municipal Government* (New York, 1919), pp. 30-31.

THE SOCIAL STRUCTURE OF THE CITY

rates of the past few decades, nevertheless the city still loses, by its high death-rate, most of what it gains through an excess of births. Apart from the infant mortality, the difference between the urban and the rural districts in the matter of death-rates is not great. Among adults it is probable that the nerve-racking tension of city life, the over-stimulation, as well as the foul air of many factories, shops, and offices, have something to do with the city's higher death-rate; but these features are easy to exaggerate.[1]

Surveying the field of vital progress as a whole, one sees clearly that the rural districts may make a greater net contribution to the growth of national population than do the cities. Where this is so, the urbanization of a country ought, in the absence of immigration, to mean a slower rate of national growth. Possibly the increasing slowness of England's decennial increase in population may be in part explained by the steady drift of the English population into the urban centres.   *The city's contribution to the national population.*

A good deal used to be said and written about the debilitating effect of urban life upon individual physique. Nothing seemed easier to prove than the superior physical development of the rural population in any country. Writers usually did not think it worth while to argue the point; they simply took for granted that city life and physical decline must inevitably go together. On the surface there seemed to be various reasons why the physical standards of the country ought to be better than those of the town, and there were no statistics to prove the contrary. Sociologists lamented the minute division of labor in urban industries which required a man to spend his lifetime in making the nineteenth part of a pin, and explained that such vocations could develop only a very small part of the worker's physical powers, whereas the rural employments encouraged versatility and all-round physical development.   *Physical virility.*   *The older notion.*

Until after the United States entered the World War we had no comprehensive body of data bearing on this matter of city life and physical degeneracy. We had never given a thorough physi-   *What the facts disclose.*

---

[1] Statistics of city death-rates must always be used with caution—especially when stated in terms of so many deaths per thousand of population. Bear in mind that outsiders who have serious ailments are often brought to the hospitals of the city. If they succumb, they go to swell the city's annual death-rate, although they were not residents and hence did not count in its population.

cal examination to any considerable part of our national population. Prisoners in jails, athletes in training, applicants for positions in the police and fire-protection services, newly enlisted men in the army and navy,—such groups of men were measured and the results put on paper; but these various classes, even when taken together, formed so small and so untypical a fraction of the whole people that any generalization from their physical measurements would have been altogether unwarranted.

Military leaders, however, in the great wars of the nineteenth century, had frequently given it as their opinion that the current notions were without any real basis, for their observation showed that regiments drawn from the cities displayed quite as much physical hardihood as those drawn from the rural districts, and sometimes more. This opinion seemed also to coincide with the figures compiled by the military authorities of France, Germany, and Italy, where compulsory military service was maintained in time of peace. In these countries several hundred thousand young men were annually summoned to do their service in the army, and were given rigid physical examinations. The results did not demonstrate any physical inferiority on the part of the city-bred man. On the contrary, the percentage of those rejected for failure to meet the minimum requirements in height, weight, or chest measure, or for deficient eyesight or hearing, was often found to be higher among the quotas which came from the country than among those which came from the towns.

Our experience during the World War.
Our experience in raising a national army during the World War threw some light upon the question so far as the population of the United States is concerned. Under the provisions of the selective service laws more than six million Americans, about five per cent of the total population, were given a physical examination during the years of 1917-1918.[1] The proportion of those rejected for full military service proved to be surprisingly high,—nearly one-fourth of all the men who were examined. According to the records of these tests, moreover, the percentage of men rejected for physical defects was slightly higher in the urban than in the rural areas, and the Provost Marshal General therefore expressed the opinion, based upon these figures, that "a

[1] This includes all who were called up for examination by local boards.

THE SOCIAL STRUCTURE OF THE CITY 59

considerable physical advantage accrues to the boy reared in the country."[1]

But this conclusion of General Crowder does not appear to be entirely warranted. The slightly larger percentage of rejections among drafted men from the cities would seem to be quite fully explained by the fact that very large numbers of physically-fit young men from the cities went into the service without being drafted, or were federalized with units of the national guard, or were commissioned as officers. In such cases they did not figure in the general records of physical examinations. Obviously the proportion of such men was larger in the cities than in the rural districts. If we credit the city with this element the discrepancy vanishes altogether. So the only warrantable conclusion to be drawn from the huge mass of statistics is that the superiority or rural over urban physique in the United States, if it exists at all, is certainly not very large. If the city is at a disadvantage in this matter, it is so slight as to be virtually negligible. The figures certainly do not afford any proof that city life is physically debilitating.[2]

A comparison of relative intelligence in city and country is something that cannot be set forth in columns of figures. We cannot measure intellects as we measure height or chest expansion. Hence we can only make a general comparison of urban with rural populations as regards the percentage of illiterates found in each, and this, of course, throws very little light on the average of intellectual attainment. The census of 1920 showed that, whereas nearly five per cent of the total population of the United States over ten years of age was classed as illiterate, the percentage in most of the cities was somewhat smaller.[3] But it is doubtful whether much dependence can be placed upon these figures even though they bear the official imprint of the census bureau. The reason lies in the methods of compiling them. The census figures of illiteracy are compiled by having the

Relative intellectual attainment.

[1] *Second Report of the Provost Marshal General on the Operations of the Selective Service System* (Washington, 1919), p. 159.
[2] For a discussion of this matter see the volume by A. G. Love and C. B. Davenport entitled *Defects Found in Drafted Men* (Washington, 1920), also the article by Rufus S. Tucker on "The Distribution of Men Physically Unfit for Military Service" in the *Quarterly Publication of the American Statistical Association*, September, 1922, pp. 377-384.
[3] This figure includes the negroes. In the white population, including foreign-born whites, less than three per cent are illiterate according to the census figures.

enumerators ask each individual whether he can write anything in any language. If he answers this question in the affirmative he is put down as "literate." No formal test is applied, and naturally the enumerators get a great many optimistic answers. The mere say-so of the individual is enough. Surely it does not require much argument to prove that statistics of illiteracy, gathered in this way, are of very little value. Indeed, they may be said to have a negative value for they serve to becloud the real situation.

Happily we do not have to depend entirely upon the census figures for data concerning this important matter. A study made by the National Education Association, through its Commission on Illiteracy, leads to more than a suspicion that the percentage of illiterates in the population of the United States is at least twice as great as the census indicates. Finally, we have the tabulated results of the tests made by the army in the case of drafted men during the war-years, 1917-1918. These show an illiteracy ratio of over 23 per cent, based on the requirement of a demonstrated ability to read and write simple English. In addition, nearly 6 per cent of the men failed so badly on the Alpha intelligence test that they were given the Beta test which was ordinarily reserved for illiterates. In a word nearly 30 per cent of the drafted men, among the million and a half to whom the test was applied, proved themselves illiterate according to army standards. Yet these men formed a pretty good cross-section of our entire national population and the test was not an unreasonable one. A man who cannot write anything on any subject or read anything in any newspaper is to all intents illiterate even though he may not be technically so according to some definitions of the term.

It may seem strange that there is somewhat less illiteracy in the cities and towns than in the country, despite the large foreign-born population which is concentrated in the urban areas, but the phenomenon can easily be explained. It is due in part to the city's superior day-school facilities and to the better enforcement of the laws relating to compulsory education. To a greater degree it is perhaps attributable to the supplementary agencies of education in which the city abounds,—the night school, the neighborhood house, and, by no means least, the daily newspaper. In the city, moreover, the pressure put upon the

THE SOCIAL STRUCTURE OF THE CITY

illiterate is greater than in the country for there is almost no city employment which does not require ability to read and write.

One may repeat, however, that although the city makes a better showing at the bottom of the intellectual ladder, this does not necessarily indicate a general average of intelligence or of education above that of the rural districts. There are some observers who believe that the city's display of erudition is only superficial, and that "scattered and unrelated fragments of half-baked information form a stock of 'knowledge' with which the townsman's glib tongue enable him to present a showy intellectual shop-front."[1] That may be true; there is no way of proving or disproving it. Yet if it be true that education is largely a matter of opportunity, there is every reason why the city should make a better showing not only in appearance but in reality. Life in the city is a continuous process of education. It tends to make men and women alert, more versatile, quicker in their mental processes, and more receptive to new ideas. The city atmosphere stimulates the sluggish mind, makes it more impressionable and quicker in response. In the city you must step lively and think lively too. But when slow-moving minds are overstimulated there is bound to be a good deal of snap judgment and shallow thinking. On the other hand, the urban communities contribute far more than their proportionate share of the leaders in all branches of the national life. One should hasten to add, however, that this does not prove early life on a farm to be a barrier in a man's climb to eminence. A large proportion of our successful men and women, whose names appear in "Who's Who," are country-born and country-bred. They are persons who migrated to the cities after having spent their formative years in the rural regions. Owing to our frequent forgetfulness of this fact the city gets a lot of credit which does not belong to it.[2]

Is the intellectual superiority of the city assumed or real?

Many sermons have been preached upon the laxity of the city's moral standards; but, like the allegations concerning the

Moral standards of cities and towns.

---

[1] J. A. Hobson, *The Evolution of Modern Capitalism* (New York, 1904), p. 339.

[2] The thirteenth edition of *Who's Who in America* (Chicago, 1924) contains an interesting discussion of the nativity, ancestry, and education of the men and women whose biographies are listed in this well-known publication (pp. 25-34). Of the 24,278 names, the cities contributed over twice as many as the rural districts in proportion to population.

inferior physical development of the city-born, these preachments rest on nothing very tangible.[1] There are no trustworthy indices of public morals, although amateur sociologists often take the divorce statistics, the number of arrests, or even the figures of illegitimate births as such. The standards of different races are never fairly comparable, nor are those of different social classes among the same people. It is true, of course, that if you study the crime statistics you will find that the cities have some explaining to do, for in these tabulations they are debited with about three times their proportionate share of all the crimes committed in the United States from year to year. But there are some things to be noted in extenuation of this rather discreditable showing. In the first place it should be remembered that rural crooks do not stay in the country; they make for the city at the first opportunity. The country youth of vicious disposition naturally seeks a field in which his sinister propensities can find better scope, and the city must bear the brunt of his later criminal record although it is not the author of his waywardness. The thief does not gravitate to the city because moral standards are lower there, but because there are more things to steal, because it is easier to dispose of stolen goods in the city, and because there is a better chance of escaping detection. Not only this but the city offers better facilities for the gambling and dissipation into which the yeggman or crook usually plunges when he had made his haul. Take the automobile thief, for example. Were he to prefer the rural district as a field of operation, he would be paying a poor tribute to his intelligence.

Bear in mind, again, that many crimes are from their very nature associated with city life and activities. Forgery, perjury, embezzlement, and business frauds of various sorts are peculiarly urban crimes; it would be altogether surprising if there were not more of them in the cities than in the rural districts. But in proportion to the amount of honest business done they are probably not more numerous in one region than in the other. Finally, it is well to remember that in the city the vicissitudes of employment have a bearing on the crime ratio. Men are at work today and out of work tomorrow; hence there is always an idle ele-

[1] For an example, see the arraignment in Josiah Strong's *Twentieth Century City* (New York, 1898).

THE SOCIAL STRUCTURE OF THE CITY   63

ment which is under temptation to get into mischief.[1] There is no such surplus of unemployed and unemployables in the agricultural regions.

We hear much nowadays about crime waves and the increased criminality of the country as a whole. These things are giving much concern to many good people. They call our attention to the fact that crimes are increasing more rapidly than population. But this fact, which appears ominous on the surface, does not necessarily indicate a declining standard of national morality. In part it points to a better keeping of criminal statistics. In part it is explained by the fact that many things are crimes today which were not so a generation ago. A good deal of it is attributable to the steady shifting of population from country to town. The crime ratio of the large cities is bound to be much greater than that of the small village; and, since our cities are growing much more rapidly than our villages, it would be strange indeed if the number of crimes did not increase with greater rapidity than the population of the country as a whole. The drift to the cities is undoubtedly responsible for much of the increase in our crime ratio, but this is not because urban growth tends to lower the moral tone of the nation. It is merely that the city, through no fault of its own, provides greater scope for that dishonest element which, whether in town or country, is governed in its action by its opportunities.

Crime waves in cities.

The truth is that we know astonishingly little about crime, its causes and its cure. Heredity, without much doubt, has something to do with the making of criminals, but just how large a part it plays we do not know. Environment is also a factor, but of unknown dimensions. Why does the crime ratio drop during a war and increase very perceptibly when the war comes to an end? Why are certain crimes more numerous at one season of the year than at others, and more common in some countries than in others? Why is crime a young man's pastime? Three-fourths of our criminals are of the male sex and under

Our inadequate knowledge of criminology.

---

[1] Those who are interested in this topic will find a readable essay on "Great Cities, and their Influence for Good and Evil" in Charles Kingsley's *Miscellanies* (2 vols., London, 1860), II, 318-345. Attention should also be called to Lord Bryce's address on "The Menace of Great Cities," printed in the *Proceedings of the Second National Conference on Housing* (New York, 1912), pp. 9-23.

twenty-five years of age. If we knew the answers to these and various similar questions we would be in a much better position to talk intelligently about crime and its causes. But the fact is that we know far less about crime than disease; we know far more about the causes of typhoid fever and malaria than about the predisposing factors in embezzlement and burglary. Perhaps the reason is that scientists have been studying the one and sociologists the other.

Ownership of property. The cities of the United States, being stronger in persons of productive age than are the rural areas, ought to have a greater income-earning power per head of population. And that is undoubtedly the case. It is certain, at any rate, that the per capita wealth of the cities far exceeds that of the rural communities. Of the total wealth of the United States, as estimated in 1920, the urban population possessed about three-fourths, which is far above its proportionate share. These reckonings, however, include personal as well as real property. If we take land and buildings as the basis of our calculation, and particularly consider the ownership of homes, we get a very different showing, for the percentage of those who own their places of abode is much larger in the rural districts. It is true that the real significance of the proportion of "farm families owning their homes," as given in the census returns (over sixty-three per cent, by the enumeration of 1920), is somewhat lessened by the fact that much of this ownership is in form rather than in fact, inasmuch as a great many farm homes are heavily mortgaged to banks and loan companies.[1] But, with all due allowance for this fact the home-owning element among the rural population of the United States is much larger than in the cities. Indeed, it seems to be a law of urban concentration that the more congested the population the lower becomes the proportion of home-owning families. If you want to find the smallest proportion of home-owners to the total number of families go to the most crowded sections of the largest cities. For the borough of Manhattan, in downtown New York, the figure is less than 3 per cent.

Property and conservatism. This marked difference in the ratio of home-owners, as between city and rural areas is one of great social and political importance. That indefinable inspiration to thrift which John

[1] The proportion of mortgaged homes in the whole country is nearly 40 per cent.

Stuart Mill called "the magic of property," and which he credited with the alchemy of turning sand into gold, is more general and more effective in country than in town. It is well known that a widespread ownership of property makes for stability and soberness in popular thought, whereas a propertyless element tends to become a proletariate with restless inclinations. The history of nations affords a good deal of evidence that urban proletariates are impatient of the slow course which social and political institutions take in working out their own evolution, and hence that the increase of the non-propertied element is likely to promote radicalism and direct action. Urban concentration means that the landless man rises to supremacy in the voting-lists, while the owner of property finds himself in a hopeless minority. This, we are sometimes told, is a dangerous situation, because the masses in the large cities are prone to be guided by their emotions, prejudices, aversions and class consciousness rather than by reason or patriotism.

On the whole, however, the history of the United States during the past fifty years does not seem to support the proposition that the propertyless element in the large cities is more radically-minded than are the people of various agricultural states where the percentage of home-owners is large. Most radical innovations in American politics, most of the clamors for economic reconstruction, have come out of the West. Make a list of the radical innovations which have been injected into American public life and politics during the past fifty years. It will be a long list—including populism, free silver, prohibition, woman suffrage, the direct election of senators, municipal home rule, the initiative and referendum, the recall, preferential voting, proportional representation, direct primaries, commission government, the city manager plan, income taxes, excess profit taxes, the short ballot, compulsory arbitration of labor disputes, federal control of child labor, blue-sky laws, farm blocs, workmen's compensation laws, minimum wage laws, executive budgets, and whatnot. How many of these had their origin, or gained their initial momentum, in the industrial centres of the country? Very few indeed. The big cities of the United States have contributed very little to political radicalism in any of its forms.[1]

---

[1] "The truth is that the industrial family is conservative in its politics as it is in its social customs. Changes are disliked and feared. Caution is

Other points of comparison.

There are many other points of view from which the urban and rural populations of the United States might be subjected to comparison, but enough has been said to show that marked differences exist in the social textures of the two. Compared from any single point of view, these differences are perhaps not of very much consequence; the mere fact that the American city is stronger in its percentage of females or weaker in its ratio of illiterates hardly suffices to give urban populations any distinctive social coloring. Taken together, however, the variations show a difference in make-up that is both great and important. It is to be remembered, moreover, that some of the most marked discrepancies, quite visible to the naked eye, are not statistically computable. Differences between urban and rural populations in their versatility of interests, in their average qualities of initiative, perseverance, and constancy, in their capacity to develop and to follow safe ideals,—these are things which cannot be set forth in mathematical ratios.

Psychological differences.

Everywhere, in all countries, the psychology of the urban crowd is different from that of the scattered millions who dwell upon the land. It must be so, for the city-dweller leads a life so crowded with impressions, each following the other with such drum-fire rapidity that no time is left for reflection. These impressions are easily made, but just as easily erased, for the city mind craves novelty and is impatient of repetitions. Its yearning is always for something new, something strange, something striking. Compare the sights and sounds of Broadway, Michigan Avenue, or Market Street with those that one sees and hears along the country lane. Compare the flaming headlines of the metropolitan daily and the shrieking poster on the city billboards with the modest captions of the rural weekly and the meek little announcement that is tacked up in the village postoffice! What a tremendous drive is made to arrest the city man's attention! He has become blasé to all that is not new and bizarre.

In the public imagination the city is a place where material motives fill the minds and govern the acts of men, a place of excessive individualism, where neighborhood feeling is almost wholly absent, and where, through the incessant shifting of the people, no neighborhood traditions ever become firmly rooted.

universal." Mary K. Simkhovitch, *The City Worker's World* (New York, 1917), p. 203.

THE SOCIAL STRUCTURE OF THE CITY 67

In the city the neighborhoods, such as they are, tend to lose all the intimacy that we associate with rural communities of similar size. Easy means of communication tempt individuals to find their friends and intimates in several neighborhoods. A city man's friends are not, for the most part, his neighbors. They are all over the city, miles apart. As a rule they are persons of his own profession, vocation, temperament, or tastes. Bear in mind that every occupation, even that of the beggar, tends in the city to become a profession, a highly-developed profession. The man without traits which differentiate him from his neighbors is the one who succeeds in the country; but the big city rewards genius and even feels a kindliness toward eccentricity. Its people, on the other hand, are restive, impulsive, intolerant of delay (yet docile enough in their continued submission to public abuses), laying too little stress upon the family as the ultimate social unit and too much upon artificial organizations that do not really take its place. If all these traits could be weighed in the balance and their intensity determined, the real extent of the city's influence upon the national life is far greater than most of us imagine.

"Don't blame the city," says a well-known American dramatist. "What the city does is to bring out what is strongest in us. . . . A man can live in a small town all his life and deceive the whole place and himself into thinking that he has got all the virtues . . . but the city strips him naked of all his disguises—and all his hypocricies—and she paints his ambition on her fences, and lights up her skyscrapers with it!—what he wants to be and what he thinks he is—and then she says to him, Make good if you can!"[1]

Don't blame the city.

It is in the great cities of the land that the extremes of life come face to face. They are the melting-pots of races and traditions. There it is that the highest culture stares down the street at unbelievable ignorance. The extremes of wealth and poverty are also there. If you desire the best in men of science, art, industry, you will find them in the great city; or if you seek the worst types of illiteracy, depravity, and indolence, you will find them there too. The city has more wealth and the country, more skill, more erudition within its bounds, more initiative, more philanthropy, more crimes, more divorces, more aliens,

The place of city in national life.

[1] Clyde Fitch, *The City* (Boston, 1915).

more births and deaths, more accidents, more rich, more poor, more wise men, and more fools. It is characteristic of city life that all sorts of people meet and mingle without in the least understanding one another. There is an east side and a west side, a north end and a south end, separated by a few hundred yards in distance, but by thousands of miles in point of view, aspirations, and conditions of life. They might almost as well be in different continents.

Into this great crucible of American municipal life the baser elements of indifference, ignorance, and greed, together with the finer elements of intelligence, public spirit, and self-sacrifice, must be poured, and out of the mass will come the composite of our citizenship. The modern metropolis is neither an Athens nor a Gomorrah; it is both rolled into one. In the rural community with its approximation to social and economic quality the problem of maintaining a reasonable standard of ideals and achievements is easier than in the city, where these things must be determined by the pull and haul of the classes and the masses.[1] That the city's influence upon the political, social, and economic ideals of the whole people ought by every effort to be thrown into the proper channel is of the most vital importance; for the urban population is far more influential than its numerical strength implies. As the population which supplies most of the national leadership and which through its press has a dominant influence upon the moulding of public opinion, it must be credited with far more than fifty per cent of the responsibility for the successes or the failures of American political life. The problems of the city are not, therefore, the problems of its own citizens alone. Their solution is of vital concern to all who value American ideals; for the ideals of a nation are determined by the most influential among various elements of its population, and being so determined, they are in constant process of change. The course of alteration is unheralded by any blast of trumpets, and it often evades the notice of trained observers. Transformations in the political or the social psychology of a people proceed insidiously. History has shown, time and again, that a general

---

[1] "The city is the spectroscope of society; it analyzes and sifts the population, separating and classifying the diverse elements. The entire progress of civilization is a process of differentiation, and the city is the greatest differentiator." A. F. Weber, *The Growth of Cities in the Nineteenth Century* (New York, 1899), p. 442.

THE SOCIAL STRUCTURE OF THE CITY 69

betterment of popular ideals may descend upon a land, like as an angel, unawares, or that a deterioration may come even as a thief in the night.

As the city, then, with all that it expresses and implies, must be the controlling factor in the national life of the future, there is no service more truly patriotic than that of helping to make it a better place to live in. True patriotism requires not only that a man shall be ready to make the supreme sacrifice for his country's salvation, but that he shall stand ever-ready to devote his time and talents to the less conspicuous but equally momentous duty of maintaining public order, protecting private property, and preserving the lives of his fellow men against the dangers which lurk in foul tenements, in unclean food, and in that whole field of civic administration whose mismanagement leaves a trail of misery through the habitations of the poor. We have no distinguished service medals for those who guard the city's health, befriend the unfortunate, and help educate the children. Is it not worthy of remark that a democracy which makes peace its great ideal should be so much more ready to glorify with decorations the soldier than even the most faithful worker in its civilian employ? Peace hath her victories; but too often the men and women who win them must go without official recognition.

True civic patriotism.

To make the city, as Henry Drummond once said, is what we are here for. He who makes the city makes the world. For though men may make cities, it is just as true that cities make men. Whether our national life is great or mean, whether our social virtues are mature or stunted, whether our sons are vicious or moral, whether religion is possible or impossible, depends upon the city. To the reformer, the philanthropist, the economist, the politician, this vision of the city is the great classic of social literature.

REFERENCES

In studying the social structure of the American city our main reliance must be placed upon the statistics gathered by the Bureau of the Census, especially those published in its volumes on *Population: Fourteenth Census of the United States* (3 vols., Washington, 1920), and on the *Composition and Characteristics of the Population* (Washington, 1922). Many interpretations and explanations of these figures can be found in the textbooks and treatises on sociology or social ethics. For a useful list of references to such books see the volume on *The City* by R. E. Park and others, cited *below*.

Among the more specialized studies, mention may be made of T. J. Jones, *Sociology of a New York City Block* (New York, 1904); John Daniels, *America via the Neighborhood* (New York, 1920); Simeon Strunsky, *Belshazzar Court, or Village Life in New York City* (New York, 1914); R. D. McKenzie, *The Neighborhood* (Chicago, 1923); Paul H. Douglas, *The Suburban Trend* (New York, 1925); Konrad Bercovici, *Around the World in New York* (New York, 1924); H. B. Woolston, *A Study of the Population of Manhattanville* (New York, 1909); R. E. Park, E. W. Burgess, and others, *The City: Human Behavior in the Urban Environment* (Chicago, 1925); C. B. Purdom, *The Building of Satellite Cities* (New York, 1925); Luther Fry, *A Census Analysis of American Villages* (New York, 1925); E. E. Pratt, *Industrial Causes of Congestion of Population in New York City* (New York, 1911); the *Report of the Country Life Commission* (Washington, 1909); the *Pittsburgh Survey* (6 vols., New York, 1909-1914), and the various other publications of the Russell Sage Foundation. Attention may also be called to J. W. Brookwalter's *Rural versus Urban, the Conflict and its Causes* (New York, 1910); G. C. Whipple's *Vital Statistics* (New York, 1917); Graham R. Taylor's *Satellite Cities* (New York, 1915); the various volumes in the series of *Americanization Studies* published by Harper and Brothers under the editorship of Messrs. Allen & Burns, and in the Century Social Science series, published by the Century Company under the editorship of Edward Allsworth Ross, especially the forthcoming volumes on *Community Problems* by A. E. Wood, *Social Statistics* by G. R. Davies, and *Urban Sociology* by Howard Woolston; also Mary K. Simkhovitch's *City Worker's World* (New York, 1917), and R. A. Wood's *Neighborhood in Nation-Building* (Boston, 1923).

CHAPTER IV

THE CITY AND THE STATE

The cities of ancient Greece were not municipalities in the modern sense. They were states, and as a rule were subject to no higher control. Athens did not have a city charter, nor did Rome. So with the great commercial cities of the later Middle Ages. They owed merely a nebulous allegiance to emperor or king. In effect they were masters of their own destinies, kept their own fleets and armies, maintained their own tariffs and were not subject to the legislative power of any superior authority. They were free cities. But the growth of national supremacy brought this freedom to an end and, everywhere the great cities passed under the domination of strong national governments. All this had come to pass long before the first boroughs were founded in the New World. In America we have never had any city-states or free cities.[1]

Early cities were free.

But this came to an end.

The American city is and always has been a local subdivision of colony, province or state. Today it is a municipal corporation created by the state, deriving all its powers from state laws, and subordinate in all its activities to the state's authority. It is one of the instrumentalities which the state uses for the more convenient administration of local government. To this end, the city is intrusted with such powers (and only such) as the state may think wise to confer, and even in such grants of power the city acquires no vested right.[2] Its authority may be enlarged, abridged, or entirely withdrawn by the state at will. In other words, the state has the right to govern the city just as it governs any other area within its boundaries. This is a funda-

Supremacy of the state.

---

[1] It has been suggested during recent years, however, that New York City and Chicago ought to be detached from the states in which they are located and admitted as separate states of the Union.

[2] More than fifty years ago the supreme court of Michigan rendered a decision in which it declared local self government to be "an absolute right" which the state could not take away. In a few other states an attempt was made to maintain the same doctrine, but without permanent success.

mental principle of American municipal law, now so well recognized that it is not open to question.¹

The modern city is its creature.
So the day of the free city has long gone by. It persists only in the dreams of idealists.² Free cities, in the old sense of the term, are quite out of keeping with the conditions of our time. The whole drift of the twentieth century is toward political centralization. Municipal freedom has steadily dwindled until we now have scarcely anything worthy of the name. The laws of the land, both in Europe and America, not only permit but actually encourage the domination of municipal policy by authorities who are beyond the control of the city itself. This steadily increasing control is resented, but the resentment does not avail to stem its progress. Many years ago the situation was summed up in a decision rendered by the foremost American authority on municipal law. "Municipal corporations," said Judge Dillon in this case, "owe their origin to, and derive their powers and right wholly from, the legislature. It breathes into them the breath of life, without which they cannot exist. As it creates, so it may destroy. If it may destroy, it may abridge and control. Unless there is some constitutional limitation on the right (i.e., in the state constitution) the legislature might, by a single act, if we can suppose it capable of so great a folly and so great a wrong, sweep from existence all the municipal corporations of the state, and the corporations could not prevent it." ³

But state supremacy is not unlimited.
But this supremacy of the state legislature in matters of municipal government is not absolute and unlimited. Two general restrictions are placed upon it: (1) those which are imposed upon all legislative freedom by the constitution of the United States, and (2) those special limitations which are contained in the constitution of the various states themselves. The federal constitution, for example, withholds from all legislative bodies, state or national, the power to take private property for public use without just compensation. And what a state itself cannot do, it obviously cannot empower any subordinate authority to do. Again, the constitution of the United States forbids the state legislatures

General limitations on state supremacy are contained in:
(a) The national constitution.

---

¹ Meriwether *v.* Garrett, 102 U. S. 472, printed in J. H. Beale's *Selection of Cases on Municipal Corporations* (Cambridge, 1911), 54.
² Brand Whitlock, *Forty Years of It* (new edition, New York, 1925).
³ City of Clinton *v.* Cedar Rapids and Missouri Railroad Co., 24 Iowa 455 (1868).

THE CITY AND THE STATE 73

to deprive any one of the equal protection of the laws. That being the case it is not possible for the legislature to confer upon city councils the right to make unreasonable discriminations—for example, in the use of their licensing power. Many other illustrations might be given to show that the various provisions in the federal bill of rights have a restraining influence upon the power of the state legislatures with respect to municipal corporations.[1]

More important, however, and far more numerous, are the limitations imposed upon the legislatures of states by their own constitutions. In the earlier state constitutions these restrictions were few; in most of them there were none at all with reference to municipal government. The legislatures could interfere with the cities almost at will, and they did. They began regulating local elections, altering the form of city government without consulting the citizens, ordering local improvements at the city's expense, and chartering various water and gas companies at the behest of special interests. These perversions of power habitually produced a reaction and by the middle of the nineteenth century the people were showing their resentment by voting into the state constitutions all manner of provisions designed to protect the cities from legislative interference. During the past fifty years this popular attitude has continued and has indeed become stronger, until it now is taken for granted that, whenever a state adopts a new constitution or revises an old one, the opportunity will be utilized to insert some new restrictions upon the state legislature in its dealings with city affairs.

(b) The constitutions of the states themselves.

As a consequence these constitutional limitations upon the freedom of the legislature to deal with city affairs are now numerous and of great variety. Many of them relate to city charters and the methods of framing them. In some states the legislature is forbidden to charter cities by special act; in others it is required to grant all charters in this way. Some state constitutions prohibit changes in city charters unless they are made with the consent of the citizens; others guarantee to the voters of cities the right to frame their own charters and to enact them into force by majority vote,—in other words, to adopt home

The nature of these limitations.

---

[1] For a full discussion see the article on "Some Limitations on the Police Power of Municipalities Imposed by the Federal Constitution" by Charles Fairman, in the *Illinois Law Review*, xix, 401-409 (February, 1925).

74 THE GOVERNMENT OF AMERICAN CITIES

rule charters. A common form of constitutional restriction prevents legislatures from giving the cities too much borrowing power, or the right to grant perpetual franchises, or authority to lend their credit to private enterprises. A full list of the things which state legislatures must not do, in relation to municipal government, would extend over several pages. Only a few of the more important restrictions can be mentioned here.

Prohibition of special charters. Clauses forbidding the legislature to charter cities by special laws have made their way into the constitutions of about three-fourths of the states, but these prohibitions have usually been found easy to evade. As long ago as 1851, for example, the Ohio constitution stipulated that the state legislature should "pass no special act conferring corporate powers," but should arrange for the government of all cities under a general law, giving this law, with its amendments, a uniform operation throughout the entire state.[1] *Ohio's experience:* This provision did not prevent the classification of cities, and in the following year the Ohio legislature enacted a general municipal code which divided all the cities of the state into two classes and with a somewhat different form of organization for each. In itself this was not seriously objectionable, but the process of dividing the cities into classes did not stop in 1852. *(1) With the classification of cities.* Further classifying took place as time went on until there were nearly as many classes as there were cities.[2] Accordingly, when the legislature desired to pass any special law for an individual city, it merely had to make the law general in form; that is, applicable to the class to which the individual city belonged.[3] It did not legislate for Cleveland, but for all cities in the first grade of class one. When it desired to deal with Dayton alone, the legislature of Ohio merely passed a general law applying to all cities in the second grade of class two. Ashtabula found itself designated as "all cities in the first subdivision of grade four in class two." In this way the constitutional provision against special legislation was entirely circumvented.

This practice continued with the approval of the judiciary until 1902, when the supreme court of Ohio lost its forbearance

---

[1] Art. xii, §§ 1, 6; art. ii, § 26.
[2] In all there were eleven classes, eight of which contained only one city each.
[3] "In all cities of the third grade, second class, having a population of 10,221 at the last census, there shall be established a board of public affairs."

THE CITY AND THE STATE

and in a notable decision declared the whole process to be unconstitutional.[1] Thereupon the legislature had to convene hurriedly in special session to enact a general code for all the cities.[2] The result was exactly what one might have expected. There were seventy-two cities in Ohio, with populations ranging from 5,000 to more than half a million. Cleveland and Cincinnati were put on the same level with Wooster and Ashtabula. Every city, even the smallest, was required by the general code to maintain a director of public service, a director of public safety, a city solicitor, a city engineer, and at least a score of other officials, many of whom had virtually no duties to perform. This, of course, was an absurdity. The larger municipalities complained that they were undermanned in officials and deficient in powers—that they could not handle their big problems within the rigid terms of the general law. Cleveland, for example, found itself unable to deal with billboard nuisances, to provide public lectures in its schools, to require the isolation of persons afflicted with tuberculosis, to do many other things which the city council desired to have done during the ten years following 1902,—and all because no general powers covering such matters had been inserted in the municipal code.[3] The smaller cities, on the other hand, found themselves burdened with much administrative machinery which they did not want and provided with many powers which they could not use.

(2) With the general municipal code.

These ten years of municipal history in Ohio demonstrated the futility of trying to deal with all cities by a uniform code when there is in fact no uniformity in the problems which the cities have to solve. Conditions which are varied cannot be

(3) With municipal home rule.

---

[1] State v. Jones, 66 Ohio 453. The "last straw" which caused the supreme court to render this decision was a law establishing for the city of Toledo a bi-partisan police board the members of which were to be appointed by the governor of Ohio. Such a flagrant defiance of the constitutional provision could not be swallowed by the court.

[2] A good summary of this code, with a narrative of the events leading to its adoption, is given in John A. Fairlie's *Essays in Municipal Administration* (New York, 1908), Chapter v. The code itself is edited, with introduction and notes by Wade H. Ellis (Cincinnati, 1909). For a statement of the circumstances which led to the adoption see the chapter on "The Municipal Crisis in Ohio" in John A. Fairlie's *Essays in Municipal Administration* (New York, 1906), and H. L. McBain's *Law and Practice of Municipal Home Rule* (New York, 1915), pp. 621-645.

[3] See the pamphlet entitled *Constitutional Home Rule for Ohio Cities*, issued by the Municipal Association of Cleveland in 1912. This pamphlet has recently been reprinted in C. C. Maxey's *Readings in Municipal Government* (New York, 1924), pp. 17-30.

made homogenous by a stroke of the pen. There is nothing to be gained, and much to be lost, by trying to standardize municipal government when no two cities are exactly alike in size, needs, or problems. The outcome of the matter was that in 1912 the people of Ohio revised their state constitution, eliminated the old provision, and replaced it by a new one which gave to all cities the right either to frame their own charters or to adopt by local referendum any general or special charter law which the legislature might pass.[1] It is under this provision that Cleveland, Cincinnati, and Dayton have adopted their city manager plans of government, something that would not have been possible twenty years ago.

What Ohio's experience demonstrates.
The experience of Ohio has been set forth in some detail because it shows that constitutional provisions which forbid special legislation for particular cities are apt to serve a negative purpose. If they can be evaded by the legislature (as they were in Ohio for fifty years) they are worthless. If they are enforced upon the legislature (as they were in Ohio from 1902 to 1912) they do more harm than good. Forcing all cities into a single straitjacket is poor policy. Buffalo may have some use for a harbor board, and Rochester also; but that is no reason why Syracuse and Utica should be burdened with similar machinery. Los Angeles may find advantage in a division of itself into boroughs, each with some local officers; but it does not follow that San Diego and Sacramento should be compelled to do likewise. The American passion for standardization ought not to kidnap our common sense in such matters.

The experience of another state—New York:
Now someone may venture this suggestion: Why not adopt a middle course? Why not group cities into three or four classes, according to their size, and embody this classification in the state constitution, thus preventing the state legislature from meddling with it? That expedient has been tried—for example, in the New York constitution of 1894. This constitution divided the cities of the Empire State into three classes [2] and provided that laws should apply to all the cities within a class. The legislature was not absolutely forbidden to enact laws applying to individual cities but the constitution provided that in any such case the

1. Constitutional classification and the local suspensory veto.

[1] Art. xviii.
[2] First class: cities over 175,000; second class: cities having from 50,000 to 175,000; third class: all cities under 50,000.

THE CITY AND THE STATE

special law, after passing the legislature, should go to the authorities of the city concerned. If the latter accepted it, the special law then went to the governor for his signature; otherwise it went back to the legislature and had to be repassed before it could go into force.[1]

How did this plan work out? To some extent it placed a damper on legislative meddling in the affairs of individual cities. Many special acts have been passed since 1894 but relatively few of them have been enacted save with the approval of the cities concerned.[2] On the other hand, the cities of New York state have asked for a great many special laws without getting them. The legislature defeated hundreds of measures which the cities introduced and when it passed such bills the governor often vetoed them. More particularly the cities were denied the right to establish the commission form of government or the city manager plan. Until 1914 the legislature made almost no concessions on such points.

In 1914, however, it yielded somewhat to the insistence of the municipalities and enacted an "optional charter law" which provided that any city of the second or third class might take its choice among six optional charters which were embodied in the law.[3] Some of the smaller cities availed themselves of this opportunity, although there was some doubt as to the constitutionality of the optional charter law and it was not until 1917 that these doubts were cleared away. But even the optional charter system did not satisfy the municipal authorities, who continued to demand that each city be given the right to select its own form of government without being compelled to choose from a prescribed list. Their persistence was ultimately successful and in 1923 a provision for municipal home rule was added to the New York state constitution.[4]

2. The optional charter system.

3. Home rule.

[1] Acceptance or rejection was decided by the mayor alone in cities of the first class, by the mayor and council in all other cities.

[2] During the years 1900-1921, for example, over 1600 measures were passed by the legislature for New York City alone, but of these only 36 became law by repassage over the mayor's disapproval. A. W. McMahon, *The Statutory Sources of New York City Government* (New York, 1923), p. 155.

[3] These six options were the commission plan, the city manager plan, and four varieties of the mayor-and-council government. *Laws of New York*, 1914, Chapter 144.

[4] See the article on "Home Rule in New York State" by J. S. McGoldrick, in the *American Political Science Review*, Vol. xix, pp. 693-706 (November, 1925). See also *below*, p. 81.

78   THE GOVERNMENT OF AMERICAN CITIES

The Chicago situation. Illinois has had some experience in the same direction, and with the same dissatisfaction, but not with a similar outcome. In this state there is a peculiar situation, Chicago being about forty times larger than the next largest city of Illinois.[1] In 1904, therefore, the Illinois constitution recognized this special status of Chicago by providing that no special law affecting that city should go into force until accepted by the municipal voters. This gave the people of Chicago an absolute veto on all special legislation applicable to their city. The plan has worked well enough as a bulwark against legislative interference, but from the nature of things it is wholly negative in its operations. It enables the city to accept or reject, but not to initiate. What the city wants, the Illinois legislature usually declines to give; what it gives, the voters of Chicago quite as frequently decline to take. The arrangement does not seem to satisfy anybody but as yet the state and city authorities have not been able to agree on anything else.

Summary: On the whole, therefore, we have not had much success in protecting cities against legislative interference by means of (a) general constitutional prohibitions, or (b) the constitutional classification of cities, or (c) giving the cities a veto (whether absolute or suspensory) on special legislation. Nor does the optional charter plan appear to be satisfactory to the cities although several states have adopted it. Briefly the plan may be explained as follows: The state legislature enacts a general municipal law with some provisions applicable to all cities of whatever size or to all cities of a single class. Incorporated in this law, or appended to it, are several fully-drawn city charters, each of a different type. Then provision is made whereby any individual city may, by vote of its citizens, adopt any one of these various charters—whichever one it prefers. In this way each city is enabled to secure a form of government suitable to its own needs; on the other hand, it is restrained from trying foolish experiments which often involve it in lawsuits and serve no purpose but to disorganize the city administration. The optional charters are framed with care and are offered to the cities with an assurance that any one of them will be found workable. Massachusetts, in 1915, adopted this plan. Its

Explanation of the optional charter system.

---

[1] Chicago has about three million people. Next comes Peoria with about 80,000.

optional charter law provides that any city of the commonwealth (except Boston) may either retain its present charter or may adopt by popular vote any one of the four general types of charter incorporated in the act. These four types or plans provide respectively for (a) a mayor and city council of nine members elected at large, with all administrative powers concentrated in the mayor, (b) a mayor and council of fifteen members of whom some are elected by wards and some at large, with a somewhat less complete concentration of administrative functions in the mayor's hands, (c) a commission of five members elected at large, without a city manager, and (d) a commission of five members with a city manager.[1] A city may vote to adopt any one of these four plans, but only one plan may be voted upon at a time, and if one plan is adopted and put into force, no vote upon the adoption of any other plan may be taken for at least four years.

In addition the Massachusetts law provides certain uniform rules as to the use of the initiative and referendum, the methods of nomination, the abolition of party designations on the ballots, the award of contracts, budget-making, accounting, and so forth, which apply to every city (except Boston), no matter which one of these four plans it may adopt. Thus the legislature sought to combine a fair measure of latitude with a reasonable degree of uniformity in matters affecting the general interest. It was also hoped that the plan would relieve the legislature from the burden of considering the numerous charter proposals which were being laid before it every year.

This hope has not been realized. In Massachusetts, and in the other states which have the optional charter system, the cities desire a larger range of selection than the options provide. They insist on having their own special needs and preferences met. Hence they keep applying to the legislature for special concessions which vary the established options and eventually the situation drifts back to the old plan of special legislation for individual cities. The optional charter plan has

[1] The Ohio optional charter law provides three options only, the commission, city manager, and mayor-and-council types of government, any one of which may be adopted at a special election called upon the petition of 10 per cent of the voters. *Laws of Ohio*, 1913, pp. 767-786. The Virginia law may be found in *Laws of Virginia*, 1914, Chapter 94. Optional charter laws have also been passed in North Carolina and a few other states.

80 THE GOVERNMENT OF AMERICAN CITIES

not taken much burden off the legislatures. Its further extension is rather doubtful.

The home-rule system. We come, therefore, to the last and most effective method of protecting cities against legislative meddling. This is known as the home-rule charter system. It originated in Missouri over fifty years ago when a constitutional provision in that state gave all cities of over 100,000 population the right to frame and enact their own charters.[1]

How a home-rule charter is framed. By the provisions of the constitution the voters of the city were permitted to elect a charter board of thirteen members,—in other words, a miniature constitutional convention,—which was empowered either to frame a new city charter or to revise an old one, its work to be submitted to the qualified voters at a regular election. During the first quarter-century following its adoption this system gained little headway outside Missouri, for in 1900 it had spread to three other states only.[2] Since this latter date, however, ten other states have incorporated in their constitutions the principle of the Missouri plan, and most of them made it applicable to smaller as well as to larger cities.[3] These thirteen home-rule states form less than one-third of the total number, yet they contain eight cities of over half a million population each (New York, Detroit, Cleveland, Los Angeles, Baltimore, St. Louis, Buffalo, and San Francisco) and about a dozen other cities with populations above the 200,000 mark. It can be said, therefore, that at least half the larger cities of the United States are now revolving more or less contentedly within the home-rule orbit.

The general practice. Among the various "home-rule" states, however, there are considerable differences in the provisions of the constitutions and the laws. In some of them it is provided that the initial step in the adoption or the revision of a city charter may be taken

---

[1] Constitution of Missouri, Art. ix, 16-17.
[2] Constitution of California, 1879, Art. xi, 6-8; Constitution of Washington, 1889, Art. xi, 10; Constitution of Minnesota, Art. iv, 36 (adopted in 1898).
[3] Colorado in 1902, Oregon in 1906, Oklahoma and Michigan in 1908, Arizona, Nebraska, and Texas in 1912, Pennsylvania in 1922, and New York in 1923. A few other states, including Maryland, Connecticut, and Florida, have provided by statute for partial home-rule. The home-rule plan still applies in Missouri to the two largest cities only; in Maryland it extends to Baltimore only; in Washington it covers only the cities of more than 20,000 inhabitants. In Pennsylvania the legislature has not yet passed the statute which is necessary to carry the home-rule provision into effect.

on petition of a prescribed number of voters;[1] in others the city council must make the first move; and in one state, Minnesota, the initiative must be taken by the district judges.[2] In all cases the actual work of drafting the home-rule charter is intrusted to a commission commonly called a board of freeholders, ordinarily made up of thirteen or fifteen members chosen by popular vote (except in Minnesota), and usually elected at large. In all the states the finished document must be submitted to the qualified voters of the city for their approval. If more votes are cast for it than against it, the charter usually goes into effect; but in a few states the charter goes to the governor who may veto it. In most cases it also goes to the legislature for final enactment but neither the governor nor the legislature are in the habit of interfering with any home-rule charter that has been adopted by the voters of the city. Amendments to a home-rule charter are usually initiated by petition and ratified by the voters, no board of freeholders being required.

New York State has a somewhat different procedure. There the drafting of a new charter may be done by the city council (with the board of estimate and the council sitting jointly if there is such a board), or the council may refer to the voters the question of establishing a special charter commission to do the work. If the latter alternate is chosen, and the voters decide in favor of a special commission, the members of the latter may be appointed or elected as the council determines, but its decision on this point must also be ratified by the voters. And when the new charter is finished there is a further reference to the voters for their approval of it. Amendments to home-rule charters, if they be of a minor or routine nature, may be made by the city council on its own authority (subject to the mayor's veto where there is a mayor), but important amendments have to be submitted to the people.[3] *The New York procedure.*

So much for the machinery by which a home-rule charter is drafted. Now comes an important question as to the powers and discretion which a charter body may exercise. To what extent *Limitations on the scope of municipal home-rule*

---
[1] The percentage varies from 5 per cent in Colorado to 25 per cent in Washington.
[2] Constitution of Minnesota, Art. iv, 36.
[3] For a full statement of the procedure see Article xii of the New York constitution as amended in November, 1923, also the *Laws of New York*, 1924, Chapter 363.

is a charter commission or board of freeholders allowed to insert in the charter whatever provisions it may think best? May it follow its own judgment in all cases. The answer to this question is *No*. Obviously the provisions of a city charter, whether of the home-rule or any other variety, must not be in conflict with the constitution or the general laws of the state. If the state constitution stipulates that city officials shall be elected, it is not possible for a home-rule charter to provide that they shall be appointed. If the state laws require that the schools shall be administered by local boards of education it is not within the powers of a charter commission to provide for the abolition of such boards and for the transfer of their work to the city council. On the other hand, where the state laws relate to some matter of purely local importance it is ordinarily within the discretion of the charter commission to adopt some different arrangement.

<small>What are "local affairs"?</small>
In a word, then, the home-rule city is said to be free to regulate its own "local affairs"; but this is not an altogether illuminating statement for it begs the question as to what affairs are *local* rather than *general* in character.[1] No clear line of demarcation has been established nor can any principle be deduced from the numerous court decisions. Matters which relate to police, elections, public utilities, taxation, and assessments have usually (but not always) been held to be of general as distinct from local importance, and when a provision of a home-rule charter conflicts with the state laws on such matters it is void. In a few constitutions an attempt has been made to specify what affairs are local in character, but it is extremely difficult to draw hard-and-fast lines of division when the interests of city and state are so closely interwoven as they have come to be.[2] Not only that but new powers are constantly coming into the field, to be exercised by somebody. Governmental authority is not a thing that can be mapped off into blocks and lots like a tract of land. It is a field that is always expanding or contracting besides constantly changing in the urgency of its exercise. There will be controversies and lawsuits whenever and wherever we attempt a pre-

---

[1] The words differ somewhat from state to state. In Michigan the term is "municipal affairs"; in New York the expression is "relating to the property, affairs, or government of cities."

[2] See the elaborate discussion of this point in H. L. McBain's *Law and Practice of Municipal Home Rule* (New York, 1916), pp. 255-321.

cise division. How carefully the allocation of powers between the nations and the states was made by the framers of the national constitution, yet what a mass of legislation has reached the Supreme Court thereon! Can we hope that a division of powers between state and city will fare better?

The home-rule charter plan, nevertheless, has some distinct merits. First among these is the fact that it enables a city to obtain the general type of governmental organization that its people desire. While it is true that the mere form or type of government is not a vital factor in determining the efficiency of a city's administration, it is equally true that no such administration is likely to be successful unless the people are in sympathy with it. A government ought to be popular as well as efficient. But governments which are imposed from above, and are not created by the action and consent of the governed, rarely become popular. The average American citizen sees no reason why he should not enjoy "self-determination" in local affairs. It is useless to argue with him that state legislators, by virtue of their wider experience, can devise better charters than he and his fellow citizens can frame. He does not believe it. If, therefore, a charter is imposed upon a city by the legislature, it will be saddled with the blame when things go wrong. There are thousands of intelligent New Yorkers who firmly believe that the source of metropolitan mismanagement is at Albany. It is astonishing how cheerfully the average citizen will tolerate mediocre government so long as it is of his own manufacture, and how vigorously he criticises anything short of perfection that is imposed upon his city from outside.

Merits of the home-rule plan:

(a) Its popularity.

Home-rule charters are homemade charters, but this does not mean that they are inferior to the legislative product. There is no reason why they should be. Legislators as a class have no special competence in making city charters. On the other hand, the citizens who constitute a municipal charter commission or board of freeholders, while they may not know much about the principles of political science, at least know their own city, its needs, its problems, and its desires. The matter being of immediate consequence to themselves, moreover, they do not go about their task in any perfunctory way. They study the charters of other cities; they get information from all quarters, and usually they consult with men who have had large experience in

(b) It insures greater care in charter-drafting.

the work of charter framing. The result is that home-rule charters are on the whole more concise, less ambiguous, and more workable in their provisions. Not only that but there is more originality in home-rule charters; those who frame them are much more ready to try experiments. Most of the new features that have come into the American municipal system in the last twenty-five years would probably have never gained their first foothold if state legislatures had monopolized the work of charter-drafting. The average senator or assemblyman likes to think that he is progressive, forward-looking, and practical; but in most cases he is nothing of the sort. The great majority of American state legislators are out-and-out traditionalists.

(c) It lessens the burden on the legislature.
A state legislature, moreover, has a great deal of work to do. It cannot devote to city charters and charter amendments the amount of time and thought that the importance of the subject demands. With the rapid growth of cities a veritable avalanche of requests for new charters or for charter amendments descends on the legislatures of the more populous states every year. In Massachusetts there are now thirty-eight cities, not to speak of at least a dozen towns which have populations large enough to qualify them as cities. At the legislative session of 1925 nearly three hundred bills were referred to the joint committees on cities, on towns, on municipal finance, and on metropolitan affairs. It is a conservative estimate that at least half of these bills were proposals to amend, in one way or another, the charter of some Massachusetts city. Every one of these three hundred bills was given a public hearing, discussed in committee, and reported favorably or unfavorably to the legislature. Is it reasonable to suppose that any legislature, in view of the other demands upon its attention, will give adequate scrutiny to so many measures of strictly local interest? Matters affecting a single city evoke very little interest save among those legislators who come from the immediate vicinity. It is their business to get what their districts desire, and they try to do it by all manner of trading on other measures. The home-rule charter system has helped to reduce the amount of logrolling at legislative capitals.

In most of our state legislatures, the rural senators and representatives control a majority. This is largely because the rural population is still predominant in most of the states, but it is

THE CITY AND THE STATE 85

also due, in some cases, to the fact that the rural districts are over-represented in the legislature.[1] This arises from the common rule that no county shall have more than a certain proportion of the entire membership in the state senate. Under the system of legislative charter-making, therefore, the up-state senators and assemblymen have the controlling voice. These men, no matter how sound their practical sense or how good their intentions, are obviously not well-versed in the conditions, problems, and needs of the urban communities.

(d) It releases the cities from bondage to the yokel.

But although they have neither special knowledge, interest, or competence in city affairs, this does not deter them from acting as though they possessed all three. The assemblyman from some village in the Catskills has no hesitancy in asserting his own opinion as to how New York City, the largest municipality in the world, ought to be governed. In general the rural legislator is suspicious of the city; he thinks of it as a place filled with foreign-born voters who allow themselves to be exploited by demagogues and corrupted bosses. He is for keeping the lid clamped down on it. Much of the legislative manhandling that the cities have had to bear can be attributed to the parochial prejudices of lawmakers who have no real conception of urban problems.

The home-rule charter system is said to have an educative value which the plan of legislative charter-making has not. The average citizen takes very little interest in what goes on at the state capital in the legislative committee rooms. The proceedings there get scant publicity. And why should he be actively interested? He knows that his voice and his vote count for nothing in the matter. What really counts is the political influence of those who have introduced the measure and are backing it upon the floor of the legislative chambers. A whispered word from the leaders of the majority party will ensure its passage or encompass its defeat,—wholly apart from the merits of the proposed charter.

(e) It promotes civic education.

But when the final decision in charter-making rests with the people, and not with the legislature, public interest is bound to become broader and more intense. Popular responsibility be-

[1] For a discussion of this rural over-representation, and the reasons for it, see W. F. Dodd's *State Government* (New York, 1922), p. 173. Mention should also be made of J. W. Brookwalter's *Rural vs. Urban, the Conflict and Its Causes* (New York, 1910).

gets popular interest. There is a world of difference between the amount of interest evoked by the two systems of charter-making. In the case of the home-rule plan the work of the local charter commission is closely followed; the newspapers give much space to its deliberations, and the whole question becomes a living issue. For weeks before the charter-election the various provisions of the document are debated and discussed at club meetings, before labor unions, at board of trade luncheons, and wherever bodies of citizens gather. It may be quite true, as sometimes asserted, that even with all this discussion, many voters go to the polls in home-rule cities with no clear idea of what they are voting for, but the amount of knowledge and interest is certainly much greater than when there is no local responsibility at all.

(f) It makes possible the divorce of municipal from state politics. Most people think it desirable to keep issues of municipal politics separate from those of the state and nation. Local elections, they feel, should be fought on local questions and not on extraneous issues of state politics. But so long as a state legislature possesses the right to interfere at will in city affairs, and so long as it adopts the policy of doing so, there is little chance of keeping state and municipal issues apart. Home-rule facilitates the separation of the two. It helps to eliminate the appeal, which, in some of the larger American communities, is so persistently made to the state legislature by minorities who want the majority compelled to do differently. Defeated in its attempt to control affairs at the city hall, the losing party turns for aid and comfort to its own friends who dominate the state legislature. New York City is overwhelmingly Democratic; the state is normally Republican. The same is true of Boston and Massachusetts. In such cases there is an obvious temptation for the Republicans to seek such changes in the city charter as will help offset their numerical inferiority. Municipal questions thus become issues in state campaigns, while state politics inject themselves into municipal campaigns. Municipal home-rule does not put a complete end to this evil but it affords a considerable measure of relief.

Objections to the home-rule charter system: The home-rule charter system, on the other hand, is open to some serious objections. Were this not so it would have been far more widely adopted. The objections, in the main, are of a practical character; they arise from the necessary inter-relation of city and state problems. The advocates of municipal home-rule are fond of applying to the city the principle enunciated in the Declaration of Independence that government ought to rest on "the consent of the governed." A sound principle, no doubt, but one that cannot be applied without reservations. If cities and towns are entitled to complete self-determination, why not also the wards of a city? Why not the precincts within the wards? Is a city of ten thousand entitled to home-rule, while a city ward of fifty thousand is denied the same right? It will be replied that wards and precincts are only artificial divisions, but so is the whole municipality. There is hardly a city in the United States whose boundaries are historic. Most of them have been changed, over and over again, by legislative enactment. In many cases there are several municipalities contiguous to one another, some large, some small, but all closely associated by the daily intercourse of their citizens. Can we say that each of these communities is entitled to complete self-determination irrespective of the effect upon its neighbors? Of course we cannot carry the principle to that extreme. Home-rule must be diluted by considerations of common interest. Like every other principle of government it must defer to the actualities. *(a) The danger of overworking the home-rule principle.*

The whole question thus becomes one of expediency. How far is it advisable in the general interest to give each city a sphere of independent action? The well-being of the whole is undeniably more to be considered than the preferences of its parts. And so long as this is the case, there can be no complete measure of municipal home-rule or anything approaching it. In many matters the city is merely the agent of the state and it is imperative that all the agencies of state government should function in a uniform way. Take the matter of local taxes, for example. The power to tax is a sovereign power, delegated by the state to the cities. It is not possible for a city, whether by adopting a home-rule charter or otherwise, to assume this taxing power for itself. Were this possible it would mean utter chaos in taxation. The city police, again, are charged with the duty of enforcing the state laws. Can we ask the state to give up all control over the enforcement of these laws? Is the safeguarding of the public health a function which can be left to the discretion of each individual city? Can we safely permit self- *(b) Home-rule is a matter of expediency.*

determination in the matter of quarantine, the reporting of communicable diseases, and the safeguarding of public water supplies? Or, take what is perhaps the best example of all—municipal borrowing. Now it might plausibly be argued that cities, like individuals, should be left free to borrow as much money as they please, provided they can get somebody to lend it; but what would happen if a city went bankrupt? The state would have to step in and help it out. Clearly no state can disclaim responsibility for what happens to its cities. Its own credit and reputation are too closely bound up with those of its urban communities.

<small>(c) The field of strictly local affairs is steadily becoming more narrow.</small>
A complete measure of municipal home-rule, therefore, is not practicable, and no state has attempted to give it. Even a large degree of home-rule is becoming less and less practicable as the growth of cities proceeds. There is no good reason why each city should not have liberty to determine its own *form* of government, assuming that it makes provision for those officers whose work is essential to the carry out of the city's functions as the agent of the state. The method of choosing the city's own officials, their general duties, and their routine methods may also be left to local determination. But the activities of the city in relation to such matters as police, public health, education, poor-relief, corrections, sanitation, elections, taxation, indebtedness, and the control of public utilities cannot be handed over as hostages to local efficiency or mismanagement as the case may be. These things are not of purely local concern under the conditions of today.

<small>Administrative, as distinguished from legislative control.</small>
What has been said in the foregoing pages has reference, more particularly, to the *legislative* control of the state over its cities; in other words, control by the enactment of codes, charters, general laws or special laws. But there is another form of control which is nowadays making considerable progress in the United States. It is commonly known as *administrative* control—a control exercised by state officials, boards, or commissions to which discretionary powers have been given by law. Those who are familiar with the governmental system of European countries need not be reminded that this form of control and supervision is very common overseas; in fact, most of the control exercised by the higher authorities over local government in France, Italy, Germany—and even in England, is of an adminis-

THE CITY AND THE STATE

trative character. Fifty years ago this type of supervision was virtually non-existent in the United States, but it began to develop during the closing decades of the nineteenth century and of late it has been expanding rapidly. Today, there are state boards and commissions of every sort assisting or supervising the work of the municipal authorities in such fields as the civil service, public health, education, public utilities, finance, and social welfare.[1] In some cases, notably in the matter of regulating public utilities (such as gas, electric lighting and street railway companies), the amount of controlling authority now vested in the hands of state boards is so great as virtually to deprive the cities of everything except the mere shadow of power.

The channels through which this administrative control is developing ought to be explained. The first step, as a rule, is to set up some state board or bureau with *advisory* functions only. Its duties are to gather information and to make this information available for cities to use. There is great need for something of this sort in many branches of municipal government. City officials often have very technical duties to perform in connection with health protection, water supply, social welfare problems, budget-making, accounting, and so forth. Yet they are mostly amateurs, without previous experience, and chosen for short terms. From all quarters they are under pressure from concerns that have materials and supplies to sell, or by pseudo-experts who urge the adoption of some new methods. It is well that there should be some source from which trustworthy information and advice may be had on all questions of material and methods, —some source from which a well-intentioned but inexperienced city official can find out what other municipalities are doing and with what results. Hence it is that state boards of health, or of education, or bureaus of fire-prevention, or departments of accounts are vested with the function of advising city officials, on matters of sanitation, school building, zoning, assessing, and the like.

How it is developed.

---

[1] Administrative control began in the field of education and was an outgrowth of the state-subsidy system. Many years ago the national government gave large tracts of land for educational purposes, and as these lands were sold the proceeds were distributed among the local school authorities. Thereupon it seemed to be incumbent upon the state authorities to see that these funds were properly spent and hence developed a system of state inspection which has gradually widened into varying degrees of control or supervision.

But the work rarely stops at this point. The state authorities presently find that although their advice is asked and given it is not always followed. They are able to point to the fact that various cities, by this disregard of good counsel, have got themselves into difficulties. Accordingly the next move takes the form of a suggestion that the state board's advice or approval be made mandatory—or sometimes that a state subsidy be withheld unless the city does things in the right way. In some cases the state authorities have plenary power to remove the local health officials, or the local assessors. In other cases the heads of the municipal police department are appointed by the state authorities and are removable by them.

Its probable expansion in the future. This slow but steady development of administrative, as distinguished from legislative control, is due to the fact that the latter falls short of our present-day requirements. Laws do not have enough resiliency. Being rigid they sometimes fall short of their desired end or else go too far and defeat their purpose. The conditions which the laws seek to regulate, moreover, are continually changing and quickly get beyond reach of the printed statute. The more thickly populated a country, and the more complex its social organization, the less efficient is the method of control by law. It is better, under such conditions, to vest the power of regulation in the hands of a board or bureau with instructions to deal with each question on its merits, subject, however, to certain general rules which the law lays down. Instead of providing by law, for example, that every city shall install a specified type of sewage disposal plant it is more practicable to stipulate that each city shall do as the state department of health may approve in its individual case. Instead of passing a uniform-accounting law for all cities it is more practicable to provide that municipal accounts shall be kept in accordance with such methods as the state bureau of accounting may approve. Administrative supervision has an elasticity which permits quick adjustment to rapidly-changing conditions. There is no doubt that we shall have much more of it in the United States as time goes on.

REFERENCES

Extensive discussions of this general subject may be found in J. F. Dillon's *Law of Municipal Corporations* (5th edition, 5 vols., Boston, 1911),

Vol. i, pp. 140-172, and in Eugene McQuillin's *Law of Municipal Corporations* (vols. i-vi, Chicago, 1911-1913, vols. vii-viii, Chicago, 1921), especially vol. i, pp. 373-564, and vol. vii, pp. 6481-6555). H. L. McBain's *Law and Practice of Municipal Home Rule* (New York, 1916) is the best book on the home rule charter system, and mention should also be made of the same author's smaller volume on *American City Progress and the Law*. An older book by President Frank J. Goodnow on *Municipal Home Rule* (New York, 1903) is still valuable. Surveys of a more general character may be found in William Anderson's *American City Government* (New York, 1925), ch. ii-iii; C. C. Maxey's *Outline of Municipal Government* (New York, 1924), pp. 14-35 and the same author's *Readings in Municipal Government* (New York, 1924), pp. 9-51; Everett Kimball's *State and Municipal Government* (Boston, 1922), pp. 374-392; F. J. Goodnow and F. G. Bates, *Municipal Government* (New York, 1919), pp. 63-148; W. T. Arndt, *The Emancipation of the American City* (New York, 1917), pp. 3-44; J. M. Mathews, *American State Government* (New York, 1924), pp. 499-518; W. F. Dodd, *Principles of American State Government* (New York, 1922), pp. 175 ff.; the Massachusetts Constitutional Convention *Bulletin* No. 11 (Boston, 1918); and the Illinois Constitutional Convention *Bulletin* No. 6 (Springfield, Illinois, 1920). See also the Second Report of the Home Rule Commission to the New York State Legislature (Albany, 1925).

For material relating to the control of the cities by higher authorities in European countries the reader may be referred to the author's *Government of European Cities* (new and revised edition, New York, 1926).

CHAPTER V

THE CITY CHARTER

What the charter is.

The city charter is a written instrument which incorporates the community as a municipal entity, organizes its governmental authorities, endows them with powers, and places various limitations upon them. It is given by, or under, the authority of the state, and ranks as a statute. As has been explained in the preceding chapter it is granted under varying constitutional limitations. The legislature sometimes bestows it by special act or by general law; in other cases it permits a city to choose a charter from among various options. And in thirteen states certain cities, or all of them, are entitled to frame their own charters under a procedure which is known as the home-rule system. We speak of the city charter as if it were a single document, just as we speak of the constitution of the United States in the same sense; but in neither case are we speaking accurately. The constitution is an original document plus nineteen amendments plus a large number of judicial interpretations which are tantamount to amendments. The charter of a city is an original document plus all the amendments, formal or otherwise, that have been added to it either directly or by the general laws. When you ask the city clerk for a copy of the charter he will give you a printed pamphlet or book bearing that title; but it does not tell the whole story. Quite as much more is usually scattered around in the general statutes and the decisions of the courts. Anything in the general laws which operates to amend the city charter is an amendment, whether it be so designated or not, and many judicial decisions are also amendments in effect.

Its legal status:

The charter is sometimes called the "constitution of the city" and, in a sense, it is entitled to be so called, especially in states where the home-rule charter system has been adopted. Like a constitution the charter forms the groundwork of government, the basis upon which the framework rests, and it is also the

THE CITY CHARTER 93

source from which the governing authorities derive their powers. But it is unlike a constitution in that it can usually be amended by a legislative body without the concurrence of the people immediately concerned. The state legislature gives, and unless restrained by constitutional limitations, it can take away. The city charter does not, therefore, possess the inherent stability of a constitution. *Its analogy to a constitution.*

On the other hand, it is sometimes said that a city charter is more analogous to the charter of a private corporation, such as a bank or a railroad. It is a document which merely empowers a group of citizens to do certain things in a corporate capacity. It conveys no grant of power that cannot be revoked. But here again the analogy is by no means exact, and indeed the differences outweigh the similarities. The city charter conveys powers which are chiefly of a governmental, and not of a business character, although some business functions are usually included. It gives various privileges and immunities which the charter of a private corporation does not grant.[1] Hence the city charter is exactly akin neither to a constitution nor to an act of incorporation in the ordinary sense. It is something between the two. Its contents resemble those of a constitution; its status is more analogous to the charter of a private company. *Its analogy to the charter of a private corporation.*

What does a city charter contain? The contents naturally depend upon the size of the city and the complexity of its governmental organization. They are also determined in part by the policy pursued in framing the charter. In some cases the practice is to include only general provisions, leaving the details to be arranged by ordinances as the city council may see fit. More often, however, many details are put into the charter itself, even minor details, with the result that the document becomes long and complicated. In general, however, a city charter ordinarily includes at least seven groups of provisions, as follows: *What a city charter contains.*

1. *Territorial Boundaries.* A statement of the city's boundaries and a declaration that the people living within these designated bounds shall form a municipal corporation, a "body politic," with the usual privileges and obligations of such a body.[2]

---

[1] See *below*, pp. 120-126.
[2] "The inhabitants of the territory which, on the fourth day of March in the year eighteen hundred and twenty-two, was comprised within the limits

2. *The Frame of Government.* Provisions relating to the frame of government, indicating what officials shall be elected and how. Sometimes the general laws of the state cover the whole matter of nominations and prescribe how elections shall be held, in which case there is no need to repeat such provisions in the city charter. It is enough to state that nominations shall be made and elections held in accordance with the general statutes, or in accordance with certain specified statutes, which are referred to in the customary way.[2] On the other hand, if it is desired to depart from the usual procedure in nominations or elections the charter sets forth the changes so far as may be necessary.

3. *Officials and Their Duties.* Provisions relating to terms of office, oaths of office, general duties of municipal officers, and sometimes their salaries. Here come also various clauses relating the division of administrative work by departments and the appointment of subordinate officers. In a large city these provisions are usually both numerous and elaborate, especially when the framers of the charter undertake to cover the whole range of departmental organization and duties.

4. *Powers.* The general powers of the municipal corporation, and of its mayor, council, boards, commission, or city manager are also indicated. Some powers are conferred on the city as such; others are vested in specified officers or boards. In a broad way these powers include the authority to enact and enforce ordinances for protecting and promoting the safety, health, morals and welfare of the people, authority to levy taxes, to make appropriations and to borrow money, to hold property, to make contracts, to undertake local improvements, and to provide various public services. All such powers are to be exercised, however, within the bounds prescribed by the constitution and

of the municipal corporation known as the town of Boston, and which, on said day, became the territory of the city of Boston, and the inhabitants of the territory subsequently annexed, as hereinafter described, are, and shall continue to be, one body politic, in fact and in name under the style and denomination of the city of Boston; and as such shall have, exercise, and enjoy all the rights, immunities, powers and privileges, and shall be subject to all the duties and obligations now incumbent upon, and appertaining to, said city as a municipal corporation." *Charter of the City of Boston,* Chapter I, Section i.

[2] This is commonly known as "inclusion by reference," the inclusion of one statute in another by referring to it. The usual method of reference is by date and chapter (or page), e.g., *Laws of New York,* 1914, Chapter 444, or *Laws of Ohio,* 1913, pp. 767-768.

THE CITY CHARTER

general laws of the state, and in accordance with a procedure which is sometimes set forth in the charter at considerable length.

5. *Business Provisions.* Almost every city charter contains some provisions which aim to ensure the use of honest and businesslike methods in the conduct of public affairs. These usually include some stipulations as to when and how the budget shall be made and voted, how the tax rate shall be determined, what audits shall be required, and how the accounts shall be published.[1] Along with these more general provisions one often finds others which relate to the advertising and award of contracts, the bonding of contractors, the disciplining of municipal employees, the inspection of materials, the making of annual inventories, and so forth. There is no end to the possibilities here.

6. *Popular Control.* Many cities make provision in their charters for popular control by means of the initiative and referendum. Some of them also provide for the recall of elective officials, by popular vote, before their terms of office have expired. In such cases it usually becomes essential to embody in the charter long sections relating to the manner in which petitions shall be filed, signatures checked, and special elections held.[2]

7. *Miscellaneous.* Finally, there must needs be some miscellaneous and transitional provisions. Among the former are clauses dealing with the pensions of city employees, for example, or their hours of labor, or vacations. It is also stipulated, as a rule, that the charter shall go into force at a certain date if accepted by a majority of the voters, but that existing officeholders shall continue until their successors are selected or appointed. There is commonly a provision that all laws and ordinances not inconsistent with the charter shall remain unrepealed, and not infrequently special mention is made of certain statutes which are definitely continued in force.

This, in a general way, is what a city charter usually contains. Most charters contain too much, too many detailed provisions.[3]

---

[1] See also *below*, pp. 328-329.
[2] For a discussion of the initiative, referendum, and recall in cities, see *below*, Chapter x.
[3] The charter of Baltimore contains about 63,000 words, that of Buffalo about 64,000, that of San Francisco about 88,000, and that of Detroit about 82,000.

96 THE GOVERNMENT OF AMERICAN CITIES

Charters tend to become too long.

This arises from the tendency to enumerate all the city's powers, one by one, and to specify the administrative departments in detail. Would it not be better to state the city's powers in broad terms and leave the administrative machinery to be created by ordinance? The framers of some recent city charters have adopted this plan. Putting details into a city charter is objectionable on several grounds: it makes the charter too long; it gives rise to more controversies concerning the exact meaning of minor provisions, and it tends to make the administrative machinery too rigid. The longer a charter, obviously, the more basis for misunderstandings and litigation. The greater the elaboration of details the greater is the opportunity for subterfuge or evasion. The average citizen does not hold it a serious offense when a municipal officeholder departs from some technical requirement which only legal experts can interpret and about which even these experts may disagree.

Can they be shortened?

On the other hand, if the administrative arrangements are left to be determined by ordinance, the charter is shortened and clarified, changes in organization and methods can be made with little delay or trouble at any time, and the incentives to evasion are diminished. Flexibility is given to the administrative system—too much flexibility, perhaps. The city council (or the commission) being permitted to change the number, organization, or methods of the city departments at its own discretion, is under temptation to make changes frequently and to be actuated by partisan motives in doing so.[1] Charter-makers have been afraid to trust city councils with so wide a range of authority as regards the mechanism of administration.

A compromise suggestion.

As a compromise it has been suggested that the city charter should restrict itself to a grant of powers and a description of the frame of government, together with a small number of general safeguards. But accompanying the charter there should be an administrative code incorporating the details of departmental organization and procedure. This code, settling all important matters of business routine, would not be so easily alter-

---

[1] When a newly-elected city government, for example, desires to turn employees out of office without running foul of the civil service rules it need only provide by ordinance for the abolition or consolidation of various departments. Then it can create new ones which will perform the old functions under a different name and with a new staff of employees. When new departments can be created at any time by ordinance there is also a temptation to increase their number in order to provide new jobs.

THE CITY CHARTER

able as an ordinance nor yet as difficult to change as are the charter provisions.[1] There is a good deal to be said for this arrangement, especially in the case of the larger cities, but it has not yet been given a trial anywhere.

In the countries of Continental Europe the practice has been to bestow upon the local communities a broad and uniform grant of powers. There is no piecemeal enumeration of the powers which a French, German, or Italian city may exercise. The presumption is always in its favor, and the central authorities have no right of intervention in local government save where such right has been expressly given to them by the general laws. The administrative courts of these countries, moreover, in controversies concerning the apportionment of power between central and local government, have almost invariably given the cities the benefit of any doubt. They maintain the doctrine that a municipality has the right to exercise any local power and to perform any local business until the contrary is shown.[2] The city does not bear the burden of proof that it possesses authority in matters of local scope; the onus is on those who deny it. In connection with its own affairs the city may do whatever it has not been forbidden to do; and the central authorities, if they claim the right to intervene in any matter of local administration, must prove that the law has explicitly given such rights to them. {The interpretation of city charters: 1. In Europe.}

In the United States the situation is reversed. The almost universal American practice has been to bestow a list of enumerated powers upon city authorities, not upon the city itself, and the courts have required strict adhesion to the express or implied terms of this enumeration. The general rule applied by the courts to the interpretation of American city charters, as stated by the most authoritative writer on this subject, is as follows: {2. In the United States.}

"It is a general and undisputed proposition of law that a municipal corporation possesses and can exercise the following powers and no others: first, those granted in express words; second, those necessarily {Judge Dillon's summary of the matter.}

---

[1] It might be arranged, for example, that provisions in the administrative code could be changed by a two-thirds vote of the city council.
[2] Questions of jurisdiction between the central and municipal authorities in Germany, France, and other Continental countries do not involve long and expensive litigation in the regular courts, but are determined promptly and inexpensively by the administrative tribunals.

or fairly implied in or incident to the powers expressly granted; third, those essential to the accomplishment of the declared objects and purposes of the corporation—not simply convenient but indispensable. Any fair, reasonable, substantial doubt concerning the existence of a power is resolved by the courts against the corporation, and the power is denied."[1]

It is on this doctrine, now commonly known as "Dillon's Rule," that the legal position of the American city is founded. To be sure there is some opportunity for the exercise of latitude in the application of the rule as stated, inasmuch as some of the words are rather elastic. One court may be more lenient than another in determining what is "fairly implied" in the provisions of a city charter, or what is "essential to the accomplishment of the declared objects and purposes of the corporation"; but in any case the presumption is against the city, which is in contrast with the established practice in Continental Europe.[2]

A comment on this difference in the rule of interpretation.

Now it is somewhat surprising that this should be the case, because central supervision of municipal government is commonly said to be more rigid in Europe than in the United States. But this is because we regard only the superficial appearances. In Europe the central control is *administrative*, not legislative in character—the two are very different things. A system of administrative supervision catches the eye more readily because large numbers of officials are required to carry it on. Legislative control of cities, being the work of senators and assemblymen who can usually divert public attention to other things, is less plainly visible but it is in fact more burdensome to the communities involved. A government of laws may be more impartial than a government of men but it is also far more unbending. Ministers, prefects, and other supervisors of local administration can use discretion, which the courts in administering the laws can not. The extreme inflexibility of the state's control over American cities, in fact as in theory, has not been fully appreciated by students of comparative government.

There is a palpable inconsistency in the rules which American

---

[1] John F. Dillon, *Commentaries on the Law of Municipal Corporations* (5th edition, 5 vols., Boston, 1911), Vol. I, Sec. 237.
[2] In England the theory and practice of the law occupy a midway position. Some powers are granted in general terms but many others are obtained by the cities individually. The attitude of the English courts has not been inclined strongly toward one side or the other.

courts have applied with reference to grants of power from the state to the nation on the one hand, and from the states to the cities on the other. The constitution of the United States contains a grant of enumerated powers to the national government, and it specifically provides that "the powers not delegated to the United States by the constitution, nor prohibited by it to the states, are reserved to the states respectively, or to the people."[1]   *A rule that does not work both ways.*

Seventeen clauses granting express powers to Congress are placed in the body of the document; an eighteenth clause provides that Congress shall have power "to make all laws which shall be necessary and proper for carrying into execution the foregoing powers, and all other powers vested by this constitution in the government of the United States, or in any department or office thereof."[2] In other words, the national government was given no broad grant of authority to deal with national affairs; it was endowed with a strict enumeration of powers and with the means of carrying these enumerated powers into effect. But the courts, as is well known, have construed these enumerated powers with great generosity. They have applied to the enumerated constitutional powers of Congress the rule of broad construction and have by that process enormously widened the area of federal jurisdiction.[3] They have stretched the simple words and phrases in such way as to give a measure of authority which the framers of the national constitution never intended to bestow upon the central government. By so doing the courts have performed a great service to the orderly expansion of American government; they have endowed the organic law of the nation with a dynamic quality which it has needed to keep it in consonance with the needs of a growing country.   *The broad construction of powers granted to the nation.*

But with reference to the enumerated powers conferred by the

---

[1] Amendment XI.
[2] Article I, Section 8.
[3] For example, the Supreme Court has held that the power "to regulate commerce with foreign nations," given to Congress by the national constitution, includes the power to prohibit such commerce. Congress did, for a time, prohibit commerce with Europe by the Non-Intercourse Act. But the state courts have usually held that the power to regulate, when conferred upon a municipal council by the city charter, does not include the power to prohibit. The Supreme Court of New Jersey, for example, held that the power to regulate the driving of horned cattle through the city streets did not confer the right to forbid their being driven through the streets at all. McConville v. Jersey City, 39 *New Jersey*, 38.

100 THE GOVERNMENT OF AMERICAN CITIES

The strict construction of powers granted to the cities.

several states on their own cities the courts have taken an altogether different attitude. Here they have shown no toleration for rules of broad construction. On the contrary they have been disposed to look upon the city as a business corporation rather than a governmental unit, and for the most part have applied the rules of strict construction under which the charters of ordinary corporations are interpreted.[1] Their action in this respect has not been without practical considerations to justify it, for in the United States the status and functions of a municipal corporation are far more akin to those of a private corporation than to those of the national government. That is a self-evident proposition. And the rule of strict construction, as Judge Dillon has pointed out, is the one that must necessarily be applied to all corporations whose activities are of a business, or even of a quasi-business nature. Bear in mind that the property-owners of a city are virtually the stockholders of the municipal corporation. Their property is assessed for the city's revenue and mortgaged for its debts. Yet they do not control the action of the corporate authorities. They are outnumbered on the voters' list by those who own no property. Were the rule of broad interpretation applied it would be possible for this propertyless majority to launch the municipal corporation into all sorts of speculative schemes, greatly increasing the indebtedness; in other words, mortgaging the property of the minority without their consent. There is no effective protection for minority stockholders save in the precise terms and rigid interpretation of the corporate charter.

The interpretation of private and municipal charters compared.

It is a general rule of legal interpretation, therefore, that the authority of a *private* corporation (such as a bank or a railroad) must never be extended to indefinite and unspecified objects but must be restrained within the express and implied powers conferred by its charter. Any doubt arising out of the terms of the charter is resolved against the company. The burden of

---

[1] This tendency did not manifest itself so clearly during the first half of the nineteenth century. During this period there were a good many instances in which the courts took a very liberal attitude toward the interpretation of specific powers granted to the cities. H. L. McBain, *American City Progress and the Law* (New York, 1919), pp. 34-36. The change in attitude was due in part, it is believed, to the gross abuse of charter powers which took place in many cities during the mid-century era, and showed itself particularly in the practice of loaning their credit to private enterprises, subscribing for stock in railroads, and so on.

proof is on it. It is allowed to exercise no power for which it cannot show specific legal authority. The same rule is applied, though not with equal rigor, to the powers of municipal corporations. A disposition to be lenient has sometimes been shown by the courts in the interpretation of those charter provisions which relate to the organization of city government or to the routine work of the ordinary municipal departments. This, as Judge Cooley once observed, is a proper concession. "Municipalities are to take nothing from the general sovereignty except what is expressly granted; but when a power is conferred which in its exercise concerns only the municipality, and can wrong or injure no one, there is not the slightest reason for any strict or literal construction with a view to narrowing its construction." But with respect to those powers which are "out of the usual range," such as the power to grant franchises, or to fix prices, or to engage in any form of profit-making enterprise, such as the ownership of a gas plant or street railway—in such matters the courts have consistently applied the rule of strict construction. They will not assume that a city possesses any such powers unless the charter is reasonably clear on the point.[1]

When, however, a grant of power has been expressly made to a municipal corporation, the manner of exercising this authority is for the municipal authorities to determine. Within reasonable bounds the manner of exercising it will not be restricted by the courts, provided, however, that no particular method has been prescribed by the charter or laws. It has been held, for example, that the power to construct a street railway carries with it the right to construct a subway. Having been given a general power to build tracks and operate cars, the city authorities are permitted to use their discretion as to whether they will put the tracks on the street surface, or below it, or above it. Power to build and maintain a market carries with it the right to lease the vacant upstairs for non-market purposes.[2] Power to provide a public water supply entitles the city to cut and sell

The manner of exercising municipal powers.

---

[1] Port Huron v. McCall, 46 *Michigan*, 565. There are indications in some of the more recent cases, however, that even in these matters the rigor of the rule is being gradually softened; but it is not to be expected that the courts will even adopt a rule of broad construction similar to that used in interpreting the enumerated powers granted by the constitution to the national government. See H. L. McBain, *American City Progress and the Law* (New York, 1919), 57.

[2] Spaulding v. Lowell, 23 *Pickering* (Mass.), 71.

102 THE GOVERNMENT OF AMERICAN CITIES

the ice that forms on the reservoirs during the winter. On the other hand it has been held that the power of a city to pave its streets does not imply the right to engage in the manufacture of bricks to be used for street paving.[1] And the power to "provide for lighting the streets" does not include the right to sell gas or electricity for private lighting.[2] The line between what is implied and what is not implied in an express power is hard to draw; and so are the bounds of a city's discretion when the express grant of a power is conceded.

<small>The difficulty of classifying the powers of a municipal corporation.</small>

Since it is the American custom to bestow municipal powers seriatim, and not by broad grant, it is difficult to classify these powers in a way which will cover the cities of the country as a whole. Powers which are given to one city are sometimes denied to another—for no assigned reason. Powers are very often conferred upon a designated board or official and not upon the municipal corporation as such. Powers are sometimes bestowed by general law and then limited by special statute. This practice of giving with the right hand, and taking away with the left, has made a rare mess of the whole matter in many municipalities. No one knows the exact range of the powers which belong at a given moment to any particular city, unless it be the head of the city's law department, and even he is not always sure of his ground. The mayor, the manager, the commissioners, or the councilmen are perpetually calling upon him for legal opinions, and what he gives them in the way of "an opinion" is often no more than hurried guesswork. To make a thorough study and give an authoritative ruling would take, in many cases, more time than his office can spare and more legal ability than it sometimes possesses. The courts are continually proving by their decisions that heads of city law departments do not know where the powers of the municipality stop. They frequently declare to be *ultra vires* the very things which the city's law department has advised the mayor or council to do.

It would therefore serve no useful purpose to insert, in this general discussion of city charters, the long list of powers usually granted to the city. Such a list, if accurately made for one municipality, would not hold true of another. If accurate

[1] Attorney-General *v.* Detroit, 150 *Michigan*, 310.
[2] Spaulding *v.* Peabody, 153 *Massachusetts*, 129.

THE CITY CHARTER

today it would not be so tomorrow, for the powers of a city are always in process of enlargement or contraction by laws, usages, and judicial decisions. Nor are all the powers on the same footing. Some are given to the city to be exercised by it as the agent of the state, without discretion. Some are given to be exercised or not as the city may itself decide. And some are given, not to the city itself, but to some designated city officer. Assuredly it is not an easy task to classify the powers of an American municipality.

A good charter is undoubtedly one of the essentials of efficient municipal administration. Not all of our troubles in past years have been due to poor charters, yet poorly-framed charters have accounted for much of it. In many instances they have been too long, too complicated, too full of legal verbiage. They have burdened cities with too much machinery. Simplification has been the most urgent need. On the other hand, it is futile to expect that a well-framed city charter or any other inanimate object will ever prove an automatic dispenser of civic blessedness. Thirty years ago it was a common saying that the *system* of city government mattered little. "It is the men that count." Carl Schurz once said that there was not a city charter in the country which would fail to bring good government if "honest and capable men" were set to work under it. He and others like him felt convinced that Pope was right in saying that the form of a government was a theme for fools to argue about. Still they could not reconcile this with the fact that when the right men happened to get elected on a wave of popular indignation, such men never managed to work any real revolution in the city's methods of doing business. That was the experience of one city after another during the last two decades of the nineteenth century. The reason is plain enough nowadays. No matter how capable or how honest an official may be he cannot do good work without adequate powers, in other words without proper tools, and it is the tools of government that the city charter must supply.

In the course of time people woke up to a realization of all this. They came to appreciate the fact that no general improvement in municipal government could ever be achieved by political campaigns which undertook merely to "turn the rascals out" and put honest men in their place. The reform

The importance of the city charter.

For a long time it was not appreciated.

of charters and laws then began to attract public attention with results that were very beneficial on the whole.

<small>Latterly it has been over-emphasized.</small>
But reformers are prone to rush from one extreme to another, and in this case they went full tilt from the idea that city charters were of little consequence to the antithesis that everything depended on them. "Give us a good charter," they began to proclaim, "and we'll guarantee to get the men." Not only the men, but the methods and results also. Whereupon the country entered an era of charter revisions, simplifications, and a general overhauling of the municipal framework. The new alchemy soon gathered a large corps of disciples, any one of whom could prescribe with a few strokes of his pen a statutory nostrum for the most malignant case of municipal misgovernment. Down to the beginning of the twentieth century almost nothing had been written on the subject of city charters in the United States. The subject was not deemed worth a chapter, much less a book. But in a few years all this underwent a change. The city charter, its form and contents, became everywhere a theme of warm controversy. More drastic revisions of city charters took place during the years 1900-1915 than had occurred in the whole half century preceding.[1]

Yet the results were not at once made manifest in a notably improved administration of the cities. Naturally so, for new charters of themselves availed little. Campaigns for civic improvement which stop short when they have gained home rule for a city, or established the city-manager plan, or shortened the ballot, guarantee results of no greater permanency than do those which cease fire when they have merely changed the personnel of city government. Neither a new charter nor a new mayor and council will carry a municipality the whole way to better things. Reform, to be permanent, must reach deeper than this. It must permeate to the voters, whose ideals and convictions provide the foundations of democratic government, whether in city, state, or nation.

<small>Neither machinery nor personnel is all-important.</small>
Let us not, however, minimize the service which can be rendered by a sensible, smooth-working charter, or the desirability of having the charter administered by honest and capable men. It is merely well to remember that these two things are not enough. Neither charters nor men are stout reeds to lean upon so long

[1] See *below*, pp. 307-308.

as the great body of citizens are treated as pawns in the game and left without vigorous and continuing agencies of political education. When the charter is unwieldy, when it diffuses responsibility, or when its provisions are too intricate for the ordinary voter to understand, the obstacles in the way of intelligent citizenship are very serious. Charter reform is, therefore, an important step in facilitating the voter's acquaintance with the facts of public business; but it is not a final step, and, as the experience of many American cities during the past ten years has shown, it is by no means an adequate one.

The purpose of a city charter is not merely to safeguard the taxpayer against extravagance and corruption, although a great many charters, old and new, seem to have been drawn with that end exclusively in view. A charter is first of all an instrument for permitting and encouraging the free exercise of that large amount of power which in every efficient scheme of self-government must be exercised by somebody. We have been proceeding on the paradox that the people may be freely trusted to choose their mayors or commissioners, and yet that these officeholders will surely abuse their authority and betray their trusts if they get the chance. We have given the power to the people, but have restricted its free exercise by the only ones through whom the people can act. Montesquieu once said that every man who gets power is prone to abuse it. He goes forward until he finds his limits. And in general the framers of American city charters have accepted this maxim. They have set limits to the power of every municipal officeholder. In doing this they have often gone too far. *What is a city charter, anyway?*

The first requirement of a good city charter is that it shall convey sufficient power to the governing officers and shall leave this authority to be exercised without placing a host of intricate and uncertain legal restrictions upon it. Direct responsibility to the people is the best safeguard against the abuse of power by public officials; in the long run it is the only dependable protection. But such responsibility must be in fact, not merely in form. Making an office elective does not guarantee true responsibility to the people. Neither does the system of nomination by direct primaries, nor the plan of taking party designations off the ballot. True responsibility involves the choice of public officials by an electorate which is fully informed about what *Its essentials.*

is going on and which is able to act on this information. People do not wilfully choose misgovernment or keep corrupt officials in office. But they often do it unwittingly, for lack of knowledge as to the true state of affairs.

If the essentials are looked after, the exact type of charter does not matter.

If this fundamental principle of all free government is kept in mind, the particular type of charter which a city adopts is not worth prolonged controversy. Adequate power with full and direct accountability can be lodged in a few hands under the mayor-and-council type of charter quite as well as under the commission or city-manager plans.[1] Which of these plans a city should adopt is a question that may best be settled by reference to local environment, needs, and traditions. With such enormous differences among American cities in matters of population, social texture, and economic problems, it would be very strange if any one organic statute should equally meet the requirements of all. Far too much emphasis has been laid upon this matter of general type or form. Energy that might be devoted to better purpose is often frittered away in controversies over the relative merits of this or that form of charter and the political machinery which it provides. Far more depends upon the skill, care, and judgment with which the various provisions of a charter are drawn than upon the particular type of city government which it establishes. And this is especially true of the administrative provisions,—those which deal with the control and organization of the several working departments and their relations to one another, with appointments and removals, with contracts and the purchase of supplies, with budget-making and audits, and with the whole field of municipal finance. These are the provisions that make possible the continuing efficiency of city government.

How a charter commission does its work.

If you observe a charter commission or board of freeholders at work you will not be surprised that this essential of good city administration often fails to materialize at its hands. The commission is usually made up of well-meaning citizens, chosen because they are widely known, and in some cases because they have been politically prominent. Few of them, as a rule, have had much experience in municipal government, or they have

[1] For the discussion of these various types, see Nathan Matthews, *Municipal Charters* (Cambridge, 1914); H. G. James, *Applied City Government* (New York, 1914); and the new *Municipal Program* of the National Municipal League (1917).

THE CITY CHARTER

had it in one branch of administration only. As a body the commission is usually at a loss how to proceed. Its first step, of course, is to elect a chairman; then it appoints a secretary whose selection is often determined by political or personal influence. Likely as not he knows even less about city charters and city problems than do the members of the commission. This is to be regretted, for the success of a charter-commission depends in large measure on having a secretary who can keep its work moving. At any rate the commission next proceeds to divide itself into committees for the study of individual provisions; the secretary is instructed to collect charters of other cities and similar data; and arrangements are made for public hearings.

Much time is wasted and very little enlightenment is obtained in the course of these public hearings. Faddists of all types come before the commission to have their say—and take their own time doing it. Officials of the city government are also invited to appear and state their views. They are somewhat better worth listening to, but what they have to say is for the most part repetition. They praise the city for what it is, declare that it is the best-governed community under the sun, commend the existing charter, and advise the commission to let well enough alone. Experts on municipal government from outside are also heard, either by request or of their own volition. Some of them are not experts in any sense of the term, but merely salesmen for a particular brand of municipal reform. "Municipal expert" seems to be a term applied to any facile talker away from home. In any event the charter commission will hear from a representative of the Single Tax Association, the Short Ballot Association, the Proportional Representation League, the National Popular Government League, the Civil Service Reform League, the National Municipal League, and all the other leagues that are marketing propaganda for their own governmental devices. The commissioners will be told how Berlin does it, or Liverpool, or Bordeaux; how Ashtabula has been redeemed by a new method of counting ballots, how Cleveland has prospered under a city manager, and how Los Angeles has decentralized by means of a borough system. They will be urged to make the ballot short by reducing the number of elective officers. They will be urged to make it long by letting initiative

The public hearings.

questions be placed upon it. One expert will tell them that proportional representation is the only system of voting that is either fair or scientific; another will reply with figures showing that as a system it possesses neither of these merits, and will explain that it takes Cincinnati two weeks to get its ballots counted under this plan.

The drafting. When the commissioners have become adequately submerged by this flood of advice and argument they get down to the immediate business in hand. There is a preliminary discussion as to the general form which the charter ought to take.[1] Much time is often spent in settling this question. Then the committees begin to submit drafts of various sections of the charter and these are discussed by the commission as a whole. Differences of opinion arise on one point after another and compromises have to be made. Eventually the various provisions, having been whipped into shape and tentatively adopted, are arranged in orderly form and in better phraseology, whereupon the commission is ready to adopt the charter as a whole. Copies are then published and the campaign for its ratification by the people is begun.

The most common faults in city charters: Most city charters are full of compromises, representing concessions made to the personal idiosyncrasies of individual commissioners. Every such compromise usually necessitates an additional section or paragraph, and that is one reason why charters are so long. Charter commissions, moreover, seem to be unduly ambitious. They have an idea that their duty is to frame a document to cover every possible eventuality. They are not disposed to leave much as a hostage to usage and good sense. It might be assumed, for example, that a city council, in the absence of its regular chairman, would select some other councilman to preside. But charter-makers do not credit the council with any such resourcefulness. They take care to

(a) Too much detail. stipulate that a chairman pro tempore shall be chosen in such cases. They provide that the council shall decide questions by majority vote, yet in the absence of stipulation to the contrary, how else does any body decide questions? It is unfortunate that all this should be the case, for experience has proved that the more intricate the provisions of a charter the

---

[1] Sometimes, however, a majority of the commissioners are already pledged to a particular type of charter.

THE CITY CHARTER

greater are the opportunities for evading them when city officials set out to evade. The ordinary citizen, who has not made a special study of these complications, is at a great disadvantage as compared with the municipal politician who, although he may be profoundly ignorant of many other things, is always a master of this. The purpose of a city charter is not merely to provide against unforeseen eventualities. It is primarily an instrument for permitting and encouraging the efficient exercise of public authority under normal conditions.

Apart from this congestion of detail a serious fault of American municipal charters has been the tendency to over-emphasize the provisions which deal with the political framework while neglecting those which relate to the city's financial and business methods. Bitter controversies have been waged in charter commissions upon the question whether the city should have nine councilmen or thirteen, whether the names should be placed on the ballot alphabetically or by lot, and whether this or that number of signatures should be needed to have some matter referred to popular vote. Yet no city has ever gained or lost good government by deciding these questions pro or con. On the other hand, cities have gained much by reason of the skill, the care, and the intelligence spent on the provisions in relation to the publicity of official proceedings, the civil-service system, appointments and removals, contracts, budget-making, transfers of appropriations, borrowing, audits and accounting, the purchase of supplies—in a word, the various provisions which relate to routine business. *(b) Too much stress is laid on the type of government.*

A good deal of crude work has found its way into city charters, although not so much of late as in earlier years. Lawyers have naturally had a large share in the preparation of these documents; for lawyers always figure prominently in the membership of legislative committees and charter commissions. It is assumed that men of this profession, even those who have devoted no particular study to municipal affairs, are better qualified than experienced laymen to determine how charter provisions should be framed. And lawyers are partial to technical phraseology. Hence it is that a great deal of legal jargon has been written into city charters, where a few simple sentences would have achieved the desired end much more effectively. The serious objection to this use of legal terminology is that the *(c) Too much technical verbiage.*

courts have often given it a meaning altogether different from that which it bears in ordinary usage.

(d) Too little attention to orderliness of arrangement.

The arrangement of the various provisions in most American city charters is poor. Clauses relating to the same topic are scattered through various sections of the document, while dissimilar provisions are sometimes incorporated under the same heading. The charter is commonly divided into chapters, and these again into sections, subsections, and paragraphs, each chapter with its own serial numbering. When an amendment is made, affecting several sections of the charter, the effect is confusing. It is much better to number the sections in a single series throughout the charter.

(e) Too much copying from other charters.

Very few city charters have anything original in them. One city copies provisions from the charter of another, which in turn has copied from something earlier. Thus the same clause may have a wide vogue, quite irrespective of the original conditions to which it was meant to apply. A good many city charters have been drafted with a much more industrious use of the scissors than of the pen, yet this is a dangerous practice, especially when clauses are clipped from different charters in which the same terms may be in different senses. It is a practice which is almost sure to result in lawsuits when the copying is done from charters of cities outside the state. Some provision in the charter of Los Angeles, let us say, attracts the attention of a board of freeholders in Minnesota. Word for word, or with a few minor changes, it is adopted by the latter. Then somebody discovers that the transplanted provision conflicts with a clause in the Minnesota constitution, and hence is invalid. It is never wise to take anything from the charter of another city without making careful enquiry. Words and phrases which have a construed meaning in one commonwealth may have quite a different construction in another. To borrow is much easier than to write anew, but in the long run it rarely saves either time or trouble. The success of the national constitution as a relatively clear and unambiguous document is in no small measure due to the fact that its framers copied almost nothing from anywhere; they made the document brief and used a minimum of technical phraseology.

Model charters.

From time to time it has been suggested that a "model city charter" might well be framed for the guidance of charter-

THE CITY CHARTER

makers. On more than one occasion, indeed, serious attempts in this direction have been made, and they have served a useful, although a somewhat limited, purpose. The practical difficulties are great and obvious because a city charter must be articulated at various points with the general laws of the state in which the city is located, and these laws are far from uniform throughout the country. In most states it will be found that such matters as the suffrage, taxation, public health, the condemnation of property for public use, the registration of births, marriages and deaths, the inspection of weights and measures, the school system, poor relief, the judicial system, the scope of municipal borrowing power—that these and many other matters are covered by the general laws. But they are not everywhere covered to the same extent or in the same way. It is almost impossible, therefore, to frame a model charter for general use throughout the country—and this apart from the consideration that cities are too varied in their size, needs and problems to be fitted to any one model. Even within the bounds of a single state this variation in size impairs the usefulness of any stereotyped draft. Nevertheless these model charters have proved useful in that they afford examples of orderly arrangement, clearness of expression, and reasonable conciseness.

REFERENCES

The most elaborate discussion of this subject is W. K. Clute's *Law of Modern Municipal Charters* (2 vols., Detroit, 1920). These two volumes contain a great deal of information but it is not very well arranged. Nathan Matthews, *Municipal Charters* (Boston, 1914) is a useful book. There is a good discussion in William Anderson's *American City Government* (New York, 1925), pp. 104-130, and reference may also be made to the discussion of the "Principles of Charter Making," by the same author, reprinted in Joseph Wright's *Readings in Municipal Problems* (Boston, 1925), pp. 151-169. The model charter of the National Municipal League, with explanatory chapters, is issued under the title *A New Municipal Program* (New York, 1919). The charter itself is separately printed in pamphlet form and can be had from the League headquarters (261 Broadway, New York City).

CHAPTER VI

LEGAL PHASES OF CITY GOVERNMENT

Unorganized and organized groups of inhabitants.

Nearly one hundred and fifty years ago an English plaintiff brought suit in the courts against "the men living in the county of Devon," claiming damages sustained by reason of defects in a bridge which it was the duty of the inhabitants to keep in repairs. Two of the inhabitants appeared in court, and for themselves as well as for their neighbors entered a demurrer; that is, they admitted the facts as alleged, but contended that they were not liable to a suit, being an unorganized body of individuals and not a body corporate. The court sustained the demurrer. The plaintiff might sue the county of Devon, it said, but not the men dwelling in the county. It did not matter that the two were the same in effect; they were not the same in the eyes of the law. "Among the several qualities which belong to corporations," the court said, "one is that they may sue and be sued; that puts them in contradistinction to other persons."[1] A municipal corporation, in a word, has a legal personality.

How municipal corporations are created.

The creation of a municipal corporation is an act of sovereign lawmaking power. In England, at common law, a municipal corporation can be created either by the crown or by parliament, but in the United States the legislature alone has this power. And in the absence of constitutional authority to do so, the legislature cannot devolve the work upon the governor, or upon a board of municipal incorporation, or upon any other body. Nor is the discretion of the legislature in creating a municipal corporation, or refusing to create one, subject to review by the courts. Nevertheless the legislature must exercise its discretion within the bounds which are set by the state constitution. If the latter provides, as it usually does, that no community shall be incorporated as a city unless it has a certain

---

[1] Russell *v.* The Men Dwelling in the County of Devon, *2 Term Reports* 667 (1788), reprinted in Beale's *Cases*, 530-532.

LEGAL PHASES OF CITY GOVERNMENT 113

number of inhabitants the legislature must conform its action to this requirement, and if it does not the courts may void the incorporation. In the absence of constitutional restrictions, on the other hand, the legislature may incorporate any body of persons, large or small, and give them much or little power as it sees fit. It can be done without the consent of the people concerned—unless the state constitution makes provision to the contrary, as in some cases it does.

Ordinarily a municipal corporation is created by some overt act, but a body of inhabitants may sometimes obtain corporate status by implication or by prescription. They are incorporated by implication when the legislature, although not expressly designating that they shall form a "body politic and corporate," empowers them to do something which only a municipal corporation can do—for example, if it authorizes the inhabitants of a certain area to elect a mayor and council, levy taxes, and borrow money. A community may claim a corporate status by prescription if the inhabitants can show that for a long term of years they have performed the duties of a municipal corporation, although without express authority. Municipal corporations by prescription have been common in England, but they are not common in the United States. *Municipal corporations by implication and by prescription.*

What are the earmarks which distinguish a corporation from an unorganized body of individuals? It may sue and be sued. But there are other earmarks of a corporation. It enjoys legal immortality. The members of a corporation may die, but others take their place and the corporation lives on. Seven or eight generations of men have come and gone in New York City since the people of that community were first incorporated as a borough in 1686, but there has been no interruption in the continuity of the municipal corporation. So there are various reasons why a body of inhabitants should seek to obtain a corporate status and become a body politic,—that is, a village, township, borough, town, county, or city. By so doing they may act as one person, they may hold property, they may make contracts, raise money, and may borrow on their common credit. *The earmarks of a municipal corporation.*

In a word those inhabitants who are transformed into a municipal corporation become endowed with various powers on the one hand and obligations on the other. Powers may be given to the municipal corporation in either mandatory or permissive *Mandatory and permissive powers of a municipal corporation.*

form. That is, the city may be invested either with powers which it *must* exercise or with those which it *may* exercise if it chooses to do so. Whether the power falls into one class or the other depends upon the intention of the legislature, and this intention is usually disclosed by the language of the enactment. If the statute provides that a city "shall" or "must" do something, the power thus conferred is mandatory and it is not within the discretion of the city authorities to refrain from exercising it; but if a statute provides that a city "may" do something, or that "it shall be lawful" for a city to do something, then the power conferred is, as a rule, permissive and the municipal authorities may or may not exercise it. This general rule does not always hold, however; for powers granted in permissive language may be mandatory in effect. The courts have in some instances held that a power conferred in permissive phraseology must be exercised if there is a clear public benefit to be derived from it.[1]

Powers may not be delegated.

But whether derived from express language or by implication, and whether mandatory or permissive in effect, no powers which are conferred may be delegated to any subordinate official or body. Powers committed to the mayor cannot be delegated by him to a board or a commissioner; powers given to the city council cannot be transferred by it to the mayor or a committee. When the veto power is given to the mayor, for example, he cannot delegate this function to some other official. When authority to fix the tax rate is given to the city council it cannot refer the matter to a committee with power. *Delegatus non potest delegare.* All this, however, does not apply to purely ministerial functions, or, in other words, to the carrying out of administrative details. The Supreme Court of the United States has held that the performance of such work by agents does not constitute an unlawful delegation of powers by a city council.[2]

The rule in Hitchcock v. Galveston.

An ordinance empowering the city engineer to make a selection between two kinds of paving material, or to determine

[1] "It is the settled doctrine in New York, for example, that where a public or municipal corporation or body is invested with *power to do an act which the public interests require to be done*, and the means for its complete performance are placed at its disposal, not only the execution of the power may be insisted on as a duty, though the statute conferring it be only permissive in its terms," Mayor of New York v. Farze, 3 Hill, 612, cited by J. F. Dillon, *Law of Municipal Corporations*, I, 466. See also the discussion of mandatory and discretionary powers in Eugene McQuillin's *Law of Municipal Corporations*, I, 836-838.

[2] Hitchcock v. Galveston, 96 *U. S.*, 341.

LEGAL PHASES OF CITY GOVERNMENT 115

the grade of a sewer, would furnish an example of delegated ministerial functions. The line between discretionary and ministerial offices is not very sharply drawn; but the essence of power must not be delegated and the disposition of the courts is to decide against delegation in doubtful cases. Any concession to a subordinate board or official which seems capable of embarrassing the regular governing organs of a city in their exercise of governmental powers, or of restraining them from a full performance of their public functions, is usually deemed an unlawful delegation.[1]

The governing authorities of the city usually put the powers of the municipal corporation into effect by enacting ordinances. Ordinances may also, in some cases, be enacted directly by the people, through the use of the initiative and referendum. Within the scope of the term *ordinance* are included "all local laws of a municipal corporation, duly enacted by the proper authorities, prescribing general, uniform, and permanent rules of conduct relating to the corporate affairs of the municipality."[2] An ordinance usually begins with the words: "Be it enacted by the municipal council of the City of ———, and by authority of the same, as follows:". It is given three readings and adopted with due formality. In most cases, after having passed the council, an ordinance goes to the mayor for his signature or veto; but this is not the case in cities which have the commission or the city manager form of government. From time to time all the ordinances of the city are revised and compiled into a single volume.

_{Municipal ordinances.}

Powers given to a city by its charter or by other statutes are usually coupled with a provision that the city council or other legislative organ of city government shall have authority to carry these powers into operation by appropriate ordinances. It is by ordinances that most cities have organized their various administrative departments. One ordinance deals with the police department, another with licenses, another with streets and street traffic, another with fire prevention, another with building regu-

_{What the ordinances deal with.}

---

[1] See the list of cases given in Eugene McQuillin's *Law of Municipal Corporations*, I, 842.
[2] Eugene McQuillin, *The Law of Municipal Ordinances* (Chicago, 1904), 2. Judge Dillon (*Law of Municipal Corporations*, II, 892) defines the term "ordinances" as including all "acts or regulations in the nature of local laws passed by the proper assembly or governing body of the corporation."

lations, and so on. Each prescribes in detail not only the way in which the department shall be organized, its personnel, and the relation of the various officers, but even the manner in which its work must be carried on.

<small>Regulations.</small>

The annual appropriations, likewise, are usually incorporated into an ordinance. By means of an ordinance, franchises are commonly granted to public service companies. In some cases the charter or other statutes gives to certain administrative bodies, such as the board of health or the tenement house commission, or even to a single official, such as the fire prevention commissioner, the power to make rules and regulations within their respective fields of jurisdiction. These are termed "regulations," not ordinances; but in general they have all the force of ordinances and as a rule they are subject to the same broad restrictions.[1]

<small>Limitations upon the ordinance power:</small>

In the exercise of their powers by ordinance (or by regulations) the governing bodies of the city are subject to several important limitations. These limitations are worth remembering, for a failure to keep them in mind has resulted in the passage of many ordinances which have subsequently been invalidated by the courts. They are not complicated, nor are they difficult to comprehend.

<small>1. General limitations.</small>

First, there are some requirements of a general nature, merely representing the application to municipal lawmaking of those common-sense principles which apply to state legislation. An ordinance must not, for example, be inconsistent with the provisions of the charter or the statute under which it is passed. When a state statute and a municipal ordinance are in conflict, the latter is invalid. It is therefore advisable, before adopting a proposed ordinance, to have it examined by the city's law department and approved as to its legality. Otherwise it may later be found to be in conflict with some state law which the councillors have overlooked. Even with the precaution of re-

[1] Both *ordinances* and *regulations*, as above defined, are distinguished from *resolutions* or *orders*. Ordinances and regulations almost invariably prescribe permanent rules of conduct or government; resolutions or orders provide temporary rules only. A resolution may ordinarily be passed by the council alone, whereas an ordinance usually requires the approval of the mayor or of the chief executive authority. The legislative powers of the corporation must, as a rule, be exercised by ordinance; its day-to-day ministerial functions may often be carried out by resolution. See the cases bearing on these points in McQuillin's *Law of Municipal Ordinances*, 4; and in Dillon's *Law of Municipal Corporations*, II, 893-896.

ferring ordinances to the law department there will be occasional conflicts.

Second. Ordinances must be enacted in keeping with the prescribed formalities. These, as laid down in the charter or in the laws, often require that the ordinance shall be published a stated number of times in one or more local newspapers before its final enactment. In the case of ordinances enacted by the use of the initiative and referendum there are many strict regulations to be observed in verifying the signatures on petitions, in calling the election, and in placing the question on the ballot. When ordinances are enacted by the city council it is usually required that they shall be formally introduced by some member, given three readings, passed by a majority vote with at least a quorum of the members present, and (in mayor-and-council cities) submitted to the mayor for approval. In some cities there is a rule that not more than one subject can be included within a single ordinance; for example, the same ordinance may not contain provisions relating to street traffic and to the sale of property for taxes. The courts will not usually hold an ordinance invalid by reason of some slight departure from the prescribed formalities; but they require, and rightly so, that a reasonable deference be paid to the established procedure. They are especially insistent upon this where the rules have been established in order to safeguard the rights of individuals.

2. Ordinances must be passed in compliance with certain formalities.

Third. Ordinances must not be arbitrary or unreasonable in their provisions; but they are always presumed to be fair and reasonable until the contrary is proved. The burden of proving unreasonableness is upon him who asserts it. There is no single test by which a court can decide what is reasonable and what is not; the determination can only be made by a scrutiny of the ordinance in question, or by a study of some specific situation to which its provisions are being applied. But so many ordinances have been successfully or unsuccessfully attacked on the ground of unreasonableness that the courts now possess a large body of precedents for their guidance. Ordinances are void if they are clearly oppressive in character; if, for example, they interfere with personal liberty to an extent beyond what is essential to accomplish the main purposes of the ordinance. It often happens, however, that an ordinance is reasonable as applied to one set of circumstances and unreasonable when applied to another,

3. Ordinances must not be arbitrary or unreasonable in their provisions.

or reasonable at one season of the year and not at another season.[1].

If an ordinance is passed by virtue of a special grant of power made to the city by the legislature, and is in accord with the terms of the grant, the courts will usually uphold its reasonableness even though they would not do so under ordinary circumstances. Questions of reasonableness, in determining the validity of city ordinances, are mixed questions of law and fact. As such they are decided by the judge and not, save in exceptional cases, by the jury.

4. Ordinances must not make unwarranted discriminations.

Fourth. Ordinances must not be discriminatory. If they confer privileges they must throw such privileges open to all who comply with the conditions. The provisions of an ordinance must apply equally to all persons in the same category. For example, it would not be a discrimination to provide that all restaurants shall be closed on Sundays while hotel dining rooms are permitted to remain open for the use of bona fide guests; but to stipulate that all Chinese restaurants shall remain closed while other restaurants are privileged to remain open would be a clear case of discrimination. An ordinance must not single out races or corporations or groups of individuals for special privilege or restriction; it must not favor residents as against non-residents, or native-born as against naturalized citizens. It must bear with an equal hand upon all persons who stand in similar circumstances. But an ordinance is not discriminatory because its restrictions, in the natural order of things, happen to fall upon single groups or individuals, they being the only ones engaged in a particular sort of business or affected by a particular set of circumstances.[2] All this may look simple enough on paper, but the sinuous line between discrimination and non-discrimination is very elusive and the courts have not ventured to frame any general rule by which it can be easily recognized.

[1] For example, an ordinance requiring that all dogs be chained indoors might be held reasonable during an epidemic of rabies but unreasonable under other circumstances. An ordinance requiring property owners to sprinkle salt on the sidewalks might be held reasonable in winter, but hardly so in summer. To provide that no openings shall be made in the street pavements at any time would be unreasonable; but it is allowable to prohibit this work during the winter months when it would be difficult to re-lay the pavements properly. An ordinance excluding motor trucks from certain streets is reasonable; but an ordinance excluding them from all streets would be held void.

[2] Soon Hing v. Crowley, 113 *U. S.*, 703.

Fifth. Ordinances must not unduly restrain trade. It is a rule of the common law that the by-laws of a private corporation are void if their effect is to procure an *unreasonable* restraint of trade. The same rule applies to municipal corporations. It is entirely allowable by ordinance to create a monopoly if the public good so requires, as, for example, in the case of a garbage-removal company. But the city council cannot by ordinance grant an exclusive franchise to any public service corporation unless it has been given, by statute, the express power to do so. It cannot, to take another example, provide that only certain contractors shall have the right to compete for the construction of public works, or that only designated firms shall have the right to sell ordinary merchandise. Within the limits of their police power the city authorities may require certain forms of business to be licensed and may exact reasonable fees for the granting of such licenses, but it cannot use its licensing power as a means of prohibition. <small>5. Ordinances must not unduly restrain trade.</small>

It will be seen from the foregoing discussion that not only are the powers of a city limited to fields expressly or impliedly plotted out for it by legislative enactment, but that even within these bounds the municipal corporation must use its authority under strict limitations. Such powers as it has obtained by general grant it must exercise in a reasonable way, without discrimination and without unwarranted interference in the common right to freedom of trade. The logical result of all this circumscription is that cities are constant supplicants at the bar of the legislature. If there be any doubt as to the scope of their powers, or as to the manner in which their authority may be exercised, the easiest course, as a rule, is to seek such additional statutory powers as will make everything clear. It is mainly to this situation that the flood of special legislation commented upon in an earlier chapter owes its existence. Not infrequently, however, the city authorities give themselves the benefit of the doubt and their action becomes a prelude to expensive lawsuits. Anyone can attack the validity of a municipal ordinance in the courts at any time. The procedure is usually laid down by statute. The court may invalidate a single provision in the ordinance, leaving the remaining provisions in effect, or it may void the whole of it if the various clauses are so related that one of them cannot be voided without effect on the others. <small>Effect of these restrictions</small>

City councils, however, often exceed their legal powers without being called to account, and this for the reason that no one happens to test the matter. It is beyond much question, for example, that many zoning ordinances (i. e. ordinances which divide the city into zones and regulate the character of the buildings that may be erected in each) contain some provisions which are beyond the city's authority to enforce. But such provisions are usually in accord with the financial interests of property-owners and the latter naturally refrain from raising the issue of legality. It is only when a zoning ordinance conflicts with the interests of the property-owner that an attack on its provisions is likely to be made.

The liability of a municipal corporation.

In all well-ordered governments power goes hand in hand with responsibility. In the nation and the state this responsibility is popular rather than legal; in other words, the government is responsible to the people at the polls, not to individuals who may desire to hale it before the courts of law. A national or state government is not amenable to suit by an individual citizen save in so far as it has voluntarily agreed to submit to the jurisdiction of the courts. This it may do and often does by statutes authorizing suits to be brought against it. A city, on the contrary, is in no such favored position. Not only is the municipal government responsible to the voters, but the corporation may be cited before the ordinary courts of justice, whether with or without the consent of its governing authorities, and may there be made the defendant in suits at law. The city is liable to be sued in actions of contract, or for the torts of its agents, or in causes arising out of its possession of municipal property. Its liability is not, however, equally complete in all three classes of actions.

1. In the matter of contracts.

In the matter of contracts the city is subject to substantially the same rules as are applied to individuals or to private corporations.[1] A suit that can successfully be prosecuted against an individual can be prosecuted against a municipal corporation. In an action for breach of contract the city can urge only the same pleas and defences that are open to the individual defendant; it has no immunities by reason of being a public corporation. It matters not whether the contract has been entered into

---

[1] The reason for this is well stated in F. J. Goodnow's *Municipal Home Rule* (New York, 1906), 106.

for a governmental or for a commercial purpose; the degree of liability for breach is the same.¹

In the matter of liability for the torts, or civil wrongs, committed by its agents or employees, on the other hand, the status of the city is not so simple. A municipal corporation, so far as the acts of its officials are concerned, stands in a dual position. On the one hand, it is part of the machinery created and used by the state in order to carry on the sovereign functions of the latter. For the improper exercise of these functions the state itself has no legal liability, nor can any legal responsibility attach to those who merely serve as its agents. The city, therefore, in so far as it is an agency of state government performing governmental functions, cannot be held responsible for the torts of its officials or employees. But the city is also a corporation, engaged in commercial or semi-commercial enterprises. It is a purveyor of water, gas, electricity; it sometimes owns and operates a street railway, as in San Francisco and Seattle. As such it is engaged in commercial enterprises and hence must assume the same liabilities as a private corporation engaged in the same undertakings.²

2. In the matter of torts.

In keeping with these general principles, a city is not liable to civil suit either for the non-exercise of the powers given to it by statute or for the manner in which it exercises them. It is not liable for its neglect to pass ordinances, or for its failure to enforce them. Such liability may be expressly imposed upon the city by law, but unless so imposed it will not be implied. For example, if an individual is injured through the failure of the city council to provide or to enforce an ordinance regulating the storage of explosives, he can recover no damages from the city treasury.³ Nor does the failure of the municipal corporation to

(a) Liability for the use of the municipal ordinance power.

---

¹ The municipal corporation may, of course, like any other corporate body, set up the defence that the contract was entered into outside the scope of its chartered powers, or that it was not made by its proper officers or agents.

² "There are two kinds of duties which are imposed upon municipal corporations: one is that kind which arises from the grant of a special power in the exercise of which the municipality is as a legal individual; the other is of that kind which arises, or is implied, from the use of political rights under the general law, under the exercise of which it is as a sovereign. The former power is private and is used for private purposes; the latter is public and is used for public purposes." Lloyd v. the Mayor, 5 N. Y., 374. See also J. H. Beale, *Selection of Cases on Municipal Corporations*, 594.

³ McDade v. Chester, 117 Pa., 414, in Beale's *Selection of Cases on Mu-*

abate a nuisance give a person who is injured by the existence of such nuisance an enforcable claim against the city, even though he has duly notified the officials of the nuisance, and requested them to abate it.[1] Most cities have ordinances regulating the construction of buildings in the interest of protection against collapse or conflagration; but if such an ordinance be not enforced and if injury to the persons or property of private individuals be caused thereby, no action for damages can be successfully prosecuted against the municipality.[2] The United States Supreme Court has gone even farther, by laying down the principle that even if a city misinterprets the scope of its statutory power and undertakes to do in a governmental capacity what it has no authority to do, it cannot successfully be sued in an action of tort.[3] The power to enact and to enforce ordinances is a governmental power, discretionary in its nature, and for negligence or mistake in connection with it the city has no legal liability.

(b) Liability for the acts of municipal agents engaged in governmental functions.

A municipal corporation must of necessity carry out its functions, whether governmental or commercial, whether public or private, by means of officials, agents, and employees; and by a general principle of law it becomes responsible for what some of them do. Certain classes of city officials and employees are engaged in purely governmental or public work; others just as clearly are employed in commercial or private undertakings conducted by the city. For the acts of the former class the city is not liable, but it is held accountable for torts committed by the latter in the discharge of their duties. A good example of the class engaged in the performance of strictly public or governmental functions is furnished by the city fire department. In the absence of express statutory provisions creating liability, the municipality is not subject to claims for damages caused by

nicipal Corporations, 583. In this case the laws of Pennsylvania had empowered the mayor and council of Chester to "prohibit the manufacture of fire works . . . by such means as to them shall seem best." But the mayor and council established no such prohibition and the plaintiff was injured by an explosion which subsequently occurred in a fireworks factory in the city. He alleged, in substance, that the city had neglected a duty, that his injury arose from this neglect, and that the city was liable to him in damages. The court held that the power to make a prohibitory ordinance was discretionary and that the city was not liable for the manner in which its discretionary power might be used.

[1] Davis *v.* Montgomery, 51 *Ala.*, 139; Kiley *v.* Kansas, 87 *Mo.*, 103.
[2] Forsyth *v.* Atlanta, 45 *Ga.*, 152.
[3] Fowle *v.* Alexandria, 3 *Peters*, 398.

the negligence or the inefficiency of the firemen.[1] Other officials and employees who are regarded as exercising governmental functions are those connected with the park department,[2] the hospital and health service,[3] and the administration of poor relief.[4] The doctrine which exempts the city from legal responsibility for negligence or inefficiency on the part of such officials often results in loss to private individuals, who are thus deprived of all effective redress. The aggrieved individual may sue the municipal employee who was immediately at fault, and may get an award of damages against him; but collecting the money from a city employee is not often an easy matter. The chances are that he has no property to satisfy the judgment.

The status of the police department is somewhat different from that of the departments just mentioned. Police officers are unquestionably engaged in the performance of a governmental or public function, and hence the city would not be liable for their defaults. But the exemption of the municipal corporation from liability for the torts of its police officers is more commonly based upon the contention that they are not municipal agents. They are, it is true, appointed by city authorities, are paid from the city treasury, and are instructed in the performance of their duties by municipal regulations. But all this does not make them municipal officers. Even in enforcing municipal ordinances the police act as agents of the state. The authority to make these ordinances "is delegated to the city by the sovereign power, and the exercise of the authority gives to such enactments the same force and effect as if they had been passed directly by the legislature. They are public laws of a limited and local operation designed to secure good order and to provide for the welfare and comfort of the inhabitants. In their enforcement, therefore, the police officers act in their public capacity and not as agents or servants of the city."[5] Being agents of the state, it

(c) Liability for the torts of police officers.

---

[1] Hafford v. New Bedford, 16 *Gray* (Mass.), 297; Taintor v. Worcester, 123 *Mass.*, 311. See also Wheeler v. Cincinnati, 19 *Ohio*, 19, and Hayes v. Oshkosh, 33 *Wis.*, 314, in Beale's *Cases on Municipal Corporations*, 618-620. See, however, the decision in Fowler v. Cleveland, which is discussed *below*, p. 126.

[2] Louisville Park Commissioners v. Prinz, 127 *Ky.*, 460.

[3] Gilboy v. Detroit, 115 *Mich.*, 121, in Beale's *Cases on Municipal Corporations*, 582; also Maximilian v. the Mayor, 62 *N. Y.*, 160.

[4] Curran v. Boston, 151 *Mass.*, 505.

[5] Buttrick v. Lowell, 1 Allen (*Mass.*), in Beale's *Cases on Municipal Corporations*, 580.

follows that the city is not their employer and is immune from legal responsibility for what they do or fail to do.

(d) Liability for the torts of agents engaged in non-governmental functions.

All the foregoing functions are clearly governmental or public. Some others are quite as clearly commercial or private. When, for example, a city owns and operates a system of water supply from which it derives revenue or profits, it becomes liable for damages resulting from the negligence or the incapacity of its employees connected with the working of the system. Its liability is the same, both in nature and degree, as that of a water company,[1] and the same rule would apply to it as owner of a gas plant, an electric lighting plant,[2] or a street railway. Municipal ownership of docks and wharves, where tolls are charged, subject the city to the same legal liabilities that pertain to a private owner.[3] It has also been held that a municipal corporation is responsible for damages caused by the faulty management of public cemeteries, markets, and bath-houses.[4] All these departments of municipal enterprise are within the range of private or commercial functions. When a city enters into a competition with private corporations it should, of course, assume responsibilities similar to those attaching to the latter. When it displaces a private enterprise in favor of municipal ownership, it ought not thereby to impair the redress available for negligent or inefficient operation. The damages in which the city may be mulcted for the torts of its employees in these branches of municipal activity may properly be made a part of the cost of operation to be covered by charges levied for the service.

(e) Liability for the torts of employees in the twilight zone.

Thus far the distinction between public and private functions is not difficult to draw, but there is a twilight zone of civic activity which does not readily and at first sight fall into either of these classes. As regards the construction and care of the streets and sidewalks, for example, the maintenance of bridges and sewers, the removal of ashes and garbage, and a few other functions, the principles governing municipal liability are not so clear. In most states of the Union the courts have held that municipal corporations are liable for negligence in the perform-

[1] Murphy v. Lowell, 12 *Mass.*, 564.
[2] Kibele v. Philadelphia, 105 *Pa.*, 41; Greenville v. Pitts., 102 *Texas*, 1.
[3] Allegheny v. Campbell, 107 *Pa.*, 530.
[4] On the detailed application of this rule, see D. A. Jones, *The Negligence of Municipal Corporations* (New York, 1892), 71.

LEGAL PHASES OF CITY GOVERNMENT

ance of their duty to keep the city streets in proper condition; but for a similar default towns and counties have been held not to be liable.[1] On the face of things there would seem to be no good reason for this distinction, and the courts have not been very successful in providing one. It is sometimes urged that the streets of cities are local thoroughfares, whereas the streets of towns and villages are state highways,—that the former are means of communication, the latter means of intercommunication; but that is true in a general way only, and scarcely in sufficient degree to warrant the broad distinctions made by the decisions. However this may be, the care of the city's streets is in most states regarded as a local responsibility and when damage results from the negligence or the incapacity of an official intrusted with this function, the doctrine of *respondeat superior* applies, and the city may be made to pay.[2]

In regard to the sewerage system the general principle, so far as the decisions may be said to establish a general principle, is that the city authorities, in planning a system of sewers, are performing a public and discretionary function and hence are not liable for injuries arising from faulty planning; as, for example, when the sewers prove too small to carry off surface water during a heavy storm. The task of keeping the sewers free from obstruction, however, and in proper repair is a ministerial function, for negligence in the performance of which the city is liable.[3] Much diversity of opinion is disclosed by the decisions bearing upon the liability of a municipal corporation for the torts of its officials and employees engaged in cleaning the streets and in removing refuse and garbage. In some cases the courts have regarded these functions as governmental and so have denied the city's liability; in other cases they have ruled that the city,

Streets.

Sewers.

---

[1] F. J. Goodnow, *Municipal Home Rule*, 144-146. See also Russell *v.* The Men of Devon (1788), in Beale's *Cases on Municipal Corporations*, 530; Mower *v.* The Inhabitants of Leicester, 9 *Mass.*, 237, *ibid.* 601; and Detroit *v.* Blackeby, 21 *Mich.*, 84, *ibid.* 603. The argument of Judge Gray on this question, in Hill *v.* Boston, (*Mass.*, 344, 369), is also very interesting.

[2] The whole question of the liability of the city in the matter of damages to property caused by changing the grade of streets is too technical to be discussed here. It is dealt with at length in J. F. Dillon's *Law of Municipal Corporations*, IV, 2920 ff.

[3] Barton *v.* Syracuse, 36 *N. Y.*, 54, in Beale's *Cases on Municipal Corporations*, 611; O'Donnell *v.* Syracuse, 184 *N. Y.*, 1, *ibid.* 611-612; also the various decisions printed in S. D. Tompson's *Cases on Municipal Negligence*, especially II, 625 ff.

126   THE GOVERNMENT OF AMERICAN CITIES

in performing this sort of work, acts in a private or commercial capacity and must therefore assume the same liabilities as an ordinary corporation or individual.[1]

A tabular view.

The whole existing legal situation may perhaps be made clearer by tabulating it in this way:

Strictly Governmental Functions.	Strictly Ministerial or Commercial Functions.	Not Clearly in One Class or the Other
1. Police	1. Water Supply	1. Street Construction and Maintenance
2. Fire Protection	2. Gas Plants	2. Sidewalks
3. Public Health.	3. Electric Light and Power Plants	3. Bridges and Tunnels
4. Schools.	4. Street Railways	4. Sewerage
5. Hospitals	5. Motor busses	5. Garbage and Rubbish Collection and Disposal
6. Poor Relief	6. Docks and wharves	
7. Corrections	7. Ferries	
8. Parks	8. Public Markets	
9. Public Recreation.	9. Public Weigh Scales	
10. Inspection of Buildings	10. Public Baths	
11. Regulation of Traffic.	11. Cemeteries	
12. Elections		
13. Licensing		

Unsatisfactory condition of the law as regards the city's liability for the torts of its agents.

The entire question of municipal liability is in a rather unsatisfactory situation. Individual citizens are injured in person or in property through the negligence of municipal employees in the so-termed governmental departments, yet no effective compensation is available to them. A hose truck, on its way home from a fire, is negligently driven across a street intersection and seriously injures an individual. The negligence of the driver may be fully admitted, but the injured individual has no ground of action against the city. Most people would agree that he has a common-sense right to compensation from the driver's employers and ought to have a legal one.[2] It is not in accordance

---

[1] See the cases cited in J. F. Dillon's *Law of Municipal Corporations*, IV, 2900.

[2] In Fowler v. The City of Cleveland, 100 *Ohio*, 158, (1919), the Supreme Court of Ohio, realizing the injustice of the existing rule, held the city liable for the negligence of an employee of the fire department. In this instance the driver of a hose truck, on his way home from a fire to the fire-station, drove the truck diagonally across a street intersection and on the wrong side of the street, striking the plaintiff and seriously injuring him. The court held that the function of fire protection was *not governmental*. In a concurring opinion one of the justices argued for the general extension of municipal liability. The decision in this case is printed in Joseph Wright's *Selected Readings in Municipal Problems* (Boston, 1925), pp. 204-212. See the interesting discussion in the *Harvard Law Review*, vol. XXIV, pp. 66-69.

But the Supreme Court of Ohio did not stand its ground. The question of liability soon came once more before it in the case of Aldrich v. The City

LEGAL PHASES OF CITY GOVERNMENT 127

with elementary justice, as the ordinary man understands it, that an admitted wrong should go unrighted because it was committed by a public employee whose name happens to be on the payroll of one city department rather than on that of another.

On the other hand, there are some difficulties in the way of establishing any doctrine of universal liability. The present policy of exemption from liability in the so-called governmental departments is clearly unjust, but would the opposite policy be any less so? When we feel any principle of law to be unfair it is a good plan to recall the mental process with which we became acquainted in plane geometry; namely, that of proving a proposition by demonstrating the absurdity of its only alternative. "For if not, let the contrary be true . . . which is absurd." The principle of non-liability, so far as it extends, is alleged to be unfair to the individual; let us assume, therefore, the contrary principle; let the city be held liable for all the negligence or incompetence of all its employees in all departments. Would less injustice, or more, result from the application of that principle?

The objection to widening the sphere of liability.

The city, for example, has now become liable for the negligence of its fire department employees. Every fire at once becomes a potential basis of a suit for damages against the city. It can be alleged that the engines were slow in getting to the fire, that the employees were negligent in attempting to put it out by one method rather than another, that their appliances were defective, or the water pressure inadequate. Witnesses, expert and otherwise, are brought forward on both sides. They disagree widely, as witnesses usually do. The questions at issue, being matters of fact and not of law, are for the jury to decide. If negligence is proved to the jury's satisfaction (and that should not be a difficult task in any municipal department) the city would be assessed in damages amounting to many thousands, and perhaps to millions of dollars; for a great conflagration runs into the

An illustration.

---

of Youngstown (106 *Ohio*, 342), 1925. The plaintiff, Aldrich, was riding in an automobile on the streets of Youngstown when he was struck by a police patrol wagon driven by a police offcer. The lower court gave him judgment against the city. The City of Youngstown appealed this decision and the Supreme Court reversed itself in the following words: "This court is of the opinion that there is no difference in principle between this and the Fowler Case, and upon its reëxamination has decided to overrule the latter." Those who are interested in this question may also be referred to the case of Kaufman *v.* Tallahassee, 94 *Southern*, 697.

millions very quickly. To satisfy the judgment special taxes would have to be levied on the property of all the citizens. That assuredly would not impress them as even-handed justice or anything approaching it, especially if the award of damages against the city were in favor of an insurance company, as would often be the case. The establishment of liability for negligence in the fire department would virtually render the city an insurer of every person's property within its jurisdiction.[1] It would make the municipal corporation a guarantor of absolute efficiency in every department. The taxpayer would be saddled with a burden which, according to the common notion of justice, does not belong to him. So we merely avoid one horn of the dilemma by becoming impaled on the other.

The present tendency.

Nevertheless the tendency in recent years has been towards the broadening in the range of corporate liability.[2] The drift of American law has been in the direction of spreading upon the whole community the cost of compensating the individual for injuries done to him from whatever source. It is not a matter of abstract justice, but merely a question of dealing with inevitable mishaps in such way as will produce the minimum of hardship. When damage is done to the person or property of a citizen, through no fault of his own, is it expedient to make him bear the entire burden? Does such action contribute to the sum of human happiness? Are not the best interests of the whole community served by "socializing" the load, spreading it out so that it will not come with more than a very slight weight on anybody? Legislators and courts are now thinking less about justice or injustice to individuals and more about the ultimate wellbeing of the entire social organism.

3. Liability of the city with reference to its property.

The legal responsibility of the city extends not only to torts committed by its officials when engaged in performing a private or commercial function for the municipality, but also to any claims that may arise from defects in city property which is not exclusively devoted to governmental purposes. When the city owns and uses buildings solely for public purposes, as the city hall, the schoolhouses, the police and fire stations, it is ordinarily not liable for damages caused by negligence in the construc-

---

[1] Wilcox *v.* Chicago, 107 *Illinois*, 334.
[2] As indicated by the passage of Workmen's Compensation Laws, for example.

tion or repair of them. If, however, the municipal authorities permit such a building to be used for other than public purposes, as for private entertainments, the city must assume liability for any injuries ensuing. This is a branch of law upon which the array of judicial decisions is at present very perplexing. The general drift seems to be in the direction of extending civic liability, even in the case of property devoted wholly to public use. Indeed, the manifest desire of the courts to give every possible security to the rights of individuals has impelled them in recent years to the policy of putting municipal corporations upon the same plane of legal responsibility as private individuals, so far as property is concerned.

A rather special field of municipal powers and duties is connected with the relations of the city to public service companies. This is a subject too extensive and too complex to be dealt with in any general discussion of municipal government; for not only does it include the scope and the limitations of municipal franchise-granting power, but it involves such important questions as the authority of the city to regulate the rates charged and the quality of the service rendered. On these points even the general principles of law, as enunciated in judicial decisions, are not easily formulated; but two rules may be laid down with some degree of assurance. In the first place, the courts have been rather reluctant to abandon the old notion that public advantage can be best secured by the competition of two or more enfranchised public service corporations operating within the same locality. Students of applied economics have long since become convinced that no permanent, effective competition in a natural monopoly, such as water, gas, electric, telephone, transportation service, can be carried on in the same area of patronage.[1] But even in recent years the courts have held that benefits will accrue to the public from competition in the operation of public utilities and hence, in the absence of express statutory authority, have denied the power of the municipalities to grant exclusive franchises. They have likewise refused to imply ex-

4. Liability of the city in relation to public service corporations.

---

[1] "There are some general principles which we wish to represent as practically the unanimous sentiment of our committee. First, we wish to emphasize the fact that the public utilities studied are so constituted that it is impossible for them to be regulated by competition." *National Civic Federation, Report on Municipal and Private Operation of Public Utilities*, (3 vols., New York, 1907), Pt. I, vol. i, 23.

clusiveness wherever any other reasonable construction of a franchise is possible, and this even when the municipality has admitted powers derived from express statutory grant.[1] On the other hand, they have not ventured to trust competition as the sole means of regulating public services. They have readily admitted the authority of the legislature (within the bounds prescribed by the federal and state constitutions) to make reasonable regulations as to rates charged and quality of service provided; but they have denied to the municipal corporation any such rights of regulation, save when it has been expressly delegated to the city by the legislature or when the power to regulate has been reserved in the franchise itself.[2]

Conclusions. Surveying the liabilities of the American city as a whole and comparing them with those attaching to the cities of Europe, one need have little hesitation in pronouncing them too narrow. In England the city has the same legal liability as a private corporation. It may be sued in the same courts and with the same freedom. In the cities of France, Germany and Italy an aggrieved individual may bring suit in the administrative courts and recover damages from the municipal treasury for the negligence or the incapacity of any city officer, no matter what his sphere of employment. In all these countries the liability of municipal corporations for the inefficiency or negligence of its officials has been a wholesome spur to good administration. An employer is more careful in choosing his employees when he knows that their errors may be costly to him, and the city is no exception. In the United States the exemption from legal liability in the case of policemen, firemen, and various other municipal employees has been a factor in our remarkable leniency towards the spoils system. If we had to pay, from the city treasury, the full price which this system costs, it would not be tolerated very long.

The life of a municipal corporation. A final aspect of the city's legal status remains to be mentioned. Municipal corporations are not created for a term of years but in perpetuity. Their existence is not terminated, nor is their identity affected by an enlargement or restrictions in territory, by an increase or a decrease in the number of inhabitants, by

---

[1] See O. L. Pond, *Municipal Control of Public Utilities*, ch. viii ("The Power to Grant Exclusive Franchises").
[2] *Ibid.*, ch. ix.

LEGAL PHASES OF CITY GOVERNMENT

any change in name, or by amendments to their charters. The repeal of an old charter and the substitution of a new one does not dissolve a municipal corporation. But where the entire territory of a municipal corporation is annexed or consolidated, the corporation is absorbed with the territory. Likewise the repeal of a city charter by the legislature without substituting another charter brings the life of a municipal corporation to an end. But the courts will never credit the legislature with an intention to repeal without substitution unless this intent is clear.

A municipal corporation can be dissolved by authority of the state and by such authority only. This involves action by the state legislature, or by the courts acting under authority given to them by statute.[1] In some states the power of the legislature to dissolve as well as to create municipal corporations is subject to constitutional restrictions. The inhabitants of a city cannot by any act of their own dissolve the municipal corporation and divest it of its responsibilities.[2] Nor is the corporation dissolved by the mere failure to exercise its functions over a term of years. Even the non-election or non-appointment of all municipal officers does not entail dissolution, for the continuance of corporate powers does not depend upon their constant exercise. The inhabitants, not the officers, constitute the corporation. Were all the inhabitants to disappear, the municipal corporation would necessarily come to an end; but that is something which does not occur in a growing country.

How municipal corporations are dissolved.

REFERENCES

The standard work on the rights and responsibilities of city authorities is J. F. Dillon, *Law of Municipal Corporations* (5th edition, 5 vols., Boston, 1911), a comprehensive, thorough, and accurate work. Eugene McQuillin's *Law of Municipal Corporations* (6 vols., Chicago, 1911-1912, and supplementary volumes 7-8, Chicago, 1921) is a later work and of virtually equal quality. Shorter treatises are H. S. Abbott, *Treatise*

---

[1] In the United States the courts have no inherent power to declare the abrogation of a city charter; but such power is customarily given to them by statutes which define the procedure to be followed. The usual procedure is by writ of *quo warranto*. The petition for such a writ, if presented by individuals, ordinarily requires the approval of the Attorney-General or some other state officer.

[2] In some states, however, the general laws provide that the inhabitants may dissolve the municipal corporation by complying with certain conditions which usually involve a popular vote.

on the *Law of Municipal Corporations* (3 vols., St. Paul, 1913); C. B. Elliott, *Principles of the Law of Public Corporations* (ed. J. E. Macy, Chicago, 1910), and R. W. Cooley, *Handbook of the Law of Municipal Corporations* (St. Paul, 1914). A brief summary of eighty-five pages under the title *Municipal Corporations*, by James Schouler, is published by the American School of Correspondence.

Three excellent case-books are J. H. Beale, *Selection of Cases on Municipal Corporations* (Cambridge, 1911); John E. Macy, *Selection of Cases on Municipal or Public Corporations* (Boston, 1911); and R. W. Cooley, *Illustrative Cases on Municipal Corporations* (St. Paul, 1913).

Special treatises which will be found useful in their respective fields are Eugene McQuillin, *Law of Municipal Ordinances* (Chicago, 1904); W. L. Williams, *The Liability of Municipal Corporations for Tort* (Boston, 1901), and Edward F. White, *The Negligence of Municipal Corporations* (Indianapolis, 1923). Mention should also be made of H. L. McBain's *American City Progress and the Law* (New York, 1918).

CHAPTER VII

THE MUNICIPAL ELECTORATE

First among the active factors in American city government is the electorate itself, in other words, the whole body of municipal voters. The composition of this body is of greater importance in the United States than in European countries, because the American electorate participates more frequently and more directly in actual government. The American municipal voter is called to the polls every year (and sometimes more than once a year), whereas the French voter casts his ballot at a municipal election only once in four years, and most of the voters in German cities only once in three years. Moreover, the American voter, when he goes to the polls, has a more difficult task to perform. He is not, like the voter in an English, French, or German city, asked to select merely one name from a short list of candidates for the city council. On the contrary, he is usually called upon to scan a ballot containing scores of names, and is expected to express his preferences in the case of several offices. *Importance of the electorate.*

Not only is the American voter required to elect the officers of city government, but wherever the system of primary elections has been adopted he is expected to nominate the candidates as well. The voters of the American city have thus a double responsibility, that of choosing the candidates and of making final selections from the candidates chosen. In the cities of no other country is this dual function imposed upon the voters. In France and in Italy the system of *ballotage* often works out to something like a primary and a final election; but in these countries the preliminary election becomes final whenever any one candidate gets a clear majority of the polled votes.[1] *Frequent tasks imposed upon the American municipal voter.*

Finally, the demands upon the American municipal voter are heavier than those placed upon the voters of European cities *The ballot's new burdens.*

[1] See the discussion of this feature in the author's *Government of European Cities* (revised edition, New York, 1926). In some American cities (in Los Angeles, for example), the primary becomes a final election in the case of any candidate who obtains a clear majority.

134   THE GOVERNMENT OF AMERICAN CITIES

because they are so often asked to decide questions submitted to them on the ballot. The use of the initiative, referendum, and recall in American cities has greatly augmented the voter's responsibility, and has made the quality of the electorate a matter of more vital importance than it used to be. It is true that municipal voters in England are occasionally asked to pass upon questions submitted to them, especially in the matter of promoting private bills in parliament; but no English city has any provision for the mandatory initiative or the recall. Popular votes are not taken on any questions of public policy in the cities of France or Italy. Some German cities, since 1918, have made provision for using the initiative and referendum but the system which they have adopted is cumbersome and virtually unworkable.

History of the suffrage in America:

1. Down to 1860.

The history of the suffrage in American cities is a long and not a very interesting story. In the colonial boroughs property qualifications for voting were virtually universal. In none of the colonies was manhood suffrage the rule. Nor was it established as an immediate result of the Revolution, although there is a widespread impression to the contrary. The Declaration of Independence asserted the unalienable natural right of all men to a voice in the conduct of their own governments, but the thirteen states which joined in the Declaration made no haste to put that doctrine into effect. They did not provide for governments based upon the consent of all the governed. With the adoption of the federal constitution in 1788, however, the reaction against property qualifications began, and the movement received some impetus from the equalitarian philosophy of the French Revolution, which had audible echoes in America. Then, in the first three or four decades of the nineteenth century came the fiercer competition of political parties and the inevitable reaching out for new voters.[1] One by one the states abolished both property and tax requirements, and by 1820 more than half of them had established white manhood suffrage, virtual or complete. But the crest of the wave came during the period 1820-1845, especially in the Jacksonian era.[2] New York, Massachusetts, Connecticut, New Jersey, Tennessee, and Delaware, one

---

[1] A good account of this development may be found in Kirk H. Porter's *History of the Suffrage in the United States* (New York, 1918).
[2] See *above*, p. 29.

THE MUNICIPAL ELECTORATE 135

after another, threw their special qualifications overboard; and when the new western territories were formed they placed their suffrage requirements on a democratic basis. Democracy thus marched with the frontier, and when it had become triumphant there, its influence rebounded back to the older communities of the East. By 1850 manhood suffrage for the white race had swept the country.

Then came the Civil War, followed by three important amendments to the national constitution. In two of these amendments an attempt was made to include the colored race within the scope of manhood suffrage, but this attempt, as will later be seen, did not prove permanently successful. Meanwhile a movement for the extension of the suffrage to women had been begun and was making slow headway. Its progress continued to be rather slow until after the turn of the twentieth century, when it gained new impetus and eventually crowned itself with success by securing the adoption of the nineteenth amendment. Manhood suffrage thus widened into universal suffrage. There can be no further widening.

2. Since the Civil War.

Today it is approximately correct, therefore, to say that every adult citizen is entitled to vote at municipal elections in the United States. It is not a strictly accurate statement, however, for there are several conditions which have to be fulfilled before adult citizens can be enrolled as voters. These conditions are not uniform throughout the United States because Congress does not determine them; they are fixed by each state at its own discretion subject only to the stipulation that no one may be excluded by reason of sex, color, race, or previous condition of servitude.

3. The final outcome.

In each state the qualifications for voting at national, state, and municipal elections are virtually uniform, although there is in most cases no constitutional barrier to their being made different. There is nothing to prevent a state legislature from imposing special qualifications for voting at municipal elections (aside from the limitations in the federal and state constitutions), and sometimes a special qualification for municipal voters has been imposed. But such requirements are very rare. We have reached a point in our electoral evolution where a man or woman, if qualified to vote at any election, is entitled to vote at them all. This would hardly be worth mention were it not that in

No dual electorate in this country.

136 THE GOVERNMENT OF AMERICAN CITIES

England a distinction is still made between parliamentary and local electors.

The present qualifications for voting:

What, then, are the specific qualifications for voting at American municipal elections? They may be summarized under the following heads: (1) citizenship, (2) age, (3) residence, (4) literacy, (5) the payment of taxes, and (6) the ownership of property. Practically all the states now impose the first three; about a third of the states have established the fourth; a few apply the fifth, and only one state (Rhode Island) retains the sixth.

1. Citizenship.

Most Americans look upon the suffrage as a *natural right* and hence as the prerogative of every adult citizen. But the suffrage is in reality a privilege, not a right. There is an important difference between the two. A right is guaranteed to the citizen by the constitution for his own benefit—the right to due process of law, for example. It is guaranteed to everyone, old or young, without exception. But a privilege is bestowed upon certain classes of citizens only, and not merely for their own benefit. It is given to be used in the service of the whole community—the privilege of practicing medicine or the privilege of performing the marriage ceremony, or of taking a civil service examination, for example. Voting is a civil privilege, bestowed upon citizens above a certain age who possess designated qualifications in the way of residence, literacy, and so forth.

A place on the voters' list is not, therefore, one of the essential attributes of citizenship. Citizenship in the United States is a matter of federal jurisdiction. Congress decides who shall become American citizens. It makes the naturalization laws. But the state legislatures determine (under certain limitations) who shall have the right to vote, and they can admit non-citizens to the polls if they choose. Until recent years, in fact, quite a few states did permit non-citizens to vote—not only in state and municipal elections but in national elections as well.[1] All but four of them, however, have now abandoned this policy. The states which still permit unnaturalized aliens to vote are Arkansas, Indiana, Missouri, and Texas. A vigorous movement to abrogate this provision is now being carried on in each of those states.

2. Age.

Without exception, all the states have adopted the old English

[1] At one time about one-fourth of all the states did it.

THE MUNICIPAL ELECTORATE

rule fixing twenty-one years as the age of political majority. As the enrolment of voters takes place some time before the annual elections, however, it is usually provided that a person otherwise qualified may have his name put on the voters' list before reaching his twenty-first birthday if the election comes after that date.

A certain minimum of "legal residence" is also required in every state. The term varies in length and usually stipulates for a certain period of residence within the state and a shorter one within the city. In most cases the minimum period of state residence is one year; but a few states have a two year requirement. On the other hand, ten states require only six months and one state (Maine) permits the residence requirement to be satisfied in three months. The period of residence in the city, or in the precinct, varies all the way from a few days to twelve months. Thirty to sixty days is the more common requirement.[1] Thus New York State requires a year in the state, thirty days in the city, and thirty days in the precinct. It should be understood, however, that the requirement refers to "legal residence," which is not the same thing as actual habitation. Ordinarily the two are the same, but it is quite possible for a man to live in one state or community and still have his legal residence in another. It is commonly remarked that a man's legal residence is where he intends it to be; but mere intent is not sufficient. There must be some actual connection between the voter and the place which he claims as his legal residence. It need not be a very intimate connection, for a voter can maintain his legal residence in a city even though he neither owns nor rents any premises there, and in fact does not visit the place for years at a time. His legal residence may be the home of some relative or friend. There must be a definite address which he not only intends to be his legal residence, but to which he has the privilege of returning after his absence therefrom. The matter is not one on which a hard and fast rule can be laid down, for much depends upon the circumstances surrounding each particular case. In the event of any controversy as to whether a citizen's legal residence is in one place or another, the courts decide. They have usually held that intent to be a legal resident must be

3. Residence.

The meaning of legal residence.

---

[1] A table showing the requirements in all the states may be found in the *World Almanac* for 1925, p. 816.

shown and that there must be some corroboration of this intent in the way of a physical connection; but they have evolved no exact definition of the form which this connection must take.¹

Legal residence and taxation.

The question is badly complicated, moreover, by the practice of permitting a man's legal residence to determine where he shall be assessed for taxes on intangible property and on income. In fact, the choice of a legal residence—for in many cases it has become a matter of choice—is often determined by a person's desire to be assessed in one state or municipality rather than another, a desire which is not unconnected with the size of the tax rate or the inquisitiveness of the assessors. A man's legal residence also determines, in some cases, the amount of inheritance taxes which his estate will have to pay when he dies, and how much of his property his widow must inherit. Wealthy men and women often find it advantageous, therefore, to maintain their legal residence in a city where the taxes are light and the assessors lenient, while spending virtually the whole of every year in some other place where both the tax laws and the officials are more severe. Knowing this propensity, indeed, some states and municipalities have altered their tax laws or put their assessments on a low basis with the idea of attracting wealthy men as legal residents.

Married women.

In the case of a married woman, her legal residence is ordinarily determined by that of her husband; but in some states it has been provided by law that a married woman, though actually living with her husband, may have a different legal residence *for voting purposes only,* and not for other purposes. This provision has been made, for example, in Massachusetts. On the whole, it is not a wise provision and opens the door to many complications. The same may be said of the federal law which permits husband and wife, although living together in the United States, to be of different citizenship.

The question of university students.

Difficult questions often arise with respect to this matter of legal residence in the case of university students. Take the case of a student who is an American citizen over twenty-one years of age. His home is at Cedar Rapids, Iowa, let us say, but he is attending the Medical School at Johns Hopkins in Baltimore. He lives in a dormitory room, intends to practice

¹ For a good discussion of the matter, see the decision in Williams *v.* Whitney (11 *Massachusetts,* 424).

THE MUNICIPAL ELECTORATE 139

in Baltimore after he obtains his degree, but is wholly dependent upon money sent to him from his Iowa home. Where is his legal residence? In Baltimore where he spends all his time and intends to reside? Or in Iowa where his "home" really is until he acquires another? Would it make any difference if he were self-supporting? In some instances the courts have held that this is the controlling factor.

In nearly one third of all the states some sort of literacy test for voting has been established by law. Connecticut, which requires that every one enrolled as a voter shall be able to read the state constitution or statutes in the English language, is the only one which allows no exemptions whatever. California, Delaware, Maine, Massachusetts, New Hampshire, New York, and several other states require that voters shall be able either to read or to write or to do both; but all grant exemptions of one sort or another.[1] These exemptions, which apply mainly to persons physically incapacitated or of advanced age, are not designed to permit racial or other discriminations, but merely to keep the strict application of the tests from resulting in hardship. Several Southern states, on the other hand, while prescribing educational tests, grant exemptions to whole classes for the express purpose of excluding colored citizens from the privileges guaranteed to them by the fifteenth amendment to the federal constitution.[2] Inasmuch as the percentage of illiterates among negroes is very large, the requirement that voters shall be able to read or write is one which, when strictly administered, shuts out a large proportion of them. It is quite effective in gaining the desired end.

4. Literacy.

But there are also many illiterate white citizens who would be excluded by the test; and for their benefit Alabama, Louisiana, Mississippi, North and South Carolina, and Virginia have provided means whereby the requirement can be easily circumvented by the white element of the population. Various devices are employed to this end. In one case the provision is that the voter must either read the constitution or "give a reasonable interpretation" thereof, the question whether the interpretation is reasonable or not resting with the white officials in charge of

Administration of educational tests in the South.

---
[1] See the *Index Digest of State Constitutions*, prepared for the New York Constitutional Convention (1915), under "Elections."
[2] G. T. Stephenson's *Race Distinctions in American Law* (New York, 1910), contains a full discussion of this matter.

the registration.¹ In other cases the "grandfather clause" was devised in an effort to exempt from the educational test all those who enjoyed voting rights before 1867 and all descendants of such voters—a mere subterfuge for giving complete exemption to all native-born citizens.² The Supreme Court of the United States, in 1914, declared this grandfather provision to be an evasion of the Fifteenth Amendment and hence unconstitutional; but meanwhile most of the illiterate white voters had become enrolled.³

In another Southern state the laws exempt from the literacy test all owners of property who have paid taxes for the year preceding enrolment. As the percentage of property-owning negroes is small in all the Southern states and the proportion of those who pay their taxes on time even smaller, it follows that not many illiterates get their names upon the rolls by the use of this exemption.⁴ It is tolerably obvious, therefore, that the educational tests imposed by various states at the South are designed not so much to purge the voters' lists of illiterates as to permit racial distinctions without violating the letter of the federal constitution. That they have done this effectively and continue to do it in spite of the action of the Supreme Court in annulling the "grandfather clause," is proved by the small negro vote cast in the Southern cities, almost without exemption.

But it is not laws alone that keep colored voters away from the polls in Southern communities. There are other ways quite as effective. Colored men and women can be excluded from the conventions or the primaries of the Democratic party, and it is at the contests for the nominations that elections are virtually decided in all the Southern states. Whoever gets the Democratic nomination is virtually certain to be elected. To exclude colored voters from a share in making the nominations is therefore more effective, as a means of disfranchisement, than keeping them away from the polls. Nor can this arrangement be declared un-

[1] Constitution of Mississippi, 1890, art. xii, 244.
[2] Constitution of Louisiana, 1898, art. cxcvii, 3-5. See also p. 114.
[3] Guinn v. U. S., 238 U. S., 347. For an excellent discussion of this whole matter, see R. C. Brooks, *Political Parties and Electoral Problems* (New York, 1923), pp. 363-370.
[4] Constitution of South Carolina, 1895, art. 11, 4. For a further discussion, see Kirk H. Porter's *History of Suffrage in the United States* (Chicago, 1918).

constitutional. The Fifteenth Amendment forbids the exclusion of colored citizens from voting at the polls but it does not forbid their being shut out from membership in a political party. Finally, if all else fails, it is usually possible to disfranchise the negro by Ku Klux or other strong-arm methods. He can be warned to keep away and he will usually do it. The fact is that most colored men and women in Southern cities are not yearning for the right to vote. A great many of them care very little whether they vote or not. Why should they, when their votes, in most cases, would not affect the outcome of the election? The controversy over the enforcement of the Fifteenth Amendment would soon subside if white politicians in the Northern states did not persist in keeping it alive.

But to return to the question of educational qualifications in general. Is it desirable that a literacy test, fairly applied and impartially enforced, should be established in all the states as a requirement for voting? New York State, since 1923, has required that all voters must present to the election officers a diploma showing that they have completed the work of an approved eighth grade elementary school, or of a higher school, in which English is the language of instruction. Or, as an alternative, they may submit a certificate of literacy issued by the state educational authorities, the board of regents.[1] It will be noted that the New York tests differ from those of every other state in that they are given by the regular school authorities and not by election officials. This means that there will be no discriminations or evasions to suit the interests of a political party.[2]

A discussion of literacy tests in general.

Would it be advantageous for other states to do as New York has done? The percentage of illiterates in the population of the United States, as has been seen, is surprisingly large.[3] It is a conservative estimate that in cities like Pittsburgh, Chicago, and St. Louis there are probably ten per cent of the voters who

[1] *Laws of New York*, 1923. Chap. 809.
[2] The work of examining applicants and giving certificates is delegated to local school superintendents and their assistants, but the test is uniform throughout the state. It involves reading a 100-word exerpt from the state constitution and writing at least ten words in English. See the article on "The New York Literacy Test," by F. G. Crawford in the *American Political Science Review*, vol. xvii, pp. 261-263 (May, 1923), reprinted in Joseph Wright's *Selected Readings in Municipal Problems* (Boston, 1925), pp. 229-230, and the further discussion in vol. xix, pp. 788-791 (November, 1925).
[3] *Above*, p. 60.

cannot read their ballots intelligently. We have no way of figuring the exact percentage, for no test is applied in these cities and if we turn to the census figures of illiteracy we find them undependable, for reasons that have already been stated.[1] Ten per cent is a considerable fraction. In most cases it is enough to determine the outcome of a municipal election. Is it right, therefore, to place the ballot in the hands of thousands who cannot read what is printed on it, or follow the discussion of the issues in the newspapers? Many years ago, in New York City, the reformers made Boss Tweed's wrath explode by covering the billboards with political cartoons. "I don't mind their literature," he growled, "for my people can't read it; but they can read these damned pictures!"

The attitude of the politicians. As a rule the politicians are vigorously opposed to literacy tests of any sort and they offer some plausible arguments in support of their attitude. People who cannot read or write often own property and pay taxes, they say. If you deny them the right to vote, it is a case of taxation without representation. Illiterates are drafted into the army when war comes. They are good enough to fight—but not good enough to vote! And what has education got to do with political intelligence anyhow? Even university graduates may be guiltless of all knowledge concerning the candidates and the issues. They often are. On the other hand, a man who has had no schooling, or almost none, may be well-posted on every phase of local politics.

The flaw in their contentions. All this sounds plausible enough, but it is largely beside the point. Suppose we carry the politician's argument to its logical conclusion. Aliens own property and pay taxes and yet are not usually permitted to vote. According to the henchman's logic they ought to be enrolled. Citizens under twenty-one years of age are liable to be drafted in time of war. Must we on that account give the ballot to them? Women, on the other hand, are not liable to military service. Does logic require that we take the ballot away from them? The arguments for illiterate voting are full of flaws. Voting has nothing to do with property owning, tax paying, or liability to military service. Whether an individual should be given the suffrage is a question which ought to be approached from the standpoint of what is best for democratic government. Does it promote the cause of honest,

[1] *Above*, p. 60.

THE MUNICIPAL ELECTORATE 143

efficient, and popular government to let illiterates vote? Surely there can be but one answer to that question. When you ask a man to mark a ballot which he cannot read, you are taking a poor way to make democracy successful.[1] Bear in mind that there is no good reason why any man or woman in an American city should remain illiterate. There are free night-schools everywhere. We compel every child to attend school for a prescribed number of years, and if anyone now grows up illiterate in an American city it is in violation of the law.

If the policy of excluding illiterates from the suffrage should become general throughout the United States there would undoubtedly be some improvement in the quality of the electorate. But we must not expect too much from any action that may be taken in this direction. Literacy tests have wrought no miracle in states which have been applying them, fairly and firmly, for more than thirty years. It should not be taken for granted, as reformers sometimes do, that the voter who cannot read or write is always an ally of crooked politics. Municipal misgovernment will doubtless continue to have plenty of friends and supporters among the well educated, as has been the case in all ages.

No state of the Union now requires either the ownership or the occupancy of property as a condition of enrolment for state elections; and only one state, Rhode Island, makes any such requirement for voting at municipal elections. In Rhode Island the right to vote for city councillors, or on matters of municipal finance, is restricted to those who own property to the assessed value of $134, or which rents for at least seven dollars per year.[2] In actual operation this restriction excludes a good many citizens who would be enrolled under a system of universal suffrage.[3] A

5. Ownership of property.

---

[1] It may be replied, of course, that the ballot can be so arranged (with party columns and symbols) that even an illiterate voter is able to understand it. That is true, so far as the voting of straight party tickets is concerned. But an illiterate voter cannot vote a split ticket (i. e., for some candidates of one party and some of another), nor can he read the referendum questions on the ballot (see *below*, pp. 242-243), and under a system of proportional voting (*below*, pp. 195-198), he is utterly helpless. Indeed, the constitutionality of proportional representation has been attacked on the ground that it imposes, in a roundabout way, an educational test for voting.
[2] The provision dates back to 1842 but was amended in 1888. *Constitution of Rhode Island*, Amendment VII.
[3] In Providence, R. I., for example (1924), there were 85,966 registered voters. Of these only 31,801 were qualified (as owners of property) to vote for city councillors; that is, only 27 per cent.

few Southern states make ownership of property a requirement for voting, but only as an alternative to some other qualification, such as ability to read and write.

6. Payment of taxes. Some other states, both North and South, require that voters shall have paid their poll taxes before being enrolled. In Massachusetts the requirement is that male voters must have been *assessed* for poll taxes before being registered—which is quite a different thing from requiring that the taxes must have been paid. In any event the poll tax qualifications has served little purpose. When it is rigidly enforced it becomes a heavy burden upon the campaign funds of the political parties, for there are many who will leave the tax unpaid until the eve of an election and then expect the party workers to provide the money. The result is that the political parties use their influence to have this requirement relaxed, or to get the taxes abated. Suffrage and taxation ought not to be conjoined, for they have no relation to each other.

Why is it unjust to impose a taxpaying qualification? In the minds of a good many people, however, there persists a feeling that somehow or other the suffrage should be linked up with taxes. This idea crops out whenever groups of business men discuss the suffrage. Why should people who contribute nothing to the municipal treasury have a voice in deciding how the money should be spent? If a man wants to be a stockholder in the municipal corporation he ought to invest some of his own money in the concern. People who pay no taxes have no real stake in the community. The non-taxpaying element is responsible for most of our civic extravagance. And much more to the same purport. But all this is mere sophistry. It rests on a false assumption. It assumes that people who pay no taxes directly pay no taxes at all. This seems to be one of our nation-wide delusions. A moment's reflection, however, ought to convince us that everybody who lives in a city is indirectly a taxpayer. The tenant pays taxes—through his landlord. The customer pays taxes—through his grocer. Every household that uses gas or electricity pays taxes—through the lighting company. Taxes are an element in the cost of everything we use or buy. There may be non-taxpayers, but they are few and far between. To exclude from voting those who do not pay taxes *directly* would be a grave injustice, the enactment of an economic delusion into the law of the land.

THE MUNICIPAL ELECTORATE 145

In all American cities there are certain disqualifications from voting. The ineligible usually include persons who have been convicted of treason or other felonies, the insane, and those who are under guardianship. In a few states the exclusion extends to all persons in receipt of public poor-relief, and to United States soldiers and sailors. Some of them also provide for the disfranchisement of persons who have been convicted of bribery at elections. In no two states are the disqualifications the same.[1]

Disqualifications from voting.

The methods of compiling and revising the voters' lists are much the same in all American cities. In most of them there is a system of personal registration. The would-be voter is required to appear before a board of registrators or election judges who hold sessions at an announced date some time before the election. On appearing before the board, he (or she) takes oath as to citizenship, age, and residence. If there is a literacy test it is given by the registration officers.[2] On satisfying the registrars the applicant is duly enrolled on the voters' list; if enrolment is refused he may appeal to the courts. In many cities a new registration takes place every year, and even oftener if a special election is held. This results in putting a large expense upon the public treasury, and is also a great inconvenience to the voters.[3] It means, furthermore, that when a citizen is absent from home during the registration period, or is ill, or forgets to register, he loses his right to vote when the next election comes.

How voters' lists are made:

1. Periodical registration.

Some of the larger cities, therefore, have adopted a system of semi-permanent registration. In Boston a voter's name is left on the list so long as he does not change his place of residence. Every year, during the first week of April, the police visit every inhabited premises in the city and list all the adults. The registrars of voters then strike from the rolls all those whose names are not on the police lists. New voters are added to the rolls by personal registration. In Detroit a complete personal registration now takes place every four years only. In some other cities a voter's name is left on the rolls until he fails to

2. Semi-permanent registration.

---
[1] For the complete list, see the table in the *World Almanac*, 1925, p. 816.
[2] Save in New York State, as has already been explained. See *above*, p. 141.
[3] The cost of registering runs from twenty to thirty cents per voter. In Chicago, for example, it amounts to about $250,000 for the whole city.

vote at two successive elections; then it is dropped.¹ Registration by proxy is permitted in a few states and in Ohio a voter can register by mail.

Protecting the list against frauds. No matter what system may be used it is difficult to protect the voters' lists from fraudulent registration. Names will be put on the lists which have no right to be there. The registrars have no way of checking up the sworn statements of applicants for enrolment. Consequently it is not hard for political bosses and their henchmen to enrol groups of "colonists," "floaters," "ringers," "repeaters," or "mattress voters," as they are variously called. These are persons with no bona fide residence in the city or the ward, but who register from some rooming-house or cheap hotel. From time to time it has been found, in the tenement house wards of large cities, that the lists are well padded with voters of this sort. Even in the smaller cities registration frauds on a large scale have sometimes been uncovered.²

Proportion of voters to population. The enrolled voters in American cities now constitute from twenty-five to thirty-five per cent of the population. It varies in different cities, depending upon various factors such as the number of unnaturalized aliens, the existence or absence of a literacy test, and the efficiency of the party machines in getting voters enrolled. Woman suffrage has not yet doubled the size of the enrolment because the number of qualified citizens who neglect to register is larger among women than among men. If every adult were a citizen qualified to vote and duly registered, the voters would constitute about half the total population, but the deductions on account of alienage, illiteracy, lack of residence, and neglect to register bring the quota of voters down to one-third or one quarter.

Some years ago it was predicted that the admission of women to the suffrage would provide the cities with a more intelligent electorate, less firmly bound by the trammels of party allegiance

---

¹ For a summary of the methods used by various cities see the pamphlet entitled *A Proposed System of Registering Voters . . . in Chicago*, issued by the Chicago Bureau of Public Efficiency in 1923.

² One of the most notorious examples was afforded by Terre Haute, Indiana, ten years ago. The evidence in this case indicated that hundreds of non-residents and dead men were enrolled. On election day they were personated by outsiders hired for the purpose. One of them testified that he voted twenty-two times, each time giving a name which had no right to be on the list.

and more ready to range itself on the right side of every moral issue. It is, of course, too early to form any definite opinion as to whether this prediction is or is not going to be justified. The ballots of women are not kept separate from those of men, hence it is impossible to determine what influence women have exerted upon the outcome of any municipal election. But so far as the superficial indications go, there is no reason to think that the extension of the suffrage to women has made any substantial change in the quality of the electorate. Women seem to be using the ballot in American cities in the way that men have used it, with no greater intelligence and certainly with no less. They are subject in the same degree to the same influences. There is as yet no indication that they are less moved by appeals to party allegiance, or to the various forms of prejudice, or that they insist upon a higher standard of honesty in public office than men have tolerated in the past. In the various municipal elections since 1920 it is difficult to find a single instance where the outcome would have been appreciably different with women excluded from the polls. Despite the expansion of the voters' lists, the Republican wards have remained Republican, and the Democratic wards have remained Democratic. There has been no overturn anywhere. Bosses have not been dethroned or rings demolished by the wonder-working powers of the Nineteenth Amendment. _{Negative effects of woman suffrage in American cities.}

All this is not to imply, however, that the extension of the suffrage to women was unwise. The adoption of equal suffrage has at least eliminated an irrelevant issue from practical politics. Sex should have no more place in politics than race or religion. The Nineteenth Amendment has enfranchised many millions of women and it is bound to develop among them an interest in public affairs which they never would have acquired so long as they were excluded from a direct share in the management of the city's affairs. Nor can we take it for certain that because women have thus far shown the same electoral characteristics as men they will always continue to do so. There is, indeed, some ground for expectation that in certain matters of public policy, such as those relating to the home, the family, and personal conduct, the new electorate will show itself more enlightened than the old.

The history of the American suffrage has been one of steady

and irresistible expansion. When the national constitution went into effect only five or six per cent of the people were qualified to vote. By 1860 the proportion had been raised to about fifteen per cent. Today it must be more than thirty-five per cent, although not all who are qualified take advantage of their opportunities. One limitation after another has been swept away by constitutional amendments and laws—religious tests, property qualifications, race discriminations, and finally exclusion on grounds of sex. Apparently we have reached the end of the expansion—for the moment at least. Today, for the first time in more than two centuries, there is no organized movement for extending the suffrage to anybody. But that can hardly be a permanent situation, for democracy can never be persuaded to stand still. What will be our next step—a further extension (reducing the age limit from twenty-one to eighteen, perhaps), or a reaction toward stricter qualifications. Among thoughtful people the tendency today is in the latter direction, but the whole history of the suffrage demonstrates that it is infinitely easier to give people voting rights than to take them away.

What we most need now, perhaps, is neither a further extension nor a contraction of the existing electorate, but more civic education for those who are already included in it. We have given astonishingly little attention to the problem of educating the voters, especially in our larger cities. We assume as a self-evident proposition that they will familiarize themselves with the organization, functions, needs, issues, and problems of their respective communities, which is exactly what a large proportion of them will not and cannot do of their own accord. In most discussions of civic improvement the necessity of instructing the people, of educating the rank and file to a knowledge of governmental problems, is treated as though it were a mere incidental. Reformers are much more deeply interested in some new type of charter, or in preferential voting, or in the extension of the civil service system. Yet the underlying essential of good city government is an interested and informed community. If the electorate remains inert, uninterested, uninformed, and unguided, it will make scant progress towards enlightened government no matter what mechanism it may use. An ignorant citizen is a far greater obstacle to effective democracy than antiquated charters, long ballots, or the spoils system. We

THE MUNICIPAL ELECTORATE 149

expect officeholders to lend an ear to public opinion, but blank minds cannot express opinions that are worth anybody's heeding. Before a voter can decide, he must know; before he can have an opinion, he must have information. How to give him this information, fully, fairly, and in a way that will make him a more enlightened voter—that is one of the most important and yet one of the most neglected problems of American municipal democracy.

REFERENCES

Interesting discussions of the right to vote, in its wider aspects, may be found in W. E. H. Lecky's *Democracy and Liberty* (2 vols., London, 1899), I, 2-38, 70-100, and Sir Henry Maine's *Popular Government* (London, 1885), chs. i-ii. There is a somewhat rambling discourse on the relations of universal suffrage to popular government in Tocqueville's *Democracy in America* (ed. D. C. Gilman, 2 vols., New York, 1908), I, ch. xiii. A. E. McKinley's *Suffrage Franchise in the Thirteen English Colonies* (Philadelphia, 1905) is a good study in its field. The best short outline of the development from strict to liberal requirements in the United States is Kirk H. Porter's *History of Suffrage in the United States* (Chicago, 1918), especially chs. ii-v, inclusive. A work of much wider scope is Charles Seymour and Donald P. Frary *How the World Votes* (2 vols., Springfield, Mass., 1918).

The relation of the suffrage system to present-day municipal problems is dealt with somewhat briefly by Professor F. J. Goodnow, *Municipal Problems* (New York, 1904), ch. vii, and more exhaustively in Lord Bryce's *Modern Democracies* (New York, 1921, 2 vols.). A well written article by G. H. Haynes on "Educational Qualifications" may be found in the *Political Science Quarterly*, XIII, 495-531; and attention may also be called to the paper on "Educational Qualifications of Voters" by J. B. Phillips in *University of Colorado Studies*, III, 55-62 (1906). The New York Literacy Test is explained by E. G. Crawford in the *American Political Science Review*, xvii, pp. 260-263 (1923), xix, pp. 788-791 (1925).

Arguments for and against restrictions upon universal suffrage are given in P. M. Pearson and E. R. Nichols, *Intercollegiate Debates*, I, 243-258; in Herbert Croly's *Promise of the American Life* (New York, 1910), 198-199; in A. B. Cruikshank's *Popular Misgovernment in the United States* (New York, 1920), and in R. C. Ringwalt's *Briefs on Public Questions with Selected Lists of References* (New York, 1911), pp. 25-30. Other sources of information are by C. W. Elliot, *American Contributions to Civilization* (New York, 1897), ch. i; H. C. Adams

Public Debts (New York, 1898), 359-366; and J. S. Mill, *Representative Government* (London, 1894), ch. viii.

On Southern suffrage laws see G. T. Stephenson's *Race Discrimination in American Law* (New York, 1910); R. C. Brooks, *Political Parties and Electoral Problems* (New York, 1923), especially pp. 363-370; J. E. Johnson, *Selected Articles on the Negro Problem* (New York, 1921), and the article by J. C. Rose on "Negro Suffrage: The Constitutional Point of View" in the *American Political Science Review*, I, pp. 17-43 (November, 1906).

The question of woman suffrage has been discussed in a great many books which cannot be listed here. Good bibliographies may be found in P. Orman Ray's *Introduction to Political Parties and Practical Politics* (3d edition, New York, 1924), pp. 576-579, and in H. Baker-Crothers and Ruth A. Hudnut, *Problems of Citizenship* (New York, 1924), pp. 482-486. Special mention, however, should be made of the article by W. F. Ogburn and I. Goltis, on "How Women Vote," in the *Political Science Quarterly*, xxxiv, pp. 413-433 (1919).

On the methods of registering voters there are short discussions in R. C. Brooks, *Political Parties and Electoral Problems* (New York, 1923), ch. xvi, and P. Orman Ray, *Introduction to Political Parties and Practical Politics* (3d edition, New York, 1924), ch. xii. The pamphlet on this subject issued by the Chicago Bureau of Public Efficiency in 1923 is very useful.

CHAPTER VIII

POLITICAL PARTIES IN CITIES: THEIR PURPOSE AND ORGANIZATION

"Governments are like clocks," said William Penn; "they go from the motion that men give them." They are mechanisms which men control. But men and women do not exercise this control as individuals. They do it in groups, in large bodies which we call political parties. The political party, therefore, is the organization through which the voter makes the expression of his will and opinions effective. Unhappily it is not always recognized as an integral factor in the process of democratic government, yet the whole history of politics can be adduced to support Lord Bryce's contention that political parties are inevitable, that no country has ever been without them, and that no one has ever shown how a representative system of government could be made to function if political parties did not exist.   *The importance of parties.*

The division of the people into political parties is the logical outcome of a simple fact, the fact that people do not all want to act alike nor yet do they all want to act differently. If they wanted to do either of these things, political parties could not originate, much less remain in existence. No matter what attitude a man may assume towards public questions, he will always get some others to go along with him—if for no other reason than that people find it so much easier to be led than to lead themselves. Political parties are sometimes defined as groups of men and women who think alike on questions of the day; but that is far from being an accurate definition. It implies that a voter's political allegiance is the outcome of his own thought and reflection, which in reality is very seldom the case. Far more often it is the result of something that has no direct relation to his own reasoned preferences. It is the outcome of the voter's ancestry, or his occupation, or his personal friendships, or the region in which he lives, or his religion, or any one of a dozen factors which may have little or nothing to do with his own mental   *Why they exist.*   *The stock definition of parties.*

volition. Party allegiance is a guise which covers a multitude of varying opinions and desires, some of them quite irreconcilable. To say, for example, that voters in Bridgeport and in Savannah necessarily "think alike on public questions" because they belong in both cases to the Democratic party—well, the mere statement of any such proposition is enough to disclose its absurdity.

Its variance with the facts.

What is it that determines the personnel of a political party? It would be difficult to enumerate all the elements which enter into its composition or to explain the motives which have induced them to wear the party's label; but a few of the more important ones may well be indicated. Every political party, in the first place, has a foundation of "regulars," as they are called. Most of these have inherited their political affiliations. They are Republicans or Democrats because their fathers and grandfathers were. Irrespective of issues or leaders or candidates, their allegiance never falters. They would support Beelzebub for mayor with the right tag pinned on him. Possibly half the adherents of the older political parties are in this category. It is not that they think alike; they do not think at all. Long before they reach the age at which they are capable of orderly thought, these individuals have had their allegiance determined for them in homes surcharged with partisanship. It is true that men and women who are Republicans by birth sometimes become Democrats by reflection, or vice versa, but the proportion of converts is far smaller than most people imagine. Were it otherwise we would not find various sections of the country remaining in the same column, one generation after another, despite complete changes in the issues that come up for decision. Heredity is a big factor in political science as in biology, but it does not obey the Mendelian law. As a rule the dominant political streak colors the entire progeny.

The varied elements which go to make up a political party.

1. The regulars.

But heredity counts for less in urban than in rural politics and there are several reasons for this: In the cities there are large bodies of foreign-born voters who naturally have inherited no strong political inclinations. They are more open to a new appeal than are the native-born whose fathers and grandfathers have handed them a tradition. Race, religion, and occupation are thus enabled to become more influential as determinants of party allegiance in the cities than in the rural areas. Person-

2. Racial groups.

alities also count for more in city than in country. Elections are more often determined by organizations and leadership than by tradition. Hence it is that a swing from one column to another is by no means out of the question in most of the large centers, even though the normal affiliation is strongly to one side.[1]

Race is a determining factor of large dimensions in American city politics, although people dislike to face the fact. In many instances the party divisions represent racial cleavage and very little else. In the Southern cities, for example, virtually all colored voters are Republicans, and for the most part the same is true of colored voters in Northern communities. Voters of Irish birth or descent in the cities of New England and the Middle States are almost unanimously affiliated with the Democratic party. In Boston, for example, fewer than five per cent of the Irish voters are normally Republican. In Philadelphia, on the other hand, there is a large Irish-Republican element. Among voters of German descent the tendency is to Republicanism, especially in the cities of the Middle West, but not strongly so. The Italians, as a race, have not gone largely into the ranks of any one political party but are well distributed, and the same is true of the Jews. Citizens of Polish ancestry tend to be Democrats, although not always. Scandinavians are strongly inclined to Republicanism but not to the reactionary brand of it. They have shown a partiality towards the more radical wing of the Republican party during recent years. The French-Canadians in the cities of New England are also heavily Republican, a phenomenon that has never been satisfactorily explained. But it is not well to generalize too broadly on this matter of race in its relation to party allegiance. Almost everywhere one will find notable exceptions to any general rule that may be laid down.

Yet the steadily-increasing accentuation of racial distinctions in American city politics is plain to the naked eye and it cannot be regarded as an auspicious development. Appeals to racial prejudice and incitement to racial intolerance are becoming more frequent and more virulent than they used to be. This is par-

[1] Such cities as New York and Boston, for example, although heavily Democratic under ordinary conditions, have occasionally gone Republican in a national election. This cannot be said of the heavily Democratic states of the South.

ticularly the case where racial and religious lines of cleavage happen to coincide, as they frequently do in cities of the Eastern States. In such cases it makes little difference whether you put party designations on the ballot or take them off, for the conflict at the polls is not usually waged on issues that can be called political.

3. Occupational groups.

Occupation is also becoming a more important factor in determining or modifying a voter's party affiliations in the larger cities. The lines of adherence are tending to assume an economic direction, with the well-to-do on one side and the less well-to-do on the other—a revival of the old Roman division between Patricians and Plebeians. There are some cities where the political complexion of any neighborhood can be accurately guessed by anyone who drives around and takes a look at the houses in which the people live. It is a case of east side against west side, tenement-house wards against residential suburbs. Not all the inhabitants of the crowded wards swing to any one political party, of course, for if they did, that party would always win; but one party usually gets the greater portion of them. It is sometimes very difficult to determine whether the boundary line follows racial or occupational motives for the two may be closely identified.

4. Religion as a factor in politics.

Religion, as has been said, is often a factor in determining the voter's political leanings but its influence is hard to gauge because people do not like to confess it openly. Nevertheless, it comes to the surface from time to time openly and boldly. Religious animosity can be turned by the politicians to their own account more easily in some cities than in others. Race and religion frequently go together, but not always. In the New England cities, for example, the voters of Irish and Polish descent, who are largely Catholic, tend to become Democrats; but the French-Canadians (who are also Catholics) are mostly in the Republican ranks, and the Catholic Italians are not monopolized by either of the two major parties. As a rule the church affiliation of a candidate will bring him support from his co-religionists in the other party, or it may lose him some votes in his own. There are always some voters who adhere to the Republican or to the Democratic party with the reservation that the candidate shall be of their own race or religion. When this requirement is not met they stay at home from the polls.

POLITICAL PARTIES IN CITIES 155

Various other forces are at work. Sectionalism is **one of them**. How a man votes is partly determined by the region in which he lives. Southern Democrats who move to the North often become Republicans in the new environment; while Northern Republicans who migrate to Southern cities as frequently gravitate into the dominant party there. A man's political tendencies are naturally influenced by the company that he keeps. From time to time, moreover, a strong leader with a compelling personality manages to swing thousands of voters to the ticket which he leads. We have had a striking illustration of this in New York during recent years. The strength and cohesion of the party machine is also a factor in keeping the ranks solid and in preventing desertions. Tammany Hall has done more than leaders or issues to keep New York City in the Democratic column. And habit is a factor which must not be left out of account. To leave one party and join another takes more initiative than a good many voters possess. The line of least resistance induces them to stay where they are. Finally, there is a small element (it probably does not exceed ten per cent of the voters) who actually "choose" one political party or the other because of a belief in its principles or policies. This is the group whose members "think alike" on public questions. It is the independent faction of the party and as such it gives the leaders the largest amount of concern.

5. Other forces.

A political party, therefore, is a composite of groups and elements. Likemindedness among all its members is perhaps the least conspicuous of all its characteristics. Some political parties, of course, come nearer to a consensus of opinion in their ranks than others do. The Socialist party is united on the principle that various services which are now in private hands (lighting plants, telephones, street railways, etc.) should be taken over and operated by the public authorities, but not all elements of the Socialist party are of one mind as to how this principle should be put into operation. On specific questions of practical policy there is almost as much diversity among Socialists as among Republicans or Democrats.

Summary.

So what is a political party? It is an association of men and women, who, by reason of ancestry, home influence, race, occupation, religion, place of abode, apathy, personal preference, and some other reasons, allow themselves to be drawn into it. That is not the orthodox definition, but it has the merit of being measurably close to the facts.

<small>No great differences in principles.</small>
Now each political party, in other words each conglomeration of diverse groups and interests, is nominally committed to certain broad principles and has an official platform. But the principles are often not clearly distinguishable from those of a rival party, and as for the platform, it is concocted with a view to satisfying everybody and hence does not usually reflect the views of anybody. Even among the "regulars," there is probably not one voter in a hundred who ever reads the platform or could give you a coherent outline of what it contains. In city elections, indeed, the party may have no platform at all. One good issue, if the party leaders can find one, is usually enough. Others would only tend to confuse it. The record and personality of the party candidate is counted upon to do the rest—supplemented of course by good organization.

<small>The two aims of a political party.</small>
Each political party in a municipal campaign has two aims, one immediate and the other ultimate. The immediate aim is to get control of the city government, for this carries with it the power to make the ordinances, to administer them, to fill the public offices and to distribute patronage. The mental vision of ardent partisans does not usually extend beyond this immediate aim. But the ultimate aim of the party is to use its control of the government in such a way as to carry its own principles into effect, assuming that it has any principles. Usually it has taken a stand on some local issue of importance—renewing a street railway franchise, or reducing the telephone rates, or reorganizing the police force—and must make at least a gesture in the way of redeeming such promises as it has made. But the people have short memories and it is not often that a political party, having gained its immediate aim, is held to a strict accountability as respects anything else.

<small>Are parties essential.</small>
Could we get along without party organizations? Perhaps we could, but the process of maintaining a system of representative government would have to be carried on very differently if party organizations or something closely resembling them did not exist. If you watch an election campaign you will notice
<small>What they do in a campaign.</small>
that it consists of a regular series of events. First, there is a stirring of public discussion about candidates. Various "feelers" are put out to see how public opinion will react. Rarely do

the party leaders commit themselves to anyone's candidacy until they have sounded the public sentiment concerning him. So some newspapers, duly inspired from the proper source, will give prominence to a rumor that So-and-So is likely to seek the party nomination. Then the bosses wait with their ears to the ground for the echoes that are sure to come. If the announcement evokes too little enthusiasm they will try another. Sometimes an aspirant will send up his own trial balloon just to show the party leaders how desirable it is for them to get aboard. At any rate it is desirable that the leaders should come to some agreement on the party's strongest man.

Then, in due course, candidates are nominated and make formal announcement of what they hope to do if elected. In national and state campaigns the platforms are framed by the party convention through one of its committees; in city elections each candidate, as a rule, makes his own pronouncements. This done, they go out and make addresses in halls and on the street corners. Pamphlets and circulars are printed and sent to the voters through the mails. Automobile parades, with cars gaudily placarded, are arranged and conducted through the streets. Publicity men are hired to grind out whole reams of stuff for the newspapers and the latter print perhaps one-tenth of what is handed to them. Even at that they give several hundred columns to a municipal campaign. By one means or another the voters are gradually worked up to a more or less intense interest, and finally the decision is placed in their hands. That is what we call a municipal election campaign. From start to finish the chain of events may cover six months or more, involving a huge amount of work on the part of many individuals, interfering with the normal routine of community life, and necessitating a large outlay of money.

Now it stands to reason that if there were no party organizations, the course of an election campaign would necessarily have to take a very different form. Candidates cannot be nominated without a concentration of effort on somebody's part; issues do not formulate themselves; the people cannot be stirred to an active interest except by vigorous propaganda conducted through the forum, the press, and a house-to-house canvass. In an age where there are so many counter attractions pressing their claims upon the public attention in urban communities,

<small>Who would do all this if political parties did not?</small>

158 THE GOVERNMENT OF AMERICAN CITIES

the interest of the people cannot be aroused without resort to every form of publicity, the more dramatic and picturesque the better. The absolute necessity of electoral organization and propaganda in some form has been demonstrated in a few large cities which have tried to eliminate political parties and put things on a non-partisan basis. The only result in most cases has been to bring forth organizations with new names, yet virtually performing the same functions as of old. They call themselves Citizens' Leagues, or Independent Voters' Leagues, or by some such name; but they nominate candidates, find or create issues, hold rallies, spend money, and do precisely what the out-and-out party organizations do. The only difference is that they commonly do all their work less effectively. You can change names, but you cannot abolish organized effort in politics so long as there are functions which only an organization can effectively perform.

A recapitulation of their useful functions.

1. Nominations.

Looking at the whole process of representative government, then, there are five useful services which political parties now render. First, they undertake the preliminary sifting of aspirants for public office. Men seek office, and they do it in such numbers that there must be some means of concentrating public attention on the ones who really have a chance. Otherwise we would have something akin to electoral chaos. In this respect the party organizations serve as an integral and useful part of the election machinery. Second, the parties (and their candidates) help formulate the issues of the campaign, or, if the issues have already been brought to the front by the natural course of events, the parties help to clarify them so that the contest between candidates becomes in effect a referendum on questions of municipal policy.[1] Third, the party organizations rouse public interest by their rallies, their pamphlets, circulars, articles in newspapers, posters, as well as by personal canvassing. This political awakening of the voters is of great importance, because electoral indifference is the besetting sin of urban democracy. Even after every possible form of publicity has been used it will inevitably be found that two or three municipal voters

2. Issues.

3. Publicity.

[1] It ought to be pointed out that this function of formulating the issues is shared by other organizations, especially in city campaigns. The chamber of commerce, labor organizations, and the various civic associations not infrequently propose action which arouses controversy and figures prominently in the campaign.

out of every ten have failed to go to the polls on election day. What would happen if there were no resort to artificial methods of stimulating the public interest? The methods which the party organizations employ are often crude, it is true, and sometimes they render a negative service to the political education of the people; but on the whole their activities provide a wholesome stimulus to democratic government.

Fourth, the party organization provides a chain which holds the various officers of city government to a joint responsibility. Municipal officers are chosen to perform widely different functions. Members of the city council are elected to enact ordinances, mayors and other city officers to administer the affairs of the municipality, and judges to help enforce the ordinances. To get the best results all three groups of public officials must work in harmony. But if each were elected independently, on his own initiative and without any reference to the others, there would be little chance of their working together. When they do work together it is usually because they have been elected by substantially the same elements among the voters. The democratic plan of government functions best when its various organs work in unison. The principle of checks and balances, whatever its value as a safeguard, would be intolerable if it meant that the different branches of the government must regularly assume an attitude of opposition to one another. A common party allegiance is a promoter of municipal coöperation, but it would be far more valuable if it did not sometimes degenerate into official collusion.

4. Responsibility.

Were there no political parties the responsibility of the public official would be altogether personal and would not endure beyond his term of office. But true responsibility should be collective and continuing. It avails very little as a practical matter to say to a municipal councilman, when his term of office expires: "You have been a disappointment; we will not honor you with reëlection." Such a penalty for unfaithfulness is altogether inadequate. Who vouched for this councilman's fitness and fidelity in the first place? It is on them that the public resentment should fall. The political organization thus becomes a bondsman, as it were, for the candidates whom it puts forward. If they make good in public office the party claims the credit; if they fail the party bears the onus. The record of the party is determined by the actions of those whom it places in public office. It must therefore exercise a reasonable amount of circumspection in choosing those for whom it stands sponsor.

5. Social service.

Finally, the party organization is equipped to render, and does render, a social service as intermediary between its own members and the governing officials. Any ward leader will readily testify that a large part of his time and energy is given to the adjustment of difficulties between individuals and the various branches of the governmental machinery. Nor is it to be imagined that this activity of the party henchmen consists solely in the obtaining of unwarranted favors, or patronage, or immunity from merited punishment. In many cases it takes the form of protection against private avarice or official oppression. The ward leader and his lieutenants often serve as a buffer between the weak and the helpless on the one hand and the soulless employer, the iron-fisted landlord, or the shyster lawyer on the other. This is especially true in large urban communities where great masses of the population are in ignorance of their rights. To such, the party leaders serve as a sort of legal aid bureau. The party machine is powerful; it is often unscrupulous and corrupt; but it is also approachable, human, and ready at all times to befriend its own people.

Why the party system is less satisfactory in urban than in rural areas.

The party system has worked less satisfactorily in the cities and has developed more flagrant abuses in them than in the states or the nation. This is true not only in the United States but in all the European countries, and there are several reasons for it. In the first place, as has been shown, the social and occupational lines are clearer in the cities than in the rural districts and these cross-cleavages tend to disarrange all strictly partisan alignments. The personality of the party leader, again, counts for more in the cities, and the allegiance of many voters is to him rather than to the party. City politics thus tend to become factional and personal. City campaigns, for the same reason, are often featured by an undue amount of mudslinging, vituperation and savage attacks on the personal integrity of rival candidates.

But the chief reason for the unsatisfactory working of the party system in our cities may be found in the fact that the party organizations in municipal politics do not usually stand on their own feet. To the average voter the issues of national politics seem to be fraught with far greater consequences than those of his own immediate community. National issues and traditions are influential in bringing individuals into the party ranks and in holding them there; local issues and traditions are not. No matter how much self-determination the city may have in moulding the frame of its own government there is no such thing as complete, or nearly complete, municipal home rule in party organization. Almost everywhere the municipal organization is looked upon as a mere subsidiary. The one notable exception is New York City where the local Democratic machine, which is popularly known as Tammany Hall, often dominates the party organization in the state.

Municipal parties, with no relation to any national or state issues, have appeared in the larger American cities from time to time, but they have rarely had a long existence. One reason for this is the absence of significant and permanent issues upon which to build a local party organization. There are, in fact, few divergences of popular opinion upon the broader questions of municipal policy. Everybody, for example, professes to agree that the city's affairs should be honestly and economically managed, that good appointments should be made, and so forth. But when it comes to determining the specific application of these principles there is no approach to unanimity. Even within the ranks of a single organization these differences of opinion appear and tend to destroy harmony. This has been the experience, over and over again, of citizens' unions, people's parties, taxpayers' leagues, non-partisan parties, or whatever their names may be. It all goes back to a fundamental fact, which is that although parties may owe their origin to issues they must depend for their subsequent momentum upon habit and tradition. And the trouble is that the problems of municipal government are so continually changing that no traditions can easily be formed. A civic program framed today is out of date the day after tomorrow. Municipal parties have other difficulties of a practical character. They are expensive to maintain and find trouble in making both ends meet, since it is much more difficult to raise funds for local than for national party organizations. This is not because contributors are oblivious to the immediate importance of city government; it is merely that local issues do not stir the patriotic fervor or arouse the enthusiasm of the average

Municipal parties.

citizen to the extent of making him put his hand deeply into his pocket.

Fusion. As a rule it is easier to put through a program of municipal reform by using one of the regular parties than by creating a separate political organization. This alliance between reform and straight partyism is called "fusion"; and several American cities (notably New York) have given it a repeated trial. But while fusion is the easiest road to success at the polls, it never produces an administration that is genuinely free from political partisanship. The regulars who provide most of the votes insist upon a preponderant share in the fruits of victory. And being well organized they commonly obtain what they demand. The new administration accordingly takes the political tint of its dominating personnel, and thereby disappoints the reformer whose support at the election was secured by professions of non-partisanship. This *mésalliance* between partyism and non-partisanship, concluded solely for practical purposes, has injected a lot of hypocrisy into American municipal politics. There has been a fusion of forces, but no fusion of ideals, for there can be none.

Outside interference in municipal party politics. Home rule in city politics is difficult to safeguard. Nevertheless the amount of interference by outside party organizations is steadily diminishing. Several things have lent their aid in this direction. The reduction in the number of elective officers is one of them. Short ballots place the political machine at a disadvantage. Small councils and elective commissions cannot be so easily manipulated as were the ponderous bodies of old. The practice of holding state and municipal elections on separate dates has also been of assistance in securing for the cities a chance to have their campaigns conducted upon local issues. Finally, the spread of civil service reform has reduced the temptation to intermeddling from above. So long as the spoils system was in full operation the state party organizations felt bound to control these lucrative fields of patronage. They needed every ounce of sustenance they could secure. The political machine does not altogether depend upon patronage for its existence; but patronage, from whatever source derived, is a most useful lubricant. Today the number of municipal offices and contracts at the disposal of the victors is much smaller than it used to be, and the interest of the state political leaders in city elections is correspondingly diminished; but the spoils are still considerable in many municipalities, quite enough to keep the interest of the higher-ups from vanishing altogether.

The American party system has acquired an astonishing measure of uniformity from coast to coast. The plan of party organization differs little from city to city; far less, indeed, than does the frame of municipal government. In Philadelphia, for example, the system of party organization is not widely different from that in Boston. The Republican party, as everyone knows, is dominant in the Quaker City. Its primal cell is the precinct, which is locally known as the district or division, there being about 1450 of these subdivisions in all. Each of these precincts has a general committee, made up of all the qualified Republican voters within the precinct, and every year they meet in caucus to choose an executive (or district) committee including a president, secretary and treasurer. This committee is responsible for the party's interests in its own little area, subject, however, to direction from the ward committee above.

There are forty-eight wards in Philadelphia, each containing from ten to eighty of these precinct divisions. Each has a ward committee made up of two delegates from every precinct, elected at a direct primary. The size of the ward committee depends, of course, on the number of precincts in the ward, hence the membership ranges from twenty to one hundred and sixty. Each ward committee chooses its own chairman who becomes ex officio the ward leader. Then comes the next step. Each ward committee appoints one delegate to the central campaign committee for the entire city, which is thus composed of forty-eight members, one of whom is chosen chairman. This central committee has final jurisdiction in all matters affecting the general interests of the party. The whole organization forms a perfect pyramid, therefore, for the central committee has jurisdiction over the ward committees and the latter have a like authority over the precinct organizations. Nevertheless the ultimate control of the whole hierarchy is vested in the Republican voters who can, by changing the precinct delegates at the primary, force a complete change in the ward and central organizations. In this way the fiction, if not the actuality, of popular control is preserved.

In Boston, where the Democrats are in the ascendancy, party

Uniformity and variety in municipal party organization:

1. Philadelphia.

2. Boston

organization also takes the ward as its unit. Once a year the enrolled Democrats in each of the twenty-two wards elect a ward committee which contains one member for every two hundred party votes. The ward committee elects its own chairman and is represented upon the city committee by one delegate, usually the chairman. There are no regular precinct committees, but when the ward chairman is efficient he arranges to place a trusted lieutenant in each of these subdivisions. The city committee, which is thus made up of twenty-two members, chooses its chairman and secretary, both of whom give their whole time to the party during the period of an election campaign and a good deal of it in the intervals between. So far as city politics are concerned, however, the solidarity and discipline of the organization have been greatly weakened by the charter amendments of 1909, which substituted nomination by petition for nomination by party primaries in the case of all elective city offices, took party designations off the ballots, greatly reduced the number of elective positions, lengthened the terms of mayor and councilmen, and laid many effective restrictions upon the distribution of municipal patronage.

3. Chicago. In Chicago there are fifty wards, and in each of them the party voters elect a ward committeeman for a four year term. This committeeman appoints a leader or lieutenant for each precinct. The fifty ward committeemen, together with some members from municipalities adjoining Chicago, make up the county committee; but the ward committeemen meet by themselves when matters affecting Chicago alone are under consideration. As a body they have charge of the party's interests both during and between election campaigns; but in Chicago as in many other large cities there are factional or personal machines within the party which assume control whenever they can. These machines have their own ward leader who may or may not be identical with the regular ward committeeman.

4. New York: Tammany Hall. By common consent the most efficient party machine in the country is the organization known as Tammany Hall.[1] It is the local organization of the Democratic party for New York County (which includes only the borough of Manhattan); but

[1] This is, of course, the name of the headquarters; but it is popularly used to personify the organization itself. A full account of the organization may be found in Gustavus Myers, *History of Tammany Hall* (2d edition, New York, 1917).

it exercises a far-reaching influence upon the party's organization in the city as a whole and even in the state. Originating in the eighteenth century as a benevolent and fraternal association, it was first known as the Society of St. Tammany. Soon, however, the organization became strongly partisan and anti-Federalist. Aaron Burr was its first prominent leader and managed to make it a tower of strength to the "Republican" party of his day. When the old Republican party went to pieces and the Jacksonian Democrats obtained their long lease of power, Tammany became a Democratic-Republican organization and it still bears this official title, although it has of course no affiliations with the Republican party of today. It has become so famous the world over as a nearly perfect piece of political mechanism that its organization and methods ought to have more than a passing mention. (a) Its origin.

The jurisdiction of Tammany extends over the twenty-three assembly districts which are included within New York County.[1] In each of these assembly districts the Democratic voters at the primaries choose delegates to a district general committee, the basis being one delegate for every twenty-five voters. The choice is made by election precincts, each precinct choosing its quota of committeemen. This district general committee is the chief party organization in the assembly district.[2] Its chairman, chosen by itself, is usually the directing figure in its operations. But in some districts two chairmen are chosen, one man and one woman. A few have no leaders but do their work through a committee of five or seven members. Where there is a single district chairman, he appoints in every election district or precinct a district captain who is the official agent of the party in the precinct and is responsible for the showing which it makes on election day. There are about 1000 of these captains. The (b) The district organization.

---

[1] These are the districts which elect assemblymen to the state legislature at Albany.

[2] The district general committee from outside its own membership also names an auxiliary committee to assist in its general activities, likewise several sub-committees from among its own members. Each district also has its clubs, usually bearing the name of some past or present district leader. These clubs maintain their headquarters the year round. From time to time they provide smokers, banquets, picnics, and so on for the members and their friends. At Christmas and on other occasions they also make gifts of clothing, food, shoes, or fuel to the poor of the district. But when an election campaign draws near, the activities of these clubs are wholly political.

captain assigns party workers in his precinct to their various tasks, as canvassers, watchers at the polls, challengers, or messengers. Each captain receives from the county committee's treasurer a sum of money to cover the expenses of this work, but is not paid for his own services. The captains form the general staff which carries out the instructions of the district central committee. They are an active body and much of Tammany's strength depends upon their work.[1]

(c) The district leader.

But the district chairman, who appoints these captains, is not the district leader, so-called. The latter, who is also chosen by the district general committee, is the district's representative on the executive of the county committee; in addition he makes the various recommendations for appointments to office, apportions whatever patronage may be allotted to his district, and exercises a considerable influence over the selection of the party's candidates. In the practical aspects of political activity the district leader is a much more important personage than the district chairman.

(d) The county committee and the executive committee.

For the whole county there is a county committee ostensibly made of all members of the district central committees sitting together. On paper this is a very ponderous body, numbering more than eleven thousand members, but as it never holds any regular meetings its size is no handicap. All its business is done by an executive committee made up of the district leaders, together with some ex officio members.[2] This executive committee is at once the regular Democratic machine of New York county and the political organ of Tammany Hall. When we speak of The Wigwam, it is this committee that we mean. The executive committee chooses its own chairman, but he is not the county leader or boss of Tammany Hall. The latter is informally elected by the high lights of the party, whether district leaders or not, and technically is only an ordinary member of the executive committee. He may not even be that. But he is by general acquiescence the dominating figure in that body and his advice, whether on matters of policy or methods, is regularly followed.

(e) The boss.

[1] All the precinct captains in each assembly district meet from time to time to discuss plans and to insure thorough coöperation as regards both aim and methods.
[2] This executive committee appoints the various standing committees which also act, within their special fields, on behalf of the dormant county committee.

Three features in this Tammany Hall organization stand out prominently. First is its ostensibly popular basis in that the voters have ultimate control. But this popular control exists in name only. Occasionally the voters overturn a district committee and oust a district chairman, but a revolt among the members of the party would have to be intense and widespread before it could compel a change at central headquarters. The directing personalities are several stages removed from direct popular responsibility. Second, the organization is cumbrous, complicated, and difficult for the ordinary voter to understand. That is what it is intended to be. The politician likes complexity; the more of it the better. People reverence the mysterious. Finally, the ramifications of the Tammany machine are extraordinarily extensive. There are in all about five thousand precincts. Figuring five workers per precinct (which is a very conservative estimate) this means at least twenty-five thousand henchmen on the lowest rung of the ladder. Committeemen, chairman, leaders, and strategists must total as many more. So here are fifty thousand active agents of the cause who form a mobile army of almost irresistible strength when pitted against almost any sort of opposition. And a great many of them are officeholders, hence their livelihood depends upon the loyalty with which they serve the organization. It is not surprising that Tammany so often wins. As an organization for winning at the polls there is nothing, the world over, that matches it in discipline.

<small>Three notable features.</small>

Many people seem to take it for granted that all the party's work is done by its regular organizations. But this is far from being the case. A candidate does not relish the implication that he is being supported by the "regulars" and by no one else. He wants it understood that his candidacy is drawing support from the independents, the business men, the labor unions, and great numbers of plain citizens who are not regularly affiliated with any party organizations. Hence, the leaders of his campaign bestir themselves to organize an All-Party Committee, or a Non-Partisan Committee, or a League of Independent Voters, not to speak of political clubs in every ward or district. These ancillary organizations are important factors during a close campaign. In general they are of two types. First there are the *ad hoc* groups which exist only on paper and are for publicity

<small>Ancillary associations, committees, and clubs.</small>

purposes alone. As a rule it is merely a matter of collecting a lot of signatures and publishing them as a proof that the committee, or league, or association with an alluring name has endorsed the candidate. The other type of ancillary organization is the political club, which is usually constituted on a neighborhood or racial basis. These clubs are real organizations, with members who come together, and often they continue in existence year after year for long periods of time. They are named after some political leader (past or present) or they have appellations which suit the fancy of the members. Thus the Hendricks Club, the Roscoe Conkling Club, the John J. Ahearn Club, the Franco-American Club, the Tipcart Club, and so forth. Each has its own hall, often with pool and card tables, and usually a couple of smaller rooms for political conferences. Members are supposed to pay monthly dues, but if they fail to do it nothing happens. The ward or district leader makes good the deficits.

But not all the political clubs are permanent. Many of them are fly-by-night affairs which come into being during the onset of a campaign and disappear on the morrow after the election. In such cases party organization provides a place of rendezvous, fits it up, and provides something to keep the habitués interested. There are "smoke talks" by various leaders, and to these affairs the members are supposed to bring their friends. There is a strong psychological reason for these organizations, because they make party allegiance concrete and personal. People who have nothing else to do in the autumn evenings appreciate a warm spot where free cigars are passed around and where any man can make acquaintances. The club member feels a sense of part-ownership in the cause. He meets the local leaders and soon gets to look upon them as friends. Young men are especially welcomed and it is by his first visit to such a club that many a man has been started on his way to the board of aldermen or the state legislature. If there is any one thing that the ward boss has mastered it is the psychology of politics, as his club-forming propensities disclose.

REFERENCES

There is no volume which deals with party organization in the cities of the United States as distinguished from party organization in the country as a whole. But there are several good books available in this latter field and all of them devote some attention to political parties in local government. M. Ostrogorski's *Democracy and the Organization of Political Parties* (new edition, 2 vols., New York, 1922), is a splendid work. The first volume deals with England, the second with the United States. Charles E. Merriam's *American Party System* (New York, 1922) contains a suggestive discussion of the subject from new angles. P. Orman Ray's *Political Parties and Practical Politics* (3d edition, New York, 1924) contains much excellent material and is well written. An exhaustive bibliography (the most useful of its sort) is appended. *Political Parties and Electoral Problems* by Robert C. Brooks (New York, 1923) is very useful for the large amount of concrete, illustrative material that it contains. A small volume on *Parties, Politics and People* by Raymond Moley (Cleveland, 1921) includes many sensible observations and comments. Mention may also be made of W. F. Johnson's booklet on *Toledo's Non-Partisan Movement* (Toledo, 1922). Frank R. Kent's *Great Game of Politics* (New York, 1923) is an extremely readable book with many shrewd comments.

Lord Bryce's *Modern Democracies* (2 vols., New York, 1921) contains some admirable chapters on the philosophy of the party system and the same is true of President Lowell's *Public Opinion and Popular Government* (New York, 1912). The same author's later book on *Public Opinion in War and Peace* (Cambridge, Mass., 1923) includes an analysis of collective opinion and its relation to parties. A. N. Holcombe's *Political Parties of Today* (New York, 1924) explains the factors which have entered into the making and re-making of American political parties, and mention should also be made of E. E. Robinson's *Evolution of American Political Parties* (New York, 1924).

Older books which deserve mention are Henry J. Ford's *Rise and Growth of American Politics* (New York, 1898), which is a brilliant piece of work; James A. Woodburn's *Political Parties and Party Problems* (New York, 1924), and last but by no means least, Alexis de Tocqueville's *Democracy in America*, of which several editions have been issued. A vigorous criticism of the party system, as a system, may be found in R. Michel's *Political Parties* (New York, 1915).

Every political party has its own set of rules and regulations, its platform, and other official publications. These explain the formal organization and set forth both principles and policies. But the actual facts of organization sometimes run far wide of the printed rules and they can only be gathered by a field study of the machine at work.

The History of Tammany Hall by Gustavus Myers (new edition, New York, 1917) is the best book on this subject. It should be supplemented by references to the other materials which are listed in P. Orman Ray's *Political Parties and Practical Politics* (see *above*), pp. 606-608. See also the references at the close of Chapter XI.

CHAPTER IX

THE METHODS OF NOMINATION IN CITIES

The two steps in an election.
There are ordinarily two steps in the election of a municipal officer—the nomination and the polling. The first step reduces the number of candidates to two or three; the second decides the winner from among these. People commonly look upon the final election as the more important of these two steps and are inclined to regard the nomination as a mere warming-up contest among the politicians. In this they are wrong. Taking the cities of the United States as a whole it can fairly be said that the primaries which decide the nominations are more potent for good or ill than are the elections which determine the final choice. It is at the primaries, not at the election, that the issue of good, bad, or indifferent municipal administration is determined in perhaps the majority of cases.

Why we have nominations.
Why is it necessary to have nominations at all? Would it not be better to give each voter a blank ballot and let him write thereon the name or names of his choice? In that way "the office would seek the man, not the man the office." There are several reasons why this simple method would not be possible. It would disfranchise thousands of voters who are unable to write legibly. It would leave the voters without guidance, and their votes would be scattered among so many candidates that no one of them would have anything like a majority. Or, as is more likely, the party organizations would take the matter in hand and in their own way would nominate candidates. That is what has happened in other countries whenever the laws have remained silent on the method of making nominations. Under a system of universal suffrage, with a highly elaborated mechanism of government, some preliminary sifting of candidates is absolutely necessary. If it is not established by the laws of the land it will be provided in some unofficial way.

This preliminary sifting of aspirants for elective office is especially essential in the cities of the United States because so

THE METHODS OF NOMINATION IN CITIES 171

many candidates come forward during the months which precede a municipal election. Nowhere else, the world over, is there such avowed willingness to serve the public—for a compensation. Whatever the deficiencies of American city government, a dearth of candidates for public office is not one of them. The reason for this seems to be fourfold. Most of our municipal offices have good salaries attached to them, which is a prime consideration with the genial fellow of wide acquaintance who has not been able to make any headway in private employment. Second, we are tolerant of the most brazen effrontery in candidates no matter how diminutive their personal qualifications may be. The multiplicity of candidates is also explained in part by the widespread feeling that rotation in office is a desirable thing; in other words, that no man ought to hold any office too long but should give others a chance. Finally, the big grist of candidates in American cities is an outgrowth of the advertising value which even a hopeless candidacy seems to carry with it. Every candidate gets himself talked about to some extent; his name goes into the newspapers; he becomes known to many who would otherwise never hear of him.

A system of nomination is peculiarly essential in the United States.

And there is always a chance that something unexpected may happen. A sudden shift in public sentiment, an issue or a slogan that happens to catch the public fancy, a wide-open split in the opposing ranks—any of these things may transform a seemingly hopeless candidate into a winner. It is a small chance, but there are those who do not hesitate to take it. At any rate it is a rare municipal office that goes unsought in America, even though it be one of very minor importance. That being the case some system whereby the field can be narrowed to a few is virtually indispensable except in those cities which have adopted the plan of proportional representation. In that case, as will be shown later, there is no need for any elimination of superfluous candidates prior to the election.[1]

In the United States during the past hundred and fifty years we have evolved several methods of nominating candidates for municipal office. At the outset the offices were few and no regular system of nomination provided by law. Until after the Revolution the methods were informal; the candidates were induced to come forward by their friends and neighbors, or in

The evolution of nominating methods in American cities:
1. The informal caucus.

[1] See *below*, pp. 195-198.

some cases by a "parlor caucus" in which the leading citizens participated, for manhood suffrage had not yet come into general vogue. There were no regular party organizations; the elective officers were unpaid; they had little power and less patronage, hence there was no deluge of candidates. The office had to seek the man.

2. The citywide convention.

But this golden age did not last forever. The cities grew in size; the number of elective offices increased; the practice of paying salaries came into existence and spread; the suffrage was widened, and party organizations began to develop. During the fifty years following the Revolution these things necessitated a formalizing of the nominating machinery. The old haphazard methods of bringing candidates into the field gave way to regular caucuses which all the voters of the respective political parties were entitled to attend. At first each political party held a single caucus for the whole city, but as the city grew larger this was not practicable. Thereupon came the next step, a caucus for each ward and a convention of delegates for the whole city, these delegates being chosen by the ward caucuses. Candidates for the city council were nominated by wards, while the party conventions put forward the candidates for mayor. This plan of regular caucuses and conventions spread to virtually all the larger cities of the country during the first half of the nineteenth century. In many of the smaller cities, however, the nominations continued to be made on a nonpartisan basis by a "citizens' caucus" to which all the voters were invited, no matter what their party allegiance.

Defects of this system.

These methods of nominating candidates for municipal office (namely, by ward caucuses and a party convention or by a citizens' caucus) continued to be used through the Civil War and for three decades thereafter. But they became steadily more unsatisfactory. One serious defect of the system lay in the fact that neither the caucuses nor the conventions were for the most part regulated by law. Each political party made its own rules concerning the manner of calling them, the times and places of meeting, and the conduct of business. This meant that the party leaders in each case virtually made the rules and controlled the procedure. Often they did this without the slightest sense of fair play but solely with an eye to their own advantage. When one faction in the party got the upper hand

THE METHODS OF NOMINATION IN CITIES 173

it would frequently call the caucuses on short notice and in out-of-the-way places which only the initiated could find. Very often they were called to meet in saloons, or in livery stables, or in other surroundings likely to discourage respectable voters from attending. A count made in New York City during the autumn of 1884 showed that two-thirds of all the caucuses were held in places where intoxicating liquors were sold.[1]

There were various reasons why the politicians liked to have the caucus held in a saloon. It helped to keep the high-brows away. It facilitated the arousing of the gang spirit and the use of strong-arm methods if necessary. It gave the leaders an environment in keeping with the methods which they were ready to employ. Finally it made certain that only a fraction of the voters could get in, for no saloon was large enough to hold them all. So word would be passed around instructing the "regulars" to come early and hold the fort. Thugs and floaters were requisitioned, when needed, from other parts of the city. Under such conditions it was easy for the boss to mount a chair, read the names of his nominees and delegates, and have them accepted with a shout.

Old-time caucus methods.

Not all caucuses were held in this fashion, of course. But whatever the environment the regulars usually had things their own way. The independent faction of the party rarely had a fighting chance. When an independent slate of nominees was put before the caucus it had to be voted upon, of course,—but there were various ways of falsifying the count. The tellers were henchmen of the regular action, named by the ward chairman or the boss. They did not hesitate to do their duty, which was to make the result of the balloting come out as the boss desired. Time and again it was apparent that a majority of those attending the caucus had been out-counted, but there was no remedy, for the laws provided none. The laws penalized fraud at the polls, but not at the caucus.

The conventions which nominated the candidates for mayor and for other city-wide offices were made up of delegates chosen in this way. If, by any chance, independent delegates managed to get themselves selected by the caucus they were subjected to all manner of pressure and sometimes to intimidation before the

The obstacles to independence.

---

[1] Theodore Roosevelt, "Machine Politics in New York City," in the *Century Magazine*, xxxiii, pp. 74-82 (November, 1886).

convention met. Large booty hinged on the control of the convention, and the machine leaders were bound not to let it pass from their hands, cost what it might. Failing all else, it was possible to nullify the selection of the independent delegates on some technicality, or to allege that their credentials were fraudulent, or to keep them out of the convention on some other pretext—for the regulars almost always controlled the committee on credentials and named the presiding officer. Looking back forty, or even thirty, years ago it is hard to believe that conditions could have been so bad as they were.[1]

Attempts to regulate the caucus and the convention by law. Obviously this situation could not be permanently tolerated. Public opinion became gradually more resentful and demanded that the laws should step in and compel either the abolition or the reform of caucuses and conventions. A beginning in the way of reform was made by enacting statutory rules which provided that due notice of caucuses should be published in the newspapers. It also enjoined that attendance should be restricted to registered voters of the ward, and that fraudulent voting or the falsifying of the count should be subject to the same penalties as at elections. This was a new departure, involving as it did a recognition of the political party as a factor in the process of electing public officials. It served to eliminate the worst of the old-time abuses. But no set of legal rules or penalties could compel the political machines to forego the advantage which they had in hand. They found various ways of "fixing" the caucuses and conventions while keeping within the law. One way was to announce the time and place of meeting as the laws provided, but to turn the clock a half hour ahead when the time approached. The leaders and their cohorts would be there and with exemplary speed would put their program through. Then, as the independents flocked in, they would be greeted with jeers. "Too late." "It's all over." "Look at the clock," and so on. Another method was to start a row about

[1] In 1896 one of the two major parties held a convention to nominate candidates for county offices in Cook county, which includes Chicago. Chicago, in fact, contains about four-fifths of this county's population. There were 723 delegates in the convention, of whom 265 were saloon-keepers, 130 were men who had served jail sentences for one offence or another, 18 were keepers of gambling houses or ex-prize fighters, 148 were political employees, and 71 had no occupation. What chance had an "independent" in that gathering? For further details see the article by R. M. Earley in the *American Review of Reviews*, XVI, pp. 322-324 (September, 1897).

THE METHODS OF NOMINATION IN CITIES 175

some point of parliamentary procedure. This squabble would then be prolonged for hours, with occasional fisticuffs, until many of the independents would get disgusted and go home. There were various ways of doing it.

In the end, therefore, public sentiment veered from a demand for the reform of the convention to a clamor for its abolition altogether. Reformers began to insist that the people be given a *direct* voice in determining the nominations, in place of the indirect and sometimes inaudible voice which the convention system afforded. During the closing decades of the nineteenth century this abolitionist sentiment grew steadily stronger until it forced the adoption of what has come to be known as the system of nomination by direct primaries. The new plan was first adopted by Wisconsin (1903) but within the next dozen years it spread over virtually the entire country.[1]

The demand for its abolition.

The direct primary differs from the old caucus and convention in two important respects.[2] In the first place it is not under the control of the political parties but is conducted by the public authorities. It is held by the regular election officials of the city in accordance with the same rules that govern the final election. There are exactly the same safeguards against fraud. Second, the primary is not a meeting in a hall or schoolroom. The voters of each political party do not come together at a stated time and place to nominate their respective candidates. They come individually, one by one, to the regular polling places and decide the nominations by marking their ballots there. The caucus and the convention were deliberative bodies. They could discuss, debate, and compromise before proceeding to a vote. But the primary is a straight yes or no, pro or con, affair.

3. The direct primary. What it is.

In order to be nominated for any elective municipal office you must first get your name printed on the ballot which is to be used at the primary. This is a simple matter; in most cases it merely involves filing a nomination paper signed by a small number of qualified voters. Then your name is printed on the primary ballot along with the names of all the other aspirants for the nomination. A primary ballot may thus contain hundreds of names.

[1] It is now used, in one form or another, by the cities of all but three or four states.
[2] In the cities of New England the primary is still commonly called a caucus, and the same is true in a few Western states.

176 THE GOVERNMENT OF AMERICAN CITIES

And how it functions.

On the date set for the primary the voters are called to the polls in their respective wards and precincts. The regular election officials are there in charge. Each voter gets a ballot, goes into one of the compartments, marks his ballot in the usual way and puts it in the box. When the hour for closing the poll arrives the ballots are counted and the results are announced. All this as at a regular election. But there are various differences between a primary and a final election as regards the form of the ballot, the scope of the voter's choice in marking it, and the number of winners who emerge at the end of the day. For bear in mind that the primary does not elect; it nominates.[1] It nominates at least two candidates for each office and sometimes more.

The three types of direct primary:

(a) The closed primary.

There are three types of direct primary—closed, open, and non-partisan. At a *closed* primary only those who are regularly enrolled as members of a political party may vote. The would-be voter at a closed primary must definitely declare his allegiance to one of the recognized political parties before he can receive a ballot.[2] A separate ballot is provided for each political party and the voter is given the ballot of the party to which he has declared his adhesion. The closed primary is the one used in most of the cities.

(b) The open primary.

A few cities, on the other hand, use the *open* primary—the cities of Wisconsin, for example. Under this system the voter makes no declaration of his party allegiance. On entering the polling place he receives the separate ballots of all the parties, which are fastened together at the top. Or, in some cases he is given a single ballot on which names of all the party candidates are printed in parallel columns, the columns divided by perforated lines. Then, in the privacy of the voting compartment, the voter detaches the ballot of his own party from the rest and marks it.

---

[1] To this statement, however, there are occasional exceptions. See *below*, p. 178.

[2] The methods of making this declaration are by no means alike in all the cities which maintain the closed primary. It may usually be done before the date set for the primary, or at the primary, as the voter prefers. Having once made a declaration the voter cannot usually change it except by going through certain formalities. The general intent is to make sure that voters who are really in sympathy with one political party shall not have a share in determining the nominations made by the other. The matter is discussed in Robert C. Brooks' *Political Parties and Electoral Problems* (New York, 1923), pp. 248-252.

THE METHODS OF NOMINATION IN CITIES 177

The closed and open primaries are alike based upon the principle that nominations ought to be made by, and in the name of, political parties. They differ only in that there is a test of party allegiance in one case and no test in the other. Both plans are open to serious objections of a practical sort, arising out of this difference. The palpable objection to the closed primary is its requirement that every voter shall have a party connection and shall declare it. Many voters do not want to be enrolled as members of any political party, while many others object to stating their party affiliations in public. The closed primary, they argue, virtually disenfranchises the independent voter. There is a widespread impression that when anyone votes the regular party ballot at the primary he is under a moral obligation to support the same party's candidates at the final election.[1] The result is that large numbers of voters stay away from the closed primaries altogether and leave the nominations to be decided by the strictly regular element in the party's ranks.

Merits and defects of each type.

The open primary is free from these objections but on the other hand it has the serious defect of making it possible for one party to influence the nominations of another. Let us suppose, for example, that there is no real contest for the Republican mayoralty nomination. The present mayor is seeking a second term and has no Republican opposition in the primary. But among the Democrats there is a spirited contest for the nomination of that party, with a probability that a strong man will be chosen to oppose the Republican candidate. Under the open primary system this affords the Republicans a fine opportunity. Their leaders can pass out the word to use the Democratic ballot and vote for the weaker of the two Democratic candidates. This practice is known as "raiding" the ticket of the other side, and both political parties indulge in it when a good opportunity comes. It is obviously an unfair proceeding because it often saddles the party with a nominee whom its own members would not have chosen. Virtually named by the Re-

---

[1] Color is lent to this impression by the wording of the declaration which the voter is required to make at the primary. In New York State this declaration is as follows: "I am in general sympathy with the principles of the party which I have designated by my mark hereunder . . . and it is my intention to support generally at the next general election, state or national, the nominees of such party for state and national offices."

publicans, he goes into the final contest as the Democratic standard-bearer, or vice versa.

(c) The nonpartisan primary.

Both the closed and the open primary, as has been said, are designed to make partisan nominations. But there are many who believe that party nominations and party designations should have no place in municipal elections.[1] In keeping with this idea, a large number of cities have adopted the *nonpartisan* type of primary as a method of nominating candidates for municipal office.[2] At a nonpartisan primary the voter has an unlimited range of choice among the names which appear on the primary ballot. These names are printed in alphabetical order, or in order determined by lot, and are not accompanied by party designations. The two candidates who receive the highest vote for any office receive the nomination and go into the final election a few weeks later. In a few cities (for example, in Chicago and Los Angeles), if any candidate receives a clear majority of all the votes cast at the nonpartisan primary he is declared elected and no final election is needed; but as a rule this type of primary is merely a qualifying heat (as it is called in the parlance of athletics) whereby the slower contestants are eliminated from the final race.

Its merits and shortcomings.

There were expectations that the nonpartisan primary would sound the knell of machine domination in municipal politics. Reformers predicted that it would put the bosses out of business. But these expectations have not been realized. In some places the nonpartisan primary has helped to erase national party lines, or at any rate to make them less distinct; but on the whole the party organizations seem to have remained as vigorous and active as ever. The major political parties cannot be ousted from municipal politics by the simple device of taking designations off the primary ballots and putting the names in alphabetical order. The voters want to know who's who in politics, and they have no difficulty in finding out. The newspapers tell them, and the information is placarded on the billboards. Or, failing this, the appeal to party loyalty can be made by the candi-

[1] They feel the same way about the election of judges in states which have no elective judiciary.

[2] For the most part these are cities which have established the commission plan or the city manager plan of government. But some large municipalities which maintain the mayor-and-council form of government have also adopted the nonpartisan primary—among them Pittsburgh, Philadelphia, Minneapolis, Boston, and Los Angeles.

THE METHODS OF NOMINATION IN CITIES 179

date in whisperings that are passed along the line among the voters. Outwardly all is nonpartisan, but in reality the leaders are diligently at work to secure the nomination of a straight party candidate. In some cases, on the other hand, a religious cleavage has replaced the old party division. Where the electorate is large and where the primary ballot contains a long array of names it is futile to expect that the voter will inform himself and make his choice independently, without guidance of any sort.[1]

The question naturally arises: has the direct primary, in any of its forms, proved to be a substantial improvement over the older methods of nomination by caucuses and conventions? Has it enabled the cities to put better men into office? These are hard questions to answer because the workings of the direct primary have differed considerably from city to city. They have even differed in the same city from one election to another. Something also depends on the point of view. A primary that results in the nomination of someone who coincides with the observer's preferences is usually put down as a success; otherwise it is branded as a failure. It is difficult to take an objective attitude in a matter where the temptation to personal bias is so strong. *Has the direct primary in any of the forms justified itself:*

In general, however, the direct primary has shown itself meritorious along several lines. It has brought out a larger number of independent candidates than usually came before the caucus or the convention. It has also brought out a larger vote for these candidates than was customarily cast for delegates under the old system. It has encouraged the non-regular element of the party to take a more active interest in the nominating process. Undoubtedly it has weakened the influence of the party leaders in the making of nominations, and this is important, for the only place a machine can be effectively beaten is at the nominating stage. So long as it can nominate its candidates *What it has accomplished.*

---

[1] The arguments for and against the use of the nonpartisan primary may be found in W. P. Capes, *The Modern City and its Problems* (New York, 1922), ch. v.; in W. T. Arndt, *The Emancipation of the American City* (New York, 1917), ch. vi; in William Anderson's *American Municipal Government* (New York, 1925), pp. 221-226; and in the article by Robert E. Cushman on "Non-Partisan Nominations and Elections" in the *Annals of the American Academy of Political and Social Science*, cvi, pp. 83-96 (March, 1923). This article is reprinted in Joseph Wright's *Selected Readings in Municipal Problems* (Boston, 1924), pp. 243-248.

it is an unbeaten machine even if it loses the subsequent election.

Undoubtedly, again, the direct primary has helped to raise the tone of local politics. It has taken the nominations out of the old roughneck environment and has at least made the proceedings orderly and respectable. Woman suffrage, of course, has contributed to the same result. It is said, and it is probably true, that although the primary has by no means eliminated bribery, corruption, and intimidation, there is far less of these things than in the old days. For this, no doubt, the new methods are not alone responsible. The general plane of electoral conduct has everywhere risen during the past twenty-five years, even in cities where the old convention system continues. The moral effect of the direct primary upon public officials has also been wholesome, for they realize that no longer is it enough to be regular and merely to satisfy the party leaders. They must gain a following among the rank and file of the voters in order to make victory certain. Yet when all is said, the fact remains that no great change has been brought about in the type of men nominated. The old convention, at its best, could do excellent work; but at its worst the nominations were unspeakably bad. The primary, on the whole, seems to have given us a better average; but the prediction that it would "draw a new and better class of men into the public service" has not been fulfilled.

Wherein it has failed:

On the other hand, the direct primary has some conspicuous defects and shortcomings. One of these (although it may sound strange to hear it set down as a defect) is the weakening of the party organizations. Many reformers would like to have us believe that anything which helps to break down party regularity is a godsend in politics. But if political parties of some type are essential to the proper functioning of all popular governments (as has been argued in a previous chapter), what is to be gained by weakening them? If parties are essential they ought to be strengthened, regulated, given an opportunity to do their work efficiently. In so far as the direct primary has weakened party discipline it has impaired party responsibility. It has made government less responsible to the people, not more responsible.

(a) Impairs party responsibility.

The direct primary is an expensive device—expensive both to the candidates and to the city treasury. To the city treasury

THE METHODS OF NOMINATION IN CITIES 181

it virtually doubles the expense of the election, making two pollings necessary instead of one. To the candidates it means a double campaign—one to get nominated and the other to get elected. Not only that but the contest for the nomination, under the direct primary system, usually develops into a rival publicity campaign. Since large numbers of voters have nothing else to guide them, they are bound to be influenced by what they see and read about a candidate's personality, his program, his views of the issues, and the prominent people who are supporting him.

(b) Has made elections more expensive.

That is as it should be, no doubt, but it means an outpouring of money by someone, for you cannot make all these things known to the voter without a liberal use of printer's ink. The candidate who is not already well known to the electorate must therefore advertise himself and get the newspapers to play him up; he must dicker with the motion-picture houses to flash him on the screen now and then; he must get hold of a radio-broadcasting station if he can and usurp the bedtime story hour for his campaign speeches; he must print and mail circulars by the thousand; and, by no means least, he must tour the city each night with a squadron of motor cars in his wake, addressing rallies or gatherings on the street corners or in halls for which he pays the rent. All this, and more, the candidate must do if he wants to put on a good campaign and make himself known to the masses of the people. Yet it is all a matter of plentiful spending. The direct primary obviously gives a decided advantage to the candidate who is already well known to the voters (either through his having held public office or for some other reason) as against the newcomer in politics.

All popular government, from its very nature, must be largely a matter of compromise. It entails a harmonizing of differences and the elimination of factional jealousies. To accomplish these ends it is essential, at times, that various elements be given representation among the party's candidates. In the old convention it was possible to get harmony in the ranks by a series of deals and dickers, but the direct primary has abolished all this. It virtually makes certain that the minority element of the party will have no representation at all. It does not produce a "well-balanced ticket." It affords no assurance that the candidates will be drawn from all over the city; on the contrary

(c) Prevents compromises.

they are likely to come from a few populous wards. Hence it is a disrupting and not a harmonizing agency.

(d) And fosters hypocrisy.

The direct primary has contributed to the vast amount of hypocrisy and insincerity which figures in our municipal politics. During the primary campaign the rival contestants for the same party nomination often go at each other in savage fashion. You will hear Box and his friends proclaim that Cox is utterly unfit for the position which he seeks. They will call him a weakling, a traitor, or a crook. But when Cox wins the nomination it is expected that Box and his friends will rally to his support and help him win the election. And in the majority of cases they will eat their words and do it. Surely this spectacle is one of the things which leads the ordinary voter to question whether there is any sincerity in municipal politics at all.

(e) The burden on the electorate.

Not least among the evils of the primary system is the burden which it places on the electorate. Most of the voters are not interested in the making of nominations, as is proved by the fact that the total vote at the primary is almost invariably far below that polled at the regular election. We are accustomed to speak of primary nominations as having made "by the people"; but they are, in fact, made by a small fraction of the people and mainly by those who are actively interested in politics—including all the city employees and their friends. The same thing was true, by the way, under the convention system. In some instances an attempt has been made to prevent minority nominations by imposing a requirement that successful candidates must receive at least a certain minimum percentage of the vote; but this merely necessitates, in many cases, the holding of a second primary. No matter what the requirements may be, the party leaders will not cease their efforts to control the nominations, and their persistence will often spell success in doing so. The average voter has other things than politics to engage his attention; he cannot give all his time and thought to the eternal vigilance of thwarting the politicians' schemes. Incessant appeals to come out and save the city from this or that impending calamity tend to make him callous, so that in time he acquires a feeling of electoral fatigue and stays at home.[1]

Summary.

In spite of its faults, however, the direct primary remains

[1] For a vigorous criticism of the direct primary the reader may be referred to Arnold B. Hall's *Popular Government* (New York, 1921).

popular in most American cities. It has lost very little ground. The party leaders do not like it and never have done so, but the rank and file of the voters appreciate the simple fact that it at least brings the nominations potentially under their control. Proposals to restore the old convention system have been greeted with no great popular enthusiasm anywhere. It is unlikely that the convention, in its traditional form, will ever be generally reëstablished; but it is quite within the bounds of possibility that informal conventions of party delegates will assume the function of recommending candidates to the people and that their recommendations will be accepted at the primary. They have already done so in many cities and in some of the states. It is also possible that the spread of the proportional representation system in cities will do away with the need for primaries.

A few cities have adopted the plan of nominating candidates by means of petitions or "nomination papers." The number of signatures is set at a figure sufficiently large to place a damper upon the undue multiplication of candidates. In Boston, for example, candidates for the office of mayor are required to file nomination petitions signed by at least 3,000 qualified voters; in the case of candidates for the city council the requirement is 300 signatures. The mayoral requirement, which has been in operation for seventeen years, has never given satisfaction and of late it has worked very badly. To obtain 3,000 signatures is a difficult undertaking for anyone who has no organized support; on the other hand, the requirement deters no one who has an organization behind him or who is able to hire canvassers at so much per signature. Such canvassers are regularly hired to go from house to house in quest of names. Many signatures are found to be those of persons who are not qualified voters and hence cannot be counted. Others are those of qualified voters who have already signed more petitions than the law allows. It is estimated that in order to be sure of 3,000 valid signatures, a candidate must file at least six thousand names. Everybody dislikes the system and it will undoubtedly be changed. The task of checking up these thousands of signatures is so great that the work cannot be carefully done in the time allowed.[1]

Nomination by petition.

[1] At the mayoralty election of 1925 fifteen candidates filed signatures,

Caucuses, conventions, primaries and petitions—all have been tried and found to have serious shortcomings in connection with the making of municipal nominations. The problem of getting the right men to stand for municipal office is still unsolved. Nor is it likely to be solved by amending or elaborating any of the processes mentioned. The more intricate a mechanism, the more likely it is to get out of order. A pre-primary convention, while it might obviate some existing difficulties, would add to the intricacies of the primary system. This being the case, it is not improbable that public opinion will veer gradually to the idea of abolishing the formalities of nomination altogether, allowing any candidate to have his name printed on the ballot at the request of a very small number of voters. There is no practical difficulty in doing this, provided a system of proportional representation is used.

REFERENCES

The latest and most comprehensive lists of material relating to the methods of making municipal nominations are those given in the concluding pages of Ralph Simpson Boots' *Direct Primary in New Jersey* (New York, 1917); in P. Orman Ray's *Introduction to Political Parties and Practical Politics* (3d edition, New York, 1924), pp. 541-551.

On the caucus and convention systems, discussions may be found in G. W. Lawton's *American Caucus System* (New York, 1885); G. D. Luetscher's *Early Political Machinery in the United States* (Philadelphia, 1903); F. W. Dallinger's *Nominations for Elective Office* (New York, 1897), and E. C. Meyer's *Nominating Systems* (Madison, 1902). Special mention should be made of chapters lx-lxii in the second volume of Bryce's *American Commonwealth,* and of the chapter on "The Convention System" in Henry J. Ford's *Rise and Growth of American Politics* (New York, 1898).

On the working of the direct primary the best source is R. S. Boots, *The Direct Primary in New Jersey* (New York, 1917). A full bibliography is appended. Mention should also be made of the long discussion entitled: "The Direct Primary,—Success or Failure?" in the *Transactions* of the Commonwealth Club of California, vol. xix, pp. 553-664 (San Francisco, 1924). A less extensive and older discussion, still of much value, is C. E. Merriam, *Primary Elections* (2nd edition, Chicago, 1909). There is also a good brief discussion in the same but in three cases the number of valid names was found insufficient. Of the remaining twelve, two withdrew after a sufficient number of signatures had been certified for them. This left ten candidates still in the field.

author's *American Party System* (New York, 1922), and in O. C. Hormell's booklet on *The Direct Primary* (Brunswick, Me., 1922). Attention may also be called to the chapters on nominating problems in P. O. Ray, *Political Parties and Practical Politics* (3rd edition, New York, 1924); J. A. Woodburn, *Political Parties and Party Problems in the United States* (3rd edition, New York, 1924); and A. B. Hall, *Popular Government* (New York, 1921). There is a volume of *Selected Articles on Direct Primaries* in the Debaters' Handbook Series (ed. C. E. Fanning, 4th edition, White Plains, N. Y., 1918).

The *Annals of the American Academy of Political and Social Science* devotes its issue of March, 1923 (Vol. cvi, No. 195) to a group of informing articles on the direct primary. Special mention should be made of the "Digest of Primary Election Laws" included in this same issue. See also the references at the close of Chapter XI.

CHAPTER X

MUNICIPAL ELECTIONS AND ELECTION PROCEDURE

Should national and local elections be held on the same day?

After the primary comes the election. In most American cities it was at one time the practice to hold the municipal election on the same day as the state and national elections, that is, on the Tuesday following the first Monday in November, but this was deemed to be an objectionable arrangement in that it inevitably brought national politics into the municipal election. So the practice of holding all elections on the same day has now been generally abandoned. Most municipal elections are held on a separate date fixed by the state laws or by the city charter. Sometimes, as in New York City and in Boston, they come on the usual November date, but in off years, that is, the years in which no national or state elections are held. In favor of holding local, state, and national elections on the same date there is the argument that this plan is cheaper and more convenient for everybody. It ensures a large vote and reduces the cost of manning the polls. But, on the other hand, it undoubtedly helps to prevent the separation of local from state and national politics. When all the elections are held at the same time the public interest is so largely absorbed by the candidates for national and state offices and by the wider issues which they represent, that the municipal candidates and problems get very little attention from the average voter. The activity of national and state party organizations in municipal politics is certain to be encouraged when identical election dates are used.[1] There is the further objection that joint elections mean long ballots, too long for busy voters to mark with proper discrimination. Inevitably they will devote most of their attention to the names at the top and will give little of it to the names at the bottom. Short ballots are essential to the proper functioning of representa-

[1] Brand Whitlock, "The Evil Influence of National Parties in Municipal Elections" in *Proceedings of the National Municipal League*, xiii, 193 ff. (1907).

tive government, yet they are impossible if national, state, and municipal officers are all chosen at the same election.

The date for the city election ought to be chosen with more care than is customarily bestowed upon this matter. It is not merely, as many people suppose, a question of picking a date which is apt to be convenient for the mass of the voters, and on which the weather is likely to be good. The elective officers of the municipality should be chosen several months before the city's new financial year begins. They should have time to be inaugurated and get the new budget in shape. Some city charters have overlooked this obvious desireratum. They elect in November, inaugurate the mayor in January, and expect him to have his budget ready by February first. It cannot be done except in a slipshod way. If the election must be held in November the city's fiscal year should not begin until May or June. *The proper date for the municipal election.*

Everywhere, throughout the countries of Continental Europe, elections are held on a Sunday or a legal holiday. There is much to be said for this practice in that it provides an election day when most voters are free. A proposal to hold municipal elections on Sunday would probably not be greeted with much favor in the United States, where Puritan traditions are still strong in spite of great ethnic changes; but the proposal to make election day a legal holiday, like Labor Day or Thanksgiving Day, would not meet with such widespread objection. On the other hand, there are those who think that we have too many legal holidays already and should not add another to the list. *Holding the election on a holiday.*

The arrangements for the election (apart from selecting the date) are usually made by the city clerk, but in some of the larger cities there are special election boards, the members of which are ordinarily appointed by the mayor with the provision that both political parties must be represented. The city clerk or the election board, as the case may be, is empowered to arrange for the printing and distribution of the ballots, for the renting of polling rooms, and for the appointment of the poll officers. These officials consist of an election judge or inspector, and one or more clerks. In selecting them the endeavor is made to give all the political parties fair representation. *Arranging for elections.*

In the selection of places for municipal polling a few points are worth remembering. Polling places should be located where *The polling place.*

they will best serve the convenience of voters; they should be at points easy to find without detailed directions; and wherever practicable, public buildings should be used for the purpose. A schoolroom makes an ideal polling place if it be available. In European cities, with Sunday elections, schools are always so used; but in America, where elections are so often held on a Tuesday, the schools are on that day in use for their regular purpose and it is not always practicable to give up a room for polling booths. When it becomes necessary to rent polling places it is advisable to secure locations which can be hired year after year, so that voters may not have to inquire where the polling places are. Buildings that are used for partisan purposes, or which have become associated in the popular mind with any partisan propaganda, are also to be avoided. Some cities have found it profitable to provide themselves with portable booths which can be set up in a public square or other convenient place for use on election day.

The ballot. Of greater importance than the time or the place of polling, however, is the form of ballot used. That it should be secret goes without saying. In the earlier stages of American political history there was oral voting; later the voters were required to write their own ballots. But the candidates and their organizations quickly adopted the practice of preparing printed "tickets" which they distributed among the voters, thus saving them the trouble of providing their own. As the number of elective officers increased, these tickets grew in size until the voter often found himself using a printed sheet with dozens of names on it. If he wished to diverge from this regular ticket or slate of candidates, prepared by his party organization, he erased one or more names and wrote in others, a procedure known as "scratching his ballot." This system remained in vogue throughout the United States until about forty years ago.

Objections to the old ballot. Now the "ticket" type of ballot was open to some grave objections. It became the custom of the party organization to provide ballot papers which, from their color or form, could be recognized even when folded, so that secrecy of voting was

(a) Encouraged straight voting. virtually destroyed. A heavy premium was put upon voting a straight party ticket, for it was a very simple thing to drop the ready-made ballot in the box without marking it; whereas the voter who wished to vary the regular slate could do so only by

erasing and writing in a way that often resulted in spoiling his ballot. The party leaders, moreover, resorted to trickery in printing these ballots. Democratic bosses, for example, would print the legend "Regular Republican Ticket" at the top of the ballot, and the first few names on the list would be those of Republican candidates, but lower down a few stalwart Democrats would have their names slipped in. The Republicans would retaliate in similar fashion. Many voters were duped in this way, by voting "tickets" which they had not scrutinized from top to bottom.

Corrupt practices of various sorts were also encouraged by this ticket system because an unlimited number of ballot papers were in circulation and some of them were bound to get into the box surreptitiously. As the tickets were printed on very thin paper, moreover, it was possible for a dishonest election official to let some voters slip two ballots into the box if they were folded to look like one. It was also possible, during the count, to take out some ballots and put in others. All sorts of manipulation is facilitated when unofficial ballots are used without a strict count kept on them. (b) Made electoral frauds easy.

To eliminate these various frauds, to relieve the party organizations of what had become a heavy expense to them, to ensure the secrecy of elections, and to encourage the practice of independent voting, the Australian ballot system was brought to the United States about forty years ago. Its introduction was strenuously opposed by practical politicians who called it a "penal colony reform," an "un-American importation," a plan of "kangaroo voting," and other hard names. But it spread rapidly and is now used almost everywhere. The outstanding feature of the Australian ballot is not its size, shape, or color, but the fact that it is *official*. Unlike the old ballot, it is printed at the public expense and is not furnished by the party organizations. The names of the candidates, of whatever political party, are placed upon it either in columns or grouped by offices in alphabetical order. Being printed by the election authorities in limited numbers these ballot are kept under careful watch in the polling room and are given out one at a time to the voters. Every ballot must be accounted for by the polling officials. When the election is over the total number must be returned to the city hall either marked, spoiled, or unused. With ballots of this The incoming of the Australian ballot.

type it is not possible to work the old forms of electoral trickery or fraud.

Ballot abuses. But the Australian ballot soon developed in America a form utterly unlike that of its ancestor in Australia. Because there were many officials to be elected, and because the various parties continued to put whole slates of candidates in nomination, it became customary to arrange in columns, according to their party affiliations, the names of all the candidates on the municipal ballot. Then came the habit of putting at the head of each column a party emblem, and below this symbol a circle in which, by making a single cross, a voter could record his vote for the score or more of candidates whose names were printed in the column underneath.[1] The original Australian ballot had none of these things. The party column, the emblem, and the circle are all features that have been engrafted upon it in America by the influence of party leaders who desired to set obstacles in the way of independent voting and to place a premium on voting the straight ticket.

The long ballot. As a result of this development, the ballot became secret but not simple. It grew long and cumbersome. The premium upon straight voting still remained. The party emblems carried a direct appeal to the partisanship of voters. The number of names upon the ballot in the larger cities rendered it impossible for the average voter to make intelligent selections, and the arrangement of the names in party columns was designed to give extra trouble, as well as impose on him the risk of spoiling his ballot, if he displayed any political independence. To vote a straight party ticket was made easy—a single cross accomplished this result; but it sometimes required the marking of fifty or more crosses to vote a split ticket. Despite the introduction of the Australian ballot, therefore, the party organizations continued to hold most of the advantages which they had acquired under the old system.

Removal of party emblems and columns. The next step in the direction of ballot reform came with the abolition of the party symbols and columns. Instead of being grouped in party-columns, the names of candidates were grouped

---

[1] Emblems of all sorts have been used. The Republicans have often used the vignette of an eagle; the Democrats a five-pointed star, the Socialists a hand with lighted torch, the Prohibitionists a fountain of water, the Farmer-Labor party a scythe and hammer. No political party is allowed to use the national flag or coat-of-arms as its emblem.

by offices, that is, according to the offices sought by them. All the candidates for mayor were placed together, all the candidates for sheriff together, and so on. Party designations were not abandoned but were now placed after each candidate's name. This was an improvement, but it assumed the voter's ability to read his ballot and hence could not well be used where illiterates were permitted to vote, as they were (and still are) in many states of the union.

Within the past twenty years the final step in ballot simplification has been taken in many cities—the removal not only of the emblems and columns but of party designations also.[1] The names go on the ballot grouped by offices, with nothing printed after them. So far as the ballot goes, there is no way in which a voter can tell whether a candidate is a Republican, Democrat, or Socialist. This step was heralded as a way of "putting the political machines out of business," and giving independent candidates a fair chance; but it has not really accomplished much in either direction. In the case of the important municipal offices the voter knows the party affiliations of the candidates. Taking designations off the ballot does not prevent his acquiring this knowledge from a dozen other sources. No party designations have been on the Boston municipal ballot for fifteen years —but does any Boston voter find himself unable to sift Democratic candidates from Republicans when he goes into the polling booth? If so, he must have kept his eyes and ears tightly closed during the weeks preceding the election! So long as party organizations exist and function, so long indeed as it is desirable that they exist and function, there is little to be gained by maintaining a pretence of nonpartisanship on the ballot.[2]

Removal of party designations.

The principal weakness of the ballot now used at elections in most American cities is not its form or arrangement but its length. The voter is called upon to do too much. He loses interest before he has finished what ought to be a one-minute task. He is confronted by too many names because too many positions are filled by election rather than by appointment. It is highly desirable, and even essential, that those city officials who have

The need for a shorter municipal ballot.

[1] Morton D. Hull, "The Non-Partisan Ballot in Municipal Elections," in the *National Municipal Review*, vi, 217-223 (1917).
[2] See the article by David Stoffer on "Parties in Non-Partisan Boston" in the *National Municipal Review*, xii, pp. 83-89 (1923).

ultimate authority to decide matters of general policy shall be directly chosen by the people, but administrative officers whose only function is to carry out the provisions of the law or the instructions of their superiors should not be chosen in this way. City comptrollers, auditors, treasurers, solicitors, superintendents of streets and the like should never be elected at the polls. Appointment is a far better and an equally democratic method of securing such administrative officials. The way to make the ballot short and intelligible is to remove from the category of elective offices those which can better be filled by executive appointment. A ballot is not an effective instrument of popular sovereignty unless it is simple enough for the average voter to mark quickly and intelligently. When it is so long, so complicated, and so unwieldy that voters are bewildered into voting a straight party ticket or fatigued into giving no attention to the candidates at the bottom of the list—then it is the party leaders and not the people who are really choosing the city officials.

How voters often spoil their ballots. Long ballots are easy to spoil, hence the proportion of spoiled ballots at an American city election sometimes amounts to three or four per cent of the total. The laws relating to the methods of marking the ballot are very strict and their provisions are sometimes mandatory. Election officials, in deciding whether a ballot is spoiled in whole or in part, are governed by these legal requirements, and so are the courts when the controversies come before them. The inspectors who count the ballots have no alternative but to throw out the ones which fail to comply with the election laws. If the laws provide, for example, that the voter shall place a cross *after* the name of the candidate it is not allowable to count a ballot where the cross has been marked before the name. But if the laws merely stipulate that the cross shall be placed *opposite* the name, it can be counted whether set before or after. In general the plain intent of the voter must be regarded if this intent is not expressed in a way which is clearly at variance with the law. Voters must not be disfranchised on technicalities,—but a specific legal requirement is not a technicality. The presumption is always in favor of counting a disputed ballot, and the burden of proof is upon the party agent who claims that it ought not to be counted.

The words "mark a cross" ought to be clear enough, yet the question what is or is not a cross has given rise to in-

MUNICIPAL ELECTIONS

numerable controversies at the polls and before the courts. The dictionaries define a cross as the intersection of two lines, but courts do not go by dictionaries and have usually held that any mark which the voter apparently intended to be a cross must be accepted as one. A line, a circle, a square, a triangle, or a check-mark will usually do. The ballot will not be counted if the mark, in lieu of a cross, is clearly intended to serve as an identifying device; for the ballot must conserve its secrecy; but what constitutes an attempt on the voter's part to mark his ballot so that it may be identified when it is being counted? The voter who signs his name or initials on his ballot renders it void, of course, but what of the voter who pencils a skull-and-cross-bones, or a fiery cross with the letters K. K. K., or a pair of crossed rifles to show that he is a former service man, or who marks a cross after the name of one candidate and writes "no good" after the name of another? What of the voter who marks his crosses in red ink after the name of each Socialist candidate and ends with the words "Workers of the World Unite!" Are such things mere eccentricities, and hence to be disregarded, or do they violate the rule that the ballot must not contain any mark which will serve to reveal the voter's identity? Many warm controversies have been waged on such matters.

How a ballot is cast. The procedure in the polling room is much the same at municipal elections all over the country. The voter, on entering the room, finds himself confronted by a railing with a gateway. Behind the railing are tables at which the polling officials, clerks, and checkers are seated. Around the wall are booths or small screened compartments, each of which has a wide shelf and a soft pencil tethered with a string. The voter, on being admitted to the enclosure (or sometimes before he is admitted), must give his full name and address. If this checks properly with a name and address on the voters' list he is given a ballot, unless he is challenged, in which case the ballot is withheld until the election inspector, or judge of the polls, or other principal officer decides the matter, which he usually does by asking the voter to take oath that he is the person whose name and address he has given. When he gets his ballot he goes into one of the booths, marks it, comes out again, and puts it in the ballot box. His name is then checked on the poll book as one who has voted and he must forthwith leave the polling room. If, in marking his ballot, he spoils it he can ask for and receive another. But he must not tear up his ballot or take it away with him. Every ballot, as has been said, must be accounted for at the close of the polls.

Voting machines. In some cities the plan of permitting the voter to record his choice by means of a voting machine has been tried with varying degrees of success. A voting machine looks something like an enlarged cash register. The keys bear the names of the various candidates; the voter steps behind a curtain and presses one key after another. The mechanism is so arranged that the voter cannot press two keys for the same office. The voting machine plan has some advantages in that it saves the trouble and expense of printing ballots; it eliminates spoiled ballots; and it prevents any tampering with the votes. It also ensures a speedy and an accurate account. On the other hand, the machines are expensive to install and maintain, particularly when several machines are needed for each polling place. Like all other complicated mechanisms, moreover, voting machines get out of order, and when they do this in the middle of an election it makes a bad mess of things. It may well be doubted that machines will ever entirely supplant printed ballots.

The preferential ballot. An inherent defect of the ordinary ballot is that it does not allow the voter to indicate more than a single choice for each vacancy. If there are five candidates for the office of mayor, let us say, the voter may mark his ballot for one of them only. He is not permitted to indicate his second choice, or his third choice, among the five. One result of this is that the successful candidate, whenever there are more than two, may be the choice of a small minority. To avoid this danger of minority control a system of "preferential voting" has been devised and is used in some cities.[1] On a preferential ballot the voter is asked to indicate in columns provided for the purpose not only his first but his second and third choices among the various candidates. The names of those candidates whom the voter does not want to support are left unmarked. In counting preferential ballots any candidate who obtains a clear majority of first choices is declared elected. But if no candidate obtains a majority of first choices, the second choices are added to the first choices and if the combined totals give any candidate a clear majority he

[1] It is sometimes known as the Bucklin system of voting.

is declared elected. In like manner the third choices are resorted to if necessary. The candidate elected by the preferential system is thus the choice of a majority in all cases, not the first choice necessarily or even the second, but one whom a majority of the voters have indicated willingness to support. The system enables the city to do away with primaries and other cumbersome methods of nomination. The chief practical objection to the preferential system is that many voters refrain from indicating anything more than their first choice, and in so far as they do this they merely revert to the orthodox system of voting, the only difference being that they use the figure 1 instead of the cross.

Preferential voting is sometimes confused with proportional representation, but the two are quite different. The former merely aims to prevent the election of a candidate who is inacceptable to a majority of the voters; the latter provides a plan whereby the majority is prevented from electing all the officials, when there are several to be chosen, and the minority is unable to obtain its due share of representation. Preferential voting can be used in the election of a mayor or any other single officer; but proportional representation can only be used when three or more persons are to be chosen to the same office at the same election, as, for example, three councillors are to be chosen from a ward.[1] The practice of asking a voter to indicate his preferences by a series of choices, rather than by a single choice, is the same in both cases; but the process of counting the votes is altogether different. Counting preferential ballots is a relatively simple task compared to the counting of ballots in accordance with the principles of proportional representation.

Proportional representation may be defined as a plan of choosing representatives in such way that all considerable groups of voters will be represented in proportion to their voting strength. Several such schemes have been devised and are used in various countries. These differ in their details but the fundamental principle is in all cases the same; namely, that representatives should be chosen by "quotas" of voters rather than by wards, or districts, or other geographical areas. Under any system of geographical representation there are bound to be groups of voters

Proportional representation.

---

[1] One sometimes hears people say, for example, that the mayor should be elected by proportional representation. But how can one official represent different political parties or other groups of voters "proportionally"?

whose numbers entitle them to one or more representatives, but who fail to elect any. There is no unity of political, social, or economic sentiment in a ward or in a district, much less in a city as a whole. Men and women who live in neighboring houses or apartments may have widely different views on public questions. Yet those who happen to be in a minority, even though they form a large minority, will probably get no representation at all so long as the ordinary process of electing officials is used. The majority will elect its entire slate. Representative government, if it means what the term implies, ought to represent not merely the majority but all elements in proportion to their numerical strength. If the Socialists form one-ninth of the voting population, they ought to have one councilman in a city council of nine members; the same is true of any element that holds definite views on public questions; for example, on municipal ownership or the single tax. The aim of proportional representation is to carry this doctrine into practice.

The "list" plan.

The type of proportional representation commonly used in European countries is called the "list" plan. It is based upon the assumption that the nominations will be made in slates or lists by the various party organizations and that most of the voters will vote the straight ticket of their respective political parties. In counting the ballots each party is entitled to a number of seats proportional to the total vote for all the candidates on its list, and in filling these seats the candidates are taken from each slate in the order of the number of votes received. No provision is made under the "list" system for transferring votes from one candidate or slate to another. By reason of its close affiliation with party nominations and party slates this plan does not appeal to the American reformer for use in municipal elections.

The "Hare" plan.

In a few American cities a different scheme of proportional representation, known as the "Hare" plan, has been given a trial in recent years. This system is not easy to explain in a few words but the usual procedure may be outlined as follows: First, the names of all candidates are printed on the ballot, not in lists or slates but individually in alphabetical order or in rotation.[1] The voter indicates his choices by marking the

[1] For an explanation of this system of rotating names on the ballot see *below*, 325, *footnote.*

MUNICIPAL ELECTIONS

figure 1 after the name of his first choice, the figure 2 after the name of his second choice, and so on. Then, when the polls are closed, the election officials compute "the quota"; in other words, the minimum number of votes needed to elect a candidate. This they do by dividing into the total number of valid votes cast the number of places to be filled, plus one, and taking the next largest whole number. For example, let us suppose that 10,000 votes have been cast and that there are seven candidates to be elected. Ten thousand divided by eight (seven plus one) is 1250 and any candidate who receives 1251 first-choice votes is declared elected. If such candidate, however, has more votes than enough to fill his quota, the surplus votes are distributed (in accordance with the indicated second choices) among candidates whose quotas have not been filled. If enough candidates are not elected by this process, the candidate with the smallest number of first choices is then dropped and his votes are distributed in the same way. This process of elimination and distribution goes on until enough candidates have filled their quotas or until the successive eliminations have left no more than enough to fill the vacant positions.[1]

This plan of proportional representation is not a model of simplicity, of course, but is not so difficult to understand as one might at first glance imagine, nor in its actual workings does it present any insuperable complications. The requirement that voters shall indicate their choices by using figures will inevitably lead to disputes as to whether a certain mark is intended to be a 3 or a 5, a 7 or a 9. When the number of candidates is not too large it is practicable to place parallel columns on the ballot headed "First Choice," "Second Choice," and so on. The voter can then indicate his preference by marking a cross at the appropriate place in each column as he does on a preferential ballot. The voter's difficulties, in any event, are small compared with those involved in counting the ballots and determin-

Is the plan too complicated?

---

[1] Proportional representation is now used at council elections in Cleveland, Cincinnati, Ashtabula, and in Boulder, Colorado. It is not provided for in the new city-manager charter of Kansas City. Provision for its use was made in the charters of Kalamazoo, Michigan, and Sacramento, California, but in each case the plan was found to be in conflict with the state constitution. On this question of unconstitutionality see William Anderson's pamphlet entitled *The Constitutionality of Proportional Representation*, issued as a supplement to the National Municipal Review, Vol. XII, pp. 745-762 (1923).

ing the result. There is a certain element of chance in this determination but mathematicians have figured that it is very small.

In the cities of Continental Europe, where the voters are regularly divided into six or seven political parties and where no one of these parties can ever muster a majority at the polls, some scheme of proportional representation is virtually indispensable. But in America, where the great bulk of the voters belong to one or the other of the two major political parties, the arguments for the plan are by no means so strong.[1] Its theoretical merits are obvious but their probable exemplification in practice is easy to exaggerate. At any rate we can form better judgment on the plan of proportional representation when it has been longer in operation.[2]

Corrupt practices at city elections.

Municipal elections afford more than the usual opportunity for corrupt practices, and various safeguards are everywhere provided against their occurrence. Such corrupt practices include personation, repeating, tampering with the ballots, and bribery. European cities have had very little trouble with the more specific forms of electoral corruption, such as padding the voters' lists, bribery, and illegal voting. Their chief difficulty has been connected with the milder forms of intimidation, including the use of sinister influence by public officials and private employers. American cities have developed a wider range of election frauds than can be found in any other country. There are various reasons for this. The bitterness of partisan campaigns in the large cities and the heavy stakes which are at issue have been an inspiration to crookedness. The floating character of the population in the crowded wards has facilitated personation and repeating. The appointment of polling officers at the behest of party bosses has often served to destroy the integrity of the ballot box. And it is only within the last twenty or thirty years that sufficiently stringent laws relating to corrupt practices have been provided in America. Illegal registration, personation, repeating, and tampering with the ballots are now

---

[1] For a discussion of the system in its practical workings see the articles reprinted in Joseph Wright's *Selected Readings in Municipal Problems* (Boston, 1924), pp. 249-268; also the pamphlet by C. C. Maxey on *Proportional Representation in Cleveland* (Cleveland, 1923).

[2] In Cincinnati, at the election of 1925, it took about two weeks to get the votes counted.

MUNICIPAL ELECTIONS 199

forbidden under heavy penalties in all American cities, but they have not yet been wholly eliminated.

Various other practices, not in themselves wrong, have been made illegal by statute because they are contrary to good public policy and tend to make an election undignified, or unfair, or unnecessarily expensive. Canvassing and the distribution of campaign literature is forbidden within a certain radius of the polling place. Campaign advertisements, according to the laws of some states, must bear the name and address of a qualified voter. Candidates are required to file with the proper authorities a statement of their campaign expenses and it is illegal to spend more than a prescribed sum even for purely legitimate purposes, such as the hiring of halls and the printing of posters. The purpose of these things is not only to render the election a dignified affair but to give every candidate, rich or poor, as nearly equal a chance as the laws can ensure. These regulations are sometimes evaded, it is true, but on the whole they are well respected both by party organizations and by candidates.

Illegal practices.

It frequently happens, in the nature of things, that some voters cannot conveniently be in their own cities on election day. Soldiers and sailors, commercial travelers, railway conductors, engineers and trainmen, fishermen, and students in universities are obvious examples. It has been estimated that in Massachusetts the number of voters who are necessarily absent from their homes on election day averages about fifty thousand. Many others, in order to cast their ballots, are put to considerable expense and inconvenience. Now it has seemed desirable to make some provision whereby those voters may cast their ballots without being actually at the polls on election day, and in some cities this has been done. The usual arrangement is that a voter who expects to be absent must apply, sometime before election date, to a designated official for a ballot. This ballot is then marked by the voter and sealed in an envelope. The envelope is attested before a notary public and deposited with the election officer, who sees that it is counted when the other ballots are counted. In some cases blank ballots may be sent by mail to absent voters who request it, and after being marked the ballots are returned by mail before election day.[1]

Absent voting.

[1] Pamphlets and mimeographed material relating to the laws which govern absent voting in the United States have been prepared by the officials of the Mail Ballot Movement (104 West Monroe St., Chicago, Ill.).

200 THE GOVERNMENT OF AMERICAN CITIES

Compulsory voting.

Compulsory voting does not exist anywhere in the United States at the present time, although it has frequently been proposed. Voting has been made compulsory, however, with legal penalties for failure to vote, in the cities of several foreign countries, notably in Belgium, in Spain, in Australia, and in New Zealand. The usual procedure is to impose a fine upon every voter who without good excuse stays away from the polls on election day, or for repeated excuses, to strike his name off the voters' list altogether. In Belgium this plan has been very successful; the number of registered voters who fail to vote is only about five per cent of the total, which is an astonishingly good showing. In American cities the unpolled vote usually ranges from twenty to thirty per cent of the total registration. The total registration, again, does not usually include more than seventy per cent of those who are eligible. Hence it is that not more than half the men and women eligible to the suffrage actually exercise it at city elections. The reasons for non-registration and non-voting are numerous—lack of interest in the city government, or in political parties, or in the candidates, forgetfulness, absorption in one's own work, lack of knowledge about how to get registered, illness, absence, fear of giving offence to somebody, and so forth.[1] It is questionable whether compulsory voting would operate in the United States as it has done in Belgium; but it might be worth while to make a trial of it.

The arguments for and against.

Compulsory voting rests upon the argument that the right to vote imposes a duty to vote. The citizen must serve on a jury in time of peace and in the army during war whether he likes these forms of public service or not. Why, then, should he be allowed to shirk his duty to vote, a duty which must be performed if democratic government is to survive? If one voter has the right to stay away from the polls, every other voter has the same right. And if all followed this policy a representative form of government could not be maintained. But there is another side to the question. The voter who goes to the polls under compulsion is not likely to mark his ballot with much discrimination, intelligence, or patriotism. Would the votes of such men and women be worth counting? It has been demonstrated by

---

[1] The best study of abstemtion from the polls, and the causes for it, may be found in C. E. Merriam and H. F. Gosnell's *Non-Voting; Its Causes and Methods of Control* (Chicago, 1924).

MUNICIPAL ELECTIONS

foreign experience that while you can drive an unwilling voter to the polls, you cannot compel him to mark his ballot properly. The chief result of compulsory voting in Swiss cities was to increase the number of blank ballots dropped into the box. It may well be argued that voting is a duty, but it is a duty which ought to be performed from motives of patriotism and not from dread of the penalties. Most citizens do not need compulsion and it is questionable whether forcing others to vote would serve any useful purpose.

In order that any system of popular voting may be permanently successful the ballot must be simple, intelligible, and secret. It must not be so long as to bewilder the voter of average intelligence, and it should afford him a reasonable chance to "split" his ballot without running a serious risk of spoiling it. A short ballot is a far more effective instrument of democracy than a long ballot. Another essential is that the polling place shall be adequately safeguarded against fraudulent practices of any sort and that the counting of votes shall be conducted with absolute honesty. A generation ago we used to hear a great deal about fraud and corruption at American elections, particularly at elections in the larger cities. These things are now less prevalent than they used to be. American elections, taking them as a whole, now compare favorably with those of any other country. Parties and candidates try hard to win; they seize every opportunity to gain political advantages over their opponents, and in so doing often travel very close to the line which separates right from wrong, but they usually manage to keep within the letter of the election laws. Transgressions may bring temporary success, but in the long run they do not pay and the politicians know it.

Summary.

REFERENCES

An excellent bibliography on Elections may be found in P. Orman Ray's *Introduction to Political Parties and Practical Politics* (3rd edition, New York, 1924), pp. 581-583. Bibliographies on related topics may be found in the same volume, pp. 583-591. R. C. Brooks, *Political Parties and Electoral Problems* (New York, 1923) contains two good chapters on this general theme.

Material relating to the ballots used in American cities is included in A. C. Ludington, *American Ballot Laws* (Albany, 1911), and in E. C.

Evans, *History of the Australian Ballot System in the United States* (Chicago, 1917).

The *Bulletins* of the Massachusetts Constitutional Convention (2 vols., Boston, 1918) contain several studies relating to election methods, namely *Absent Voting* (No. 23); *Compulsory Voting* (No. 24); *Preferential Voting* (No. 27), and *Proportional Representation* (No. 28). Each bulletin contains a select bibliography on the subject. The Library of Congress, Legislative Reference Division, issued in 1916 a sixteen-page pamphlet containing a summary of the statutes and constitutional provisions relating to *Absent Voting*, then in force. Josiah H. Benton's volume on *Voting in the Field* (Boston, 1915) deals with absent voting in war time.

Among standard publications on the subject of proportional representation the most useful are J. R. Commons, *Proportional Representation* (2nd edition, New York, 1907), J. F. Williams, *The Reform of Political Representation* (London, 1922), and J. H. Humphrey's *Proportional Representation* (London, 1911); and there is an interesting chapter in H. L. McBain and Lindsay Rogers, *The New Constitutions of Europe* (New York, 1922), pp. 83-116. Short articles describing the operations of proportional representation in various American cities may be found in the files of the *National Municipal Review*, 1916-1922, *passim*. Special mention should be made of the trenchant criticism of the system contained in Professor H. L. McBain's article on "Proportional Representation in American Cities," *Political Science Quarterly*, Vol. xxxvii, pp. 281-298 (June, 1922). The current progress of the movement is recorded in the *Proportional Representation Review*, issued quarterly at Haverford, Pennsylvania.

The best book on the short ballot is R. S. Childs, *Short Ballot Principles* (New York, 1911). A small volume on the short ballot is included in the Debaters' Handbook Series (compiled by E. D. Bullock, White Plains, N. Y., 1915). The *Bulletins* of the Illinois Constitutional Convention (Springfield, 1920) contain a brief study of the subject with special application to Illinois conditions, entitled *The Short Ballot* (No. 5). Mention should also be made of the pamphlet on *The Short Ballot* issued by the National Municipal League and of the *Outline of a Model Election System* published by the same organization.

The matter of corrupt practices at elections is discussed in P. O. Ray's *Political Parties and Practical Politics* (see above), pp. 202-232, with bibliographical references, pp. 570-572, and in Charles Seymour and Donald P. Frary, *How the World Votes* (see above), Vol. I, pp. 246-265.

CHAPTER XI

PRACTICAL POLITICS

The party organizations in the cities have a great deal of work to do. An efficient organization does not leave it all until the weeks which precede the election. It begins far in advance by getting new voters naturalized. The alien rarely takes the initiative in becoming a citizen. He does not know how to do it. He waits until some worker in the lower ranks of the ward organization (usually one of his own race) comes to him. The party worker then obtains the date of the alien's arrival in the United States, and figures out the period which must still elapse before the newcomer can be admitted to citizenship. In well-organized wards a canvass for non-citizens is made every year. The work is done by the younger henchmen who are starting to win their spurs. It is a job that calls for very little experience but for a great deal of patience and tact. A good many foreigners dislike to give the information. They are afraid that it may have something to do with taxes or military service. {Work of the party organizations: 1. Getting aliens naturalized.}

In due course, if he proves coöperative, the alien is taken to the clerk of the court and his "first papers" are procured for him.[1] This is a simple matter, but they give him no right to vote. He must wait until he has obtained his final papers, or letters of citizenship, and getting these is not so simple. To obtain them the alien must file a formal petition and submit to an examination on his knowledge of American government. This test is given by an agent of the bureau of naturalization. The applicant must also produce a certificate from the immigration authorities certifying the time and place of his arrival.[2] He must then appear in open court accompanied by two wit- {The procedure.}

---

[1] Officially these first papers are known as the *Declaration of Intention*. They may be obtained at any time after the alien's arrival in the United States, provided he is eighteen years of age or over. No witnesses are required.

[2] This is not necessary in the case of aliens who came prior to June 29, 1906.

nesses, both citizens of the United States, who are ready to swear that he has been five years in the country. And he must answer satisfactorily such questions as may be put to him by the presiding judge concerning his antecedents and loyalty.

One can readily appreciate that most immigrants need guidance through this elaborate process, and it has become the business of the ward organizations to furnish it. Agents of the party organization help him to make out his petition; they get him coached for the tests; they hunt up his witnesses, and they are at his side in court when the hearing takes place. Finally, if need be, they pay his naturalization fee for him. It is easy enough to see how all this interest and assistance can be utilized to place the new citizen under obligations to the party. Its emissaries have befriended him without charging him for it. All they ask is his vote on election day.

2. Getting voters registered.

The next job of the party organization is to get its full strength registered on the voters' lists. This also involves a certain amount of circularizing and canvassing. Left to themselves it is astonishing how many eligible voters in large cities would remain unenrolled. Apathy and ignorance are responsible in the case of many who live in the poorer sections of the city. They know that they must register but they don't know where to go or what to do. So the organization gets after them. It does not confine its work to advertisements in the newspapers or printed notices sent through the mails. The workers in the organization are given definite blocks of territory to cover and are instructed to register everybody who seems likely to vote the party ticket. They do it with a zeal which sometimes results in putting names on the lists which have no right to be there. One of the ways in which a young party worker can bring himself to the favorable attention of the ward leader is by getting a large number of voters registered. Registration is fundamental, for an unregistered voter is valueless to the party. To win an election you must first get your own people on the voters' list. Not infrequently a municipal election is won before the first ballot is cast. The organization clinches its victory at the registration offices.

Getting your own voters on the rolls is only half the job, although it is the more onerous half of it. Keeping the other side's names off the list is also a desideratum. Consequently it behooves an efficient organization to have its watchers at the registration centers where they can object to the enrollment of those whom the rival workers bring in. Objections may be urged on grounds of immature age, non-citizenship, or insufficient residence in the city or ward—the last is the most common objection. The registration officials decide whether an objection is valid or not, and they often do it in a partisan spirit. For this reason it is usual to require that both political parties be given representation on the board of registration. Unseemly brawls have sometimes occurred in the registration rooms when a close contest on election day is impending.

Next comes the work of nominating the party's candidates. In cities which use the direct primary or the system of nomination by petition, the party leaders and committees are supposed to stay neutral, to keep their hands off, and to let the "free and independent voters of the party" make their own choice. This, however, is a theory which rarely finds much exemplification in practice. Neutrality in any sphere of city politics is virtually unthinkable to members of a party organization, no matter what the laws may say. The organization, through its leaders and workers, can rarely be induced to keep out of primary fights. On the contrary, if it dares to do so, the organization frames a slate which is satisfactory to itself, puts the names on the primary ballot, and energetically tries to secure the nomination of its own candidates. It does these things quite openly in some cases, but good strategy more often dictates that the whole process be screened by professions of non-interference. For there is always a danger that some section of the party will raise a clamor against the "handpicking" of candidates and may cause a breach in the ranks which cannot be healed. A party organization always prefers harmony to discord, and it will go through the gestures of neutrality if harmony does not seem to be attainable in any other way. In such cases, however, the word will be quietly passed along the line that So-and-So is not "regular," or that Somebody Else is "not acceptable to the organization," and these whisperings prove quite as effective as any open show of opposition.

No slate of candidates is ever exactly what it seems to be. A veil of pretense is almost always hung up to obscure the realities. There is surprisingly little candor in a primary campaign.

3. Picking the candidates and getting them nominated.

The show of neutrality.

The smoke screen in party campaigns.

Candidates pose as sterling independents on the stump and then confer each evening with party bosses in a back room on some side-street. Party organizations sometimes make an open show of opposition, half-hearted of course, in the case of candidates whom they are trying through every possible subterranean channel to help. Bismarck once said that he never believed anything in politics until it was officially denied. When a ward leader issues an official statement that his machine is neutral the voters may well be on their guard. In the vocabulary of the boss there is no such word as neutrality.

Why the organization does not keep its hands off.
Yet the party organizations, leaders, and bosses can hardly be blamed for their disinclination to be neutral. The outcome of the primary is of deep and direct concern to them. Whoever is nominated, the organization will have to back him for election. It will have to sing his praises, raise money for his campaign expenses, induce hundreds of people to work for him as volunteers, and guarantee that he will make a good mayor or alderman or whatever he aspires to be. Is it surprising that the leaders should dislike the prospect of having to do all this for somebody who is not of their own ilk, not congenial to them, and does not think in their own terms? If necessity demands, they will make wry faces and do it, as Boss Platt did when he found no practical alternative to the acceptance of Theodore Roosevelt as the Republican candidate for governor of New York State; but it is not often that the leaders of the organization let themselves get into such a situation. They demand, and in most cases make good their insistence, that the candidate shall be somebody "whom the whole party can get behind" and who can be depended upon "to recognize his obligations" in case he is elected.

In a way they are perfectly right about this. Winning a municipal election is a matter of good organization, good candidates, and good issues. The party supplies the organization and selects the candidates; the candidates in turn provide the issues. That is the normal procedure, although it may be set askew by an insurrection in the party from time to time. Poor organization or poor issues may defeat good candidates, and the converse is also true. In order to have all three up to a winning standard, there must be team play. In the last analysis that is why the party organization is bound to have an influential voice in selecting the candidates, no matter what the theory of the nomination procedure may be.

After the primary comes the election campaign, usually extending over a period of four or five weeks. During this interval there is a great deal of intensive work to be done by the party organization. These campaign activities on the eve of an election are of a varied character but they may all be included under the following eight heads: (a) informing the voters concerning the party's candidates and program; (b) assailing the candidates and program of the other side; (c) arousing enthusiasm and making it appear that the party's candidates are going to win; (d) dickering for the support of leaders, groups, and individuals who are not already committed to the support of either party; (e) forming clubs and other secondary organizations to promote the party's interests during the campaign; (f) canvassing and getting pledge cards signed; (g) getting the full party vote polled on election day, and (h) raising the money to pay for all this.

4. Conducting the campaign.

Among these various activities the first two are usually conjoined. A headquarters is established somewhere downtown and from this center the flow of publicity is launched. It customarily begins with various "statements" or interviews by the candidates or by the party leaders. These the newspapers are expected to print as news, without expense to the organization. Regular advertising matter is also prepared and inserted, but not so much of it as a generation ago because political advertisements use up a lot of money. They must be displayed on the front page if possible, and must be large enough to attract attention, all of which is expensive when newspapers with big circulations are concerned. A single, relatively small, advertisement in a big city newspaper often costs two or three hundred dollars. To advertise in several papers, day after day, throughout the campaign, means a big bill. On the other hand, the newspapers are expected to print summaries of what is said at the numerous mass meetings or rallies, and all of them do it without cost to the candidates because their readers are supposed to be interested. Ostensibly these summaries are prepared by newspaper reporters who attend the meetings, but in most cases they are written by the publicity staff at the party headquarters. A well-organized and efficient publicity machine will furnish every newspaper with more stuff than it can possibly use. Sheets known as "flimsies"

Publicity work.

The newspapers.

containing the high spots in all the speeches are handed to the newspapers before the speeches are delivered. Each publicity staff thus keeps close watch on the rival camp to see that claims issuing therefrom are promptly denied. Charges must be met with counter charges. If it announced that the betting-odds favor one candidate someone must be sent out with money to swing them the other way if he can. Each new publicity move of the other side must be checkmated as quickly as possible. If it cannot be done through the newspapers it must be accomplished in some other way. On the morning of a recent municipal election, in a large Eastern city, one of the newspapers appeared with a flaming headline which announced that a certain candidate had already conceded his rival's victory. There was no time to contradict this statement through the newspapers, so a large number of motor trucks were hired and were rushed through the city streets bearing huge placards: "The headline in this morning's ——— is a lie."

Billboards. In municipal campaigns the billboards are used to a considerable extent, but this form of advertising has also become rather expensive. Billboard space in good locations is costly. Cardboard posters bearing the candidate's picture, with an appropriate slogan, cost less to prepare and can be placed around in shop windows where they catch a good many eyes. Circulars are sent through the mails to the voters in most municipal campaigns, and when skilfully prepared they form an effective method *Campaign "literature."* of appeal. This material is commonly known as campaign literature; but as "literature" it does not rank very high. The essential thing is that the appeal shall be brief and snappy. It should be sent to the voter in a sealed envelope and must avoid the appearance of mere advertising matter. The cost of printing, folding, addressing, and mailing these circulars is about six cents apiece, hence the sending of a single appeal to all the voters of a large city involves an expenditure of many thousand dollars.[1]

The movies and the radio. Two new devices for reaching the voters are coming into steadily growing use, namely, the motion picture and the radio. The motion picture houses afford an advertising medium of

[1] On the voters' list of the city of Boston at the present time there are about 240,000 names. A single appeal through the mails therefore costs about $14,500.

great possibilities, but the owners have thus far tried to keep clear of partisan alliances. Only to a slight extent have they been ready to include campaign propaganda among the preliminary features which precede the regular pictures. The radio, on the other hand, can be far more easily brought into use. Broadcasting stations are ready to put a candidate "on the air" whenever he is willing to pay the price. This price varies with the popularity of the station. At a recent Boston election the rates were from twelve to fifteen dollars per minute. This may not seem excessive, yet a candidate who used this method of appeal, ten minutes each evening, for the three weeks of the campaign, found that it cost him the tidy sum of $2500, or one-quarter of a whole year's salary.

The successful conduct of a campaign is not merely a matter of advertising. It requires not only that the voters be informed but that they be aroused to enthusiasm in the party's behalf. They must be impressed with the vital importance of the election and quickened in their loyalty to the cause. Most of the mass meetings, rallies, and parades in municipal campaigns are not designed to inform the voter but to stir up his emotions. This is particularly true of the street-corner rallies which have become so common in recent years. They doubtless have a considerable part in acquainting the people with the fact that an election campaign is on, but as for converting voters from one side to the other their value is not commensurate with the energy expended. The same is true of the automobile parades and torchlight processions, the red fire and the brass bands, the campaign buttons and the placards which adorn the backs of motor-cars during the days preceding the election. They are appeals not to human reason but to the human emotions. *Meetings and rallies.*

Some of the most effective work which the organization accomplishes during the campaign is not visible to the onlooker at all. It takes the form of bargainings and manœuvers for the support of various leaders or racial groups or other "interests" in the city. Here and there are key men who control varying groups of voters. Such men are well known to the party leaders, and a drive is always made for the ones who can be swung into line. They customarily have their price. In many cases it is merely a matter of which side will promise most in the way of recognition or patronage. Very often the amount of influ- *"Back-room bargains."*

ence which these group leaders can exercise is grossly overestimated, and they get more for their support than it is worth.

Truckling for the "labor vote" and other organized elements. This is especially true of men who claim to control "the labor vote" or certain sections of it. There are such men in every large community. They bargain for patronage on the basis of votes which they assume that they can influence. But as a matter of fact the labor vote, so-called, is not deliverable by any man or set of men. Those who promise even modestly in this connection are rarely able to deliver. Threats to throw the labor vote against this or that party organization are mostly meaningless. It is easier to consolidate the business men than the workers when it comes to a showdown. Yet politicians, although they know all this, stand in awe of the labor bogie. It is possibly because those who claim to control the labor vote are so aggressive and so voluble.

Canvassing. Canvassing the voters individually is perhaps the most effective of all campaign methods, but it consumes more energy than the party organization can spare, except in the smaller cities. To some extent volunteer canvassers are available, but for the most part the men and women who do this work have to be paid for it. Even with a large corps of canvassers it is difficult to cover a whole city in a few weeks. The canvassers must not only be persevering but tactful; otherwise they may do more harm than good. Pledge cards are often given to them and these the voters are asked to sign. Every seasoned campaigner recognizes the great value of canvassing, for it affords a reliable guide to the general drift of public sentiment. It enables the leaders to ascertain where the weak spots are and where there is most need for additional work. The one deterrent to canvassing on a city-wide scale is the large expense involved.

Other campaign activities. There are divers other activities of a minor sort which engage the attention of headquarters. Campaign buttons are sometimes distributed to all who will wear them. "Straw votes" are manipulated and announced as indicating a landslide. An attempt is sometimes made to control the "atmosphere" so that it will carry an aroma of victory. Many voters are fickle in their political allegiance. They want to be with the winners. It is desirable, therefore, to create a premonition of victory if it can be done. And it can be done. No matter how absurd the pre-election claims of a candidate there are some who will believe them. The newspaper which keeps reiterating that victory is certain, by a large margin, will convince many unsophisticated readers. There are some people who imagine that a candidate cannot lose if the betting-odds are reported as being heavily in his favor.

No two municipal campaigns are ever conducted in exactly the same way. The emphasis given to one feature or to another depends upon the character of the electorate, the drift of public feeling at the moment, the personality of the chief candidate, and the amount of money available. To conduct a hoopla or hoorah campaign takes a lot of money and assumes that the candidates are of the hard-hitting, he-man type. If funds are low, and if the candidates are of the mollycoddle variety, it is better to use the gumshoe or whispering methods which every practiced politician knows how to employ. In some cities an attempt is invariably made to arouse racial and religious animosity by setting afloat every sort of absurd rumor or insinuation. The length to which this sort of thing is carried in some of the larger municipalities would be incredible were it not so plainly a matter of record. It goes far beyond the bounds of common decency.

Variety in municipal campaigns.

The campaign having been brought to a close, the culminating task of the committees and leaders is to see that the full strength of their supporters is brought to the polls on election day. This is primarily the work of the precinct or ward committees, but it is conducted by them under central supervision. The routine, when well handled, is about as follows: For each precinct a printed list of voters is obtained from the registration officials, and on this list the ward or precinct chairman checks the names of those whose votes can probably be depended upon. Two or more checkers are named to be at the precinct throughout the hours of polling, usually taking turns at their work. The checker's work is to keep tally of all those who vote and to make prompt report of how things are going. This he does at intervals to the ward or city headquarters as the case may be. He may do it by telephone, but more often the ward leader or one of his lieutenants drives around from precinct to precinct obtaining a report from each checker.

5. *Getting out the vote on election day.*

To every precinct, moreover, one or more automobiles are assigned, each appropriately placarded. In the early hours of the day these are used to convey such voters as are known to be

The division of labor.

212 THE GOVERNMENT OF AMERICAN CITIES

aged or infirm; later the cars are sent after the merely forgetful. Towards mid-day it will appear that in some precincts the voters are turning out well, while in other precincts a very small vote is being polled. The ward leader, accordingly, shifts some workers and automobiles from the former to the latter; if his entire ward is running below its normal vote he may call upon the city headquarters for more helpers and these will be provided from some other ward where the need is less urgent. One of the marks of good precinct or ward leadership is the polling of a full vote for the party candidates. When a leader fails at this point it is time to replace him.

3. Financing the campaign. It must not be supposed, however, that the foregoing routine is regularly adhered to at all municipal elections, or that it works with machine-like precision from top to bottom, from headquarters to ward and from ward to precinct. In some wards the organization is always more efficient than in others; in some the problem of getting out the vote is much less difficult than in others. The result is that some precincts may be left without any checkers or conveyances at all. A good deal depends upon the degree of public interest that has been worked up and the amount of money available. Many workers volunteer their services and to some extent automobiles are loaned by friends of the candidates; but the job of getting out the vote is greatly facilitated when money is available to pay for additional helpers and conveyances. Each ward leader, accordingly, receives from the city headquarters a certain allowance for this purpose. The amount depends upon the size of the ward, the influence of the ward leader at headquarters, and the relative opulence of the campaign treasury. The money is distributed a day or two before the election and the distribution is invariably accompanied by a good deal of grumbling, for the amount is never quite up to expectations.

How the money is raised. How is this money obtained? In a large city the amount needed is considerable, running far into the thousands and even into the hundreds of thousands. A mayoralty campaign in New York City costs Tammany at least a million dollars under favorable conditions. In Chicago there are about two thousand precincts, so that even with an allowance of only one hundred dollars per precinct the total outlay would be about two hundred thousand dollars. An aggressive campaign would cost several

PRACTICAL POLITICS

times that sum. The financing of a municipal campaign becomes, therefore, one of the chief concerns of the candidate, his committees, and his party organization. It must be well planned in advance.

So each party organization has a treasurer and usually a finance committee. At an early stage in the campaign this finance committee, whose members are chosen for their assumed proficiency in money-raising, send out a circular to all who are regarded as potential contributors. The list of those who have given something in previous campaigns is used as a basis, but new names are added as suggested by members of the committee or by the candidates. These circulars bring in a variable amount, depending upon the degree of interest in the election and the popularity of the ticket. But the response to mere circulars is never sufficient to fill the chest, and follow-up letters have then to be sent out. These letters are more direct and more personal than the circulars; they are customarily signed by some member of the committee who is personally known to the prospective contributor. This appeal usually adds a good deal more to the fund, but still not enough. So, finally, the method of personal solicitation is brought into play. Members of the finance committee, or the treasurer, or one of the candidates, or somebody else connected with the organization will telephone to those whose contributions have not yet arrived, or will even go to see them in person. In a close campaign the money-raising effort takes on all the characteristics of an organized drive with no let-up in it until election day comes. *The finance committee.*

Contributions, large and small, come from a variety of sources. The candidates themselves or their close friends are supposed to head the list with substantial donations, provided they can afford to do so. In the process of picking and grooming its candidates the machine never disregards their relative opulence. The party leaders, before they warm up to any man's candidacy, always want to know how he rates financially. Can he finance his own campaign, in whole or in part? Has he well-to-do friends who will see him through? Or must the organization assume the laborious task of raising funds for him? There are questions which come to the front of the politician's mind when the names of various aspirants are suggested in the first instance. The man with a long purse has a decided advantage *Who provides the money?*

over all others not so fortunately placed. This is not because the politicians prefer a rich candidate *per se* but simply because it is great relief, in any hard campaign, to have the whole problem of financing off their minds. It leaves them more time for campaign work.

The variety of sources. But neither the candidate nor his personal friends can ordinarily provide the entire amount needed. Other sources must be tapped. Office-holders who have been elected or appointed by the influence of the organization are often assessed a proportion of their salaries. The civil service laws commonly forbid this, but such laws are circumvented by merely calling for a "voluntary" contribution which officials know to be in fact a demand. To the spoilsman in office an invitation from the party leader is an invitation from royalty, not to be declined. Contributions are also solicited and come regularly from contractors and others who have dealings with the city or expect to have. Public utility companies were fair game in the old days; they were virtually blackjacked into giving large sums for self-protection, sometimes to both parties or candidates in order that they might be safe whoever won. The laws now forbid such contributions in most American cities, but here again evasion is not difficult. Some official of the company or someone unofficially connected with it makes the contribution in his own name. The amount is charged on the company books as advertising, legal expenses, promotion of business, charity, or anything that looks unsuspicious. Finally, the list of campaign contributors will include many men and women who give in varying amounts from varied motives. Some are inspired by the desire to promote what they believe to be the well-being of the community. Others are actuated in whole or in part by considerations of self-interest which may not be apparent on the surface. Men and women act from curiously mixed motives, especially in politics. Many contributions are actuated by obligations or aspirations known only to the contributors.

Restrictions on campaign contributions. The laws have endeavored in recent years to place a curb upon excessive campaign expenditures in two ways: first, by requiring that lists of contributors be published, and, second, by fixing the maximum amount which a candidate (or in some cases his organization) may spend. These laws have not proved very effective, partly because they are indifferently enforced, and partly because they do not reach those roundabout methods of raising and spending money which all political wiseacres know how to use. No legal restrictions, for example, can prevent a candidate's friends from spending money directly out of their own pockets on his behalf. The amounts expended in this way may be far in excess of what is disbursed through the regular channels.

When the election is over, there remains the final function of the party organization. This is the duty of "advising" the successful candidates after they are installed in office. The leaders expect to be consulted in all matters of official policy, such as appointments and the distribution of patronage. To some extent the candidates may be pledged in advance; it is rarely indeed that any mayor or councilman goes into office without some pledges, expressed or implied. In any event the party leaders and committees expect "recognition," which means that they want to be consulted in all matters directly connected with the party's welfare. The way in which this recognition shall be given is sometimes determined before the election by an informal understanding between the candidate and his leading supporters. Anyhow, the man who owes his election to the party and who expects further advancement from it, must strive to keep the organization in a satisfied frame of mind. He may follow his own judgment as to how this can best be done, but he will usually find his path smoother if he defers to the advice of the organization on all important questions of appointments and patronage.

7. Dividing the spoils.

Much has been written about the boss in politics, the man of mystery who manipulates the campaign from behind the scenes. But he is not a man of mystery. "The boss in politics," as Theodore Roosevelt once said, "is just like any other kind of boss." His business is to get a job done and he uses whatever means are most readily at hand. There have been bosses in rural districts, plenty of them, but on the whole it is in the cities, especially in the larger cities, that bossism has flourished. The terms leader and boss, organization and machine, are often used synonymously but not properly so. The party leader occupies a position which is established and recognized by rule or custom, and sometimes by the laws of the land. He is chosen in a prescribed way and has certain well-defined responsibilities. But the boss creates his own position, determining its powers and

Some unofficial aspects of the party system.

The boss and the machine.

its obligations alike. He is a ruler by the divine right of the strongest. The party organization, again, is an official affair, open and above-board in its make-up, if not always so in its methods. In theory, and sometimes in fact as well, it is responsible to the party voters. But the machine is a purely personal affair, made up of a boss and his satraps. Its aim is to absorb power and patronage for the benefit of the few. We should keep these distinctions in mind, but often do not. Men rail against party organizations and party leadership, when it is machines and bossism that have drawn their animosity. Party organizations and party leaders are essential: we cannot get along without them. But machines and bosses are the excresences of the party system which actually divert it from the fulfillment of its proper functions.

Why machines and bosses exist. Why do we have machines and bosses in American municipalities but not in the cities of Europe? That is not an easy question to answer. The chief reason, as commonly stated, is that "we have so many foreign-born voters in America." But this explanation does not explain why Boston, with a very large foreign-born population should remain undominated by bossism while Philadelphia and Cleveland, with relatively smaller proportions of alien-born, are regularly subjected to boss domination. Nor does it seem that density of population, rapidity of growth, illiteracy, or the avarice of public service corporations have had much to do with it. All these things exist in European cities but have not produced boss rule. They exist in the larger cities of Canada, just to the north of us, yet bosses have not developed there. The prevalence of bossism in so many American cities appears to be due to the complexity of the party mechanism, the multiplicity of elective offices, the blanket ballot, and the absence of the right political traditions. Too much machinery in the form of caucuses, conventions, primaries, petitions, and committees is one reason. Too much machinery in the form of mayors, councils, boards, commissions and departments is another. Too much patronage in the form of contracts, appointments, jobs and perquisites is a third. The boss is with us because we have made things easy for him.

Evolution of the boss. How does a boss become a boss? He does it by a natural process. Here is a young man who becomes interested in politics, sometimes before he has reached voting age. He begins by volunteering as a precinct worker. His first assignment is to gather a list of aliens who are eligible for naturalization, or to round up unregistered voters, or to act as an outside checker at the polls on election day. He proves himself a hustler and does his first job well, whereupon he attracts the notice of the precinct captain, or ward boss or district leader—any one of the higher ups. They are always on the lookout for young hopefuls. In one way or another the young worker broadens the range of his acquaintance and perhaps becomes the leader of a small group or gang. This makes him doubly worth recognition. When the time comes he is given more important work to do, such as supervising the work of getting voters registered or acting as the district leader's right hand man. At this point, in most cases, the embryo boss connects with the public payroll. He gives so much of his time to politics that he can hold no ordinary job. So the ward leader gets him a place as a time-keeper in the public works department or as deputy clerk at the county court house— any position that pays a salary without requiring special competence or fidelity. But it must be a position which allows enough free time for political work.

The oncomer is now ready to climb another rung in the ladder. His bread and butter are assured—for the moment. He attaches himself solidly to some leader whose fortunes seem to be on the rise, and as the latter goes up, he goes with him. He becomes a precinct executive and in time gets control of the ward if things come the right way. From this point forward it is a matter of natural selection, the survival of the fittest. If he is more courageous, more resourceful, more industrious, more adroit, and more fortunate than the other ward bosses in the city, he gradually rises to primacy and gets the whole municipality under his sway. In most cases it is a long climb and a weakling never survives it.

If you study the bosses who have reigned in American cities during the past fifty years—Tweed, Kelly, Croker, Murphy and Olvany in New York City; Roger Sullivan, Lundin, Powers, Kenna and Coughlin in Chicago; "Fingy" Connors in Buffalo; McNichol, McManes, the Vare brothers and Durham in Philadelphia; Stone and Rasin in Baltimore; Cox and Hynicka in Cincinnati; Maurice Maschke in Cleveland; "Abe" Ruef in San Francisco; "Doc" Ames in Minneapolis; Butler in St. Louis; Kent

Some notable city bosses.

Parrot in Los Angeles; Flinn and Magee in Pittsburgh; together with other bosses of the second magnitude, you will find that they do not conform to a type. The list includes both native-born and foreign-born, well-educated and semi-illiterate, stern and amiable, fighters and compromisers, silent and garrulous, honest and crooked,—men of every conceivable sort. There is not a single quality that every one of them possesses in common. Nor is there a common method pursued by those who succeed in the realm of bossdom. Every boss devises his own methods. Some rise and rule by brute force, others by diplomacy and shrewd compromising. Among the henchmen of every boss, a legend grows up like the Napoleonic legend, and all sorts of qualities are pinned on the demigod. The public imagination accepts it all as gospel.

Rings. Groups of bosses, or of bosses and their satellites, are known as rings, hence the Tweed ring, the Gas ring, the Courthouse ring, and divers others. A boss prefers to rule alone, for the inclination of all power is toward despotism. Montesquieu was right when he said that every man who gets power is under temptation to abuse it. Then others become jealous of him. In a big city the boss finds his authority so expansive that he must sometimes take others into partnership. Then decisions are reached by conference and all goes well until the partners fall out, as they frequently do, for it is hard to agree upon an equitable division of the spoils.

The cure for bossism. Much has been written about the cure for bossism in American cities, but very little of it has gone to the root of the problem. The trouble goes deeper than personalities. It goes deeper than methods of nomination or vote-counting. Fifteen years ago it was predicted by reformers that "the direct primary will put an end to bossism," but it has not done so. Today there are enthusiasts who tell us that proportional representation will do it. One can safely predict that it will not. Neither will the initiative and referendum, nor woman suffrage, nor the city manager plan. The cure for bossism must strike at the primary source of the boss's power, which is the patronage that he controls. So long as the boss can get good jobs for his friends, he will have friends aplenty, and so long as he has large numbers of friends he will have power at the polls. The first step in eliminating the spoilsman is to get rid of the spoils. Civil service reform has accomplished something in this direction, but the system needs to be expanded and greatly improved. Patronage in the form of contracts or in the purchase of supplies must be put on a non-political, competitive basis—a thing that is extremely difficult to do. Elective offices should be reduced in number, made more conspicuous, and endowed with a clearer responsibility to the people. Leadership should be encouraged at every point, for leadership there must be, and if we do not provide it through official channels the boss will see that it is provided at his own behest. Unhappily we have frowned on leadership. Lest the mayor should be a real leader we have hedged him with all sorts of restrictions. Then the boss steps in to fill the gap. In drafting city charters there has been a holy horror of "concentrating too much power in the hands of any one man." But the boss and his friends have no qualms of conscience along that line. If power is left lying around loose they seize it. It should not be left for them to take. That, in the last analysis, would seem to be the cure for most perversions of the party system.

REFERENCES

In addition to the books mentioned at the close of Chapter VIII there are many others which deal with party methods, party finance, bosses, machines, rings, and political corruption. An excellent list may be found in P. Orman Ray's *Political Parties and Practical Politics* (3rd edition, New York, 1924), pp. 564-568, 570, 592-594, 605-612.

Special mention should be made of Frank R. Kent's *Great Game of Politics* (New York, 1922), Brand Whitlock's *Forty Years of It* (New York, 1925); Samuel P. Orth's *The Boss and the Machine* (New Haven, 1918); W. L. Riorden's *Plunkitt of Tammany Hall* (New York, 1905); R. C. Brooks' *Corruption in American Politics and Life* (New York, 1910), and the same author's *Political Parties and Electoral Problems* (New York, 1923), especially Chapters ix, xii; Theodore Roosevelt's *Autobiography* (New York, 1920); Lincoln Steffens' *The Shame of the Cities* (New York, 1904); W. M. Ivins, *Machine Politics in New York City* (New York, 1897); W. E. Weil, *The New Democracy* (New York, 1912), ch. viii; Tom L. Johnson *My Story* (Cleveland, 1913); W. B. Munro, *Personality in Politics* (New York, 1924); H. H. Curran's *John Citizen's Job* (New York, 1924); H. F. Gosnell's *Boss Platt and His New York Machine* (Chicago, 1923); Clement G. Lanne's *Travelling on the Democratic Donkey* (Rochester, 1925); A. P. Paine, *The Tweed Ring* (New York, 1905); and Raymond Moley, *Parties, Politics and People* (Cleveland, 1921).

CHAPTER XII

URBAN PUBLIC OPINION

What popular government involves.

In a democratic government all power is assumed to emanate from the people. The government is deemed to be at all times under their control. But how do the people exercise this control? Through what channels do they assert their sovereignty? It stands to reason that the people, in a literal sense, cannot govern themselves. There is no such thing as government by the whole people, and never has been, for it is the essence of government that some shall lead and others follow. Government by the whole people would not be government but chaos. The very term government implies that some shall govern and others shall be governed, that some shall command and others obey. It is a two-sided affair.

Aristotle's six types of government.

More than two thousand years ago the greatest political scientist of all time, Aristotle, divided governments into three normal forms and three perverted forms, or six types in all. First there is monarchy, the Rule of One, which in its perverted form becomes tyranny. Second, there is aristocracy, the Rule of a Few, which sometimes degenerates into oligarchy. And, finally, there is democracy, the Rule of the Many, which may be perverted into the rule of the mob. This is a striking classification, and at first glance it seems to cover the ground. It has been incorporated into all the textbooks of political science during the past two thousand years.

They are all reducible to one.

But when you come to study this classification more closely you find that it does not tally with the facts. The world has never seen six forms of government, or even three forms. It has never seen but one form of government—the Rule of the Few. Monarchy is not the rule of one; it is the rule of a few who exercise power in the monarch's name. Even the most absolute monarch, so-called, has his advisers and courtesans who control his mind and will. Aristocracy is the rule of the few who exercise the power in their own name, as the barons of England did at Runnymede. Democracy, with all due respect to the dictionaries, is not the rule of the many but the rule of the few who exercise power in the name of the people. All government, as Lord Bryce has well said, is the Rule of the Few. It is an aristocracy of royal favor, or of birth, or of wealth, or of military control,—or more commonly in our day,—of politicians.

Nothing is more striking, indeed, than the ease with which at all periods of history, from ancient Rome to modern Moscow, the few have ruled the many. Even the dictatorship of the proletariate, when stripped of its sophistry, is the rule of the few. It must inevitably be so. In every government, no matter how democratic, a few people must be called upon to serve as the immediate custodians of power. There is too much power for any one man to wield unshared. There is too little for equal division among all. That is why government, in order to be government, must give to a small percentage of the people the function of exercising political authority. So the chief practical problem of all government is this: How can these few custodians of power be most effectively controlled by the people whose agents they are? Every other problem is an offshoot from this one. *The fundamental problem of popular government.*

There are three ways in which the people of the city are supposed to control their mayor, aldermen, councillors, commissioners, and other elective officers. The first channel of control is through the influence of public opinion, which supposedly exerts a continuous pressure upon all officeholders and holds them to a sense of popular responsibility. Second, the people control their government by their action in nominating and electing the chief officeholders of the municipality. The ballot is the symbol of their sovereignty. And, finally, the people of many cities have provided themselves with a third means of controlling their government; namely, the right to do it through the initiative, referendum, and recall. They have reserved to themselves the right to propose and adopt laws directly, without the intervention of representative legislators. They have furthermore reserved the power to reject laws which their representatives have enacted. Likewise they have in some cases asserted the right to recall or dismiss any elective official whose work is not satisfactory to them. These are the three methods by which the ultimate power of the people is assumed to be exercised. To what extent are they adapted to the end in view? *Three ways in which the people try to control their government.*

The first way: Public opinion.

Public opinion is not an easy thing to define, although the term is one that slips easily from anybody's tongue. In order to have public opinion there must be a coincidence of individual opinions covering a sufficient number of persons, and preferably a majority of them. Not necessarily a majority, however, for public opinion is more than a matter of numbers. The *intensity* of the opinions is quite as important. Public opinion is a composite of numbers and intensity. A minority of the people if they feel intensely on any subject, will outweigh a majority if the latter are lukewarm in their opinions. The aggressive, outspoken element among the people exercises an influence upon the moulding of public opinion which is more than proportionate to its numerical strength.

What it is.

Public opinion is often assumed to be a spontaneous emanation from the group mind, the mind of the multitude, which of course it is not. It does not arise phoenix-like from the cogitation of the populace. For the most part it is a manufactured product. It is usually the result of active effort on the part of a relatively few people who are carrying on a campaign of education, as they call it. In every city, and on all important questions, there are conflicting currents of opinion; but they are not allowed to flow their own course until one proves stronger than the other. Propagandists take a hand in retarding one stream and accelerating the other. A shrewd New York politician once said that "the man who hires the hall is the man who makes public opinion." There is a good deal of truth in this remark. It is not only the man who hires the hall for a propagandist gathering, but the man who pays for space in the newspapers and on the billboards, the man who manipulates the broadcasting station, and the man who builds up an organization for promoting a cause. These are the men who have the largest share in the making of public opinion. There are times, however, when no amount of organized effort and propaganda will avail to stem the drift of public sentiment in a given direction. The emotions of the people become profoundly stirred now and then by some occurrence and nothing prevails to quiet their clamor for action. But under normal conditions every wave of public opinion is set in motion and kept in motion by the efforts of a relatively few busy men and women who are engaged in the work of selling their own ideas to the people at large.

URBAN PUBLIC OPINION

Now the governing authorities of the city are supposed to keep their ears to the ground and to be guided by this public opinion; but it often is a very difficult thing to ascertain. What they hear is a babel of voices crying out in discordant tones. The newspapers are said to reflect public opinion, and some of them try hard to do it, but in general they are not safe guides to follow. In many cases what a newspaper reflects is the sentiment of its own constituency, its subscribers or its advertisers, and sometimes nothing more than the inclinations of its editors or owners. In a newspaper office the wish is father to the thought. The editor is actuated by the same motives which counselled the prophets of Ahab when they told him to go up and smite the men of Gilead hip and thigh. Nor are the resolutions passed by chambers of commerce, civic associations, labor organizations, or federations of women's clubs, to be depended upon as reliable indications of what the people think or want. Usually they are inspired by a few members of the organization and are perfunctorily adopted in the name of the rest. A chamber of commerce may have a thousand members, or even several thousand. This large membership, obviously, does not consider and determine the chamber's attitude on most questions. A small committee is usually given the matter for consideration, and in due course makes its recommendation. This recommendation is then adopted at a slim meeting of the membership and it put forth as the opinion of the whole organization.

Every public official, moreover, receives a lot of letters (signed or anonymous) commending him for this thing or berating him for that. One might think that he would be influenced if he found all these letters expressing the same attitude, one way or the other. But experience has taught him to know better. He has learned that the man or woman who makes a practice of writing letters to the newspapers or to public officials is invariably one whose judgment is very little to be relied upon, and he is also aware that some organized personal interest, animosity, or resentment is usually behind the missives which come to his desk. Brand Whitlock, when he was mayor of Toledo, found that more protests and complaints reached his desk in Monday morning's mail than at any other time during the week. So many people had nothing better to do on Sunday than to reflect upon the shortcomings of others! "Tuesday was not so bad," he says,

How it is reflected.

Newspapers.

Resolutions.

Letters.

"and by Wednesday the atmosphere had begun to clear; by Thursday and Friday everyone seemed to be attending to his own business and letting the faults of his neighbors go unnoted or at least unreported, and Saturday was a day of such calm that one's whole faith in humanity was miraculously restored." [1]

The "phantom public." Public opinion is so nebulous a thing, especially in our polyglot urban communities, that some students of the subject have been almost constrained to feel that no such thing exists. It is phantom, they say, a will-o'-the-wisp which leaders of the people are trying to divine and follow, but fail.[2] In a large city the issues of public policy have become multifarious and require a high degree of intelligence to comprehend. They have gone above the heads of the masses. It is not an *opinion* that the populace holds concerning these complicated matters; but merely a hunch, as it is colloquially called. There is some basis for this point of view, no doubt, but it should not be pressed too far. What passes for the *vox populi* is sometimes a stuttering, stammering, discordant thing. It is an endeavor to make articulate a curious medley of prejudices, whims, and aspirations. But in all this confusion a process of clarification is going on, and in the end certain opinions, or sets of opposing opinions, emerge. The process is expedited by a number of factors, among which the most important are propaganda, traditions (or mental stereotypes), and leadership.

Propaganda as a factor. Let us look for a moment at each of these factors. Propaganda is not only the most aggressive but probably the most influential of all the factors which mould the urban public opinion today. I use the term propaganda in no disparaging sense. Call it civic education if you prefer, for the difference between downright propaganda and a campaign of popular education is all in the way you look at it. When you want something done, and work vigorously for it, you are engaged in a campaign of education. You think yourself a public-spirited citizen, for you are trying to educate the voters to a realization of what the welfare of the city requires. But when the other fellow pursues the same course in behalf of some project which you do not like, you denounce his activity as pernicious propaganda and feel it your duty to warn the unwary voter against being misled by it.

[1] *Forty Years of It* (new edition, New York, 1925), pp. 230-231.
[2] Walter Lippman, *The Phantom Public* (New York, 1925).

In either case the purpose is the same, and so are the methods used. Propaganda is no new thing in government, but it has become a conspicuous feature of modern political life for two reasons: first, because the agencies of propaganda have enormously multiplied in our cities, and second, because it is no longer possible for any man in public office to inform himself, on his own initiative, concerning all the problems that come to him for solution. Do you imagine for a moment that any councilman can, by his own efforts, become familiar with the merits of thousands of proposals during his term at the city hall? Of course not. In order to get him even mildly interested in your ideas you must go to him both in print and in person. You must make him believe that thousands of people are clamoring for this proposal of yours, and that the voters of his own ward are especially concerned about it. In a word, you must focus your pressure upon the individual officeholders and unless you do this your measure will never get very far.

Very few people realize what an extraordinary development we have had in the means whereby propaganda can be carried on nowadays—in the facilities for impressing one man's mind with the ideas of other men. Think how difficult it must have been in ancient times to get any reform accomplished! Ideas and opinions travelled slowly, for they could be spread only by word of mouth. But the invention of printing, the development of the postal service, the telegraph, telephone, and radio; the enormous output of books, magazines, pamphlets and circulars; the growth of the newspapers in size and circulation; the billboards which greet the eye everywhere; the multiplicity of lectures, meetings, forums and discussions; the numberless organizations, associations, leagues, and clubs; the tremendous resort of the people to motion-picture houses; the orgy of radio broadcasting;—all this has made it possible for the ideas of one individual to be brought within a few hours to the eyes and ears of millions. The agencies of urban propaganda were never so plentiful as now, never so easy to use, and never so effective in what they are able to accomplish.

Among these agencies of propaganda, so far as exerting an influence upon city government is concerned, the newspapers still hold first place, although they are probably not so influential as they were a generation ago. The daily newspaper of today, *The newspapers as Propagandists.*

with its artful headlines, its insinuating cartoons, its trenchant editorials, and its adroit handling of news, is still a potent factor despite the tendency of politicians to belittle its influence. On this matter I have sought the views of men who have been through many strenuous municipal campaigns, sometimes with the newspapers on their side, and sometimes with the newspapers against them. It is their conviction that while the newspapers, as agencies of political propaganda, are not so influential as they are commonly supposed to be, their power is far from negligible. A study of the mayoralty campaigns in several large American cities during the past twenty years, notably in New York, Chicago, Boston, Pittsburgh, and Indianapolis, seems to indicate that there is very little connection between newspaper support and success at the polls. Candidates have been frequently elected in these cities with practically the entire press arrayed against them. The same is true of measures submitted to the people at referendum elections. Not long ago, for example, the voters of Chicago rejected by a very large majority a street railway ordinance which had the virtually unanimous support of the newspapers of that city. Every Chicago newspaper except one was strongly in favor of the ordinance; it was also backed by the chamber of commerce and virtually every important civic organization, yet the people were not impressed. A fair statement of the part which newspapers play in municipal politics was made to me by one battle-scarred veteran when he said, "On the whole I would rather have the newspapers with me than against me, but it's the publicity, not the support or opposition, that counts. If the newspapers give me enough space I don't care what they say. Their opposition helps just as much as their support in getting my name before the public, and that is what I want."

Something depends, of course, upon the aggressiveness with which the newspaper give their support to a man or a measure. Mere editorial advocacy, that is, propaganda confined to the editorial page of a newspaper, counts for very little. Not one newspaper reader in ten ever glances at the editorial columns. And those who do read newspaper editorials are for the most part people who think for themselves. They are but mildly influenced. In the countries of Continental Europe the editorial attitude counts for a great deal more, because the political editorials appear on the front page and are usually signed by some widely-known journalist.

On the whole there is more independence among urban than among rural newspapers, but few in either class are nonpartisan. The average American reader does not want the uncolored truth about political matters. He is himself a partisan and he prefers his news served up to him with the right flavor. When he takes up his morning journal, and props it against the sugar bowl at breakfast, he likes to find something that will put him in good humor for the rest of the day. The newspaper's job is to make its readers happy. It is all well enough to say that the newspapers ought to print the unvarnished truth, but the unvarnished truth has about the same selling quality as ice in the Arctic circle. And in any event there are reasons why the inside story cannot be laid bare in the columns of the press. Sometimes the newspapers do not know the facts and cannot get them. Sometimes they know the facts but have obtained them from confidential sources and hence cannot make them public. All experienced politicians are well aware that if you want to keep the truth out of the newspapers the best way is to give it to them in confidence. Sometimes, again, a newspaper is in possession of facts and is entirely at liberty to print them but does not do it because such action might antagonize some powerful interest, political or financial, which the newspaper is disinclined to offend. More often, however, a newspaper gets the facts and prints them, but with a toning-down or a touching-up which helps to make them innocuous. It is here that the "re-write" man, as he is called, gets in his work. His job is to take the copy that comes over the wires or is brought to the editor's desk, and give it the proper coloring. It is here also that the maker of headlines can give a story its proper twist. Many readers get their entire impression from what they see at the top of the column, and all readers get their initial impressions there. Headlines inevitably determine the orientation of the reader to what is printed below. There is more propaganda in the headlines than in the news itself.

Propaganda and the news.

In addition to these regular organs of public opinion there are the specialized publications whose sole and avowed purpose is to promote some particular cause, and which exist for that purpose alone. Their name is legion. There is scarcely a public

The specialized publications.

movement of any sort that does not have its own official organ. No one has ever counted them all, but the total must run into the thousands. Every reform crusade has its own vehicle of propaganda—civil service reform, divorce reform, ballot reform, tax reform, reform of the courts, reform of the colleges, reform of public morals, reform of everybody but the reformer himself. Some of the organizations which champion these various causes are active bodies with thousands of bona fide members recruited from every class. They represent an honest endeavor to mobilize some branch of public opinion in behalf of a more or less worthy cause. But others are merely straw organizations with high-sounding names and with virtually no membership lists at all. A few individuals or corporations, sometimes a single individual supply all the money that is necessary to keep the organization going. The entire equipment consists of a paid secretary and a supply of letterheads. Very often the individuals behind these organizations are men who would not dare come out into the open. Their prominence would be fatal to the cause, for their self-interest in the project would be transcendently apparent. So they conceal their identity behind a hollow organization and it does the talking for them. They call it the League for Honest Government, or the Independent Taxpayers' Association, or the Public Franchise League, or the All-Citizens' Federation for Public Welfare, or by some such alluring title. The paid secretary is on hand at every public hearing "to present the organization's point of view." He is merely a screen for the little handful of propagandists who pay his salary.

The lobby. Then there is the lobby. We are accustomed to associate lobbying with legislatures, but city halls have their lobbies too. Every day you will find the propagandists of this, that, or the other cause waiting their turn in the mayor's anteroom. You will find them outside the door of the council chamber, or even on the inside. Their function is to promote the interests of those whom they serve—be it the public service corporations, or the labor unions, or the large taxpayers, or the city employees, or some other civic organization. Assiduity in pressing their cause helps to atone, in many cases, for a lack of merit.

New agencies of propaganda: Two new agencies of propaganda have come rapidly to the front within the past few years and are crowding into the field which the newspapers formerly monopolized. These two channels of propaganda are the cinema and the radio. The development of the motion picture industry during the first quarter of the twentieth century has been a phenomenon almost without parallel in economic history and the end is not yet. In a single large city there are hundreds of motion picture houses with a combined attendance that runs into the tens of thousands daily. Obviously there are unlimited possibilities in this field for the exercise of influence upon the public mind. Thus far, however, relatively little use has been made of the screen by organizations of a political character. This is partly because the politicians and lobbyists have not yet fully awakened to the possibilities of the motion picture houses as centers for the city-wide diffusion of ideas. They are, of all men, the slowest to adopt a new technique. There is a common impression that practical politicians are alert-minded, receptive to new ideas, and eager to adopt any improved method of campaigning. Nothing could be further from the truth. When the politician changes his ways it is always with reluctance and regret. The failure to make greater use of the cinema for urban political propaganda is also due, in part to the unwillingness of the motion picture industry, to allow itself to be used as a channel of propaganda. There are exceptions, of course, but in general the screen has been neutral in politics.

1. Motion picture houses.

It quickly ceases to be neutral, however, when its own interests seem likely to be affected by a proposed action of the public authorities. We have had several good illustrations of this during the past decade. In Massachusetts, for example, a law providing for state censorship of films was submitted to a referendum a few years ago. The legislature had enacted this law and it was assumed that the people would endorse the legislature's action, for public opinion seemed to be strongly in favor of the measure. Then the motion picture houses started their campaign. In virtually every house throughout the state they began each performance by flashing on the screen their reasons why people should vote against the censorship. It was very adroitly and persuasively done, with the result that a swing in public opinion was soon discernible. At the polls the people defeated the measure by an overwhelming vote. On various other occasions and in different parts of the country the motion picture houses have been able to turn the scale where their own interests seemed to be threatened in an indirect way. Take the so-called "daylight saving" laws, for example. Even in the industrial states, where the agricultural vote is relatively small, the farmers have sometimes been able, with the assistance of the lighting companies and the motion picture industry, to prevent any tinkering with the clock.

All in all there seem to be great possibilities in this field, especially in view of the fact that the control of the motion picture industry is concentrated in relatively few hands. Four or five large producing companies and distributing agencies control the greater part of it and the tendency is towards a further consolidation. This, of course, is not the case with the newspapers. There are some affiliated newspapers under unified control, but in the totality of American journals these chain-newspapers form an inconsiderable minority. No matter what public issue may arise we can always count upon a division of sentiment among the newspapers, often a very marked division. It is not possible to enlist the newspapers unitedly in any cause unless it be a wholly non-partisan and non-controversial one. But there is no such disintegration of control in the case of the picture houses and it is quite conceivable that the next generation will encounter here the most formidable of all propagandist agencies.

2. The radio.

The radio is yet in its swaddling days, but its capabilities in the way of influencing the public mind are already apparent to thoughtful men. Literally millions of people hear the voice of the President when he delivers his public addresses, probably more of them than read it in the newspapers. Certainly no single newspaper, however large its circulation, can reach so wide a constituency as the broadcasting station commands. Is it possible to make any forecast concerning the part which the radio is likely to play in the future dissemination of ideas, the education of the people, and the moulding of public opinion? To what extent will it be utilized by those who want to bring pressure to bear upon the public authorities? Candidates for municipal office are already using it to some extent and they will undoubtedly do more broadcasting of their appeals as time goes on, if only for the reason that it is the cheapest way of reaching large numbers of people in the shortest interval. Here is a channel of propaganda which cannot easily be monopolized, however, by any single interest or controlled by the promoters of any single cause.

The amount of propaganda in the cities is obviously far greater than in the rural districts. But its influence is not proportioned to its quantity. The city-dweller becomes so inured to it that its penetrating power is diminished. He is under such an incessant stimulus that much of what he hears or sees can make no lasting impressions on him. A small item in a rural newspaper may be remembered by readers for months, but the flaming headline in a metropolitan daily is forgotten in a couple of days. Impressions are easily made upon the mind of the urban populace but they are just as easily erased. They do not harden or accumulate because the urban mind dislikes repetition and craves novelty. From the whirlpool of propaganda, ever-changing in purpose and form, it is surprising that a consensus of opinion ever emerges at all. *Urban and rural propaganda compared.*

A second influential factor in moulding the minds of the people is tradition. The world in which the average New Yorker or Bostonian or Detroiter lives is after all a very small one. From his own daily experience he knows little about what is going on a few blocks away. There are those who live in the West End but do not visit the East Side once a year. They know nobody there, and are quite happy about it. Yet every citizen is expected to visualize the life of the city in all its phases, to know how all its people live, and to form opinions on community-wide problems. He cannot be guided by knowledge, for he does not possess it. In such circumstances he must perforce be guided by his mental stereotypes, as Walter Lippman calls them—the pictures (sometimes far removed from realities) which have been graven on his mind by reason of his social heritage or his environment. These stereotypes are not ideas. They are not principles. They have not been thought out. They are attitudes or inclinations of mind. They are merely silhouettes without any of the details filled in. *The influences of tradition on urban public opinion.*

When the busy man in the large city is confronted with a new problem he usually relates it, first of all, to this general inclination, preference, prejudice, or obsession that is already in his mind. If one course of action seems to fit his crude philosophy he favors it; if it does not he reacts unfavorably. Thus the man who has stamped upon him the dogma that taxes ought to be reduced will customarily approve any action that involves a reduction of municipal expenditures, and he will do this without enquiry as to the wisdom of the particular curtailment. This is because it fits his mental picture. And because it does not fit he will react against any proposal to spend more, no matter what the social gain may be. The attitude of the average voter towards franchises, increased license fees, higher pay for city employees, holidays for policemen, expenditures for public celebrations, and all such concrete proposals is not usually the result of his reflection. Get his "point of view," as we call it, and you can predict the rest.

Now there are more points of view represented in the city than in the rural area for the reason that viewpoints are largely the result of inheritance and occupation. There is a greater diversity of racial inheritance and of occupation in the city than in the agricultural region. People approach a problem from a larger number of angles. A general agreement, or anything approaching it, is very much more difficult to obtain. Thus it is that although the population of a city may undergo a great transformation no change in public policy necessarily results because the newer elements are not able to unite in establishing a new tradition to displace the old.

Take an illustration. Why is it that there are no professional league ball games in Boston on Sundays as there are in Chicago or St. Louis? Why are there no Sunday afternoon newspapers? Certainly not because the population of Boston is more sabbatarian than are the populations of the other cities named. Boston's attitude on this matter is a hangover from the past; it is a sign that the Puritan tradition remains a factor in the moulding of the city's public opinion. We say that public opinion rules the city, but this does not necessarily imply that public policy is decided in accordance with the reasoned convictions of living men. Not merely the evil that men do lives after them; all the strong traditions of one generation are passed on and in a degree enslave the public opinion of the next. What we call democracy, therefore, is to an extent necrocracy—or government by the graveyards.

Leadership in relation to urban public opinion. Public opinion is also influenced by leadership. Every idea, cause, or movement is likely to produce its leader, big or little, through whose personality it can be made manifest. The leader

typifies the cause and makes it concrete for the multitude. The
average mind does not easily get hold of an abstraction, or at any
rate does not grow enthusiastic about it. A personality is more
real. There are thousands who supported Roosevelt's "my
policies" without any clear conception of what those policies
were. They were attracted to Roosevelt by Roosevelt, not by
his policies. The same has been true of New York's more
recent favorite son, Governor Smith. Voters by the thousand
will follow a leader on issues relating to a street railway franchise, as they followed Tom L. Johnson of Cleveland, without
the slightest conception of the technical questions involved.
They will take his slogan as a gospel text. When a leader has
once firmly established himself in the confidence of his followers there are always large numbers of people who will take
their opinions ready-made from him.

Leadership plays a larger part in moulding urban than rural *Urban and rural leadership compared.*
public opinion because the issues in the large city are difficult to
unravel. What ordinary citizen, for example, can form for himself an intelligent opinion on the merits of a zoning ordinance or
the extent to which the appropriations in a municipal budget
should be segregated? There is not much to do, in such matters,
but to choose leadership and follow it. I once asked a successful leader of his people in a downtown ward why the voters
always took his word on every sort of public question, no matter
what its nature. He replied, "It ain't because I've got more
brains than they have, but because they know I've never sold
my people out." It is not superiority of mental apparatus that
enables the few to lead in the moulding of public opinion; it is
rather a reputation for unswerving loyalty to a common cause.

Authoritative political leadership is an essential of sound *Why true urban leadership is rare.*
municipal democracy. It is necessary in order to induce some
sort of consensus out of the welter of propaganda and pressures.
Yet we have made the development of true leadership in American cities very difficult and to that extent have impaired the
rule of an opinion which is truly public. We have done this
by adhering to the principle of checks and balances. The man
who is elected mayor cannot always be a real leader, even when
he has the personal qualities, because he needs the concurrence
of the city council for some of his most important acts. In
such case his actions are not dictated by what he deems best

but by what he deems most practicable. On the other hand, the growth of leadership in the council has been stunted by the retention of the ward or district system and by the strength of the current notion that there should be rotation in office—that when a councilman has served for a few years he should retire and make room for someone else.

The development of leadership in the cities has also been retarded by the premium which we place upon the outward amenities, some of which involve a lot of cant and hypocrisy. It is not good form for anyone to announce, in this country, that he feels himself qualified to be a leader of public opinion and is going to try his hand at leading it. He must disclaim any such ambition and intention. All who are not leaders are in the habit of scolding about leadership and calling it dictation. "I never tell my people what they ought to think," a successful politician once told me. "I just get somebody to suggest it to them and keep myself in the background." That statement, while not exactly a confession of candor, disclosed a knowledge of urban psychology. People are willing to follow a leader but do not want to be told so.

Again, it is not in accord with the amenities that a man should seek public office no matter how well-qualified he may be or how capable of serving as a leader of public opinion. "The office should seek the man," it is said, "and not the man the office." Many people believe it. It is true that the office sometimes goes seeking the man,—about as often as a burglar goes looking for a policeman. The man who wants to be a councilman or mayor must go out after the place, in nine cases out of ten, but in so doing he should affect a show of indecision and reluctance. Out of deference to the popular idiosyncrasy he ought to explain that candidacy means a great sacrifice to him, but that he has yielded to the insistence of his friends and has consented to be "drafted." Now why should all this quackery be insisted upon? It deceives nobody. There is nothing unworthy in seeking office at the hands of the people. Among the things that make for good leadership is a frank avowal that one is willing to lead.

Leadership is essential to the making of public opinion. Leadership is essential to the emergence of public opinion. Issues do not propound themselves. Somebody must acquaint himself with the facts, call public attention to them, and propose a remedy. By so doing he makes himself a leader of public opinion. Others will interpret the facts differently and propose some other remedy. They, too, will become leaders of opinion. For no matter what interpretation of the facts a man may give, or what remedy he may propose, he will find some people to agree with him. Out of this general rivalry one current of opinion will gain more force than the others and become in time the preponderant opinion. This may be because a majority hold it, or because a minority has absorbed it with great intensity. When an opinion has become preponderant we call it public opinion. It is not necessarily the opinion of the majority. Much less it is necessarily the opinion of the average man. It is the opinion that by reason of its own intrinsic merit, or as the outcome of propaganda, or because of its consonance with a predominant tradition, or through its championship by competent leaders, or by reason of all these things combined,— the opinion that has emerged with the power.

Lord Bryce has said that three classes of persons, in different degrees, have to do with the making of public opinion.[1] First, there are those who seriously occupy themselves with public affairs,—whether as legislators, mayors, newspaper editors, heads of civic leagues, ward leaders, bosses, or even city employees. All are politicians by vocation or by avocation. Their total number is hardly one per cent of the population, but their influence is great because they know the facts better than the rank and file of the people, and when they hold opinions they hold them earnestly. The second class consists of those who take a cursory but not an active interest in public affairs. They are the intelligent, observant, thoughtful citizens who ordinarily do not care about what goes on at the city hall but who sit up and take notice whenever something of unusual significance occurs. They are only half-asleep, and can easily be aroused. Finally, there is the residue of men and women who are wholly indifferent to political issues or personalities, whose daily reading on such matters never goes below the headlines, and whose thinking in this field is negligible. So far as this class has any opinion on matters of public policy it is derived from inheritance or from the occupational milieu to which the members belong. It is here that one finds the largest non-voting element. Those who

The three classes which make public opinion.

[1] *Modern Democracies* (2 vols., New York, 1921), vol. i, p. 156.

are in the third class do little to mould public opinion, but as Bryce says they sometimes help "to swell its volume." They are far more easily attracted to a personality than aroused by an issue.

<small>How can public opinion be discerned?</small>
There is no accurate barometer of public opinion, not even an election, for the outcome of an election may be determined by circumstances quite apart from the preponderant opinion of the people on any one of the assumed issues. When the people elect a mayor who favors the extension of the civil service system it may be in spite of his stand on this question, not because of it. The personal magnetism of the candidate, or his superior organization, or the lack of popular confidence in his opponent, may be much more decisive than the issues that he represents. Bear in mind that an election often gives the people a choice between two candidates neither of whom they want. It rarely gives them clean-cut issues for decision. You can count the votes, when the last ballot has been polled, but you cannot count the motives behind the votes.

<small>Public opinion and the politicians.</small>
The best way to find out how the people feel on any question is to go out among them, among all sorts and conditions of the people and talk with them. "Talk is the best way of reaching the truth," says Lord Bryce, "because in talk one gets directly at the facts, whereas reading gives not so much the facts as what the writer believes or wishes others to believe." To be able to talk with men of all types, to elicit their reactions and to discern the drift of the public inclination before it becomes apparent to the unpracticed eye—that is the work of the skilled politicians. Some of them do it better than others, but they all try to do it. This quest for a line on the public mentality is not always dictated, however, by a desire to conform the work of government to the popular desire. Quite as often it is actuated by the hope of sensing an incipient drift and diverting it before any harm can be done. Politicians tell us that they want to be guided by public opinion, but as a rule they have no such desire. They want public opinion to be guided by them.

<small>Summary.</small>
Anyone who makes a study of urban public opinion will soon realize how little of it is either truly public or true opinion. He will soon disabuse his mind of the egalitarian notion that all citizens contribute equally to the making of it. He will find that what frequently passes for public opinion is created, fash-

ioned, and marketed by particular groups of interested men who fit their propaganda to the mental silhouettes of the populace and sell ideas like merchandise through a system of brokerage which we call leadership. Considering the way in which it is developed, can we accept the platitude that public opinion rules or ought to rule the city? Can we depend upon it as a means of holding the Few to a strict accountability?

REFERENCES

Much has been written in recent years on public opinion and its relation to government. Among outstanding books are A. Lawrence Lowell, *Public Opinion and Popular Government* (New York, 1913), and *Public Opinion in War and Peace* (Cambridge, 1922); Walter Lippman's *Public Opinion* (New York, 1922) and *The Phantom Public* (New York, 1925); and M. P. Follett's *The New State: Group Organization the Solution of Popular Government* (new edition, New York, 1920). Shorter discussions may be found in Arnold B. Hall's *Popular Government* (New York, 1921), ch. ii; Arthur N. Holcombe's *foundations of the Modern Commonwealth* (New York, 1923), pp. 30-39; C. E. Merriam's *New Aspects of Politics* (Chicago, 1925), ch. iii-vi; and in the various works on *Social Psychology* by William McDougall, E. L. Bogardus, Floyd N. Allport and others.

CHAPTER XIII

THE INITIATIVE, REFERENDUM, AND RECALL

Why direct legislation seems necessary. The object of all popular government is to let the people rule, yet it has been shown in the last chapter that the pressure of public opinion is not in itself sufficient to achieve this end. Public opinion is too nebulous a force to be authoritative. So we have recourse to a second agency of popular control over the governing authorities; namely, that which is provided by the system of nominations and elections. The people endeavor to assert their sovereignty by nominating and electing representatives—a mayor, city councillors, members of the school board, and so forth. Representation is commonly thought to be a very dependable means of giving expression to the will of the people, but as a matter of fact it is not always so, and for three reasons.

Undependability of representative legislation. For one thing, the ballot takes no account of differences in the intelligence or the intensity with which it is marked. Every vote has the same value. Ballots are counted, not weighed. Wise men and foolish are absolutely equal in the polling booth, although they are equal nowhere else. All men are certainly not equal in the amount of influence which they exert upon the outcome of an election. In the second place, the election is determined by a plurality of votes; it is not necessary that the successful candidate shall have a majority. So "representatives of the people" regularly go into public office despite the fact that more votes have been cast against them than for them. While this is the case there is an absurdity in designating the representative system as a perfect machine for carrying the will of the people into effect. Very often an election carries into effect the reverse of the popular will as expressed by a majority. More people sometimes vote against a candidate than for him (in a three-cornered election) yet he goes into office and proceeds to rule as though he possessed a popular mandate. Finally, the elections come at stated intervals, sometimes two or four years apart, and during the period between elections the voters have

THE INITIATIVE, REFERENDUM, AND RECALL

no direct control over those whom they have chosen. An exception to this, in cities which have made provision for the recall, will be noted a little later.

When we say, therefore, that the people of a city control their government through the election of representatives we are stating a half-truth only. To a degree, and under certain conditions, they do exercise an effective control in this way, but it is by no means a complete or a continuous control. There has long been a feeling that the representative system affords only a partial assurance of official responsibility and ought to be supplemented by a direct channel of popular intervention. Hence our recourse to the newer agencies of democracy as they are called,—the initiative, referendum, and recall.

These agencies of popular government may be defined and described as follows: The initiative, as used in the cities, is an arrangement by which any sufficient group of voters may propose a new charter, or a charter amendment, or a change in the ordinances, and may require that such proposal (unless adopted by the city council or commission) shall be submitted to the people at the polls. If ratified by a majority, the initiated proposal goes into operation with the force of law. The initiative thus enables the voters to frame and adopt any legal measure by direct action, without the aid of their representatives. It is a positive instrument of popular rule. *The initiative, referendum, and recall defined.*

The referendum, on the other hand, is a device whereby a stated proportion of the voters may require that any measure which has been passed by the city council or city commission shall be withheld from going into force until the people have had an opportunity to accept or reject it by popular vote. It is a species of popular veto, enabling the voters to override the action of their representatives. A measure which is submitted to a referendum does not go into effect if a majority of the votes is cast against it.

The recall, finally, is a process by which a designated number of voters can demand the immediate removal of an elective officeholder and can have the question submitted to the voters for their decision.[1]

It is only about thirty years since the initiative and refer-

---

[1] In a few cases the recall may also be applied to the city manager, who is not an elective officer but is appointed by the city council.

240 THE GOVERNMENT OF AMERICAN CITIES

Their development in America. endum, in their present form, made their appearance in America. But in a broader sense they go a good deal farther back. The right of the people to petition for redress of their grievances, which is the essence of the initiative, is coincident with the very beginnings of American government. And the referendum is as old as the New England town meeting; as old, indeed, as the Teutonic folkmote. For nearly three hundred years the referendum in some form or other has been an American institution, and ever since the Revolution its sphere has been widening. Many American cities used it throughout the latter half of the nineteenth century in connection with charter amendments, municipal borrowing, and the restriction of the liquor traffic. But this employment of the referendum was occasional and sporadic, being restricted to certain designated fields of legislative action. Not until the end of the century did the movement for city-wide direct legislation begin to reach fruition.[1]

During the years intervening between 1900 and the outbreak of the World War, however, the spread of the initiative and referendum in American cities was very rapid. The spread was undoubtedly aided by the general reorganization which took place in the municipal system during the period, involving the substitution of the commission and city manager plans for the older type of government in a large number of municipalities. The initiative, referendum, and recall seemed to furnish a useful balance-wheel for these simplified forms of municipal organization which were viewed with suspicion in many quarters. So the newer forms of city government and the newer agencies of popular control spread together over the country, each helping the progress of the other. Today there is provision for the use of the initiative and referendum in more than three hundred cities of all sizes, including many large municipalities such as Cleveland, Cincinnati, Denver, Detroit, San Francisco, Los Angeles, Seattle, and St. Louis. During the past ten years the movement has slackened considerably and few additions to the list have been made.

Reasons for their rapid spread. How is this rapid spread of the initiative and referendum in American cities, as contrasted with those of Europe, to be accounted for? Three reasons, at least, may be given by way of

---

[1] The first American city charter to provide for the regular use of the initiative and referendum was that of San Francisco, 1898.

THE INITIATIVE, REFERENDUM, AND RECALL

explanation. One is the decline in the caliber of American municipal officeholders, especially in the quality of aldermen and councillors. The powers of city councils in the United States, as will be indicated a little later on, have been steadily reduced during the past fifty years. With diminished powers the councils have failed to attract men of energy and intelligence as they did in earlier days. It is no wonder that the people, in watching the work of their city councils, should have made up their minds that they could do no worse themselves—and might do a great deal better. The second reason may be found in the habit of evading responsibility which state legislatures and city councils acquired during the latter years of the nineteenth century. When difficult questions confronted these bodies it became the common practice to seek an easy solution by "putting the matter directly up to the people." Ostensibly this was a mark of the lawmaker's confidence in the wisdom of the electorate; in reality it was a mere ruse by which supine legislators sought to evade and usually succeeded in evading their own responsibilities. At any rate, the practice of voluntarily submitting matters to the judgment of the voters became more and more common until it was only a short step to the principle of compulsory submission. A third reason may be found, perhaps, in the simplification of city government that has taken place in the United States during the past twenty-five years. Commission government and the city manager plan, while possessing obvious merits in the way of simplicity, are open to the popular objection that they concentrate a great deal of power in very few hands. The initiative, referendum, and recall supply a ready means of weakening the force of this objection in that they provide an agency of electoral control over the concentration of power. The movement for the simplification of municipal machinery has thus carried the process of direct legislation along with it as a safeguard.

In using the initiative and referendum there are rather elaborate formalities to be complied with, and these vary in different cities. The first step in the use of the initiative is the framing of a petition accompanied by a proposed charter amendment or ordinance. This may be done by any group of voters, but initiative petitions are usually started by some society or organization —a chamber of commerce, labor federation, or civic league, for

Their workings explained:

1. The initiative.

example. A stated number of signatures to the petition must be obtained, the minimum being usually fixed at from ten to fifteen per cent of all the enrolled voters or of the voters who voted at the last city election. These signatures are obtained in various ways—by holding meetings, by a house-to-house canvass, or by placing copies of the petition in stores, banks, and other places where people may sign them. When enough signatures have been obtained, the petition, accompanied by the proposed measure, is presented to the proper authorities at the city hall (usually the city clerk, or the registrar of voters), who count the names and check them with the voters' list. If they find that the petition fulfills all requirements, they so certify, whereupon provision is made for submitting the measure to the voters at the next election, unless the city council passes it in the meantime. If the next election is too far away the measure may be submitted, in some cities, at a special election called for the purpose; but special elections are expensive and hence are avoided whenever possible. To inform the voters concerning the various measures which are to appear on the ballot, it is the custom in many cities to have an explanatory pamphlet prepared and mailed to every voter some days prior to the election. These pamphlets contain the texts of the various proposals and also, in some cases, a summary of the arguments for and against their adoption. At the election the voters mark their ballots with a cross under the words *Yes* or *No* which are set opposite each measure.[1]

2. The referendum or protest. When it is desired to invoke the referendum upon any measure which has been passed by the city council of its own volition, a petition is circulated for this purpose by any group of interested voters. If enough signatures are obtained (usually the same number as is required in the case of the initiative), the petition is filed at the city hall; the signatures are then checked up and certified; and the question of acceptance or rejection is placed on the ballot. Meanwhile the measure is withheld from going

[1] The question appears on the ballot in this form:

Shall Ordinance No. 47,105 regulating the maximum gross weights of vehicles and loads operated or moved upon the public streets be adopted?	YES
	NO

THE INITIATIVE, REFERENDUM, AND RECALL

into operation, unless it be an emergency measure in which case a referendum may not be invoked.[1] This method of invoking a referendum on enacted measures was originally known as "the protest," a good term which unfortunately did not persist.

Ordinarily a referendum does not take place on any measure unless petitioned for, but there are some exceptions to this rule. Occasionally in city charters there is a provision that certain matters—such as franchises and bond issues—must be submitted to the people irrespective of any petition or protest. The city council, moreover, may of its own accord refer matters to the people. The popular vote in most cases has no legally binding effect on the council but is for the latter's guidance only.

The initiative and referendum have now been used on a considerable scale in many cities for fifteen years or more. In some cities as many as thirty questions have been submitted to the voters at a single election. At the outset, when the system was new, the voters displayed an active interest in the questions, even when they were numerous, but when the novelty began to wear off this interest noticeably declined. Electoral indifference was also encouraged by the practice of submitting questions of minor importance, such as the salary of some individual city officer or questions involving technical amendments to the city charter. At the San Francisco election of 1921, for example, twenty-three questions were put on the ballot, of which all but one were charter amendments. They covered a wide range of matters, most of them unrelated to each other and of such nature that no one who had not carefully studied the existing city charter could understand them. Together they filled an election pamphlet of thirty-one pages.[2] It is not surprising that the average voter fails to display an active interest or to exercise much discrimination when confronted with a task of that sort. Happily the voter has hit upon his own remedy in such cases. In self-defense he has adopted the slogan, "When in doubt, vote *No*."

Merits and defects of the system.

New devices do not always attain the ends which their proponents desire. It has been so in this instance. The initiative and referendum were urged upon the cities by the progressive

They have proved more conservative than was expected.

---

[1] The council, as a rule, decides whether the measure is an emergency one or not. It has sometimes abused this privilege.

[2] E. L. Shoup, "The Initiative and Referendum in Thirty-Six American Cities" in *National Municipal Review*, XII, pp. 610-615 (October, 1925).

elements, so-called. Their advocacy brought terror to the conservative soul. It was assumed, as a matter of course, that once all sorts of people were allow to vote on all sorts of questions there would be an end to stability and rationalism in government. Business, property, and (most of all) the public utilities would be at the mercy of the popular caprice. On this basis the conservatives fought the movement in its early stages and expended a great deal of energy in trying to combat the progress of these "revolutionary innovations," which they declared to be utterly subversive of orderly government. The progressives, on the other hand, and the other professed friends of the common man, welcomed each advance of the initiative and referendum as a victory for the people over the vested interests.

Only a dozen years have passed since this fight was on, but they have brought enlightenment to both sides. The "forward-looking men" are now wondering why they ever put so much faith in these devices; the conservatives are amazed that they should have fought the movement at all. For the initiative and referendum have not proved to be revolutionary in any sense; on the contrary they have been of at least equal value to the conservative cause and probably more than that. "The people," as one disillusioned radical laments, "would rather purr than scratch."[1] They are too cautious by half. They insist on being shown. They have not scrupled to reject, by large majorities, proposals for adopting the single tax, for rushing into municipal ownership of public utilities, for giving pensions to city employees, and so forth. Not only that but their action at the polls can be influenced by skilful propaganda,—and propaganda is merely a matter of using brains and money. The vested interests have both. The same advantages that have so often enabled them to control the election of mayors and councillors seem equally potent when used to secure the adoption or the defeat of some measure on the ballot. It is for this reason that many radicals have lost faith in "direct democracy" and are suggesting that we might get along better with less of it.

It is asserted that the process of direct legislation has an edu-

[1] See the interesting article on "The Dancing Bear," by Frederic Nelson, in the *New Republic* (May 27, 1925), in which the writer resigns himself to the thought that "the folly of mankind is no new thing" and concludes that the populace is merely "a dancing bear which cavorts to the tune which the exploiters sing."

cative value in that it encourages the voters to become better informed about municipal affairs and to take a more intelligent interest in what is going on at the city hall. The line of reasoning usually followed in support of this proposition is plausible enough. So long as everything is decided by a body of councilmen or commissioners, it is argued, the people as a whole are not likely to display any direct interest in the proceedings. The surest way of promoting popular interest in political problems is to give the people the direct responsibility for deciding them, and not merely a vicarious power exercised through representatives. It is pointed out, moreover, that the practice of mailing a pamphlet of information to every voter on the eve of election assures a certain amount of education upon the issues. Even if it be true that a good many of these pamphlets go into the waste basket, it is nevertheless beyond question that just as many and possibly more are read by the voters.

Their educative value.

Now it may be granted that if there is any electoral device which can be depended upon to make the whole citizenship more enlightened and more interested, the arguments in favor of using it would be very strong indeed. For civic education is the basis of all permanent governmental reform. The most serious indictment of the American municipal system is not its toleration of antiquated charters or lax business methods or incompetent officeholders. These things are merely the outcroppings of electoral indifference. The underlying cause to which most of our municipal ills are attributable has been the failure to interest the people and to keep them interested in questions of municipal policy. If, then, a frequent resort to the process of direct legislation serves to make the voter more civic-minded, as the friends of the initiative and referendum are fond of asserting, it would be hard to think of a stronger argument in favor of their plan.

Has this amounted to anything?

To what extent has this claim been substantiated by the experience of the past twenty-five years? Has the use of the initiative and referendum in American cities during this quarter-century contributed to the political education of the people? Do the voters, as a class, know more about municipal problems and display a more intelligent interest in those communities which make free use of direct legislation than in those which do not? If you seek on this question the opinions of those who are at the vantage points of observation, you will get them in considerable variety. There is some ground for the belief that the system of direct legislation does foster electoral interest in public questions; but not greatly so after the novelty has worn off. The average voter is not capable of sustained enthusiasm; he soon finds the task of crystallizing his own opinions to be a good deal of a bore. That is not surprising, for to most men the process of individual thought and reflection is hard work. It is very much easier to let some organization consider the various questions in all their bearings and tell its members what to do. That is what customarily happens. The party leaders, the chamber of commerce, the citizens' association, the labor federation, the league of women voters, and various other bodies are the ones that make up the voter's mind for him. Thousands of voters affiliated with these various organizations find such recommendations a sufficient guide, without further study; hence the amount of political education which percolates through to the individual is relatively small. He responds to the influence of suggestion and reiteration, rather than to the promptings of his own reason. He has seen everywhere, on the billboards, in the newspapers, and on the windshields of automobiles the legend "Vote *No* on Question Ten,"—and he does it.

Their guarantee of good faith. The process of direct legislation, it is claimed, affords a guarantee that charters and ordinances will be framed by those who wish them to be successful,—which is not always the case in the process of representative legislation. The motives of those who bring measures before the city council, or who support them there are not always easy to fathom, nor are they in all cases what they superficially appear to be. The same is true of the motives which dictate the making of amendments to measures when they are before the council for consideration. City councils have often gone through the motions of complying with a popular demand, while taking good care to put jokers in the ordinance. They do not, as a rule, commit the folly of killing popular measures in the open by the use of steam-roller methods. They find it more advantageous to use the artifices of treacherous friendship. Under the pretext of agreeing to a reasonable compromise, or series of compromises, it is often possible for any strong element in the city council to dictate the virtual emasculation of popular measures.

Now the process of direct legislation affords very little oppor-

THE INITIATIVE, REFERENDUM, AND RECALL 247

tunity for the insertion of jokers as a means of turning a good ordinance into a bad one. Every measure goes to the people as originally framed by its friends. Those who desire its rejection must come out into the open. Incidentally, it is claimed, this promotes a popular respect for the laws. One reason why people so often manifest a deficient respect for the ordinances of the municipality may be found in their knowledge of the way in which these enactments have been passed. They are well aware that intrigue and subterfuge have figured in the process. But measures enacted by the initiative and referendum bear the stamp of specific public endorsement. They are the handiwork of the public themselves and hence have a strong claim to be respected.

Do they encourage popular respect for law?

It would be interesting, but not easy, to discover the extent to which this claim is borne out by the actual experience of American cities. Laws and ordinances relating to the manufacture, transportation, and sale of intoxicating liquors, for example, have been treated with a good deal of disrespect in American cities during the past few years. Is there any ground for the belief that this antagonism, among certain elements of the population, would have been less widespread or less intense if the policy of prohibition had been endorsed by popular vote rather than by legislative action? It may well be doubted. Local prohibition by popular vote, when cities had it, did not obtain any more loyal acquiescence than national prohibition by constitutional amendment. The very people who make the laws are often the first to offend. Lawlessness seems to be inspired by something more fundamental than the mere mechanism of lawmaking. We have waves of it now and then, especially after great wars and in times of economic depression.

The claim is made that direct legislation results in the adoption of charters and ordinances which are better drawn, less ambiguous in their terminology, and more satisfactory as instruments of government than are the products of representative lawmaking. At first glance this may seem a strange claim to make, since the drafting of such measures is a technical task which on its face ought to be as well, or even better, performed by the city councilmen than by any group of petitioners among the people. But the fact is that in neither case is the work done by amateurs. The ordinances which come before the city council are not drafted by the councilmen themselves. They are prepared, as a rule,

Do they promote better-law-drafting?

by the city's law department. And ordinances which accompany the initiative petitions are not framed by the petitioners but by lawyers whose assistance is secured for the purpose. So the question simmers down to the relative skill and intelligence of the city's law department, on the one hand, and the legal advisers of the petitioners on the other. In this connection it should be borne in mind that appointments to the city's law department are, as a rule, political appointments. Party service generally counts for more than legal skill and expertness. The law department, moreover, is almost always overburdened by work, especially in the larger cities; hence there is a temptation to do things in slipshod fashion. It is not difficult for any group of men to obtain, at a relatively small outlay, more intelligent and more painstaking service in drafting an ordinance than the council obtains from the city's law department. The petitioners can at least obtain service from some lawyer whose heart is in the work, and that counts for a good deal.

It is sometimes said that the initiative and referendum give the masses of the people a means of breaking the power of the professional politicians. In proof of this our attention is called to the vigor with which the professional politicians have opposed the whole process. But this opposition is not of great significance. The politicians, as a rule, oppose anything that is new. They have learned the rules of the game and do not want them changed. At any rate it is urged that here is a way in which the people can loosen the grip of the boss, the ring, or the machine if they see fit to do it. As a theoretical proposition this may be true, but it has found very little confirmation in practice. The party system has been almost wholly unaffected, either in its good or its evil features, by the use of the initiative and referendum.

Some serious objections: The advantage which they give to organized interests. On the other hand, these two decades of experience with the initiative and referendum in American cities have disclosed some serious objections to the process of direct legislation. First among these objectionable features is the ease with which the system can be used by any well organized group to promote its own selfish advantage. In politics, as in war, mere numbers do not prevail against superior organization and discipline. Property and wealth can be mobilized, and they are quickly mobilized whenever their interests appear to be threatened. As between an organized minority which possesses the wealth, and an unorganized majority which possesses the votes, there need be little question concerning the outcome in four elections out of five. You can give every citizen an equal vote yet come far from giving everyone an equal political influence. The acceptance or rejection of any question on the ballot will always depend, in large measure, upon the relative facility with which its supporters and opponents are able to organize, upon the degree of unity in their ranks, and upon the amount of money they are respectively able to spend upon a "campaign of education" which is merely a synonym for expensive and aggressive propaganda.

When, therefore, a proposal has to do with the immediate interests of any well organized group, whether it be organized capital, organized labor, or organized partisanship, the chances of its adoption are greatly increased. If the proponents, moreover, are able to spend large sums of money in a campaign of advertising, the chances of success are still greater,—and advertising is largely a matter of spending money. Its results are closely proportioned to the amount expended. By persistent and effective advertising you can "sell" an idea to the people as easily as you can sell a breakfast cereal or a patent medicine. This being the case, it is clear that the measures which have the least chance of success at the polls are those which concern the good of the average citizen who has neither an organization to champion his cause nor unlimited funds to spend in moulding public opinion.

Take the question of motion-picture censorship, for example. What an uphill fight it is to get laws and ordinances covering this matter adopted by the people at the polls! The reason is that the motion-picture interests are almost always opposed to censorship regulations and they have ideal facilities for carrying on a campaign of propaganda. To use these facilities costs them virtually nothing, but when the other side tries to offset this campaign by counter-propaganda in the newspapers the cost is prohibitive.

A second shortcoming of the initiative and referendum, as disclosed in the cities of the United States during the past twenty years, is their repeated failure to obtain *majority* decisions at the polls. Most of the arguments for direct legislation start with the assertion that "the will of the majority" ought to prevail— which is a self-evident proposition. But what usually does pre-

<small>Their failure to prove an agency of majority rule.</small>

vail is the will of the minority. Not ten per cent of the measures enacted by the process of direct legislation in American cities have had an actual majority recorded in their favor. Forty per cent of the registered vote, under normal conditions, is always sufficient to adopt a measure; even thirty-five per cent is ample as a rule. Measures have been carried, not infrequently, with less than thirty per cent of the registered voters pronouncing in their favor. The reason for this is not far to seek. Many voters stay away from the polls, and of those who attend the election considerable numbers are interested only in the candidates and not in the questions. So they pay no attention to the mass of printed matter at the bottom of the ballot.

"But what of it?" the friends of direct legislation reply. "The voters have their opportunity; if they do not avail themselves of it by going to the polls and marking all the questions on the ballot, they have nobody but themselves to blame." That is true; it explains but hardly justifies a system of minority law-making. To urge that a political device would function properly if the people were differently-minded does not conduce to the solution of the problem. Many evils in government would right themselves if people would only do differently. Were it not, indeed, for the perverseness of the voters our system of representative lawmaking would never have fallen into disrepute and there would never have been any call for direct legislation. Political institutions must be judged in the light of their relation to human nature as it is. Whether the initiative and referendum would work better if human beings were differently constituted is hardly worth quarrelling about. The important thing is that in actual practice what purports to be the verdict of a majority is the verdict of a minority, sometimes a small minority. The retort that this is the people's own fault leads us nowhere. In the last analysis all the weaknesses of government are the people's fault.

The limitations of the *Yes* and *No*.
Direct legislation is subject to the essential limitations of the categorical. A referendum is merely a call for the *Ayes* and *Nays;* it affords no opportunity for ascertaining the voter's entire opinion on any subject. We are sometimes told that direct legislation is merely an elaboration of the methods used for nearly three hundred years by the New England towns, and in a sense that is true. But in one very important particular the analogy

THE INITIATIVE, REFERENDUM, AND RECALL 251

fails. The town meeting has always afforded opportunity for discussion, for compromise, and for the amendment of any proposal. The referendum calls for a straight vote on the "previous question"; that is, upon the questions as it stands on the ballot. It assumes that every voter is ready to say *Yes* or *No* to any question which may be placed before him. The unthinking voter may be prepared to do this, but very few intelligent voters find themselves able to give exact expression to their opinions by the simple expedient of marking with a cross. This is especially true when the question is one which raises more than one issue and carries various implications, as referendum questions sometimes do. When, therefore, a voter marks his ballot affirmatively he does not always mean that he approves the proposal as it stands. Very often he means that having to choose between two evils he has decided to take what seems to be the lesser. To say that direct legislation "gives the people what they want" is taking a great deal for granted. Not infrequently it offers them a choice between two alternatives, neither of which they want or would take if they could avoid it.

Yet we should not lay too much stress on this objection. It is easy to say that legislatures and city councils can "deliberate," while the people at the polls cannot; but anyone who is familiar with the actual work of legislative bodies knows full well that they do astonishingly little deliberating. Ordinances are often put through city councils without being read (except figuratively) and certainly without their provisions being understood. City councils can compromise and secure a meeting of divers minds, but as a rule they do not. The majority often puts its measures through by a simple *Yea* and *Nay* vote, rejecting all amendments and even limiting debate. There is in truth a good deal of the categorical about the work of representative lawmaking.

There are other objections to the initiative and referendum. These devices are said to be un-American and out of tune with the spirit of our institutions, both of which they are not. On the other hand, they are expensive in operation, because it costs money to circulate petitions, check the signatures, count ballots, and hold elections. They necessarily tend to lengthen the ballot when we ought to be striving to make the ballot short. Certainly there is nothing to be gained by reducing the number of candidates on the ballot if we merely use the space (and more) to

Other objections.

print questions. The masses of the people are slow of comprehension. They read slowly and think slowly when they think at all. Many referendum ballots assume a far greater amount of mental alertness and breadth of knowledge than the majority of voters possess.

Nature of the questions submitted.   Go over the list of questions submitted to the people of San Francisco, Los Angeles, Portland and other cities during the past fifteen years. They relate to such matters as daylight saving, water filtration, abolishing one-man cars, fixing street railway fares, franchises, gas rates, excess condemnation, jitney bus regulation, the purchase of land, the selling of electric power, the salaries of officials, pensions, censorship, hours of work for city employees, and so on. Many of them raised issues of a technical character on which no thinking man could form an opinion without considerable data and study. In most cases no questions of general policy were concerned, but merely some matters of administrative method. It seems absurd that we should employ experts to manage the city's water or power plants but should refer to the people various problems which even these experts find difficulty in solving.

The future of the initiative and referendum in America.   In general, the initiative and referendum have neither fulfilled the hopes of their friends nor justified the fears of their opponents. Direct legislation has not put an end to the power of political bosses, or destroyed the party system, or transformed electoral indifference into popular enthusiasm. On the other hand, it has not thrust cities into the clutches of demagogues or wrecked the foundations of government. It has not proved socialistic in any sense. Ordinances passed by means of the initiative and referendum have been, on the whole, no better and no worse than those passed by city councils. The strong probability is, if one may venture a prediction, that less use will be made of direct legislation as time goes on. This does not mean, however, that the process will be altogether discarded. The people are likely to keep it as a safeguard. There is no good reason why they should not do so. The impeachment procedure, as provided in the national and state constitutions, for example, is cumbrous and expensive. If used at frequent intervals it would work more harm than good. But as a weapon of last resort, for use in emergencies, its value is unquestionable. In like manner the initiative and referendum will doubtless have their chief

THE INITIATIVE, REFERENDUM, AND RECALL 253

value, as time goes on, in providing the voters with a spur which they can drive into the flanks of the city council when an urgent need arises.

The recall is usually, but not necessarily, linked with the initiative and referendum. Each can be used without the other. As has been said, it is the right of a designated number of voters to demand the immediate removal of any elective officeholder and to have this demand submitted to the voters for decision. Thus it applies to men and not to measures. A petition for removal is drawn up and circulated for signatures; and when enough signatures have been obtained they are presented to the proper authorities, who thereupon hold an election to decide the matter. The petition usually states the reasons for requesting the officeholder's removal before the expiration of his term. If a majority of those who vote on the question are in favor of the removal, the officeholder vacates his post at once; if the demand for a recall is rejected, he continues in office. Provision for the recall was first established in Los Angeles (1903) and during the past twenty years it has been adopted in many cities in different parts of the country. Several city officials have been removed at recall elections. Nevertheless the recall has been used more sparingly than anyone expected at the time of its introduction. No figures, so far as I am aware, have ever been compiled to show how many recall elections have been held in American cities during the past twenty years or what proportion of these elections have resulted in the removal of city officials. The number of attempts has probably not exceeded a hundred and fifty, of which not more than half seem to have been successful. An average of three or four recalls a year would seem to indicate a very conservative use of the procedure.

The recall: how it operates.

There is one aspect of the recall procedure that ought not to be overlooked, namely, the incentive which it provides toward the lengthening of official terms. In American cities we have always been skeptical of long terms for public officers. We believe in keeping government "near the people," by compelling mayors and councilmen to stand for reëlection every year or two. But where the recall procedure is available the arguments for a short term lose most of their force. The official, even though elected for a four or a six year term, is kept amenable to those who have chosen him.

One important aspect of it.

REFERENCES

A list of material relating to the initiative and referendum, published prior to 1915, is included in W. B. Munro, *Bibliography of Municipal Government* (2d edition, Cambridge, 1915), pp. 48-55. Since that date the most useful additions to the literature of the subject are J. D. Barnett, *Operation of the Initiative and Referendum in Oregon* (New York, 1915); Arnold B. Hall, *Popular Government* (New York, 1921), especially pp. 120-143; W. F. Dodd, *State Government* (New York, 1922), pp. 502-545; Samuel Peterson, *Democracy and Government* (New York, 1919), pp. 235-275; the Massachusetts Constitutional Convention *Bulletin No. 6* (1917), and the Illinois Constitutional Convention *Bulletin No. 2* (1920). Other references may be found in E. N. Snow's *Bibliography of Books and Articles on the Initiative, Referendum and Recall*, issued by the Legislative Reference Section of the New York State Library (Albany, 1924).

The debates on the Initiative and Referendum at the Massachusetts Convention have been printed in a separate volume of over a thousand pages (*Debates in the Constitutional Convention*, Vol. II, Boston, 1918). These debates covered every phase of the subject and brought forth every conceivable argument that could be adduced on either side of the controversy. The development of direct legislation, with summaries of referenda votes, is recorded in the monthly issues of the *National Municipal Review*. The Debaters' Handbook Series contains a volume of *Selected Articles on the Initiative and Referendum*, compiled by Edith M. Phelps (3d edition, White Plains, N. Y., 1914). Some interesting observations on the whole subject are set forth in Bryce's *Modern Democracies* (2 vols., New York, 1921), Vol. II, pp. 417-434. William Anderson, *American City Government* (New York, 1925), chap. xi; J. St. L. Strachey's *The Referendum* (London, 1924), and R. C. Brooks, *Political Parties and Electoral Problems* (New York, 1924) also deserve mention.

The workings of the recall are described in the Massachusetts Constitutional Convention *Bulletin No. 26* (with bibliography). D. F. Wilcox, *Government by All the People* (New York, 1912) gives the arguments for it (pp. 196-310) and Arnold B. Hall, *Popular Government* (New York, 1921), pp. 203-240, gives the arguments against. The law relating to the power of removal or recall may be found in Judge Dillon's *Commentaries on the Law of Municipal Corporations* (5th edition, 5 vols., Boston, 1911), Vol. II, pp. 779-823.

CHAPTER XIV

THE FORMS OF CITY GOVERNMENT

In every European country there is a uniform system of city government. Virtually all the cities in each of them are governed alike. Accordingly, when you understand the general frame of municipal government in one English city you know all you need to know about the rest. Liverpool has the same type of government as Leeds, and Leeds has the same as Sheffield or Manchester. In France the uniformity is as just as great. There is no essential difference between the governments of Marseilles, Bordeaux, Lyons, Rouen, Dijon, and all the other French cities with the exception of Paris. Every city, town, and village in France (with the exception of the capital) is rated as a "commune," and each commune in France has a simple government consisting of a mayor, one or more adjoints, and a municipal council. Italy, Belgium, Spain, and the other European countries pursue the same policy. Each has a general municipal code which sets up a single type of government for all the cities, whether large or small. Europeans see no reason why individual cities should go off on their own tangents, setting up whatever form of local government seems best to themselves. What is good for one city, they assume, ought to be good enough for the others.

The uniformity of types in Europe.

There is another outstanding feature of the municipal system in the various European countries, namely, the absence of any experimenting with new types of city government. Great changes in population and in problems have taken place in Europe during the past half century but the general outlines of municipal organization have come through with almost no change whatever. English cities of today have their mayors, aldermen and councillors with almost precisely the same powers, responsibilities and relations that these officials possessed ninety years ago. The cities of France, all of them, have exactly the same type of government that was given to them after the establishment of the Third Republic in 1870. Germany has been transformed from

Another contrast with America.

an empire to a republic within the past decade, yet the general structure of city government in the various German states has not been substantially changed. The spirit has altered considerably, but the form has not. In a word there has been very little experimenting with new types of city government in any country of Western Europe during the past half century.

<small>There is no American type of city government.</small>
But when we turn to the United States there is a different story to tell. Here we have no uniformity and we have had endless experimenting. There is no American type of city government; there is not even a California type or an Ohio type. Even within the bounds of a single small state like Rhode Island there are variations in the form of city government. No two cities, indeed, throughout the whole expanse of America have exactly the same municipal organization, or, if they have, it is merely by accident. When you study the government of Buffalo you get no inkling as to the form of government in Boston, or Chicago, or Cleveland. Each of these four cities, as a matter of fact, has its own peculiar type of government quite different from that of the others. Buffalo has the commission form; Boston has a mayor with a weak council; Chicago has a mayor with a strong council; and Cleveland has the city manager form of government with proportional representation. It is for this reason that foreign students find the American municipal system so difficult to understand. They are bewildered by the variety of types and forms. Yet there is no need to be concerned over this extreme diversity, for the type of organization is not the vital thing in city government. Two cities with very dissimilar forms of organization may in fact be administered almost alike. In the spirit of their government, in methods, in fundamentals, in all that really counts—in these respects there is far more uniformity among American cities than the surface indications would imply.

<small>The diversity of forms in the United States:</small>
During the past twenty-five years the United States has served as the world's chief laboratory for experiments in local administration. Since 1900 we have tried more experiments in this field than have been undertaken by all other countries of the world put together. And the process of experimentation is by no means at an end. We are still in the midst of it. Hardly a week passes by without the announcement that some American city, big or little, has decided to abandon its existing form of government in order to give some other form a trial. This, of course, is not to

THE FORMS OF CITY GOVERNMENT 257

be deplored, for it is only through the method of experimentation that progress comes. We have learned much from our municipal experience during the past twenty-five years,—more than we did in the whole century preceding.

Now the cities of the United States began their history with a single, fairly uniform type of government. There was a single governing organ, an elective council in which the mayor was merely the presiding officer. Later the mayor became an independent official, the chief municipal executive, elected directly by the people and having powers of his own. Thus came into being the mayor-and-council type of government which spread over virtually the entire country and held sway during the nineteenth century. This scheme, it will be remembered, was modelled on the general plan of national government and its cornerstone is the principle of division of powers. Chicago, Philadelphia, Los Angeles, and many smaller cities retain it at the present day. As chief executive of the city, the mayor possesses the veto power, and the right to initiate certain appointments, but the council is the governing authority of large importance and virtually controls the finances of the municipality. For lack of a better name this arrangement may be called the "limited executive" type of mayor-and-council government and its general structure is illustrated by the diagram on the next page. *1. The original form,—limited executive.*

It will be noted that the mayor has authority to appoint the chief officials of the city (with some exceptions), but that most of his appointments must be confirmed by the city council before they can become valid. He also has the power to veto ordinances and resolutions of the city council, but his veto may be overridden by a two thirds vote of that body. On the other hand, the council has the initiative in ordinance-making and controls the appropriations. In some instances (as in Chicago) it actually prepares the annual budget, through one of its committees, and the mayor has nothing to do with appropriations until after the council is through. In other cities the estimates which form the basis of the appropriations are presented to the council by the mayor. *Its salient features.*

It is often asserted that this plan of city government has the merit of making the mayor and the council serve as a check upon each other and thus preventing the accumulation of too much power in the hands of either. It provides a safeguard against *Its merits and faults.*

258 THE GOVERNMENT OF AMERICAN CITIES

dishonesty and malfeasance on any large scale, we are told, because one organ of city government is always standing watch on the other. Power is a check to power. There may be some force in this contention, although the value of checks and balances in local government has been heavily over-estimated. On the other hand, the limited-executive type of municipal administration has disclosed a good many grave defects. The most seri-

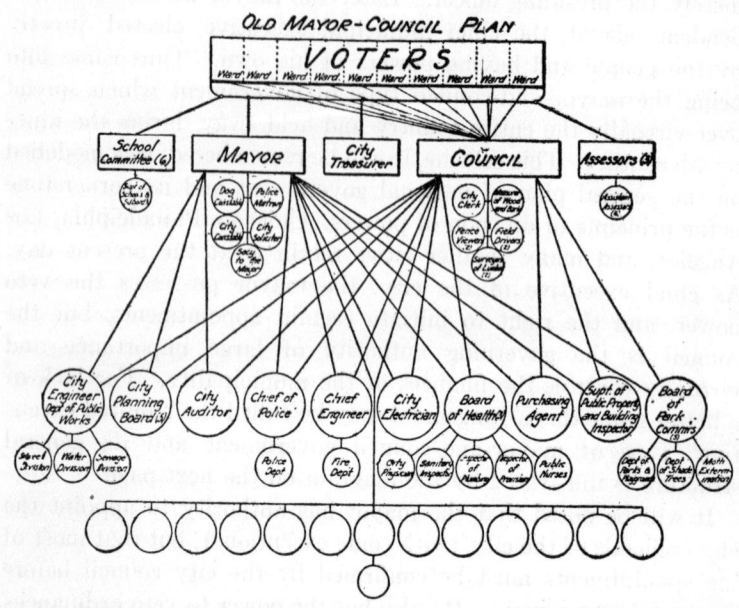

ous is to be found in the fact that division of powers inevitably means division of responsibility. Take the matter of appointments, for example. When the mayor is permitted to make them without the necessity of obtaining the council's confirmation, he becomes directly responsible to the people for his actions. He cannot evade responsibility for poor selections. But when the council shares the appointing power with him there is no such concentration of credit or blame. The limited-executive form of government has been provocative of friction and deadlocks between the executive and legislative branches, leading often to compromises in which the public interest has suffered. The mayor, elected by the whole people, is looked upon as the outstanding city officer and is expected to take summary action

THE FORMS OF CITY GOVERNMENT

whenever the occasion calls for it. But he is held in check by the councilmen, each of whom is chosen by his own ward or district. He must conform his actions to their demands and to that extent he is not a free agent.

During the later years of the nineteenth century the people in some of the cities grew impatient with this type of government. They felt that there was too much pulling and hauling, too much tugging at the mayor's coat-tails when he set out to fulfil the expressed desires of the people. From time to time the voters put strong men in the mayor's office, only to find that their action availed little because the concurrence of ward politicians in the city council was necessary for almost every important executive act. So municipal reformers came to the conclusion that the independent powers of the mayor ought to be enlarged; and they began to urge this idea upon legislators and charter commissions wherever a change of city government was under discussion. They made slow progress at the outset but by dint of persistence they ultimately succeeded in persuading a few cities to curtail the council's powers. The results seemed in these instances to be favorable and eventually the "strong-executive" type of city government was adopted by a considerable number of cities. Today it exists in New York, Boston, Detroit, and many smaller municipalities. The essential features of this type of government are indicated by the chart or diagram which the reader will find on the next page.

2. The strong-executive type of mayor-and-council government.

It will be observed from this diagram that the strong executive plan of government departs from the older system in several important particulars. The mayor directly controls the whole field of administration. He appoints all the heads of departments and holds them responsible to himself alone. He does not need the council's permission to appoint or remove. His position is like that of the President in relation to the heads of the national departments. If anything goes wrong in municipal administration the mayor has the power to set it right. Likewise, under this plan of government, the mayor prepares the annual budget and submits it to the council. The council, however, is not always free to change the budget at will; in some cities it is not permitted to increase the appropriations under any circumstances; its authority is confined to making reductions if it sees fit. And even in such cities its action is subject to the mayor's

Its chief features.

260   THE GOVERNMENT OF AMERICAN CITIES

veto. Thus the council is ousted from all share in administration and becomes a mere ordinance-making body. In most cases it has also been reduced in size and its members are elected by the city as a whole, not by wards or districts.

Its advantages and defects. The advantages of the strong-executive plan are easy to appreciate. This arrangement puts an end to the old-time delay and

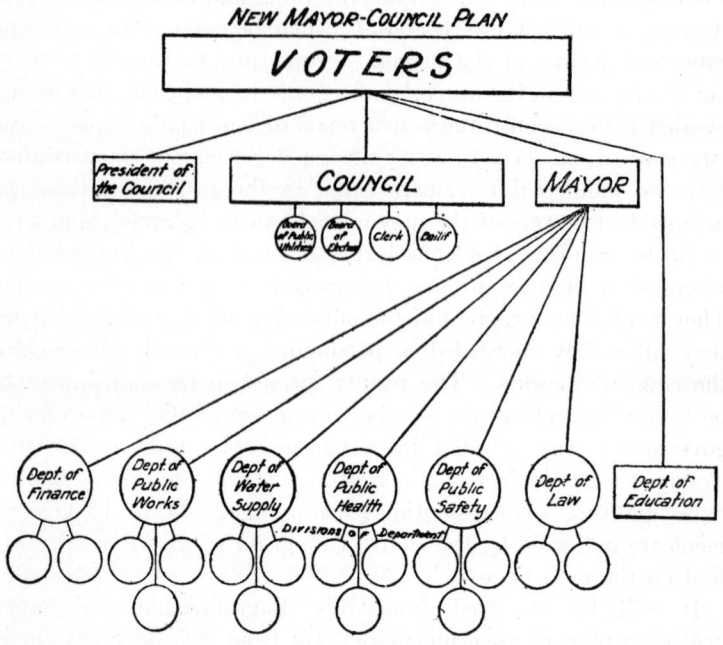

friction, for all administrative power is centralized. It gives the mayor a range of power that is commensurate with his position as chief executive. With the right type of mayor in office it assures the city an efficient administration. But the strong-executive plan of municipal government has the defects of its qualities. It reduces the council to semi-impotence and by so doing inevitably lowers the quality of its membership. Capable men will not become candidates for council when this body has no important functions to perform. The large powers given to the mayor, and the extensive patronage that he can distribute, are in the nature of a temptation to build up a strong personal or political machine, thus helping to ensure his own re-election. In some cities this danger is guarded against by a legal provision

THE FORMS OF CITY GOVERNMENT

which debars a mayor from being his own immediate successor in office; but this provision does not prevent his passing the office to one of his close friends whom he can continue to control. Mayors of the wrong kind will succeed in getting themselves elected from time to time, and when this happens under the strong executive plan, nothing stands between the city and a virtual dictatorship. Still, with all its faults and dangers, this form of government is superior to the older scheme of administration by checks and balances.

The foregoing were the only two types of city government existing in the United States down to 1900. Then a wholly new and somewhat revolutionary scheme of municipal organization made its appearance in Galveston, Texas. Although devised to meet a local emergency, and not intended to be permanent, this plan found such favor that it spread widely over the whole country during the next ten years. It is commonly known as the commission form of government. Today this type is established in Buffalo, New Orleans, St. Paul, Omaha, and many smaller municipalities. Its general features may be diagramatically set forth as follows:

3. The commission plan.

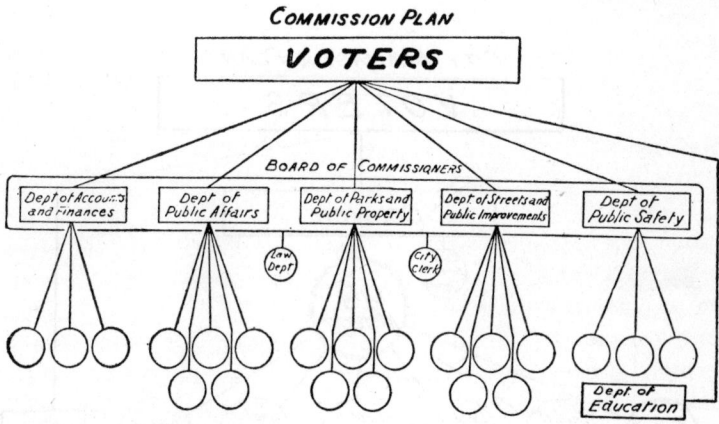

Simplicity is the keynote of the commission plan. Five commissioners are elected by the people of the city and they exercise all authority of whatever sort. There is no separation of executive and legislative functions. Each commissioner takes immediate charge of some one administrative department, but is subject to supervision and control by his fellow-commissioners. The

Its outstanding features.

same men prepare the budget, levy the taxes, spend the money, and appoint all officials. Thus the principle of checks and balances is relegated to the discard, utterly and absolutely. The commission plan became for a time the most popular and widely-praised form of city government in the country. It appealed to the imagination of the ordinary citizen by reason of its clean-cut simplicity. But it soon proved to have defects as well as merits and its career of conquest came to an end. During recent years there has been some reaction away from it. The story of the commission plan, its origin and spread, its achievements and its shortcomings, will be narrated in a later chapter of this book.

4. The city-manager type. Finally there is the city manager plan. It is the newest of the four types of government, having originated less than fifteen years ago. Several cities claim to have originated this scheme, but Dayton, Ohio, was the first large municipality to give the plan a trial. Other cities quickly followed Dayton; the city manager plan spread widely and it is still gaining converts. Cleveland, Cincinnati, Kansas City, and Rochester have adopted it within the past few years. Here is the city manager plan as it is customarily delineated:

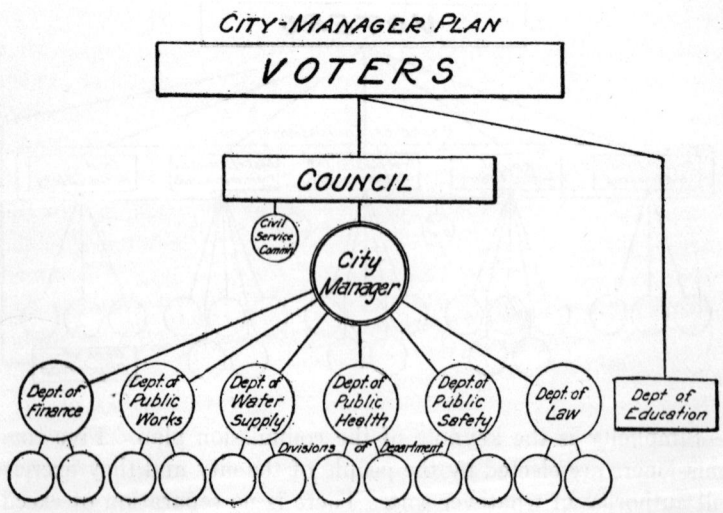

Its characteristics. Advocates of the city manager plan are fond of asserting that it is a business type of government, that it equips the city

THE FORMS OF CITY GOVERNMENT

with the same effective mechanism that is possessed by a well-organized business corporation. The people, as the stockholders of the municipality, elect a small council, commission, or board of directors. This body, in turn, appoints a city manager who directly controls all departments of administration. All responsibility is headed upward and inward to a common center. The city manager plan unifies the powers of government, yet it aims to preserve a separation between policies and routine, between planning and executing, just as a business organization does. In a word the plan rests upon the assumption that city government is business and not politics or philanthropy. This brief outline of the plan will at once suggest the drift of the arguments which are usually advanced in its favor, but there are some practical objections to the city-manager plan as will be indicated a little later on.

These are the four general types of government now functioning in the cities of the United States. No one of them can be designated as the best plan, irrespective of local needs and conditions. A good deal depends on the size of the city, its local traditions, and the nature of its problems. Two of the four types, however, seem to be losing ground at the present time—the limited-executive and the commission plans. The other two types are gaining steadily. They are gaining for the reason that they secure a concentration of power and responsibility which the other forms do not. The strong-executive and the city-manager plans both integrate authority, yet they do it by quite different methods, for the voters directly choose the mayor in the one case while the council appoints the city manager in the other. Not only this, but it is always taken for granted that the mayor will be a layman, whereas the city manager is assumed to be a professional, chosen because of his special training and experience in administrative work. This is a broad and fundamental difference. Summary.

Now the foregoing brief discussion of the various types of government may well suggest this question: Is the *form* of a government worth arguing about? Does it make much difference whether a city adopts one type of government or another? There are two opinions on this matter. Many students of the science of government have been inclined to accept the famous dictum of Edmund Burke that "the form of a government reaches

Is the *form* of government important?

but a little way." It is merely a scheme on paper, Burke said, and everything depends upon the men who put it into operation. There is something to be said for this point of view. Laws do not function in a vacuum. Governments are not automatons— to be wound up and left to run without care or direction. The human equation is always a large factor in rulership. It is a self-evident proposition that men of the wrong type can make any plan of government function badly, no matter what its intrinsic merits may be.

One view.

But this is only one side of the picture. There is a considerable body of opinion which holds that the form of a government is by no means of negligible importance. On the contrary it is deemed to be the real determinant of success or failure. "Give the city a workable form of government, embodied in an up-to-date charter," it is said, "and everything else will take care of itself,—men, methods, and results." It is all right to talk about putting good men in office, but no matter how good the men may be they cannot do satisfactory work unless provided with proper tools, and it is the charter that supplies them with the tools of their trade. The form of a government determines whether the men whom the people elect to office shall have power and opportunity, or whether they shall be checked and hampered at every turn. From this point of view it is argued the charter reconstruction is the first essential step towards a permanent bettering of municipal administration. Shorten the ballot, simplify the framework of city government, separate administration from politics, place experts in charge of the city's business—do these things and the problem of personnel will take care of itself.

Another view.

Here, after all, is the vital problem. How can we get good men into public office? And, having got them there, how can they be encouraged and enabled to produce results? There is a traditional Yankee way of answering a difficult question, which is by asking another—in this instance the question would seem to be: Why don't we have enough good men in municipal office already? It is everywhere conceded that we do not. The ablest men in any American community rarely become candidates and are even more rarely elected. Our city councils are full of men to whom no sophisticated citizen would entrust any private business of his own. Why should that be the case? The clumsiness of the municipal mechanism is in part responsible. When there are

The vital problem.

THE FORMS OF CITY GOVERNMENT 265

many officials to be elected the average is almost certain to be low. When the nomination procedure is complicated and irksome it serves to deter from candidacy all except those who make politics their profession. When the ballot is long, and when the names are arranged in party columns, it puts a handicap upon anyone who does not surrender his conscience to the party organizations. Finally, when the frame of government is badly constructed, with powers widely scattered into many hands, no participation in it is likely to attract men above the level of mediocrity. To improve the type of officeholder you must first raise the prestige of the office, which can only be done by endowing it with an adequate range of power.

So the form of government is not merely a matter for fools to argue about. The machinery of government is not constructed of laws alone, or of men alone. It is a composite of both. The two, moreover, are interdependent. A good form of government will more readily attract men of the right type into its service; it will also facilitate their work after they have been placed in public office. Conversely an unwieldy form of government serves to repel those whose participation is most to be desired, or if they do take office it ties their hands. This is not an empirical proposition, for it has been fully demonstrated by the experience of American cities that the more intricate and uncertain the provisions of a city charter, the more extensive are the opportunities for shunting inefficients upon the public payroll and for keeping them there despite all manner of incompetence. The rings and the bosses, the caciques and the bagmen of the ward organizations, one and all they dislike nothing more than to see the form of city government simplified, with power and responsibility concentrated in fewer hands. Its complications are to them a valuable asset, for everything that tends to make a government intelligible to the average citizen helps to take it out of the citizen's control. *Conclusion.*

Throughout the United States there is a traditional aversion to placing power in the hands of a few, howsoever they may be selected. Whenever the attempt is made to reduce the city council in size, to abolish superfluous boards, or to concentrate more authority in the hands of outstanding officeholders we are invariably met with the protest that government is being removed from the control of the people and made .less representative. *The fear of the few.*

Every attempt to simplify city government encounters this objection. There exists in the American mind a fixed delusion that the more officials you elect the more truly democratic your government is bound to be. The contrary would be more nearly true. The people really control their government in inverse ratio to the number of names on the ballot. All sound popular government is government by the few. When it becomes government by the many it ceases to be truly responsible. So the vital question is how most wisely to choose the few, give them sufficient power and hold them to a strict accountability. All the problems which relate to the form of government head themselves into this outstanding one.

REFERENCES

A discussion of the forms of city government in the United States may be found in Joseph Wright's *Readings in Municipal Problems* (Boston, 1924), pp. 151-169, William Anderson's *American City Government* (New York, 1925), pp. 310-340; W. P. Capes, *The Modern City and Its Problems* (New York, 1922), pp. 100-177; and C. C. Maxey's *Readings in Municipal Government* (New York, 1924), pp. 52-115. A brief discussion of the subject was prepared and issued by the Chamber of Commerce of the United States in 1923. See also the references at the close of the next three chapters.

CHAPTER XV

MAYOR-AND-COUNCIL GOVERNMENT

A. THE MAYOR

Among the four types of American city government the mayor-and-council form is the oldest. It was borrowed from England and adapted to the conditions and preferences of a new country. For a long time it was the only type of city government existing in the United States, but it underwent a gradual evolution in the course of which two species of mayor-and-council government were developed. The differentiation was based upon the amount of power lodged in the hands of the mayor. It may be well, therefore, to consider briefly the origin and growth of the mayor's office, for this development profoundly affected the whole American municipal system during a period of over one hundred years. *The oldest of the four types.*

The office of mayor originated in France, migrated to England, and was brought from England to America during the seventeenth century. For a time, in the new environment, the office was of little importance because no attempt was made to separate administrative from legislative functions. The sole organ of borough administration in colonial America was the borough council. Sometimes the mayor was appointed by the governor of the colony in which the borough was located; in other boroughs he was chosen by the councillors from among their own number; and in a few instances he was elected by popular vote, although this method was never in any borough a regular practice.[1] He held office for a single year but was frequently reappointed, and he served without pay. But he had no special powers. He was the presiding officer at meetings of the borough council and had a vote like the other members, but he had no veto over the council's actions and no authority to nominate or appoint borough officers. In a few colonial boroughs, notably *Evolution of the American mayoralty:*

1. In the colonial era.

---

[1] In New York he was appointed by the governor; in Philadelphia he was chosen from among the aldermen; only in the smaller boroughs was he ever elected, and even there not very often.

in New York and Albany, he was intrusted with certain minor functions, such as the licensing of taverns, the supervision of the market, the determination of petty suits at law, and the holding of coroner's inquests; but the pre-Revolutionary American mayor was not in any sense an independent administrative officer like his descendant of the present day.[1]

<small>2. After the Revolution.</small>

Nevertheless power soon began to drift into his hands. The Revolution and the adoption of the national constitution brought in a new theory of administration, which gradually wrought a change in the position and powers of the mayor. Ample evidence of this change appears in the Baltimore charter of 1797, which provided that the mayor should be chosen for a two-year term, by a miniature electoral college, the members of which were to be elected by the voters of the city, two from each of the eight wards. Only property owners were eligible to the office and the mayor was to receive an annual salary.[2] In all this the influence of the so-termed federal analogy appears very plainly. Even more distinctly it was shown in the extent and nature of the powers which the charter intrusted to the mayor. In the first place, the mayor's veto here made what is presumably its first appearance in a city charter; for one of the provisions permitted the mayor to veto any ordinance or resolution of the Baltimore council, with the limitation, however, that the veto might be overridden by a three-fourths vote. In the second place, the mayor was invested with certain powers of appointment, but his authority in this direction was closely restricted by the requirement that he must take all his appointments from lists submitted to him by the aldermen. Finally, by the terms of this charter, the mayor was charged with the enforcement of all the city ordinances; he might call for financial statements from the officers of the city treasury at any time, and he was authorized to make recommendations to the city council.

<small>The gradual assumption of new powers:
(a) The naming of the council's committees,</small>

Various other American cities obtained new charters during the closing years of the eighteenth century and the first two decades of the nineteenth, but none of them went so far as Baltimore in bending to the influence of the federal analogy. Even without changes in the city charter, however, the mayor

---

[1] For a more detailed statement of powers vested in the colonial mayor, see J. A. Fairlie's *Essays on Municipal Administration* (New York, 1908), 68-69.

[2] See *above*, p. 26.

MAYOR-AND-COUNCIL GOVERNMENT

frequently managed to increase his own authority. One way of doing this was afforded by his power to appoint the various committees of the city council. The city charters did not empower him to do this; it came from the council's own rules of procedure. Committees were necessary and the council merely authorized the mayor (as its presiding officer) to appoint them as a matter of convenience. The committees had no final powers, and at the outset had very little to do; but as the cities grew in size and as the council's business became more complicated, their work developed considerable importance. Having gained the power to appoint these committees, the mayor kept it and in this way was able to exert an influence upon the various branches of administration. When Josiah Quincy was mayor of Boston, for example (1823-1828), he made himself chairman of all the important committees; he presided regularly at their meetings, and virtually dominated their work.

From the power to name committees it was neither a long nor an illogical step to the power of appointing the regular administrative officials of the city, and mayors were presently given this right. At first its exercise was made subject to confirmation by the council, but even this check upon the mayor's discretion was eventually shaken off. Step by step during the middle decades of the nineteenth century the council lost and the mayor gained. In most cities he ceased to preside at the council meetings, withdrew to the seclusion of his own office, and took advice from his own political friends. When he had occasion to deal with the council he did so by sending written messages after the fashion of presidents and governors. Mayors lost no opportunity to stress this analogy, far-fetched though it was. Appealing to the established practice in state and national government, they sought and secured the right to veto the council's acts. With this advance the mayoralty was no longer a subordinate but a co-ordinate branch of the city government.

(b) The appointing of administrative officials.

How is the growth of the mayor's authority during the nineteenth century to be accounted for? Easily enough; the shifting authority from the council chamber to the executive office gained its impulse from two sources. On the one hand, there existed a popular conviction that the city council, being a deliberative or legislative body by nature, should not be permitted to control the administrative affairs of the municipality. Insofar as this

Why the mayors increased their powers during the nineteenth century.

conviction prevailed the mayors were bound to gain, for the administrative functions of American municipalities were expanding more rapidly than their purely legislative requirements. The inclination to follow a principle, so characteristic of the American mind in political matters, dictated that the new administrative functions, as they arose, should be given to the mayor. There was also a very practical consideration, namely, that the councils were doing their work badly while the mayors were performing their own functions fairly well. Councils delayed and evaded; mayors acted promptly and in the open. This greater efficiency of the mayor's work was natural, for councilmen and aldermen were elected by wards, invariably on a partisan ballot, and often by methods in which corruption played a large part. The councils, again, were unprovided with any official leadership, and the absence of recognized leaders within their own ranks gave the ward boss his opportunity. The subservience of the aldermen to invisible influences became everywhere apparent. Handicapped in these various ways the council was bound to lose in its rivalry with the mayor, and lose it did at one point after another. By the close of the nineteenth century the mayor had captured most of the strategic positions; he had become the head of the municipal system in fact as in name.

The movement went farther in some cities than in others.

Now, while this development of the mayor to a dominating position in American municipal administration can be clearly followed when one views the country as a whole, it never proceeded so far in some cities as in others. In places like New York, Detroit, and Boston the powers of the mayor have dwarfed into insignificance the authority of the municipal council; but in cities like Chicago and Philadelphia this is by no means the case, for the councils of these cities still retain a large measure of control over the administrative branch of city affairs. Hence it is impossible, in describing the position and powers of the mayor in American cities, to say anything broadly or without large reservations. There is, in fact, hardly a single statement concerning the jurisdiction of mayors in this country that would hold true of all the cities, and very few statements that would apply to even a majority of them. Nevertheless, the essential features of the mayor's office and its relation to the city council can be set forth in general terms, with due allowance for local conditions.

MAYOR-AND-COUNCIL GOVERNMENT 271

The American mayor (unlike his prototype in England and in France) is elected by direct popular vote. Candidates are nominated by the same procedure as is established in the various cities for the nomination of the other elective officers; the election is everywhere by secret ballot and a plurality of votes (except in a few cities that have adopted the system of preferential voting) is sufficient to elect. The term of office varies from one to four years. Some cities in New England continue the annual term, a relic of town-government days; but most middle-sized places throughout the country, and probably a majority of the entire number of whatever size, have a two-year mayoral term. Nearly all the larger cities have lengthened the mayor's term to four years. Among the latter are New York, Philadelphia, Detroit, Chicago, St. Louis, Boston, and Baltimore. Ordinarily the mayor is eligible for re-election but in a few cities he is not permitted to succeed himself.[1] This prohibition is intended to keep him from using the patronage of his office in building up a personal machine with the purpose of continuance in office.

The American mayor of today.

1. How he is chosen.

To be eligible for election to the mayoralty of an American city one must in all cases be a qualified voter. But in a few cities a minimum term of residence in the city is also exacted. Several cities have a minimum age limit, which is customarily fixed at thirty years. A few cities still retain the requirement that the mayor must be an assessed taxpayer. But no city requires the most important of all qualifications, namely, that the mayor shall have had some prior administrative experience.

2. Who are eligible.

Still, as a matter of practice, the men who are elected to the office are usually drawn from those who have already served the city in some other official capacity. In the larger cities this does not seem to be so common as in the smaller ones. It is not that men who have had no prior political experience are very often chosen as mayors of the larger cities; but the experience that most of those elected have had is not municipal experience. More often they are men who have become prominent in state or national politics. In a large city, the tenure of a subordinate city office does not give the occupant much publicity. Men who serve in such posts do not command the public eye or ear. They can become better and more favorably known by serving the

The prior experience of men who are usually elected.

[1] In Philadelphia and in Boston, for example.

nation or the state, or even the party organizations. Another good recruiting ground for mayoralty candidates is the office of the district attorney because this position affords a fine opportunity for getting into the newspaper headlines and making one's name known to the whole community.

Mayoralty elections. American mayoralty elections a generation ago were almost everywhere fought out on strictly partisan lines. Candidates were nominated by party conventions and were elected by the strength of the party organizations. The same is still true in some cities, but the maintenance of party discipline in municipal contests has become increasingly difficult during recent years. This is due to the spread of the non-partisan primary, the removal of party designations from the municipal ballot, and the simplification of the ballot in other ways. It is also the outcome of a popular disinclination to be guided in local elections by party principles or party platforms. The voters of American cities are nowadays inclined to be influenced by the personality of the candidate quite as much as by the label of any political party. Municipal campaigns are becoming less partisan and more personal. With increasing frequency it nowadays happens that Democratic cities elect Republican mayors and vice versa. In city elections there is a larger element of party independence than in state or national campaigns. The dominant party cannot be sure of winning with a weak candidate.

The mayor's powers:

1. In relation to the city council.
The powers which attach to the mayor's office are not easy to state in concise form, since they differ considerably from one city to another. They depend upon whether the city has the limited-executive or the strong-executive type of government. The mayor is commonly spoken of as an executive or administrative officer with no share in the legislative work of the city, but this description does not tally with the facts. It is true that he is rarely a member of the city council, but this does not prevent his having an important influence upon the council's action. For one thing, he may recommend measures to the council at any time. This he may do by personally appearing before it or by sending written communications. Of course the right to recommend does not in itself mean much, but it is a poor mayor who does not have some active supporters among the councilmen. These councilmen are consulted before the recommendations go forward, so that the mayor is able to feel out the prospects

MAYOR-AND-COUNCIL GOVERNMENT 273

before he acts. And in any case the average councilman stands to gain very little, either for himself or for his constituents, by incurring the mayor's displeasure. If he can bargain his support of the mayor's proposals for something tangible in the way of patronage he is under a strong temptation to do it. Hence, whatever the theory of the office may be, the actual influence of the mayor, even in matters of a strictly legislative nature, must not be disregarded by anyone who desires to know how the city's affairs are really handled, whether in the chamber or the ante-chamber. Through his intermediaries the mayor is sometimes a very influential participant in the making of municipal ordinances.

The right to send communications to the council gives the mayor one channel of influence over the course of municipal ordinance-making. But he has another channel of influence which is vastly more important. This is his right to veto the council's actions. The qualified veto power, as it exists in most American cities, is fashioned after the device which the framers of the federal constitution worked out in 1787 and which has since found its way into practically all the state constitutions as well. The usual provision in a mayor-and-council type of charter is that every ordinance, resolution, or order which has been duly voted upon must go to the mayor for his approval. If he approves the measure, he appends his signature and it goes into effect. But if he does not approve he returns the measure to the council unsigned, with a statement of his objections. This he must do within a prescribed number of days, otherwise his approval is taken for granted. When the measure comes back to the council, the latter takes a vote on the question of repassing it over the mayor's veto, the usual requirement for repassage being a two-thirds majority. Under normal conditions this is a difficult requirement to meet and the mayor's veto usually stands. The possession of this power has contributed greatly to the dominating influence of the mayor in all matters of municipal legislation. *The mayor's veto power.*

What are the merits of this executive participation in the process of municipal lawmaking? A distinction should be made, in any attempt to answer that question, between the mayor's right to recommend and his right to veto. The former is a power to which no serious objection can be raised, inasmuch *Merits and defects of the veto system.*

as the right to petition the council and to suggest action is one that every citizen possesses. That being the case, there is no good reason why it should be denied the mayor. But the veto stands on a different footing. It was devised by the framers of the national and state constitutions as a part of the mechanism of checks and balances. It was intended to provide a safeguard against the development of legislative tyranny. It was an application of Montesquieu's dogma that "power should be a check to power." Then, from the national and state constitutions, the veto worked its way down into the municipal system where no conceivable danger of legislative despotism existed at all. The natural safeguard against any serious abuse of governmental powers in the cities is the supremacy of the state, for the state legislature can apply the brakes when needed. The extension of the executive veto to city government was pure imitation, undictated by any real need or sufficient reason.

We have had a large experience with the veto power in cities the past hundred years, and many illustrations of its usefulness can be brought forward. Undoubtedly it has promoted the interests of honest and economical government in many cities upon numerous occasions. Without having this weapon at hand honest mayors would not have been able to prevent the wasteful granting of franchises, or the journeyings of council committees upon expensive junkets, or the multiplication of needless positions on the city payroll—all of which they have throttled at times by the use of their veto power. But a potential instrument for good can usually be transformed into an agency of harm; and the mayor's veto power has just as often been used unfairly, unwisely, or even corruptly. The mayor who sets out to browbeat a city council into submission, or to make political trades with it, finds in the veto a useful weapon. By vetoes or threats of vetoes he can bulldoze a council until its members are ready to seek terms and talk compromise with him. Mayors have actually done this in many cities and on numberless occasions. In such pitched battles between the mayor and the council the public interest stands little chance to gain. Business is delayed, the ultimate compromise satisfies nobody, and worst of all is the evasion of responsibility which the counter-play facilitates. The merits of the particular issue are always lost in the bedlam of recriminations and personalities.

MAYOR-AND-COUNCIL GOVERNMENT 275

Among the mayor's administrative powers the most important is that of making municipal appointments. It is still the practice, in many cities, to elect by popular vote certain heads of departments and members of boards, but the number of officials chosen in this way is much smaller than it used to be. There is a strong popular conviction that certain financial officers—the city comptroller and the city treasurer, for example,—ought to be directly elected in order that they may be free from collusion with higher authority. Members of the school board are also elected by popular vote in most cities, this method being maintained in order to ensure a representation of all classes in the determination of educational policy. The school board, in turn, appoints the superintendent and other school officials. With these and some other exceptions, however, the power to name the chief administrative officials of the municipality rests with the mayor. The mayor's appointing authority has been steadily widening in those cities which retain the mayor-and-council form of government. In commission governed cities, all appointments are made by the commission; under the city-manager plan of government, the making of appointments devolves upon the manager.

2. The mayor's appointing power.

When appointments are made by a city commission or by a city manager no confirmation by any other authority is usually required. But the mayor does not always have this freedom. In cities of the limited-executive type the mayor's appointments go before the city council for confirmation by that body and do not become valid until so ratified. This procedure is another illustration of the influence which the example of the national government has exerted upon city charters in the United States. The plan of senatorial confirmation in the case of presidential appointments has some distinct merits, but the analogous arrangement with respect to appointments by mayors has worked rather badly. This is largely because entirely different traditions have determined the practice of confirmation in the two spheres of government. The Senate of the United States, although constitutionally free to confirm or reject all presidential appointments at will, has used its prerogative or rejection sparingly. Not one appointment in a hundred, on the average, has been denied confirmation. In the case of members of the cabinet it has almost always confirmed the President's selections as

Restrictions upon this power.

a matter of course.[1] The Senate has taken the rational ground that since the President is responsible for the conduct of executive officers he ought to have a free hand in the selection of his immediate advisors and associates. City councils have developed no such tradition. They confirm or reject as the spirit moves them. If the mayor and the majority of the council's membership belong to the same political faction, appointments are usually confirmed without hesitation, no matter how poor their quality may be; but when these two organs of government are at variance the power to reject will be freely used upon good and bad appointments alike. Experience shows this to be the rule, although there are occasional exceptions.

<small>Defects of the system of council confirmation.</small>
The requirement of council confirmation was intended to place a check upon any mayor who might set out to build up a personal machine by placing his strongest supporters in immediate control of the city departments, with large amounts of patronage at their disposal; but it has not accomplished much in that direction. On the whole it has not prevented the making of partisan or inferior appointments. Council confirmation has afforded no security against the spoils system; on the contrary it has rather encouraged the bestowal of public office as a reward for partisan service. City councils, to a greater extent than mayors, have been under boss domination. In order to get their appointees confirmed, mayors have had to deal with the unseen hands behind the council. The worst vice of the system is the way in which it lends itself to the evasion of responsibility for unpopular appointments. When the press and the public cry out against any such action the mayor proclaims that the fault is not his, that he could not leave the office unfilled and that he was formed to appoint the obnoxious individual because the council would not confirm anyone else.

But despite the hollowness of the results obtained from aldermanic confirmation, cities are not easily persuaded to give it up. They are abandoning it very slowly. New York abolished the requirement in 1901; Boston followed eight years later. But Chicago, Philadelphia, St. Louis, Baltimore, and Los Angeles still retain it. The same is true of many smaller cities. There is a deep-seated conviction in the popular mind that it is dangerous to give the mayor a free hand in the making of appoint-

[1] There have been only three exceptions in the past hundred years.

ments, yet this conviction finds little or nothing in American municipal experience to support it. The wrong sort of mayor will manage to get the wrong sort of men into office, confirmation or no confirmation. New York and Chicago, under altogether different charter provisions, afforded good illustrations of this a few years ago. On the other hand, the right sort of mayor, in his endeavor to make the best sort of appointments, is almost certain to find the requirement of confirmation a serious obstacle in his way. It is an arrangement which affords inadequate protection against the bad and furnishes no incentive to the good. It is merely one of our various mechanical substitutes for official honesty, intelligence, and patriotism.

The third outstanding function of the mayor in many American cities (but not in the majority of them) is that of preparing a statement of estimates, revenues and expenditures, for submission to the council in the form of a tentative budget. Originally this duty was everywhere regarded as a legislative function, to be performed by the city council through its committees. It is still so regarded in English municipalities and in some American cities as well. But nowhere in American government has this plan of budget making given satisfaction and least of all has it done so in those cities where members of the council are chosen by wards. In such cases the process of budget-making has usually resolved itself into a chaos of sectional grabs. Even where the councilmen are elected at large the plan has lent itself to the evasion of responsibility for extravagant expenditures. There has developed in recent years, accordingly, a disposition to designate budget-making as an executive function and to vest it in the hands of the mayor. In a few cities it has been given to a special budget-making board with the mayor as chairman.[1] But whether the budget is prepared in the first instance by the mayor alone, or by a board constituted for this purpose, it must in all cases be submitted to the city council for its approval. To that extent the voting of appropriations remains a legislative function.

3. Powers in relation to municipal finance.

But the discretion of the city council or board of aldermen with respect to changes in the tentative budget, as laid before it, is not always unshackled. In New York the aldermen can

His relation to the budget.

[1] For example, the Board of Estimate and Apportionment in New York City.

reduce or strike out but cannot increase any item or insert any new appropriation. If they reduce or strike out any item, their action is subject to veto by the mayor, whose veto cannot be overridden in such cases save by a three-fourths majority. In Boston the council can take no action upon the budget submitted to it by the mayor other than to strike out or reduce items, and even here the mayor's veto applies and cannot often be overridden. In Philadelphia the council is free to amend the tentative budget as it pleases, the mayor's veto power being the only check upon its discretion. In Chicago the budget is prepared in the first instance by the finance committee of the city council, with the help of the comptroller, and is voted by the council before it goes to the mayor. The latter may veto the budget as a whole, or any part of it, but may not increase or reduce any item.

In the smaller cities the functions of the mayor, as regards the control of appropriations, display even more variation than in the larger ones just named. But the tendency is to place the preparation of the budget in the hands of the mayor and to reduce, step by step, the council's power to make additions to it after it has left the mayor's office. The right to strike out or to reduce items in a municipal budget is a hollow prerogative from the council's point of view. City councils, as a rule, are not greatly interested in eliminating or cutting down expenditures. Most councilmen are seeking public improvements for their own districts, or other things which involve increased outlays; they see no reason why money should be left in the city treasury when it might be "put into circulation." So, when the city council or board of aldermen is restricted to the power of making reductions, it can usually be counted upon to make no changes in the budget at all. Nevertheless, the right to reduce taxation is there if they want to exercise it, and the hallowed principle that "no taxes shall be imposed upon the people save by action of their representatives" is in theory preserved. For does not the tax rate depend upon the appropriations; and does not the council, by its acquiescence in the appropriations, assume the responsibility for fixing it? Meanwhile the real responsibility for both appropriations and the tax rate belongs, in many American cities, to the mayor.

Finally, the mayor has a variety of miscellaneous functions

and duties, including many of a social nature. He is charged with the general duty of "supervising" the administrative work of the municipality, but unless he has adequate power with respect to appointments, removals, and appropriations, this general grant of authority to supervise does not amount to much. The duty of approving contracts is also, in some cities, imposed upon the mayor; but charter provisions relating to the award of contracts have now become so strict that he no longer possesses much discretion in this field. Social duties of a varied character, welcoming distinguished visitors to the city, speaking at all manner of public and semi-public functions, listening to deputations and individuals who come with grievances or with requests and recommendations,—these things take up a great deal of the mayor's time. They leave him all too little for the careful and orderly consideration of strictly official business. *4. Miscellaneous powers of the mayor.*

The mayor's position as a party leader, or as the head of a political or personal machine, also provides work for him to do. No inconsiderable portion of his time, in some cities, is devoted to "keeping his political fences in repair." Some mayors give most of their time to political conferences, attending social functions and getting into the public gaze as much as possible. Others spend their working hours at a desk in an inner office and go out among the people as little as is practicable. Mayor Mitchel of New York pursued this policy, attending strictly to official business all day and every day. People soon began to say that he was cold-blooded as an icicle, a martinet, a recluse, a poor mixer. Mayor Tom L. Johnson of Cleveland went to the other extreme. He argued that a quarter of an hour each day was time enough for any mayor to spend at his desk, enough to sign important documents and to give general instructions. A competent secretary could do the rest. The mayor's place, according to Johnson was "out among the folks." Mitchel was by far the better mayor, but he failed to get himself re-elected while Johnson did it three times. *The mayor as a party leader.*

Although the salary which attaches to the mayor's office is fairly liberal, it rarely suffices to cover the numerous and heavy demands upon him. Very few honest mayors leave office with an increased bank balance, but they retire much richer in worldly experience. Getting elected costs something—often a good deal. Even though most of the campaign fund is con- *The drain on the mayor's purse.*

280   THE GOVERNMENT OF AMERICAN CITIES

tributed by personal friends or by political supporters, the personal expenses of the candidate are bound to be considerable. While in office a mayor is beset with requests for contributions from every source. Every philanthropic enterprise requests his endorsement and subscription. It is difficult to refuse them all, or even most of them, without acquiring a reputation for stinginess which it is good politics to avoid. It is a great asset to be rated by the people as generous and a good fellow. This makes for success at the polls while a reputation for counting the pennies does not. So the mayor who tries to do all that he is asked to do, and yet make both ends of his official salary meet, is bound to have a hard time of it.

Earning money on the side.

On the other hand, the opportunity to use his official position for private gain, directly or indirectly, is always open to any mayor who possesses a sufficiently flexible conscience. It is always possible for the chief executive of a large city to make considerable money in a roundabout way while keeping within the letter of the statutes. He can become a silent partner in some legitimate business enterprise, the success of which depends in part upon the friendliness of the public authorities,—a sewer-digging company, for example. He can use his advance information concerning proposed public improvement to dabble in real estate through the intermediary of his relatives or close friends. He can obtain tips on profitable investments from men in financial circles who desire to gain or to hold his favor. The channels of potential profit are many; whole pages might be filled in an enumeration of them.

A high office which is often poorly filled.

The exacting duties of the mayor's office, particularly in the bigger cities, call for a high degree of intelligence and judgment, a knowledge of men, and for habits of personal industry. But the method by which mayors are selected does not lend itself to the choice of men possessing these qualities. Personal popularity, even though it be of the bizarre type, counts for more at the polls than administrative capacity. The man who catches the ear of the people with an array of promises, or an ingenious appeal to their prejudices, is almost certain to get more votes than the one who disdains this method of electioneering. The mayor's position calls for a skilled administrator; what the city gets is a skilled politician. Even in the largest cities, where the mayor's powers are great and where so much depends upon

MAYOR-AND-COUNCIL GOVERNMENT

the making of wise selections, it is not often that the chief executive post goes to one who would be intrusted with any large amount of authority or responsibility in the field of competitive business. Surprisingly few men of broad gauge ability are ever elected. This is proved by the fact that they go no higher.

The office of mayor ought to be a training school for higher positions in the service of the state and nation, but it has not been so. During the past forty years we have had nearly three hundred mayors in the twenty largest cities of the United States. Exceedingly few of this large number obtained national reputations by reason of their skill or service, and these conspicuous exceptions merely illuminate the general rule. Grover Cleveland served one term as mayor of Buffalo on his way to the White House. Newton D. Baker, Secretary of War from 1916 to 1921, was twice mayor of Cleveland. Brand Whitlock was four times elected mayor of Toledo before his appointment to the diplomatic service. Calvin Coolidge, early in his long political career, served as mayor of Northampton, Massachusetts, but this episode had nothing to do with his later advancement in state or national politics. Senator Couzens of Michigan was once mayor of Detroit. A few others, less well known, might be mentioned if one were making a complete list. Some ex-mayors in different parts of the country have obtained a modest degree of distinction as state officials, judges of state courts, or congressmen, but even here the proportion of the total is small. How many mayors of New York, Philadelphia, Detroit, Cleveland, St. Louis, Boston, or Baltimore have risen to the post of governor during these forty years? In Chicago the promotion has happened only once during that time. Yet this ought to be the natural order of advancement. A term as chief executive in a great city ought to be the best possible preparation for the subsequent performance of executive duties in the state.

It has not been a good stepping stone.

Why is it that American mayors so rarely manage to go any farther upward in the public service? One reason is to be found, no doubt, in the fact that the mayor's office does not usually attract the type of man whose personality appeals to the rural voter. The garish brand of popularity which seems to count in the downtown wards does not make much impression upon the people of the upstate counties. The rural voter mistrusts the city, its motives, its methods, and its mayors. It is not a mere

Why mayors so seldom go further in politics.

accident that the political completion of the larger cities is so often different from that of the states in which they are located. The urban and the rural voter are inclined to look at things from different angles. The type of candidate that appeals most strongly to the one does not usually appeal to the other.

The popularity which carries a mayor into office, moreover, is as fleeting as a meteor. It may vanish in a day and in any event is likely to do so long before his term comes to an end. No mayor can satisfy everybody, especially among the politicians who hover on his flanks. The people of the whole city look to him for what they want and blame him for what they do not get. As a rule they give little attention to the work of the city council; it is the leadership and the patronage that interests them. In the state and national governments the legislative bodies bulk large; the public eye is turned towards them much of the time; they are convenient depositories for any responsibility the executive may desire to avoid. But in the cities this is not the case, at any rate not to the same extent. The mayor cannot so readily plead in avoidance, stand neutral, or evade. He must come out squarely on one side or the other, which means that he must create antagonisms. It may be replied that by taking firm ground and shouldering responsibility a mayor will gain as well as lose followers. This ought to be the case, but as a matter of practical politics it usually is not. Many of the questions upon which a mayor must pass final judgment do not interest the people of the city as a whole. They are of deep concern to neighborhoods, or to certain elements of the population, or to particular individuals. It is quite easy for a mayor to create many centers of resentment without gaining any counterbalancing appreciation from the citizens at large. That, indeed, is what the honest and capable mayor often succeeds in doing. He gains a reputation for being "no man's man" by diminishing his own strength as a vote-getter. Party leaders do not place a high valuation on the political availability of any mayor who follows his own counsel and pays no attention to the political consequences of his acts. They prefer one who is tractable, regular, easy to reach,—an "organization man."

So the mayor who harbors an ambition to go higher on the political ladder finds himself on the horns of a dilemma. If he works in harmony with the party leaders, the independents will set him down as boss-ridden or a "machine man." If he does not work in harmony with them, he will incur their wrath and opposition. In either case he lessens his chances of success as a candidate for any other public office.

Still we have had many notable mayors in our larger cities during the past forty years, men of strong and sometimes picturesque individuality. William J. Gaynor who served as mayor of New York City during the years 1910-1914 was successful in making himself a national figure. During his campaign for election he promised the voters that if he went to the city hall they would never have one dull, uninteresting day during his term. He was elected and kept his promise. Every day there was something worth a newspaper headline, although Mayor Gaynor was sometimes hard pressed to provide it. He was a great admirer of Epictetus, whose famous maxims he quoted almost daily for the intellectual refreshment of jaded New Yorkers. On the other hand, although elected by Tammany he was no henchman but formed his own convictions and never disdained to express them. New York has had many worse mayors than Gaynor and few that were better.

<small>Some notable mayors:</small>

<small>William J. Gaynor.</small>

Samuel M. Jones of Toledo, known far and wide as "Golden Rule" Jones, was, perhaps, the most striking American mayor of his time. He owned a factory, ran it according to the golden rule, but made it pay dividends nevertheless. It is hardly a tribute to our ethical standards that when he announced his candidacy on a golden rule platform the whole country laughed aloud and branded him as an eccentric. Theodore Roosevelt had the same platform, but he called it a "square deal" and nobody was amused. It makes a difference how you say the thing. Jones, at any rate, was elected and tried to put his precept into operation. He agreed that it would take a thousand years to do what he planned, and he did not live that long. His mantle descended to Brand Whitlock who combined practicability with idealism and left a record which entitles him to high rank among the mayors of his generation.[1]

<small>Samuel M. Jones.</small>

One might write a good deal that is interesting about the municipal kings of the past half century, but this is hardly the place for it. Seth Low of New York was a scholar in munic-

<small>Other mayors.</small>

---

[1] For Whitlock's appreciation of "Golden Rule" Jones see his *Forty Years of It* (new edition, New York, 1925).

284   THE GOVERNMENT OF AMERICAN CITIES

ipal politics and so was George B. McClellan who reigned by the grace of Tammany during the years 1906-1910. The two Carter Harrisons of Chicago, father and son, were skilled politicians who knew how to keep their fences up. Rudolph Blankenburg of Philadelphia and Henry Hunt of Cincinnati showed how hard it is for the temperamental reformer to make a satisfactory mayor. The redoubtable A. D. Ames ("Doc" Ames) of Minneapolis was the most resourceful and the least scrupulous of them all. He was mayor and boss combined. One can find infinite variety among the municipal executives of the past fifty years.

The future of the mayor's office will be interesting to watch. For fifty years it has been steadily gaining in power; today it has no counterpart in any other country. The mayor of New York City is the most powerful municipal officer in the world. Within his own sphere he is as nearly absolute as any monarch could be. He has more real power and patronage than pertains to the governor of any American state. One may hazard a query as to where this concentration of power will lead us if it keeps on.

B. THE CITY COUNCIL

Relations of mayors and councils.

The mayor is an outstanding figure in all cities that have the mayor-and-council form of government, yet in no American municipality is he all-powerful. The council is always to be reckoned with—to some extent. There was a time in American municipal history when the council was the chief and in fact the only governing organ of the city, but it has long since ceased to be the sole organ, and in some places it is no longer the dominant one. Still, in spite of its decline in power the council retains a remnant of its old importance and in many places it has a good deal more than minor functions to perform.

Importance of the council in earlier stages of municipal development.

The importance of the council as an organ of local government during the earlier stages of American municipal development arose from the fact that the colonial boroughs adopted the system of municipal government which then existed in England, a system in which the council ruled the town. It chose the mayor and made him its presiding officer, but it permitted him to do nothing without its own consent. American cities took this arrangement as a starting point and gradually moved away from it. As the mayor gained, the council lost. From being the chief factor in city government it slowly dropped to the status of a coördinate branch and in some cases to even less than that. Its old-time administrative functions were absorbed by the mayor. Its power to pass ordinances was curtailed by the interference of the state legislature. Its legislative authority was abridged by the introduction of the initiative and referendum. The history of the American city council during the past forty years is an almost uninterrupted chronicle of retreat.

Now it may be doubted whether this decline of the city council in the American municipal system has been altogether fortunate. No similar emasculation of the municipal legislature has taken place in any other country. While it is undoubtedly true that the larger part of what we call municipal government is administrative rather than legislative in character, it does not follow that general questions of administrative policy ought to be decided by the mayor or by any other administrative officer. In corporate business organizations all such questions are decided by the board of directors. So, in the conduct of public affairs, there are many matters of broad concern which ought to be decided by a board of the people's representatives. They ought to be decided, indeed, by a body which is large enough to represent all important elements among the people. And these fundamental matters, such as the levying of taxes, the voting of appropriations, and the borrowing of money affect the whole course of municipal policy.[1] *Comment on its decline:* *One important result.*

There is another aspect of the matter. When control over matters of general policy is taken from the city council it almost inevitably drifts into the hands of the state legislature. That is what has happened in many of the larger American cities; the council has been reduced in power until good men are no longer attracted to it. Then, when any question of large importance comes up we hear the business men of the city say: "This is too big a matter to be handled by a weak city council such as ours; it ought to be entrusted to a special commission or to the state authorities." As a practical matter there are only two alternatives. The policy-determining function in cities may be devolved upon the city council, or it may be arrogated by the *Another by-product of it.*

[1] For strong presentation of the case in favor of the city council see the article by E. Dana Durand on "Council Government versus Mayor Government" which is reprinted in Joseph Wright's *Readings in Municipal Problems* (Boston, 1924), pp. 331-350.

state legislature. There is no middle course. No city lets the mayor fix the tax rate, or appropriate money, or authorize loans. These are powers which, according to the American traditions of government, must be exercised by a body of representatives, by a legislature. The only question is which legislature—by that of the city or that of some larger area. Reducing the city council to a cipher is one of the surest way of transferring local government from the city hall to the state capitol.

Variety in the structure of American city councils.

In describing the organization and powers of the American city council it is impossible to convey a correct impression by using such general terms as are used abroad. We cannot say that American city councils are organized thus and so, or that they have such and such powers, for no two of them are alike. An accurate description of the New York board of aldermen would not in the least fit the city council of Detroit, nor would a citizen of Pittsburgh recognize the San Francisco board of supervisors as having any counterpart in his own community. There is a great variation all over the country in the size of the councils, in the methods of selecting their members, in their relations with the mayor, in council procedure—and most of all in the powers which the city councils possess. These differences are even greater than they used to be, for charter changes have been very numerous during the past twenty years and they have conformed to no general principle as respects the place of the city council in city government, unless it be the principle that the council's authority should be diminished wherever practicable.

Single and double chambers.

In most American cities the council now consists of a single chamber. Twenty-five years ago the bicameral system was very common; a great many of the more important cities maintained an upper chamber commonly known as the board of aldermen and a lower chamber which was usually designated as the common council. This arrangement, which provided the cities with too much legislative mechanism, was staunchly defended for many years on the ground that it provided a safeguard against hasty and unwise action. But the evils which went with it, as disclosed by the painful experience of one city after another, were eventually felt to outweigh its merits and the telescoping of municipal chambers has been going on steadily in recent years. Among the twenty largest cities of the United States, not one maintains the dual system; among the smaller cities the proportion is relatively small.[1] The widespread adoption of the two-chamber plan of council organization in the earlier part of the nineteenth century was another indication of the attempt to mould the government of the cities along lines marked out by the nation and the states. It was an unwise move in the first place; but not until the cities developed in size did the error become generally recognized. By that time the double chamber had firmly anchored itself as a municipal institution and its elimination has been a slow process.

The size of the council is not necessarily proportioned to the size of the city, although it happens that the two biggest American municipalities have the largest councils—New York with seventy-one and Chicago with fifty. St. Louis has twenty-nine councilmen and Boston has twenty-two. Philadelphia, although as large as both these cities put together, has only twenty. Only in rare cases do city councils have more than twenty members.[2] The tendency everywhere during the past thirty years has been to reduce the council in size as well as in power. There is a feeling that fifteen councilmen can do better work, with less waste of time and talk, than is likely to be done by a council of fifty.

Size of city councils.

On the other hand, the city council ought to be large enough to provide adequate popular representation, for unless this is the case there will be a persistent outcry from the unrepresented elements. Large enough to be fairly representative and small enough to do its work without suffering from unwieldiness—those are the essentials. The council should be big enough to attract councillors of varying types but not so big that it will degenerate into a debating society and thus repel from candidacy those who have no time to waste. At what point can this happy mean be found? In smaller cities one councillor for each 10,000 population ought to suffice. In the larger cities this ratio would make the council an unwieldy affair. Boston has one councillor for every 40,000 population; Philadelphia one for every 80,000; Chicago one alderman for every 55,000, New York one for every 90,000, and Detroit one councillor for every 100,000 population.

How large should a city council be?

[1] The chief survivors of the bicameral system today are Providence, Louisville, and Atlanta.
[2] The principal instances are Minneapolis (26 councillors), Milwaukee (31 councillors), Cleveland (25 councillors), and Providence (10 aldermen and 40 councillors).

This may seem to be a large block of people for one representative to represent, but bear in mind that every congressman, on the average, has a constituency of 250,000.

The term and remuneration of councilmen.

The usual term of councilmen in the United States is two years, but four-year terms are the rule in some cities, and three-year terms are not unknown.[1] In some cases a proportion of the membership retires annually. As a rule any qualified voter may be elected. In most of the smaller cities no regular salaries are provided (occasionally there is a fee per meeting), but in the more populous communities the practice of paying a stated annual remuneration to each member of the council has become general. The wisdom of this policy has been the theme of much controversy. On the one hand, it is pointed out that a councilman who takes his duties seriously must give a considerable portion of his time to the city. He must serve on committees and sub-committees. He must be at the beck and call of voters in his ward or district. Men who have themselves and their families to support cannot do this if there is no pay attached to the office. Or, if they do consent to serve, they are under a strong temptation to recoup themselves in some roundabout way—by getting contracts for their friends or by accepting sinecure positions on the payroll of some private corporation which is looking for favors from the city. When a city gives its councilmen or aldermen no salaries it is surprising how many of these officials manage to find some sort of private employment which yields good pay with no onerous duties. On the other hand, if a substantial salary is provided, the position of councilman is likely to be sought by professional politicians for its emoluments alone. It becomes a job worth seeking and worth holding. Some cities have tried the compromise of paying a moderate sum, not enough to make the position a shining mark for the political pot-hunters but sufficient to remunerate any honest citizen for the time which he gives to the city. But like most compromises this one does not appear to have given satisfaction to anybody.

Methods of electing councilmen:

There are several methods of choosing members of the city council, namely, election by wards, election at large, election by a combination of the two foregoing plans, election at large after

[1] For a table showing the term and method of electing councillors in various cities see William Anderson's *American City Government* (New York, 1924), pp. 352-353.

nomination by wards, election by preferential voting, and election according to the principles of proportional representation. Election by wards was practically universal fifty years ago and is still the practice in many municipalities. Under the ward system the city is divided into areas which are supposed to be approximately equal in population, and each of these elects one, two, or three councillors. Chicago has fifty wards, with one alderman from each. Philadelphia has twenty districts with one councillor from each. Wards or districts are purely arbitrary divisions, and their boundaries are altered from time to time as the population of the city changes. This redistributing sometimes affords an opportunity for gerrymandering or boundary manipulations in the interest of local politicians.

1. The ward plan.

Elections at large is the second plan. Ward lines are disregarded, and the councilmen are chosen by the voters of the entire city. This is a common method in the smaller cities; it is used by a few of the larger communities as well—notably in Detroit, Pittsburgh, San Francisco and Seattle. As a rule the whole council is not chosen at the same time but is partially renewed every year or every two years.

2. Election at large.

Both election by wards and election at large have something to be said in their favor, and both are in some respects open to objection. The ward system gives the voter a short and simple ballot; it ensures the representation of all sections of the city; it places in the council men who may be presumed to know the needs of their respective localities, and it makes virtually certain that both political parties will be represented in the council's membership. Among its defects it fosters a spirit of localism and lessens the emphasis upon the interests of the city as a whole. The American city is something more than a hodgepodge of neighborhoods; it is more than the sum of its wards. On all important issues there is, as a rule, a city-wide sentiment which will manifest itself if given a fair chance. The ward system breaks this into segments and helps to destroy its effectiveness. The councilman who owes his election to one ward will almost inevitably make its interests his own. If he represents the first ward, why should he concern himself with the interests of the ninth? His task is to obtain the largest number of advantages, in the way of public improvements, for the ward which elected him and to which, in due course, he will appeal for re-

Merits and defects of each plan.

election, if he wants to be re-elected. He is safe so long as he succeeds in getting appropriations for his own locality; he will not be turned out of office even though he lose the confidence and respect of nine-tenths of the voters in every ward but his own. If he helps his fellow-aldermen to get something in their districts, it is because he wants their assistance in getting something for his own. So the work of the council degenerates into a mêlée of trading and logrolling; the councilman who refuses to join in it will merely find his own district slighted; his opponents at the next election will raise a hue and cry that the district needs a more aggressive man. The ward councilman has a narrow duty to perform, hence the voters of the ward are likely to choose a narrow man, intellectually and politically, to perform it. For such a man it is not a long step from the representation of *local* interests to the representation of *private* interests; from serving the ward to serving some corporation, some contractor, some party boss, or some group of individuals who happen to be influential in the ward.

The ward system, moreover, often prevents the majority of the voters from getting control of the council. To get control of the council it is only necessary to win a majority of the wards, not a majority of the voters in the whole city. Wards are supposed to be approximately equal in population, but quite often they are not. Sometimes they are gerrymandered, and even when they are equal at the outset they may become very unequal within a few years by the shifting of population. Thus it frequently happens that although one political party can carry the city at large it finds that its ward councillors are in a minority.

The system of election-at-large is free from most of these objections. It helps to make the council's work a reflection of the entire municipal sentiment; it tends to draw better men into the list of candidates, and it encourages them to take a broad view of civic questions after they are elected. It raises the whole tone of the council's deliberations. In order to gain election and to secure re-election at the hands of the whole people, a man must have something more than the favor of his own immediate neighborhood. All this is to the credit of the system, but there are items on the debit side as well. If councillors are elected at large they may come almost entirely from a few sec-

MAYOR-AND-COUNCIL GOVERNMENT

tions of the city, some wards being regularly left without representation. All of them may be, are likely to be, from the dominant political party. The party which has a majority among the voters will nominate and elect its entire slate, leaving the minority unrepresented. This is not a mere possibility; it actually happens. Taking party designations off the ballot does not seem to prevent it.[1] Such a denial of representation to certain sections of the city and to the minority party is regarded as a real grievance by those who are immediately concerned. The system of election at large also increases the cost of securing election to the council because every candidate must conduct a city wide campaign. For these reasons two large cities (Boston and Los Angeles), which gave the plan a fair trial over a considerable term of years, abandoned it in 1925.

Is there any way in which the advantages of election-at-large can be secured without encountering these practical objections? Several plans have been tried. The simplest is the expedient of providing that although councilmen shall be elected at large, each must be nominated from a different district. This method has been tried in St. Louis and some other cities but has accomplished nothing worth while. Another plan is to divide the council into two sections, electing a part of the membership at large and a part by wards, say half the members by each method. The difficulty here is that a considerable enlargement of the council becomes necessary, for if the city has fifteen wards it must have a council of thirty members. Sometimes this objection has been overcome by having fewer and larger wards, or by diminishing the number of councillors elected at large. Milwaukee, for example, has twenty-five ward councillors and six councillors elected at large. Baltimore elects three councillors from each of six wards and only one at large. The preferential ballot, it was hoped, would provide a solution of the problem by allowing each voter to express on the ballot his first, second, and third choice among candidates, thus making possible a fair representation of the minority, but experience with it has

3. Combining the two plans.

4. Preferential voting.

---

[1] In Boston, for example, the Republicans form about 40 per cent of the total body of voters. Under the system of election at large only one Republican ever managed to get himself elected to the city council during the entire decade 1915-1925. In the latter year the ward system was restored and the Republicans at once elected nine councillors out of twenty-two.

292 THE GOVERNMENT OF AMERICAN CITIES

5. Proportional representation. been disappointing.[1] A system of election in accordance with the principles of proportional representation is receiving a trial in several American cities including Cleveland, Cincinnati, and Rochester. It aims to surmount the objections commonly raised against both the ward system and the system of election at large. There are indications that it will be successful in doing so. The plan has been explained in a previous chapter and need not be further discussed here.[2]

How a city council organizes. When a new city council has been elected its first duty is to meet and organize. This it does on a date fixed by the city charter. Thereafter the frequency of meetings depends upon the amount of work to be done. As a rule city councils meet regularly once a week or once a fortnight, but special meetings may be held when required. Business does not accumulate during prolonged intervals between sessions, as in the case of a state legislature. There are a few cities—Chicago and San Francisco are the most conspicuous examples—in which the charter authorizes the mayor to assume the post of presiding officer, but as a general practice the council is empowered to choose one of its own members for this duty.[3] He is commonly known as the president of the city council and has the usual powers of a presiding officer. The city clerk acts as clerk of the council and is usually chosen by it.

The rules of procedure. City councils everywhere determine their own rules of procedure, but in the United States this freedom is often circumscribed by provisions which have been incorporated in the city charter for the purpose of putting an end to sharp practices. The rules, which are usually printed in a small handbook for use by the members, have tended to become tricky and technical. The newly-elected councilman, until he masters the various twists and turns of procedure, is at a great disadvantage. The purpose of the rules, both in legislatures and councils, is to expedite business, to insure a fair and open consideration of measures, and to give the minority a square deal. As the rules are applied, however, they sometimes fail to achieve any of these pur-

[1] See the discussion of this in the chapter on Municipal Elections, *above*, pp. 194-195.
[2] *Above*, pp. 195-198.
[3] In New York City the president of the board of aldermen is chosen by the voters of the city at large, and the same is true of the president of the city council in St. Louis.

poses. When the minority members of the council desire to obstruct business, the rules make it too easy for them to do this, but when the leaders of both factions are agreed on any point the same rules facilitate the passage of measures without any real consideration at all. By "unanimous consent," or by a suspension of the rules, the council can rush important matters through its calendar at a single session with no opportunity for public protests to be heard. Then, by a well-known trick, reconsideration can be blocked. It is for this reason that the procedure of the council is now being determined, to an increasing extent, by definite provisions in the city charter.

Most of the routine work which a city council has to do is performed through standing committees. When there are two branches of the council, there are joint committees made up of members from each branch; but if either chamber has special functions apart from the other, that branch will also have some separate committees of its own. In a large city the council will have from a dozen to twenty committees, each made up of from three to nine members. The Chicago city council has no fewer than twenty-two regular committees; the San Francisco board of supervisors has nineteen. This means that each councilman must serve on two or three committees, and sometimes on a half dozen of them. The Boston city council, prior to 1925, had nine members and fifteen committees. This would seem to be the *reductio ad absurdum* of committee work. Some council committees are very influential bodies, with many questions of real importance to consider. Perhaps the most important is the finance committee, or the committee on appropriations; but the standing committees on ordinances, streets, police, health, water supply, sanitation and fire protection also have a great many important matters to deal with every year. The committees on publicity, statistics, pensions, sinking funds, public celebrations, and contingencies, have, for the most part, only perfunctory duties and often hold no meetings at all. In addition the council sometimes meets as a committee of the whole. This is sometimes done to facilitate the consideration of business, but quite as often the purpose is to exclude the public from the council's deliberations. City charters often provide that "all sessions of the council shall be public"; but this requirement is rarely applied to meetings of committees, hence the council when it

<small>The council's committees.</small>

<small>Division of work among them.</small>

desires to sit behind closed doors need only resolve itself into a committee of the whole.

<small>How committees are chosen.</small> How are council committees chosen? In a few cities (including New York and Chicago) a committee of selection is chosen by the whole body at the beginning of each year to frame a slate of regular committees; in San Francisco the committees are named by the whole council (board of supervisors) directly; but in most other cities they are named by the president of the council. This last named arrangement gives the presiding officer a great deal of patronage because the various councilmen desire places on major committees and there are not enough places to go around. Hence it is that the president of the city council sometimes gains his place by promising committee-chairmanships or places on important committees to those councilmen who are ready to vote for him. The committee slates, accordingly, are more often framed with a view to the fulfilment of the new presiding officer's pledges than with a purpose to secure upon the committees men who are best qualified to deal with the special matters that will come before them. Not only that but it is unusual for a councilman to serve two successive terms upon the same committee. A change in the party complexion <small>Weakness of the system.</small> of the council, or even a change in presiding officers, involves a general shifting of committee memberships. Every councilman, moreover, is looking for promotion to a more important committee or to a chairmanship. Consequently there is a reshuffling with the result that rarely does anyone stay on the same committee long enough to gain a good knowledge of the things with which it has to deal. Most members of these council committees have a real interest in the matters which come up for discussion at the meetings; they are impatient of details, bored by prolonged hearings, unwilling to investigate any question thoroughly, and intolerant of expert advice. This is not altogether surprising because so much of the committee work is routine in character and does not seem to be either interesting or difficult. Yet the fact remains that the council's own work is largely determined by the efficiency of its committees. It is in the committee rooms that both the best and the worst work is done.

<small>Powers of city councils:</small> The powers of the American city council defy any attempt at concise summary. In no two cities are they exactly alike and

MAYOR-AND-COUNCIL GOVERNMENT

even in the same city they change from time to time as the result of special legislative enactments. In most municipalities, however, except those which have adopted commission government, the powers of the council represent a residuum; they are no more than the remnants of a once-comprehensive jurisdiction which has been steadily dwindling during the last forty or fifty years. Such powers as still remain may be conveniently classified under the two heads of legislative and administrative authority; but as the former group is much the more important it should, for purposes of study, be divided into various subsidiary divisions.

The legislative powers of city councils extend, first of all, to such matters relating to the general structure of municipal government as are not provided for in the city charter or the general statutes. It may be laid down as a common rule of law that when any power belongs to a municipal corporation, and the city charter is silent as to the manner in which such power shall be exercised, the city council may determine the matter. This it usually does by ordinance; in other words, by enacting a local law or by-law. As a rule the city charter and the statutes cover all the essentials of municipal organization. They determine the structure of city government, the terms of officers, their compensation, and their duties; but if the general laws fail to make detailed provisions on such points the city council may do so by ordinance.

1. Legislative:
(a) Ordinances dealing with the structure of government.

In the second place, the legislative powers of the city council usually include the right to pass ordinances in exercise of the municipality's police power. Within this rather broad field is comprised suitable local legislation for the protection of life and property, as well as for the preservation of the public health and morals. Ordinances relating to traffic in the streets; the establishment of fire limits and the regulation of fire hazards; building laws; sanitary and health regulations; ordinances providing for the inspection of goods offered for sale or for standardization of weights and measures; restrictions upon the storage of dangerous materials; bill-board regulations; rules governing theatres and other places of amusement;—all these afford examples of the exercise, by legislation, of the local police power. Authority to make some of these regulations is now and then intrusted to some special administrative board. Traffic in the

(b) Ordinances under the police power.

streets, for example, may be put within the jurisdiction of the street commissioners or of the police authorities; the making of sanitary regulations is often turned over to the municipal board of health. But when such disposition has not been made by the city charter or by other statutory enactment, the power to regulate all these matters by ordinance belongs to the city council, subject, of course, to the general restrictions governing the validity of municipal ordinances.[1] In the larger cities the tendency has on the whole been to take more and more of this authority away from the council and to vest it in the hands of the administrative authorities. State laws, moreover, are steadily trenching upon the field, in some cases leaving very little to be handled by any city authority.

(c) Ordinances dealing with city finance.

The city council's legislative powers, again, include various matters connected with municipal finance. In most cities the council determines the annual tax rate, but it does not decide what property may be levied upon, this matter being almost always fixed by state law. The council often, but not always, grants exemptions and abatements in taxation matters. It also makes the annual appropriations. Sometimes these appropriations are put together into a budget and laid before the council by one of its own committees; more often the list is prepared by the mayor, and in a few cities, including New York, by a board of estimate and apportionment.[2] But however the appropriations may originate, they can become effective only with the assent of the council. The charters of a few cities, notably those of New York and Boston, provide that the council may in no case increase items in the budget and shall not even have a free hand in decreasing appropriations laid before it. In New York, for example, changes in the budget even by way of decrease may be made against the will of the mayor only by a three-fourths vote of the council; in Boston the council may in no case increase the estimates and, save with the mayor's approval, may reduce them only by a two-thirds vote. In most other cities the council may augment or diminish the appropriations, subject, of course, to a veto of such action by the mayor. The city council, again, continues to be an important factor in the exercise of the city's borrowing powers. All loan orders, whether authorizing

[1] See *above*, pp. 116-119.
[2] For a further discussion of this matter see *below*, pp. 453-454.

temporary or bonded indebtedness, must as a rule have its assent. The council, it is true, is not the only authority possessing the power to issue bonds on the credit of the city. Not infrequently the legislature gives this right to water boards, park boards, or other administrative boards. In general, however, borrowing projects must go before the council for consideration and in many cities they must also be approved by the voters at a "bond election" before any permanent indebtedness can be contracted.

Within the council's legislative jurisdiction, likewise, falls the determination of many general matters relating to the public utilities. As a rule the city council has authority, usually under stringent limitations prescribed by the state constitution or by statute, to grant such franchises to public service corporations as the convenience of the citizens may require, and to determine the duration of and detailed provisions of such franchises. On the whole, no municipal power has been more grossly abused than this. It is as a franchise-granting authority that the city council has often done its worst. Accordingly, in keeping with the usual policy of depriving subordinate authorities of any power which they show a disposition to abuse, many states have put stringent limitations on the franchise prerogative of the city councils. Sometimes by constitutional or statutory enactments they have forbidden the council to grant franchises for a longer period than twenty or thirty years, or they have made all franchise-votes of the council subject to a referendum. Sometimes, again, the legislature has arrogated to itself a part of the franchise-granting power and exercises it directly. The rôle of the city council in this field has everywhere become less important than it used to be. On the other hand, when the city itself owns and operates any public service, such as a water or a lighting plant, the council usually possesses the right to regulate by ordinance the terms and incidents of such service. In most cases the service is entrusted to a special board of commissioners and the council merely determines broad matters of general management. (d) Ordinances dealing with the public utilities.

Finally, there is a considerable group of miscellaneous matters to which the general legislative power of the city council extends and which are exercised by passing orders or resolutions rather than ordinances. These do not lend themselves to easy classification, but they include such things as the fixing of locations for city buildings, the acceptance or rejection of permissive powers (e) Minor legislation.

granted to the city by statute, the adoption of "orders" requesting the mayor or other administrative authorities to supply information, the holding of investigations, the passing of resolutions which indicate the city's attitude in matters of pending legislation, and so on.

The output of ordinances. Despite its narrowed authority, therefore, the average city council deals with a great variety of matters and it is not surprising that its annual output of municipal ordinances, orders, and resolutions is very large. The revised ordinances of Chicago make up two solid volumes of over a thousand pages each. Every year a good-sized folio document is required to promulgate new ordinances and amendments to old ones. No limit is fixed either by law or by public opinion to the number of ordinances that a city council may enact on matters within its purview; the only requisites are that the measures shall all be enacted in due form and shall not be unreasonable or oppressive in character but general in their application and consistent with the national and state constitutions as well as with the general or special laws. A city ordinance is the lowest rung in the ladder of jurisprudence. It must not be in conflict with any one of the five superior grades of law, namely, the federal constitution, the federal laws, the state constitution, the state laws (including the city charter) and the common law. How can one tell whether some proposed action of the city council is repugnant to any one of these? Only a lawyer can give an accurate answer to such a question, and he cannot do it until after he has made a study of the matter. Even then he cannot always be sure of his opinion. City councils rarely act on any new project without first getting an opinion as to legality from the city's law department. As for the ordinary citizen, he is presumed to know both the laws and the ordinances of the community in which he lives, notwithstanding the fact that they are numbered by the thousand!

2. Administrative powers. So much for the council's legislative authority. In the second place there are the administrative powers of city councils. As a matter of political theory city councils ought to have no administrative power, but as a matter of fact they do possess a good deal of it and in many cities this part of their work is of much importance. In some cities, both large and small, the council still retains the right to make appointments to certain municipal offices, but the number of such posts has been dwindling.[1] In most cases the appointments are now made by the mayor but with the provision that they must be confirmed by the city council before they become valid. This is the case in Chicago, Philadelphia, and Los Angeles, for example, but not in New York or Boston. In the latter cities the mayor does not need the council's consent. The merits and faults of council confirmation have been already discussed,[2] but wherever it exists it gives the council a power of great importance. Indeed, the chief difference between the limited-executive and the strong-executive type of city government is that the council can control the mayor's appointments in the one and cannot in the other. *(a) Appointments and confirmation of appointments.*

In some cities the council's consent is also essential before certain contracts can be awarded—such as contracts for street lighting or for garbage removal. Most city councils have the right to require stated reports from the various administrative departments when they choose to do so. These powers are not intended to give the council any right of interference in the direct administration of city departments, but not infrequently they have been made to serve this purpose. As the official records have more than once disclosed, a large part of the time of a city council may be spent in discussing questions relating to increases in the pay of city employees, or hours of labor in the municipal service, or the purchase of supplies—all of which lie outside its proper sphere. What the council cannot bring about as a body, moreover, individual councilmen usually manage to secure. They spend their time besieging the mayor and the heads of departments to appoint their friends to places on the city payroll, to give out minor contracts to political supporters, or to order supplies from favored stores. If heads of departments, trying to perform the duties laid upon them by law, refuse such appeals, their official lives are made miserable by attacks at council meetings. In this fashion the wrong sort of councilman is often able to exert an influence in departmental administration which the city charter never intended him to possess. *(b) Other administrative functions.*

The reason, of course, is not far to seek. The councilmen are interested in patronage, and patronage is administrative, not legislative. Councilmen who confine themselves strictly to legislative work find little that excites their real interest and equally *The quest for patronage.*

---

[1] The city clerk, for example, is usually chosen by the council.
[2] See *above*, pp. 275-277.

little opportunity to augment their own political strength. It is not often that anyone wants a favor by way of an ordinance. What a councilman's friends and supporters want him to get for them are jobs, contracts, orders for merchandise, and special privileges, all of which are known by the general name of patronage. The power to influence the patronage is what the councilmen in most cases are after, and they reach for it hungrily even when charter provisions have tried to put it far beyond their grasp.

What the principle of separation of powers has involved.

The principle of separation of powers, as applied to local government, has come to mean that the city executive shall have most of the honor, the power, and the patronage, while the city legislature (the council) shall have what is left. The whole trend has been in the direction of reducing the council to a body which makes a few ordinances from time to time, passes the appropriations with no power to increase them in amount, authorizes borrowing when necessary, and importunes the mayor for the crumbs of patronage that drop from his table.

A continued decline is probable.

It is unfortunate that this should be the case, yet one is reasonably safe in predicting that under the mayor-and-council form of government the council is likely to reach an even lower plane as time goes on. The limited-executive type is slowly giving way to the strong-executive type. This seems inevitable so long as we continue to take power away from the councils because the quality of their membership is so poor, and thus lower the quality still further. It is not a vicious circle that is being followed but a downward spiral.

City councils and boards of aldermen in the larger cities do not embody a very high type of intelligence or of fidelity to a public trust. Make a list of the membership, showing the occupation of each, and you will find for the most part an array of vocations which do not prefigure competence or success as the world reckons it. Make a table showing the amount of taxes which the councillors or aldermen pay into the city treasury each year. The total will probably be less than the annual salary of the lowest-paid stenographer in the poor-relief department. The council chamber attracts few men of initiative, resourcefulness, substance, and education. It offers them, under present conditions, too little scope for effective service to the community.

REFERENCES

On the mayor's share in the mayor-and-council form of government the best book is Russell M. Story's *American Municipal Executive* (Urbana, 1918). Various autobiographical volumes, notably Brand Whitlock's *Forty Years of It* (new edition, New York, 1925), and Tom L. Johnson's *My Story* (New York, 1911) contain interesting material on the actual work and problems of the mayor's office. A series of biographical sketches, covering several recent mayors, may be found in the files of the *National Municipal Review* for 1926.

There is a good chapter on the city council in William Anderson's *American City Government* (New York, 1925), pp. 341-387, and a discussion of the subject may also be found in C. C. Maxey's *Readings in Municipal Government* (New York, 1924), pp. 56-79. E. Dana Durand's notable essay on "Council Government versus Mayor Government" is reprinted in Joseph Wright's *Selected Readings in Municipal Problems* (Boston, 1925), pp. 331-350. A series of articles on American city councils may be found in the files of the *National Municipal Review*, 1924-1926.

CHAPTER XVI

THE COMMISSION FORM OF GOVERNMENT

The old system of city government by checks and balances.

In the last chapter an outline has been given of what may be termed the orthodox form of American city government. This mayor-and-council type of government rests firmly upon the principle of "separation of powers" even as the national and state governments rest upon it. The idea that executive and legislative authority ought to be kept separate is one that permeated every field of American government during the nineteenth century. It was carried into the government of even the smallest cities—where its application was an absurdity. The doctrine of separation of powers, or of "checks and balances" as it is more often called, was devised as a safeguard against tyranny in national governments. It was based on the ancient fear of kings. It was never intended to be used for anything else, and certainly not as a means of securing efficiency in local administration. Yet so strongly did this principle become embedded in minds of the American people that until about twenty-five years ago hardly anyone ventured to question its validity. It developed into a sort of biological inheritance, accepted by one generation after another. Every schoolboy learned that the chief desideratum in all government was to keep each branch of it balanced and checked and separated. Otherwise some official might find himself endowed with power to act on his own initiative and responsibility!

The first departure from it.

So far as city government is concerned no dent was made in this doctrine until after the turn of the twentieth century. Even then the shift in public opinion was brought about by an accident. No city avowedly repudiated the principle of checks and balances, but one municipality, on the morrow of a great disaster, provided itself with a plan of government in which the principle found no recognition. This city was Galveston, Texas, which in 1901 established what has since come to be known as the commission form of government.

THE COMMISSION FORM OF GOVERNMENT

Galveston is the chief seaport of Texas and one of the leading commercial centers of the South. Its population in 1900 was about 37,000, of whom nearly a fourth were negroes. The government of the city was no better, and perhaps no worse, than that of many other American communities of its size and type. The old Galveston charter provided for a mayor, various elective officials, and a board of aldermen (elected by wards), each with independent powers. Each was intended to be a check upon the others. Elections were conducted on a partisan basis and the Democratic candidates invariably won by a large margin. There was no merit system of appointment, no executive budget, no provision for the use of business methods in the city departments. All varieties of municipal mismanagement were cheerfully tolerated at the city hall. Politicians monopolized the offices; they put their own friends on the city payroll; the debt was large; the citizens got poor service; and the accounts never balanced at the end of the year. Annual deficits were the rule, and these were regularly liquidated by the issue of bonds. Thus the shortcomings of each administration were passed along to the next. The city debt was increased three million dollars during the years 1890-1900 by this practice of borrowing to cover annual shortages. From time to time the heavier taxpayers and the business organizations raised an outcry against the way in which the city's affairs were being conducted, and on more than one occasion started a "reform" movement, but the practical politicians were well intrenched behind their barrier of checks and balances, hence the insurrections accomplished nothing. After a number of these futile attempts to get a "business administration" into office, the better elements of the citizenship became discouraged and resigned themselves to the conclusion that municipal government was an affliction which must be borne because there was nothing else in sight.

Galveston's experience.

Then the disaster came. On September 8, 1900, a hurricane drove in from the Gulf of Mexico and carried a tidal wave over the city. Bridges were swept away, streets were torn up and great strips of wood-block pavements floated off to sea like life rafts. The water supply and sewer systems were put out of commission and badly damaged; the lighting plant was wrecked; schoolhouses and fire stations were demolished by the violence of the tidal impact. When the waters receded the city was a

The tidal wave of 1900 and its sequel.

desolation of rubbish and sand. More than one-third of all its shops and dwellings had been destroyed. About six thousand persons, more than fifteen per cent of the population, lost their lives. Twice as many more were injured or rendered homeless.

This overwhelming disaster naturally put the existing city government to the severest kind of test. It was imperative that relief on a large scale should be organized; that the streets and public buildings should be rebuilt; the water, sewerage, and lighting plants restored, and adequate measures taken (such as the building of a sea-wall) to prevent recurrence of the catastrophe at some future time. But the existing city government, as anyone might have foreseen, proved itself helpless and hopeless when brought face to face with so stupendous a task. Its utter incompetence was quickly revealed, as a flash of lightning illumines the earth on a dark night. While the city lay prostrate its mayor and aldermen fell to wrangling as to who should have the contracts for clearing away the ruins! Meanwhile an exodus of the surviving population began; people sold their properties to speculators at sacrifice figures and crowded the outgoing trains. The city treasury was empty, of course, and the treasurer had to default the interest on the city debt when it became due. Under such conditions it was apparent that no new funds could be obtained from banks or investors for relief, for reconstruction, or for any other purpose. The city was to all intents bankrupt and there seemed no alternative but to place it in the hands of a receiver like a bankrupt railroad or factory.

<small>The new plan for governing the stricken city.</small> It was at this point that some of the city's leading business men stepped in. Ignored by the politicians in the years preceding the disaster they were now called upon to save the situation. That is what often happens. In times of good fortune and tranquillity the politicians are allowed to run things in their own way, but when war or famine or disaster of any kind comes there is a shout for the big business men, the trained executives, to come and serve as food administrators, or fuel administrators, or wherever the most critical needs may be. Fortunately there existed among the merchants, manufacturers, bankers, and shippers of Galveston an organization which had been formed to secure the improvement of the harbor, and this body was prevailed upon to step into the breach. A committee representing the business men of the city hurriedly drafted a plan for the

THE COMMISSION FORM OF GOVERNMENT 305

temporary abolition of the old municipal system and the substitution of government by a state commission. "It is a question of civic life or death," they said.[1] This proposal, in the form of a special statute, was presented to the Texas legislature and in April, 1901, was enacted.

At one stroke the measure abolished every branch of the old municipal organization. In place of the mayor, aldermen, boards, and officials, it set up a commission of five citizens with pretorian powers.[2] The commission was authorized to pass ordinances, to make appropriations, to levy taxes, to borrow money, to administer the various departments, to grant franchises, to award contracts,—in a word to exercise all the powers of the municipal corporation. A noteworthy feature of the Galveston plan was the stipulation that the commissioners should apportion the various functions of administration among themselves, each commissioner becoming the head of a department.[3] Legislative and administrative functions were thus combined in the same hands, the old doctrine of checks and balances being simply ignored out of existence.

An outline of it.

It should be made clear that this plan was not intended to

[1] In a statement accompanying the measure its sponsors set forth the gist of the matter as follows: "We believe that municipal government, as it has been administered in this community for the past twenty years, is a failure. It did not require the storm to bring a realization of this fact, but it brought it home with greater force upon us. We are seeking relief from the municipal destruction and despair staring us in the face. It is a question with us of civic life or death. . . . We are asking for a charter placing the entire control of the local government in the hands of five commissioners, designed to benefit the people rather than to provide sinecures for politicians."

[2] As originally passed by the legislature in 1901 the statute provided that three of the commissioners should be appointed by the governor of Texas and two elected by the voters of Galveston. But after the commission had been constituted in this way, and had begun its work, the constitutionality of the statute was attacked in the courts. The Supreme Criminal Court of Texas, in March, 1900, held that the legislature had no power, under the Texas constitution, to authorize the appointment of municipal officers, with powers to exercise police jurisdiction, by the governor of the state (*ex parte Lewis*, 45 *Texas Criminal Reports*, 1). Thereupon the legislature amended the Galveston charter making all the commissioners elective and the voters of the city forthwith elected the three commissioners who had been in office by virtue of the governor's appointment. In its final form, therefore, the Galveston plan provided for the election of five commissioners by the voters of the whole city.

[3] Four departments were created, namely, finance and revenue, water and sewerage, police and fire protection, and streets and public works. One of the commissioners was placed at the head of each. The fifth commissioner was named mayor-president and took no department but was charged with a general supervision over the entire field of administration.

Success of the venture.

provide a permanent scheme of city government for Galveston, much less a model for adoption by other cities. It was an emergency arrangement, devised to meet a situation where the question of "civic life or death" was involved. The Texas legislature consented to it reluctantly, with a tacit understanding that when normal conditions had been fully restored the old form of government would be re-established. This, however, was not what happened. The success of the Galveston commission was so notable that the citizens were much impressed by it. In a remarkably brief space of time the commission secured from Congress its help in the construction of a great breakwater, and as a further precaution it raised the ground level of the entire city. It repaved the streets, reconstructed the public buildings, and put the municipal utilities into service again. All this necessitated the floating of large loans; but by drastic economies in the current expenses of the city the commission was able to keep the tax rate within bounds. Sinecure offices were abolished; various channels of leakage and waste were closed; the city's business methods were improved, and the whole administration toned up. Within five years Galveston was a far better community than it had been before the storm. So astonishing was the improvement that all thought of restoring the old municipal system disappeared.

Nation-wide interest in the Galveston plan.

Meanwhile the "Galveston plan" attracted attention in other communities. Newspapers and magazines interested themselves in this miracle of municipal administration. Some of them sent special correspondents and write-up men to get what seemed to be a good story, the story of a city that "came back,"—and Galveston presently became the most widely advertised place in the country. Municipal reformers in other states took up the cue, for here was an opportunity to talk facts, not theories. What had been done in Galveston, they argued, could be done elsewhere. In many cases they found ready listeners and the plan began to spread. Des Moines was the first northern city to follow Galveston's lead.[1] From the Iowa capital it moved both east and west, overturning the old municipal system like a setup of ninepins.

---

[1] The Des Moines plan differed somewhat from that established in Galveston and was generally regarded as an improvement over the latter. It provided for the nomination of the commissioners by a non-partisan primary, for civil service reform, and for the initiative, referendum and recall.

THE COMMISSION FORM OF GOVERNMENT 307

The spread of the commission plan during the years 1907-1914 was extraordinarily rapid. Politicians who had grown accustomed to the traditional apathy of the people in matters affecting city government were frankly bewildered. They protested, as usual, that the plan was dangerous, un-democratic, socialistic, un-American, a return to the ancient Greek form of government by tyrants. But public opinion did not pay much heed to these jeremiads, and in one city after another the voters adopted the new plan when they got the opportunity.[1] Mayors, councils, and boards retreated as though they were sections of the Hindenburg line. In 1910 more than a hundred cites of all sizes had established the commission form of government; two years later the number had more than doubled; in 1914 the total had passed four hundred.[2] There had never been anything like it in American history. For a time it seemed like an impending general sweep of all the cities, both little and big. But presently the stampede began to lose its momentum and the movement came to a halt during the war years, 1918-1919. Since that time the

Its spread elsewhere.

[1] Many of the states enacted general laws permitting any city to adopt the commission form. Today there are only four states (New Hampshire, Vermont, Rhode Island, and Delaware) in which the establishment of commission government is not authorized by general law.
[2] The appended chart shows the course of the movement:

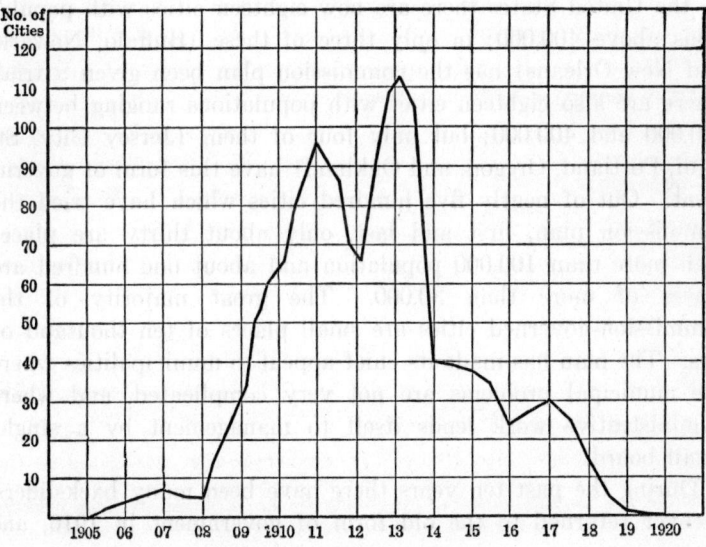

commission form of government has made relatively few converts. It has, in fact, lost ground and is still losing. The drift of public sentiment is now running towards the city manager plan, an outgrowth of the commission form, which will be explained in the next chapter.

<small>Sections of the country in which it made most progress.</small>
It is interesting to note the sections of the country in which the commission plan of city government made its greatest progress. Although originating in Texas it did not make much headway among the cities of the southern states, taking them as a whole. Its chief strength developed in the Middle West, in New England, and on the Pacific slope. In the Middle Atlantic states, with the exception of New Jersey, it did not gain much ground. The same is true of the South Atlantic region, with the exception of South Carolina. In the Southwest, particularly in Kansas, the commission plan caught the favor of the people, as it also did in the Northwest; but in neither of these regions was there any clean sweep of the old charters. Pennsylvania and New York seemed to be relatively impregnable. This unevenness in the degree of welcome accorded to the new plan in different parts of the country is not easy to explain for there were various currents and cross-currents at work.

<small>Present status of the commission plan.</small>
It is significant, moreover, that the commission plan made its greatest gains in the smaller and medium-sized communities. In the United States there are now eighteen cities with populations above 400,000; in only three of these (Buffalo, Newark, and New Orleans) has the commission plan been given a trial. There are also eighteen cities with populations ranging between 200,000 and 400,000; but only four of them (Jersey City, St. Paul, Portland, Oregon, and Oakland) have this form of government. Out of nearly five hundred cities which have tried the commission plan, first and last, only about thirty are places with more than 100,000 population and about one hundred are places of more than 30,000. The great majority of the commission-governed cities are small places of ten thousand or less. The plan has made its chief appeal to municipalities where the municipal problems are not very complicated, and where administrative work lends itself to management by a single, small board.

<small>The reaction.</small>
During the past ten years there have been many backsliders. Denver returned to the old form of government in 1916, and

THE COMMISSION FORM OF GOVERNMENT 309

its example has been followed by several smaller cities; but Buffalo and St. Paul, some years later, defeated proposals to abolish the commission plan.[1] In general there has been no widespread tendency to restore the old mayor-and-council system; the inclination is to move forward to the commission-manager or city-manager plans of government, thus taking what many believe to be the logical next step toward a more efficient plan of municipal organization.

While the commission plan is not uniform in all the cities working under it, the variations are of relatively small consequence. The essential feature of the plan is a commission of five members elected by the people.[2] The commissioners are elected at large for a term of two or four years and are usually paid for their services.[3] One of the five commissioners serves as chairman of the commission and is customarily given the title of chairman or mayor.[4] According to the original commission plan, as established in Galveston, the chairman or mayor was given no veto power and no authority to make appointments; his duties were to preside at meetings of the commission and to keep an eye on the general course of the administration, nothing more. This arrangement has not been strictly followed by other cities, some of which give the mayor additional powers.[5] In any event each commissioner (usually including the mayor) takes charge of a group of administrative functions. As there are only five commissioners, there can be only five departments or groups of departments, no matter how numerous or varied the city's administrative activities may be.[6]

General features of the plan.

[1] In Buffalo the attempt was negatived by a municipal veto of a legislative act to abolish the commission plan. In St. Paul the proposal was defeated at the polls.
[2] Occasionally the membership is fixed at three or seven; but five is the usual number.
[3] The salary varies with the size of the city. In New Orleans the mayor receives $10,000 and the other commissioners $6,000 each; in Buffalo the figures are $8,000 and $7,000; in Galveston $2,000 and $1,800.
[4] It was originally intended that the commissioners, after their election, should choose one of their own members as chairman or mayor. The more common practice now is to have the people choose the mayor directly.
[5] In some cases the mayor has been given the veto power, as in St. Paul, or the power to appoint the city officials, as in Houston, Texas.
[6] The usual grouping is somewhat as follows: Public Works, Public Health, Public Safety, and two other groups which may be either Accounts and Finance, Public Affairs, Public Property, Public Utilities, or Public Welfare. Various combinations of functions are possible. The apportionment of duties among the commissioners may be done in any one of three ways, namely, by the direct election of commissioners to specific commis-

It is now more than twenty-five years since the commission plan originated in Galveston and more than twenty years since it made its way into various other cities. This interval has been sufficient to afford the system a fair trial under diversified conditions and to permit some appraisal of the results obtained. Those who have observed the workings of the plan at close range will not deny that it has some real merits and some serious defects —which is a roundabout way of saying that it is like most other governmental devices. There is this to be said of the commission plan, however; its advantages are on the surface where they can readily be appreciated by the average voter, while its defects do not become apparent at first glance. It is an instrument of government which does not seem to improve with use.

What are these advantages and defects? The most obvious merit of the commission plan is its simplicity. It eliminates the diffusion of powers and responsibilities which the mayor-and-council type of city government has often carried to an extreme. There is but one governing authority,—the commission,—all municipal powers are exercised by it alone.[1] There are no checks and balances in commission government. The value of this simplicity and concentration is self-evident. Public attention, like a spotlight, can be focussed upon one governing body, for there is only one. There is no shifting of responsibility from one body of officials to another until the people lose sight of it altogether. There is no opportunity for a lot of officials to point fingers at one another and say, "It's you, not me" when things go wrong.

Being simple, the commission plan of government is intelligible. One does not need to dig into learned treatises or write a thesis in order to understand it. Mayor-and-council government, complicated by the existence of numerous administrative boards, is wholly untelligible to the masses of the people, and even students of political science do not always find it easy. As for the average citizen he does not know where the municipal authority rests, or how it is shared by the various checks and balances. He is bewildered by the seeming confusion of mayor's vetoes, aldermanic confirmations, executive independence, council supremacy sionships, or by vote of the commission, or by the mayor. The second plan is the one most commonly used.

[1] An exception is usually made in the case of the schools which remain in the hands of a separate board.

THE COMMISSION FORM OF GOVERNMENT 311

over appropriations, committee hearings behind closed doors, and urgent business bandied here and there from one office to another with nothing done. Government ought to rest on the consent of the governed; but people cannot give a willing consent to that which they do not understand. Government ought to be responsible to the people; but no government can be responsible unless it is intelligible. The professional politicians do not want government simplified. They want it kept mysterious. The more obscure the provisions of a city charter, and the more complicated the processes of government, the easier it is for them to pursue their traditional policy. Their chief objection to the commission plan is that it let in the light.

The mayor-and-council plan is based upon the doctrine that the city's business is government, while the commission plan goes on the principle that the city's government is business. The aim of one plan is to protect the people against the concentration and abuse of power; the purpose of the other is to lodge authority where it can be promptly and decisively used. And obviously if "city government is business" one can easily argue that the right way to conduct it is by electing a small board of directors and giving them sufficient power. Starting with this hypothesis, and stated in this form, the argument for the commission plan has a plausibility which appeals to shallow-thinking men and women, and indeed it proved very persuasive in many a charter campaign during the years 1908-1915.

2. It has sought to provide a "business" government.

But is it, after all, a sound argument? Does it not take too much for granted? The government of a city is not "business and nothing else." [1] It is a combination of government, business, and philanthropy. And anyhow the commission plan does not conform to the principles of business management. Every well-organized business has a single directing head; it is not managed by five commissioners with equal powers. The members of a board of directors do not divide the administrative duties among themselves; they delegate such duties to a president, a manager, or a superintendent. The commission plan makes no provision for single-headed, unified direction of city affairs. On the other hand, it can fairly be said that the commission plan, by placing a single body in complete and undivided control of all the city departments, has both encouraged and

[1] See Chapter xxi, *below*.

facilitated the use of better business methods in city administration than were practicable under the plan which it displaced.

3. It has improved municipal standards.

The commission form of government has set new standards of harmony, promptness and publicity in the handling of the city's affairs. A very wise man once said that "in a multitude of counsellors there is wisdom"; but it was not city councillors that Solomon had in mind when he gave this proverb to the world. A multitude of councillors and other officials, each sharing in the determination of municipal policy, is a far better guarantee of a palaver than of collective wisdom. Five men can do business where fifty cannot. The more numerous the members of a governing body the greater is the temptation to the use of obstructive tactics and the greater, also, is the likelihood that matters will be settled in secret conclave by a few. Under the commission form of government it is relatively easy to secure the harmonious, expeditious, and public transaction of business. No form of government, however, offers an absolute guarantee that public affairs will be conducted in this way, and the experience of the past twenty years has proved that even five commissioners can form cliques, play politics, sacrifice the public interest to personal ends, and do business behind closed doors.

4. But has not changed the type of elective officeholder.

When the commission movement was spreading like wildfire through the country, fifteen years or more ago, its more enthusiastic advocates predicted that the new system would enable the cities to draw better men into the municipal service. The mayor-and-council form of government, they said, provided too many elective offices and by so doing placed a premium on mediocrity. No city can elect forty or fifty officials at a single election without finding some duds in the lot. It is a commonplace of practical politics that voters will not exercise discrimination when a long list of candidates is set before them at the primaries or the polls. But with the number of elective offices reduced to five, it was said, the situation would be different. The five commissionerships would appeal to the best men of the community, to men who had made a success of their own affairs. But this prophecy, like many others in the literature of reform, has not been very amply fulfilled. The caliber of municipal officeholders is not a thing that lends itself readily to any form of statistical computation, but there is plenty of evidence to prove that the adoption of commission government has not brought a "new type" into the municipal service.¹ Politicians of the common variety have been elected in commission-governed cities, plenty of them. The nonentity with a pleasant smile and a hearty handshake is still in evidence—the "ideal vote-getter" whom Elbert Hubbard once defined as "a candidate who can say, do, and be nothing." Nor is this surprising. Elective offices under any plan of municipal government go to men who have a wide acquaintance and who are willing to hustle for votes. Popularity and persistence will help a man to win at the polls, whether he be one candidate among five or among fifty. It is probably true, nevertheless, that the general average has been raised by reducing the number of offices to be filled, and in any event it is beyond all reasonable doubt that the commission plan affords even mediocre men a better opportunity to achieve results after they have been elected. It is the testimony of men who have held office under both systems that the commission plan, with its concentration of power and responsibility, makes officeholders more conspicuous and more sensitive to public opinion, that it affords more incentive to good work and a more favorable opportunity for doing it.

When municipal reformers set out to convince the people that some new governmental mechanism ought to be adopted, they usually predict that the change will reduce expenses, lower the tax rate, and give the city a greater return for a smaller outlay. Such promises, in nine cases out of ten, merely create expectations which cannot possibly be fulfilled. It is a reasonably safe prediction to make in any city, at any time, that taxes will keep on going up no matter what form of government is adopted. City government is conducted under the inexorable "law of increasing costs per capita." ² This is because the citizens in all progressive communities are insatiable in their demand for more service, and better service, no matter what it may cost. The adoption of the commission plan has not enabled cities to reduce their expenditures, and no one should ever have committed the folly of promising that it would do so.

5. Nor has it reduced taxes.

But having discovered that the expenditures keep rising in

¹ A study of the personnel in ten cities, some years ago, showed that of 50 commissioners then in office, no fewer than 36 had held some elective or appointive municipal position under the mayor-and-council form of government which preceded.
² See *below*, pp. 409-410.

spite of the change, the supporters of the new plan content themselves nowadays with the assurance that although commission government does not mean a lower tax rate it gives the taxpayer "more for his money." This may or may not be true. There is no way of comparing what two communities obtain for their respective outlays, for in no two of them are conditions exactly alike. The quality of a city's administration is largely a matter of opinion. When you point out that one city is paying more money per capita for its police or fire protection than these things cost in some other city of the same size, you are met with the ready excuse that the problem is far more difficult or that the service is correspondingly better. The claim that the commission form of government has enabled cities to get more for their taxes is one which can neither be proved nor disproved. It may be true; more likely it is not.[1]

6. On the other hand, it has not facilitated corruption.

But if the commission plan has hardly measured up to what its more ardent friends anticipated, it is equally true that the pessimism of those who opposed the innovation has also proved to be without basis. The latter predicted that the plan would enable small cliques of politicians to get control of the city funds and to use them corruptly. Three commissioners, in collusion with each other and in league with the bosses, could plunder the city like a Tweed ring—there would be no checks and balances to hinder them. But the fact is that nothing of the sort has happened anywhere under commission government. There has been no more bossism in commission-governed cities than in other communities. Dividing power into many hands, as was done in the old days, does not afford a safeguard against collusion and crookedness. It is easier, as a matter of practical politics, for a few bosses to manipulate a large elective body than a small one. The people can watch three men more easily than thirty. Security against corruption and malfeasance can best be provided by choosing a small number of officials, holding them to a strict accountability and compelling them to do their work in the public eye. As for the objection that the commission

[1] In 1916 the United States Bureau of the Census made a study of tax rates, expenditures, and debts in a selected group of cities, some having commission government and some the older form. The results were inconclusive. In the commission-governed cities the expenditures were relatively smaller; but the per capita indebtedness was greater. Bureau of the Census *Comparative Financial Statistics of Cities Under Council and Commission Government* (1916), p. 9.

THE COMMISSION FORM OF GOVERNMENT

plan is undemocratic, un-American, and contrary to "sound principles of government"—all this may be dismissed as street-corner oratory. These epithets have been applied at one time or another to the Australian ballot, the merit system, the nonpartisan primary, the initiative and referendum, woman suffrage, prohibition, and fifty other reforms. Anything that a politician does not like is undemocratic and un-American.

There are, however, some substantial objections to the commission form of government which the experience of the past two decades has made plain. First and most important among these is its failure to effect a real concentration of administrative responsibility. The commission is a five-headed municipal executive, a pyramid without a peak. It has the weakness which characterizes all types of board-government in that it easily becomes a house divided against itself. The five commissioners often fail to agree, and the temptation is for three of them to combine against the remaining two.[1] This is what has happened in many cities. It is also an essential weakness of the commission plan that although each commissioner is given charge of a department his colleagues can overrule him on any point. And when they interfere, the commissioner in immediate charge of a department regards it as an unwarranted intrusion and is free to disclaim responsibility, whereupon we have the old confusion re-installed.[2]

Defects of the system:
1. Lacks executive unity.

This is an organic defect, not a merely incidental one. It is a weakness inherent in the plan itself; it does not arise from the jealousy and sensitiveness of the officials whom the people elect. The various city departments cannot be treated as separate entities and managed independently without reference to one another. There must be some co-ordinating supervision. When a commission of five men undertakes to dictate how each of its own members shall manage his own department all harmony goes a-glimmering. You cannot combine unified control with

---

[1] See the article on "The Weaknesses of the Commission Plan," by C. M. Fassett, in *National Municipal Review*, Vol. IX, pp. 642-67 (October, 1920). This article is reprinted in C. C. Maxey's *Readings in Municipal Government* (New York, 1924), pp. 85-92.

[2] "One commissioner has been given an appropriation for an auto truck and proposes to buy it from a dealer who has helped him at election time. Other commissioners know that this truck is a poorly built vehicle and unfit for the purpose for which it was intended, but, aware that a like occasion may arise in their own departments, they are not likely to interfere with the purchase and the city's interest suffers." *Ibid.*, p. 645.

departmental independence. The commission plan is fundamentally unsound in that it makes no provision for a strong mayor, a city manager, or any other individual apex of control and responsibility. Doubtless it is better to distribute administrative power among five men than among fifty-five; but to concentrate it in the hands of one man, holding him duly responsible for its exercise, it better still. Plural executives rarely give satisfaction; they have shown their weakness in county administration throughout the United States, and in the New England towns they are breaking down whenever the community grows large enough to create difficult administrative problems.

2. Is not adequately representative.

So a commission of five members is too large to assure the unified and harmonious direction of the city's business affairs. On the other hand, it is too small to serve satisfactorily as a legislative body in any large community. The body which enacts the ordinances, determines the tax rate, votes the appropriations, authorizes loans, and decides other questions of general policy should be large enough to reflect in its membership the more fundamental variations of opinion among the people. This does not mean, of course, that it should be large enough to represent every shade of opinion, political, racial, religious, social, and geographical. A council or commission chosen on that basis would be too big and unwieldy. How large a city council of commission ought to be in order to serve as a trustworthy mirror of public opinion depends upon the size and character of the community. In cities of 30,000 population or less a body of five members ought to be sufficient, and it is among such municipalities that the commission plan has had its greatest vogue. But in large communities it is difficult to see how any adequate representation of substantial interests can be accorded in a body of only five members. The suggestion will be made, of course, that five men can reflect public opinion just as well as fifty if they try to do it, and that is undoubtedly true. But the voters will never be convinced that they are actually represented in a body which contains nobody from their own neighborhood or their own class. When nobody from the east side, or from the north end, or from across the river is to be found among those who direct the course of municipal policy it is futile to argue with the east-siders or the north-enders or the transriparians that this absence of local representation is a matter

THE COMMISSION FORM OF GOVERNMENT 317

of no consequence, because their interests are being fully looked after by broad-minded men who live in other ends of the city. You may be stating the truth, but they will not believe you.

Another practical objection to the commission plan is that it encourages administration by amateurs. It does not abet but actually discourages the placing of capable and experienced officials at the head of the various city departments. Each commissioner, as has been said, becomes individually responsible for some branch of city administration,—be it public works, finance, health, education, or social welfare. It was contemplated in the original commission plan that the commissioners themselves would have no special qualifications for administrative work and that they would devolve the bulk of it upon experts. But this expectation has not been realized. In the general haziness as to what duties a commissioner ought to perform, men have often been chosen because they possessed some pseudo-qualifications for the position in sight.[1] The practice of paying each commissioner a substantial salary has also had an influence in expanding the functions of these officials far beyond what they were originally intended to be. To make a show of earning his salary each commissioner feels naturally that he ought to be the real and not merely the nominal head of his department. Most cities, moreover, cannot afford to pay two salaries for the same work—one salary to the commissioner of public health, for example, and another to a qualified public health expert. In that case it keeps the elective commissioner and does without the expert. The members of the commission, accordingly, are tempted to go beyond their depth, and to try their inept hands at problems which are quite beyond the competence of any layman. Laymen cannot be transformed into experts by the alchemy of a ballot-given designation. Jersey City, some years ago, chose an undertaker as its commissioner of health; in Topeka the commissioner of public utilities was a barber by trade; in Houston, Texas, a machinist became commissioner of finance.[2] There

3. Does not encourage the use of experts.

[1] This has been particularly the case in cities where the commissioners are elected directly to the headships of designated departments. Under the original commission plan all the commissioners were elected on an equal footing; then, after election, they divided the departments among themselves. But some cities did not like this arrangement so they provided that the designation of each commissioner to a specified department should be made by the people at the polls.

[2] For some further examples see Raymond B. Fosdick, *American Police Systems* (New York, 1920), p. 176.

is no reason, of course, why the pursuit of any honest occupation should debar a man from service as a *representative*, but the capable management of a municipal department like streets, water supply or health, demands something more than honesty and good intentions.

<small>4. Has sometimes failed to go far enough.</small>

To ensure the permanent bettering of municipal administration it is essential not only that the frame of government be simplified, and the responsibility centralized, but that accounting and financial methods be improved, the merit system extended, opportunities for corruption and wastage eliminated, publicity introduced into all the departments, business methods adopted, and measures taken for arousing the interest of the people in municipal issues. These far-reaching reforms, it stands to reason, cannot be brought about by merely changing the type of government. The framers of commission charters have been inclined to overlook the elementary fact that success or failure in obtaining full value for public expenditures does not depend wholly, or even largely, upon the election of five men in place of twenty-five. In large measure it is related to the way in which city officials are required to do their work. In every branch of the city's business, whether it be the keeping of accounts, the making of budgets, the letting of contracts, or the borrowing of money, there are right ways and wrong ways of doing things. Left to themselves the laymen will usually choose one of the wrong ways, not from sheer perverseness, but because they do not know any better. Put an amateur in charge of any technical enterprise, from paving a street to dealing with a criminal, and if he hits upon the right way it will be by miracle. The wise architect, when he plans a building, leaves nothing to imagination or surmise on the part of those who are to do the work. On the contrary, he prepares plans and specifications covering even the minutest details, and he expects these details to be followed. Those who plan systems of municipal government cannot be so precise, but they have left too many important things as a hostage to chance or happy accident.

<small>The future.</small>

In view of the organic and incidental shortcomings which the commission plan has disclosed in actual operation it is quite unlikely that our cities, especially the larger ones, will find emancipation from their troubles by adopting it. Many small communities will doubtless retain the plan, and will continue to find it advantageous; but such places can get along with any form of government provided it is simple. Among cities of 100,000 population or more it is not probable that the commission form of government will make new converts. It is weak at the very point where a plan of government must be strong in order to facilitate the solution of those complicated problems which confront great urban committees today. Let it not be concluded from all this, however, that the commission movement has failed to render a great service to the cause of municipal reform in the United States. It embodied a protest against the old order, and as such it was exceedingly effective. It compelled American cities, both big and little, to clean house. By its phenomenal spread it taught a lesson that will not soon be forgotten. It showed the politicians that the rank and file of the voters, when driven to it, will not scruple to wipe the slate clean and begin anew, and that they will not be deterred from this drastic action by calling a plan of government hard names. The commission movement worked a complete revolution in the governments of several hundred American communities, and a partial revolution in the governments of quite as many more. It set things going in the right direction.

REFERENCES

Books and pamphlets relating to commission government, issued prior to 1915, are listed in the author's *Bibliography of Municipal Government* (Cambridge, 1915). The Library of Congress, Division of Bibliography, issued in 1920 a thirteen-page *List of References on Commission Government for Cities*. Later references may be found in the *Annual Bulletin* of the Public Affairs Information Service, and the *Annual Cumulation* of the Readers' Guide to Periodical Literature, both published by the H. W. Wilson Co., New York.

The most comprehensive treatise on the subject is T. S. Chang's *History and Analysis of the Commission and City Manager Plans of Municipal Government* (Iowa City, 1918). Attention may also be called, however, to the survey in *Bulletin No. 12* of the Massachusetts Constitutional Convention (Boston, 1918), in William Anderson's *American City Government* (New York, 1925), pp. 320-325; and in L. T. Beman's *Current Problems in Municipal Government* (New York, 1923), pp. 233-372. This last-named volume contains an elaborate bibliography (pp. 245-268). Mention should also be made of the discussion in W. P. Capes, *The Modern City and Its Government* (New

York, 1922), pp. 126-149, and likewise of the chapters on the topic in A. M. Kales, *Unpopular Government in the United States* (Chicago, 1914), pp. 139-180. A brief but vigorous criticism of the commission plan may be found in Raymond B. Fosdick's *American Police Systems* (New York, 1920), pp. 174-186.

A study of the actual workings of the commission plan is included in Henry Bruère's *New City Government* (2d edition, New York, 1916). In 1916 the U. S. Bureau of the Census issued a special report containing *Financial Statistics of Cities under Council and Commission Governments*.

The draft of a model commission-government charter may be found in Nathan Matthews, *Municipal Charters* (Cambridge, 1914).

The rules of law relating to the adoption of commission charters are given in W. K. Clute, *The Law of Modern Municipal Charters* (2 vols., Detroit, 1920), also in Vol. VII of the Supplement to Eugene McQuillin's *Treatise on the Law of Municipal Corporations*, pp. 6440-6480.

CHAPTER XVII

THE CITY MANAGER FORM OF GOVERNMENT

We come now to the latest among types of government in American cities—the city manager plan. It grew out of the commission form of government, as a logical evolution, when the latter disclosed two serious shortcomings. These two fundamental defects of commission government, as indicated in the preceding chapter, are its failure to make provision for a unified central control over the entire administrative work of the city and its practice of putting the various city departments under the supervision of men who have no technical qualifications but who nevertheless try to do the work of experts. Almost from the very outset these weaknesses began to show themselves. It was soon discovered that harmonious and efficient municipal administration could not be achieved by the simple device of electing five men, giving them high sounding titles, and making them sit in public session at a round table. Fixing responsibility and focussing the public gaze on a weak man does not make him a strong man. Calling a man Commissioner of Public Works or of Public Welfare does not guarantee that he will be an expert in either of these fields. It more often leads to nothing better than cephalic elephantiasis in the man upon whom the resounding title is bestowed. The result was that personal rivalries within the commission's membership, with each commissioner striving to gain the largest share of public applause, often balked the development of any constructive leadership. City government, after all, does not consist merely in settling questions which have attracted great popular interest; the larger part of it has to do with matters of humble routine in which the public does not seem to have any interest.

When the weak features of the commission plan began to be widely and plainly disclosed, charter-makers turned once more to the analogy of corporate business. They soon diagnosed the trouble to their own satisfaction: it arose from the fact the

The city manager form grew out of the commission form.

It aimed to correct the weaknesses of the latter.

commission government was not what it claimed to be. It professed to be a "business" government with a "board of directors" chosen by the "stockholders of the city." But boards of directors in business concerns do not assume the actual functions of administration, either collectively or as individuals. They employ a general manager to do this for them. And having assured themselves that this manager is the right man for the job, they give him reasonable freedom in the selection of his subordinates, in the planning of his work, and in the handling of routine as he deems best. The directors merely look to him for results, and so long as these are satisfactory neither the board nor any of its members ever interferes with his methods of getting them. If, therefore, it is desired to equip the city with a business government, why is it not best to follow the business analogy to its logical conclusion. Why not provide that the commission, instead of trying to perform the work of administrative supervision through its own members, shall employ a general manager for this purpose? That is the angle from which the leaders of reform in some American cities approached the problem about a dozen years ago and developed the city manager plan.

Beginnings of the city manager plan in Dayton.
The first important city to carry the managerial idea into effect was Dayton.[1] It is sometimes said that Dayton, like Galveston, was driven to the adoption of the city-manager plan by reason of a great emergency, but this is hardly an accurate statement. It happened that the new plan of government was adopted in Dayton immediately after the inundation of the city by a flood (1913) which caused a great destruction of life and property, thus creating an emergency which the existing municipal authorities found themselves unable to handle. Affairs for the moment were so badly disorganized that the governor of Ohio declared martial law within the city. Not only so, but he commissioned Dayton's most prominent business man a colonel in the national guard and set him to do what the mayor and council had failed to do.[2] But the movement for the reorganization

[1] The plan really originated in Staunton, Virginia, the birthplace of Woodrow Wilson, but attracted no considerable attention until Dayton took it up.

[2] Mr. John H. Patterson, head of the National Cash Register Company. He became chairman of the charter commission subsequently, and was mainly instrumental in persuading his colleagues to draft a commission-manager form of charter.

THE CITY MANAGER FORM OF GOVERNMENT

of Dayton's municipal system had been started some months before the inundation and was already well under way when the latter came. The disaster merely gave the movement new vigor. At any rate a charter commission of fifteen members was at once elected in accordance with the home-rule provisions of the Ohio Constitution (which had been adopted in the previous year), and this charter board set to work without delay. One of its first decisions was to frame a charter providing for the commission form of government with the addition of a city manager. The conscious aim was to secure the merits of the commission plan while keeping clear of its defects.[1] By dint of hard and steady work on the part of the charter board, the details were worked out in a remarkably short space of time; the charter was then submitted to the people of Dayton and adopted by a large majority, the vote in its favor being more than two to one. It went into effect on January 1, 1914.

The essential features of the Dayton plan may be briefly summarized. All municipal authority was vested in a commission or small council of five members elected at large on a non-partisan ballot for four-year terms. An election was to be held every two years, and at each election two or three members, as the case might be, were to be chosen. A non-partisan primary was provided for the making of nominations, and the name of any voter might be placed upon the primary ballot by a petition bearing the signatures of at least two per cent of the registered electorate. The candidate who polled the highest vote at the election when three commissioners were chosen was to take the title of mayor and to preside at all meetings of the commission, but to have the same voting power as the other members. He was given no veto over the acts of the commission and no special administrative functions. Although chosen for a four-year term, each member of the commission (including the mayor) was made subject to recall by the voters at any time after serving six months. But the petition for a recall required the signatures of at least twenty-five per cent of the registered electorate, a requirement which obviously made the procedure rather difficult. The commission, after the fashion of a board of directors, was

Essential features of the Dayton experiment.

---

[1] See the statement which accompanied the charter: "We have taken a step in advance of the commission-governed cities and provided a remedy for the generally-acknowledged defects of such form."

to hire a city manager, an expert in municipal administration, and was empowered to go outside the city for him if it chose. Then it was to let him manage the administrative affairs of Dayton subject to its own general supervision.

Its rapid spread. This "business" type of government, on its adoption by Dayton in 1914, seemed to strike a popular vote. The phrase city manager caught the public imagination; it was self-explanatory. Many cities which had been operating under the commission form of government seized upon the new plan as the next logical step forward. Some of them made the change by charter amendment; others merely provided by ordinance that the commissioners, instead of doing the work themselves, should employ a manager to do it. Cities which had looked askance at the commission type of government because of its known weaknesses became converts to the plan in its new and improved form. The idea spread widely and rapidly, being in part helped and in part hindered by the war. During the war-years the cost of city administration mounted everywhere and taxes had to be greatly increased. This gave rise to restlessness among the taxpayers and to a demand for administrative changes in the interest of economy. Many cities were induced to adopt the city manager plan by the promise that it would help keep municipal expenses down. On the other hand, the movement was to some extent slackened by a natural disinclination to make radical changes in government at a time when the energies and thoughts of the voters were so completely absorbed by the national emergency.

Its present extent. At any rate the city manager plan kept spreading during the war period and after it. Even yet its momentum continues and it is by no means certain that the crest has passed. The number of cities which have adopted the manager plan, or some variation of it, now exceeds three hundred; but the great majority of them are small communities with populations under ten thousand. The list includes four cities of over 300,000 (Cleveland, Cincinnati, Kansas City, and Rochester), and about fifteen other cities ranging from 50,000 to 300,000.[1] About six million people are now living under city manager government.

Cleveland, with a population of about a million, is the largest

---

[1] The full list may be found in the *City Manager Magazine*, vol. vii, pp. 195-205 (March, 1925). Additions to the list are noted in each monthly issue of the same publication.

THE CITY MANAGER FORM OF GOVERNMENT 325

city under the city-manager form of government. There the plan went into force on January 1, 1924. The charter provides for a city council of twenty-five members elected from four districts. Candidates for the council are nominated by petitions which must be signed, in each case, by at least five hundred voters residing in the district. If a voter signs petitions for more than one candidate his signature is invalid except as to the petition first signed. The nominating petitions are filed and verified at the city hall, and if the valid signatures are found to be sufficient the candidate's name is printed on the ballot in an order determined by rotation.[1] No party designations appear on the ballots. The four councilmanic districts are mapped out in the charter but after each decennial census the city council is empowered to divide the city into districts anew, and to designate the number of councilmen to be assigned to each, with the limitation, however, that no district shall have more than nine or fewer than five councilmen. At present two districts have seven councilmen, one has six, and one has five. Councilmen must be residents of the district from which they are chosen. They are elected for two years, but may be recalled from office at any time after six months of service. They are paid $1800 per year.

Cleveland's city manager charter.

The council.

The city council chooses a presiding officer from its own membership and he has the title of mayor. But he has none of the independent powers which pertain to the chief executive office in mayor-and-council cities. He is merely the presiding officer of the council, and the official head of the city for ceremonial purposes; but in time of emergency he may take command of the police if such action be necessary.

The titular mayor.

---

[1] The charter provision for this rotation of names on the ballot is as follows: "The ballots for each district shall be printed in as many series as there are candidates for the council in such district. The whole number of ballots to be printed for the district shall be divided by the number of series and the quotient so obtained shall be the number of ballots printed in each series. In printing the first series of ballots the names of candidates shall be arranged in alphabetical order of their surnames. After printing the first series the first name shall be placed last and the next series printed, and this process shall be repeated until each name shall have been printed first in one series. The ballots so printed shall be combined in tablets to be supplied to the various polling places. Each tablet shall contain substantially the same number of ballots from each series, and, so far as practicable, the ballots shall be combined in such manner that two or more from the same series shall not be together in a tablet." *Cleveland City Charter*, Sec. 162.

What the council does.

The council is the city's legislative organ. Subject to various limitations imposed by the city charter it determines its own rules of procedure. By majority vote it enacts the ordinances, makes the annual appropriations, and determines all general questions of municipal policy. Ordinances passed by the council must be withheld from going into force for forty days and must be submitted to the voters for acceptance or rejection if during this interval a referendum petition signed by voters equal in number to ten per cent of the total vote cast at the last preceding municipal election is filed against the ordinance. Ordinances may also be initiated and submitted to the people by any 5000 registered voters. The commission appoints no officers except the city manager, the city clerk and his assistants, the three members of the civil service commission, and the members of the city planning board. Nor does it have any immediate control of departmental administration. Individual members of the council are not placed in charge of departments as in commission-governed municipalities. On the contrary, the council is expressly required by the provisions of the charter to choose a city manager and to vest in him the actual work of supervising the administrative departments. It is forbidden "to dictate or attempt to dictate" in the case of appointments or removals under consideration by the manager.

The city manager.

The city manager is chosen by a majority vote of the council and holds office for no fixed term. He may be removed at any time. It is provided that "he shall be chosen solely on the basis of his executive and administrative ability and need not when appointed be a resident of the city." No member of the city council is eligible for appointment as city manager. Opinions as to what constitute "executive and administrative ability" may well differ widely; and there is nothing to keep the city council from appointing, if it so desires, some local man whose qualifications are political only. This does not mean, however, that the provision as to definite administrative qualifications is either futile or superfluous. It gives the right sort of council a valid defence against political pressure when the members make up their minds to observe the spirit of the provision. The office of city manager carries a substantial salary; it is fixed by the city council and is the most highly paid position in the municipal service.

THE CITY MANAGER FORM OF GOVERNMENT

The usual powers of the city manager may be grouped under four heads. *First*, he is the council's advisory expert on all questions of municipal policy. He attends its meetings, takes part in the discussions (but does not vote), and provides the council with such data as it may need in reaching decisions. His immediate subordinates, the heads of the various administrative departments, have the same right. Thus they are the connecting links between the legislative and administrative branches of the city government. In this advisory capacity a city manager who knows his business and possesses the right personality can exert a great deal of influence. *Second*, the city manager is the council's agent for conserving law and order, enforcing the ordinances and carrying the council's decisions into effect. In this respect he inherits a function which belongs to the mayor in mayor-and-council cities. *Third*, he has the right to appoint and remove all municipal officials except the few already mentioned, who are chosen by the council. But the city manager does not have entire discretion in this field. He must make appointments under civil service regulation in so far as the latter apply. It should be mentioned, however, that some cities have the city-manager plan without any civil service rules. Where civil service regulations exist they usually give the city manager a free hand in selecting the heads or directors of departments, but require that appointees to all subordinate positions shall be taken from lists supplied by the civil service board. Subject to the same restrictions he has the right to suspend or to remove appointive officials. In a few cities (in Pasadena, California, for example) it is required that the city-manager's appointments to the higher positions must be confirmed by the council before becoming valid. This is wholly at variance with the spirit of the city-manager plan. *Fourth*, the city manager takes final responsibility for the conduct of the various municipal departments; street, police, fire protection, and the rest. It is his duty to instruct the directors or heads of these departments, to secure a proper interlacing of their functions, to investigate complaints concerning their work, and to compose any differences which may arise among them. In a word, he controls the various activities like the general manager of any business concern, but the city council is given power to investigate his work at any time.

328   THE GOVERNMENT OF AMERICAN CITIES

The departments.

In order to facilitate this work of direction and supervision it is usually provided in city manager charters that all administrative activities shall be grouped into a designated number of departments. The number in most cases is five, this being a survival of the commission plan out of which the city manager type of government has grown. City manager charters sometimes go further, as in Dayton, and prescribe what bureaus or divisions shall be established within each department, thus giving an unnecessary rigidness to the whole administrative organization. As a rule, however, the arrangement of departments and bureaus is not fixed by charter provision but is left to be dealt with by ordinance. In Cleveland, for example, it is provided that "there shall be a department of law, a department of finance, a department of public utilities, and such other departments and offices as may be established by ordinance."[1] This is the better plan. In any event each department has a head appointed by the city manager and each is divided into two or more divisions; the latter are in charge of officials with appropriate designations. Thus the concentration of administrative responsibility is complete; all the lines converge inward and upward.[2] Heads of divisions or bureaus are responsible to the heads of departments; these are in every case responsible to the city manager; he in turn is accountable to the representatives of the people.

Business methods.

So much for the essentials of city manager government. What of the routine procedure, the business methods, and the securities against extravagance or corruption? City manager charters devote a good deal of attention to these things and rightly so, for they are of great importance. In the model city manager charter prepared by the National Municipal League nearly half the provisions relate to the methods of routine administration—to such matters as appropriations, budget making, special assessments, borrowing, accounting, audits, contracts, centralized purchasing, franchises, the control of public utilities, annual reports, and so on. In the Cleveland city charter no fewer than 119 out of 185 sections are devoted to such provisions.

It is impracticable, of course, to give a digest of these various provisions, but a few outstanding features deserve emphasis. It is worth noting that the duty of preparing a preliminary esti-

---

[1] Section 37.
[2] See the chart on p. 262.

THE CITY MANAGER FORM OF GOVERNMENT 329

mate of the year's expenditures is imposed upon the city manager. He obtains figures from the officials whom he has placed in charge of the various municipal departments, puts these together in orderly form, and submits the whole list, accompanied by his own estimate of revenue, to the city council for its consideration. The council considers these figures in detail with the city manager present.[1] The city manager, indeed, is entitled to be present at all meetings of the commission "except when his removal is being considered." When his estimates are under discussion either he or his subordinates explain the various items, particularly those which represent an increase over the figures for the preceding year. The council may decrease or increase any item at will. It may strike out any estimate or insert a wholly new one. And when the council has finished its work of reviewing the budget it votes the appropriation ordinance as a whole; thereupon it has nothing further to do with the individual appropriations. The spending of the money is under the control of the manager.

Except for purposes of inquiry and investigation, moreover, the members of the council must deal with all branches of the city administration through the city manager and through him alone. Any violation of this provision is sometimes made a punishable offence. The council alone can authorize the borrowing of money, but in many cities an affirmative vote of the people is also necessary before bonds can be issued. City manager charters provide, as a rule, that all supplies shall be bought through the central purchasing agency; that contracts shall be let by open competition; that the accounts of all departments shall be kept in a uniform way; that no members of the council shall have any business dealings with the city, and that all its meetings shall be open to the public.

The purpose of the city manager plan, in a word, is to establish a real pivot of administrative authority and to place this under expert control. On the other hand, it seeks to avoid the "one-man government" which has developed in mayor-and-council cities. The city manager has no right to settle any question of general policy at his own discretion, but mayors possess this authority over a wide range. It aims to encourage, although it

The spirit of the plan.

---

[1] See the provisions for elaborate detail embodied in Section 63 of the Cleveland charter.

cannot guarantee, a reasonable security of tenure in office, thus making more practicable the carrying out of projects extending over a term of years. It leaves the lines of responsibility unmistakably clear. It endeavors to establish, as between experts and laymen, the type of relationship which prevails in all well-managed non-public enterprises. The provision that the city manager shall have the right to be present at all meetings of the council makes for frankness and fair dealing. A manager who is really master of his job ought to have little difficulty in wielding a large influence in the commission's deliberations. Knowledge is power. It is power in public as in private life. The city manager plan is an improvement upon the commission form of government in that it provides a better basis for co-operation and harmony. It permits the enlargement of the legislative organ from five to seven, nine, twenty-five, or as many members as may be desired; thus opening the way to the broad and diversified representation which the people of large cities desire. Incidentally, it creates a new profession, that of the trained municipal administrator, which has long existed in Europe but is new to America.

In general one may sum up its outstanding features by saying that it combines separation of *functions* with unification of *powers*. It makes the short ballot practicable. It uses an expert chief administrator as the apex of the whole administrative system. It re-establishes the council in ultimate control of municipal policy. It conforms to John Stuart Mill's dictum that "the business of an elective body is not to do the work, but to see that it is properly done." It points the way, in theory at least, to a combination of democracy and efficiency, two yokefellows that rarely drive together.

How the plan is working. It is yet rather early to make an inventory of the results which the city manager plan has achieved, but some merits and defects have already disclosed themselves with sufficient sharpness to warrant a word of comment. The placing of a manager at the head of the city's administration has unquestionably tended to unify the work of the various department and to eliminate friction among them. It has paved the way for the introduction of better budget-making methods in the smaller cities, as well as for improved accounting, the centralized purchasing of supplies, and the honest awarding of contracts. Floating debts have been wiped out in many cities and expenditures kept within the appropriations. There has been a noticeable improvement in administrative routine, in the methods of reckoning unit costs, and in the fixing of regular salary schedules for city employees. For the most part the plan seems to be maintaining its hold on the confidence of the voters, although the complaint is sometimes heard that city managers give so much attention to matters of "efficiency" that they get out of touch with the every-day sentiment of the people. Thus far it has not met with the usual experience of organic governmental reforms—high hopes at the outset and disillusionment after a few years of actual trial. In cities where the attempt has been made to abolish the city manager plan and restore the mayor-and-council form of government, the attempt has usually failed.[1] Such antagonism as exists is usually directed against the personality or methods of the manager, not against the plan itself.

On the other hand, the adoption of the city manager plan has not enabled cities to lower their tax rates, or to make any appreciable reduction in annual expenditures, or to cut down their bonded indebtedness. It has accomplished some of these things in individual cities, but not in general. It has not always eliminated the evil of deficits at the end of the fiscal year. The excuse is offered that no form of government could have availed to prevent the increase of municipal tax rates and indebtedness during the past half dozen years, and there is much force in that contention. Save in a very few instances the city manager plan has not yet had a full and fair trial. We have yet to see what it can accomplish under normal conditions. *What it has failed to do.*

One thing, however, has become plain enough; namely, that the city managers are themselves destined to be the biggest factors in determining the ultimate success or failure of the plan. The framers of the Cleveland charter realized this and insisted that the council should have an absolutely free hand in selecting the best man available, either from inside or outside the city. Most other communities have pursued the same course, giving their commissions or councils a like discretion. It is in accord *The personal equation in it.*

---

[1] Nevertheless there are in all about 50 cities, big and little, in which the plan has been tried and abandoned. Most of these, however, are cities in which the office of city manager was established by ordinance and not by charter. The largest cities which have abandoned the city-manager plan are Akron, Altoona, and Nashville.

with the spirit of the plan that a non-resident shall be chosen without any hesitation if he seems to be the best man in sight; likewise that he shall be paid a salary in keeping with his attainments and that when installed in office he shall be left there so long as his work proves satisfactory. There is assuredly no fault to be found with these ideals; it would be an admirable thing if they could be transformed into realities. But the practical question is whether American cities, as their electorates are now constituted, are going to live up to them.

Some serious obstacles:

1. The difficulty in finding good managers.

Dayton began in 1914 by setting a good precedent. The commission went outside the city in making its first appointment, chose a man of unquestioned administrative ability, and voted him a salary of $12,500 per year—nearly three times what it had paid the mayor under the old form of government. Other cities displayed the same liberality and for a time there was a brisk demand for competent men. The demand, indeed, greatly exceeded the supply, because no training school for city managers existed nor was there any private vocation which could be looked upon as properly fitting men for the exacting duties of the new position. The well-trained city manager ought to know something about municipal government, law, engineering, and finance, about sociology and economics, and a good deal about human nature. He must needs possess an encyclopedic mind —and the series of all-inclusive minds which began with Aristotle came to an end with Benjamin Franklin. The cities, therefore, found it necessary to select managers on the basis of their general qualifications. Graduates of engineering schools were preferred, on the theory that most of the city manager's work would relate to the supervision of physical services—streets, buildings, water supply, sewerage, and parks. Sometimes, however, a lawyer was appointed to the post, or a banker, or occasionally someone whose only profession was that of a public officeholder. The larger places, when the plan got well under way, began to draw their managers from the smaller communities, choosing men who had made a success of their managerial duties in towns. The prediction was made that the plan would work out as in Germany, where burgomasters have moved by promotion from one community to another.

But it soon became apparent, unhappily, that neither the appointment of outsiders, nor high salaries, nor permanence of

THE CITY MANAGER FORM OF GOVERNMENT 333

tenure was destined to be an invariable feature of city manager government. In some cities the clamor for a local man was not long in making itself heard. Protests began to be voiced against the idea of "bringing in a carpet-bagger to run the city." "Why go afield for a manager when there are plenty of competent men at home?" The spirit of localism is stronger in the United States than in other countries; it shows itself in a multitude of ways and cannot easily be broken down. So the appointing authorities have felt themselves constrained, even against their own best judgment, to take this prejudice into their reckonings. Although Dayton went to Cincinnati for its first manager, it found its second one at home. The Ashtabula council chose one of its own members as its first manager; for its second appointment it selected the local postmaster. Cleveland, despite its unlimited range of choice, took one of its own citizens. Examples could be multiplied, although the habit of selecting a local man is not yet general by any means. Cincinnati, for example, went to Washington for its first manager. 2. The clamor for a "local man."

Sometimes the issue is brought to the front at the municipal election by a demand that candidates for election as councilmen shall pledge themselves to choose some resident of the municipality and not go outside. This is a pledge which candidates, for tactical reasons, often feel obliged to make. In a few cases, the attempt has been made to exact from candidates a promise that, if elected, they will vote for some designated individual; in which case the main issue at the election is whether this man or that man shall be ultimately chosen manager,—the council thus degenerating into a sort of electoral college with its action determined in advance. In one or two instances by this procedure the people have really elected the city manager at the polls; the council merely ratifying their choice when the time came.

The same is sometimes true as respects the removal of a city manager who is already in office. By making certain appointments he gives offence to some element among the voters, or he creates animosity by insisting that affairs be conducted in an efficient way. Most people do not like governmental efficiency when it runs counter to their own ideas of what ought to be done. Every capable city manager finds it necessary to do, almost every day, things which displease somebody somewhere. He 3. The insecurity of tenure.

must deny requests for street improvements, or for jobs in the city service, or for holidays to municipal employees. Presently he finds himself assailed by the local politicians. Then candidates pledged to vote for his removal are brought into the field at the next election. Whereupon the manager becomes the main issue —shall he be kept or dismissed?

4. The attitude of the practical politicians.

This way of choosing and dismissing city managers, if it should ever become general, would bring the plan to grief. Administrative skill and experience cannot be secured in American cities by any form of popular election. Elections are determined by personal popularity, breadth of acquaintance, membership in a sufficient number of lodges and other organizations, assiduity in keeping one's name before the public, readiness to make promises—by all sorts of qualities which have no relation to administrative competence. The poorest type of administrator may be the strongest candidate for public office. Men are usually elected because they are good vote-getters, and for no other reason. Hence it is to be feared that insistence on the appointment of a local man will mean, in the long run, the selection of some local politician who is influential enough to promote the election of his friends as members of the city council. If the people will tolerate it, politicians will electioneer for the office of city manager as they have electioneered for the office of mayor; they will organize and build up political machines; they will trim and sidestep; they will endeavor (as they have always done) to see that men of forthright and independent attitude are not elected to the council.

From a pledged-in-advance or ring-controlled city council it would be but a short step to the direct election of city managers by the people. If it ever becomes apparent that the councilmen are not free agents, the people will insist on taking the choice of the city manager in their own hands. They will supplant indirect by direct election. This is not a prophecy; it is merely a statement of what has always happened in similar circumstances. In America when the voters do not like the way officials are nominated or elected by their representatives, the remedy is to have the people do the job themselves. That is why we changed the method of choosing senators; that is why the direct primary has replaced the party convention. It is essential to the preservation of the city manager plan, therefore, that the choice of the manager be made by councilmen who are unpledged and hence free to select either an outsider or a local man as they may deem best. No system of appointment can ever achieve satisfactory results if the appointing authority is reduced to the mere function of registering decisions which have been made for it by others.

The nearest analogy that we have had to the appointment of a manager is to be found in the organization of the public school system. In every American city there is a school board or board of education, the members of which are (with a few exceptions) chosen by popular vote. This board, while exercising a general control over all questions of educational policy, deputes the actual administration of the schools to a superintendent who is in effect the board's educational manager. In choosing their superintendents the school boards have had no hesitation in going outside the city; they feel no obligation to select a local man. What they seek is a man whose qualifications are such that he can manage the schools efficiently and economically, without friction or turmoil. On the whole, they have succeeded in securing such men and in making the school superintendency a professional career, not a politician's job. But in some cities the demand for a local man in this post has made itself felt as an issue in school elections and almost always with results that have been detrimental to the best interests of the educational system. One of the best ways to keep local politics out of the school system is to put the administration of the schools in the hands of a man who has no local affiliations. What is true of the school superintendent is equally true of the city managership.

A good analogy.

The greatest problem of city manager government is to get the right manager, and no city can hope to obtain a competent manager unless it is prepared to pay the price. It must pay a higher salary than it was accustomed to pay its mayor. But local sentiment often recoils from doing this. A business corporation with an annual turnover of a few million dollars does not hesitate to pay its manager twenty to twenty-five thousand dollars in salary each year, but the people of the city balk at doing anything of the sort. Dayton paid its first manager $12,500 per annum but this action was made the basis of continual criticism on the part of the labor leaders and when the time came to choose a new manager the salary was reduced to $7500.

5. Unwillingness of cities to pay the price.

Cleveland fixed the managerial salary at the unprecedented figure of $25,000 per annum, and thus far have kept it there despite widespread grumbling on the part of the politicians that it is too high. The first city manager of Pasadena received $12,000; the second dropped to $8000. Grand Rapids went from $10,000 to $6000 during the years when all salaries in private business were moving higher. Other cities have encountered the same obstacle. There are many voters to whom twenty-five thousand dollars looks more like a fortune than a salary. If you assure them that business corporations pay their managers even more than this, they will reply that it is more than they are worth, and that if managers got less the workmen would get more. The average voter thinks of the city manager in terms of work rather than in terms of responsibility. The position looks to him like a soft berth, no more difficult than that which the mayor has been occupying. He does not realize the breadth of difference between a political expert and an expert of any other variety.

The qualities which a good city manager ought to have. It is readily demonstrable, of course, that the position of city manager requires professional and personal qualities of a high order and that it demands from the incumbent a degree of administrative capacity which would command a high scale of remuneration in private employment. The successful city manager must not only be well versed in the technical phases of city administration; he must have energy and good judgment; he must be able to get along with his superiors and with his subordinates.[1] Men possessing these qualities are none too plentiful; their services are worth a good deal to large corporations. They will not serve the city for less; on the contrary, they are almost certain to insist upon more, for private employment offers promotions and a permanence which the serv-

---

[1] In the (October, 1924), issue of the *National Municipal Review* a "vocational psychologist" reports the results of a "job analysis" which he made in order to find out the qualifications which a man ought to have for the work of a city manager. These, he writes, are the "qualities which are considered essential for the vocation": 1. High General Intelligence for Abstract Subjects. 2. Pleasing Personality. 3. Leadership. 4. Liking for All Kinds of Persons. 5. Intellectual Sympathy. 6. Liking for Responsibility. 7. Ability to Stand Criticism. 8. Ability to Persuade Others. 9. High Ethical Standards. 10. Technical Training. It is significant that technical training is placed last and least important in the list! For a much better "job analysis" in this field see the monograph cited on p. 339, footnote.

ice of the city does not. Thus far the profession of city manager has given very little indication that it affords a promising career. More than half the men who have entered it since 1914 are already out and at something else. Relatively few have managed to stay in the same office more than three or four years. Many have found the responsibilities too onerous, or the salaries too low, and accordingly have taken the first good opportunity to transfer into private employment.[1] Not a few have proved unsatisfactory and have been dismissed, in some cases without proper reason.

It is not surprising, however, that dismissals from office have been frequent. Many managers, appointed solely on their technical qualifications, have shown themselves to be deficient in the personal qualities needed. Colonel Henry M. Waite, the first city manager of Dayton, once expressed the opinion that a successful manager "must be an executive, must know how to handle men, must be fair and just, must be firm and polite, and must have the courage of his convictions." This is a large order to fill on a salary of three or four thousand dollars a year, especially when cities insist that the appointee shall be a man of technical education and experience as well. It is easy enough to obtain, at almost any figure, an official who knows something about the technical end of road building, or sewer construction, but who lacks competence as an executive or organizer. For a modest salary a city can also obtain the services of somebody who possesses a fair degree of administrative capacity but who has no competence as an engineer. To obtain an official who is strong in both capacities, who can get results without creating antagonisms—that is a far more difficult problem.

Too many city managers have been strong-headed, untactful, visionary. The most common ground for dismissal has been inability to work harmoniously with the council or with its committees or with the heads of departments whom the manager has himself appointed. In some cases the newly-appointed managers have found a hostile attitude among the subordinate officials which they have not been able to overcome. In a few cases

Why some of them have failed.

---

[1] "Taking as typical the group of managers who left the profession in 1923 we find that 58 per cent left because of private business interests which offered them better salaries. It is proverbial that cities as employers will rarely compete in salaries with those paid by private enterprise for the same service." City Managers Association *Yearbook*, 1924, p. 13.

the trouble has been due to the failure of the city manager to deal tactfully with the newspapers and the public. The city manager is a busy man. He cannot spend time making himself popular as mayors are in the habit of doing. Some cities have tried as many as three different men in three successive years and found each unacceptable. It is often difficult to tell where the blame should be placed.

Some city managers have made a speedy failure because they could not resist the temptation to take a hand in local politics. This temptation, of course, is hard to resist. A manager, for example, proposes some public improvement which he believes to be very urgently needed by the city. The city council accepts his recommendation and asks the voters at a special election to authorize the issue of bonds in order to secure the necessary funds. But before the people will authorize the loan they want to know all about the proposal. And who is better fitted to explain it than the manager? He originated the project; he has the facts and figures. So he lets himself be persuaded to explain it in the local newspapers, to advocate it at a luncheon given by the chamber of commerce or the rotary club. At these gatherings he is expected to answer questions about it and to make reply to any objections that may be raised. Sometimes he manages to start a large-sized controversy in which he is forced to make himself a leader of the bond-issue forces. Then everybody who is on the other side feels aggrieved. No man can go through a contest of this sort without making some political enemies.

Who provides the community with leadership under this plan?

It is essential, then, that the city manager shall keep clear of local politics, but if so who is to supply the community with its political leadership? Good democratic government must rest upon something more than mere mechanical efficiency. It postulates a vigorous interest on the part of the people, an interest in city issues, in city politics. This popular interest will demand leadership and will find leadership.[1] If it does not find leadership inside the established city government it will find it outside. The city manager, accordingly, finds himself in a difficult position. The people look to him for what he cannot give except at the risk of making his own position insecure.

[1] For a further discussion of leadership in politics see the author's *Personality in Politics* (New York, 1924), ch. iii.

THE CITY MANAGER FORM OF GOVERNMENT 339

Certain it is, in any event, that the fault has not been all on one side. City councils have often been unreasonable and unjust in their dealings with managers. In many cases they have not lived up to the spirit of the plan; they have claimed all the credit when things have gone right and have been quite ready to make the manager a scapegoat when things go wrong. In some instances they have undermined the morale and discipline of his subordinates by a campaign of rumors and whisperings. The manager comes to the city a stranger, unacquainted with its people, its politicians, its civic organizations, its self-seekers, hobby-riders, cranks, and crotchets. He must tread warily, and even though he exercise extreme caution he is likely to stumble at times. The position is one for which a man cannot be educated and trained through the ordinary channels. Experience is the only thing that can teach a city manager what to do and what to avoid, but in the process of acquiring his experience he may make some bad mistakes and be dismissed. The city manager ought to be given more leniency and consideration than both councilmen and people have usually accorded him. It takes time and forbearance to build up a new profession.[1]

A difficult career at best.

Serious difficulties have arisen and are bound to keep arising with respect to the precise limits of the city manager's powers. The city charter usually provides that the council shall not interfere with the city manager in the performance of his duties; some charters go so far as to make any such interference punishable by the courts.[2] But stringent provisions of law do not much avail unless the councilmen are ready to observe them in spirit. When a manager is trying to retain a precarious hold on his position a mere hint from the council may be as a command

A fundamental weakness of the whole system.

---

[1] See the interesting monograph by Joseph Cohen on "The City Managership as a Profession," issued as a supplement to the *National Municipal Review* (July, 1924).

[2] Take the following drastic provision from one city-manager charter, for example, "Neither the council, nor any of its members, shall dictate the appointment of any person to office or employment or prevent him from exercising his own judgment in the appointment of officers or employees in the administrative service. Except for purposes of enquiry the council and its members shall deal with the administrative service solely through the manager, and neither the council nor any member thereof shall give orders to any of the subordinates of the city manager either publicly or privately. Any such dictation, prevention, orders or other interference on the part of a member of the council with the administration of the city shall be deemed a misdemeanor, and upon conviction thereof the member so convicted shall be fined not exceeding one hundred dollars, and may, in the discretion of the court, be removed from office." *Charter of Norfolk, Va.*

from on high, not to be disobeyed. The commissioners need not violate the charter by open interference; they can easily make veiled suggestions or let their desires become known in some roundabout way. They can tell the newspaper reporters, for example, that while the council desires the manager to have a perfectly free hand a certain appointment would be very pleasing to the council majority. A manager who keeps his ear to the ground will get a good deal of information through subterranean channels.

Seekers of jobs and favors often go directly to members of the council, not to the manager. They know the routes of indirect influence. Politicians will wink and remind you that while the manager appoints the officials it is the council that appoints the manager. The laws can prohibit any direct interference with the manager's appointments but they cannot prohibit the council from dismissing him when he fails to heed the hints that come to him. This privilege of dismissal is one which cannot be abridged without throwing away the keystone of city manager government. And so long as the council has complete freedom to employ and dismiss the city manager he cannot be unmindful of its wishes in individual cases, no matter how these may be communicated to him.

It must inevitably be so, for the members of the council are not protected against pressure from the public. It is natural that they should reflect the public attitude toward the actual work of administration, which is what they are elected to do. A plan of local government which lodges administrative powers in the hands of an appointive officer may be sound in principle but it is bound to encounter many obstacles of a very practical sort, at least until such times as traditions of administrative independence become firmly established in America, as they have been in England. Theoretically the power of an elective body to appoint and dismiss an administrative official at will is not inconsistent with the exercise of a large measure of independence by the latter. Of this English cities afford a striking illustration. But whether it is practicable in American cities still remains to be proved.

The outlook.

On all these matters, however, the temptation to venture anything in the way of predictions ought to be resisted. The city manager plan is yet in its experimental stages. The lapse of another half-dozen years will demonstrate, probably beyond much question, whether the various difficulties which it is now encountering can or cannot be overcome. The world has had no previous experience with a municipal system of precisely this type. The city manager plan was not transplanted from Germany although it bears some resemblance to the system of burgomaster administration long established in that country. It is the American plan of corporate business organization adapted to the use of the city. It is a plan that school boards have used for many years. There is nothing un-American about it; it is an indigenous product of the soil. On paper the city manager form of government has much to commend it, but it is never possible to ascertain, except by prolonged trial, whether the practice of a government will run close to its design. Nothing is easier to make than an "ideal" plan, and nothing is harder than to apply the idealism. On the other hand, wise men have often argued that American cities might greatly improve the efficiency of their government is they would only place trained experts in charge of it, and here is a scheme that gives them the opportunity to do just that. The awkward fact remains, however, that under no plan of democratic government can the employment of experts be made compulsory against the wishes of the voters, or against the will of those whom the voters elect. The city manager plan provides a means, but it unhappily does not guarantee the attainment of the end. It is "not the only one for reaching the end in view, but it is the best that has yet been proposed for American cities and the one most in harmony with the spirit of our institutions."

REFERENCES

The most useful sources of information on the development and status of the city manager plan are the ten annual *Yearbooks* of the City Managers' Association, 1915-1924. This yearbook has now been replaced by the *City Manager Magazine* which appears monthly but with an enlarged "annual number," equivalent to a yearbook, each March. This publication contains a great deal of data and many informing articles, chiefly from city managers themselves.

A loose-leaf *Digest of City Manager Charters*, edited by Professor R. T. Crane (New York, 1922), has been published by the National Municipal League and can be procured from that organization (261 Broadway, New York City). The same league's *New Municipal Pro-*

gram (ed. Clinton Rogers Woodruff, New York, 1919) contains the draft of a model city-manager charter, with various chapters explaining its provisions. A new edition of this volume is now in course of preparation. Mention should also be made of the pamphlet on *The Story of the City Manager Plan* and other informing material issued by the same organization.

Descriptions of city-manager government, its origin, organization and workings, may be found in H. A. Toulmin, Jr., *The City Manager* (New York, 1915); C. E. Rightor, *The City Manager Plan in Dayton* (New York, 1919), and T. S. Chang, *History and Analysis of the Commission and City Manager Plans* (Iowa City, 1918). The last named work contains a long list of references. There are briefer discussions in William Anderson's *American City Government* (New York, 1925), pp. 325-339; C. C. Maxey's *Outline of Municipal Government* (New York, 1924), pp. 59-68; the same author's *Readings in Municipal Government* (New York, 1924), pp. 92-116; Joseph Wright's *Readings in Municipal Problems* (Boston, 1924), pp. 386-407; W. P. Capes, *The Modern City and Its Government* (New York, 1922), pp. 150-177; A. B. Gilbert, *Modern Cities: Their Methods of Business* (New York, 1918), pp. 170-199; Everett Kimball, *State and Municipal Government* (Boston, 1922), ch. xxv; and *Bulletin No. 13* of the Massachusetts Constitutional Convention (Boston, 1918).

In the Debaters' Handbook Series there is a volume of *Selected Articles on the City Manager Plan*, edited by C. E. Mabie (New York, 1918). Attention should also be called to E. A. Fitzpatrick's *Experts in City Government* (New York, 1918).

In 1920 the Library of Congress issued a *List of References on the City Manager Plan*.

CHAPTER XVIII
THE ADMINISTRATIVE DEPARTMENTS

The administrative department as a self-standing factor in city government, independent of the municipal council, not chosen by the latter, and not made up of members from it, is also an exclusively American institution. Like many other features in the American system of urban government, it is a by-product of that undue stress which was, during the nineteenth century, laid upon the principle of division of powers in local, as in state and national, affairs. It has been shown in a previous chapter that, during the colonial era and for an interval after the Revolution, legislative and administrative functions were not divorced in the cities of this country. The city council had charge of both; and throughout the first four or five decades of the nineteenth century the various tasks of local administration as they confronted the cities were given over to standing committees of the council. That was the plan pursued in England, whence the cities of the United States first derived their frame of government, and it remains unaltered in English municipalities to the present day.[1]

{The independent administrative department an American institution.}

In England the system of administering each branch of the city's business (such as streets, parks, health, police and fire protection) through the agency of a council committee has been satisfactory, but mainly for the reason that the committee does not attempt to do the work. It merely sees that an expert does it. The same system would have functioned in the cities of the United States if a similar policy had been pursued by the committees. Unfortunately it was not. With the spoils system in full force the council placed at the head of each service men who had no expert competence, who knew no more about the work than the councilmen themselves, and hence to whose advice

{Its evolution in the United States.}

{1. Council committees.}

[1] The way in which this plan of department administration by council committees works in the cities of Great Britain is explained in the author's *Government of European Cities* (new edition, New York, 1926).

the committee have no special heed. The committees undertook to settle the details of administration in the health, police, fire, parks and all other departments. They developed a tradition altogether different from that which has existed in English cities. Their methods did not lead to any catastrophes, of course, so long as the cities remained small, with simple administrative problems to handle; but with rapid growth and increasing complexity the whole arrangement broke down, as anyone might have foreseen.

2. The elective boards.

Then came a new administrative experiment. The various departments were turned over to separate boards, usually of three or five members. It was assumed that a special water board, a police board, or board of health would do better than a council committee, the members of which were elected by wards and had to transact all business by logrolling methods. Unhappily, however, it was arranged to have the members of these boards elected by popular vote, this being a concession to the democratic spirit of the times. The result was that the boards, in their personnel and methods, did not prove to be much better than the committees. They were not able to cope with the need for more efficient public services in the rapidly-growing municipalities.

3. The appointive boards.

Accordingly, still another shift was made. The boards were made appointive by the mayor, it being anticipated that in this way more competent men could be secured. Popular election, it was said, must inevitably fill the boards with good fellows who will do favors for their friends but have no competence in handling administrative work. Appointment, on the other hand, would allow the mayor to pick capable men irrespective of their vote-getting qualities. "When you want representation, elect; when you want skill, appoint." That was the saying which embodied the philosophy of the change.

4. The single commissioner.

On the whole, the outcome was a marked improvement. More competent men were secured for administrative work in many American cities. Not always, however, for when the wrong sort of mayor got into office he usually filled the various boards with his own henchmen and thus built up a personal machine with which he tried to perpetuate his own lease of power. And in any case there were some departments in which the work did not lend itself to board management, the police and fire

THE ADMINISTRATIVE DEPARTMENTS 345

departments more particularly. It was all well enough to have these departments managed by an unpaid board of three or five citizens so long as the departments were small and the work of a non-technical character. But with the expansion of the police force to hundreds of men and with the increased complexity of police technique the board system functioned much less efficiently. The great handicap of a board is the opportunity that is given for disagreement when prompt and decisive action is needed. So the board system began to give way in certain departments, being replaced by a single official—a police commissioner, fire commissioner, superintendent of streets, and so on. This movement has been going on during the past twenty-five years and is still proceeding.

As respects management, therefore, we have had four stages in the evolution of the administrative department—the council committee, the elective board, the appointive board, and the appointive commissioner. It is not to be imagined, however, that these stages were clear-cut, or that they can be marked off into definite periods. Some cities preceded others into each of the last two stages. Administration by council committees has almost entirely disappeared, but here and there you will still find elective boards. School boards, of course, are generally elective, but the school department has always occupied a special position. Appointive boards are still numerous at the present day, particularly in the smaller cities and they have some merits as will later be explained.[1] The general tendency, however, is to put a single commissioner at the head of each department, with certain exceptions such as schools, city planning, and poor relief.

Summary.

Hand in hand with this development a great expansion of municipal functions has taken place. The typical American city of a hundred years ago had volunteer constables, a volunteer bucket-brigade, cobblestone pavements, wooden sewers, and no public water supply but the town pump. Council committees, however inefficient, could manage utilities of that sort. Even at the time of the Civil War there were relatively few full-time salaried employees. The rural village of today has relatively as much administrative machinery as was needed by cities seventy-five years ago. But as the cities grew the services ex-

How administrative functions have grown concurrently.

---

[1] They are also common in some larger cities such as Detroit and Los Angeles. See *below*, pp. 353-354.

panded, new functions were undertaken (such as street cleaning, public recreation, health centers and all the rest), more employees were needed, and more supervision.[1] It was this that forced the evolution of administrative organization through its various stages. And there can be little doubt that the continued increase in functions will compel further adaptations. The amount and variety of the administrative work which the large American city now has to do is something that the ordinary citizen has no conception of. Just run through the index of a municipal report, all the way from "abattoirs" to "zoological garden" and get some idea of it.

Some fundamental questions of administrative organization.

Now this steadily-increasing amount and variety of administrative work which must be performed in every large city naturally makes the problem of departmental organization a difficult one. How many administrative departments should a city have? What principles should be followed in apportioning the work among them? On what principle should a large department (such as public works) be divided into bureaus and divisions? Should departments be placed in charge of boards or single commissioners? How should the department heads be selected? Should they be qualified experts? Should they be appointed under civil service rules? How can we keep men of the right sort on the city payroll and men of the wrong sort off? Good city administration, by general consent, is a matter of both systems and men. What system will best help to get the men? These are questions that come up for discussion wherever new city charters or charter amendments are under consideration. Their timeliness entitles them to all the thought they have been getting, and more.

The starting point.

It would be sheer folly, of course, to determine by general rule the number of administrative departments that a city should have. It would be like requiring that every house ought to have five, or seven, or ten windows without regard to its size, use, or orientation. A city has a varying number of administrative functions to perform, the number depending upon its size, its resources, and the extent to which it has branched out into new fields of public service. Some cities own and operate their lighting plants and street railways; some do not. The wider

[1] For a further discussion of this growth in functions, see *below*, Chapter xxi.

THE ADMINISTRATIVE DEPARTMENTS 347

the scope of a city's activities the more administrative machinery it needs. This ought to be a commonplace, but it is not, as witness the "model" schemes of administrative organization which are periodically put forth for the guidance of all cities whatever their size or problem. The commission plan, as has been shown, is the most conspicuous transgressor in this respect.[1]

Two considerations, it may be suggested, ought to be influential in determining the distribution of administrative work among city departments. They are as follows: First, the number of departments should not be increased beyond what is necessary for the efficient conduct of the city's business. Second, functions which are similar should be placed in the same department, while those which are dissimilar should be kept in different departments. *Two basic aims.*

The first of these two propositions will hardly be disputed. The distribution of administrative work on too elaborate a scale leads to a waste of effort. There is a law of diminishing returns which begins to operate at a certain point in the subdivision of administrative labor; beyond this point (whatever it may be) the multiplication of departments does not facilitate but hinders the proper conduct of the city's business. Twenty-five years ago most American cities had too many departments. Some have too many yet. Boston, for example, has about forty departments, or separate agencies under some other name; New York and Chicago have thirty each; Detroit has about twenty; Philadelphia has eleven, and Buffalo only five.[2] *Keeping the number of departments down.*

In some cities the number of departments has been considerably reduced; the process of reduction and consolidation has gone so far, in fact, that there is danger of its overreaching itself. The evil of having too many departments is being replaced by the evil of having too few. Administrative reformers have a habit of assuming that the consolidation of two departments into one always makes for efficiency, no matter how far the process may be carried. But merging two departments into one accomplishes no useful end if it means that widely different functions are thereby grouped together under a single head. There would be no sense in putting poor-relief, prisons, play-

[1] *Above*, p. 309.
[2] It is not always easy to give the exact number because sometimes a department is not listed under that name but is called a commission, or an office, or some other name.

grounds, pensions, and printing together because they all begin with *p;* yet some cities have made similar combinations for reasons which appear to be very little better.

The objections to mergers.
The objection to putting unrelated matters into the same department is that some of them, when this is done, are certain to be neglected. The head of the health department, to be worthy of his place, should be primarily interested in public health matters. Unless he is an uncommonly versatile man he will not be interested, for example, in tree planting, free legal aid, the regulation of billboards, employment bureaus, the inspection of weights and measures, the censorship of amusements, or any one of a dozen other functions which, however secondary they may seem, ought to be given proper attention by someone whose personal interest they can command. If these functions, therefore, are thrown into the health department, or into any other department, for the mere reason that the general administrative scheme provides no suitable place for them elsewhere, they are likely to be accorded very little attention by the head of the department. On the other hand, it is obvious that a city cannot maintain a separate department for every municipal function, big or little. No one would suggest, in smaller cities at any rate, the maintenance of individual departments for the issuing of building permits, the removal of garbage, the repairing of sidewalks, the compilation of statistics, or the abatement of nuisances. These things must be combined with something else. So the problem is a practical one, to be solved by listing all the functions, classifying them, grouping those which from their nature can be conveniently and properly grouped, and deciding the number of departments in that way. It may be eight, ten, a dozen, or even more in large cities.

How to settle the matter.
Charter makers usually begin with this problem at the wrong end. Their first step should be to make an inventory of what the administrative authorities are expected to do. This inventory will provide a surprisingly long list in any large city—fifty or sixty distinct administrative functions at least.[1] Most of them, however, will fall readily into seven or eight functional

[1] A list compiled for the city of Detroit in 1921 gives 184 separate functions, ranging from auto repairs to venereal clinics. See *below*, p. 408. This list has been reprinted in William Anderson's *American City Government* (New York, 1925), pp. 404-405.

THE ADMINISTRATIVE DEPARTMENTS 349

groups, such as finance, public works, public safety, public health, poor relief and correction, education, parks and recreation, and public utilities. But there will be some which do not seem to belong in any one of these functional groups and yet are not of sufficient importance to have departments to themselves. Some administrative activities, moreover, seem to have equal affiliations with two departments. Take the work of establishing, equipping, and supervising playgrounds, for example. Where does this properly belong—with parks and recreation, or with education? Should public playgrounds and athletic fields be under the jurisdiction of the park department or the school board? Either disposition may be defended with plausible arguments. The work of acquiring the land for recreation purposes, improving it and caring for it, is closely akin to the customary work of the park department. Considered as physical property there is no great dissimilarity between a public park and a playground. Regarded from the standpoint of its activities, however, the playground is an educational institution and as such links itself up closely with the works of the schools. A playground without supervision falls far short of its highest service. Supervision is the aspect which should have the emphasis, and being a form of instruction it can best be provided by the school authorities. In some cities the playgrounds have been grouped with parks; in others they have been tied up with the schools; in others, again, they have a department to themselves.

So with many other matters on which more than one department may have a claim. Does the management of a municipal cemetery, for example, belong properly to the park department or to the health department? Should "parkways" be regarded as parks or as streets for administrative purposes? Is garbage collection a matter of public health or of public convenience? On the determination of this question depends its proper place—whether in the health or the public works department. What of the public library? If a city is to have only seven or eight departments the public library cannot have a department to itself. Where should it go? Some argue that, being an education institution, the public library should be administered by the school board. Should the censoring of motion pictures be entrusted to the police, or to the park and public recreation departments, or to the school authorities, or to a separate board?

Specific questions which arise.

These are practical questions; they certainly cannot be answered by stating any formula that will hold good for all cities. It is a good deal easier to say that "departments should be based on a functional classification" (as the efficiency experts tell us), or that "related functions ought to be kept together" than to decide what the relationships really are.

<small>Determining whether functions are related.</small>
In determining whether functions are related in fact and not merely in appearance, one should look primarily at the nature of the problems which are encountered in performing them. In some branches of the city's work the chief problems are of an engineering, technical, and constructional character. In this respect water supply and sewage disposal are closely allied, even though superficially they might seem to be at opposite poles. The one brings to the city a something that is essential to life and health; the other takes away from the city a large volume of waste which is dangerous to life and health. But this superficial dissimilarity is of no real consequence when it comes to determining whether the two departments should be combined. Different in aims, they are alike in their problems. They dig ditches, lay pipes, run pumps, employ large amounts of unskilled labor—both of them. Various groups of municipal functions, again, have to do with the problems of finance, or of instruction, or of personal contact and supervision. Each has its own bonds of kinship. Police and fire protection have an intimate relationship in that both are concerned with the public safety, both are organized on a semi-military model, and both have as one of their most difficult problems the maintenance of discipline in the ranks. But there is no relationship between police and poor relief, or between sanitation and public libraries, for example, whether in purpose, methods, or problems. Such municipal functions call for administration by officials who are altogether different in training and aptitudes.

<small>The relation of departments to one another.</small>
Whether the number of departments be small or large it is also essential that they be properly articulated. The work of administering a city is an entity; a rather complex entity, it is true, but nevertheless a unified enterprise. No part of it should be aloof from the rest. No department, to borrow a war metaphor, should "march with its flanks in the air." Every branch of the municipal administration should be linked to a common center; the lines of control and responsibility should converge

upward and inward. The whole scheme should take the form of a pyramid, with the mayor or city manager at the apex, the city employees at the base, and the hierarchy of officials coming between. Each group of employees should have a foreman or chief; the latter, in turn, should be under direction from the head of a bureau or division, and the heads of divisions should be responsible to the head of the department. Finally, all heads of departments ought to be responsible to the mayor, the city commission, or the city manager.[1] This, however, is not what one usually finds in cities which have the mayor-and-council form of government. Some heads of departments are chosen by the mayor and are responsible to him; others are directly elected by the people and are not controllable by the chief executive. The result is that the two groups often work at cross purposes. The elective head of a department desires to make a reputation for himself by devising his own policies and pursuing his own methods. His lodestar, too often, is the ambition to get himself elected mayor some day. Why, then, should he exert himself to make the present mayor's administration a conspicuous success? Unless the heads of all departments are responsible to a common center there can be no unity of program.

A generation ago the board system of departmental management was widely used in American cities. This was in part due to a popular impression that municipal administration ought to be bi-partisan; that the minority political party ought not to be excluded from a share in it. In a board of three or five members both parties could be represented, whereas in a department with a single head, no dual representation could be afforded. The work of bi-partisan boards proved very unsatisfactory, however, for the membership almost invariably lined itself up three against two, or two against one. The plan was especially objectionable, when applied, as it often was, to the police, fire, and health departments, in all of which there is need for prompt and decisive action. Dissensions among members of the boards reflected themselves in loose discipline all the way down. During the past twenty years, therefore, the cities have been replacing police boards, fire boards, and boards of health by single com-

How a department should be headed: The board system.

---

[1] There are a few exceptions, e.g., the school department or the city-planning department, which may for good reasons be left outside the main scheme.

missioners. But some of them still retain the board plan, for virtually all departments. Los Angeles is the most conspicuous example among the larger municipalities, having no fewer than seventeen administrative boards. Every important branch of the city's business is managed by a board of five members— police, fire protection, health, water and power, library, parks, playgrounds, even pensions. Detroit comes a close second with twelve administrative boards, but police, fire protection, and recreation are under single commissioners.

Objections to it. There is very little to be said for the board system in departments where executive rather than deliberative action is called for. In the matter of fire protection, for example, there is no need for a representation of varied interests or for deliberation on matters of general policy. The general policy of a well-organized fire department is the same everywhere. The whole problem is one of maintaining efficiency of apparatus and personnel. On the face of things there is no better reason for putting a board in charge of the fire department than for setting a group of five generals at the head of an army. A unified command is equally desirable in both cases.

Where it fits. On the other hand, there are certain departments which, from the nature of their work and problems, are by no means so obviously unsuited to the board system. The school department is perhaps the best example. Unrestrained control of educational policy should not be given to any one official, whether layman or expert. In the community which supports the public schools there is bound to be a variety of opinion and sentiment on questions of educational policy and it is proper that these diverse points of view should be represented. Among all departments of American municipal administration the school department, taking the country as a whole, has been the most honestly, economically, intelligently, and progressively managed. It is there that scandals have been fewest, wastefulness the least prevalent, and progress the most notable. The American municipal taxpayer comes nearer to getting a hundred cents in value for every dollar of expenditure in this department than in any other. This is due in part, perhaps, to the fact that it has been somewhat easier to eliminate the spoils system from school administration than from the other departments of the municipal service. But it is not without significance that the school de-

THE ADMINISTRATIVE DEPARTMENTS 353

partment is the only one which has succeeded in establishing and maintaining that combination of lay supervision with professional management which is so characteristic a feature of municipal administration in European countries. The superintendent of schools in American cities is the only administrative officer who occupies a status and exerts an influence comparable to that of the permanent city officials abroad.

The board system is still rather generally used in the administration of poor relief, and to the work of this department it lends itself very well. Municipal public libraries in American cities are also for the most part in charge of boards, and board supervision is commonly applied to public utilities, city planning, and recreation as well. It is the only fair plan, moreover, in the case of the department which has charge of registering voters and conducting elections, inasmuch as bipartisan representation needs to be accorded here. But in departments other than those mentioned, the preponderance of argument favors the single commissioner plan. The latter means concentration of responsibility, greater promptness in action, and a better morale among subordinates. *Its present extent of use.*

Still the board system is perhaps in greater disfavor than it deserves to be. People are inclined to see only its shortcomings and to overlook the fact that board administration, under certain conditions, has a good deal to recommend it. When continuity of policy, for example, is a desideratum in any department (as it is in the case of public works) the board system provides a means of securing it. When a single commissioner goes out of office and a new one comes in there is likely to be a change in plans and methods. The new commissioner feels that he must signalize his advent by taking the department out of the old ruts. He does not want to display his lack of initiative by merely taking over where his predecessor left off. Old plans are therefore thrown aside and new ones announced. But before the new commissioner brings these plans to fruition his term comes to an end; he gives way to someone else and the process of substituting still newer methods is repeated. When public works are undertaken by a board, on the other hand, the members do not all go out of office at once and there is an element of continuity. One member retires and is replaced, but the others hold over and carry the old traditions along. This *Its merits.*

is a consideration of some importance in departments where drastic reversals of procedure are likely to involve the city in heavy expense.

Other alleged advantages. The board system is sometimes defended on grounds of economy. In small cities, or in certain departments of large cities (such as poor relief or public libraries), it is usually possible to obtain, without remuneration, the part-time service of interested citizens, thereby saving the salaries which would have to be paid to full-time department heads. One frequently hears the assertion that expert officials, giving undivided attention to their work and keeping a sharp outlook for leakages, can easily save the city the amount of their salaries. That is theoretically true. But as a matter of experience it has too often been found that when cities abolish unpaid boards and replace them by salaried heads of departments they do not always manage to get service that is expert in character or diligent in saving money. Too often the replacement of an unpaid board by a single commissioner merely adds to the public payroll another professional politician who devotes to the work of the department less intelligence, less thought, and less time than it received from members of the unpaid board.

Our long process of experimentation with different methods. It is a serious defect in the American system of municipal administration, and one which has frequently been commented upon by foreign observers, that we have thus far failed to devise a satisfactory method of selecting the paid heads of departments. We have tried at least eight methods—election by the people, appointment by the city council, appointment by the mayor with council confirmation, appointment by the mayor without council confirmation, appointment by the mayor subject to the approval of a civil service commission (the Boston plan), appointment by the governor, appointment by a commission, and appointment by the city manager. The first two plans proved intolerable. The third is not so bad but has serious practical defects. The success of the fourth depends wholly upon the ideals of the mayor, and these have left a good deal to be desired. The fifth plan has availed little in the way of improvement, and the sixth is unpopular because it involves a clear departure from the principle of municipal home rule. Appointment by an elective commission has not appreciably raised the standard, and the last plan, appointment by the city manager,

THE ADMINISTRATIVE DEPARTMENTS 355

has not yet been tried long enough to show what it can produce in the way of permanent results.

Not one of these various methods has been successful in securing men of acknowledged competence for the management of the city's business affairs. It is true, of course, that men of high capacity are sometimes obtained, but it is not the rule. In no large city can it be said that political considerations have been eliminated or even reduced to a secondary place in determining the selections. They are still the controlling factor in the majority of American cities of all grades. In many instances the departmental heads who are in charge of such important functions as street paving, sanitation, water supply, parks, and public buildings, are men whose only experience is of the political type, and who would not be entrusted with equal responsibilities in any field of private business. These men, in the larger communities, are spending millions from the public treasury. They have hundreds, sometimes thousands, of city employees under them. Yet it is a commentary upon their business ability that when the head of a department loses his position through a change of mayors he sometimes has a hard time finding a job at half the salary anywhere outside the public service.

The present situation.

The successful head of a city department must be honest, fair-minded, and willing to work. He should be willing to exert authority and to assume responsibility for it. He should be able to keep harmony in his department, to maintain discipline among his subordinates without being disliked for it, and to deny unwarranted favors without provoking animosity. He should be a good judge of what the public wants and hence able to discern before he does a thing whether it will prove popular or unpopular. In a word he ought to be a good leader of men, a good organizer, and a good fellow. But this is not all. No amount of personal magnetism will make a department head successful unless he knows the technique of his job. Technical training and experience are highly desirable in all cases, and for the best results they are essential.

Qualities needed in a department head.

It is easy enough to set down on paper the attributes which a good department head should possess, but no one expects, as a practical matter, to find them combined in a single individual. No individual so richly endowed would be willing to serve as the head of a municipal department, for he could turn his rare

They are rarely obtained.

combination of qualities to much more profitable use in some field of private business. The only practicable choice, as a rule, is among men who have some of the qualifications but are lacking in others. One possible appointee may be well qualified by education and training but entirely untried as an organizer and wholly inexperienced in dealing with the public. Another may be a tactful, resourceful, and popular fellow who can be depended upon to keep his co-workers happy but whose professional standing is next to nil. And there will be applicants who represent all the grades of fitness and unfitness between. As a general rule it will be found that the political pressure is in inverse ratio to an applicant's own personal qualifications.

Can we devise a better plan than most of those now in use?

Is it not practicable to devise some plan whereby more capable officials can be secured for the higher administrative posts in American municipalities? The superintendent of schools is always an expert in his line; no mere politician without education or experience is appointed to this post. Is it not possible to place such departments as health, public works, parks, and poor relief in charge of officials similarly qualified? Europe, as has been said, affords us no guidance in this direction, for we have tried Europe's method and found it a failure. Civil service enthusiasts contend that heads of departments, like subordinate officials, should be selected by straight civil service competition, but no American city has as yet given this plan a comprehensive trial and until some municipality is courageous enough to try this experiment it is not possible to say what its actual merits or defects would be.

Ordinary civil service will not do.

The proposal to choose the heads of departments by straight civil service competition does not look altogether promising, however, for the reason that no competitive tests can possibly measure the essential qualities which these officials ought to possess. It would not be difficult, of course, to determine by competitive examination the relative knowledge, education, and experience of various applicants. But these are not the only qualifications that the head of a municipal department ought to have. He should be temperamentally qualified for the delicate task of getting along smoothly with the public; he must be tactful, an organizer, able to work with others, and capable of winning the confidence of all concerned. These various qualities are not closely related to either knowledge or skill, and no one has yet devised an objective method of testing men for such qualities as initiative, soundness of judgment, power of coöperation, ability to keep a level head in emergencies, capacity to get work out of workers, or, with all due respect to the psychologists, broad intelligence. These things must be judged subjectively by giving some higher authority the function of rating them on a basis of his own personal knowledge.

During the past sixteen years a plan of non-competitive selection under the supervision of the civil service authorities has been given a trial in Boston. The mayor in all cases takes the initiative in selecting the department heads. Having made his tentative selection, however, he must submit the name of the proposed appointee to the Massachusetts Department of Civil Service, which is a state board of three persons appointed by the governor and hence quite outside the mayor's control. This body, if it finds that the proposed appointee is "qualified by education, training, and experience" for the work which he is expected to do, issues a certificate to that effect and the appointment then becomes valid. But if it does not find him to be so qualified, the appointment falls through and the mayor submits some other name. There is no formal competition and no one can be appointed except on the mayor's nomination. The only function of the civil service board is to veto any appointment which does not fulfil the stated requirements. In practice the plan has not measured up to expectation. The civil service authorities have interpreted the words "education, training and experience" in a very lenient way. They have made a good many rejections for obvious unfitness; but they have also accepted many appointees whose qualifications would not have passed muster if judged by the usual standards outside the public service. When the requirements for appointment to public office are stated in general terms they do not count for much. The head of the law department should be a lawyer, of course, and city charters so specify; but there is a world of difference among lawyers. The commissioner of public health ought to be a physician; but it is quite possible to be a doctor of medicine and still have the merest smattering of knowledge concerning public health and sanitary problems. On the other hand, there are practical difficulties in the way of requiring that heads of departments shall have qualifications which are set forth in

Boston's experiment.

detail. Character is the foundation of success, everywhere and at all times; but no man has yet been able to write an acceptable definition of what that word means.

What the civil service reformers now propose.

Civil service reformers have suggested that whenever a department head is to be chosen, the civil service commission should appoint a temporary examining committee of three laymen, all of whom are recognized experts in the same or in some closely related field. This committee of selection would then consider all the applications, devising and applying such tests as it might see fit, and reporting the results to the appointing authority. The conclusions of the committee would not be based upon relative technical proficiency alone, but would take into account the personal qualifications of the various applicants. Each applicant would be rated in order of general merit.

An objection to it.

This proposal has a good deal to commend it, but the objection commonly put forward is that it would break down the responsibility of the chief executive. When you compel a mayor or a city manager to work through lieutenants whom he has no initiative in selecting, and whose ideas may differ widely from his own, you cannot put the blame on him when things go wrong. It will be recalled that the President is given a free hand in the selection of his cabinet, and that the Senate rarely declines to confirm any head of a department whom the President may choose, although it has a constitutional right to do so.[1] The reason is that the constitution makes the President responsible for the faithful execution of the laws and this obligation cannot be fulfilled without giving him power to choose his own immediate subordinates. City charters usually place upon the mayor or the city manager a like obligation to see that the ordinances are enforced and the orders of the city council carried out. He cannot be held to it if required to work through men whom he has not chosen and in whom he may have no confidence.

The problem is still unsolved.

We have not yet found a good solution of this problem—how to put good men at the head of the city departments without breaking down the principle of executive responsibility. Nor have we completely solved another problem, that of protecting them against removal on improper grounds. It avails little for one mayor to place competent men in charge of the departments if his successor has a free hand to turn them out again. Not only

[1] See *above*, p. 276.

that but the insecurity which attaches to the higher administrative positions has served to make them unattractive in the first instance. The headship of a city department, as a rule, leads nowhere. It provides a man with a livelihood for a few years and then leaves him to shift for himself. It might be advisable to have heads of departments appointed for longer terms, but when a newly-elected mayor or a newly-appointed city manager makes up his mind to be rid of an official there is not much to be gained by using the compulsion of the law to prevent his doing so. Without the mayor's support a department head can rarely accomplish anything. What we need is a tradition of permanence, a habit of leaving men in office so long as they do their work satisfactorily. That tradition has been developed in American business organization but not yet in American government.

The internal organization of a municipal department is also a matter of considerable importance. In large cities, and particularly in those departments which have a variety of work to do, a division of labor and responsibility within the department becomes necessary. Departments are therefore broken up into bureaus and these again into divisions and sections when necessary. The department of public works, for example, may divide itself into bureaus of engineering, streets and bridges, water supply, sanitation and sewerage, lighting, parks, and buildings. The bureau of water supply may include two or more divisions, such as construction, maintenance, and finance. The finance division may have an accounting section, a section which deals with the collecting of water bills, and so on. Each bureau has at its head a deputy commissioner, superintendent, or bureau chief; each division or section has a divisional chief or foreman. These officials are now appointed in many cities by competitive tests under civil service rules. The general principles which apply to the division of administrative functions among departments should also govern the allocation of work among bureaus and other subordinate entities. But the details of organization cannot be determined by any general rule. These will vary in different departments. There is and can be no standard plan of internal organization applicable to them all. *The internal organization of city departments.*

It will be found, for example, that a certain type of work is common to several departments, or divisions, or bureaus. Legal *Line and staff work.*

360   THE GOVERNMENT OF AMERICAN CITIES

work or engineering work will serve as illustrations. The street department, park department, water department, buildings department are all concerned at times with the purchasing of lands and the various legal formalities involved. Should each department have its own legal expert to handle this work? Obviously that would mean duplication and waste. One central law department usually serves them all. Similarly these various physical departments have to do with the making of surveys and plans. Should each have its engineering bureau? As a rule a central engineering department functions for them all. So with departmental purchasing. In a word there are certain functions which have to be distributed and there are others which can be centralized.

An illustration. All this can be made plain, perhaps, by taking a concrete example. Let us suppose that the city desires to erect a new fire station. First of all, the land necessary for a site must be bought. But the fire department obviously has no official who is equipped to carry on the real-estate negotiations, sign an agreement of sale, and approve the deed to the city. So the law department is intrusted with this work. Then plans and specifications for the building have to be prepared. Here is where the city engineer's department comes in. And money must be raised by taxation or by loan to pay for both the land and the building. Likewise the bills have to be approved for payment. This brings the financial officers of the municipality into the job. A fire department, in a word, must call on at least three other departments, when it desires to have certain undertakings accomplished in an economical way.

A military analogy. Sometimes a military analogy is used to make this point clearer. In the army a distinction is made between "line" and "staff" work. Line work is distributed among infantry, cavalry, artillery, air forces, and so on. Staff work, such as is done by the quartermaster or ordinance corps, is not distributed; on the contrary, these two organizations function for all the line divisions. Similarly such departments or bureaus as law, finance, records, engineering, purchasing, statistics, research, auditing, and so forth represent the staff work of the municipality, while street paving, construction of buildings, sanitation, policing, fire protection, water supply and such things constitute the line functions which have to be widely distributed.

THE ADMINISTRATIVE DEPARTMENTS

The matter may perhaps be graphically illustrated by taking the organization of a public works department and showing its functional distribution in a general way.

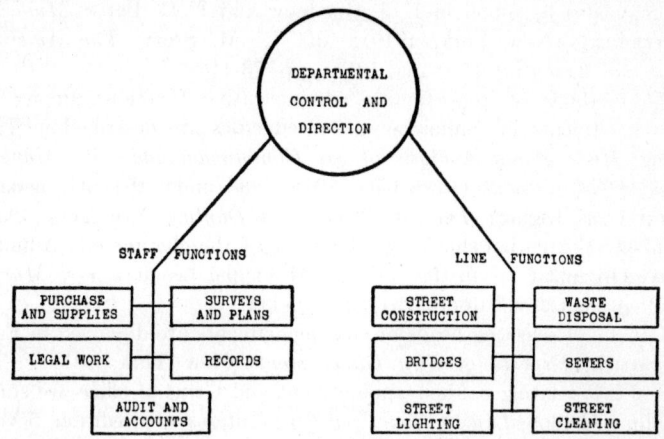

At the left are functions which can be performed for the public works department by divisions and bureaus in other departments—by the survey division of the city engineer's office, for example. At the right are functions which must be performed under the exclusive direction of the public works department itself.

This introduces a serious obstacle to the unification of responsibility, for where staff work is concerned the head of the line department does not exercise full control over it. But this is not an insuperable obstacle provided the responsibility of all departments to a common chief executive is maintained. On the other hand, even though all the lines of administrative responsibility converge inward and upward, there may be wastefulness of energy and funds through an injudicious distribution of work among departments, an unscientific intra-departmental organization, or a failure to concentrate staff work adequately.

This division makes the problem of internal organization more difficult.

REFERENCES

The departmental organization of fourteen typical American cities, big and little, is shown by a series of charts in W. P. Capes, *The Modern City and Its Government* (New York, 1922). The principles of departmental organization are discussed in Henry Bruère, *The New City Gov-*

ernment (2d edition, New York, 1913), in William Anderson, *American City Government* (New York, 1925), pp. 422-453, and to some extent in Morris L. Cooke, *Our Cities Awake: Notes on Municipal Activities and Administration* (New York, 1912). Briefer discussions of the subject may also be found in F. J. Goodnow and F. G. Bates, *Municipal Government* (New York, 1919); and R. M. Story, *The American Municipal Executive* (Urbana, 1918), pp. 73-113.

The methods of apportioning administrative functions among the five departments in commission-governed cities are described in T. S. Chang, *History and Analysis of the Commission and City Manager Plans of Government* (Iowa City, 1918), and under the city manager plan in C. E. Rightor, *The City Manager in Dayton* (New York, 1909), pp. 57-208. Mention should also be made of the chapter on "Administrative Organization" in the National Municipal League's *New Municipal Program* (New York, 1919), pp. 119-144.

Methods of selecting heads of city departments are discussed in E. A. Fitzpatrick, *Experts in City Government* (New York, 1918). The rules of law relating to their appointment and terms of office are stated in John F. Dillon, *Law of Municipal Corporations* (5th edition, 5 vols., Boston, 1911), Vol. I, pp. 664-668. Mention should be made of the various administrative surveys published by the New York Bureau of Municipal Research, particularly those of San Francisco, Rochester, Denver, and Indianapolis. Special attention should also be called to the elaborate report on *The Government of Cincinnati*, edited by Lent D. Upson (Cincinnati, 1924). The organization of departments in European cities is explained in W. B. Munro, *The Government of European Cities* (new edition, New York, 1926).

CHAPTER XIX

MUNICIPAL EMPLOYEES AND THE CIVIL SERVICE SYSTEM

One of the difficult problems in any large business enterprise is the labor problem. In so far as the city is engaged in enterprises of a business nature it has similar difficulties to face. Indeed, the proper handling of its labor force, skilled and unskilled,—the handling of it in such way as to reconcile efficiency with humane considerations—that is a problem which makes mayors and city managers prematurely old. How should city employees be hired, at what rates, and what privileges should they have? How can discipline among them be maintained? Should they be allowed to organize? How can their relentless demands for more pay and fewer hours of labor be resisted? And when those who serve the city become old and useless how can they be taken care of—that is, without putting too heavy a burden on the city treasury. These, and many other similar questions, make up the American city's labor problem.

The labor problem.

The cities of the United States are spending for all purposes about two billion dollars per year, of which more than half goes for salaries and wages. This huge sum provides a livelihood for about 700,000 employees. Now it is a common complaint that the cities do not obtain anything like full value for this payroll expenditure and the complaint has a good deal of justification. It is pretty generally conceded that municipal employees are less industrious and give less value for their wages than do those engaged by private corporations. The only question is how much less. Some competent observers have figured that city labor is on the average eighty per cent efficient; but most heads of departments would regard this percentage as far too high. The fact is that the relative efficiency of city employees is not the same in all branches of work. It is usually highest in the school department and lowest in those forms of public service where large amounts of unskilled labor are

Waste in the payroll.

employed,—in the street cleaning department, for example. Striking an average, it would probably not be unfair to say that the American city does not get more than sixty cents on the dollar for its payroll expenditure.

It is over emphasized.

Critics of our municipal system will call this figure too high, but they have been inclined to exaggerate the slothfulness of those who hold city jobs. Having no reliable data upon which to base a comparison between public and private employments, the average citizen is guided to conclusions by what he happens to see. On his way to work in the morning he sees a decrepit old fellow feebly pushing a refuse-cart along the pavement, picking up a scrap of paper here and there and covering the ground at the rate of half a block an hour. He assumes that this is what goes on in all branches of the public service—a dollar's worth of work for four or five dollars a day. It does not occur to him that the oldest and least capable among city employees are usually assigned to the street-cleaning division. When an employee has grown old in the service and is no longer able to do an eight-hour stretch with pick and shovel, the city must either find a pension or an easy job for him. Frequently it has no regular pension system and hence must resort to the other alternative. It turns the payroll into a pension list.

The reasons for the waste.

Yet with all proper allowance for these exaggerated impressions based upon casual observation it cannot be denied that the problem of obtaining a fair return for its labor expenditures is one that cities have not yet been able to solve. The reason can be summed up in three words—the spoils system. It will be replied that many cities have abolished this system by the introduction of civil service reform, and in a formal sense this is true. They no longer, openly and flagrantly, give jobs to incompetents for purely political reasons. A prominent Boston politician has recently been narrating his autobiography in a series of newspaper interviews. Speaking of his early career he says, concerning an old-time political friend: "I worked hard for him and he paid me by getting me a job on the city." Today we do not put it in those words, nor is the thing done so directly. The job-seeker in many cases must make his approach to the payroll in a roundabout way through channels which the civil service laws prescribe.

It is easier to abolish the spoils system than to get rid of the spoils spirit. The latter remains. Many city employees still look upon political pull as their chief asset and defense. They depend upon it for promotion, for assignment to favored locations, for overtime work at high rates of pay, for extra holidays, and for the forgiving of sins. The adoption of the merit system has by no means dissociated politics from municipal employment, not even in cities where the civil service rules are most rigidly administered. Reformers sometimes ask the question: "Why can't the city get work from its employees the way private enterprises do?" It is a sign of the reformer's political innocence. There are some good reasons why the city has not been able to do it.

The spoils system and the spoils spirit.

Remember, in the first place, that the city employee occupies a dual position. He is a worker—but he is also to an extent his own employer because he has a vote and helps elect those who are set over him. All city employees are inveterate voters; they come close to a hundred per cent attendance at primaries and elections. The direct and indirect political strength of the public employees in American cities is nowhere less than ten per cent and is probably twice as much in some communities. Here is a solid bloc which the mayors and city managers must take into their reckonings. These officials, who stand in the position of ultimate employers, are in part dependent for their continuance in office upon the good will and favor of their employees. To retain the political support of these employees they are sometimes forced to sacrifice what they know to be the best interests of the municipality. For the city employees, whether organized or not, are a unit in protecting their own interests,—which cannot be said of the rest of the people. Their pressure is strong beyond what their numbers warrant. It is not necessary for the city employees to strike in order to gain their ends. They can go to the polls and change their employers, for in many cases they hold the balance of power. That is one important difference between the organization of public and private business.

The dual position of city employees.

There is another difference. In every private business enterprise, the management has to meet the competition of rival concerns and hence is compelled to maintain a certain standard of labor efficiency. Failure to do this will result in diminished earning-power and perhaps in bankruptcy. But the city authorities are subject to no such competitive inspiration. They set

The lack of standards.

their own standards. And no matter how low these standards may be, a city is never driven out of business by its competitors, nor into the bankruptcy court by its creditors. Even if its streets are ill-kept and badly lighted, its public buildings shabby, its sanitation defective, its death rate high, and its police corrupt,— the city nevertheless keeps on doing business. If it fails to make both ends meet, it borrows money. If it cannot repay the debt when due, it borrows more money. When the treasurer of a bank absconds with the funds the bank closes its doors, but when a city treasurer is found short in his accounts the tax rate comes to the rescue. The manager of a factory, when he fails to earn a dividend, cannot pacify his stockholders by dilating upon the wickedness of his rivals or by praising the enlightened character of his own work. But public officials are able to exculpate themselves for almost any form of incompetence by starting a partisan controversy. The pocket-nerve controls the muscles of business. The body politic may be an organism, as some students of political theory have assured us, but if so it lacks this nerve in its anatomical structure.

The dependence on subordinates. No matter how capable or how diligent the head of a city department may be he cannot obtain full value for departmental expenditures so long as his associates or his subordinates are unable or unwilling to give him full support and coöperation. There are so many details to be handled that he must rely upon the judgment and counsel of his chief subordinates, each of whom is presumed to have special familiarity with some branch of the department's work. They, in turn, must devolve important duties and decisions upon inspectors and foremen. In the public works department, for example, the specifications for street construction are necessarily prepared by subordinates and submitted to the head of the department for his approval. The latter cannot check up every item and make certain that there are no crevices in which a slippery contractor may find refuge. If a department head should try to scrutinize such details he would have no time for anything else. Then, when the contract has been awarded and the job is in progress, he must depend upon his subordinates for rigorous inspection to ensure that the contractor lives up to his specifications. If these inspectors happen to be corrupt or negligent the city will find itself paying good money for scamped work, no matter how honest

MUNICIPAL EMPLOYEES

the head of the department may be. It is not enough to make a department efficient at the top. Public money will continue to be wasted so long as the municipal service is incompetent or ill-disciplined in its lower grades.

Low standards of labor efficiency to some extent are due to the methods by which the city's workers are recruited. Originally the favor of a politician was the only passport to employment and in some cities this is still the case. In others there are civil service rules which require that positions be filled either by open competition or, in the case of ordinary manual labor, by priority of application. This merit system has made headway during the past forty years, but on the whole its progress has been slow because the power of the politicians has been unitedly thrown against it. Down to about 1885 the spoils system was so deeply entrenched that its overthrow seemed impossible. Nevertheless civil service reform has succeeded in dislodging it from a considerable part of the national, state, and municipal administrations. *Civil service reform as a remedy.*

The purpose of the merit system, or civil service reform, is twofold. It seeks to prevent the appointment of persons who are clearly unqualified and whose selection represents the liquidation of political indebtedness. But a merely negative purpose is not a sufficient foundation upon which to build an improved public service. Hence the second aim of the merit system is to provide a means whereby qualified applicants may be recruited and certified to the appointing authority. That is the constructive service which it undertakes to render. *Twofold purpose of the merit system.*

In some features the civil service or merit system differs from city to city, but its general operations are about as follows: Whenever a subordinate position is to be filled, the mayor or other appointing officer calls upon the civil service commission to send him an "eligible list," or list of persons who have qualified for appointment. If the commission has recently held competitions for positions of this class it will have an eligible list on hand. For example, if the position is that of policeman, fireman, clerk, or stenographer, there is usually no delay in sending an eligible list, because examinations for these posts are held frequently. But if some unusual position is to be filled, such as that of bacteriologist in the water department or chief cataloguer in the public library, it is often necessary to hold a special *How it operates.*

competition. Public announcement is made; applications are received; special examiners are appointed when necessary, examination papers are made out; the tests are taken by the various applicants; and the results are figured. Candidates who have made the best showing are then certified, and the appointment must be made from among them. Ordinarily the appointing officer may select at his own discretion anyone on the eligible list.

The nature of the tests. It should not be assumed from this brief description, however, that civil service competitions take the form of written examinations like those given in school or college. They are competitions rather than examinations in the narrow sense, and of a distinctly practical nature. The tests are closely related to the work which the applicants will have to do in case of appointment. Candidates for positions as stenographers are required to receive dictation and transcribe it. Rapidity, accuracy, and neatness are taken into account in determining the order of merit. Civil service tests for policemen assume the form of physical examinations, questions on elementary law, on local geography, and on the duties of a policeman. The examiners find out what qualifications a position demands and then try to devise a set of questions which will determine these qualifications. In the case of technical positions it is the practice to enlist the aid of experts in framing the questions and in grading the answers. The civil service commission, it should be made clear, does not make the appointments but merely certifies the names of those who are eligible. In many cities it is provided that no one who is not a bona fide resident may be certified as eligible.

Adaptation of the tests to the position. There is a great deal of difference in the nature of the various competitions. In most cases a certain amount of weight is given to general education and experience, as indicated by the diplomas and testimonials which each applicant presents. Knowledge of technique and practical ability are tested by written and oral examinations. Personality is rated on a basis of an interview with the examiners. These various tests are weighted according to some scale such as 30 for general education and experience, 50 for technical competence, and 20 for personal qualities. It is desirable that leeway be given for a rating on personal qualities, but it obviously opens the door to favoritism if the examiners are susceptible to political influence.

MUNICIPAL EMPLOYEES

In the case of high positions, of a special or technical sort, it is the practice in some cities to give a non-competitive test when the appointing authority asks for it. This merely involves a scrutiny of the applicant's qualifications to see whether he measures up to the requirements. The justification for this is that sometimes a well-qualified man will accept a position on that basis, whereas no applicants of any such qualifications would appear for a public competence test. Non-assembled competitions are also held in some cases. In such cases the candidates do not come together but send in their records, samples of work, etc., and the examiners rate them on this evidence.

Non-competitive tests.

Ordinarily, when an appointment is made from the civil service list it is probationary for a period of six months or a year. At the end of this interval the appointing authority may discharge the new official or employee and may ask for another. But if the probationary period has been concluded the employee, if continued, goes on the permanent force and may not thereafter be discharged except in accordance with the civil service regulations.

For the honest and impartial administration of the merit system it is essential that the civil service commission shall be so organized as to be immune from direct political pressure. This immunity is not easy to ensure but various methods of securing it have been given a trial. In Massachusetts there is one civil service commission for the entire state.[1] This state board includes a commissioner of civil service and two associates, all of whom are appointed by the governor. No Massachusetts city has its own municipal civil service commission; when any post within the classified service is to be filled, the city authorities call upon the state authorities to certify the necessary names. The palpable objection to the Massachusetts plan is that it infringes the principle of municipal home rule, as this principle is commonly applied throughout a large portion of the United States. But in essence it is nothing more than the extension of a practice which has been commonly followed (and is not regarded as an infringement upon local autonomy) by states which lay great stress upon the sacred privilege of municipal self-determination. Examinations for teachers' certificates are in many of these states conducted by state boards of education and

The civil service commission: how organized:

1. The Massachusetts plan.

---

[1] The same is true of New Jersey.

no one who is not so certified can be appointed to any teaching position in a city school. If the certification of teachers can properly be made a state function, why not the certification of other municipal officials and employees such as playground supervisors, probation officers, library assistants, for example? The question, after all, is one of expediency, not of principle. In Massachusetts the plan of state examination has had the advantage of removing the civil service system from the direct control of the local politicians; but it is not at all certain that it would work out this way in other jurisdictions. The state politicians might use it for their own benefit.

2. The Illinois plan.

In the cities of Illinois, and in those of most other states which make provision for civil service rules in their cities, a very different plan of administering the merit system is in use. The mayor of each city (or the commission, where there is one) appoints a civil service board, usually of three members. Each member ordinarily serves for three or six years and one member retires annually or biennially. Sometimes it is provided that both political parties shall be represented on the board. Under certain conditions the mayor may also remove members of the civil service board or commission. These municipal commissions function within their respective cities; they conduct the local competitions and are not subject to the supervision of any state authority. This method is more considerate of home rule sensibilities, but it is unsound in principle and has not been found satisfactory in practice. The civil service commission is assumed to act as a check upon the mayor. But how can it properly fulfil this function when it is virtually under his control? It is in accordance with an elementary and universal trait of human nature that civil service commissioners appointed by the mayor will try to meet his desires by straining both the letter and spirit of the law as far as they will go. Persons not properly qualified will be slipped into classified positions when the mayor insists upon it. This can be done by holding non-competitive examinations, or by authorizing "temporary" appointments ("permanent temporaries" they are facetiously called) without any examinations at all, or by otherwise stretching the commission's power to make exceptions in special cases. In one or another of these ways patronage will be allowed to masquerade in the garb of merit. A recent investigation of the subject has shown that nearly all the strictly municipal commissions are honeycombed with politics.[1]

3. The Philadelphia plan.

Some cities endeavor to keep the civil service commission out of the mayor's reach, while preserving the principle of home rule, by vesting the appointment of the commissioners in the hands of the city council. This is the arrangement in both Philadelphia and Denver, and there is a good deal to be said in its favor. The Philadelphia civil service commission consists of three members chosen for four years by a majority vote of the city council. They are not removable by the mayor nor are they in any direct way subject to his control. Unfortunately, however, American municipal experience does not warrant the expectation that civil service commissioners chosen by city councils will consistently reflect a high standard of integrity or non-partisanship. As an appointing authority the American city council has proved a failure. The average councilman, especially if he be a ward or district representative, is not interested in civil service reform or in reform of any sort. He is far more concerned, as a rule, about getting jobs for clamorous supporters. The civil service commission which insists upon a strict adherence to merit, paying no heed to the hints, suggestions, recommendations, and protests of councilmen will sooner or later find itself replaced by one whose members are more amenable. No one who has observed the habits of American city councils can fail to be driven to that conclusion.

4. The New York plan.

There is still another method of administering the civil service laws in cities; namely, the New York plan, which attempts to combine local management with central supervision. Each of the sixty cities in New York State has its own civil service board appointed by the mayor. These local boards conduct the civil service tests and prepare the eligible lists. But their work is under the supervision of a state civil service commission appointed by the governor. The latter prescribes the general rules; it may investigate the work of any local commission and may even remove the latter from office. The value of this plan is proportioned of course, to the thoroughness and impartiality with which the state commission performs its supervisory duties, and

[1] See the report on *The Character and Functioning of Civil Service Commissions*, issued by the Governmental Research Conference (1922), pp. 23-35.

in New York this has not always been very strict. Competent supervision involves about as much work as actual administration of the civil service rules.

Results of the system. The merit system of selecting city officials and employees, despite the ineptitude with which it has too often been administered, has demonstrated itself to be a vast improvement over the older method of distributing responsible positions among party workers. Where civil service rules have been intelligently and impartially applied they have closed the door to one of the most iniquitous of all political practices, that of treating public office as a thing to be bargained for like merchandise, its price being determined by the law of supply and demand. The merit system has honestly sought to substitute fitness for favoritism and open competition for political manipulation. No one nowadays has the hardihood to assert that all men are endowed with an equal capacity to perform the technical duties which arise in connection with the city's accounting, sanitary, health, and constructional work. The marvel is that any such doctrine should ever have gained currency. The issue today is a purely practical one: admitting that the appointees ought to have special qualifications, how can we best make sure that no one deficient in these qualifications shall be selected? The system of civil service competition, with all its shortcomings, affords a reasonable degree of assurance on this point. If anyone has honest doubts on this score he can speedily resolve them by comparing the administrative personnel of those cities which have applied the merit system with that of other cities which have not.

Some obstacles that it has encountered: The progress of the merit system would have been more rapid were it not for the mishaps and obstacles which any far-reaching reform is sure to encounter. It was put on the market under an ill-chosen name; for there are few expressions in the English language less inspiring than "civil service reform." It has had the misfortune to be imposed upon unwilling officers. Its aim is to make mayors and other appointing authorities do what most of them would not do if they could avoid it. It is maintained by the strength of statutes and the decrees of courts, not by the power of public sentiment or the influence of tradition.

1. Public indifference. The indifference of public opinion, when raids upon the merit system are in progress, has been illustrated by the ease with which amendments to the civil service laws have been enacted for the special benefit of men who have been in the military or naval service. In many instances these "veterans' preference" laws have virtually destroyed the merit principle and have compelled the appointment of some men who have no qualifications except that they went into the army under the draft laws when they could not avoid it. *Dulce et decorum est pro patria vivere*—when the work is light and the pay is good. If public sentiment were not so indifferent to civil service reform, this breach in the merit system would never have been possible.

But if the public is somewhat indifferent to the strict application of the merit principle, the politicians are not. Failing to prevent the enactment of civil service laws, they endeavor to control the boards and commissions which are entrusted with the administration of these laws. To this end they bring pressure to bear upon governors or mayors and often secure the appointment of civil service commissioners who are ready to "administer the system liberally." This pressure is the more difficult to withstand because the leaders of both political parties join in it. Party platforms pay lip-homage to the principles of civil service reform but in many instances its destinies have been committed to the care of unenthusiastic or even hostile hands. <small>2. Political pressure.</small>

Civil service commissions have had to work with the tools at hand. Written and oral examinations, supplemented by testimonials, records, and general information gleaned in various ways, have been their chief reliance. Every sort of test has been tried in some city or another—written tests, oral tests, physical tests, performance tests, character tests, intelligence tests, experience tests, and so-termed "practical" tests. Some commissions require that applicants shall have had a definite amount of preliminary training or experience before being admitted to the examinations; others make the competition a wide-open one to which even those who have no chance of success are admitted. In any case the civil service system is handicapped by the unreliability of the tools available. Formal examinations and tests, no matter what their character, cannot be relied upon to sift the best from the second-best. There are no known tests by means of which one can unerringly determine, from among a roomful of candidates, the two or three who rank highest in firmness, initiative, honesty, tact, leadership, common sense, resourcefulness, personality, and general intelligence. Yet <small>3. Inadequacy of the tools.</small>

these are the qualities which are greatly to be desired in public officials. No amount of technical proficiency will spell success in either public or private employment if a man be deficient in all of them. Those who have had much to do with college examinations can well appreciate the necessary limitations of any system based upon questions and answers. Examinations have their only justification in the fact that thus far we have found nothing better. No matter how intelligently they are planned or how "practical" they may be, they rarely uncover more than one thing—the ability of the candidate to pass them. And this may or may not be related to their ability to do other things.

4. Labor's attitude. In labor circles there is a feeling that the merit system is "undemocratic" in that it affords an undue advantage to those applicants who have had a high school or college education. This objection is especially urged in the case of clerical positions. Young men and women who, through straitened circumstances, have been compelled to leave school and go to work at an early age are apt to find the civil service tests too difficult. This means that they are debarred from employment in positions to which the merit system applies. For obviously the candidates who have gone through high school or college are at a great advantage in being able to write legibly and correctly, to make the most of what they know, and to keep their wits about them at the examination. Taking examinations is an old story with them. They are in other respects well equipped and score higher on the rating for general education; so they go to the top of the list, while the candidates who were "too poor to get much schooling" gravitate to the bottom. The politicians are continually sobbing about the injustice of this situation.

But why shouldn't the educated young man or woman be allowed to take the advantage which comes from greater knowledge and intellectual proficiency? And why shouldn't the city get the benefit of it? Public education, if it is worth the enormous sums we are spending on it, ought to yield some return to the public which pays the bills.

5. Results in the choice of mediocrities. The merit system, one often hears it said, is a promoter of mediocrity in the public service. It shuts out the worst but fails to get the best. It has filled the municipal service with appointees who have just enough intelligence to pass the tests and no more.

These men and women, if they had more ambition and ability, would be in some form of private business. As it is, they fall back upon the public service as offering the most pay for the least effort. By dint of coaching and repeated trials they eventually manage to pass the civil service tests and are appointed. Thereafter their work is done with one eye on the clock; the height of their idealism being to keep from being suspended or dismissed. They become routineers, knowing only one way of doing their work and always opposing any new way. They oppose the whole weight of their inertia to all progress in methods or mechanism.[1]

This indictment, so often framed by public officials, is much exaggerated, yet it is not altogether without foundation. The civil service competitions are not patronized by the ambitious young men and women of the community. To them public employment does not promise a secure and profitable career. Consequently the service must draw, for the most part, from among those who find difficulty in measuring up to the standard of private employment. Compared with private industry the public service is better paid at the bottom but more poorly paid at the top. Common laborers, messengers, clerks and bookkeepers get more remuneration for less work in the city's employ than they can usually obtain elsewhere. But superintendents, skilled technicians, and engineers are usually underpaid by the municipality, hence they are continually dropping out into private employ. In a word the municipal service is a sort of sifter which tends to keep the poorest and let the better ones go. For this situation the merit system is not to blame, inasmuch as the civil service authorities do not fix the scale of salaries.

But it is a fair criticism upon civil service commissions that they have concentrated their attention too exclusively upon the work of examining candidates and have laid too little stress upon the importance of recruiting a better grade of applicants. They merely examine those who come, overlooking the very important fact that if all the candidates are of a poor grade there is no form of examination which will pick good ones from the lot. Still the root of the trouble may be found in the failure of the city to make its service permanently attractive. This it

The need for better recruiting.

---

[1] For a criticism of civil service personnel, based on experience in public office, see F. C. Howe, *Confessions of a Reformer* (New York, 1925).

could do if promotions and salaries, as well as appointments, were made to depend upon merit. Meanwhile, and until this is done, the work of recruiting better material for the public service ought to have more attention. There has been some contact with trade schools, with schools which give stenographic and clerical training, and with other institutions which are natural recruiting grounds. But there ought to be some contact with the colleges where the best material for the public service is being diverted to the professions and to private business.

<small>Promotions in the municipal service.</small> The greatest obstacle to the successful working of the merit system is the existing system of promotion. No method of making appointments will secure the best results so long as it is accompanied by a plan of promotions based upon political influence or personal favoritism. The service is a blind alley for the man without a pull. This is still the situation in most American cities. Increases in pay or advancement in rank are not usually determined by examinations, or by efficiency records, or by other objective test; hence the incentive to real effort is lacking. Why should a young man work hard in a city engineer's office when he knows that some politician's friend of inferior ability is likely to be promoted over his head after the next election? This is the main reason why the atmosphere at the city hall is permeated with inertia. Promotions, like appointments, should be based upon merit and upon merit alone. Yet it is far easier to say this than to devise a promotional system based upon merit. In promotions the personal equation ought to count for more than in appointments. An employee is not entitled to promotion unless he has shown a coöperative spirit as well as ability. Some cities maintain efficiency records which take into account the quality and quantity of work performed, punctuality, general conduct, errors and omissions, as well as the personal opinions of foremen, bureau chiefs, and heads of departments. Ratings based upon these records are used in determining who shall be promoted and when. On the whole, however, this plan of promotion based upon efficiency records tends to become mechanical and seems rarely to be popular with either the higher officials or the employees.

The time has come for American cities to accept some lessons in personnel administration from the field of private employment. Almost every large industry now maintains an employment or personnel department charged with the function of securing employees of the right type and seeing that they are not improperly discharged. These employment departments have made a great advance in their technique during the past ten years; their work has succeeded in reducing the labor turnover in all large industries. It has been suggested, therefore, that cities should reconstruct their civil service departments along similar lines, particularly by insisting that the single commissioner at the head of this department shall have a "knowledge of the science of modern employment administration." It is further proposed that this employment commissioner should take over, as in the case of private enterprises, some responsibility for the health, the working conditions, the recreation, and the general welfare of the municipal employees.[1] In a few cities a start along such lines has already been made.

Personnel work: a lesson from private employment.

The merit system is concerned not only with appointments and promotions but with dismissals. In the absence of civil service regulations the employees are for the most part subject to removal without any assigned cause. Under the merit system the usual requirement is that no official or employee appointed under civil service rules may be discharged except on specific charges made in writing, and on such charges he is entitled to a hearing. In some cities this hearing takes place before the mayor or the head of the department who makes the dismissal; in others it is held by the civil service commission. In the latter case the commission is sometimes authorized to decide whether the charges have been sustained, and if it finds that they are not, to reinstate the employee. Occasionally there is a right of appeal to the courts. The mere requirement that charges be filed and supported at a public hearing may not seem to afford much protection against unjust dismissal, but in practice it does provide a considerable means of security. Mayors and heads of departments will put up with a good deal rather than comply with this procedure. The dismissed official is sure to strike back by making counter-charges and attacking the work of his former superiors. He will have a lawyer for his counsel at the hearing;

Dismissals.

---

[1] For a further consideration of this matter see A. W. Procter, *Principles of Public Personnel Administration* (New York, 1921); the Report of the Governmental Research Conference on *The Character and Functioning of Municipal Civil Service Commissions* (1922); and the *Report of the National Municipal League's Committee on Civil Service* (1923).

witnesses will be summoned, and before the matter is closed some high explosives may be set off. Every city employee who keeps his eyes open and his ears alert is bound to accumulate truths and half-truths which make spicy reading when unfolded in newspapers. There are skeletons in every city hall closet. No mayor desires to run the risk of providing his political enemies with ammunition by permitting these public hearings to be held frequently during the course of his administration. For this reason it is sometimes hinted that incompetent and intractable employees keep their positions by reason of what they know, not by reason of what they do.

Standardization of work and pay.

Much dissatisfaction among municipal employees is caused by the haphazard methods of relating work and pay. Rarely is there any standardization of positions or salaries. Men who do exactly the same work may be rated as clerks at two thousand dollars a year or as bookkeepers at twenty-five hundred. Women are put down as stenographers, typists, secretaries, or clerks, not according to the work they do but according to the caprice of the department heads. In most cities there is no standard rate for each designated form of service. The ordinary laborers in all the departments commonly get a fixed rate of four or five dollars per day, but for those higher up on the payroll every department is a law unto itself. What a city official or employee receives in salary or wages at any given time depends upon a number of things, among which political influence, personal favoritism, legislative action, good luck, length of experience, and individual competence figure in varying degrees. American cities, taking them as a whole, have had no comprehensive or consistent policy in the matter of salaries or wages. Although civil service commissions are sometimes empowered to classify positions they find great difficulty in doing this without creating a lot of jealousy and resentment among the more favored employees. Every city employee believes in the standardization of positions and salaries provided the schedules are standardized upward—nobody wants standardization downward.[1]

The difficulties concerned.

Various plans of employment-and-salary standardization have been worked out and a few cities have put them into operation. Chicago was the first, about a dozen years ago. All the employees

[1] For a discussion see W. C. Beyer, "Employment Standardization in the Public Service," *National Municipal Review*, vol. ix, pp. 396-398 (1920).

MUNICIPAL EMPLOYEES 379

of that city were classified according to the nature of their work and the length of their service, a standard rate of compensation being fixed for each. Other communities followed Chicago's example. But the general increases in the cost of living which accompanied the war threw schedules and standards out of joint. Cities felt that substantial increases in the pay of employees were warranted by the higher living costs and it seemed expedient to deal more generously with employees in the lower ranks than with those higher up. Men with families on their hands were deemed to be deserving of special consideration irrespective of their work or experience ratings. Remuneration cannot be easily standardized either in public or in private employment so long as the purchasing power of the dollar keeps fluctuating. It is not enough, in any event, to adopt a plan of salary standardization and leave it to take care of itself. Evasions will multiply unless watchfulness is maintained. Favored employees will be classified as foremen, inspectors, or timekeepers when the nature of the work does not warrant such classification. Clerks who do the most routine work (who merely make out the monthly water bills, for example) will be rated as bookkeepers or accountants in order that they may obtain more than the standard rate of remuneration established for ordinary clerical service. A plain stenographer will blossom overnight into a "confidential secretary" or will be given some other title that looks like a warrant for higher pay—with no change in duties. To protect the city against such abuses it is essential not only that the civil service authorities be empowered to determine the proper classification of employees but that they also examine the payroll. Discretion in this matter cannot be safely left to the heads of departments.

It is the habit of economists to tell us that the rates of remuneration, in all forms of employment, depend fundamentally upon the law of supply and demand. But in so far as workers become thoroughly organized they are less susceptible to the immediate influence of this law. Municipal employees are now well organized, under some plan or other, in most of the larger cities of the United States. The higher officials (police chiefs, park superintendents, engineers, etc.) have their own national organizations but these are in no way affiliated. Even the city managers have their association. The subordinate employees are

The organization of municipal employees.

organized by departments and they usually (though not always) affiliate with kindred organizations of workers in private employment. Thus the teamsters and chauffeurs in the employ of the city are members of a union which links up with the similar bodies drawn from the service of private contractors. These organizations of municipal workers have in many cases obtained charters from the American Federation of Labor and are under its jurisdiction. The work of organizing has been so vigorously carried on that the great majority of those who are on the city payroll are now organized. In Boston (1925) the unionization and outside affiliation includes not only the laborers and foremen in practically all the city departments, but the library employees and many of the school teachers. It does not, however, include the policemen and firemen who are organized but with no outside affiliation. Where the outside affiliation exists it is usually with the American Federation of Labor or with the National Federation of State, City, Town, and County Employees' Unions.

Some basic questions involved. Questions concerning the right of municipal employees to organize, to bargain collectively, to affiliate with national organizations, and to enforce their demands by means of a strike have been much discussed during recent years. The right of these employees to organize for the promotion of their own interests is generally conceded. No serious objection has been urged against the formation of local organizations under local control. But there is no such censensus of opinion concerning the right of all organized municipal employees to affiliate with national federations and thereby subject themselves to a measure of outside control. Even wider is the disagreement as to whether such organizations of municipal employees should possess the right to strike as a means of enforcing their own demands or as a method of showing their sympathy with the demands of some affiliated organization.

The ordinary workers. An intelligent answer to this question seems to require that a preliminary distinction be made among the various classes of municipal employees. Some of them are engaged in work which can be interrupted, for a time at least, without grave menace to the public safety. The cessation of work in the public parks or on street construction may result in monetary loss to the city and inconvenience to the citizens. But the degree of loss or inconvenience is not greater than when public utilities under private operation (the telephone, lighting, or street railway services) are tied up by a strike of the workers. It would be a doctrine hard to maintain that while motormen and conductors may resort to a strike for the enforcement of their demands, the employees in the parks and paving departments may not.

But there are certain branches of municipal administration in which the interruption of service involves not only monetary loss and public inconvenience but exposes the whole community to serious danger. This is the case when a police or fire department goes on strike, leaving the city a prey to yeggmen and incendiaries. Under such conditions the municipality is left powerless to fulfil the most elementary functions for which it was created, the protection of life and property. The right of doctors and nurses to walk out of the city hospital, leaving the sick to suffer unattended, can hardly be called a self-evident right. It is not a right that inheres in humanity. Even amid the inhumanities of war the combatants assert no such right in relation to their enemies. In any event the proposition that the safety of the whole people stands above the economic interests of any class, whether of workers or employers, is not open to debate, argument, or arbitration. A government cannot debate or arbitrate its own right to perform the functions for which it was created. *The special services.*

Another difficult question concerns the obligations of the city to its employees when they have grown old in the service or have become incapacitated. There is no legal obligation, to be sure, but people seem to feel that there is a moral one. The easiest, and at the same time the most costly way of fulfilling this obligation is to keep men on the payroll after they have outlived their usefulness. That is what most cities have done. Today, however, some of them have come to an appreciation of the wastefulness involved in this practice and have taken hold on the pension problem in a fair spirit. Many cities have partial pension systems covering certain classes of officials and employees such as school teachers, policemen, and firemen. In the other departments they give allowances on retirement where the service has been notably meritorious or where the aged employee's friends can bring sufficient political influence to bear. During the past ten years a number of cities have established pension sys- *Pensions for municipal employees.*

tems covering all branches of their service and it is probable that other cities will follow.

Comprehensive pension systems covering all classes of city employees, and resting upon a basis which is equitable both to the employee and the taxpayer, are among the most urgent needs of the American city today. The old arrangement has been not only unfair but extravagant. Aged employees cannot be summarily dismissed and left to shift for themselves, thus becoming a burden on their relative or recipients of public charity. No city can pursue this method as a settled policy; the humanitarian sentiments of the people will not tolerate it. Mayors and councilmen cannot justify it before their constituents. The only alternatives are to provide a pension system or to make the payroll serve the purpose—and of these two alternatives the former is far cheaper in the end. Keeping a lot of superannuated employees on the payroll is not only expensive in itself but it exerts a slackening influence upon the work of younger men. It slows up the whole department.

<small>Recent progress in this field.</small> American cities would have established comprehensive pension systems long ago were it not for the practical difficulties which stand in the way. Should the employee contribute something to the pension fund, or should the pension be a free gift from the city? What should be the pension age? Some men are decrepit at sixty, while others are capable of doing a good day's work five or even ten years later. Should pensions be given only to those who have served for twenty or thirty years; if so, what about the men who entered the service late in life and cannot be dismissed without being left penniless? What provision should be made for the widows and children of employees who die in service before reaching the pension age—especially where they have contributed to the pension fund? In any event a general pension system is bound to involve a city in large expenditures. Workers outside the public service do not usually take kindly to public pension schemes. They cannot see the justice of providing pensions for men who have held steady jobs in the public service at good rates of pay, who have never been out of work, and who are generally regarded among their fellows as a favored class. For this reason, municipal pension schemes, when submitted to the people at the polls, have often been defeated and this despite the fact that the entire political strength

of the city employees has been mobilized in their favor. The American municipal voter requires further education in this field. Nevertheless, in spite of these difficulties, several large cities have been successful in adopting sound municipal pension systems within the past few years.[1]

It is worthy of remark that although the American people spend a round billion each year to maintain the public schools, they spend nothing (or next to nothing) in specific education for the public service. There are schools of military and naval training, but there are no publicly supported schools for the training of men and women in the work of postmasters, internal revenue officers, police commissioners, paving inspectors, probation officers, park foremen, assessors, and the like. To some extent municipal officials in the technical bureaus (water analysis, engineering, health laboratories, and so on) are trained in the regular institutions of technical and professional education, but they form but a small part of the entire municipal personnel. The same is true of school teachers, who form a larger element, and of librarians, accountants and draftsmen. In some of the larger cities there are municipal training-schools for policemen and firemen. But as respects the majority of men and women on the city's payroll they receive no special training in their duties before entering the municipal service. {The training of municipal employees.}

A few schools of training for the public service have been established under private auspices and they have served a useful purpose. The most conspicuous of these is the National Institute for Public Administration, formerly the New York Bureau of Municipal Research. It aims to train men in such things as budget-making, administration, organization, personnel work, and municipal research. But no close correlation between preliminary training and public can be effective unless the training schools are conducted as municipal institutions and unless the cities are ready to take the graduates whom the schools turn out. It has been suggested, over and over again, that the universities ought to provide courses of study leading to positions in the public service and a few American universities have done something in that direction. But there are three difficulties in {Training schools now in operation.}

[1] On the principles of a pension system see Paul Studensky's *Pensions in Public Employment* issued as a supplement to the *National Municipal Review* (April, 1922), and Lewis Meriam's *Principles Governing the Retirement of Public Employees* (New York, 1918).

the way,—first the disinclination of capable young men to enter a career which as yet seems unpromising; second, the aversion of cities to the appointment of anybody from outside their own boundaries, and third, the obvious difficulty of fitting anybody for responsible executive positions in the municipal service by means of academic instruction alone. If the first two obstacles could be surmounted, the third might not prove to be insuperable.

Training employees after they enter the service.

More urgently to be desired than training *for* the public service is training *in* it. The lawyer, the physician, the teacher does not get all his training in the law school, the medical school, or the school of pedagogy. His whole career, if it be a success, is one of learning and training. So it ought to be in the municipal service. In the ranks of the subordinate municipal employees there are hundreds of young men and women who, with proper encouragement, would become experts in their line and well qualified for promotion. But the best among them are not sought out or encouraged or aided in any way. There are lectures and extension courses for those who work in banks and business offices, for school teachers and for nurses. But there are none, or almost none, for municipal assessors, surveyors, accountants, park planners, playground instructors, paving foremen, traffic officers and all the rest.[1] Small wonder it is that so many city officials and employees allow their ambitions to become atrophied. Go into any city hall. You will find there any number of employees who do their work like automatons, who find no joy in it, and whose sole ambition is get an increase of pay or an extra holiday. If the morale of city employment is low, the city is largely to blame for it.

REFERENCES

General discussions of this subject may be found in William Anderson's *American City Government* (New York, 1925), pp. 454-500; in C. C. Maxey's *Readings in Municipal Government* (New York, 1924), pp. 169-214; and in Joseph Wright's *Selected Readings in Municipal Problems* (Boston, 1925), pp. 454-499. Mention should also be made of a chapter in W. P. Capes, *The Modern City and Its Problems* (New

---

[1] See the discussion of "Training Municipal Employees," by Dr. J. J. Reilly, printed in Joseph Wright's *Selected Readings in Municipal Problems* (New York, 1925), pp. 465-473.

York, 1922), entitled "Making Municipal Officials Efficient" (pp. 26-42), and a chapter on "They Who Serve the City" in Morris L. Cooke's *Our Cities Awake* (New York, 1918), pp. 97-120.

The history of the civil service reform movement in Great Britain and the methods now used in the British national service are dealt with in Robert Moses, *The Civil Service of Great Britain* (New York, 1914). Mention should also be made of the *Fourth Report of the Royal Commission on Civil Service* (London, 1914), and of W. A. Robson, *From Patronage to Proficiency in the Public Service*, issued by the Fabian Society (London, 1922). For the United States the history of the movement is narrated in C. R. Fish, *The Civil Service and the Patronage* (New York, 1905), and W. D. Foulke, *Fighting the Spoilsmen* (New York, 1919). Mention should also be made of the booklet entitled *A Sketch of the Merit System*, by Edward C. Marsh, issued by the National Civil Service Reform League (New York, 1922), and of the article on "The Civil Service in Post-War Readjustment" in the *Annals of the American Academy of Political and Social Science* (March, 1919).

As to the present workings and future developments of the merit system in American cities the most useful pamphlets are the report on *The Character and Functioning of Municipal Civil Service Commissions in the United States*, issued by the Governmental Research Conference (1922) and the *Report of the Civil Service Committee*, issued by the National Municipal League (1923). Another good source of information is L. F. Fuld, *Civil Service Administration* (New York, 1921). A monthly journal *Good Government*, is the organ of the National Civil Service Reform League (8 West Fortieth St., New York), and contains much current material. The annual *Proceedings* of the Assembly of Civil Service Commissioners are also valuable.

On questions relating to pensions for municipal employees, reference may be made to the *Report of the New York Commission on Pensions* (3 vols., New York, 1916); the report of the Boston Finance Commission on *Municipal Pensions*, Vol. XVII, pp. 85-112 (Boston, 1922); the *Report of the Milwaukee Pensions Laws Commission* (1920) and the National Municipal League's report on *Pensions in Public Employment*, printed in the *National Municipal Review*, Vol. XI, pp. 97-124 (April, 1922); also to F. Spencer Baldwin's "Retirement Systems for Municipal Employees" in *Annals of the American Academy of Political and Social Science*, Vol. XXXVIII, pp. 6-14 (July, 1911). The latest general treatise on the subject is Lewis Meriam's *Principles Governing the Retirement of Public Employees* (New York, 1918), to which an elaborate bibliography is appended.

Problems relating to classification of functions, promotions, standardization of work and pay, and so forth, are discussed in A. W. Procter, *Principles of Public Personnel Administration* (New York, 1921). Mention should also be made of the *Standard Specifications for Personal Service* issued by the New York (City) Bureau of Personal Service (1917); the reports on *Standardization of Public Employment* prepared by the New York Bureau of Municipal Research (Part I, 1915; Part II, 1916); and of W. C. Beyer's article on "Standardization of Salaries in American Cities" in the *National Municipal Review*, Vol. V, pp. 266-272 (April, 1916).

The rules of law relating to municipal employees in classified positions are set forth in John F. Dillon's *Law of Municipal Corporations* (5th edition, 5 vols., Boston, 1911), Vol. I, pp. 684-735.

CHAPTER XX

THE MUNICIPAL COURTS

The term which stands at the head of this chapter is somewhat misleading. In the United States there are no municipal courts in the sense that there are municipal councils or municipal boards. The courts of the city are part of the state's judicial machinery; their organization and procedure are determined by state law, and their decisions may be appealed (in most cases) to the higher courts of the state. This is true even in cities where the judges of the municipal courts are paid from the municipal treasury, and when their work has mainly to do with the enforcement of the city ordinances. Hence it is not accurate to say that in the United States we have three sets of courts—federal, state, and municipal—although these three designations are used as a matter of convenience. There are only two sets of courts, those of the nation and those of the states. Municipal courts, police courts, justice courts, district courts, county courts, and so on, are all of them integral parts of the state judiciary. They are subordinate state courts.

Place of the municipal courts in the American judicial system.

But although the courts of the city are subordinate tribunals, or lower courts as we usually call them, this does not mean that they are of little importance, or undeserving of attention from students of municipal government. On the contrary, the organization and work of the city courts ought to have much more consideration than our lawmakers have been devoting to such matters. For these courts come into a peculiarly close contact with the masses of the people, and particularly with the foreign-born populations of the cities. These groups rarely come into any relation with the higher courts of law. It is from the local courts, and more particularly from the police courts, that they obtain their conceptions of what justice or injustice means. In considerable measure their ideas as to the honesty and humanity of city governments are derived from their all-too-frequent contact with the police, the police judges, the bail brokers, and

Their importance.

the assistant district attorneys. The justice that these lower courts administer is the only kind of justice that great masses of our people ever get a chance to know.[1] And hence it is that if the courts of the city are venal, or susceptible to partisan influence, the whole underworld is sure to find it out. Not only will it make the discovery but it will act upon the principle that justice is purchasable and that crimes can be committed without fear of due punishment.

That is what has happened, from time to time, in some American cities. The pressure of political and other sinister influences upon the local courts, or upon the office of the prosecuting attorney, has resulted in perversions of justice, especially in the way of discrimination between offenders of the same class. At times it has also resulted in a degree of leniency to habitual malefactors which menaces the public safety. Why is it that the courts of American cities give the criminal a better run for his money (when he has the money) than he gets in the courts of any other country? The answer, however brief it be, must carry us back to the early days of American history.

Evolution of the municipal courts:

1. In colonial times.

When the earliest American boroughs were chartered in colonial days there was no clear distinction between legislative, executive, and judicial functions. In colonial New York and Philadelphia the same mayor and aldermen exercised all three. They made the local by-laws and regulations; they enforced them; and they sat on the bench to punish violators. They were ex officio justices of the peace, with power to try both civil and criminal cases. This was merely the English system of borough government transplanted to the new world. It remained without substantial change until after the American Revolution.

2. After the Revolution.

After the Revolution, and more particularly after the adoption of the national constitution, there developed a strong conviction that the three functions of government should be separated and kept separate. The men who made the laws should not be allowed to sit on the bench and administer them. The safeguarding of individual liberty seemed to require that councils and courts be confined within their own spheres of jurisdiction, each forming a check on the other. Gradually, therefore, the judicial functions of the mayor and aldermen were allowed to lapse, or were taken away. These functions were given to mag-

[1] On this topic see R. H. Smith, *Justice and the Poor* (New York, 1919).

istrates or recorders appointed or elected for this work alone. The process was expedited by the growth of business in the larger communities during the first half of the nineteenth century. It became impossible for mayors and aldermen to perform court service; they had too many other things to do. Moreover, they were not lawyers, as a rule, and as the legal system became more complicated with the growth of the cities they found increased difficulty in threading their way through the technicalities. At any rate the function of presiding over the local courts was gradually transferred from the regular municipal authorities to officials who had more time and more legal knowledge. Even yet, however, the municipal system retains a few traces of this earlier fusion of administrative and judicial functions. In some cities the mayor is still ex officio a justice or magistrate and is entitled to preside over the municipal court when the regular police judge is absent.

Another important feature came in on the heels of the Revolution; namely, the provision of elaborate constitutional safeguards for the rights of the individual when brought before the courts. During the colonial era there were no rigid guarantees of trial by jury, the right of appeal, and moderation in punishment. But the new state constitutions, adopted after the Revolution, contained long lists of them. These stipulations reflected a general feeling that courts would become tyrannical unless held to the strict observance of certain fundamental civic rights. Hence the multifarious provisions that juries must be used, that appeals from lower to higher courts must be allowed, that accused persons must be permitted to have counsel, that no one could be put on trial for a serious offence without having first been indicted by a grand jury, that excessive bail should not be required, or unusual punishments inflicted. These various constitutional provisions were motivated by the right spirit, no doubt, but almost from the first they slowed down and made more difficult the efficient administration of justice in the lower courts. Incidentally they made it more essential that these lower courts should be linked up with the higher state courts and should be equipped with judges who knew their business, for otherwise there would be endless appeals and reversals.

The constitutional restraints.

In other words, the emphasis on individual liberty entailed a gradual specialization of municipal court work. No general

390   THE GOVERNMENT OF AMERICAN CITIES

3. The influence of the frontier.

reconstruction took place; it was a slow development, beginning in the larger Eastern communities where the need was greatest and then spreading to the smaller ones. At the outset the magistrates or justices of the municipal court were usually appointed by the city council, or by the governor of the state. But as new communities developed in the western part of the country the practice of electing these magistrates and justices was adopted and spread. It was a manifestation of the frontier spirit—the desire to keep judicial administration close to the people. From the West the practice edged its way back into the states of the East and found considerable favor in some of them but not in others. That is why the method of choosing municipal judges is so far from uniform throughout the country. In some cities they are appointed by the mayor, in others by the governor of the state, while in most places they are elected by the people.

4. The geographical division of municipal courts.

Meanwhile, during the nineteenth century, the cities kept growing in population, and the work that had to be done by the local courts piled up correspondingly. It grew at a more than proportional rate. Litigation always increases more rapidly than population. It might almost be said that it increases as the square of the census figures. Accordingly a single municipal court soon found itself overwhelmed in a growing city and a division of work became imperative. But this division was not made on a functional basis, at least not at the outset. When the municipal court found itself swamped with business there was no creation of another court to absorb some of its functions—for example, by taking over all minor offences, or all civil cases. Instead the practice was to divide the city geographically, establishing a municipal court in each section, and each having jurisdiction of the same range. In the course of time a large city might have six or seven of these sectional courts. Along with the geographical disintegration, however, there was some division of work by functions. In various cities a separation between civil and criminal cases was made, with different lower courts for each. In some western cities the division was based upon the type of law administered—one court enforcing municipal ordinances and the other hearing cases brought under the state laws. The latter is in every sense a state court although its jurisdiction may be confined to the municipality. By these divi-

THE MUNICIPAL COURTS

sions of courts and jurisdictions a further divergence from uniform practice was brought into the municipal court system.

Today it is impossible to make any general statement that would hold true of municipal courts throughout the country. These courts are known by a variety of names—district courts, police courts, recorder's courts, justice courts, and so on. They have magistrates or judges who are sometimes appointed and sometimes elected. The terms of these officials range all the way from life to a couple of years. Usually, but not always, they must be "learned in the law," but any lawyer, however slim his knowledge of jurisprudence, is eligible. In the larger cities they hold court each morning and their jurisdiction depends upon what the laws have assigned to them. As a rule it covers violations of the city ordinances, minor offences against the state laws, preliminary hearings in serious cases, and civil controversies where the amount or the issue is not of large consequence. But let it be repeated that no general statement will hold true, or nearly true, in this field. The organization, the jurisdiction, and the procedure of the municipal courts (using this term in its broader sense) must be mastered, if at all, by studying the subject in a single city.
The present situation.

The administration of justice in American municipal courts has been far from satisfactory. This is fully admitted by all who have had to do with them. There are several reasons for this continuing situation, but the first reason has been disclosed in the historical sketch just given. The development of our municipal courts has been for the most part unguided and unplanned. They have evolved under the pressure of growth in business, each stage in their evolution being dictated by a desire to meet an immediate need in the easiest way. They have developed along lines of least resistance. In most large cities their jurisdiction is not adapted to the needs of today; they have too little authority and are burdened with a cumbersome procedure. In some cities there are a dozen justices of the peace with power to hear cases, each without reference to the others. There is no coördination of their work save the small amount provided by the higher courts through rulings on appeals.
Reasons for the unsatisfactory conditions in municipal courts.

Sometimes you will find in a large city (as in Boston, for example) six or seven courts sitting in different parts of the municipality, hearing cases of the same sort, yet each independent
The disintegration in some cities.

of the others and with no effective coördination of their work. The same offence may be differently penalized, depending upon the section of the city in which it is committed. Obviously, when a court is required to deal with all sorts of cases—violations of the traffic rules, assaults, robberies, and even small civil claims—it cannot become highly competent in handling any of them. Court work has become a big business and demands efficient organization like any other big undertaking. The efficient administration of justice in large cities is no longer something that can be attained by putting any lawyer on the bench and expecting him to deal wisely with every sort of offence. It has become a specialty which calls for specialized competence.

The unification of judicial work.

In keeping with this idea several of the largest cities—including New York, Chicago, Detroit, and Cleveland—have now unified their judicial organization by establishing a single tribunal, with its work divided among several branches each of which handles cases of a single type. In this way the advantages of specialized judicial administration are sought to be obtained. In Chicago, for example, there is a single court with a chief justice and thirty associate justices. These justices are assigned to hear definite classes of cases—traffic cases, juvenile offences, cases involving domestic relations, criminal cases, civil cases, and so on. They confine themselves to these specialties. They see to it that the same offence is not dealt with according to varying degrees of severity in the different parts of the same community. A similar unification and specialization has been effected in other cities and ought to be brought about in all of them.[1]

The plan of the American Judicature Society.

The American Judicature Society has prepared a model plan of judicial administration for use in larger cities based upon the principle of a single court with its work apportioned among five divisions.[2] It is proposed in this plan that each division should have a presiding justice whose duty, in addition to hearing cases, would be to assign the other judges within the division to their respective branches of work. The five presiding judges

---

[1] For a discussion of this matter, with specific examples, see the *Journal of the American Judicature Society*, vol. vi, pp. 19 ff. (April, 1922).

[2] The five divisions are as follows: (1) equity, (2) probate and domestic relations, including divorces and juvenile offences, (3) civil cases with juries, (4) non-jury civil cases, (5) criminal cases. This fifth division might have a dozen justices, each sitting in a different part of the city.

of divisions, together with the chief justice of the municipal court, would exercise a general supervision over the workings of the entire judicial machinery. Justices might be transferred from one division to another in order to relieve congestion at any one point. The adoption of this plan, or something like it, would greatly improve and unify municipal court work in the larger cities.

No reform in municipal court organization will greatly avail, however, if the local justices are selected in such way as to preclude the choice of capable, honest, and impartial men. The plan of popular election is widely used in the cities of the United States and it is supported by a widespread conviction that it is the only way of keeping the courts "close to the people." But popular election, as experience has shown, does not always mean that the people do the choosing; in many cases their only function is to ratify a choice made for them by a few political bosses or by powerful economic interests which have selfish ends to serve. It has even happened that law-breaking elements, through their control of the party machine, have virtually dictated the nomination and election of judges favorable to themselves. Conspicuous instances of partisanship and crookedness on the municipal bench have led to demands for the abolition of the elective method and the substitution of an appointive judiciary.[1] It ought to be added, however, that in those cities where the local bar association exerts a powerful influence over the choice of candidates, and where judges with good records are re-elected as a matter of course, the elective plan has achieved tolerably good results. *The selection of judges.*

But the practice of appointment, exercised through the ordinary channels, would not ensure the elimination of politics and personal favoritism from the municipal courts. Mayors and governors are themselves partisan and at times subservient to special interests. A stream will rise no higher than its source; a partisan or corrupt executive cannot be relied upon to appoint an upright judge. Mayors and governors are not primarily con- *Is appointment better than election?*

[1] "It is impossible to escape the conclusion that in a metropolitan district with one hundred thousand voters and upward, the selection of judges by the electorate is practically impossible. It is equally certain that the judges in such a community must be selected by some appointing power. The real and only question is: What is the best method of appointment?" Albert M. Kales, *Unpopular Government in the United States* (Chicago, 1914), pp. 234-235.

cerned with the functioning of the local courts in any case; their work and responsibilities are chiefly of an administrative nature. On the whole, however, the plan of appointment has proved to be more satisfactory than the plan of election. The longer the term for which municipal judges are elected, moreover, the better has this method seemed to work. It has been suggested that municipal judges ought to be appointed by the judges of the higher state courts, who are themselves elected,[1] or that the people of the city should elect the chief justice only, leaving him to choose his associates as a President chooses his cabinet. There are serious practical objections to both of these proposals and they have not yet found adoption anywhere in the United States.

Qualities essential in a municipal judge.

But whatever the method of selection it is generally assumed that no one can be a capable judge of a municipal court unless he is a lawyer by profession and it is everywhere required, either by statute or custom, that those who are elected or appointed shall have this qualification. In certain branches of municipal court work, if not in all of them, this is a necessary provision. No layman is qualified to handle equity cases, or to sit with a jury in civil controversies, even in a local court. To permit this would mean innumerable appeals and the wholesale setting aside of judgments. Even in the handling of minor criminal cases and elementary knowledge of the substance and the forms of law is essential. But successful work on the bench of a police court does not depend upon legal scholarship alone. The common sense of the police justice, his knowledge of human nature, his ability to grasp the essentials of every case that comes before him—these are the things that count. The magistrates of New York City have before them every year more than 150,000 cases ranging from serious felonies to minor infractions of the traffic rules. It requires no small amount of worldly wisdom to deal fairly with this enormous grist of cases.

Relieving the congestion in the regular municipal courts:

Is there no way of relieving the regular municipal courts from the congestion of cases? To some extent it can be done by transferring certain classes of cases to special tribunals which make provision for handling them expeditiously. Small civil claims afford a good illustration. A landlord raises the rent and a

[1] For an argument in favor of this method see Dorman B. Eaton, *The Government of Municipalities* (New York, 1899), pp. 444-445.

tenant refuses to pay; a customer claims that she is overcharged for groceries; a workman claims that some pay due him is being withheld. Thousands of such controversies, each involving only a few dollars, arise in every city. When brought into the regular courts they not only clog the calendar but they are costly to all concerned. Many cities, therefore, have established small claims courts with a minimum of technical procedure. Controversies involving small amounts can be brought into these courts and quickly determined, virtually without any costs. They relieve the regular courts and promote the dispensation of justice to those who otherwise would be denied it.

1. Small claims court.

In European cities much of the load has been taken off the regular municipal courts by setting up tribunals of arbitration and conciliation. Much of the litigation that arises in cities can be avoided by bringing in the parties and having them state their respective grievances to some impartial arbiter. We have had no considerable development of such arbitration in this country although the regular judges often suggest, when contestants come before them, that they try to agree on a settlement or refer the matter to some arbiter. If they take such advice it obviates not only the need for issuing writs or making arrests but the delay and expense of having a jury hear all the evidence.[1] We might well learn something from the experience of European cities in this field.

2. Courts of conciliation.

The administration of criminal justice in American cities has suffered grievously by reason of the ease with which cases may be appealed from the municipal police courts, and the frequency with which convictions are set aside on technical grounds. The whole trend of judicial administration in the higher courts has been so strongly directed toward safeguarding the right of the individual that the safety and welfare of the community are often menaced.[2] It has been said that a criminal trial, according to American procedure, is "a game in which the defendant is given every possible chance to escape, fair or unfair, while every possible obstacle is placed in the way of the prosecution." This is overstating the matter, but it is beyond question that

The abuse of the right to appeal.

---

[1] In Detroit the recorder's court maintains a complaint division which tries to settle cases before they are brought up by regular process. It has had remarkable success in adjusting controversies.

[2] See Moorfield Storey, *The Reform of Legal Procedure* (New Haven, 1911).

American methods of criminal procedure give the criminal more avenues of escape than he would get in any other country. The absurdities which clever but conscienceless attorneys have successfully spun to defeat the ends of justice are almost beyond belief.[1] One of the urgent needs of today is that of rendering these miscarriages of justice impossible. All the states should do what more than half of them have already done; namely, provide by statute that no police court decision shall be overturned by reason of technicalities which do not affect the substantial merits of the case or the plain constitutional rights of the defendant.

The slowness with which the wheels of justice move. The most conspicuous feature of judicial procedure in American cities is its slowness. Weeks, months, even years sometimes elapse before ordinary cases are finally cleared from the docket. Cases are on record in which the defendant has been able to prolong the hearings over five or six years. These delays are almost always to the advantage of the accused. They make it easy for him to play on the sympathy of the jurors. In its excitement over fresh crimes the public forgets all about the old ones for which no one has been punished. Thus it becomes possible for the prosecuting attorney to let cases drop, or to place them on file, or otherwise to accord a measure of leniency which public sentiment would never have tolerated when the details of the offence were fresh in mind. Why is it that we have so dilatory a procedure? It is partly because Americans borrowed their system of judicial process from England in the days before England undertook a judicial reform. Our courts are still working, to some extent, under the spell of English methods as they were a century or more ago. The delays, postponements, and continuances which this obsolescent method makes possible can only be avoided by radical simplifications in the whole system of judicial procedure.

A contrast with Europe. The far more expeditious handling of cases in the municipal courts of England, France, Germany, and other European countries has been commented upon by American lawyers. The procedure of these courts is summary in character, and even compli-

---

[1] It is figured that for every person convicted in an American municipal court not more than one in ten ever pays the full penalty (be it fine or imprisonment) imposed upon him. Suspended sentences, probation, appeals with a remission in the higher courts, paroles, etc., all contribute to this outcome.

THE MUNICIPAL COURTS

cated cases are tried quickly. Appeals are relatively infrequent, and they are heard without long delays. The judges deny all motions which aim at delay for delay's sake, and in so doing they can count upon support from the highest courts of the land. But in America the history of a criminal is often a long record of hearings, rehearings, continuances, postponements, exceptions, motions in arrest of judgment, appeals, pleas for a new trial, and all the other pleas of delay or evasion that the resourcefulness of the defendant's lawyers can devise.

Divers evils connected with the administration of municipal justice have developed at the courthouse but are outside the control of the courts. Shyster lawyers who haunt the place and prey upon the unfortunate are responsible for much of the aversion which attaches to the administration of local justice in the mind of the masses. They are on the spot whenever an arrest is made or a prisoner brought in, volubly advising the offender concerning his "constitutional rights" and offering to defend him in court. The fees which these men charge are stretched to the utmost limit that the traffic will bear, and the service which they render is rarely of much value. Their methods often serve to prejudice judges and juries against those whom they represent. And when a lawyer of this stripe loses his case he usually does not scruple to assure his client that the court was prejudiced, partisan, or corrupt. In this way a false impression concerning the integrity of the municipal courts has been spread through the poorer sections of the city. Time and again we have had evidence, in the course of legal investigations, that unfortunates have been fleeced by dishonest attorneys and the blame diverted to the court. *Justice and shyster lawyers.*

The politicians are likewise busy around the courthouse corridors. The first thing that some habitual offenders do, on being arrested, is to get in touch with the local senator, assemblyman, alderman, or city councillor. The latter is beseeched to interview the prosecuting officer, the judge, or the magistrate before the case is called. As a rule they respond—for the doing of favors is one way of getting votes. In almost any large city you will find dozens of local politicians around the courthouse lobby each morning. They are there, for the most part, to see that justice does not take its regular, evenhanded course. Prisoners sometimes boast to the police that they have influence *Justice and the politicians.*

398 THE GOVERNMENT OF AMERICAN CITIES

enough to prevent the imposition of any penalty, and the court records indicate that their assertions are not always without basis. In the crowded sections of large cities the local politician, be he ward boss or alderman, is daily called upon to get bail for somebody, or have his case placed on file, or pay his fine. It is through the doing of such unforgetable favors that the politician builds up his machine. Prosecuting attorneys and magistrates, it must be remembered, are human beings. With them, as with other men, it is far more agreeable to forgive than to punish. When a prisoner gets undeserved leniency no one has any cause to complain but the public—and the public does not get interested until things become very bad.

Public defenders. To some extent these abuses are being mitigated by the appointment of officials known as public defenders, whose duty it is to represent in court those accused persons who are too poor to engage competent lawyers. The public defender receives a salary from the city and his services are free to anyone who, *Legal aid bureaus.* when brought into court, declares himself unable to pay a lawyer. In civil cases much assistance has been rendered to the poor by the legal aid bureaus which have been established in many of the larger cities. These bureaus are maintained by private contributions and by the volunteer services of young lawyers. Anyone can go to the legal aid bureau, state his grievance, and be competently advised for a nominal fee or no fee at all.

The bail system. Serious abuses have sometimes arisen in connection with the furnishing of bail. The constitution of the United States, and those of most of the states, stipulate that "excessive bail shall not be required" from persons accused of crime. Subject to this general limitation the amount is left to the discretion of the courts. Bail is furnished by having somebody file a bond, or by depositing cash with the clerk of the court. Where a bond is given, the bondsman must swear that he has sufficient property to cover in case of default. Then, if the accused person does not appear when called for trial, the bail is forfeited. Applicants for bail are so numerous in the larger cities, however, that a class of professional bondsmen and bail brokers has grown up, ready to provide bail for anyone if they are paid for it. And when the defendant absconds they often manage to evade or compromise the forfeiture. It is by reason of the professional bondsmen that many criminals are let out on bail and are enabled thus to continue their depredations. Many crimes are committed by men who ought to be in custody, and who would be were it not for abuses in the system of giving freedom on bail.

It is commonly said that crime is a "social disease," and there is a certain amount of truth in this assertion. Many crimes are committed by feeble-minded persons or by persons of sub-normal mentality. Where this is the case the court should know the fact and make disposition of the case accordingly. In some of the larger cities the courts are provided with an expert in psychiatry upon whom they can call for assistance in this respect. Many crimes, again, are caused by defective home conditions—by the maladjustment of the youth to his home environment. Hence the desirability of having some machinery through which the court can be informed of these conditions and can be guided by this information in deciding what to do. If home conditions are at fault there is not much to be gained by sending a first offender back to his home and family unless the situation can be remedied.

Crime as a social disease.

Much might be written on the various phases of modern penology such as probation and probation officers, the parole system, improvement in jails, the segregation of prisoners by type, indeterminate sentences, prison self-government, and so on, but this is not the place for it. These things relate to the entire system of judicial administration and not to the municipal branches of it alone. Moreover, they would occupy far more space than is justifiable in a general survey of municipal government. But all of them are interesting; all of them have merit; and all of them are readily susceptible of abuse.[1]

We hear a great deal about crime waves, and the lack of respect for law among the people of the United States. It is doubtless true that there is more mischief floating around in America than in any other civilized country; but the United States is a big country, a new country, with a scattered and heterogeneous population. It is unfair to make comparisons with England or France where the population is homogeneous and where legal traditions have been long established. To some extent our high crime ratio is a result of that impatience with legal trammels which marks the American temperament. It is,

Crime waves.

---

[1] For books on these topics see the references in the author's *Municipal Government and Administration* (2 vols., New York, 1923), vol. ii, p. 238.

in part, a relic of the old frontier influence which has colored so many aspects of American life. In larger part, more probably, it is due to deficiencies in the machinery which we have provided for the prevention and punishment of crime. It has been said, and it is probably true, that American democracy has made its poorest showing in the administration of criminal justice. But how may this situation be bettered? First of all, by studying it carefully. We have had very little research in this field. Apparently there is need for an improvement in the methods and the personnel of law enforcement, for better court organization, for specialization under unified supervision, for simpler procedure, and for more competent judges. But before we can point the way to remedial action of a definite sort we must know what the real causes of the existing troubles are. They are probably not what they superficially appear to be. Drastic and radical reforms, if undertaken without a thorough study of the fundamental causes, usually do more harm than good. We should bear in mind also that the human equation is even more important in this than in other branches of city government. Much depends on the system, but more depends upon the attorneys, prosecutors, judges, and magistrates who administer it. To revolutionize a system of organization and procedure is easy enough, but to raise the standards of personnel, to promote sound traditions, and to maintain the integrity of all who are connected with the administration of justice—these are far more difficult things to achieve.

REFERENCES

Brief discussions of municipal courts and their procedure may be found in William Anderson, *American City Government* (New York, 1925), pp. 604-628; H. G. James, *Local Government in the United States* (New York, 1921), pp. 352-357; F. J. Goodnow and F. G. Bates, *Municipal Government* (New York, 1919), pp. 228-250, and W. F. Dodd, *State Government* (New York, 1922), pp. 341-359, *passim*. There is a good chapter on "Municipal Courts" in John F. Dillon's *Commentaries on the Law of Municipal Corporations* (5th edition, 5 vols., Boston, 1911), Vol. II, pp. 1115-1136, and an excellent account of police court powers may be found in Eugene McQuillin's *Treatise on the Law of Municipal Corporations* (Vols. I-VI, Chicago, 1911-1913; Supplementary Vols. VII and VIII, Chicago, 1921), under the head of "Actions to Enforce Police Ordinances." *The Municipal Index* (1925) contains a good survey of "The Administration of Justice in the Modern City and County" by E. H. Sutherland, adapted from the same author's *Criminology* (New York, 1924). Roscoe Pound's article on "The Administration of Justice in a Modern City," *Harvard Law Review*, Vol. xxvi, pp. 302-328 (1913), is the most useful short discussion of the subject.

There is a great deal of new and interesting data in the report on *Criminal Justice in Cleveland* (Cleveland, 1922), and in R. H. Smith's *Justice and the Poor* (New York, 1919). Attention should also be called to the various articles in the *Bulletin of the American Judicature Society*, a full list of which is printed in Vol. viii (April, 1925). A discussion of simplified municipal court procedure, by R. S. Saby, in the *American Political Science Review*, Vol. xviii, pp. 760-772 (November, 1924) also deserves mention.

CHAPTER XXI

CITY GOVERNMENT AS BUSINESS

The annual report of the city's business operations. Every year the city issues a printed volume, its pages well-packed with figures. This publication is known as the city's annual report; it contains a statement of revenues and expenses, a general description of the work done by the various departments, and various tabulations showing the city's net indebtedness. Occasionally it is illustrated by diagrams or charts showing the growth of expenses and indicating where the money has gone. Sometimes there is a sheet of assets and liabilities. An attempt is made to have this report look businesslike, but not always with much success, and in any event it is dry reading except for statisticians. Among average citizens very few ever glance through these columns of figures or even look at the charts, and still fewer understand what they mean.

Its inadequacies. As a matter of fact these figures and diagrams sometimes do not mean very much. Not infrequently they are intended to conceal or gloss over, rather than to uncover or explain. In order to show a low per capita cost, for example, the estimated population of the city is placed too high—being figured on school attendance or water consumption or something other than the census returns. You can always illustrate, by graphs and diagrams, that the per capita cost of city government is not increasing—provided you pad the estimated figures of population sufficiently. This is what some western cities have regularly done.[1] Or, again, the balance sheet is doctored up to show a vast margin

---

[1] A favorite plan is to figure the estimated population from the number of water-consumers or telephone subscribers, or street railway fares. In 1920, when the last federal census was taken, the city had 52,000 population, let us say. The city authorities reckon, however, that it must now (1926) have at least 80,000 because the water consumption has increased more than 50 per cent since 1920 and the telephone company reports an even greater percentage of increase in its subscribers. But the flaw in the figuring comes from the fact that water consumption and telephone-users increase much more rapidly than in direct proportion to population. So do bank clearings, post office returns, and all the other data upon which optimists at the city hall base their estimates of population.

CITY GOVERNMENT AS BUSINESS 403

of assets over liabilities. This is done by including, as assets, the estimated value of all the city's streets, reckoned in proportion to the value of abutting property. An absurd proceeding this is, of course, for if the streets were sold the abutting property would have no such value. The streets of a city represent "assets" that could not possibly be realized upon as an offset to liabilities, hence a balance sheet which lists them as assets is altogether misleading.

On the other hand, the annual report of a city often omits the information that the student of municipal affairs would be most glad to have at hand. It rarely gives things in terms of unit-costs. Hence you may spend hours in the study of a water department's report, endeavoring to make out whether it had a surplus or a deficit, and yet not find what you are after. If you want to know what street paving has cost the city per square yard, the street department's annual report is about the last place to look for it. Many of these reports are mere transcripts of figures from the auditor's report, unenlightening to anyone but the auditor himself. Still we are making progress in this matter. Municipal reports are much better than they used to be; in some cases they have been made both comprehensible and interesting. In most cities, however, the methods of preparing the annual report are still defective and the figures are sometimes two or three years out of date when they leave the printer's hands.

Its omissions.

Glance through one of these annual reports, selecting for this purpose one of the best of them. You will be tempted to ask yourself the question: "Why do they call these activities *government?* Here are whole pages of figures relating to such matters as the construction of public buildings, the paving of streets, the building of sewers, the management of a water plant, the lighting of streets, the purchase of supplies, the awarding of contracts, the hiring of labor, the borrowing of money, the auditing of accounts, and so forth. The city of Boston buys water at wholesale, sells it at retail to the people, and makes a profit. The city of Detroit operates a street railway system and claims to be making it pay. Other cities manufacture gas or electricity and sell it at what they allege to be a profit. Others, again, buy cemetery land by the acre and sell it by the square foot, or they collect rubbish at so much per load, or they rent stalls in

Business vs. government?

markets, or engage in other forms of strictly commercial enterprise. Why do we insist on calling such things *government?* They are simply business operations in every sense of the term. They would be carried on by private corporations if the city had not entered the field. And if they are business operations, why shouldn't they be handled as such, in accordance with business methods by an organization that is competent to deal with them in this way?

It is largely business.

There is something to be said for this point of view. Many years ago Judge Dillon pointed out that "a city is not so much a miniature state as it is a business corporation." A large part of the work that its officials perform is of a business rather than a governmental nature. To the task of making laws and enforcing them the officials of the municipality now devote a relatively small portion of their time. The great majority of city officers and employees are engaged in rendering social and economic services—teaching in the schools, preserving public order, caring for the public health, supervising playgrounds, building streets, inspecting markets, safeguarding the water supply, removing waste, putting out fires, managing a lighting plant, buying books for the public library, and figuring tax bills. These services ought to have no political or partisan flavor. There is a right and a wrong way of performing them, but no Democratic or Republican way. The main thing is that the work shall be done, as similar work is done under competitive conditions, with intelligence and honesty. We have had too much government in business and not enough business in government.

The business analogy should not be pressed too far.

Nevertheless there is danger of pressing this business analogy too far. The aim of private business is to make a profit; the purpose of municipal administration is not merely to make a profit but to promote the collective interests of the citizens without reference to monetary gain. The city's mission is not to make money but to spend money. Business should produce a surplus, but government does well when it makes both ends meet. In any event government must be conducted in compliance with the desires of the voters, whatever these desires may be, and must give them what they want. Business can be managed without scrupulous heed to public opinion, but municipal administration cannot. Even though popular sentiment be headstrong and unwise, it cannot be set at naught. The desires of the people must ultimately prevail even though they may not conform to what the experts prescribe as the best or the cheapest.

Government by the best people, in other words, is not necessarily the best government. Nor is cheapness in itself a criterion of efficient administration. The city is not a voluntary corporation; it is a compulsory association into which the citizen is born. He does not join it of his own volition. That is another fundamental difference between a municipal and a business corporation which is too often overlooked. It is because of this differentiation that the municipal authorities are obliged to be governed by social motives which do not actuate the ordinary business concern. They cannot do their planning in terms of dollars and cents, profit and loss, unit costs, and outlay per capita. They must reckon with the prejudices, the traditions, and the caprice of the electorate.

The strength of these social considerations is not the same, of course, in all departments of municipal activity. Some things lend themselves, practically without reservation, to the use of business terminology and business methods. This is largely true of the physical activities, such as the construction and maintenance of public improvements. But it does not hold true in equal degree of those municipal departments which have mainly to do with human relations; for example, poor relief, correction, and public recreation. Only to a limited extent can such departments be organized and conducted on a "business basis" without the danger of creating a hostile public sentiment. Success or failure in the administration of these departments cannot be demonstrated by pointing to columns of figures or by applying purely objective tests of any sort. It is a matter of good and humane service, something which cannot be measured by the devices of accountants and statisticians. *The conflict of political and social motives.*

It is not accurate, therefore, to say that "city government is simply business." It is that and a good deal more. It is a combination of business, philanthropy, and government. That is what makes it so difficult. If the city were merely a business corporation, with functions exclusively of a business nature, the problem would be simple. A small board of directors and a general manager would be all the organization necessary. On the other hand, if the city were simply a governmental unit we would merely need to reproduce in miniature the political frame *Points of approach and points of view.*

of the state or nation. But unhappily the city is neither the one nor the other; it is both. Its activities are both governmental and commercial; and the courts take cognizance of this distinction, as has been seen, in determining the city's liability for the torts of its employees.[1]

Much depends on your point of view. If you look merely at the departments of police, fire protection, health, and finance, you will conclude that the city's work is largely governmental. If you focus your eyes on the departments of public buildings, streets, lighting, and water, you will be moved to say that its functions are largely commercial. But in addition the city cares for the poor, maintains a house of correction, provides band concerts and neighborhood dances, pays for a public library, and sets off fireworks on the Fourth of July. Looking at these functions, to the exclusion of the others, you might aver that the city's work is of a social welfare or eleemosynary character. The truth is that every modern city has varied functions to perform, some of them widely different in scope and nature. Obviously it is difficult to create a scheme of organization that will be equally efficient in performing them all.

Functions and organs. We are sometimes told that "the functions in the long run determine the form," and that the city's administrative organization must be developed accordingly. If this is true, then the city must develop a variety of organs, channels and instrumentalities through which to carry on its work and these will differ according to the nature of the work to be done. It may find that a large unpaid board is the best agency for supervising the public library or for dispensing public charity, while a single, full-time highly-paid commissioner is the only efficient instrumentality for controlling the fire department. Naturally so, for there is the widest possible difference between the functions concerned. From time to time you will be told that "all unpaid boards should be abolished," because they are cumbrous and unbusinesslike. But it is yet to be demonstrated that the ideal organization for a department of public poor relief, or for a public library, is exactly akin to that of a packing plant or a cotton factory.

Organizations of business men, such as chambers of commerce,

[1] See *above*, pp. 121-122.

boards of trade, and merchants' associations, have been prone to over-emphasize one aspect of the city's municipal operations— the one that naturally comes nearest to their own interests. They try to arouse the electorate to the need for a city administration conducted "on business principles," with a better regard for "efficiency and economy"—all this to be secured by a segregated budget system, the standardization of work and wages, a pay-as-you-go policy, and such things. These appeals have not proved to be very effective, on the whole, and the reason is not far to seek. They betray a poor conception of mass psychology. Business men may like the term "efficiency," but the average worker does not. To his mind it connotes piece-work, time-clocks, and speeding up. It doesn't inspire him to give three cheers. On the contrary, his first reaction to the business man's program is usually unfavorable. A business administration of the city's affairs, so far as he can judge from the administration of banks, factories, shops or railways, does not promise much to his personal advantage. It is unfortunate that this should be so, for the worker is the one who really has most to gain from the stoppage of public waste and inefficiency. He is the one who suffers most from its continuance. But unhappily he does not realize it.

A wrong conception of electoral psychology.

Nor is it surprising that he should fail to do so. The scope and variety of the city's activities are beyond his limited knowledge. Can one urban voter in a thousand make even a fair guess at what it costs to supply water per million gallons, or how many acres of park land the city owns, or what the city's net indebtedness is, or how much granite block pavement costs per square yard, or what the flaming arc-lamp on the nearest corner costs per year? And so on through a thousand questions which men can answer in relation to their own affairs but cannot even estimate in relation to the city's. What the city is doing for its citizens is quite beyond the grasp of the average man, save in its most general outlines. It is beyond even the best-informed among the people. That being the case it is altogether inevitable that the bulk of the people should be guided by partyism, prejudice, inertia, class consciousness, or something other than personal knowledge.

The activities of the modern city cover a wide range and they are steadily increasing. A few years ago a little pamphlet was issued, showing the functions in one of our largest cities.¹ Detroit, the municipality in question, was incorporated as a city in 1824. It had then a mayor, a city council, a municipal court, a city treasurer, a city attorney, a police department, a fire department, a street-grading department, and a school board. There was no public water supply, no sewerage system, no street lighting, no street paving; there was not even a high school. But all these were added during the thirty-five years following the incorporation of the city. At the outbreak of the Civil War, therefore, the city government of Detroit was engaged in about twenty different municipal activities. The population of the place had grown to 45,000 and the taxes amounted to about four dollars per capita.

After the Civil War was over, Detroit grew at a more rapid rate, as did many other cities of the middle west. Fifty years from the date of its incorporation it passed the 100,000 mark; its municipal activities had increased to more than thirty; and its taxes had risen to nearly ten dollars per capita. This seemed to be a notable growth but it was nothing to what the next fifty years were destined to bring. The close of the nineteenth century saw Detroit's population tripled; it was about 300,000 in 1900. The varied municipal activities now numbered more than eighty, and the per capita tax levy was nearly thirteen dollars. Finally, we have the extraordinary expansion of Detroit during the past twenty-five years. Associating its fortunes with the motor industry, the city has had a phenomenal advance; its population is now well above a million, and its municipal authorities are engaged in nearly two hundred activities of all kinds, ranging from garbage collection to free evening lectures, and from educational research to the censorship of motion pictures. Significantly enough, its per capita tax rate has risen to about forty-five dollars. During this latest period, therefore, Detroit increased its municipal activities more than 125 per cent, its population more than 250 per cent, and its total tax levy more than 1000 per cent.

The story of other rapidly growing American cities, if it were written, would be much the same. The progress of industry is

[1] *The Growth of a City*, issued by the Detroit Bureau of Governmental Research (Detroit, 1922). See also the article by Lent D. Upson on the same subject in *The American City*, vol. xxvii, pp. 407-410 (November, 1922).

CITY GOVERNMENT AS BUSINESS

centripetal in its effect upon population; it brings great masses of people together into relatively small areas. This means congestion, and congestion creates new problems which the city authorities must grapple with and solve. That is why we have added city planning, zoning, street widening, traffic regulation, and such things to the list of municipal activities. The progress of industry has also been accompanied, more happily, by a rise in the standard of living among the workers—with more leisure and a desire to use it in agreeable ways. This has brought with it a general demand for public libraries, museums, playgrounds, athletic fields, band concerts, free evening lectures, public bathing beaches, and even neighborhood dances, held in school buildings and financed from the public treasury. We have also had, during the past few decades, an increased emphasis upon the city as a humanitarian agency. It is becoming, more and more, a great and generous philanthropist. Hence its health centers, milk distribution depots, outdoor clinics, free dispensaries, detention homes, tuberculosis camps, district nurses, mother's pensions, free school books, and all the rest. Finally, the progress of the applied sciences has made possible all manner of improvements in the technique of the great physical services, such as street paving, cleaning, and lighting, water supply, waste disposal, and fire protection. All such improvements result in greater specialization and increased cost. *The public demand for more service.*

From this it becomes apparent why municipal government is conducted under "the law of increasing cost per capita." In other words, the larger the city the greater is the cost, per person, of providing the various services which the people insist upon having. This, of course, is not the case with most business enterprises. The bigger the enterprise the less it costs to produce each unit of goods or services. In a small bookbinding establishment, for example, the cost of binding will be so much per volume. But if the establishment grows twice as large and binds twice as many books per day, the cost per volume will be less, not more. In municipal administration the reverse is true. A small city finds that it costs so much per citizen for police and fire protection, streets, school, poor relief, and so on. But if the city becomes twice as large, with twice as many people in it, the cost of these things per head of population is altogether likely to go up, not down. Or to put it more concretely—suppose the cost of gov- *The law of increasing costs per capita.*

ernment and administration in a city of 50,000 people is a million dollars per year, or about twenty dollars per capita. One might think, at first glance, that if the population were to double and become 100,000, the expenses would not keep pace and the cost per capita would be less than twenty dollars. That, however, is not what happens. When the population doubles, the expenses are usually a good deal more than doubled—sometimes tripled or quadrupled. The cost per head of population becomes thirty dollars, forty dollars, or even more.[1]

The difficulty in reducing taxes.

Men who are candidates for municipal office often promise that if they are elected they will reduce the city's expenditures, and the voters believe them. But these promises are very rarely, if ever fulfilled. It is true that where money is being wasted the cost of administering the city's affairs can sometimes be reduced by shutting down on this wastefulness, but the amount of actual waste in city government has been exaggerated. The only way in which municipal expenditures can be substantially reduced is by abandoning some of the work which the city does. The legitimate and essential costs of government are bound to increase as a city grows in size. When people work to make the city bigger and more prosperous, they should not forget (although they usually do) that this growth will mean heavier outlays and higher taxes.

[1] This may be illustrated by the figures of current expenditures per head of population in some typical American cities of various sizes. These figures of population are for the year 1920; the statistics of per capita cost are those compiled by the United States Bureau of the Census in its *Financial Statistics of Cities*, published in 1921.

	Population 1920	Per Capita Current Expenditures (1921)
New York	5,620,048	$44.81
Chicago	2,701,705	36.69
St. Louis	772,897	31.92
Toledo (Ohio)	243,164	26.49
Fall River (Mass.)	120,485	24.91
Camden (N. J.)	116,309	22.44
Utica (N. Y.)	94,156	21.32
Peoria (Ill.)	76,121	20.53
Allentown (Pa.)	73,502	19.33
Mobile (Ala.)	60,777	17.54
Lancaster (Pa.)	53,170	15.52

It is not to be understood, of course, that the size of the city *invariably* determines its per capita expenditures. On the contrary, it occasionally happens that the per capita cost in one city is lower than that of a larger one near by. But in general the rule holds that per capita costs tend to increase with growth of population.

CITY GOVERNMENT AS BUSINESS 411

How often we hear speakers at chamber of commerce banquets say that "if we had more industries in the city, more people and more buildings going up," there would be more property to assess for taxation, and the general tax rate could thus be reduced. It sounds plausible enough; but it will not stand analysis. More industries, more buildings, and more people would provide more resources from which to draw the city's revenue, it is true; but they invariably bring with them a demand for more police, better fire protection, better street pavements, more parks and playgrounds, more and better service all along the line. A community in this respect is like an organism. In its lower and simpler forms it has few and simple needs. The small village does not require professional police or firemen. One or two constables and a volunteer fire brigade for the work. It does not require an elaborate system of water supply and public lighting. But when the village becomes a city, it needs these things and more besides. Its life becomes more complex, its needs more diversified, and its administration more costly. It is futile to expect a declining tax rate in a growing city. If the tax rate keeps coming down in any community, it is a bad sign.

A widespread delusion concerning the relation of city growth to the tax rate.

And in any event we should not concentrate our attention on the problem of reducing expenses and taxes. We should not condemn public officials solely because the tax rate goes up or commend them because it comes down. A large portion of a city's annual expenditure is "uncontrollable"; in other words it cannot be reduced no matter how much the municipal authorities may wish to diminish it. Interest on the city debt must be paid, for example, and this sometimes amounts to twenty or thirty per cent. A city must provide in some way for protecting property against fire, for maintaining law and order, for lighting the streets, and for keeping its streets in repair. It is not practicable for the city authorities to abandon any of these functions. The best that can be done is to manage them more economically, and the amount that can be saved in this way is much less than the average citizen realizes.[1] It is more than offset, as a rule, by the rising cost of labor and supplies as well as by the need for better service in all the city departments. There is no solid ground for the expectation that taxes in American cities will

A low tax rate is not the only goal.

---

[1] The chart on the next page, for a typical large city, shows where the taxpayer's dollar goes.

412   THE GOVERNMENT OF AMERICAN CITIES

come down; the probability is that they will keep going up. The law of increasing costs is fundamental in public finance.

The city's revenues.   Taking all the cities of over 30,000 population in the United States (and there are about 275 of them) the current expenses are now (1926) about $30 per capita.[1] They range from less than twenty dollars in the smaller places to more than fifty in the largest ones. All this money comes from the pockets of the people. The city government, as such, produces no wealth. It merely enables others to produce it. How is the money obtained? Nearly 70 per cent of it, on the average, is secured by direct

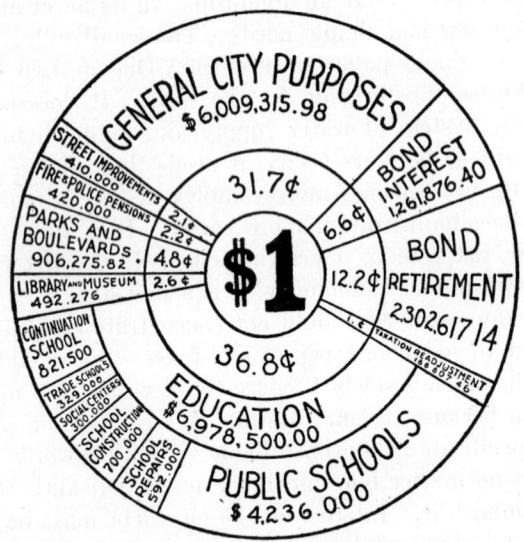

property taxation; the balance comes from fees, fines, licenses, business taxes, poll taxes, special assessments, profits from municipal water or lighting departments, and miscellaneous sources. Taxes, therefore, are the city's main reliance—more particularly taxes on property.

Limitations on the taxing power.   But cities are not permitted to tax as they please. The power to tax involves the power to destroy, hence it is subject to strict limitations imposed by the general laws. Of itself, indeed, a city has no power to tax. Its power is derived from the state in

---

[1] This includes interest on the municipal debt but does not include "outlays," i.e., permanent improvements paid for by loans, or the cost of maintaining the self-supporting public enterprises such as water supply.

CITY GOVERNMENT AS BUSINESS

which it is located. It comes from the state legislature by express grant, and never does it come in wide-open form. There are always some limitations as to what may be taxed, the methods of taxing, the purpose of the tax, and sometimes as respects the maximum rate. In general the city is allowed to tax land and buildings, tangible personal property (such as merchandise, machinery, and furnishings), and usually intangible personal property, such as stocks, bonds, notes and mortgages. In some states, however, there is a state income tax which takes the place of local taxes on intangibles. Cities are also permitted, in some cases, to levy poll taxes and taxes on business enterprises. But in any event no tax can be legally imposed by the city unless the subject of the tax, be it property, persons, or business, has been allocated to it by the state. The state laws also prescribe how the tax rate shall be fixed, how values shall be determined for taxation, and how the tax shall be collected. Very little is left to local discretion. In the exercise of its taxing power the city acts as the agent of the state and sometimes is required to turn over a portion of the proceeds to the latter.

Relatively few cities have been left free to fix their annual tax rates as they deem best. Almost everywhere there are tax limits imposed by the state constitutions or by the state laws. Usually the limit is fixed in terms of so much per thousand of assessed valuation—for example, ten dollars per thousand. Then the city must keep its levy within the figure. But the limit is not always so simply expressed or so easily calculated. It is often complicated by provisions which stipulate that interest on the city debt, and various other payments, need not be figured within the tax limit. The purpose of a municipal tax limit is to protect the city against extravagance but on the whole it has proved of doubtful value as a safeguard. In some way or other the city authorities generally manage to get the money when they need it. If a tax limit stands in the way they raise the assessed valuations, or borrow for current expenses, or leave deficits to pile up year after year.

Before a tax on property is levied there must be an assessment; *The assessment.* in other words, an appraisal or valuation is made by assessors who go about the city and set down tentative figures respecting each parcel of property, after which the owner has a right to protest if he deems the assessment too high. Such protests are usually heard and determined by a board of revision. The work of fairly assessing property is difficult and on the whole has not been well done. The assessors have rarely possessed adequate qualifications for the work and in many instances have owed their appointment to political considerations. The situation is gradually improving, however, and the work of assessing property is now being better done than it used to be.

To make fair valuation of real estate is difficult, but not impossible, for the reason that the property is in plain view for the assessors to see. In the case of intangibles, such as stocks and bonds, there is the additional difficulty that arises from concealment. The assessors do not know what securities a man keeps in his safe-deposit box, nor can they find out unless he chooses to tell them. What they do in most cases is to make a guess at it. They assess him so much and see if he lodges a protest. If he does not, they are likely to raise the assessment the next year, and so on until the taxpayer makes a storm about it. Concealment of intangibles is encouraged by the fact that the laws usually require such property to be taxed at the same rate as lands and buildings—a provision which is grossly unfair because it means that the owner of the stocks or bonds must give up, in taxes, perhaps half the income received from them. The general property tax thus fails to reach a great deal of the wealth owned by the citizens, a form of wealth which is increasing at a rapid rate year after year.

Alternatives to the general property tax.

It is desirable, accordingly, that the practice of levying a uniform or general property tax be abandoned. In some states this has already been done. One alternative is to put intangible property in a class by itself, with a lower tax rate than that applied to real estate. Another is to tax the *income from*, rather than the *value of*, intangible property. In the latter case the state authorities levy the tax and distribute the proceeds to the cities. Individuals are required to make sworn returns showing their annual income, thus obviating the danger of any concealment on a large scale.

Sources of revenue other than taxation.

There is need for new sources of revenue in American cities. Real estate is now being too heavily burdened. In some cases an amount equal to half the net income from business or residential property is being collected in taxes. In order to prevent a further increase in this burden the cities have been diligently

CITY GOVERNMENT AS BUSINESS 415

searching for new sources of income but not with great success. Some of them are imposing business taxes, that is, taxes levied upon trades, professions, industries, and so forth in proportion to the volume of business or on some other basis. A good deal of income is being obtained, here and there, by the taxing of public utilities such as privately-owned gas and electric plants, telephone companies and street railways. Chicago derives considerable revenue from a wheel tax on automobiles using the city streets. Many cities, especially in the western portion of the country, manage to pay for street improvements by levying special assessments upon the owners of abutting property. It has been suggested that the cities should levy an excise of say one per cent on all retail sales—which would bring in a large revenue—but there are practical difficulties in the way. There are, indeed, objections to any new form of tax. Yet the stern fact remains that cities must have more revenue and it will have to come from the taxation of property unless some other lucrative sources are found.

How is the tax rate determined? First of all the assessors turn in their lists showing the valuations. Then the estimates of expenditures for the year are compiled. This is done by asking the heads of all departments to make a tabulated statement of what they will require. The estimates, submitted in this way, are gone over carefully and embodied in a document known as a budget. This is quite an elaborate document showing on the one hand the estimated expenditures for interest on the city debt, for schools, police, street maintenance, public health, and all the rest. On the other hand, it indicates the probable income from fees, permits, licenses, and all such sources apart from taxation. The difference between the two will show the amount that has to be raised for taxation. In a word you have so much property to be taxed, and so much money to be raised by taxing it. It is merely a problem in simple arithmetic. Dividing the one by the other gives you the tax rate.

How a tax rate is fixed.

But the process of fixing the tax rate for the year is not quite so easy as the foregoing paragraph might indicate. Much time is usually spent on the estimates, paring them down wherever practicable. A reserve for emergencies must be provided. Some taxes will prove uncollectible and an allowance (known as an overlay) must be made for this contingency. Care must be

416   THE GOVERNMENT OF AMERICAN CITIES

taken to keep the tax rate within the statutory limit, if there is one. As a rule there are several tentative calculations of the tax rate, with successive revisions of the estimated expenditures, before it is finally announced.

Budget methods. Much attention has been given in recent years to improving the budgetary methods in American cities.[1] Good practice requires the early completion of the estimates on standardized forms, their submission to the mayor, city manager, commission, or to a committee of the city council in intelligible form, their scrutiny with provision for public hearings, and their final adoption, item by item, with proper safeguards against the expenditure of appropriations for any other purpose than that intended. All contingencies cannot be foreseen a year ahead, hence some transfers of money must be made possible. But the process should be hedged with adequate restrictions. No two cities have exactly the same budget procedure, nor is there any ideal way of handling this important phase of the city's business; but there are numerous wrong ways of budget-making and slovenly practices connected with the work which are bound to prove costly unless they are avoided.

When the budget has been finally adopted, the appropriations are available to be spent by the various departments. When bills are presented they go to the comptroller or auditor. He charges them against the appropriation and sends them to the city treasurer who issues his checks in payment. Thus there are three officials concerned: the head of the department who certifies that the bill has been properly incurred; the auditor who makes sure that there is an appropriation available to be drawn upon, and the treasurer who pays out the money. Even so, there are times when the city pays for what it does not get.

The usual allocation of expenditures. The city's chief business is to raise and spend money. Spending thirty dollars per capita, and doing it efficiently, is no small job in a city of a hundred thousand or more. How is the money distributed? The proportions vary from city to city, but in general from fifteen to twenty per cent goes for interest on the city debt. Another twenty-five to thirty per cent goes for education. Police and fire protection take ten or fifteen per cent addi-

---

[1] For a full discussion see A. E. Buck, *Municipal Budgets and Budget Making* (New York, 1925), and R. Emmett Taylor's *Municipal Budget-Making* (Chicago, 1925). A good bibliography may be found in the latter volume.

CITY GOVERNMENT AS BUSINESS 417

tional; health protection requires a good deal less. Streets, charities, parks, "general government," and so on take the rest. In general the cost of the various services has been increasing all along the line but much more rapidly in some departments than in others. Education has had the most rapid growth among all branches of local expenditure during the past dozen years. The people, apparently, are willing to have this rapid increase continue. There is a feeling, and it is probably justified, that the taxpayer gets more real value for his money from the school department than from any other.

Not all the city's expenditures are defrayed out of current income, however. Improvements of a permanent character, when not financed by special assessments, are paid in whole or in part by borrowing money. Bonds are issued and sold on the city's credit. The justification of municipal borrowing is that future taxpayers, who will have the use of permanent improvements (such as parks, public buildings, or bridges), should share in the cost. The borrowing, of course, should not be for a longer term than the useful life of the improvement. It is accounted good practice to issue the bonds in serial form, that is, in such way that some of them will fall due and be paid each year from current revenues. In any event the city is not given a free hand in borrowing money. As a rule it is restricted as to the purposes for which it may borrow and as to the length of the term for which the bonds may be issued. In many cases each bond-issue must be approved by the voters before becoming legal and sometimes more than a majority vote at the polls is required. In most of the states there are constitutional or statutory debt limits above which cities may not incur indebtedness even with the approval of the voters. Such limits are usually fixed in terms of the total assessed valuation—say five per cent of this total. If the entire assessed valuation of property within the city is a hundred million dollars it would in that case be allowed to incur a total debt of five million. Some borrowings, however, come "outside the debt limit," notably those connected with self-supporting municipal enterprises such as the water supply or the municipal lighting plant.

Obtaining funds by borrowing.

Debt limits.

The principles to be followed in municipal borrowing do not differ fundamentally from those pursued by well-managed business corporations. Money should not be borrowed for current

Principles of municipal indebtedness.

expenses—but many cities have pursued that practice, on occasions. Debts should not be incurred for ordinary replacements or alterations in the case of existing improvements—the renovation of a city hall, for example. Nor should money be borrowed for constantly recurring expenses, such as the purchase of fire apparatus, even though such additions to the city's plan may have a useful life of several years. On the other hand it is clearly impracticable for a city to follow a "pay-as-you-go" policy as respects all its outlays. Expenditures that are of a non-recurring character, such as the acquisition of land and the construction of a new park, or of a new city hall, or a public library, or a high school ought to be financed by equitably spreading the burden of cost upon those who will benefit.

Competition among cities.

The mayor of a large American community, in a recent inaugural address, said that "cities, like business concerns, are competitors with one another." If one city lets its taxes and indebtedness become too high it will be at a disadvantage, in attracting industries, as against other cities that have conducted their financial affairs more cautiously. To a certain extent that is true. But industrial growth depends upon many other factors than tax rates and net debts. Some cities seem to wax mightily in spite of the most flagrant financial mismanagement. Cities are in competition to a degree, but not to the degree that competing industries are. When they mismanage their business they do not inevitably lose trade by reason of it. If a bank gives its customers poor service they transfer their patronage to some other bank. When a subscriber does not like one newspaper he is at full liberty to stop reading it and buy some other journal. But when a city lays poor pavements at high prices, or omits to provide playgrounds, or has a corrupt police force, the average citizen cannot pick up his belongings and go somewhere else. In that sense he does not get the benefit of any inter-city competition.

Politics and business standards.

A word in conclusion. Standards in government, we are sometimes told, should be brought abreast of our standards in business. The answer is that in some matters they are already abreast, and even ahead. The spoils system is still rampant in some fields of business. The promoter who gets control of 51 per cent of the stock in a business corporation has no compunctions about throwing the old crowd out and putting his own friends in their places. Nepotism is resented in politics, but in business it is so common as to be hardly worth mentioning. Aldermanic junkets are frowned upon by public opinion, but big business still tolerates them, not to speak of banquets for directors and favors of all kinds for their friends. A public officer who accepts a sum of money for the doing of that which it is his duty to do is a grafter and finds himself indicted by a grand jury; but the banker who accepts a commission for negotiating a loan to a customer sometimes regards that action as part of an honest (and profitable) day's work. The city officials hesitate to sell out the worker's cottage for arrears of taxes, lest it be accounted an example of man's inhumanity to man. But it is good business to foreclose a mortgage in the same circumstances. "As I have learned more about private business," says Henry Bruère, "I have come to the conclusion that there are not many things you do in private business that can be done similarly in public business." Least of all can you apply private standards.

REFERENCES

There is an interesting chapter entitled "Is City Government a Business?" in W. P. Capes, *The Modern City and Its Problems* (New York, 1922), pp. 43-53. Chapters on municipal functions and on the financial aspects of city administration may be found in William Anderson's *American City Government* (New York, 1925). The second volume of W. B. Munro's *Municipal Government and Administration* (2 vols., New York, 1923) deals with all the various phases of municipal administration from art to zoning. References will be found at the end of each chapter.

CHAPTER XXII

MUNICIPAL REFORM AND REFORMERS

A broad definition of reform.

Municipal reform is the term used to designate any kind of organized agitation which has for its aim the improvement of existing conditions in some branch of local administration. It is one of the most comprehensive phrases in the vocabulary of political science, comprising as it does a great variety of separate agitations which start from sources widely apart, profess different purposes, and employ very dissimilar means of carrying their respective programs into effect. Movements for the simplification of municipal machinery, for direct primaries, for improvements in the ballot, for the introduction of the initiative, referendum, and recall, for proportional representation, for displacing patronage by the use of the merit system, for new budget methods, for greater uniformity in municipal accounting, for the replanning of streets, for the extension of playground facilities, for improved housing conditions, for better law enforcement, for remodelling the system of municipal taxation, and for a host of other changes in the existing system of city government or administration—they are all lumped together under the inclusive name of reform. It matters not that some of these movements are contradictory; that there is, for example, a necessary antagonism between the short-ballot agitation, which seeks to ease the ballot of its present burdens, and the propaganda for direct legislation, which seeks to make the ballot more cumbersome by putting questions on it. However antagonistic to one another they may be, all projects of civic betterment, from whatever source they may come and whatever their merits, are branded as "reforms," and those who urge them are called "reformers."

Why people dislike the term.

It is not surprising, then, that reforms and reformers are in rather poor repute with people in general. The public imagination has come to regard the reformer as a busybody who lends his support to any new scheme, however visionary, and who goes on the principle that whatever is, is wrong. The newspaper cartoons picture him as a lean, cadaverous individual in semi-clerical garb, carrying a large umbrella and looking as though there was a bad smell at the end of his nose. Brand Whitlock once defined reformers as people who "feel a deep responsibility for the shortcomings of others." Theodore Roosevelt, although he was himself the most notable reformer of his day, regarded them as the "lunatic fringe" of human society. Roosevelt was a police reformer, a civil service reformer, a reformer of big business, and a would-be reformer of the Republican party, yet he had an abhorrence of the term. Woodrow Wilson also disliked the title, but he was none the less a reformer in every sense of the term. He reformed the tariff, the banking system, and the system of national defence. He tried to reform the world's government and make it safe for democracy. Grover Cleveland, a generation ago, and Abraham Lincoln a generation preceding him, were both of them reformers although they did not call themselves by that name. The fact is that all men of progressive outlook are reformers, and all progress comes by way of reform. The names may be in disfavor, but the thing itself ought not to be.

In general, municipal reformers are of three types. First, there is the public officeholder, or the man in active politics, or the careful student of municipal affairs who realizes from his own experience, or from his own study, the need for various changes in governmental machinery or methods. He wants these changes made, but has no delusions as to the practical difficulties. He is ready to go forward a step at a time. He will take a half loaf if he cannot get a whole one. Usually he dislikes to be called a reformer and prefers to be known as a man of constructive ideas, or a "forward-looking man" (to use Woodrow Wilson's phrase), or something of the sort. It is through men and women of this type that most improvements in municipal administration have been brought about during the past fifty years. Reformers of this type have been patient, persevering, practical. They have bided their time and gained results. May their tribe increase! *Three types of municipal reformer:* *1. The applied idealist.*

Second, we have the large group of men and women who are sincerely interested in some specific reform, such as the city manager plan, the extension of the merit system, or the installation of better business methods at the city hall. As a rule they *2. The specialized reformer.*

know what they are talking about, and to a certain extent they appreciate the practical difficulties involved. But their interest in reform in rather narrowly specialized and they often get things out of proper proportion. Some civil service reformers, for example, would have you believe that if everybody in public office could only be selected by competitive examinations, the political millennium would be at hand. Yet reformers of this second type have been well organized and persistent. A Tammany henchman once said that they were "like queen hornets. They sting you once and then they die." He was wrong, as history proves. The ballot reformers, charter reformers, tax reformers, police reformers, housing reformers, and reform hornets of a dozen other brands have been buzzing around for forty years. They have stung the politicians repeatedly. Much credit is due them for what they have accomplished through sheer persistence in the face of great difficulties.

3. The professional reformer.

Finally, there are the militants, the crusaders, the professional reformers, the ones whom Roosevelt had in mind when he spoke of the lunatic fringe. They are ready to champion anything that is drastic, from the single tax to the padlocking of dance halls. It is their obsession that the common good can be achieved by fiat of law. They desire that the statute book shall be a reflection of their own moral yearnings. They stand always for economy, efficiency, law enforcement at all hazards, Sunday observance, paternalism, regulation, and above all things, order. Reformers of this type have done a great deal to make the old virtues unattractive. They have done harm to the cause of reform by their extreme views and unbending ways. Although they constitute a small minority among reformers these extremists manage to get themselves very much in the limelight and they color with a blue shade the whole rainbow of reform.

The men and women who make up this third group of reformers ought to interest the student of psychology, for their minds work in a curious way. They begin with the assumption that they are right. Their proposals must be sound, they reason, else reformers would not be championing them. And thus it follows, as the night the day, that if you decline to join the cause you are deficient in civic patriotism. It matters not that there are difficulties, seemingly insuperable, in the way. Nor does it matter that reform proposals, even when they prove practicable, usually fail to function as anticipated. The militant reformer idealizes his reform. If he feels that it is "sound in principle" he cares little about the practical aspects of it.

Reformers of all types try to advance their respective causes by organization and propaganda. They form leagues, associations, federations, societies, and clubs. These organizations are of almost endless variety. Some of them are of nation-wide scope and include thousands of members. They aim at the betterment of conditions in all American cities. The outstanding organization of this type is the National Municipal League, a body which has existed for more than thirty years, during all of which it has contributed materially to the enlightenment of opinion on municipal affairs. Its membership is drawn largely from the two upper groups of municipal reformers, and more especially from that portion of the citizenship which, while not holding public office, is disposed to keep a close and intelligent eye upon those who do. The League has not sponsored any single reform or group of reforms. It has lent a hand to every project that looked both practicable and promising. It has been a clearing house for information and ideas. Its chief service has been the dissemination of knowledge concerning the facts of municipal government.[1]

Reform organizations:

The National Municipal League.

Another reform organization on a nation-wide basis, and with a comprehensive program, is the American Civic Association. Its interest has been mainly devoted to the physical improvement of cities—by better planning, zoning, the elimination of billboards, and the smoke nuisance, the development of park systems and the preservation of natural recreation spaces. The monthly periodical known as *The American City* is not the official organ of this association, although its interests cover the same field and more. It gives a great deal of attention to matters connected with the physical aspects of municipal progress and is in all respects a valuable publication.[2]

The American Civic Association.

Second, there are various organizations which, although main-

---

[1] Its publications include the *National Municipal Review* (published monthly), various *Supplements* to this publication, books and monographs on subjects of current interest, technical pamphlets, digests of charters, model charters, pocket folders, leaflets, and clipping sheets.

[2] Mention should also be made of the *Municipal Index* which is issued annually by this periodical and contains a great deal of useful material. For a list of "National Organizations serving Municipalities and Local Civic Groups" see the *Municipal Index* for 1925, pp. 511-513.

Specialized organizations. tained on a nation-wide basis, do not sponsor any general program of reform but devote their energies to the promotion of some one particular cause. Such are the National Civil Service Reform League, the Short Ballot Organization, the National Popular Government League, and the Proportional Representation League, which bend their entire energies to the extension of the merit system, the reform of the old-style ballot, the spread of the initiative and referendum, and the adoption of proportional representation, respectively. The first of these bodies maintains a national headquarters but also works through state and municipal organizations. The others function through national headquarters and field agents. Being much more specific in their programs they are able to obtain results which are more direct and more tangible, if perhaps no more important in the long run, than organizations which spread their interest over wider fields. They are aggressive and persevering in their campaigns of education, and have not been daunted by obstacles of any kind. On the whole, their actual success, as indicated by the laws that have gone upon the statute-books through their efforts, constitutes much more than a profitable return for the time, patience, and money expended. This is in part due to the fact that such organizations have been able to mobilize their efforts upon what for the moment seems to be a vulnerable point. Wherever, for example, a new city charter is being framed, the energies of the Civil Service Reform League or the Short Ballot Organization, or the other Leagues, are deflected to that point and remain centered there until they gain their point or are defeated.

Professional organizations. A third class of organizations, though not adopting the nomenclature of reform, is none the less an active agent of municipal betterment. Within this class are included the various bodies of city officials or other professionals which have been organized for mutual information and the exchange of ideas. There is the City Managers' Association, for example, with a membership which includes most of the men who are serving in this office. There are organizations which include most of the city engineers, the health officers, the police chiefs, the park executives, the librarians, and the school superintendents, respectively.[1] There

[1] A full list, with the name of officers, may be found in the annual issues of the *Municipal Index*.

are other associations whose memberships are not drawn mainly from among city officials but from professionals whose work touches city government—as, for example, the National City Planning Conference, the Governmental Research Conference, the National Conference of Social Work, the American Waterworks Association, and the American Public Health Association. All such organizations are professional or semi-professional in character; their chief object is not the promotion of any specific reform or set of reforms, although they are interested in particular phases of municipal administration. Their chief purpose is to bring people of kindred interests into contact with one another and to serve as clearing-houses for the exchange of new ideas. At their meetings, which are held annually or oftener, papers upon matters of technical interest are presented and discussed. The service rendered by bodies of this sort in broadening the horizon of city officials is of great value.

All three classes of organizations mentioned in the foregoing pages,—namely, those which work for the improvement of municipal conditions in general, those which give their attention to improvement in one specific direction, and those which afford opportunity for the officials of one municipality to learn what other cities are doing,—all these are bodies whose activities are broader than the bounds of any single state or municipality. They are national associations. Another type of reform organization of which there are numerous examples is the state league of municipalities. Leagues of this sort have been formed in many of the states—including California, Illinois, Indiana, Iowa, Kansas, Minnesota, Texas and Wisconsin.[1] They represent the cities in each state and their gatherings are mainly attended by city officials. In the main they have been interested in protecting the city against state interference and in getting favorable legislation for all the cities of the state. Likewise there are many other organizations which function on a state-wide basis but confine their interest to a narrower field. Among such are state health associations, tax associations, and public health leagues. To make a complete list for the whole country would be quite a task. As a rule the organizing begins locally, that is, a small association for some specific purpose is organized in a single city.

Leagues of municipalities.

---

[1] In New York the organization is known as the State Conference of Mayors. For a full list see the *Municipal Index* (1925), pp. 513-514.

Then similar associations are established in other cities, one by one. Presently someone suggests that, having all the same purpose, these organizations should form a state league or federation, and this is done. It enables a concentration of strength when needed.

Local reform bodies.
This brings us, finally, to the reform organizations which function in a single city. There are literally hundreds of them in every large municipality—if one includes every organization which is engaged in work of a constructive sort. Some are municipal reform organizations in the strict sense of the term, that is, they are directly concerned with the reconstruction of city government in some of its features. They are active in politics, but they are not all active to the same degree, nor do they use the same methods of gaining their ends. Sometimes the Municipal Reform League, or Good Government Association, or Municipal Voters' League is to all intents a political party. It either nominates or endorses candidates in municipal campaigns. It raises and spends a campaign fund. In other cases the organization merely publishes information concerning the candidates, this information being gathered by the League's agents. In other cases, again, the reform organizations make an alliance with one of the regular political parties—as the Citizens' Union has done in New York City on several occasions. The methods depend upon the size of the organization's membership, the amount of money that it has available, and the local campaign situation. There are times when a municipal reform organization holds the balance of power and can swing the election to one side or the other. Politicians usually proclaim aloud that civic leaguers and "goo-goos" count for nothing, and that their support is a liability rather than an asset; but they know better and will tell you so in private.

The host of "service" organizations.
Aside from the avowed municipal reform organizations there is the great host of local improvement associations, chambers of commerce, boards of trade, women's clubs, church federations, parent-teachers associations, real estate boosters, neighborhood societies, welfare societies, luncheon clubs, and whatnot. All of them profess a desire to serve the community. All of them have aims of a civic character. Nearly all of them come forward from time to time with proposals for consideration by the city authorities, and delegations from them are constantly pressing

MUNICIPAL REFORM AND REFORMERS

some form of municipal betterment. Each association has its own specialty. One is concerned with increasing the city's trade or bringing new industries to it, another with promoting real estate values, another with tax reduction, another with playgrounds and places of recreation, another with the abatement of the billboard nuisance, another with the problem of laying adequate restrictions upon public-service companies, another with the reform of municipal accounting, and so on. The methods pursued are adapted to the ends in view and they differ just as widely. No two are alike. Some have hundreds of members, others a mere handful. Some hold regular meetings, others come together only when there is need for it. Some devote all their attention to public affairs, while others are only interested on occasions. Some, like the Rotary and Kiwanis Clubs, prefer to lunch; others, like the Chamber of Commerce, prefer to dine. All of them have to hear speeches whether they like it or not. There is no subject on which more oratory has been lavished than the welfare of the city. If words could accomplish it we would have entered the millennium long ago.

All such organizations, of course, need money for their work, and they usually obtain it from membership dues or from general subscriptions. The total amount gathered in this way must be enormous each year; yet the tangible results that come from its expenditure are astonishingly small. One reason is that much of the money is spent in ways that are ineffective. Salaries and clerical expenses devour most of the income which the average reform organization is able to secure. A secretary is employed, and the salary of this official, together with office rent, may absorb most of the year's revenue. Many reform organizations regularly present the spectacle of a secretary who spends most of his time gathering money and then uses most of the money to pay for the time he has spent in gathering it. Some reform associations seem to take it for granted that their mere existence constitutes a public service; at any rate, the lethargy which their paid officials frequently display would not be tolerated even among municipal employees, slow as the latter may be. Our larger cities abound in organizations which bear impressive names, and whose officials from time to time put themselves forward as the spokesman of important elements in the community, when as a matter of truth, many of them do not

The financing of reform.

possess a corporal's guard of members and perform no public service worthy of the name.

The wastefulness of reform methods.

Municipal waste through the inactivity of public officials and through the failure of different departments to work in harmony has become proverbial. Yet it may be questioned whether public office-holders have displayed these shortcomings in a greater degree than that shown by civic-welfare organizations as a whole. The overlapping of effort among them is notorious. At times they are extremely jealous of one another. Every large city has organizations at work in the same field without the slightest reference to one another. They are in each other's way. Often there is every reason why two organizations should unite into one, thus saving both time and money—but they rarely do it. Large sums are spent in sending out circulars, or in advertising, most of it in a conventional, ineffective way. One of the first reforms needed in most large cities is a reform of these reforming organizations.

Research bureaus.

In enumerating the organized forces of civic improvement one should make particular mention of the various bureaus of research now in operation in a dozen or more of the larger cities of the United States. These institutions, organized more or less closely upon the model of the parent bureau in New York City, are a development of the last two decades in American municipal government. Sometimes they are supported by private contributions and are under the control of citizen trustees or directors. In other instances they are maintained by public funds and are under official direction. In either case the bureau is an institution for the thorough study of actual conditions in its own city; it possesses a staff of investigators who probe their way into every branch of the municipal service and emerge with data upon which they base recommendations for improvement.

These bureaus take it upon themselves to act as public advisers in matters that are, for the most part, too complicated and too technical for the public to understand and form opinions upon without assistance. Their very existence, in fact, rests on the idea that the greater part of the city's business is technical, and hence that the city's treasury commonly suffers more from leakage due to inefficient methods than from official dishonesty. They assume, quite properly, that before these leakages can be stopped their exact locations must be disclosed, and believe that this is a task involving patient study by trained men. After the sources of waste have been plainly indicated to the voters by convincing evidence, public opinion, they declare, may be trusted to exert all the pressure that is needed to effect a reform. In a word, the bureau of municipal research aims to provide an effective center of trustworthy information and to bring this information to the ears of every citizen by a persistent and usually a somewhat original publicity campaign.

Taking all these organizations together,—national, state, and local, political, semipolitical, and nonpolitical,—the battalions of reform make up an impressive brigade. Why have they not accomplished more? Why does city government, in spite of their efforts, leave so much to be desired? These are questions easier to propound than to answer, but some of the superficial reasons for the habitual failure of reform to achieve tangible results are not far to seek. *Why have reform organizations not accomplished more?*

In the first place, until recent years, most reform movements approached city government from a wrong angle. They assumed that the existing machinery was not seriously defective, but that the trouble lay with the men who were in control of it. In their eyes, therefore, the obvious remedy was to oust from office those whose incompetence or lack of integrity had befouled the administration, and to put capable, honest, high-principled men in their place.[1] Not the *reconstruction* but the *purification* of municipal politics was long the goal of reform. But campaigns which started with this assumption found themselves confronted with great practical difficulties. For one thing, men in office were not easy to dislodge; on the contrary, they fought to the last ditch. And they had well-organized political machines behind them. "Turn the rascals out," was the reformer's slogan. But it was easier to call them rascals than to beat them at the polls. For another thing the "honest, public-spirited, capable, and well-trained men" whom it was deemed so imperative to put into office did not always come into the fight. They were hard to draw into politics, and rarely proved to be good campaigners when they got there. Hard to nominate, they were still harder to elect. Now the existence of this situation should have been *The old angle of approach.*

[1] Recall, for example, the remark of Carl Schurz that there was "not a municipal government in this country, on whatever pattern organized," which would "not work well when administered by honest, public-spirited, capable, and well-trained men."

proof to the leaders of reform that there was something wrong with their program. There are times, no doubt, when circumstances may be such as to deter capable men from willingly entering the service of the city. But when that situation becomes normal, when year by year the efficient service of society involves too heavy a personal sacrifice for the well-intentioned citizen,—then the trouble cannot lie elsewhere than in the conditions under which the service has to be performed. The cause of reform was long misguided, therefore, by the notion that municipal ills were personal matters, whereas in point of fact they lay far beyond the mere personnel of city government and required for their eradication a change in the framework.

The sterility to which it led. Efforts inspired by the belief that individuals and not institutions were at fault naturally led to sterility in results. At times the reformers managed to elect their nominees; whereupon they held a banquet, congratulated both the winners and themselves, and went home to enjoy the promised new era in city affairs. But the new era was not forthcoming. The new mayor and aldermen, however capable and honest, found that they could not do good work with the tools at hand. The political shackles imposed upon them by law, the maze of restrictions on every hand, and the small modicum of real power, all combined to thwart the new administration. In a whole term of office, therefore, the reformers were usually able to accomplish no more than some penny-saving improvements which were far from redeeming the preëlection promises so freely made by reform campaigners.[1]

The new angle of approach. In due time, however, the need of charter reform obtained recognition, and movements for the simplification of municipal machinery began. New York made a start during the last decade of the nineteenth century, and other cities like St. Louis, San

[1] "In almost every American city the people, at one time or another, have grown weary beyond endurance of partisan misrule and extravagance and have given expression to their indignation through some form of citizen's movement, and good men of clean records have been given control of city affairs. What has been the result? The new officers have invariably found a system of government so honeycombed with the greed and selfishness of partisan politics and their actions so hampered by state legislation that no permanent good could be done. The people were impatient for results, and when not forthcoming, their enthusiasm waned, the tidal wave of reform receded, the politicians quietly planned the next campaign, and the unworthy and incompetent resumed control of the great public estate." T. C. Devlin, *Municipal Reform in the United States* (New York, 1896), p. 13.

MUNICIPAL REFORM AND REFORMERS 431

Francisco, and Boston, followed. In the smaller communities the striking success of the commission form of government sent its echoes to all sections of the country. Municipal reform thus entered a new phase, and one which gave promise of far more in the way of achievement. Not only the leaders of opinion but the rank and file of municipal electorates began to realize that true reform is not merely a question of putting capable and honest men in office, but rather one of making the offices attractive to capable and honest men. They began to see that they could make public office attractive only by attaching to it an opportunity for real, unrestricted, constructive service to the community, and that they could do this only by renouncing, first of all, that slavish allegiance to the old political formulas which had done nothing but misguide.

The magnetism of power is so great that few men in any community can resist its attraction; but it must be real power and not merely the form of it. If the pattern of city government becomes such as to afford to every elective officer those great opportunities of service which go with power, most of the difficulties which beset the paths of reform organizations in earlier years will disappear. Reform has gained in effectiveness as it has become impersonal, organic, and reconstructive. It has made great headway everywhere. Unlike the guerilla warfare of earlier days, the charter reform campaigns of the last two decades have been well worth the efforts expended in them. *And a new outcome.*

The years 1865-1895 have been called the Dark Ages of American municipal government, and they deserve the name. They were the days when our cities, in point of consistent maladministration, had none elsewhere to rival them. Tweed Rings, Gas Rings, County Rings and other plunderbunds reigned unashamed. In municipal misgovernment America led the world. We contributed to the English tongue such new words as boodle and graft because we needed them to describe existing practices and could find nothing suitable in the dictionaries. But the last thirty years, 1895-1925, are equally entitled to be known as the Civic Renaissance, for these three decades have seen an almost unbelievable improvement all along the line. Municipal government in the United States is no longer the "conspicuous failure" that James Bryce called it in his notable work on the American Commonwealth. It has been improved to a revolutionary de- *A contrast in eras.*

gree. And the municipal reformer has had much to do with this miracle. He has kept up the fight decade after decade, and by sheer persistence has crumbled the old order bit by bit. Were Schurz and Curtis and Nast and the other embattled reformers of a generation ago to rise from their graves they would be amazed at the change. They would find that even Tammany has become respectable. Let us hope that the renaissance will last.

Can the new order be made permanent? To secure even temporary improvements in city administration is good, but to make them permanent is better. Reform which aspires to finality must not content itself, therefore, with a mere reorganization in the political framework of municipalities. To assume that a good charter and a staff of capable officials are the only things essential to an efficient and thrifty municipal administration is to overlook the fact that many of the city's difficult problems are questions of business and not of government. Even the best city charter provides but a small part of the mechanism necessary to solve these problems correctly; the rest of the apparatus, which includes the whole interior of administration, must be sought within the range of general powers conferred by the charter. It is just here, as has already been noted, that the shortcomings of municipal administration have been most numerous and most costly. When a private corporation proves successful in the conduct of affairs, the reason is not usually to be found in the scope of powers conferred upon it by its charter, or even in the capacity or honesty of the men who sit upon its directorate, but rather in the efficiency of its internal organization, in the skill with which it has adjusted the various parts of the business machine, and the ability which it has shown in putting the right subordinates in the right place.

If the city desires administrative success, it must seek it in the same way. Reformers must realize, therefore, that a final solution of the chief municipal problem of the American city, that of getting full value for the city's expenditures, depends upon more than the mere enunciation of sound political principles in city charters. If this has been said before it will bear repetition, for no other maxim of municipal science is more often disregarded. There has been too much belief that good government can be ensured by adopting a scheme, a principle, or a slogan. Good government, in any community, has to be earned by years of industry, vigilance, sacrifice, and civic education. It can be had in no other way.

From the experiences of the past thirty years our reform organizations can draw good lessons for the future. They should find some means of ensuring better team play among themselves. They should bear in mind that politics is a practical art rather than a science. The reason why the average politician can master it is that he learns by experience. The reformers should also remember that no matter how worthy a cause may be, it cannot succeed without making converts from the ranks of the people. It will succeed in proportion to its hold on the citizenship. The reformer should never permit himself to be drawn into personal recriminations, for in this field the politician is sure to get the better of him. Personalities are here today and gone tomorrow; it is the system of government that ought to be the focus of reformers' attack or solicitude as the case may be. Finally, there is need for more realism in circles of reform. The reformer must be satisfied at times with the half of what he would like to obtain. He should keep in mind the fable of the hare and the tortoise—letting the politicians play the part of the hare. It is better to go out for a single playground, and get it, than to insist on "a comprehensive, fully-planned system of recreation"—and get nothing. It is better to win with a pretty good candidate than to lose with a paragon of excellence heading the ticket. It is better to compromise and save part of a good law than to stand pat and lose the whole of it. Finally, it is well for the reformer to keep his courage. During the past thirty-five years he may have lost many battles, but he has been winning the war.

Lessons for the future.

REFERENCES

The literature of municipal reform is extensive. Such of it as was published before 1915 may be found in the author's *Bibliography of Municipal Government*. Publications since that date may be found by going through the files of the *National Municipal Review*.

CHAPTER XXIII

THE CRITERIA OF GOOD CITY GOVERNMENT

Government as it appears to the average citizen.

It is not always easy to tell whether a city government is good or bad. No city is ever as well governed as it ought to be; on the other hand, no city is ever so badly governed as its critics would have us believe. Throughout the country there are all degrees and varieties of good and bad city government. In determining the place which a city occupies in this scale, moreover, people are guided largely by their prejudices on the one hand or by their partisanship on the other. They decline to believe that the city is badly governed when their own friends are in power. The government of other cities, or of their own city when conducted by officials of an opposing party, is self-evidently an inferior variety of government. No matter how good a city government may be by all the outward signs, there are some who will tell you that it is the worst on earth. No matter how bad it may be, by all the surface indications, there are others who will try to convince you that there is none better.

Its quality depends on his prejudices.

People judge the quality of a city's government in accordance with their own prejudices or partialities for the reason that they have no objective tests to apply. In the old days, when the government of the community was a relatively simple affair, the average citizen knew his rulers and could keep an eye on what they were doing. He knew whether his taxes were going up or down, whether the streets were kept clean and the laws obeyed. But now, in the larger centers, all this has got far beyond him. Two-thirds of the citizens know nothing about the tax rate. They are not property owners, and although they pay taxes indirectly (through landlords and merchants), most of them do not realize the fact. And as for the efficiency of the various city departments—such as police, fire protection, public works, schools, and all the rest—the average citizen can see but a small part of the work and even as respects this small fraction he is

THE CRITERIA OF GOOD CITY GOVERNMENT

hardly competent to form an opinion of his own. How can he tell, for example, whether the city has the form of charter most suited to its needs, whether the departments are properly organized, whether there are too many drones on the municipal payroll, whether the budget system is functioning smoothly, or whether the per capita cost of his city's government is higher than it ought to be? Even well educated and well informed citizens are frequently unable to make up their own minds on such matters.

What we need, accordingly, is a series of nonpartisan tests or criteria by which the efficiency of a city government can be fairly measured. We know that a railroad is being efficiently managed if the fares and freight rates are low, the service good, and the profits high. No railroad, if inefficiently conducted, could satisfy these three tests. We know that a bank is being efficiently managed if it keeps drawing business away from its competitors and increasing the annual dividend to its own stockholders. But the city—by what tests can the goodness or badness of its government be appraised? Not by the growth of its population, or by the size of its tax rate, or by the amount of its funded debt. Nor yet by the splendor of its public buildings, the cleanness of its streets, or the integrity of its police. All these things are of some significance, but they reach only a little way. German cities, before the war, kept their streets spotless and their policemen honest—but they were sadly deficient in municipal democracy and grossly neglected some of the social welfare branches of community administration. A city with well-paved streets and no housing laws is not a well-governed city. A city with honest policemen and no public playgrounds is in the same category. To judge a city government fairly, we must apply a rather long series of criteria extending over the entire field of municipal activities—legal, political, social, and economic. To use a metaphor of the open road one might say that a city administration is not functioning well unless it hits fairly on all four cylinders. The legal powers of the municipality may be adequate; it may have a generous measure of home rule, and yet be unable to keep its politics clean. It may have honest men in public office and yet be unprogressive in its administrative methods. Honesty and efficiency do not always go together. By what tests can a city be fairly judged?

The need for some objective criteria.

But rigid formulas cannot be laid down.

Now there are obvious dangers in laying down any series of formulas where so broad a range of functions is concerned and where the conditions are so widely variant. All cities are not equally easy to govern. In some of them, by reason of their physical or social structure, the problem is more difficult than in others. That being the case, the use of a rigid yardstick in measuring the efficiency of government, in all cities of whatever size or character, would be clearly unfair. The criteria, if used at all, must not be too definite and they should be somewhat flexibly applied. With this reservation, they may serve a useful purpose. They will at least direct attention to the vital things in community administration.

A suggested series of twenty-five tests:

There will be differences of opinion, quite naturally, as to these objective tests of good city government. No one, however intensively he may have studied the operations of American municipalities, is qualified to lay down a definitive series of rules to which they should conform. The best that can be done is to indicate certain general questions which the intelligent citizen may ask and answer in relation to his own local government. And if he can honestly answer all of them in the affirmative, he may rest assured that the mechanism is sound in its essentials. If the government of his city, under such conditions, is not what he desires it to be, the only counsel to be given him is one of hope and patience. The following questions, therefore, are suggested as an aid to the citizen's survey of his own government.

1. How much genuine home rule?

1. Do the constitution and laws of the state afford the city a reasonable amount of freedom in the management of its own affairs? A reasonable amount of municipal freedom does not necessarily involve home rule, as this term is commonly understood. It does not require that the city shall have the right to frame and adopt its own charter. Municipal home rule, as has been pointed out in a previous chapter, may mean much or little.[1] In some states it is hardly more than a pleasing phrase. A city may be given the right to make its own charter and still be hedged by so many restrictions that this right amounts to very little. In determining the degree of freedom from state interference which a city enjoys, one should regard the traditions and the facts, not merely the letter of the constitution and the laws.

2. Is the city charter a document sufficiently concise and

[1] *Above*, chap. iv.

THE CRITERIA OF GOOD CITY GOVERNMENT 437

intelligent to be within the comprehension of those who have to do their work under its provisions? In other words, does it confine itself to fundamentals or is it cluttered with details and minor provisions of all sorts? Is it really a charter or does it attempt to usurp the ordinance-making authority of the municipality? Is it a constructive document which aims to facilitate the work of honest and capable officers, or are its provisions for the most part checks and balances, framed on the assumption that the people will elect incompetents, and designed to forestall the inevitable results of popular folly,—in other words, to protect the people against themselves? Are the provisions of the charter worded in such language that he who runs may read and understand?

2. The city charter.

3. Is the structure of city government simple, does it provide for a sufficient concentration of responsibility and at the same time ensure responsiveness to the will of the people? These qualities are not peculiar to any one form of government. The mayor-and-council type of government can be made as simple as any other. The city manager plan, although often criticised for its lack of responsiveness, is not intrinsically deficient in that respect. The commission plan of government does not readily lend itself to a full concentration of responsibility, yet many cities have achieved it under this plan. In a word, the type of government is not the sole consideration. The real question is: does the structure of city government, whatever its type, combine the qualities of simplicity, concentration, and responsiveness to a sufficient degree?

3. The frame of government.

4. Is there adequate provision for the control of the government by the people? Many cities have endeavored to make such provision by means of the initiative, referendum, and recall. These agencies of control have merit, as has been shown, but they do not by any means provide an absolute insurance against official irresponsibility. Nor, on the other hand, can popular control of the government be stigmatized as inadequate because a city has made no provision for initiative petitions, referenda, or the recall of elective officers. There are reformers who do not hesitate to brand a city charter as a poor affair whenever they find no provision for these things in it, but they would find difficulty in pointing out any American city that has attained good government through the mere possession of these instru-

4. Popular control.

mentalities or has lost it through the lack of them. Adequate popular control can be secured in a variety of ways, some of which will be suggested in the next few paragraphs.

5. How many elective officials? 5. Are the elective positions few and outstanding? The method of electing officials by popular vote should be used to fill only those positions which carry policy-determining functions, which are conspicuous, and on which the public attention can be focussed. This ensures a short and wieldy ballot. When you ask the voter to choose a dozen or more officials at the same election you are taking one of the best ways of making his government irresponsible. The short ballot is the best of all agencies for promoting discrimination on the voter's part and hence insuring the responsiveness of his government to him. Some would add that the ballot, besides being very short, should contain no party designations, but that is a matter on which there may be legitimate differences of opinion. Long and cumbrous ballots are in any case to be avoided, which can only be done by reducing the number of elective officers.

6. Concentration of administrative responsibility. 6. Are all the regular administrative officials of the city directly chosen by and responsible to the chief executive authority? Officials whose duties are not concerned with the determination of policy but are of a purely administrative character should be appointed. The chief executive officer of the city, be he mayor or city manager, should have undivided power of appointment and removal, without the confirmation or concurrence of any other authority and subject only to the civil service regulations. Unless this is done there can be no centralization of administrative authority. Make a chart showing the way in which the administrative service is organized. Do all the lines converge inward and upward? If not, the scheme of organization is prima facie defective.

7. The terms of office. 7. Are the terms of office long enough to give elective officeholders an opportunity to demonstrate what they can do, and are they short enough to hold these officials to a strict accountability? In general the terms of office for mayors and councilmen have been too short. They should in no case be less than two years. Four years is in most cases a better term, but longer terms than this would probably be unwise. Even with four-year terms there is something to be said for having the recall procedure available in case of need.

THE CRITERIA OF GOOD CITY GOVERNMENT 439

8. Is the legislative organ of the city large enough to be representative, yet small enough to function smoothly? Large city councils waste time in futile discussion. Not being able to get business done in the council chamber, they refer it to committees. These committees do much of their work in executive session, behind closed doors, with no publicity given to the motives which influence their recommendations. They are subjected to various forms of pressure which would not be exerted in the open. It is desirable that the city's organ of lawmaking and policy-determining should be small enough to avoid the necessity of relegating important matters to any subordinate body. In English cities the committee system works satisfactorily because a good tradition has long since become established. In America the people are suspicious of council committees, and with good reason, for they have not contributed much to the efficiency of government in municipalities. A city council of seven, nine, or eleven members can get along without delegating much of its work, but a council of twenty or thirty members cannot. Care should be taken, however, to avoid the other horn of the dilemma, which is the fault of making the council small to the point of inadequate representation. There is no virtue in cutting the council to a membership of five or seven if this means that various important elements in the population of the city must go unrepresented altogether.[1] *8. Size of the city council.*

9. Does the city's departmental organization conform to sound administrative practice? More specifically, is the number of departments no greater than the work requires; does each department possess functions which are well worked out and related in character,—or is there too much machinery, with the resultant duplication and friction? There is no ideal number of administrative departments and no model plan for organizing them. But there are certain principles which a sound departmental organization ought to follow.[2] *9. Plan of departmental organization.*

10. Are the subordinate officials and the employees of the municipality appointed and promoted on a merit basis and are they adequately protected against removal without cause? There are only two methods of selecting and advancing public employees, namely, the spoils system and the merit system. The *10. Merit system.*

---

[1] For a discussion of this question see *above*, pp. 287-288.
[2] For a statement of these principles, see *above*, pp. 346-348.

latter has its shortcomings, no doubt, but it is steadily being improved and the improvement inevitably will continue. The objections to the spoils system are fundamental and inherent; they cannot be eradicated by any change in administrative methods. In the case of the merit system, on the other hand, it is merely a matter of overcoming various practical difficulties, perfecting the mechanism, and making it function more flexibly.

11. Morale of the working force. 11. Are the city employees paid fair wages according to an equitable classification of work? A great deal of injustice is embodied in the payrolls of most American cities. Some employees are paid too much; others too little. Different salaries are often fixed for work of precisely the same character. The favored employees get the soft berths and this is disastrous to the morale of the whole working force. Everybody resents favoritism except those who are the recipients of it, and they inevitably form a small fraction of the whole. Is there a standard classification of work and wages with a direct connection between the two?

12. Pension system. 12. Is there a system of pensions for disabled or superannuated municipal employees, resting on a sound actuarial basis? It is an axiom of practical politics that a city must take care of its employees when they become disabled in the service or too old for further duty. If there is no pension system they will be kept on the payroll and given full wages for nominal work. This is a highly expensive method of meeting a moral obligation and in the long run is far more costly than an out-and-out pension plan. It is not only more expensive but much less satisfactory to all concerned.

13. Contracts. 13. Are all important contracts awarded by fair competition, openly advertised, without regard to any considerations other than the city's best interest? It is not enough that the city charter shall contain general stipulations providing for the advertisement of contracts and for competitive awards. There are various ways of evading such general stipulations.[1] The real question is whether the awards are fair in fact or whether there is a mere gesture of compliance with the law accompanied by subterfuge or trickery. Unfairness in the award of municipal contracts cannot be completely eliminated by any form of

---

[1] For a discussion of these various ways see the author's *Municipal Government and Administration* (2 vols., New York, 1923), vol. II, pp. 59-63.

THE CRITERIA OF GOOD CITY GOVERNMENT 441

statutory prohibition. It is a matter of good traditions and official honesty.

14. Is there a system which ensures the rigid inspection of all contract work being done for the city, and is this inspection performed without fear, favor, or affection? It avails little to draft specifications carefully and to award contracts honestly if there is no effective follow-up to ensure that the terms of the contracts are observed. There has been more waste in cities through lax or dishonest inspection than through the award of contracts by favoritism, although both things usually go together. The award gets public attention while the work of inspection does not. For that reason the latter needs to be particularly emphasized. *14. Inspection of public work.*

15. Are the appropriations made in accordance with a sound system of budgetary procedure? This involves the use of proper forms for the submission of estimates, a reasonable amount of segregation among the items of expenditure, a workable plan for the scrutiny of the estimates by qualified examiners, and a series of public hearings before the budget is adopted. In general, it is desirable that the responsibility for having the budget prepared for submission to the legislative body shall be entrusted to the chief executive of the city. But it is also important that no item of appropriation shall become effective until it has received the legislative body's approval. Apart from these general considerations there are many subsidiary tests of a good budgetary procedure. What arrangements are made for providing the departments with funds pending the adoption of the budget? How are transfers made from one appropriation to another during the course of the fiscal year? What means are employed to prevent the head of a department from exhausting his appropriations before the year is out? Does the budget make adequate provision for unforeseen and emergency expenditures? In a word, is the procedure such that it functions smoothly and promotes economy or does it lead the city officials into financial snarls and produce deficits with ominous frequency? *15. Budget procedure.*

16. Are the city's revenues adequate for the work which its people expect their municipal government to perform? There are various devices for keeping the cost of city government within bounds, but one of the least effective is the plan of providing in the city charter that the tax rate shall not be fixed above a *16. Are revenues adequate?*

certain point—say ten dollars per thousand of assessed valuation. When the people demand more service, or better service, and when they elect officials to provide it, these officers will find the revenue, no matter what the charter may provide. They will jack up the assessed valuations, or borrow money to pay current expenses, or merely let a deficit accumulate. No statutory device will avail to keep the people of a city from having what they want. There is only one way to accomplish it—which is by taking the suffrage away from them. That being an unpractical step the alternative is to let them bear the brunt of their own extravagance and learn by experience that good things cannot be had without sacrifice. To manage a city's affairs agreeably to the demands of the citizens is a task which, however economically performed, requires a steadily increasing amount of annual revenue, most of which must come from taxes. There should be reasonable leeway in obtaining the funds needed.

17. Borrowing policy.

17. Does the city pursue a sound policy in the matter of borrowing? Sound policy in this field of municipal finance involves at least the following practices: (a) no borrowing to meet current expenses, or to meet expenses which are of a regularly recurrent character;[1] (b) no borrowing for a longer term than the estimated life of the improvement (e.g., fire station, schoolhouse, bridge, or street pavement) for which the loan is raised; and (c) adequate provision for amortizing or paying off the bonds when they fall due. These provisions may be made by the creation of sinking funds or by issuing the bonds in serial form, the latter method being by all means the better one. It goes without saying, moreover, that the funds obtained by borrowing should be strictly conserved for the purpose intended and not diverted to some other enterprise.

18. Central purchasing.

18. Is there an arrangement by which supplies required by the various city departments are purchased under competitive conditions, in accordance with rigid specifications, through a central purchasing agency? Much waste has resulted from the common practice of permitting each department to buy coal, oil, automobiles, gasoline, stationery, and office supplies independently, each patronizing a favored concern and obtaining

---

[1] The purchase of fire apparatus, for example. This is not strictly a "current" expense, for the apparatus lasts several years, but it is an expenditure that recurs (for some new apparatus) almost every year.

THE CRITERIA OF GOOD CITY GOVERNMENT 443

merchandise of poor quality at a high price. It is desirable that the buying should be done by a central purchasing authority which prepares definite specifications as to quality, and calls for bids from all who desire to do business with the city. Standard specifications for supplies of every sort are now available and many of the best-governed cities use them regularly.

19. Does the per capita cost of the various services, such as policing, lighting the streets, maintaining the schools, and caring for the poor, compare favorably with similar costs in other cities of about the same size and character? Cost per capita is not always a fair basis of comparison. Too much reliance should not be placed upon it. A higher per capita cost in any department may be fully warranted by the special conditions of an individual city—for example, the per capita cost of street lighting will necessarily be high in a city that has long, wide stretches of residential highway not closely built up. Still, it is always interesting and useful to compare cities on this basis and also on the basis of their relative costs per acre of area, per thousand dollars of assessed valuation, or per mile of streets. When a city stands high in all these tabulations there is presumptive evidence of over-expenditure. *19. Per capita costs.*

20. Is the outlay for service in the various departments reckoned in terms of unit costs, and are these unit costs reasonable when compared with figures, similarly compiled, in other cities of about the same size? Conditions and problems may differ from city to city; in one municipality there may be more difficulty in meeting the public demands than in another; but such units as a square yard, a ton, a gallon, or a kilowatt are the same everywhere. If a designated type of street pavement, laid in accordance with standard specifications, costs one city a certain amount per square yard, there is no good reason why a neighboring city should pay twenty, thirty, or forty per cent more. Comparing unit costs is one of the best ways of discovering leakages. It should be a universal practice in cities, but relatively few of them use it regularly. *20. Unit costs.*

21. Is there a system of audit and financial control which ensures that all income is duly accounted for, and that no money is spent (a) without a specific appropriation, (b) without satisfactory evidence that the account has been approved by the department concerned, and (c) save in accordance with the laws, *21. Audits and financial control*

the city charter, and the ordinances? It is a fundamental rule of sound municipal finances that no bills should be paid from the treasury until an appropriation therefor has been made by the appropriating authority; that is, the city council or the city commission. The only exceptions are those cases where the state law makes a payment mandatory, irrespective of any appropriation. It is the function of the city comptroller or auditor to see that this principle is observed. It is not his duty, however, to determine whether the bills presented to him have been wisely incurred. The approval of the department which incurred the bill is ordinarily sufficient unless the auditor has reason to believe that there has been some error or crookedness. In order to help departments keep within their appropriations, the comptroller or auditor should inform them, at monthly intervals, concerning the amount of balances available.

22. Municipal reporting.

22. Are the reports issued by the city intelligible and informing to the ordinary citizen? Most municipal reports are not. People, as a rule, are not interested in figures unless they are bedded in reading matter. Accordingly, the city's annual report should describe, in simple language and in an interesting way, the major activities of the year. Matters of routine administration should be given very little space. Illustrations and diagrams should be freely used. Some cities now issue their reports in admirable form and these might well serve as models to other municipalities.

23. Civic organizations.

23. Is the city provided with civic organizations which follow closely what is going on in official circles and take a constructive part in the shaping of public policy? The work of governing a city should not be left entirely to the men and women whom we elect at the polls. The public officials cannot supply all the initiative and all the ideas. They should not be expected to do so. Chambers of commerce, boards of trade, labor unions, civic leagues, and other organizations ought to foster discussion and focus the attention of the whole people upon what goes on at the city hall. They should have committees at work studying the various problems of the community and thus be in a position to suggest ways of meeting difficulties as they arise. In every city there are hundreds of competent men and women who for various reasons cannot give their full time to the public service but who will gladly give a portion of it through work on un-

THE CRITERIA OF GOOD CITY GOVERNMENT 445

official committees. Does the city government make full use of these advisory agencies, or does it repel even the most constructive suggestions as an intrusion upon the prerogatives of the elect?

24. Are the organs of public opinion (particularly the newspapers) independent and helpful to the cause of civic education, or are they partisan to the point where they gloss over or conceal what the electorate has a right to know? Newspapers can be great constructive forces in any community. In many cities they are. What the average voter knows, or thinks he knows, about the government of his city comes mainly from the newspapers. A fearless newspaper, relentless in its quest for the facts, and thoroughly fair in its presentation of them, is the best friend of good government that a city can have.

24. The organs of public opinion.

25. Finally, are the people of the city manifesting a live interest in civic questions? Does a large proportion of the enrolled vote come out at every election, or do large numbers of voters regularly remain away from the polls? What is the popular attitude between elections? Does the civic conscience stay awake or does it go to sleep? The alertness of the electorate is often looked upon as the least among all the criteria of good government, whereas it is the foremost and the most trustworthy of all. No form of charter, no scheme of departmental organization, and no system of checks and balances can ever secure good government for a city if the people as a whole have not been awakened to the fact that eternal vigilance is the only insurance against the abuse of power. The most serious indictment of the American municipal system is not its complexity, or its toleration of incompetents in public office, but the existence of a widespread civic apathy among the masses of its people.

25. Are the people really interested?

At any rate, here are twenty-five suggested criteria of a good city government. They are not intended to form a complete or definitive list. There are others equally applicable, and equally searching when applied. No two students of municipal government would agree as to what tests are the most vital and the most dependable. The foregoing are merely suggested as yardsticks which may be applied to the outstanding features of city government. They may afford a starting point for someone who can make a better list.

It should be borne in mind, moreover, that no test is automa-

The value of criteria. tically impersonal and that none can be applied with entire impartiality. Somebody has to apply the test, whatever it is, and he will always be influenced to some extent by his own temperamental leanings. It is far easier to ask the question: "Does the city pursue a sound policy in the matter of borrowing?" than to answer it Yes or No. There are all degrees of soundness in this field of municipal policy. No city maintains an absolutely clear record in its borrowings, and indeed a temporary departure from sound principles may sometimes be quite justified. Political and economic theories must reckon with the realities of government and finance. So what we call criteria of good government are little more than guide posts which show the right direction. Their value, if they have any, is in directing the citizen's mind towards the fundamental things when he becomes bewildered by the mass of details and inconsequentials. They help him get back to first principles.

REFERENCES

No one, so far as I am aware, has undertaken to work out a complete and definitive series of criteria covering the whole field of municipal government and administration. Dr. Charles A. Beard, in his *Municipal Government of Tokyo* (New York, 1923), makes some excellent suggestions along this line, but he is dealing with a single city, and one in which conditions are different from those of America. The more recent survey of *The Governments of Cincinnati and Hamilton County* (Cincinnati, 1924), directed by Dr. Lent D. Upson, carries the process a good deal farther. In studying the work of each municipal department, the investigators in this instance set out to "determine the fundamental principles that should govern the conduct of the governmental activity studied, to examine the activity as to conformity with these principles, and to draw such conclusions as mature judgment and experience warranted" (p. 35). This book may be commended, therefore, to the attention of those who desire to follow up an interesting phase of the subject.

CHAPTER XXIV

THE GREATER CITIES

Twelve American cities in 1920 had populations exceeding a half million each.[1] That is more than can be said of any other country in the world. These twelve cities contained somewhat more than sixteen million persons in all, or about fifteen per cent of the entire national population. By sheer force of numbers, by their leadership in business and finance, by the power of their daily press, and by their position as centres of skill and intelligence these great aggregations are exerting, for good or ill, a profound influence upon the national life. Their government is a matter not merely of local but of national concern. *A land of great cities.*

When a city grows to be a place of half a million or more it encounters various problems that do not arise in smaller municipalities. It becomes a planet around which various residential and industrial satellites begin to revolve. Each of these may have its own municipal identity and its own local government. These communities which range around the large municipality impose upon it great burdens of cost which they do not share. They insist upon transit facilities in and out, police protection, parking space in the streets, and places of recreation—all at the expense of the big central municipality. There is a social and economic unity to the whole area, but often without political integration. *Some problems connected with growth.*

The relations of city and county also become more of a problem when the city grows beyond the half million mark. A small city occupies only a portion of the county, but the large municipality may spread over the whole of it, or even over several counties. Then arises the question whether two sets of officials, or even more than two, ought to continue exercising authority within the same area. Such action involves not only a dupli-

[1] They were as follows: New York, 5,612,151; Chicago, 2,701,212; Philadelphia, 1,823,158; Detroit, 993,737; Cleveland, 796,836; St. Louis, 772,897; Boston, 747,923; Baltimore, 733,826; Pittsburgh, 588,193; Los Angeles, 575,410; San Francisco, 508,410; Buffalo, 505,875.

cation of effort and expense but the probability of friction between the county and city authorities. Hence it has been found desirable, and practicable in certain cases, to consolidate the city and county governments. This has been done in Denver, in San Francisco, and to a large extent in Boston.

Finally, when a city becomes sufficiently distended in area and in population there is an inevitable demand for some arrangement which will keep its government from getting too far away from the people of the various neighborhoods. There is a clamor for the revival of ward representation, or for the division of the city into boroughs with a devolution of some municipal functions upon the borough authorities. In other words growth beyond a certain size appears to popularize the federal idea in municipal as in national government, or at least some concessions to the principle of federalism. It seems not improbable that the growth of the greater cities, during the next half century, will be accomplished by devising some method of uniting the surrounding municipalities into a federal system rather than by annexing them outright.

Four great American cities as illustrations. In order to give some idea of the arrangements under which the greater American municipalities of today are governed, four cities have been selected. New York, Chicago, and Philadelphia are taken as the three largest cities in the country. Boston, according to the census returns, is not the fourth largest; but this is because the census figures are based upon population within the municipal boundaries. These, in the case of Boston, have been fixed within such narrow limits that there is a much larger population immediately outside than within. Municipal Boston has a population of only 800,000 or thereabouts, but metropolitan Boston includes about 1,800,000. And it is the metropolitan area that really counts when one is talking about a city as a problem in government, for it is the people who come into the city during the daytime and evening hours that accentuate many phases of the problem. The difficulty of financing and efficiently administering a city government does not depend upon the number of "legal residents" but on the number of people who actually throng its streets and participate in its daily life. In Boston the daytime population exceeds a million by a considerable margin. And in any event, whether it be the fourth largest American city or not, its government embodies certain features

THE GREATER CITIES

(some of them virtually unique) which deserve consideration here.[1]

I. NEW YORK [2]

New York, the metropolis and the commercial gateway of the new world, may still be second to London in population, but it is first in the scope of its municipal operations. It raises more revenue and spends more money, for example, than any other city on earth, more, indeed, than many of the smaller nations. In population and resources it is not merely a city but a commonwealth in itself. Only three states of the Union have populations exceeding that of New York City; in wealth it surpasses all of them except, of course, the State of New York itself. More than half the population of New York State, moreover, is concentrated in New York City. *The American metropolis.*

Founded by the Dutch in the earlier part of the seventeenth century, New York (then New Amsterdam) organized in 1656 its first municipal government, consisting of burgomasters and schepens. The infant community was small in area and small in population, having at this time less than a thousand inhabitants. But even at the outset it was a cosmopolitan place, for there were said to be "men of eighteen different languages" in the town. Then, as ever since, it numbered among its people the fortune-hunters of many nations. *The beginnings of New York.*

In 1664, however, the English captured the place and changed its name from New Amsterdam to New York, and in the following year a proclamation by Governor Nichols changing the municipal organization was issued. This replaced the burgomasters and schepens by a mayor, aldermen and sheriff, but even *Earlier political development.*

---

[1] In 1926 the Massachusetts Legislature discussed a measure providing that for census purposes Boston should be taken to include the entire metropolitan district, approximately as shown on p. 478. It is understood that the United States Bureau of the Census is willing to make the enumeration of 1930 on this basis.

[2] The various histories of New York City are listed in the author's *Bibliography of Municipal Government* (Cambridge, 1915). Mention should also be made of the historical monographs by Edwards and Peterson (see below, p. 450, footnote.) A volume on the *Municipal Government of the City of New York*, by A. G. Baker and A. H. Ware (New York, 1916), is now somewhat out of date but still useful. Another small volume entitled *Our City—New York*, by Frank A. Rexford and others (New York, 1924), is intended as a textbook for high school use. The Brooklyn *Eagle* issues each year a useful *Guide to the Municipal Government of the City of New York*.

450   THE GOVERNMENT OF AMERICAN CITIES

with the new names there was little change in either the spirit or the routine of municipal government. The official records, from 1664 to 1673, were mainly written in Dutch. The mayor and aldermen, who were appointed from year to year by the governor, met once a week to "make such peculiar laws and orders as they Judged Convenient for ye Well Governing ye Inhabitants," as well as for the trial of offenders.[1] They formed a council and a court combined.

The Dongan charter (1686).

But as the community continued to grow, the burghers in 1686 petitioned Governor Dongan for a new charter conferring wider powers and privileges. The result was the granting of a charter which bears the governor's name.[2] In general this charter set up a municipal corporation similar to that which existed in most of the English boroughs in the closing years of the eighteenth century. The mayor continued to be named by the governor, but the aldermen, councilmen (or assistants as they were sometimes called), and constables were henceforth to be elected annually by the "inhabitants of each ward." The city consisted of six wards, each of which chose one alderman and one councilman. Both the aldermen and the councilmen sat with the mayor in the same body, which continued to exercise both administrative and judicial powers.

The Montgomerie charter (1731).

This document continued to be the groundwork of New York's municipal government until 1731, when Governor Montgomerie issued a new charter confirming the old privileges of the corporation and making some important additions. The Montgomerie charter, with changes made by statute from time to time, remained in force for more than a century. The city received various new powers, but the mayor was still to be appointed by the governor. It was not until 1821 that the election of the mayor was given to the council, from whom it passed in 1834 to the people. The council was also, at the latter date, divided into two chambers. The state constitution confirmed the Montgomerie charter in 1777, and it remained in force until 1836.

Charter changes during the nineteenth century.

During the next sixty years many changes were made by the state legislature in the government of the city, most of them due to its steady and rapid growth. By the census of 1800, New

[1] A. E. Peterson and G. W. Edwards, *New York as an Eighteenth Century Municipality* (2 vols., New York, 1917), I, 10.
[2] Although it bears date the 27th of April, 1686, it was virtually in force on December 10, 1683. *Ibid.*, p. 14.

THE GREATER CITIES

York had a population of about 60,000; in 1850 it had passed the half-million mark. Important charter revisions were made in 1849 and in 1857. Finally, in 1873, following the exposure of the Tweed Ring, the city government was considerably altered. The council was once more reduced to a single chamber, to be called the board of aldermen, while a new body, known as the board of estimate and apportionment, was established.

Meanwhile the adjacent areas outside the old city limits became thickly settled and organized their own municipal governments, Brooklyn, for example, and Long Island City. After prolonged negotiations these were incorporated (1897) into the greater City of New York which has henceforth comprised five boroughs, Manhattan, Brooklyn, Queens, Richmond and The Bronx. This consolidation made a new charter necessary and a state commission was appointed to prepare this document. Their draft of a charter, enacted in 1897, was accepted by the legislature, but it was found somewhat defective in operation and had to be revised. The amended charter, which went into effect on January 1, 1901, remains in force at the present day. It is a formidable document, containing nearly 350,000 words, which in printed form make up a volume of over a thousand pages.

The amalgamation of Greater New York.

The charter of 1901.

The home rule amendment which was added to the New York State constitution in 1923, and the home rule law which was passed under its provisions in the following year, constitute an important amendment to the charter of the metropolis.[1] Under this home rule law the Board of Estimate becomes the upper chamber of the municipal legislature,—an interesting reversion to the bicameral system. The two legislative bodies, Board of Estimate and Board of Aldermen, acting concurrently, have power to enact local laws and charter amendments of a routine or minor character, without submitting them to the state legislature or to the people. For important amendments to the charter, or for the adoption of a new charter, a referendum to the people is required.

The home rule law of 1924.

Greater New York is made up of Manhattan Island, which now forms the Borough of Manhattan and the County of New York; the former City of Brooklyn, now the Borough of Brooklyn, which covers all of Kings' County; Staten Island, now the Borough and County of Richmond; part of Long Island, east

Present extent of the greater city.

[1] See *above*, p. 81.

of Brooklyn, now the Borough and County of Queens; and the area above the East and Harlem Rivers on the mainland, now called the Borough and County of the Bronx. The entire area of these five boroughs is about 300 square miles; the population is now (1926) estimated at about six millions. These five boroughs differ widely in population. Manhattan and Brooklyn have each more than two million, while Richmond has less than 150,000.

The Mayor. The mayor of New York is elected by popular vote for a four-year term. He may be removed by the governor on charges after a hearing, and the governor's action is not subject to review. He is the city's chief executive and as such is charged with the general duty of enforcing all laws and ordinances. He is responsible for the entire municipal administration except the department of finance and the departments under the control *His powers.* of the five borough presidents. He appoints all the higher administrative officials (except in these departments), and in most cases may remove them at any time. No confirmation by the board of aldermen or other body is required. Subordinate officials and employees are chosen, for the most part, under civil service rules. He has the right to veto any order or resolution of the board of aldermen but this veto may be overridden by a two-thirds vote. If, however, the vetoed order involves the expenditure or borrowing of money, a three-fourths vote is necessary. The mayor is the presiding officer of the board of estimate and apportionment, having three votes in that body on all questions coming before it. He is ex-officio a member of several other boards and commissions.

The city-departments. The city's administrative work is performed, in the main, by various municipal departments covering the entire city; but to some extent it is delegated to the presidents of the five boroughs. There are twenty-nine administrative departments under the mayor's control. He appoints their heads, whether boards or single commissioners. The most important of these departments are headed by the president of the board of taxes and assessments, the corporation counsel, the board of education, the police commissioner, the fire commissioner, the commissioner of street cleaning, the commissioner of water supply, gas and electricity, the commissioner of parks, the commissioner of plant and structures, the commissioner of docks, the commissioner of health, the

THE GREATER CITIES

tenement house commissioner, the commissioner of public welfare, the commissioner of correction, and the civil service commission. Some of these officials, for example, the members of the board of education, are appointed for a definite term; but most of them hold office during the mayor's pleasure. The heads of two departments, the comptroller and the city clerk, are not under the mayor's control. The former is elected by the people and the latter by the board of aldermen.[1]

Before passing to a consideration of the organization and work of these various departments, something should be said about the board of estimate and apportionment. In its present form the board dates from 1901, although a body with the same name has existed in New York for more than a half century.[2] It now consists of eight members, all *ex-officio,* and elected for four-year terms. The mayor is the chairman and has three votes on all

The Board of Estimate and Apportionment.

Its composition.

[1] CHIEF OFFICERS OF GREATER NEW YORK.

Officers	How chosen	Term of office
Mayor	Elected by people	4 years
Assistant to the mayor	Appointed by mayor	Pleasure of mayor
Comptroller	Elected by people	4 years
Director of the Budget	Appointed by mayor	Pleasure of mayor
Chamberlain	Appointed by mayor	Pleasure of mayor
Corporation counsel	Appointed by mayor	Pleasure of mayor
Police commissioner	Appointed by mayor	5 years
Borough presidents	Elected by people of borough	4 years
Commissioner of water supply, gas and electricity	Appointed by mayor	Pleasure of mayor
Commissioner of street cleaning	Appointed by mayor	Pleasure of mayor
Commissioner of plant and structures	Appointed by mayor	Pleasure of mayor
Commissioner of parks	Appointed by mayor	Pleasure of mayor
Commissioner of public welfare	Appointed by mayor	Pleasure of mayor
Commissioner of correction	Appointed by mayor	Pleasure of mayor
Fire commissioner	Appointed by mayor	Pleasure of mayor
Commissioner of docks	Appointed by mayor	Pleasure of mayor
Civil Service Commission	Appointed by mayor	6 years
President of the board of taxes and assessments	Appointed by mayor	Pleasure of mayor
Members of board of education	Appointed by mayor	7 years
Commissioner of health	Appointed by mayor	Pleasure of mayor
Tenement house commissioner	Appointed by mayor	6 years
Commissioner of licenses	Appointed by mayor	Pleasure of mayor
Aldermen	Elected by people	2 years
City Clerk	Elected by board of aldermen	6 years

[2] It was copied by Boston but speedily abandoned.

questions. The comptroller, the elective head of the department of finance, is a member and also has three votes. The president of the board of aldermen (who is elected by the voters of the whole city, not by the aldermen) is a third member and has three votes. The other five members are the presidents of the various boroughs who are elected by the voters of these boroughs. The Presidents of Manhattan and Brooklyn have two votes each; the presidents of Queens, Richmond, and The Bronx have one vote each. The eight members of the board have, accordingly, sixteen votes in all, and the three members who are elected by the voters of the whole city control a majority of these votes.

Its functions.
The chief functions of the board of estimate and apportionment are as follows: (1) to prepare each year tentative budgets of revenues and expenditures for submission to the board of aldermen; (2) to pass upon all proposals for municipal borrowing; (3) to investigate and authorize all requests from the various departments for the transfer or modification of budget allowances; (4) to determine all grants of franchises; (5) to investigate and act upon all larger questions of public improvements, and all resolutions of local improvement boards relating to assessable local improvements and to see that they conform to good city planning; (6) to determine all matters relating to new positions in the city service; all transfers of employees; the elimination of positions, and changes in the salaries of department employees, (7) to serve, in a way, as the upper chamber of the municipal legislature, while the board of aldermen forms the lower chamber. For the more effective carrying out of those functions the board maintains five bureaus and about a dozen standing committees; its detailed work is carried on by these subordinate bodies but the board itself has final jurisdiction in the matters enumerated.

The city's budget.
By all means the most important among these various functions are the preparation of the tax budget and the granting of franchises. The tax budget is so called because it contains a list of the appropriations which are to be defrayed chiefly from taxes.[1] This budget totals more than $425,000,000 per year. It is compiled, first of all, by the director of the budget, from estimates submitted to the board of estimate and apportionment by the

[1] Appropriations of money obtained by the sale of bonds are considered at various times during the year.

various departments. The procedure, as set forth in the city charter, is quite elaborate and includes the preparation of a tentative budget upon which hearings are held. After these hearings the budget is adopted by the board of estimate and apportionment with such changes as this board may deem advisable. It then goes to the board of aldermen. The latter may eliminate or reduce any item which is not fixed by law, but it cannot insert any new item or increase any appropriation already there. Even when the board votes to eliminate or reduce an appropriation its action is subject to the mayor's veto, and this veto stands unless overridden by a three-fourths vote.

No franchises can be granted in New York City for a longer term than twenty-five years, with a renewal privilege of twenty-five years. An exception is made in the case of subways, where franchises may be for fifty years, with a twenty-five year renewal in addition. Franchises of every kind are now granted exclusively by the board of estimate and apportionment, except that certain franchises for rapid transit lines also require action by the public service commission, which is a state-appointed body. This commission supervises the rates of public utilities with the exception of transportation companies. The latter are supervised by a transit commission. *Franchises.*

Something should be said about the chief administrative departments. The comptroller is the head of the department of finance. He is elected by the voters at the same time as the mayor and for the same term. He is also subject to suspension or removal by the governor on charges after a hearing. As the chief financial officer of the city he has general charge of collecting the municipal revenues, of the audit of accounts, of borrowing and of making payments. His department is divided into various bureaus, and one of them, under the control of the city chamberlain, has the custody of all the city's funds. The chamberlain is, thus, the city treasurer, and although his bureau is within the department of finance, and subject to the supervision of the comptroller, he is appointed by the mayor. The comptroller is a member of the board of estimate and apportionment, and has three votes in that body. Next to the mayor he is the city's most important administrative officer. *The department of finance.*

The department of taxes and assessments is in charge of a board consisting of seven commissioners appointed by the mayor.

456   THE GOVERNMENT OF AMERICAN CITIES

The department of taxes and assessments.

One of the commissioners is designated president of the board. The chief function of this board is to assess all property for purposes of taxation. This property includes real estate (whether owned by individuals or by corporations), franchises, and taxable, tangible personal property (such as merchandise, machinery, bank stock and moneyed capital owned by individuals). Special assessments are levied by a board of three assessors appointed by the mayor.

The police and fire departments.

The police department of New York is under the control of a commissioner appointed by the mayor for a five-year term and removable by either the mayor or the governor. The commissioner has more than thirteen thousand men of all ranks under his command. The fire department, with seven thousand men, is also in charge of a commissioner appointed by the mayor, but his appointment is not for any designated term. Fire prevention as well as fire protection comes within the jurisdiction of this department. The city and district prisons are supervised by a department of corrections.

The department of water, gas and electricity.

The municipal utilities are under the control of a department of water, gas, and electricity. This department has a single commissioner at its head. It has jurisdiction over the sources and distribution of water supply, and the collection of water rates. It provides for the lighting of streets, parks, and public buildings, and has certain control over the transmission of gas and electricity in or under the streets. It has charge of the inspection of electric installations in all buildings.

The board of education.

The board of education, which controls the public schools of the city, consists of seven members appointed by the mayor for a term of seven years. At the expiration of each term appointments are made for seven years.[1] This board, which performs much of its work through committees, determines all matters of general educational policy. The city, however, is divided into forty-eight school districts in each of which there is a local school board made up of five members appointed by the president of the borough in which the district happens to be, together with one member of the board of education and the district superintendent ex officio. These local boards make reports and recommendations twice a year to the board of education. Direct man-

---

[1] Two members are appointed from the borough of Manhattan, two from Brooklyn, and one from each of the other three boroughs.

agement of the schools rests with a board of superintendents, which consists of city superintendent of schools and eight associate superintendents, all of whom are appointed by the board of education.

The foregoing are some of the most important administrative departments, but they form only a small portion of the total list. Health, sanitation, welfare, streets, docks, plant and structures, all suggest other departments which are by no means subordinate in the scope or importance of their functions. Administrative power, all along the line, is finally centred in the mayor so far as all these departments are concerned and the departmental heads are all responsible to him. *Other departments.*

In the matter of subordinate appointments, however, the civil service laws impose a check upon the freedom of both the mayor and the departmental authorities. These rules require appointments to be made from a list submitted by the civil service commission. This commission consists of three members who are appointed by the mayor but are not removable by him without the concurrence of the state civil service authorities. Certain positions are exempt from civil service rules, chiefly those of a policy-determining or confidential nature. Positions of a minor nature are filled by non-competitive tests and all applicants for jobs as city laborers are put on the eligible lists in order of their application as soon as they have passed the physical examination. *Civil service.*

Mention has been made of the fact that some administrative functions are performed by the presidents of the five boroughs. These presidents are elected every four years by the voters of their respective boroughs. In a way they are local mayors, responsible for borough improvements and administration. Each has charge of highway and sewer work, the care of certain public buildings, and the enforcement of building regulations within his borough. The management of this work is performed, for the most part, in each borough by a commissioner of public works whom the president appoints and may remove at pleasure. Each borough is divided into districts with local improvement boards made up of the aldermen from each district. The borough president is *ex officio* a member of each of these local improvement boards. In Queens and Richmond the borough presidents also have charge of street cleaning and waste collection. *The borough presidents.*

Local school boards, as has been said, are appointed by the presidents in all the boroughs.

The five borough presidents likewise, as has been indicated, are members of the board of estimates and apportionment, having in some cases two votes and in others one vote each. Each borough president is also a member of the board of aldermen.

The board of aldermen. The board of aldermen, which is the chief legislative organ of the city, consists of a president elected by the voters of the whole city, sixty-five aldermen elected from aldermanic districts every two years, together with the five borough presidents, making seventy-one members in all. The head of every city department is entitled to a seat, but not to a vote, at meetings of the board and must attend when required.

Its powers. Although some of the board's principal powers have been whittled away by successive charter amendments, its authority is still of considerable importance. It makes, amends and repeals all ordinances and has a general control over water rates, street traffic, building regulations, and market tolls. Without the board's permission no contract exceeding one thousand dollars can be awarded save by open competition. It may reduce or eliminate any items in the budget except those which are specifically exempted from its control, and its assent is necessary for the issuance of certain bonds. The board elects the city clerk and the commissioners of elections, but it no longer has any authority over franchises or licenses, and its action on other matters is subject to veto by the mayor. Today it is only the ghost of a legislative body.

Where the chief power resides. Surveying the government of New York City as a whole it may seem to have needless complexity, being neither a unified nor a federated type of local organization. In so far as powers over the administration are centred at the City Hall (as most of them are) the government is of the unified type; but in so far as they are decentralized among the various boroughs the government of the city has a touch of federalism. The explanation of all this is to be found in the city's history. New York is a federation of cities by origin, but the federal idea is utterly swamped by the centralization which dominates the great city of today. The real pivot of municipal power is the mayor. He, with the board of estimate and apportionment, is the chief factor in the determination of all municipal policy. The borough presidents merely represent concessions, and not very generous ones, to the principle of local representation.

The world has never seen a greater nor a more difficult experiment in democratic local government than that which the history of New York City represents. Two powerful forces lend themselves to factional politics and political demoralization. On the one hand, there is an enormous cosmopolitan population, absorbed in its own affairs, only partially Americanized, and naturally lending itself to political exploitation. On the other, there is the massing of great wealth and boundless ambition, a standing incentive to extravagance, intrigue, and corruption. The cause of honest government is about equally menaced from both sides. Nevertheless the government of New York City has been relatively better, and its administration in general more efficient, than that of the average American city during the last twenty-five years.

Conclusions.

II. CHICAGO [1]

Among the greater cities of the world, Chicago is one of the youngest. The exact date of its first settlement is not known, nor need it concern us. The place had a population of only three hundred and fifty in August, 1833, when application was made for incorporation as a town. A town government, consisting chiefly of an elective town board, was set up and a period of rapid growth at once began. By 1835 the population had risen to 3264, and in 1837 the town applied for a city charter. This was an era of "boom cities"; new settlements all through the Middle West capitalized their future growth, and a whirlwind of speculation in city lots swept over this section of the country.

Early history of Chicago.

By the charter of 1837 the government of the city, which then extended over an area of about ten square miles, was vested in a mayor and ten aldermen, who together constituted the common council. Both the mayor and the aldermen were elected an-

The charter of 1837.

[1] The best source of information on the early development of Chicago's government is S. E. Sparling, *Municipal History and Present Organization of the City of Chicago* (Madison, 1898). In 1906 the League of American Municipalities issued a booklet containing a historical essay on "Chicago, A Review of its Governmental History," by Hugo S. Grosser, City Statistician. The Chicago *City Manual* contains a good deal of information concerning the present organization of city government. The Chicago Bureau of Public Efficiency has issued pamphlets dealing with the unification of local authorities. The *Year Book* issued by the Chicago *Daily News* gives a good account of current municipal affairs.

nually by the voters, but the privilege of voting was restricted to those citizens who paid property taxes of three dollars per year or more. But in 1841 this tax qualification was abolished and manhood suffrage took its place. In the same year the number of aldermen was increased to eighteen and they were henceforth chosen for two years, one half of them retiring annually. The mayor was merely the presiding officer at meetings of the common council, having no independent administrative powers. The council made all the appointments and settled all questions of municipal policy until 1847, when the positions of city attorney, city collector, and city treasurer were made elective.

Meanwhile the city kept growing rapidly. Its population had risen in 1850 to about 30,000 and a revision of the charter seemed desirable in order to provide improved administrative machinery. The charter of 1851 enlarged the power of the mayor. It gave him the right to veto ordinances of the council, subject to the repassing by majority vote. With the concurrence of two-thirds of the council the mayor might now remove certain city officials. But the council still remained the chief organ of government. Much of its work was performed through its own standing committees which the mayor, as presiding officer, now acquired the right to appoint. All the chief administrative officials continued to be elected by popular vote until 1857 when some of them were made appointive, the appointments to be made by the mayor with the approval of the council. This charter marked a swing towards the development of mayoral predominance, although it did not go so far as was the case in some other American cities at the time.

The charter of 1863. The charter of 1857 was soon amended by the legislature of Illinois. Special laws applying to Chicago crowded one another on the statute book year after year. They were so numerous that a consolidation became necessary and revision of the city charter once again became necessary in 1863, when Chicago's population had risen to more than 140,000. The mayor's term was now extended to two years. This charter, frequently amended, served the city until after the great fire of 1871.

The general charter law of 1872. In 1870 the state of Illinois adopted a new constitution in which there was a provision forbidding all special legislation for cities. This made necessary the framing of a general municipal charter which the legislature enacted in 1872. This charter was

THE GREATER CITIES

to apply to all cities incorporated after 1872 and to any already incorporated city that might decide to adopt it. Three years later, in 1875, the citizens of Chicago by a small majority voted to reincorporate under this general charter law. This law restored to the city council some of the powers that it had lost, and made the mayor its agent in the carrying out of municipal policy. Its adoption, moreover, put an end for nearly thirty years to the old form of legislative interference in Chicago's affairs, although the legislature sometimes achieved the same end by enacting optional acts or by passing amendments to the general law in such a way that these amendments would apply only to cities of over 100,000 population, that is, to Chicago alone. On the whole, however, Chicago suffered less from legislative interference during the years 1875 to 1904 than most other large cities of the country.

In this latter year (1904) a change in the situation was made. Chicago now so far overtopped the other cities of Illinois that its government could properly be regarded as a separate problem. Accordingly the state constitution was amended so as once more to permit special legislation for Chicago, but only with the proviso that no such special legislation takes effect until after it has been accepted by the voters of the city at a referendum. Chicago does not have municipal home rule in the usual sense, but its citizens have some protection in this way against hostile legislation. *The constitutional amendment of 1904.*

Since 1904 Chicago has continued under the operations of the Illinois general charter law, but various changes have been made by the legislature and accepted by the voters. A new charter was submitted to the people but rejected by them in 1907. A certain amount of flexibility exists in that the Municipal Act of 1872 grants to the city councils of all Illinois cities a large amount of authority to create, alter, and abolish municipal departments as well as to define the duties and fix the salaries of municipal officers. The chief difficulty at the present time, from an organic standpoint, is the large number of relatively independent local authorities who now operate within the city limits but are not a part of the regular city government. There are numerous boards of this sort (trustees of the sanitary district, board of education, library board, various boards of park commissioners, and so forth). A complete unification of these local authorities would *Present charter situation in Chicago.*

462 THE GOVERNMENT OF AMERICAN CITIES

be highly desirable, but this cannot be had without extensive changes in the state constitution and the adoption of a new city charter.[1]

The mayor. The mayor of Chicago is elected for a four-year term and is re-eligible.[2] Nominations are made at a primary election and party designations are used on the ballots. Owing to the fact that the city has no consolidated charter, the functions of the mayor are difficult to enumerate, but his powers are smaller than those of the chief executive in New York, Philadelphia, or Boston. He appoints all the chief administrative officers of the city except the city clerk and the city treasurer, but such appointments require confirmation by the city council (aldermen). He may also remove any official whom he appoints, but must report to the council in ten days his reasons for the removal. If the mayor's action is disapproved by a two-thirds majority of the council the dismissed officer is reinstated. The mayor also possesses the right to veto any ordinance or resolution of the council, subject to a reversal of his action by a two-thirds vote. He may veto, in this way, any item in the list of city appropriations. By the general municipal law of Illinois the mayor is entitled to preside at all meetings of the city council and is also authorized to make recommendations to the council at any time. When presiding at council meetings, he has no vote except in case of a tie. The mayor also has power to examine or inspect the books, records, or papers of any municipal department.

The city departments. The chief administrative departments in Chicago are: finance, public works, police, fire, health, law, buildings, electricity, public service, and supplies. Each of these departments is in charge of a commissioner or other single head appointed by the mayor.[3] There are about twenty departments of less importance. In addition there is a "board of local improvements," made up of five members appointed by the mayor, whose duty it is to pass upon all proposed street improvements before the plans are laid before the city council for its approval. This board also determines what special assessments shall be levied in payment for such

---

[1] See *Bulletin No. 11* of the Illinois Constitutional Convention, entitled "Local Government in Chicago and Cook County" (Springfield, 1920).

[2] A concise outline of Chicago's Municipal Organization, by Dr. F. D. Bramhall, may be found in the *Cyclopedia of American Government*, vol. 1.

[3] They do not all, however, bear the title "Commissioner." The head of the police department is called the "General Superintendent of Police," and the head of the law department is the "Corporation Counsel."

street improvements. The mayor also appoints the board of education (eleven members), the nine trustees of the public library, the civil service commission of three members, and various other heads of departments.

The department of finance includes three principal officers, the city comptroller, city treasurer, and city collector. The comptroller is the head of this department, which has the general custody of all city revenues [1] (but not the assessment or collection of taxes) and the disbursing of all expenditures. The comptroller is the fiscal agent of the city, and as such has charge of all deeds, leases, and other papers relating to municipal property. He also has charge of bond issues and the payment of interest upon the city debt.

Department of finance.

The department of public works includes jurisdiction over streets, water supply, sewerage, and maps. The department has charge of the construction and maintenance of all public improvements, such as streets and alleys, bridges, viaducts and docks, markets and public buildings. It has charge of the harbor, the sewers and sewage works, the maintenance of water supply and the collection of water rates. These functions are performed through several different bureaus, of which the most important are the bureaus of engineering, streets, water, sewers, and maps. But all local improvements which are paid for in whole or in part by the levy of special assessments do not come within the jurisdiction of the public works department until they have been completed and accepted by the city. Parks are not within its control except small parks and playgrounds. They are managed by several independent boards.

The department of public works.

One of the striking features of Chicago government, in fact, is this multiplicity of local authorities not directly embodied in the regular frame of municipal administration. Cook County, although more than ninety per cent of its population is contributed by the city of Chicago, has its own independent government. Taxes for city purposes are assessed and collected by the county authorities, who also have charge of poor relief and elections. The Chicago Sanitary District, which includes the entire city and a fringe of territory outside, is a separate municipal unit, with its own borrowing powers. The nine trustees of this Sanitary District, elected by popular vote, have charge of the

The multiplicity of local authorities.

[1] The city treasurer, however, is the immediate custodian of public funds.

great drainage canal which carries off the city's sewage. There are also three great park districts, two of them in charge of boards appointed by the governor of Illinois, the third under the supervision of a board appointed by the circuit judges of Cook County. Each of these boards has entire control of the planning and maintenance of all parks in its district. Apart from the city council and the board of education there are twenty different boards and commissions, each vested with authority to spend money. The result is an increase of overhead costs, and a lack of close coöperation in the conduct of public business. The number of elective officials is also excessively large; at some general elections the voters are called upon to choose more than fifty persons, including national, state, county, and city officials, judges, and trustees of various sorts. The result is a ballot of confusing dimensions. Each local authority, moreover, is assigned a separate tax rate by state law with no provisions for central control. The various rates are added together and the whole levy is then assessed and collected by the county authorities, who, in turn, distribute the proceeds to the various governmental units. No common budget is, therefore, possible. Efforts have been made in recent years to improve this condition of affairs by the consolidation of all the various administrative authorities operating within the city, but these efforts have not yet been successful.[1]

The school department. The board of education constitutes a municipal corporation and is in most respects independent of the city council, although its eleven members are appointed by the mayor. It purchases the land for school buildings, erects schools, equips them, appoints the teachers, fixes their salaries, and prescribes the curriculum. The maximum tax rate which it may ask the county to impose for school purposes is fixed by state law.

The city council. The Chicago city council, the members of which are called aldermen, is made up of fifty members, one from each of the wards for a two-year term. All are elected and retire together. Until 1919 nominations were made by means of party primaries, but at the November election of that year the voters accepted an act providing for non-partisan elections. The new system involves a preliminary election for which candidates are

---

[1] See the pamphlet entitled *Unification of Local Governments in Chicago*, prepared by the Chicago Bureau of Public Efficiency, January, 1917.

THE GREATER CITIES

nominated by petitions, signed by not less than two per cent of the number of votes cast for aldermen in the ward at the last aldermanic election. If no candidate receives a clear majority at this preliminary election, a supplementary election is held at which the two highest candidates are voted upon. The preliminary election takes place at the end of February; the final election (when necessary) at the beginning of April. Provision is made that the names of candidates shall rotate on the ballot, so that each name shall appear at the head of an equal number of ballots, thus giving no one an advantage over the others. The Chicago city council has wider powers than the legislative branch of the government in any other large American city. Included are nearly one hundred different items of authority, as listed in the Illinois municipal code and its amendments, but the entire category of powers may be concisely summarized under the following heads: *Its composition.*

Its powers.

(a) *Financial.* As there is nothing in Chicago which corresponds to New York's board of estimate and apportionment, the city council has complete control of the city budget.[1] Each year the estimates are sent by the various heads of the city departments directly to the comptroller, who, in turn, submits them in unified form to the council. Here they are referred to the council's finance committee, which, after due revision of the items, lays before the council an appropriation bill. The council may then increase or reduce any item or insert any new appropriation, subject to the mayor's veto.

(b) *Franchises and Public Utilities.* The power to grant franchises for all locations in the city streets resides in the council. Important franchises are, as a matter of recent custom, however, referred to the voters for their approval.[2] Since 1913 the council has had very little to do with the regulation of public utilities. The Public Utilities Commission, a state body, now possesses this field of jurisdiction, regulating the rates charged for gas, electricity, and telephone service.

---

[1] As already pointed out, however, this budget does not include expenditures for the local administration of justice, for poor relief, for parks, or for the sanitary district. The school and library budgets are included but are never changed from the original requests as made by the respective boards.

[2] For example, the proposed traction franchise of 1925 which the voters rejected by a large majority.

(c) *Control of Departmental Organization.* In most of the larger American cities the administrative organization is prescribed in the charter or by law; in Chicago the city council is empowered, through its own ordinances, to remodel the municipal departments as it may see fit. With a few statutory exceptions it may abolish departments altogether, or consolidate them, or establish new administrative positions. It fixes practically all municipal salaries, including those of the mayor and aldermen. In this respect Chicago is conspicuously a "home rule" city. Its administrative framework has a potential flexibility which is rare on this side of the Atlantic.

(d) *Miscellaneous.* In addition, the Chicago city council possesses most of the routine functions which are vested in municipal legislative bodies. It enacts ordinances for the regulation of building construction, the protection of the public health, the speed of vehicles and the use of the streets, the sale of food, the licensing of various trades, and so forth. It exercises, in a word, the "police power" of the city.

Its procedure. The council meets weekly, except in the summer months, and the mayor has the right to preside at all meetings, but has no vote except in case of a tie. He has, however, what is much more effective than a vote, namely, the right to veto the council's acts. The detailed work of the Chicago city council is performed by standing committees, of which it has about twenty. These committees are not appointed by the mayor as presiding officer, but by a steering committee which the council itself selects, and which under the new non-partisan organization of the council is made up of five members. The first ten wards choose one member of the steering committee, the second ten wards another, and so on.

In the cosmopolitan character of its population, Chicago is a world city; but in every other respect it is about the most thoroughly American city we have. Although a congeries of municipal areas (school districts, park districts, sanitary districts, etc.) it is a single economic unit—served for the most part by one giant water plant, one gas company, one electric lighting company and one street railway system. Although in every sense a metropolis, the metropolis of the American West, a centre of wealth and culture, with a highly advanced civilization, it is nevertheless in many respects a frontier city still. Its people are as militant in politics as in industry or commerce. No city of the New World is more energetically alive.

III. PHILADELPHIA [1]

Although Philadelphia was founded in 1681 and laid out in 1683 it did not become a chartered borough until ten years later. This charter of 1691 left the legal status of the community somewhat indefinite. No record of government under this charter has been preserved, but in 1701 William Penn issued a new document which was a substantial confirmation of powers bestowed ten years before, and placed the corporate rights of the "city" beyond the range of controversy. This charter established a municipal corporation under the name of "The Mayor and Commonalty of Philadelphia," consisting of a mayor, a recorder, eight aldermen and twelve common councillors. The mayor was chosen annually from among the aldermen by joint vote of the aldermen and councilmen. The latter were chosen for life, and when a vacancy occurred it was filled by the remaining aldermen and councilmen. In other words, the method of choosing officials was by co-optation, not by popular election. The charter of 1701 remained in operation until 1776, when the city was occupied by British troops and the old form of municipal government suspended. It remained suspended until 1789, when a new charter was granted by the Pennsylvania legislature.

Early history.

The charter of 1701.

The charter of 1789 abandoned the "close corporation" type of government and created a modern municipality. The mayor, aldermen, and councilmen were retained, but each of the latter were increased in number. Fifteen aldermen were to be chosen for seven-year terms by the *freeholders* or property-owners of the city, while thirty common councilmen were to be for three-year terms chosen by the *freemen*. The latter category included not only property-owners but those householders who had personal property worth fifty pounds. The mayor was chosen annually by the aldermen from among their own number and was the presiding officer of the council in which both aldermen and councilmen met together.

The charter of 1789.

The charter of 1789 established a representative form of

[1] On the history of Philadelphia the reader may be referred to E. P. Allison and Boies Penrose, *Philadelphia*, 1681-1887 (Baltimore, 1887), and J. R. Young (editor), *Memorial History of Philadelphia* (2 vols., New York, 1895-1898).

468   THE GOVERNMENT OF AMERICAN CITIES

Philadelphia's government during the nineteenth century.

municipal government, although the suffrage was still closely restricted. Amendments were soon forthcoming. In 1796 the aldermen were reduced to twelve and the councilmen to twenty. Provision was made that all should be elected by the freemen. Heretofore the aldermen and councilmen sat together; after 1796 they met separately, the aldermen forming the Select Council and the councilmen the Common Council. As time went on, moreover, these two councils assumed many executive functions and virtually controlled the administrative affairs of the city through their own committees. The scheme of administration became cumbrous and complicated. Nor was any simplification made in 1854, when the boundaries of the city were widened. Philadelphia from 1789 to 1887, despite many changes in charter details, remained under what was substantially a council type of government.

The Bullitt Act of 1887.

In this latter year (1887) a new charter, commonly known as the Bullitt Act, went into effect. This charter transferred executive powers to the mayor, made him the chief administrative official of the city, and forced a complete readjustment in the city government. The two councils were retained as the legislative organ of the municipality and were enlarged, the select council to forty-seven and the common council to about double that number.[1] The mayor was given large powers of appointment, but in most cases subject to confirmation by the select council. His veto could be overridden by a three-fifths vote in both chambers; in a few specified cases a two-thirds vote was required.

The new charter.

This scheme of government, despite its growing unwieldliness, remained in operation, with various minor changes, until 1919, when the Pennsylvania legislature enacted a revised municipal charter for Philadelphia and also a series of laws regulating elections in such way as to make the will of the people more direct and effective at the polls. These measures were passed after a severe struggle waged by the Citizens' Charter Committee of Philadelphia. In general their result has been the simplification of the city's government, the strengthening of the civil service system, and the ousting of the municipal contractor from his time-honored hold upon the community.[2]

---
[1] In 1918 the numbers had become 48 and 97 respectively.
[2] Data concerning the present municipal organization of Philadelphia

THE GREATER CITIES

According to the charter of 1919 the mayor is designated as the chief executive of the city. He is elected by popular vote for a four-year term and is not eligible for immediate reëlection. His salary is left to be fixed by ordinance, with the provision that it shall not be increased or diminished during his term of office.

Its provisions:
The mayor

The powers of the mayor are extensive. He is charged with the enforcement of the city ordinances. He appoints the heads of all important municipal departments subject to confirmation by the city council. He may make recommendations to the city council on any subject and has the right to veto any ordinance or resolution passed by the council, subject to repassage by a three-fifths vote. The mayor prepares the annual budget for submission to the city council, but the council may increase or reduce any item in this list of appropriations, or may insert new items. The mayor's power of veto extends, however, not only to the budget as a whole but to individual items in it. He may order the accounts of any department to be audited at any time. The mayor has the powers of a magistrate, may issue warrants, cause arrests to be made, and in time of emergency may take immediate command of the city's police department. It is further stipulated that the city council shall not pass any ordinances directing or interfering with the exercise of the mayor's executive functions.

His powers.

The charter established eleven regular municipal departments as follows: public safety, public works, public health, public welfare, wharves, docks and ferries, city transit, city treasurer, city controller, law, civil service, and receiver of taxes. It provides that no department shall be created other than those named, but the city council is given power to reorganize, from time to time, any of these eleven departments. The council may not, however, direct or interfere with the departments in the discharge of their routine functions. Each department is in charge of a director appointed by the mayor, usually for a four-year term, but subject to confirmation by the city council. Exceptions are made in the case of the city treasurer, the city controller, and the receiver of taxes, each of whom is selected by

The city departments.

may conveniently be found in the *Year Book and Citizens' Manual of Philadelphia*, published annually by the *Evening Bulletin*. Mention should also be made of the booklet subtitled *Philadelphia's Government*, published by the Philadelphia Bureau of Municipal Research in 1924.

the people, and also in the case of the civil service commission, which consists of three members elected by the city council.

The city council. The charter of 1919 abolished the old two-chambered municipal legislature of one hundred and forty-five members, replacing it by a single council made up by the election of one or more councilmen from each of the various state senatorial districts. Each such district has the right to elect one councilman for every 40,000 assessed voters and an additional councilman for each additional 40,000 voters of major fraction thereof. The present council (1921) consists of twenty members. Councilmen are prohibited from holding any other office under the city, county, state, or federal governments. This has put an end to the old practice of dual officeholding.

Its authority. The council has the usual powers of a municipal legislature. It enacts the ordinances and by its control of the appropriations determines the tax rate. This tax rate must be so fixed, however, that it will produce sufficient funds to cover the year's financial programme. The council also authorizes all borrowing, but no money may be borrowed on long-term bonds unless certified as for a capital outlay.

The civil service system. The classified civil service is stated by the charter to include all officials except those elected by the people, directors of departments and assistant directors, a few other important officials, and those persons who hold emergency or temporary appointments. All positions except those above excepted are filled from lists prepared by the civil service commission. This commission segregates all the positions in the classified service into three groups known as the competitive class, the exempt class, and the labor class. The first includes all positions above that of unskilled labor for which competitive tests are practicable. The second category includes those posts to which appointments may be made without examination because competition has been found impracticable, but the commission in all such cases must first by a public hearing determine that persons possessing the usual and requisite qualifications cannot be had by open competition. The exempt class also includes the chief assistant to the head of each department, one secretary or clerk appointed by the mayor, and one secretary or clerk appointed by the head of each department. The labor class includes ordinary unskilled laborers who are listed in the order of their application and given preference according to such rules as may be made and promulgated by the civil service commission.

Removals from all city positions are forbidden except after a written statement of the reasons has been furnished to the person removed and an opportunity for a written answer given. The statement and answer to it are to be incorporated in the records of the civil service commission. Dismissal of police officers or firemen may take place only after the dismissed official is given a public hearing before the civil service commission or before a person or board appointed by it.

Removals from office.

A strenuous endeavor has been made to divorce municipal business from partisan politics, both by the foregoing civil service arrangements and by charter provisions which prohibit any city officer or employee from taking an active part in any political convention or serving as a member of any party committee or actively participating in any election campaign by soliciting campaign contributions or otherwise. Any taxpayer may bring proceedings to enforce these prohibitions. Much of the public work (such as the collection and disposal of ashes and garbage) which prior to 1919 was performed by contractors is required by the charter to be hereafter undertaken by the city's own employees, unless a majority of the council, with the approval of the mayor, shall affirmatively decide to continue the old system.

An attempt to secure non-partisan administration.

Contemporaneously with the Philadelphia charter of 1919 the Pennsylvania legislature amended and greatly improved the existing laws relating to the registration of voters and the machinery of elections. The registration of voters was simplified. The work is in charge of a state board appointed by the governor, thus taking the whole system from the control of the local politicians. Improvements in the methods of conducting the primary elections were also made, and provisions adopted to secure for the voters a free opportunity to express their will at the polls. It may be regarded in some parts of the country as a matter for surprise that any such legislation should be needed at this late day; but those who are familiar with the political machinations of the contractors' ring in Philadelphia during the three decades preceding 1919 are aware that these men through their control of the registration, primary, and election machinery were able on many occasions to defy and thwart the will of the electorate. That condition of affairs has now passed away.

Electoral reforms of 1919.

472 THE GOVERNMENT OF AMERICAN CITIES

Conclusion. Surveying these changes as a whole, it is apparent that Philadelphia has made a notable advance in its scheme of city government. The charter of 1919 was an epoch-marking piece of legislation. Containing less than 25,000 words it is one of the most concise documents of its kind possessed by any American city. It may be true that "Philadelphia has the reputation of being more inseparably welded to the idols of corruption than any other great American city,"[1] but in recent years it has been making efforts to live that reputation down. Its people were for a long time patient and forbearing. Lincoln Steffens once referred to them as "corrupt and contented." They paid good money for sham mahogany in city buildings and vile service in public places. Spasms of reform during four decades accomplished very little in the way of permanent improvement. But the spark of ambition would not be quenched, and today Philadelphia is far from being the worst-governed large city in the country.

IV. BOSTON [2]

The town of Boston. The history of Boston goes back to about 1630, when settlers under the auspices of the Company of Massachusetts Bay established themselves on the stern and rockbound Atlantic coast. Presently a town government was organized, with a town meeting serving as the sole governing organ at the outset. Then, as the town developed, selectmen and other officers were chosen. A movement for a borough charter began as early as 1650, but nothing came of it, and Boston remained a town throughout the colonial era.

Boston's first city charter. After the Revolution the system of government by town meeting became increasingly cumbrous, but although several attempts were made to abandon it, the old plan of government remained in existence until 1822 when the increase of population, which had now risen above 40,000, rendered its further continuance impracticable. A city charter was accordingly obtained from the legislature in that year.

---

[1] D. F. Wilcox, *The Government of Great American Cities* (New York, 1910), p. 244.

[2] On the municipal history and government of Boston the following references will be found useful: Josiah Quincy, *Memorial History of the Town and City of Boston* (Boston, 1852); Nathan Matthews, *City Government of Boston* (Boston, 1895); *Boston, 1822-1922*, a centennial volume issued by the city in 1923; C. P. Huse, *Financial History of Boston* (Cambridge, 1916); and the *Boston Year Book* (Boston, 1924).

THE GREATER CITIES

The charter of 1822 established a municipal government consisting of a mayor, eight aldermen elected at large, and a common council of forty-eight members—four from each of the city's twelve wards. The mayor, elected by the people, was given powers of small importance. Although enjoined by the charter to "be vigilant and active at all times in causing the laws for the government of the said city to be duly executed and put in force," he was clothed with none of the powers necessary for the performance of these duties. In other words, the charter of 1822 gave Boston a frame of government substantially like that which had existed for many generations in the commercial boroughs of England. The governing power lay with the board of aldermen and the common council. The mayor had no veto over their acts, made no appointments, and had no control over the city administration except such as was derived from his vote in the board of aldermen, where he was the presiding officer.

From 1822 to 1854 the executive business was in the hands of council committees, a plan which became more and more unsatisfactory as the city grew larger. The inadequacy of the old charter in this and other respects became a matter of common admission, and in 1854 a revision was obtained.[1] This revision did not, however, transfer the predominance of administrative power to the mayor, although it gave him a qualified veto over all actions of the aldermen and councilmen. It also permitted him to remove appointive officers, but the power of appointment remained with the council.

The charter revision of 1854.

As the city continued to grow, during the next thirty years, the difficulty of conducting its various branches of administration by means of council committees became annually more apparent. Various commissions considered the matter of a new charter and the subject was frequently discussed in the Massachusetts legislature, but it was not until 1885 that any definite action was taken. In that year several drastic amendments were made, chiefly in the way of increasing the mayor's powers.

The charter amendments of 1885 transferred all the executive powers of the city to the mayor, to be exercised by him through various officers and boards under his supervision and control. It gave the mayor the power to appoint practically all important officials of city administration and gave him authority to re-

Increase of executive powers in 1885.

[1] Nathan Matthews, *City Government of Boston* (Boston, 1895), p. 167.

move such officials for cause. It prohibited the aldermen and councilmen from interfering in any manner in the employment of labor, the making of contracts, the purchase of material, or the handling of administrative business in general. The veto power of the mayor was somewhat extended and henceforth included the right to disapprove separate items in appropriation measures. Hitherto the mayor had been a member of the board of aldermen and had presided at its meetings. By the amendments of 1885 these rights were withdrawn and the divorce between the executive and legislative branches of the city government was made practically complete.

<small>Other changes.</small>
The amendments of 1885 were followed by various other enactments during the next half-dozen years, and these various measures, taken together with the legislation of 1885, practically amounted to a new charter for Boston. The mayor, who was still elected for a one-year term, controlled the administrative affairs of the city. The board of aldermen and common council retained their full legislative functions, but subject to the mayor's veto and also to the general laws which circumscribed with increased strictness the financial discretion of the city council. The board of aldermen now consisted of thirteen members elected annually at large, while the membership of the common council, which had been fixed at forty-eight by the charter of 1822, was now raised to seventy-two members and ultimately increased to seventy-five members, or three from each of the twenty-five municipal wards.

<small>The so-termed "new charter" of 1909.</small>
Under the foregoing charter provisions the affairs of the city were conducted until 1909, when another series of amendments were put into effect. This change came as a result of a thorough investigation which was made during the years 1907-1909 by a body known as the Boston finance commission. This commission was nominally appointed by the mayor but in reality consisted of one member representing each of the important civic organizations of Boston, such as the chamber of commerce, the real estate exchange, the central labor union, etc. In the course of its investigation many instances of extravagance, waste, and inefficiency were brought to light. The commission recommended that the whole frame of city government should be simplified and that the principle embodied in the charter amendments of 1885 should be carried to its logical conclusion. The Massachusetts

legislature in 1909 adopted this recommendation and made several important alterations in the city charter, some of which were put into effect at once and others referred to the voters of Boston for their decision. These alterations were so sweeping as to actually constitute a new charter.

Since 1909 the term of the mayor has been four years. Nominations are made by petitions which must bear the names of 3000 qualified voters. The mayor is not eligible for reëlection at the close of his term. Provision was made in the charter amendments of 1909 for the recall of the mayor by majority of the registered voters, but this provision was found to be unworkable and it was subsequently repealed. The system of nomination by filing 3000 signatures has tended to multiply candidates. At the election of 1925 there were no fewer than ten candidates who qualified for places on the ballot—but two of them did not manage to get 3000 votes at the polls.

<small>Present government of Boston: 1. The mayor.</small>

The powers of the mayor under the present Boston charter may be briefly summarized as follows:

<small>His powers.</small>

1. *Appointing power.* Nearly all the heads of departments and members of boards are appointed by the mayor and removable by him. The principal exceptions are the police commissioner, who is appointed by the governor of Massachusetts; the members of the licensing board; and the members of the finance commission, all of whom are similarly appointed. When the mayor nominates a head of a department or a member of a board he must transmit such nomination to the state department of civil service with a certificate stating that the appointee is "qualified by education, training, or experience" for the position to which he is nominated. If within thirty days the state department of civil service finds the mayor's appointee to be qualified, it so certifies and the appointment becomes at once effective. No confirmation of the mayor's appointments by the city council is necessary.

2. *Veto power.* Any act, resolution, or order of the city council is subject to the mayor's veto and this veto may not be overridden by two-thirds vote or otherwise. It is decisive and final.

3. *Financial powers.* No proposal to spend money (except from the proceeds of loans) may be originated except by the mayor, and no expenditure proposed by the mayor may be increased by the city council. Each year a list of appropriations is prepared under the supervision of the mayor and transmitted to the city

council, where any item may be reduced, subject to the mayor's veto. The council may not, however, increase any item or insert any new item. On the other hand, the council may originate loan orders but most proposals to borrow money, as a matter of practice, originate with the mayor. His control of expenditures is, therefore, of an almost complete character.

4. *Miscellaneous.* The mayor has various powers of a miscellaneous sort, particularly in relation to the awarding of contracts. Members of the city council are prohibited under stringent penalties from interfering with the mayor in the conduct of his executive functions or with the management of the various administrative duties. But this prohibition is very frequently and flagrantly honored in the breach.

2. The municipal departments.

There are about thirty municipal departments in Boston, a larger number than is to be found in other American cities. This is in part due to the fact that, many years ago, heads of departments were exempt from civil service regulations. When, therefore, it was desired to give some influential politician a secure position without putting him to the strain of a civil service competition, a new department was usually created for this purpose. Since the charter amendments of 1909 there has been no further multiplication of departments and, indeed, there has been some reduction. At the present time the chief departments are as follows: law, public works, police, fire, parks, city treasurer, city clerk, city auditor, building, assessing, collecting, health, hospitals, schoolhouse, infirmary, penal institutions, library, elections, printing, and supply. With the exception of the city clerk, who is elected by the council, and the police commissioner, who is named by the governor, the heads of all these departments are appointed by the mayor and removed by him.

3. The city council.

The city council of Boston has consisted since 1925 of twenty-two members elected for a two-year-term, one councilman from each of twenty-two districts. Nominations are made by petitions bearing the signatures of at least 300 qualified voters. The ballots at Boston municipal elections bear no party designations. The order in which the names of candidates appear on the ballot is determined by lot.

Its powers.

Since 1909 the powers of the Boston city council have been relatively unimportant. Its functions are confined to legislative matters only, and even in this field its jurisdiction has been greatly circumscribed by the activity of the state legislature, which has assumed the function of legislating for Boston in nearly all important matters. The city council still passes ordinances relating to such matters as the inspection of buildings, housing, etc.; it makes all the appropriations for city expenditures on the recommendation of the mayor, but may not make any changes in these estimates by way of increase; its consent is necessary for all municipal borrowing and for the purchase of land by the city; and certain important long-term contracts require its approval. On the other hand, all resolutions and orders of the council are subject to absolute veto by the mayor.

An interesting feature of Boston government is the presence of certain state officials exercising what would ordinarily be called strictly municipal functions. One of these is the police commissioner, who is named by the governor of Massachusetts for a five-year term and who has full charge of the appointment, removal, and discipline of the police force. Whatever appropriations are requested by the commissioner must be granted by the mayor and city council. It is provided, however, that all increases in the number of the force or in the rates of remuneration must be concurred in by the mayor before becoming effective. The licensing board of three members is also appointed by the governor and is not subject in any way to the control of the municipal authorities. Originally this board was vested with power to grant or withhold licenses for the sale of intoxicating liquors, and its establishment as a state commission was intended to take this question out of city politics. At present its jurisdiction is confined to the licensing of common victuallers, billiard rooms, bowling alleys, and so forth. *[State control: 1. Police. 2. Licenses.]*

Another state board which operates within the city is the Boston finance commission. It consists of a chairman and four members, all of whom are appointed by the governor, one each year for a five-year term. The chairman receives a salary, but the other members are unpaid. It is the duty of this commission to investigate and report upon any question of municipal efficiency or economy which may seem to require investigation and to report its findings to the mayor, city council, or the state legislature. It has power to summon witnesses and to require the production of documents but has no authority to put its find- *[3. The finance commission.]*

ings or recommendations into effect. Its functions are those of inquiry only. On the whole, the finance commission has proved a vigilant guardian of the taxpayers' interests.

The school system. The school system of Boston is under the supervision of a school committee consisting of five members elected at large. Nominations are made by petition and no party designations appear on the ballot. The term of each committeeman is four

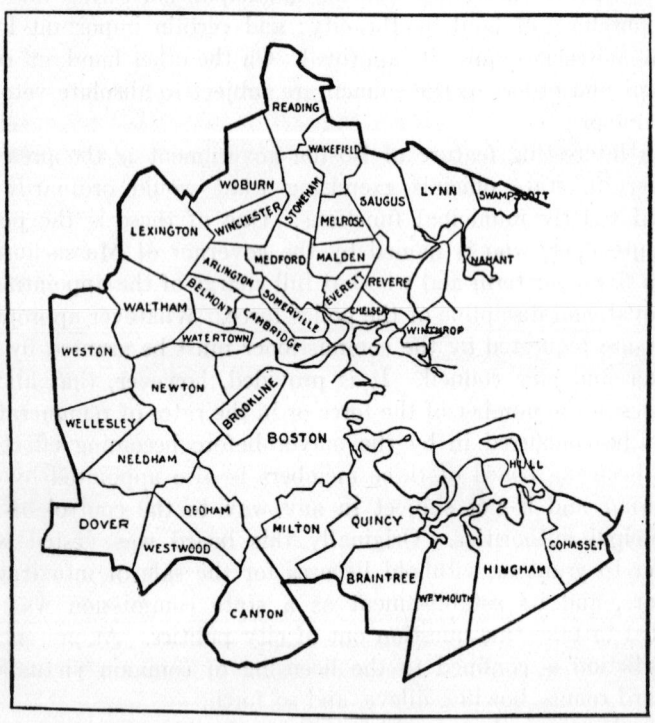

years. This committee has the appointment of teachers and other school officials; it has full charge of the general programme of elementary and secondary education; and its minimum appropriations are fixed by state law. The buying of land for school buildings and the erection of schoolhouses are matters which are not intrusted, however, to the school committee. They are in charge of one of the regular municipal departments known as the schoolhouse department, which is under the jurisdiction of the mayor.

THE GREATER CITIES

In one respect Boston is unique among the large cities of the country. It is a classic example of what the sociologists call a "conurbation"; in other words, a large number of urban aggregates, all situated in territory that is physically contiguous and all of it virtually forming a single economic unit as shown by the map on the preceding page. *The special problems of Boston.*

Boston, in this larger sense, is a metropolitan community formed by the simultaneous expansion of many neighboring cities and towns. These have grown out towards each other until they have reached a social and economic (but not a governmental) coalescence in one continuous urban area. How to reconcile political disintegration with this coalescence is Boston's most difficult problem. Within a dozen miles of Boston there are no fewer than thirty cities and towns, each with its own independent municipal administration. Under such circumstances a considerable degree of state intervention is inevitable because many questions (such as fire prevention, public health, rapid transit, etc.) must be handled with a view to the common interest of all these communities, and not with special reference to the needs of Boston alone. As there is no metropolitan authority with general jurisdiction over all these various communities, the state legislature naturally assumed this function. For many years a movement has been on foot to create a Greater Boston which would include all these surrounding municipalities and have a population of something more than a million and a half. The conflict of local interests, however, has thus far proved to be a barrier to any such achievement.

In the whole world, at the present day, there are about thirty-five "greater cities," each with a population exceeding one million. The United States has eight of them—or nearly one-fourth of the total. We have in this country only one-twentieth of the world's population; but a far larger proportion of the world's great cities. This gives Americans an especial interest in the problem of metropolitan government.

INDEX

Abbott, Edith, *Immigration: Select Documents and Case Records*, 51.
Abbott, H. S., *Treatise on the Law of Municipal Corporations*, 132.
Absent voting, 199. See also Elections.
Adams, H. C., *Public Debts*, 150.
Administrative control, of cities, in America, 88-90; in Europe, 98.
Age, distribution of city populations according to, 47-49.
Agriculture, relation of, to city growth, 6-7.
Akron, Ohio, importance of the rubber industry in, 7.
Aldrich v. City of Youngstown, 127.
Alien immigration, effect on cities of, 49-52.
American City, The, 423.
Allegheny v. Campbell, 124.
Allison, E. P., and Penrose, Boies, *History of Philadelphia*, 25, 44, 467.
Allport, Floyd, N., *Social Psychology*, 237.
American Academy. See Annals of the American Academy.
American Civic Association, its work as a reform organization, 423.
American Federation of Labor, affiliation of municipal employees with, 380.
American Judicature Society, model plan of municipal court organization prepared by, 392-393.
American Political Science Review, 401.
Ames, Adelbert D. ("Doc"), mayor and boss of Minneapolis, 284.
Anderson, William, *American City Government*, 20, 45, 91, 111, 179, 254, 266, 288, 301, 319, 342, 348, 361, 384, 400, 419; "The Constitutionality of Proportional Representation" 197.
Andreas, A. T., *History of Chicago*, 44.
Annals of the American Academy of Political and Social Science, 185, 385.

Antin, Mary, *The Promised Land*, 51.
Appeal, the right of, from decisions of municipal courts, 395-396.
Appointments, municipal, by mayors, 275-276; powers of city councils in relation to, 299. See also Civil Service, Employees.
Aristotle, classification of governments by, 220.
Arndt, W. T., *The Emancipation of the American City*, 91, 179.
Assessment, of property for taxation, 413-414.
Attorney-General v. Detroit, 102.
Audits, municipal, 443-444.
Australian ballot, the, 189-190.

Baker, A. G., and Ware, A. H., *Municipal Government of the City of New York*, 449.
Baker-Crothers, H., and Hudnut, Ruth A., *Problems of Citizenship*, 150.
Baker, Newton D., mayor of Cleveland, 281.
Baldwin, F. Spencer, "Retirement Systems for Municipal Employees," 385.
Ballot, form of the, in municipal elections, 188-192; rotation of names on, 325. See also Elections, Short Ballot.
Baltimore, charter of 1797, 26-27, 268.
Barnett, J. D., *Operation of the Initiative and Referendum in Oregon*, 254.
Beale, J. H., *Selection of Cases on the Law of Municipal Corporations*, 72, 122, 123, 125, 132.
Beard, Dr. Charles A., *Municipal Government of Tokyo*, 446.
Beman, L. T., *Current Problems in Municipal Government*, 319.
Bemis, E. W., *Local Government in the South and Southwest*, 44.
Benton, Josiah H., *Voting in the Field*, 202.
Bercovici, Konrad, *Around the World in New York*, 70.

Beyer, W. C., "Employment Standardization in the Public Service," 378; "Standardization of Salaries in American Cities," 386.
Birth rate, in American cities, 54.
Blankenburg, Rudolph, mayor of Philadelphia, 284.
Board system, in municipal administration, merits and defects of, 351-354.
Board of Estimate and Apportionment, in New York City, 453-454.
Boards of Freeholders, organization and work of, 106-107. *See also* Charters, Home Rule.
Bogardus, E. L., *Social Psychology,* 237.
Bonds, municipal, 41.
Boots, Ralph Simpson, *Direct Primary in New Jersey,* 184.
Boroughs, American, in the colonial era, 21-25.
Borrowing, municipal, 417-418.
Bosses, in city politics, 215-216. *See also* Practical Politics.
Boston, first charter of, 22; party organization in, 163-164; budget system in, 278; size of city council in, 287; civil service confirmation of mayor's appointments in, 357-358; unionization of municipal employees in, 380; present system of government in, 472-478; metropolitan district of, 478-479.
Boston Finance Commission, *Report on Municipal Pensions,* 385.
Boston Year Book, 472.
Bramhall, F. D., "Chicago's Municipal Organization," 462.
Brooklyn Eagle, *Guide to the Municipal Government of the City of New York,* 449.
Brookwalter, J. W., *Rural versus Urban, the Conflict and its Causes,* 70, 85.
Brooks, R. C., *Political Parties and Electoral Problems,* 140, 150, 169, 176, 201, 219, 254; *Corruption in American Politics and Life,* 219.
Bruère, Henry, *New City Government,* 320, 361; on the ethics of business, 419.
Bryan, W. B., *History of the National Capital,* 45.
Bryce, James (Viscount), *The American Commonwealth,* 4, 184; *Modern Democracies,* 5, 149, 169, 235, 254; quoted, 151, 236.
Bücher, Karl, *The Industrial Revolution,* 19.

Buck, A. E., *Municipal Budgets and Budget Making,* 416.
Budgets, municipal, powers of mayor in relation to, 277-278; methods of compiling and adopting, 416, 441. *See also* Finance.
Bulletin of the American Judicature Society, 401.
Bureau of the Census, *A Century of Population Growth,* 45; *Statistics of Cities of Over 30,000,* 45; *The Statistical Abstract,* 45; *Population: Fourteenth Census of the United States,* 69; *Composition and Characteristics of the Population,* 69; *Comparative Financial Statistics of Cities Under Council and Commission Government,* 314, 320.
Bureaus of municipal research, 428-429.
Business, city government as, 402-419.
Buffalo, commission form of government in, 308.

Campaigns, municipal, methods used in, 207-211; raising funds for, 212-214.
Capes, W. P., *The Modern City and its Problems,* 179, 266, 319, 342, 361, 384, 419.
Caucus, the use of, in city elections, 172-173.
Chang, T. S., *History and Analysis of the Commission and City Manager Plans of Government,* 44, 319, 342, 361.
Charters, of colonial boroughs, 21-22; of cities, in the United States, 92-112; provision for administrative departments in, 348-349; the reform of, 430-431. *See also* Home Rule.
Chicago, the founding of, 3; party organization in, 164; budget system in, 278; size of city council in, 287; present government of, 459-467.
Chicago Bureau of Public Efficiency, *Proposed System of Registering Voters . . . in Chicago,* 146, 150, 459; *Unification of Local Governments in Chicago,* 464.
Chicago City Manual, 459.
Chicago Daily News Year Book, 459.
Childs, R. S., *Short Ballot Principles,* 202.

INDEX

Cincinnati, city manager government in, 324.
Citizenship, and the suffrage, 136.
City council, relation of mayor to the, 272; organization and powers of, 284-301.
City manager form of government, chart illustrating, 262; explanation and criticism of, 321-342.
City Managers' Association, 424.
City Manager Magazine and Year Book, 324, 341.
Civic organizations, their part in municipal affairs, 444-445. *See also* Reform.
Civil service, early history of the, 38; operations of the, in American cities, 367-376.
Civil Service Reform League, 424.
Clerget, Pierre, "Urbanism", 19.
Cleveland, the city manager form of government and proportional representation in, 324-327.
Cleveland, Grover, mayor of Buffalo, 281.
Clinton *v.* Cedar Rapids and Missouri Railroad Co., 72.
Closed primaries, 176-177.
Clubs, political, in municipal election campaigns, 167-168.
Clute, W. K., *Law of Modern Municipal Charters,* 111, 320.
Colonial Laws of New York, 22.
Commerce, relation of, to city growth, 9.
Commission form of government, chart illustrating the, 261; explanation and detailed criticism of, 302-320.
Committees, appointment and work of, in city councils, 293-294.
Commons, J. R., *Races and Immigrants in America,* 51; *Proportional Representation,* 202.
Commonwealth Club of California, *Transactions,* 184.
Compulsory voting, 200-201.
Conciliation, courts of, 395.
Confirmation, of mayor's appointments, 275-277.
Constitution of the United States, restrictions on legislative freedom of cities in, 72.
Constitutions, of the states, in relation to cities, 73-74.
Contracts, liability of municipal corporations for, 120-121.
Conventions, nominating, in city elections, 173-175.

Cooke, Morris L., *Our Cities Awake: Notes on Municipal Activities and Administration,* 361, 385.
Cooley, R. W., *Handbook of the Law of Municipal Corporations,* 132; *Illustrative Cases on Municipal Corporations,* 132.
Coolidge, Calvin, mayor of Northampton, 281.
Council. *See* City Council.
Corrupt practices, in municipal elections, 198-199.
Courts, municipal, organization and work of, 387-401.
Couzens, James, mayor of Detroit, 281.
Crane, R. T. *Digest of City Manager Charters,* 341.
Crawford, E. G., "The New York Literacy Test", 149.
Croly, Herbert, *Promise of the American Life,* 149.
Crime, prevalence of, in cities, 62-64; the problem of preventing, 399-400.
Criteria, of good city government, 434-446.
Cruikshank, A. B., *Popular Misgovernment in the United States,* 149.
Crowder, Major-General Enoch, Provost Marshal General, on urban and rural physique, 58-59.
Curran, H. H., *John Citizen's Job,* 219.
Curtis, George William, civil service reformer, 432.
Cushman, Robert E., "Non-Partisan Nominations and Elections," 179.
Cyclopedia of American Government, 462.

Dallinger, F. W., *Nominations for Elective Office,* 184.
Daniels, John, *America via the Neighborhood,* 70.
Davies, G. R., *Social Statistics,* 70.
Davis *v.* Montgomery, 122.
Dayton, Ohio, origin of the city manager plan in, 322.
Death rates, comparative, in cities, 55-57.
Debaters' Handbook Series, 202, 342.
Debt limits, municipal, 417.
Delegation of powers, in city government, the rules of law relating to, 114-115.
Departments, administrative, organization and functions of, in cities, 343-362. *See* also Civil Service.

Des Moines, Iowa, commission form of government in, 306.
Detroit Bureau of Governmental Research, *The Growth of a City*, 408.
Detroit, charter of 1824 in, 29; growth of municipal functions in, 408.
Devlin, T. C., *Municipal Reform in the United States*, 430.
Devon, the men of, case of, 112.
Dillon, John F., quoted, 72, 100, 404; *Commentaries on the Law of Municipal Corporations*, 90, 98, 114-116, 125-126, 131, 254, 362, 386, 400.
"Dillon's Rule", 98.
Direct legislation in cities, 238-253.
Dismissals, of municipal employees, 377-378. *See* also Spoils System.
Disqualifications from voting, 145.
Dissolution, of municipal corporations, 131.
Dodd, W. F., *Principles of American State Government*, 85, 91, 254, 400.
Douglas, Paul H., *The Suburban Trend*, 70.
Drummond, Henry, on the importance of cities in the national life, 69.
Durand, E. Dana, "Council Government versus Mayor Government," 285, 301.

Eaton, Dorman B., *The Government of Municipalities*, 394.
Economic base, relation of the, to city growth, 11-13.
Electorate, municipal, in the United States, 133-150. *See* also Suffrage.
Elections, municipal, 186-202. *See* also Ballot, Nominations, Proportional Representation.
Electoral divisions or wards, 289-292.
Eliot, C. W., *American Contributions to Civilization*, 149.
Elliott, C. B., *Principles of the Law of Public Corporations*, 132.
Employees, municipal, the liability of cities for the torts of, 122-128; appointment, tenure, and work of, 363-386.
Europe, city charters in, 97; municipal courts in, 396-397.
Evans, E. C., *History of the Australian Ballot System in the United States*, 202.
Expenditures, municipal, chart showing the distribution of, 412.

Fairchild, H. P., *Immigration; A World Movement and its American Significance*, 51.
Fairlie, J. A., *Essays in Municipal Administration*, 23, 45, 75, 268. *Municipal Administration*, 45.
Fairman, Charles, "Some Limitations on the Police Power of Municipalities Imposed by the Federal Constitution," 73.
Finance, municipal, powers of the mayor in relation to, 277-278; powers of city council over, 296-297; law of increasing costs in, 409-410.
Fish, C. R., *The Civil Service and the Patronage*, 385.
Fitch, Clyde, *The City*, 67.
Fite, E. D., *Social and Industrial Conditions in the North during the Civil War*, 31.
Fitzpatrick, E. A., *Experts in City Government*, 342, 361.
Follett, M. P., *The New State: Group Organization the Solution of Popular Government*, 237.
Ford, Henry J., *Rise and Growth of American Politics*, 169, 184.
Forms of city government, 255-266.
Forsyth *v.* Atlanta, 122.
Fosdick, Raymond B., *American Police Systems*, 317, 319.
Foulke, W. D., *Fighting the Spoilmen*, 385.
Fowle *v.* Alexandria, 122.
Franchises, rules of law relating to the granting of, 129-130; in New York City, 455.
Fry, Luther, *A Census Analysis of American Villages*, 70.
Fuld, L. T., *Civil Service Administration*, 385.
Functions, of city governments, 126; of political parties, 158-159.
Fusion, in New York City, 162.

Galveston, Texas, origin of the commission plan of government in, 303-304.
Gary, Indiana, the remarkable growth of an industrial satellite, 8.
Gas Ring, the, in Philadelphia, 218.
Gavitt, J. P., *Americans by Choice*, 51.
Gaynor, William J., mayor of New York City, 283.
General charter laws, 75.
General property tax, 414.
Gilbert, A. B., *Modern Cities: Their Methods of Business*, 342.

INDEX

Gloucester, Massachusetts, the "economic base" of, 11.
Goodnow, Frank J., *Municipal Home Rule*, 91, 120, 125; *Municipal Problems*, 149.
Goodnow, F. J., and Bates, F. G., *Municipal Government*, 56, 91, 361, 400.
Gosnell, H. F., *Boss Platt and his New York Machine*, 219.
Gould, E. R. L., *Local Government in Pennsylvania*, 44.
Governmental Research Conference, *The Character and Functioning of Municipal Civil Service Commissions in the United States*, 371, 377, 385; work of the, 425.
Grand Rapids, Michigan, dependence of, on a single industry, 7.
"Grandfather clause," the, 140.
Grants in aid, or state subsidies, to cities, 89-90.
Gras, N. S. B., *Introduction to Economic History*, 19.
Greece, the city states of, 1.
Greenville v. Pitts, 124.
Grosser, H. S., *Chicago: a Review of its Governmental History*, 44, 459.
Growth of cities in the United States, 27-28, 41-42.

Hall, Arnold B., *Popular Government*, 182, 185, 237, 254.
Hamilton, Alexander, on the industrial growth of the nation, 3.
Hare plan of proportional representation, 196-197.
Harrison, Carter, mayor of Chicago, 284.
Harrison, Frederic, "The City as It Is and as It Might Be," 20.
Haynes, G. H., "Educational Qualifications," 149.
Heads of departments. See Departments.
Hitchcock v. Galveston, 114.
Hobson, J. A., *The Evolution of Modern Capitalism*, 61.
Holcomb, W. P., *Pennsylvania Boroughs*, 44.
Holcombe, A. N., *Political Parties of Today*, 169; *Foundations of the Modern Commonwealth*, 237.
Hollander, J. H., *Financial History of Baltimore*, 44.
Home rule, municipal, 80-88. See also Charters.
Hormell, O. C., *The Direct Primary in Maine*, 185.

Howe, F. C., *Confessions of a Reformer*, 375.
Howe, W. W., *Municipal History of New Orleans*, 45.
Hull, Morton D., "The Non-Partisan Ballot in Municipal Elections," 191.
Humphrey, J. H., *Proportional Representation*, 202.
Hunt, Henry, mayor of Cincinnati, 284.
Huse, C. P., *Financial History of Boston*, 472.

Illegal practices, in city elections, 199.
Illinois, special position of Chicago in constitution of, 78; civil service system in cities of, 370.
Illinois Constitutional Convention, *Bulletins*, 254, 462.
Illiteracy, in city and country compared, 59-61.
Immigration, effects of, on municipal politics, 52-54.
Implication, the chartering of cities by, 113.
Income taxes, in cities, 414.
Indebtedness, municipal, 417-418.
Industry, the relation of, to city growth, 7-9.
Infant mortality, in cities, 56-57.
Initiative and referendum, in cities, the workings and results of, 238-253.
Interpretation, the, of city charters by the courts, 100-101.
Ivins, W. M., *Machine Politics in New York City*, 219.

Jackson, Andrew, and the spoils system, 29-30.
James, H. G., *Applied City Government*, 106; *Local Government in the United States*, 400.
Jefferson, Thomas, on the growth of industrial centers, 3-4.
Jenks, J. W., and Lauck, W. Jett, *The Immigration Problem*, 51.
Johnson, J. E., *Selected Articles on the Negro Problem*, 150.
Johnson, Tom L., mayor of Cleveland, 279; *My Story*, 219, 301.
Johnson, W. F., *Toledo's Non-Partisan Movement*, 169.
Jones, D. A., *The Negligence of Municipal Corporations*, 124.
Jones, Samuel M. ("Golden Rule" Jones), mayor of Toledo, 283.
Jones, T. J., *Sociology of a New York City Block*, 70.

Kales, A. M., *Unpopular Government in the United States*, 319, 393.
Kansas City, Missouri, the city manager form of government in, 324.
Kauffman v. Tallahassee, 127.
Kent, Frank R., *The Great Game of Politics*, 169, 219.
Kibele v. Philadelphia, 124.
Kimball, Everett, *State and Municipal Government*, 91, 342.
King, Clyde L., *The History of the City Government of Denver*, 45.
Kingsley, Charles, *Miscellanies*, 63.

Lanne, Clement G., *Travelling on the Democratic Donkey*, 219.
Larson, L. M., *Financial and Administrative History of Milwaukee*, 45.
Lawton, G. W., *American Caucus System*, 184.
Leadership, in relation to public opinion in cities, 233-235.
Leagues of municipalities, in the several states, 425.
Lecky, W. E. H., *Democracy and Liberty*, 149.
Legal aid bureaus, 398.
Legal phases of city government, 112-132.
Legal residence, as a qualification for voting, 137-139.
Leonard, J. W., *History of the City of New York*, 44.
Liability, of municipal corporations, 120-130.
Library of Congress, Legislative Reference Division, *Absent Voting*, 202; *List of References on Commission Government of Cities*, 319; *List of References on the City Manager Plan*, 342.
Lippman, Walter, *The Phantom Public*, 224, 237; *Public Opinion*, 237.
List plan, of proportional representation, 196.
Literacy, as a qualification for voting, 139-140.
Lloyd v. the Mayor, 121.
Lobby, the, in municipal politics, 228.
Los Angeles, early history of, 3; rapid growth of, 11.
Love, A. G., and Davenport, C. B., *Defects Found in Drafted Men*, 59.

Low, Seth, mayor of New York City, 283-284.
Lowell, A. Lawrence, *Public Opinion and Popular Government*, 169, 237; *Public Opinion in War and Peace*, 169, 237.
Ludington, A. C., *American Ballot Laws*, 201.
Luetscher, G. D., *Early Political Machinery in the United States*, 184.

Machines, political, in cities, 216-219.
McBain, H. L., *The Law and the Practice of Municipal Home Rule*, 35, 75, 82, 91; *American City Progress and the Law*, 91, 100, 101, 132; "Proportional Representation in American Cities," 202.
McBain, H. L., and Rogers, Lindsay, *The New Constitutions of Europe*, 202.
McClellan, George B., mayor of New York City, 284.
McConville v. Jersey City, 99.
McDougall, William, *Social Psychology*, 237.
McGoldrick, J. S., "Home Rule in New York State," 77.
McKenzie, R. D., *The Neighborhood*, 70.
McKinley, A. E., *Suffrage Franchise in the Thirteen English Colonies*, 149.
McMahon, A. W., *The Statutory Sources of New York City Government*, 77.
McQuillin, Eugene, "Urban Life and Modern Civilization," 20; *Treatise on the Law of Municipal Corporations*, 44, 91, 114-115, 131, 319, 400; *Law of Municipal Ordinances*, 115-116, 132.
Macy, John E., *Selection of Cases on Municipal or Public Corporations*, 132.
Maine, Sir Henry, *Popular Government*, 149.
Marriage rate, the, in urban communities, 54-55.
Marsh, Edward C., "A Sketch of the Merit System," 385.
Massachusetts, workings of the optional charter law in, 79-80; civil service system in the cities of, 369-370.
Massachusetts Constitutional Convention, *Debates*, 254; *Bulletins*, 91, 202, 254, 319, 342.

INDEX 487

Mathews, J. M., *American State Government*, 91.
Matthews, Nathan, *City Government of Boston*, 44, 472, 473; *Municipal Charters*, 106, 111, 320.
Maxey, Chester C., *Outline of Municipal Government*, 20, 91, 342; *Readings in Municipal Government*, 20, 75, 91, 266, 301, 315, 342, 384; "Proportional Representation in Cleveland," 198.
Mayor, position and powers of the, in American cities, 267-284.
Mayor-and-council form of government, in the United States, 257-260; detailed description of, 267-301.
Meriam, Lewis, *Principles Governing the Retirement of Public Employees*, 383, 385.
Merriam, Charles E., *American Party System*, 169, 185; *Primary Elections*, 184; *New Aspects of Politics*, 237.
Merriam, C. E., and Gosnell, H. F., *Non-Voting; Its Causes and Methods of Control*, 200.
Metropolitan areas, the government of, 447-479.
Meyer, E. C., *Nominating Systems*, 184.
Michel, R., *Political Parties*, 169.
Mill, J. S., *Representative Government*, 150; quoted, 330.
Milwaukee, report on pensions, 385.
Missouri, origin of the home rule charter system in, 80.
Mitchel, John Purroy, mayor of New York, 279.
Moley, Raymond, *Parties, Politics and People*, 169, 219.
Montesquieu, Baron, quoted, 115.
Motion pictures, the use of, for propaganda in municipal campaigns, 208-209, 228-230.
Moses, Bernard, *The Establishment of City Government in San Francisco*, 44.
Moses, Robert, *The Civil Service of Great Britain*, 385.
Municipal corporations, the rules of law relating to, 112-132.
Municipal Index, The, 401, 423-425.
Municipal Program. See National Municipal League.
Munro, W. B., *Bibliography of Municipal Government*, 45, 254, 319, 433, 449; *Government of European Cities*, 91, 133, 343, 362; *Personality in Politics*, 219, 338; *Municipal Government and Administration*, 399, 419, 440.
Murphy v. Lowell, 124.
Myers, Gustavus, *History of Tammany Hall*, 30, 32, 164, 169.

National City Planning Conference, 425.
National Civic Federation, *Report on Municipal and Private Operation of Public Utilities*, 129.
National Civil Service Reform League, *Good Government*, 385.
National Education Association, estimate of illiteracy made by, 60.
National Industrial Conference Board, *Report*, 51.
National Institute of Public Administration, 383.
National Municipal League, *New Municipal Program*, 106, 111, 342, 361; *Outline of a Model Election System*, 202; *Digest of City Manager Charters*, 341; *Story of the City Manager Plan*, 342; report of civil service committee, 385.
Nationality, distribution of population according to, in cities, 49-51.
Naturalization of aliens, 203-204.
Negro, the disfranchisement of the, in Southern cities, 139-141.
Nelson, Frederic, "The Dancing Bear," 244.
Newark, New Jersey, commission form of government in, 308.
New Orleans, commission form of government in, 308.
New York v. Ordrenan, 35.
New York Bureau of Municipal Research, 362, 383; *Standardization of Public Employment*, 386.
New York Bureau of Personal Service, *Standard Specifications for Personal Service*, 386.
New York City, early history of, 22, 24; party organization in, 165-166; present government of, 449-458.
New York Constitutional Convention, *Index Digest of State Constitutions*, 139.
New York State, municipal home rule in, 81; *Report of Home Rule Commission*, 91; literacy tests for voting in, 141; civil service system in cities of, 371-372.
Newspapers, the influence of, in city election campaigns, 207-208, 223-228.
Nominations, in cities, 170-174.

Nonpartisan primaries, 178.
Non-Voting, the causes of, 200.

Ogburn, W. F., and Goltis, I., "How Women Vote," 150.
Ohio, experience of, with general charter system, 74-76.
Open primaries, 176-177.
Ordinances, the rules of law relating to, 115-120; liability of municipal corporations for defects in, 121; powers of city councils to pass, 295-298. *See* also Regulations.
Orth, Samuel P., *The Boss and the Machine*, 219.
Ostrogorski, M., *Democracy and the Organization of Political Parties*, 169.
Ownership of property, by population of urban and rural areas compared, 64-65.

Paine, A. P., *The Tweed Ring*, 219.
Park, R. E., Burgess, E. W., and McKenzie, R. D., *The City*, 11, 20, 70.
Parties, political, organization and work of, 151-169; methods used by, 203-219.
Patterson, John H., and the city manager plan, 322.
Pearl, R., and Reed, L. J., *Predicted Growth of Population of New York and Its Environs*, 19, 45.
Pearson, P. M., and Nichols, E. R., *Intercollegiate Debates*, I, 149.
Penn, William, quoted, 151.
Pensions, for city employees, 381-382.
Personnel work, in city employment, 376-377.
Peterson, A. E., *New York as an Eighteenth Century Municipality Prior to 1731*, 22.
Peterson, A. E., and Edwards, G. W., *New York as an Eighteenth Century Municipality*, 44, 449-450.
Peterson, Samuel, *Democracy and Government*, 254.
Petitions, as a means of nominating candidates for municipal office, 183-184. *See* also Initiative.
Petty, Sir William, *Essays on Mankind and Political Arithmetic*, 43.
Phelps, Edith M., *Selected Articles on the Initiative and Referendum* (Debaters' Handbook Series), 254.
Philadelphia, early charter of (1789), 25-26; party organization in, 163; budget system in, 278; size of present city council in, 287; civil service system in, 371; present charter and government of, 467-472.
Philadelphia Bureau of Municipal Research, *Philadelphia's Government*, 469.
Phillips, J. B., "Educational Qualifications of Voters," 149.
Physique, effects of city life on, 57-59.
Pirenne, Henri, *Mediæval Cities*, 19.
Pond, O. L., *Municipal Control of Public Utilities*, 130.
Pope, Alexander, quoted, 103.
Population, distribution of, in modern cities, 46-50; ratio of voters to, 146; methods of estimating, 402; of larger American cities, 447. *See* also Growth of Cities.
Port Huron v. McCall, 101.
Porter, Kirk H., *History of the Suffrage in the United States*, 134, 140, 149.
Pound, Roscoe, "The Administration of Justice in Modern City," 401.
Powers, of municipal corporations, 102-103, 113-115; of mayors, 272-279; of city councils, 294-300.
Practical politics, under urban conditions, 203-219. *See* also Parties.
Pratt, E. E., *Industrial Causes of Congestion of Population in New York City*, 70.
Preferential voting, 194-196; in city council elections, 291-292.
Prescription, the chartering of cities by, 113.
Primary, the direct, its use in cities as a means of nominating elective officers, 175-183.
Procedure, rules of, in city councils, 292-293.
Procter, A. W., *Principles of Public Personnel Administration*, 377, 385.
Propaganda, in municipal campaigns, as a means of influencing public opinion, 224-226; in referendum elections, 244-245.
Property, liability of municipal corporations in relation to, 128-129; as a qualification for voting, 143. *See* also Ownership of Property.
Proportional representation, explained, 195-198; as a means of improving city councils, 292.
Proportional Representation Review, 202.
Providence, Rhode Island, breadth of the "economic base" in, 12; ef-

INDEX 489

fect of property qualifications for voting in, 143.
Provost Marshal General, *Second Report on the Operations of the Selective Service System,* 59.
Public defenders, 398.
Public opinion, nature of, and methods of influencing, in cities, 220-237.
Public service corporations, legal questions relating to, 129-130. *See also* Franchises.
Public utilities, powers of city councils in relation to, 297. *See also* Franchises, Public Service Corporations.
Purdom, C. B., *The Building of Satellite Cities,* 70.

Qualifications for voting, in city elections, 136-148.
Quincy, Josiah, mayor of Boston, 44.

Race, the distribution of urban populations according to, 49-51; relation of, to political affiliation, 152-154.
Radicalism, among city populations, 65.
Radio, the use of, in city election campaigns, 209, 230-231.
Ray, P. Orman, *Introduction to Political Parties and Practical Politics,* 150, 169, 184-185, 201-202, 219.
Recall, the use of, as applied to municipal officers, 253.
Reform, early history of municipal, 39-41; of municipal courts, 393-396; of municipal government in general, 420-433. *See also* Civil Service, Short Ballot.
Registration of voters, 145-146; party workers in relation to, 204-205.
Regulations municipal, 116. *See also* Ordinances.
Reilly, J. J., "Training Municipal Employees," 384.
Religion, as a factor in politics, 154.
Reports, municipal, 402-404; the improvement of, 444.
Residence, as a qualification for voting, 137-139.
Revolution, American, its effect on borough charters, 25-26.
Rexford, Frank A., *Our City—New York,* 449.
Rhode Island, qualifications for voting in, 143.

Rightor, C. E., *The City Manager Plan in Dayton,* 342, 361.
Rings, in city politics, 218.
Ringwalt, R. C., *Briefs on Public Questions with Selected Lists of References,* 149.
Riordon, W. L., *Plunkitt of Tammany Hall,* 219.
Roberts, Peter, *The New Immigration,* 51.
Robinson, E. E., *Evolution of American Political Parties,* 169.
Robson, W. A., *From Patronage to Proficiency in the Public Service,* 385.
Rochester, New York, city manager form of government in, 324.
Roosevelt, Theodore, 44; "Machine Politics in New York City," 173; quoted, 215-216; *Autobiography,* 219; on the "lunatic fringe" of reform movements, 421.
Rose, "Negro Suffrage," 150.
Ross, E. A., *The Old World in the New,* 51.
Royal Commission on Civil Service, *Fourth Report,* 385.
Rural exodus to cities, nature and causes of, 41-42; continuance of, 49.
Russell Sage Foundation, *Report of the Country Life Commission,* 70. *The Pittsburgh Survey,* 70.

Saby, R. S., on simplification of municipal court procedure, 401.
St. Louis, size of the city council in, 287.
Satellite cities, 8.
Scharf, J. T., *History of St. Louis,* 44.
Schouler, James, *Municipal Corporations,* 132.
Schurz, Carl, on the importance of the human equation in government, 103, 429 *n.*
Sex, the distribution of urban population by, 47.
Seymour, Charles, and Frary, Donald, P., *How the World Votes,* 149, 202.
Shaw, Albert, *Local Government in Illinois,* 44.
Short ballot, 191-192.
Short Ballot Organization, 424.
Shoup, E. L., "The Initiative and Referendum in Thirty-Six American Cities," 243.
Simkhovitch, Mary K., *The City Worker's World,* 66, 70.

Small Claims Courts, 394-395.
Smith, R. H., *Justice and the Poor*, 388, 400.
Snavely, Charles, *History of the City Government of Cleveland*, 45.
Snow, E. N., *Bibliography of Books and Articles on the Initiative Referendum and Recall*, 254.
Social structure, of modern cities, 46-69.
Soon Hing v. Crowley, 118.
Sparling, S. E., *Municipal History and Present Organization of the City of Chicago*, 44, 459.
Spaulding v. Lowell, 101.
Spaulding v. Peabody, 102.
Spencer, D. E., *Local Government in Wisconsin*, 44.
Spoils system, origin of the, 29-30.
Sprague, H. H., *The City Government of Boston, its Rise and Development*, 44.
State v. Jones, 75.
State, relation of the city to the, in earlier period, 34-36; at the present time, 71-91.
"Straw votes," the political value of, 210-211.
Steffens, Lincoln, *The Shame of the Cities*, 219.
Steiner, Edward A., *From Alien to Citizen*, 51.
Stephenson, G. T., *Race Distinctions in American Law*, 139, 150.
Stoffer, David, "Parties in Non-Partisan Boston," 191.
Storey, Moorfield, *The Reform of Legal Procedure*, 395.
Story, R. M., *The American Municipal Executive*, 34, 301, 361.
Strachey, J. St. L., *The Referendum*, 254.
Strong, Josiah, *The Twentieth Century City*, 62.
Strunsky, Simeon, quoted, 10; *Belshazzar Court, or Village Life in New York City*, 70.
Sutherland, E. H., "The Administration of Justice in the Modern City and County," 401.
Studensky, Paul, "Pensions in Public Employment," 383.
Subsidies, or grants-in-aid, from state to local authorities, 89-90.
Suffrage, the, in American cities, 134-148.

Tammany Hall, the organization of, 165-169.
Taxation, municipal, 411-414.

Taxes, the payment of, as a qualification for voting, 144-145.
Taylor, Graham R., *Satellite Cities*, 19, 70.
Taylor, R. Emmett, *Municipal Budget Making*, 416.
Tennyson, Alfred (Lord), quoted, 49.
Tocqueville, Alexis de, on the probable effects of city growth in America, 4; *Democracy in America*, 149, 169.
Thompson, S. D., *Cases on Municipal Negligence*, 125.
Torts, of municipal employees, the city's liability for, 121-128.
Toulmin, H. A. Jr., *The City Manager*, 342.
Traditions, the influence of, upon city government, 231-232.
Training schools, for the public service, 383.
Tucker, Rufus S., on the Provost Marshal General's conclusions concerning urban and rural physique, 59.
Tweed Ring, in New York City, 36, 218.
Types of city government, described, 255-266.

Unit costs, of municipal work, 443.
University of Pennsylvania, Wharton School of Finance and Economics, *The City Government of Philadelphia*, 44.
Upson, Lent D., *The Governments of Cincinnati and Hamilton County*, 362, 446; "The Growth of a City," 408.

Veto power, of the mayor, 273-274.
Voters, proportion and qualifications of, in cities, 133-150.
Voters' lists, how compiled, 145-146.
Voting machines, 194.

Waite, Colonel Henry M., first city manager of Dayton, Ohio, 337.
Ward system, 289-290.
Warne, F. J., *The Tide of Immigration*, 51.
Weber, A. F., *Growth of Cities in the Nineteenth Century*, 19, 45, 68.
Weil, W. E., *The New Democracy*, 219.
Whipple, G. C., *Vital Statistics*, 70.
White, Edward F., *The Negligence of Municipal Corporations*, 132.

INDEX

Whitlock, Brand, mayor of Toledo, *Forty Years of It*, 72, 219, 224, 283, 301; "The Evil Influence of National Parties in Municipal Elections," 186; quoted, 223-224, 281, 421.
Wilcox v. Chicago, 128.
Wilcox, D. F., *Municipal Government in Michigan and Ohio*, 44; *Government by All the People*, 254; *The Government of Great American Cities*, 472.
Williams v. Whitney, 138.
Williams, J. F., *The Reform of Political Representation*, 202.
Williams, W. L., *The Liability of Municipal Corporations for Tort*, 132.
Williamson, C. C., *The Finances of Cleveland*, 45.
Wilson, J. G., *Memorial History of the City of New York*, 44.

Wilson, Woodrow, on reformers, 421.
Wisconsin, the open primary in, 176.
Woman suffrage, 146-147.
Wood, A. E., *Community Problems*, 70.
Woodburn, James A., *Political Parties and Party Problems*, 169, 185.
Woods, R. A., *The Neighborhood in Nation-Building*, 70.
Woolston, H. B., *A Study of the Population of Manhattanville*, 70; *Urban Sociology*, 70.
Wright, Joseph, *Selected Readings in Municipal Problems*, 20, 111, 126, 141, 179, 198, 266, 285, 301, 342, 384.

Year Book and Citizens Manual of Philadelphia, 469.
Young, J. R., *Memorial History of Philadelphia*, 367.